The Death Penalty
Constitutional Issues, Commentaries, and Case Briefs

D1573198

The Death Penalty

Constitutional Issues, Commentaries, and Case Briefs

Third Edition

Scott Vollum
University of Minnesota, Duluth

Rolando V. del Carmen
Sam Houston State University

Durant Frantzen
Texas A&M University, San Antonio

Claudia San Miguel
Texas A&M International University

Kelly Cheeseman
Messiah College

Routledge
Taylor & Francis Group

LONDON AND NEW YORK

First published 2005 by Anderson Publishing

Published 2015 by Routledge
2 Park Square, Milton Park, Abingdon, Oxon OX14 4RN

and by Routledge
711 Third Avenue, New York, NY 10017, USA

Routledge is an imprint of the Taylor & Francis Group, an informa business

Acquiring Editor: Pam Chester
Editorial Project Manager: Ellen S. Boyne
Project Manager: Priya Kumaraguruparan
Designer: Russell Purdy

Library of Congress Cataloging-in-Publication Data
The death penalty / Scott Vollum, Rolando V. del Carmen, Durant Frantzen, Claudia San Miguel,
    Kelly Cheeseman.–Third edition. p. cm.
1. Capital punishment–United States. I. Vollum, Scott, 1970- author. II. Del Carmen, Rolando V.
    author. III. Frantzen, Durant, author.
    KF9227.C2D4117 2014
    345.73'0773–dc23

                            2014001186

British Library Cataloguing in Publication Data
A catalogue record for this book is available from the British Library

ISBN 978-1-4557-7633-7 (pbk)

We dedicate this edition to our co-author Kelly Cheeseman. We will remember her sense of humor, dedication to her students, and her passion for her profession. Kelly will be greatly missed.

Contents

Preface to the Third Edition

Much has changed in the legal world of the death penalty since this book was first conceived in 2003. Over this span of 10 years there have been more than 500 executions and 1,175 new death sentences. During this period the United States hit and surpassed the 1,000-execution post-*Furman* milestone (1,347 executions as of October 1, 2013). But during that same time, the rates of death sentences and executions have declined precipitously. Six states have abolished the death penalty—five since the last edition of this book—and several others are considering doing so. There also have been 42 exonerations of individuals on death row who were found to be innocent, including six due to DNA testing.

By all measures, the popularity and use of the death penalty is on the decline. Increasing awareness of the flaws and failures of the death penalty system, as well as increasing concerns about the financial costs of the death penalty, seem to have played a role in this decline, as has the now virtually universal availability of true life sentences. That being said, we still remain one of the most prolific nations in terms of executions and the only Western nation to carry out executions at all. Furthermore, though it seems to be occurring in only a shrinking minority of jurisdictions, the death penalty continues in earnest in some states and localities. Texas surpassed 500 executions this year; states such as North Carolina, which has had no executions since 2006, are taking measures to revitalize and expand the death penalty and speed up executions. The death penalty remains a criminal sanction that presents us with many contradictions and controversies and increasingly evokes ambivalence among lawmakers and the public alike.

Violence in the United States has also declined significantly over the last decade, though it may be hard to tell given that we are presented with increasingly stark images of violence on a seemingly daily basis. Highly publicized cases of extreme and mass violence seem to have proliferated in the last few years, often drawing attention as capital or potentially capital cases. Just in the last two years, there has been a terrorist bombing at the Boston Marathon as well as twelve mass shootings, including a particularly horrific massacre of young children in a grade school in Newtown, Connecticut. Though many of these violent acts end with the offender's suicide, in cases in which the offenders live, such as the man who opened fire in a Colorado theater killing 12 people and injuring another 58, or one of the men who set off the bombs in Boston, the death penalty enters the public consciousness almost immediately. Both of these cases are still in progress at the time of this writing, so it is unknown whether they will result in death sentences. But there is no denying that cases such as these challenge us to think very hard about violence and killing and, by extension, the death penalty. When we are faced with horrors such as these, it is easy to understand why the death penalty persists. It is also easy to understand why the death penalty often evokes great emotion and conflict in our society.

The death penalty remains a hotly debated topic in the United States and a potent public policy in certain locations. In much of the United States, the public continues to support it and, in some cases, demand it. However, it also continues to be a lightning rod of sorts, drawing attention to many of the problems and controversies within criminal justice. Issues of cost, public safety, deterrence, retribution, justice, wrongful conviction, rehabilitation, redemption, race, and discrimination are illuminated through the magnifying glass that is the death penalty. As such, we believe that an understanding and analysis of the legal and constitutional issues surrounding the death penalty serve the broader objective of better understanding the criminal justice system. It is our hope that, throughout this book, we have served this objective and that we have provided insight into the often complex and confusing world of the U.S. Supreme Court and its death penalty jurisprudence.

In this revised third edition, we have again maintained the overall structure and much of the content from the prior two editions. But there is also much that is new and improved. We present eight new case briefs and discuss many more new cases throughout the book, recalibrating our commentary on the major constitutional issues in line with the ever-evolving jurisprudence. We also added to the coverage of important peripheral legal and social issues, such as racial disparities in the criminal justice system, life sentences for juveniles, public opinion, wrongful convictions, and state trends in abolition of the death penalty.

Over the last five years, Supreme Court activity in terms of death penalty cases did not take on the same pace or volume that it had in previous decades. However, the legal developments, issues, and challenges—many of which have stemmed from prior Supreme Court decisions—have flourished and will likely continue to spur further involvement by the Court for the foreseeable future.

Scott Vollum, Ph.D.
Duluth, MN
October 1, 2013

The case briefs added in the third edition are:

Chapter 4: The Mentally Impaired and the Death Penalty
Bobby v. Bies (2009): Reassessment of mental retardation for the determination of eligibility for the death penalty.
Ryan v. Gonzales/Tibbals v. Carter (2013): Competence to assist counsel during appellate processes.

Chapter 7: The Right to Effective Assistance of Counsel and the Death Penalty
Wood v. Allen (2010): Counsel's failure to present evidence of mental retardation in capital mitigation.
Maples v. Thomas (2012): Counsel's failure to meet a filing deadline and "cause" to excuse a consequent procedural default.

Chapter 8: Due Process and the Death Penalty
Cone v. Bell (2009): Procedural default of habeas corpus claim following a lack of proper review by a state court; application of the *Brady* rule when evidence was suppressed.
Connick v. Thompson (2011): Section 1983 lawsuit based on wrongful conviction and establishing liability of state agents.

Chapter 10: Appeals, Habeas Corpus, and the Death Penalty
Stewart v. Martinez-Villareal (1998): The AEDPA's successive petition restriction and the filing of successive habeas corpus petitions when previous petitions were dismissed as premature.
Skinner v. Switzer (2011): The use of Section 1983 lawsuits to compel DNA testing in claims of actual innocence.

Preface to the Second Edition

The death penalty, in the context of the United States Constitution and the Supreme Court, is constantly evolving. In this, the second edition of *The Death Penalty: Constitutional Issues, Commentaries, and Case Briefs*, we try to reflect this evolution by presenting the most recent Supreme Court cases and the issues inherent in them that have occurred in the years since we published the first edition of this book. As I write this preface, we have just come off the longest hiatus in executions since the death penalty was reinstated following the Supreme Court decision in *Gregg v. Georgia*. This informal moratorium resulted from the Court's decision to consider the constitutionality of the execution method of lethal injection. The case was *Baze v. Rees*, one of the most recent among the new cases analyzed and discussed in this book, and the Court held that lethal injection is a constitutionally permissible method of execution. The first execution since September 25, 2007, was carried out on May 6, 2008, when William Earl Lynd was executed in Georgia by lethal injection at 7:51 P.M. As I write this, Mark Schwab is scheduled to be executed by lethal injection in Florida for the rape and murder of an 11-year-old boy; it will be the tenth execution of the year. There are more than 20 executions scheduled to take place over the coming months.

Over the last several years executions have slowed, but the Supreme Court's consideration of constitutional issues pertaining to them certainly has not. During the four years since the first edition of this book was published, the Supreme Court has made significant decisions about, among other things, racial disparity in capital jury selection, mental impairment as a mitigating factor in capital sentencing, standards of effectiveness of legal representation for capital defendants, jury instructions pertaining to aggravating and mitigating evidence, evidence of actual innocence in habeas corpus petitions, and, most recently, the constitutionality of lethal injection as a method of execution and the constitutionality of the death penalty in cases of the rape of a child when the victim is not murdered. The makeup of the Court has also changed in the years since this book was first published. Chief Justice William H. Rehnquist has been succeeded by new Chief Justice John G. Roberts, and Justice Sandra Day O'Connor has been succeeded by Justice Samuel Anthony Alito Jr. Justice Alito's first death penalty opinion was in *Holmes v. South Carolina* (briefed in Chapter 8), and Chief Justice Roberts has written several opinions in death penalty cases and penned the plurality opinion in *Baze v. Rees* (briefed in Chapter 11).

Although the structure and much of the content in this second edition remains the same as in the original edition, there is much that is new and revised. There are 17 new cases briefed and many more new cases discussed throughout the book. The added case briefs are:

Chapter 3: Racial Discrimination and the Death Penalty

> *Miller El v. Dretke* (2005): Racially disparate questioning in jury selection
> *Snyder v. Louisiana* (2008): Exclusion of prospective black jurors without racially neutral explanations

Chapter 4: The Mentally Impaired and the Death Penalty

> *Singleton v. Norris* (2003): Forcefully medicating an inmate for competency in order to be executed
> *Tennard v. Dretke* (2004): Mental retardation as mitigating factor when unrelated to crime
> *Panetti v. Quarterman* (2007): Mental competency to be executed

Chapter 6: Juries, Jurors, and the Death Penalty
> *Uttecht v. Brown* (2007): Trial court judge's role in death qualification

Chapter 7: The Right to Effective Assistance of Counsel and the Death Penalty
> *Rompilla v. Beard* (2005): Counsel's failure to make a reasonable effort to contest evidence supporting a death sentence
> *Schriro v. Landrigan* (2007): Defendant's interference with counsel's strategy and the presentation of mitigating evidence

Chapter 8: Due Process and the Death Penalty
> *Deck v. Missouri* (2005): Shackling of a capital defendant during sentencing phase of trial
> *Holmes v. South Carolina* (2006): Introduction of third-party guilt evidence

Chapter 9: Aggravating and Mitigating Factors in Death Penalty Cases
> *Kansas v. Marsh* (2006): Death sentence when aggravating and mitigating factors are equal in weight
> *Brewer v. Quarterman* (2007): Statutory restrictions on jury instructions regarding the consideration of mitigating factors

Chapter 10: Appeals, Habeas Corpus, and the Death Penalty
> *Nelson v. Campbell* (2004): Right to bring a lawsuit challenging the method of execution
> *House v. Bell* (2007): Habeas corpus appeals on the grounds of actual innocence
> *Lawrence v. Florida* (2007): Suspension of AEDPA's statute of limitations while awaiting habeas corpus decision

Chapter 11: Evolving Standards of Decency and the Eighth Amendment's Ban on Cruel and Unusual Punishment
> *Baze v. Rees* (2008): Constitutionality of lethal injection as a method of execution
> *Kennedy v. Louisiana* (2008): Constitutionality of the death penalty for nonhomicide cases of sexual assault against a child

Only one case brief has been removed (the 2003 case of *Miller-El v. Cockrell* has been replaced by the more recent 2005 case of *Miller-El v. Dretke*). Discussion surrounding past cases and the rich history and lineage of Supreme Court decisions in capital cases has been preserved but has been supplemented by numerous new decisions and updated information on the many related death penalty issues. In the end, we believe that the second edition of this book significantly strengthens and bolsters what was already a valuable and unique book and offers the reader the most comprehensive and up-to-date collection and consideration of constitutional issues and Supreme Court decisions pertaining to the death penalty.

Scott Vollum, Ph.D.
Harrisonburg, Virginia
July 1, 2008

Preface and Introduction to the First Edition

Death as a form of punishment was used in the United States even before the American colonies became a republic. For a long time, the death penalty was—and still is—an option available to the state when dealing with serious offenders, and the public accepted it as such without many legal or political challenges. In recent times, however, issues have arisen concerning the constitutionality and wisdom of this ultimate sanction. This has spawned numerous court cases, decided over several decades, that have sought to declare this form of punishment unconstitutional, or that attempted to refine and polish some of its features. These cases and what they say are the focus of this book.

Constitutionality and the wisdom of imposing the death penalty are two separate issues, although they tend to be treated as one in some quarters. Constitutionality is an issue addressed and resolved by the courts, while the wisdom of imposing it is a political question to be resolved by political decision-makers who represent the public. This book focuses on the constitutionality issue. Whether the death penalty is wise or desirable as a form of punishment is for political entities to eventually determine and resolve.

Numerous books and articles have been written on the death penalty. This book seeks to add a legal dimension to existing literature by bringing together all the major cases decided by the United States Supreme Court on the death penalty. The first case decided by the Court on the death penalty was *Wilkerson v. Utah* in 1878. The cut-off date for the cases briefed in this book was July 1, 2013. A total of 72 cases are briefed here. As in any project in which choices are involved, subjectivity played a role in determining which cases from among the many decided by the Court are sufficiently important to justify inclusion among the briefed cases. That determination, including the "Top Ten Most Significant Death Penalty Cases," was made by the authors based on their familiarity over the years with death penalty cases.

THE BOOK'S PURPOSE AND AUDIENCE

This text is written to fill a need for a book that gathers and synthesizes all the legal issues related to the death penalty, bringing together both fundamental presentation and discussion of these issues with short case briefs of key Supreme Court cases. There is no such book available to the general public at present, except perhaps those used in law schools and in full case form. It classifies the death penalty cases according to legal issues, provides a commentary on the various subtopics, and then presents legal materials in an easy-to-digest and understandable form. The main audiences of the book are undergraduates and criminal justice practitioners. The book should also prove useful, however, for anyone who has an interest in the legal issues surrounding the death penalty.

THE BOOK'S CONTENT

The book consists of 12 chapters, subclassified into four parts.

Part I (Chapters 1 and 2) introduces the history of the death penalty and then discusses the foundation cases of *Furman v. Georgia* and *Gregg v. Georgia*.

Part II (Chapters 3, 4, and 5) focuses on constitutional issues and specific groups. These groups are those discriminated against because of race, mental impairment, or due to their having committed serious crimes at a young age. These offenders are treated differently by the Court.

Part III (Chapters 6, 7, 8, 9, 10, and 11) constitutes the major thrust of the book. It addresses constitutional issues such as the role of juries and jurors, the right to effective assistance of counsel, the right to due process, aggravating and mitigating circumstances, appeals, habeas corpus, and the concept of evolving standards of decency.

Part IV (Chapter 12) addresses the current death penalty issues and trends in the United States, including the flaws in its administration of which awareness and acknowledgment seem to be growing rapidly. The trends of declining use of the death penalty are discussed, asking what they might foretell about where things are headed in regard to this controversial criminal sanction. We end with a consideration of this possible future of the death penalty in the United States.

FORMAT

Every chapter starts with commentaries on the general case law on a subtopic, followed by a chart of the cases briefed in the chapter, and then the case briefs. The case brief approach to the study of law is deemed more effective for undergraduates and field practitioners who do not have the time or the inclination to go into a prolonged reading of United States Supreme Court cases. A case brief acquaints the reader with the case by summarizing its facts, issues, reasons, and holding. This is done in the interest of brevity, but hopefully not at the expense of accuracy.

A WORD ON LEGAL REFERENCING AND ACCESS TO ORIGINAL CASES

Every case briefed in this book contains a case citation. For those who may need some guidance in understanding case citations, the legal citation used in this book is similar to those used in law books and articles. To illustrate, let us use the following citation: *Gregg v. Georgia*, 428 U.S. 153 (1976). *Gregg v. Georgia* is the case title, 428 refers to the volume where the case starts, U.S. means the United States Reports (the official government publisher of United States Supreme Court cases), 153 refers to the page where the case starts, and 1976 refers to the year the case was decided.

Anyone who wants to read the case of *Gregg v. Georgia* as originally printed may therefore go to any law library, pull out Volume 428 of the United States Reports, then go to page 153, where the case starts. Some Supreme Court decisions are short, while others are very long.

The original decisions of the United States Supreme Court in these cases are readily available on the Internet. To find these cases, go to the Supreme Court's Website at www.supremecourtus.gov and click on "Opinions," then the year of the decision. If more research is desired on a case, perform an Internet search, then choose the U.S. Supreme Court decision from the many results. There will likely be many entries on that case, including the decisions of the lower courts that were appealed and commentaries on the case. Make sure the case is the U.S. Supreme Court decision and not that of the trial court, the court of appeals, or of a state supreme court.

About the Authors

Scott Vollum is an Assistant Professor in the Department of Sociology-Anthropology at the University of Minnesota, Duluth, where he primarily teaches classes on violence, the death penalty, restorative justice, criminological theory, and research methods. He conducts research and writes on a variety of topics related to the death penalty, including attitudes about the death penalty and experiences of those impacted by it (e.g., condemned death row inmates, co-victims of capital murder, and death row exonerees). He also conducts research on and writes about moral disengagement, restorative justice, violence against animals, and crime and justice in popular culture.

Rolando V. del Carmen retired in May 2011 as Distinguished Professor of Criminal Justice (Law) in the College of Criminal Justice, Sam Houston State University. He has authored numerous books and articles in various areas of law related to criminal justice. His book, *Criminal Procedure: Law and Practice*, has been translated into Japanese, Korean, and Chinese and is used extensively in the United States and some Asian countries. He has won all three major awards given by the Academy of Criminal Justice Sciences. He has taught numerous graduate and undergraduate classes in law and has been a mentor and friend to many of his students.

Durant Frantzen is Associate Professor of Criminology in the College of Arts and Sciences at Texas A&M University, San Antonio. His research focuses on offender reentry and recidivism, domestic violence policy, and the death penalty. He teaches courses on forensic psychology, statistics, victimology, and comparative systems in criminal justice.

Claudia San Miguel is an Associate Professor of Criminal Justice within the Department of Public Affairs and Social Research at Texas A&M International University in Laredo, Texas. Her research focuses on the trafficking of women and children, dating violence, domestic violence, and various policing issues. She recently traveled to England, Poland, Sweden, Austria, and Spain to help form collaborative relationships with their antitrafficking task forces. She has also taught courses for the Department of State in Roswell, New Mexico, on global human trafficking at the International Law Enforcement Academy.

Kelly Cheeseman Dial was Associate Professor and Chair of the Criminal Justice Program at Messiah College in Grantham, Pennsylvania. Until her untimely death during the production of this book, her research interests included female offenders, prison deviance, correctional officer stress and job satisfaction, institutional corrections, the death penalty, ethics, and sexually deviant behavior.

Acknowledgments

The authors would like to thank their families, friends, colleagues, and students. The work required to bring this book to fruition quite simply would not have been possible if not for their support and encouragement. We also express gratitude to the staff at Elsevier Publishing, particularly Pam Chester and Ellen Boyne. Pam was an early advocate for the publication of this revised edition and worked with the authors through the early stages of its development. Ellen guided us and provided valuable feedback and assistance through the writing and revision process. We greatly appreciate their insight, guidance, and assistance, without which the third edition of this book would not have happened.

Online Resources

Thank you for selecting Anderson Publishing's *The Death Penalty: Constitutional Issues, Commentaries, and Case Briefs,* Third Edition. To complement the learning experience, we have provided online tools to accompany this edition.

Interactive resources can be accessed for free by registering at: www.routledge.com/cw/vollum

Table of Cases

Note: Page number followed by *b* indicates boxes, *t* indicates tables, and *np* indicates footnotes.

Top Ten Most Significant Death Penalty Cases

10. ***Lockett v. Ohio***, 438 U.S. 586 (1978). Death penalty statutes must allow for consideration of mitigating factors regarding the character or history of a defendant as well as the circumstances of the offense.
9. ***Payne v. Tennessee***, 495 U.S. 149 (1990). Victim impact statements pertaining to characteristics of the victim and the emotional impact of the crime on the victim's family do not violate the Eighth Amendment and are admissible in the sentencing phase of a trial.
8. ***Baze v. Rees***, 553 U.S. 35 (2008). Lethal injection does not violate the Eighth Amendment's prohibition of cruel and unusual punishment and is thus a constitutionally permissible method of execution.
7. ***Lockhart v. McCree***, 476 U.S. 162 (1986). Prospective jurors whose opposition to the death penalty is so strong as to prevent or impair the performance of their duties as jurors at the sentencing phase of a trial may be removed for cause from jury membership.
6. ***McCleskey v. Kemp***, 481 U.S. 279 (1987). A statistical study suggesting racial discrimination in the imposition of death sentences does not make the death penalty unconstitutional. What is needed is that "petitioner must prove that decision-makers in his case acted with discriminatory purpose."
5. ***Ring v. Arizona***, 536 U.S. 584 (2002). "The decision whether or not to execute a defendant must be made by a jury. A judge may not alone make a determination of aggravating circumstances and thus elevate a punishment to death. Such aggravating circumstances are 'the functional equivalent of an element of a greater offense' and therefore must be determined by a jury as required by the Sixth Amendment."
4. ***Atkins v. Virginia***, 536 U.S. 304 (2002). "The execution of mentally retarded defendants is a violation of the Eighth Amendment's prohibition against cruel and unusual punishment."
3. ***Roper v. Simmons***, 543 U.S. 551 (2005). Imposing the death penalty on juveniles who commit crimes at age 16 or 17 constitutes cruel and unusual punishment prohibited by the Eighth Amendment.
2. ***Furman v. Georgia***, 408 U.S. 238 (1972). The death penalty is unconstitutional; it violates the Constitution's equal protection clause and the prohibition against cruel and unusual punishment.
1. ***Gregg v. Georgia***, 428 U.S. 153 (1976). Death penalty statutes that contain sufficient safeguards against arbitrary and capricious imposition are constitutional.

The Death Penalty: Past and Present

1

CHAPTER OUTLINE

I INTRODUCTION

The history of the death penalty in the United States may be divided into two historical periods: the period prior to the 1976 seminal decision in *Gregg v. Georgia* (1976)[1] and the period after *Gregg*. This chronological division, based on the two historical periods of the death penalty, reflects the most significant change made by the Supreme Court regarding the constitutionality of the death penalty. However, to fully appreciate the profoundness of the Court's decision in *Gregg* and to understand why *Gregg* is the point at which to differentiate between the two periods, an analysis of the historical roots of the death penalty must be undertaken.

---

[1]*Gregg v. Georgia*, 428 U.S. 153 (1976).

This chapter first presents a brief overview of the history of the death penalty from colonial times to 1971. Specifically, it first explores the virtual importation of the death penalty from England to the colonies and examines the early justifications for the death penalty. It also discusses early movements to abolish the death penalty that were inherently influenced by the Age of Enlightenment. Parts of this chapter examine the constitutional issues that were important prior to *Gregg*. Additionally, because of the Court's repeated use of the Eighth Amendment's proscription against cruel and unusual punishment in determining the constitutionality of state death penalty sentences, this chapter discusses the high court's early interpretation of the Eighth Amendment. The chapter also briefly explores the Court's decision to use the Eighth Amendment despite the fact that it was not made applicable to the states until 1962.[2] Finally, the chapter also explores the current state of the death penalty. Although it will be covered in more depth later in the book, this chapter provides an overview of recent state decisions to abolish or repeal the death penalty as well as recent Court and circuit court decisions.

II A RETROSPECTIVE ANALYSIS OF THE DEATH PENALTY
A The Colonial Period

The first recorded execution in America occurred in 1608,[3] but the death penalty's formal and legal foundations were not firmly established until later in the seventeenth century, when European settlers formed permanent colonies in the New World after the 1620 s. In colonial America, the penalty of death was typically imposed on those who engaged in crimes such as murder, adultery, bestiality, witchcraft, and blasphemy. Although the colonies' codifications of laws and accompanying penalties differed, most state codes were reflective of religious beliefs, and thus the death penalty was justified on religious grounds. For instance, biblical arguments in favor of the death penalty were evident in the capital laws of the Massachusetts Bay Colony. Strongly influenced by the Mosaic Code of the Old Testament, known for the retributionist doctrine "an eye for an eye," the Bay Colony's 1641 *Body of Liberties* (the penal code) prescribed the penalty of death for violation of 13 laws: idolatry, witchcraft, blasphemy, murder, manslaughter, poisoning, bestiality, sodomy, adultery, man-stealing,[4] false witness in capital cases, conspiracy, and rebellion. Interestingly, the crimes listed in the Body of Liberties were accompanied by their biblical references in the Old Testament.[5]

The harshness that characterized the penal code of the Massachusetts Bay Colony was relatively lenient in comparison to the many crimes (more than 50) punishable by death in England during the same period. In addition, compared to the other colonies such as Virginia, Maryland, Georgia, and Carolina, which imposed the death penalty for crimes committed only by indentured slaves, the Bay Colony's capital laws were quite lax. However, by the eighteenth century, support for the death penalty in all of the colonies grew as immigration to the New World increased substantially and public order was threatened. The death penalty grew almost by necessity because the colonies lacked adequate

---

[2]The Eighth Amendment was incorporated to the states in the 1962 case of *Robinson v. California*, 370 U.S. 666 (1962).
[3]This was the execution of George Kendall, a European colonist who was hanged for the crime of "spying for the Spanish." In Hugo Bedau and Paul Cassell (eds.), Debating the Death Penalty (Oxford: Oxford University Press, Inc., 2004).
[4]Man-stealing is akin to kidnapping.
[5]Bryan Vila and Cynthia Morris (eds.), Capital Punishment in the United States (1997), pp. 8–9.

long-term facilities to incarcerate offenders.[6] Despite such issues, the number of capital crimes increased because of the demands of the English Crown, which had renewed its control over the colonies during this time. The English Crown insisted that the colonies follow its example and revise their penal codes to include 200 crimes punishable by death.

B The Age of Enlightenment and the Early Movement to Abolish the Death Penalty
1 From Europe to the Colonies: The Impact of Enlightenment

While the colonists were struggling to control the massive immigration movement to the New World during the eighteenth century, Europe was at the height of a philosophical and intellectual movement known as the Enlightenment. The Age of Enlightenment, which began a century before, was spurred by the writings of naturalistic philosophers who were instrumental in dispelling spiritualistic or religious notions that human beings were born with fixed or innate personality traits.[7] For example, John Locke, one of the most influential philosophers of the time, articulated the notion of sensationalism, which claimed that humans were shaped not by the spiritual world but rather by their sensory reactions to the external environment. In his book *Two Treatises on Government* (1690), Locke also rejected the idea that government was the creation of God and instead supported the principle that the government derived its authority from the people.[8]

Locke's writings, and those of other philosophers such as Montesquieu and Voltaire, generated great changes in intellectual and philosophical thinking in Europe by introducing the notion that humans had the mental capacity, or the *rationality*, to create a form of government that protected the rights of the people. The writings of these Enlightenment philosophers eventually generated changes in the administration of justice, particularly with regard to the death penalty. Their writings influenced Italian philosopher Cesare Beccaria to advocate for the abolition of the death penalty.[9] Beccaria, who wrote *An Essay On Crimes and Punishment* (1764), believed that a punishment should be proportionate to the crime committed or to the harm that was inflicted on society. He also believed that too severe a penalty, such as death, may provoke an individual to engage in lesser forms of crime simply to avoid capital punishment. Thus, rather than deterring crime, the death penalty, according to Beccaria, may encourage lesser forms of crimes. In addition, he argued that "the death penalty served as an example of barbarity rather than a deterrent to it, because it sanctioned the taking of human life—the very act it was intended to deter."[10] As alternatives to the death penalty, Beccaria proposed incarceration among several humane and proportionate forms of punishment.

In the colonies, the Age of Enlightenment served as an impetus for revolution and independence. Influenced greatly by Locke's notion that a government should be altered or abolished by the people if it was not fulfilling its duty to protect natural rights such as life, liberty, and property, the colonists expressed their displeasure with the English Crown in the Declaration of Independence and subsequently declared war. However, with much concern about the beginning of the Revolutionary War,

---

[6]*Id.*

[7]Mark Lanier and Stuart Henry, ESSENTIAL CRIMINOLOGY (2d ed. 2004).

[8]J.W. Peltason and Sue Davis, UNDERSTANDING THE CONSTITUTION (15th ed. 2000).

[9]Beccaria did believe that the death penalty was useful in some situations, such as when there was a need to protect the security of a nation or government. In Piers Beirne, *Inventing Criminology: The "Science of Man" in Cesare Beccaria's Dei delitti e delle pene.* CRIMINOLOGY, Vol. 29(4):777–820, 1991.

[10]Bryan Vila and Cynthia Morris (eds.), CAPITAL PUNISHMENT IN THE UNITED STATES (1997), p. 16.

other Enlightenment ideals, such as those proposed by Beccaria, did not seep into the colonial main-stream until after the war. It was not until 1779 that Thomas Jefferson first advocated punishments in proportion to crimes committed. Jefferson, who advocated abolishing the death penalty for all crimes except murder and treason, believed that imprisonment might be able to reform offenders. He also opposed the death penalty because executions would greatly decimate the number of able-bodied men who were needed for various laborious tasks. In *A Bill for Proportioning Crimes and Punishment* (1779), he proposed that:

> *capital punishments, which exterminate instead of reforming ... should be the last melancholy resource against those whose existence is become inconsistent with the safety of their fellow citizens ... [capital punishments] also weaken the state by cutting off so many who, if reformed, might be restored sound members of society, who, even under a course of correction, might be rendered useful in various labors for the public, and would be living and long continued spectacles to deter others from committing the like offences.*[11]

Several years after the Articles of Confederation were adopted in 1781, a few states began to slowly abolish the death penalty for certain offenses, such as robbery and rape, but continued to retain executions for offenders who committed murder or treason. Pennsylvania in 1786, for instance, no longer imposed the death penalty for crimes such as burglary, robbery, or sodomy.[12] The first true movement to completely abolish the death penalty, however, was spearheaded by Dr. Benjamin Rush in 1787. Rush, a signer of the Declaration of Independence, urged a reconsideration of the death penalty as well as punishments that were imposed for retributive or vengeful purposes. He declared that "laws which inflict death for murder, are . . . as unchristian as those which justify or tolerate revenge."[13] Because of a belief that jails and other penal facilities of the time were contributing to the corruption of offenders rather than deterring them from committing crime, Rush also argued in favor of the creation of a penal institution that not only incarcerated offenders in solitary cells but also allowed offenders an opportunity for reform through penance. Together with a group of Pennsylvania Quakers, Rush formed the Society for Alleviating the Miseries of Public Prisons in 1787, and in 1790 the first penitentiary was established in Pennsylvania.

2 Changes in the Death Penalty from 1790–1950

The early abolitionist movement pioneered by Rush and the Pennsylvania Quakers prompted several states to modify their death penalty statutes. The first significant change was the introduction of statutes that distinguished first-degree murder from second-degree murder. Although the distinction between first- and second-degree murder was already in practice in England, the state of Pennsylvania in 1793 was the first to make such a distinction by executing only those who committed murder in the first degree. First-degree murder included crimes such as premeditated murder and the killing of a human being during the commission of a felony (arson, burglary, rape, robbery). Conversely, second-degree

---

[11]Thomas Jefferson, *A Bill for Proportioning Crimes and Punishments* (1779). In Bryan Vila and Cynthia Morris (eds.), Capital Punishment in the United States (1997), pp. 16–18.

[12]In Hugo Bedau and Paul Cassell (eds.), Debating the Death Penalty (2004), p. 22.

[13]Benjamin Rush, *An Enquiry into the Effects of Public Punishments Upon Criminals and Upon Society* (1789). In Bryan Vila and Cynthia Morris (eds.), Capital Punishment in the United States (1997), pp. 20–23.

murder, which was punishable by imprisonment, included crimes such as manslaughter or the killing of another without malice or premeditation.[14]

The second significant change in the death penalty was the discontinuance of public executions. As a feature of the death penalty in both England and the colonies, it was customary to execute an offender in public in order to achieve the greatest deterrent effect. However, the gathering of large crowds to witness an execution had the unintended effect of increasing crime. For instance, captivated groups of witnesses were suitable targets for petty thieves who found it convenient and easy to practice their trade. Additionally, executions had the effect of inciting riots and disorder, which not only placed a strain on limited law enforcement resources but also contributed to a growing fear of crime.[15] Although public hangings provided lucrative business opportunities not only for thieves but also for vendors who sold food and tickets for admission, witnesses were susceptible to injuries due to the unsafe conditions of viewing stands. In 1827, "one crowd was so dense at an execution in Cooperstown that several spectators were injured when a viewing stand collapsed."[16] Accordingly, several states found it prudent to execute offenders behind prison walls. The first state to end public executions was New York in 1834, followed by Pennsylvania and New Jersey. By 1845 almost every state had ended public executions.

Eliminating mandatory death sentences was the third significant change. A common feature in the colonies (and later the states) was for the death penalty to be automatically imposed when a defendant was found guilty of first-degree murder. Thus, no state allowed a jury to determine whether the penalty of death was justified. However, in the 1830 s, the abolitionist movement urged a reconsideration of mandatory death sentences. In 1838, Tennessee was the first state to end mandatory death sentences. Tennessee was also the first state to allow a jury the option of imposing the death penalty for a convicted murderer. In the years following the decision made by the state of Tennessee, other states slowly began to abolish mandatory death sentences. By the end of the nineteenth century, 20 additional jurisdictions had eliminated mandatory death sentences.[17]

The fourth significant change in the death penalty was the method used to execute offenders. From England to the first European settlement in the colonies, hanging was the preferred method of execution. Undoubtedly, both in England and the colonies, the popularity of hanging could be attributed to the fact that it was the most inexpensive and easiest way to punish offenders who committed capital crimes.[18] However, hanging was also preferred because of its deterrent effect. The belief was that:

> *Hanging inflicted a signal indignity on the victim in a uniquely conspicuous fashion. It displayed the victim to the onlookers in a most ignominious and abject of postures and would thus be likely to enhance the deterrent effect of his punishment on anyone who might be tempted to do what he had done.[19]*

---

[14]Hugo Adam Bedau, *An Abolitionist Survey of the Death Penalty in America Today*. In Hugo Bedau and Paul Cassell (eds.), DEBATING THE DEATH PENALTY (2004), p. 16.

[15]In Bryan Vila and Cynthia Morris (eds.), CAPITAL PUNISHMENT IN THE UNITED STATES (1997), p. 33.

[16]Deborah W. Denno, *Is Electrocution an Unconstitutional Method of Execution? The Engineering of Death Over the Century*, 35 WM. & MARY L. REV. 551, 564 (1994).

[17]Robert M. Bohm, DEATHQUEST (3d ed. 1993).

[18]Michael C. Cokley, *Whatever Happened to That Old Saying "Thou Shall Not Kill?" : A Plea for the Abolition of the Death Penalty*, 2 LOYOLA J. PUB. INT. L. 67 (Spring 2001).

[19]*Id.* at 83.

In the 1840 s, abolitionists began to campaign for more humane forms of execution. Although they would have favored the complete abolition of the death penalty, many abolitionists were content with modifying torturous and painful deaths, especially when there was evidence that "numerous botched attempts and many cases of lingering death"[20] plagued so many hangings. The first state to look into a more humane form of execution was New York. In 1899, New York, which was also the first state to legally sanction hanging as a method of execution, introduced a new and more humane form of execution: the electric chair. The quest for a painless death eventually led to the use of lethal gas, or the gas chamber, as a form of execution. In 1921, execution by lethal gas became another acceptable form of execution.

In addition to these four significant changes in the death penalty, several other notable events occurred during this time. The Bill of Rights was ratified in 1791, and the Fifth and Eighth Amendments affirmed the colonial practice of executing capital offenders. In 1847, prior to the U.S. Civil War, Michigan became the first state to abolish the death penalty for all crimes except the crime of treason. In 1852, Rhode Island outlawed capital punishment for all crimes, including treason, and in 1853 Wisconsin followed the example set by Rhode Island. In the mid-nineteenth century, the abolitionist movement that was started by Benjamin Rush had diminished in support due to preoccupation with the Civil War. However, after the Civil War, the abolition movement again gained momentum. Between 1907 and 1917 six states (Kansas, 1907; Minnesota, 1911; Washington, 1913; Oregon, 1914; South Dakota, 1915; Missouri, 1917)[21] completely abolished the death penalty, and three other states (Tennessee, 1915; North Dakota, 1915; Arizona, 1916) modified their statutes to limit executions to offenders who committed either treason or the killing of a law enforcement officer or prison official. The beginning of World War I and intensified fears about the emerging war caused five out of the six states that had previously abolished the death penalty to reinstate it by 1920. From 1920 to 1940, the death penalty received unprecedented support. In the 1930s, more offenders were executed than in any other decade in U.S. history—an average of 167 deaths per year.[22]

III **EARLY SUPREME COURT DECISIONS ON THE DEATH PENALTY**

The Bill of Rights has not been found to prohibit the practice of executing offenders found guilty of capital offenses, except for during a brief period from 1972 to 1976 as a result of the *Furman v. Georgia* (1972)[23] decision. The Bill of Rights, principally the Fifth Amendment, apparently permits the use of the death penalty as long as "no person shall be held to answer for a capital or otherwise infamous crime, unless on a presentment or indictment of a Grand Jury" and as long as no person is "deprived of life, liberty, or property without due process of law." The Eighth Amendment does not clearly bar the use of the death penalty per se but only prohibits the imposition of cruel and unusual punishments. Because both the Fifth and Eighth Amendments do not expressly prohibit the use of the death penalty, legal scholars contend that the inclusion of these two amendments in the Bill of Rights was necessary to

---

[20]*Id.* at 86.
[21]Robert M. Bohm, DEATHQUEST (3d ed. 1993).
[22]Death Penalty Information Center, *History of the Death Penalty*, September 20, 2004, pg. 5. Available at: www.deathpenaltyinfo.org/article.php?scid=15&did=410#Earlyand-Mid-TwentiethCentury.
[23]*Furman v. Georgia*, 408 U.S. 153 (1972).

prevent judicial arbitrariness in imposing the death penalty—a common practice in England before and during the time of the writing of the Constitution.

Because the death penalty was an acceptable form of punishment, there was little need for the Supreme Court to address the issue of its constitutionality. Thus, the Supreme Court refrained from making any declarations regarding the constitutionality of the death penalty until 1878. When the Supreme Court finally broke its silence, its decisions reinforced prevailing concepts that the death penalty was constitutional. These early decisions included interpretations of the Eighth Amendment's prohibition against cruel and unusual punishments and marked the beginning of a long series of cases addressing legal issues involving the death penalty.

A *Wilkerson v. Utah:* **Death by Firing Squad**

The first death penalty case ever to be decided by the Supreme Court was *Wilkerson v. Utah* (1878).[24] In *Wilkerson*, the issue before the Court was not the constitutionality of the death penalty per se but rather its method of execution—in this case, death by firing squad. Although executions by firing squad were common under military law,[25] Utah was the first territory in the United States to include this method of execution in its death penalty statute. Since 1851, prior to Utah becoming a state, the General Assembly of the territory of Utah had decreed that "when a person shall be found guilty of murder . . . and sentenced to die, he, she or they shall suffer death by being shot, hung, or beheaded."[26] The inclusion of three forms of execution was distinctive for its time because most of the other states preferred to execute offenders only by hanging. Although Utah resorted to hanging convicted murderers, the first execution by firing squad was not carried out until 1861. By the time Utah became a state in 1896, it had executed 14 offenders, 11 of whom were executed by firing squad.

When Wallace Wilkerson was convicted of a capital offense (premeditated murder) and sentenced by the court to be executed by firing squad, Utah had not yet been granted statehood. Moreover, when Wilkerson was sentenced to be executed, Utah had repealed the law that had allowed for three forms of execution. In 1876, Utah repealed the section of its death penalty statute that offered three methods of execution, and the newly adopted statute did not provide any guidance as to which specific method of execution should be imposed on those found guilty of capital offenses. However, the new statute included a provision that authorized the court to decide such issues. Convinced that the repeal of the law prevented Utah from using a firing squad to execute him, Wilkerson petitioned the Court to overturn his sentence, arguing that death by firing squad violated the Eighth Amendment's cruel and unusual punishment clause. The Court disagreed and ruled that "in view of the fact that the laws of the Territory contain no other specific regulation as the mode of executing such a sentence, the court here is of the opinion that the assignment [of death by firing squad] . . . is no grounds for reversal of the judgment of the court below."[27] The Court noted that because executions by firing squad were common practice in the territory of Utah, there was nothing unusual about Wilkerson's sentence.

---

[24]*Wilkerson v. Utah*, 99 U.S. 130 (1878).
[25]Michael C. Cokley, *Whatever Happened to That Old Saying "Thou Shall Not Kill?" : A Plea for the Abolition of the Death Penalty*, 2 LOYOLA J. PUB. INT. L. 67 (Spring 2001).
[26]Christopher Q. Cutler, *Nothing Less Than the Dignity of Man: Evolving Standards, Botched Executions and Utah's Controversial Use of the Firing Squad*, 50 CLEVE. ST. L. REV. 335, 340 (2002–2003).
[27]*Wilkerson v. Utah*, 99 U.S. 130, 131 (1878).

The Court's decision to uphold the use of a firing squad to execute capital offenders was significant because it marked the beginning of the high court's death penalty jurisprudence. Although the decision was expected in light of the overwhelming support for the death penalty, the Court's use and interpretation of the Eighth Amendment was interesting. Historically, the Eighth Amendment only applied to federal sentencing practices, because the Bill of Rights was initially introduced for the sole purpose of curtailing the power of the federal government but not the power of the states. Consequently, the states at the time of the *Wilkerson* decision were not bound by the first 10 amendments to the Constitution. The applicability of the provisions of the Bill of Rights to the states was not an issue until after the ratification of the Fourteenth Amendment in 1868, which holds that "no state shall make or enforce any law which shall abridge the privileges and immunities of citizens of the United States; nor shall any state deprive any person of life, liberty, or property without due process of law; nor shall deny to any person within the jurisdiction, the equal protection of the laws." In the 1920s the Court approved the applicability of some of the provisions of the Bill of Rights to the states and did so by carefully selecting which amendments to incorporate. It was not until 1962 that the Eighth Amendment was held binding on the states via the Fourteenth Amendment's due process clause.

Because the Eighth Amendment was not applicable to the states until 1962, *Wilkerson* represented a unique legal paradox because the Court opined that the amendment's prohibition against cruel and unusual punishment applied to the states and even to territories of the United States. The Court declared that although each state and territory "may define offenses and prescribe the punishment of offenders," all states and territories were "subject to the prohibition of the Constitution that cruel and unusual punishments shall not be inflicted [emphasis added]."[28] The Court also stated, however, that "cruel and unusual punishments are forbidden by the Constitution, but . . . the punishment of shooting as a mode of executing the death penalty for the crime of murder in the first degree is not included in that category, within the meaning of the Eighth Amendment."[29] By 1890, the Court reconsidered its rationale of using the Eighth Amendment in death penalty cases.

B *In re Kemmler:* Death by Electrocution

In 1890, the Court addressed the constitutionality of using electrical current to execute capital offenders in *In re Kemmler* (1890).[30] Unlike its decision in *Wilkerson*, the Court in *Kemmler* explicitly said that the Eighth Amendment was not applicable to the states. The Court therefore did not use the Eighth Amendment (cruel and unusual punishment) but instead used the Fourteenth Amendment (due process clause) to uphold the constitutionality of using the electric chair. The Court ruled that the amendment "was not designed to interfere with the power of the state to protect the lives, liberties, and property of its citizens, and to promote their health, peace, morals, education and good order."[31] Therefore, the Court held that the state of New York did not violate Kemmler's due process rights under the Fourteenth Amendment when it sentenced him to die by electrocution, because it was merely preserving the lives of other citizens.

---

[28]*Id.*
[29]*Id.*
[30]*In re Kemmler*, 136 U.S. 436 (1890).
[31]*Id.*

The constitutionality of using electrocution as a method of execution in *Kemmler* was challenged as a violation of the due process clause of the Fourteenth Amendment. But when Kemmler first appealed his death sentence, the legal issue used in state court was not the due process clause. Instead, it was the cruel and unusual punishment clause of the Eighth Amendment and a similar provision in the New York constitution. A change in legal strategy was employed after unsuccessfully trying to prove that electrocution was a form of cruel and unusual punishment under both the U.S. Constitution and the state's constitution.

Kemmler's difficulty in proving that electrocution was a form of cruel and unusual punishment may have been partly attributable to several reasons. First, at the time of his death sentence, electrocution was believed to be the most humane way to execute capital offenders. Electrocution as a method of execution was instituted by New York in 1888 when it adopted the Electrocution Act to overcome the cruelty and inhumanity of executing capital offenders through hanging. Several years prior to the formal adoption of the electric chair, the governor of New York argued before the legislature that "the present mode of executing criminals by hanging has come down to us from the dark ages, and it may well be questioned whether the science of the present day cannot provide a means for taking the life of such as are condemned to die in a less barbarous manner."[32]

Other reasons for Kemmler's failure to prove that electrocution was cruel and unusual may have been the politics and financial forces in New York at the time of Kemmler's first appeals. When Kemmler appealed his death sentence, a battle had intensified over the appropriate electrical current (AC, alternating current, or DC, direct current) to use in bringing about the death of a convicted capital offender. Direct current was discovered by Thomas Edison in 1880 and used for the first time to provide electricity for a small residential area in New York. The current, although considered safe, was deemed to be limited in its capacity to provide electricity to the entire city of New York. Experimentations in alternating current, performed by George Westinghouse, began in 1884. With a lower cost to consumers, alternating current was gaining popularity over direct current.[33] Alternating current was also more powerful in that it was capable of providing more electricity to the entire city.

When debates ensued about which current to use in electrocutions, direct current was disfavored because it was believed to lack the potency needed to bring about instantaneous death. Because alternating current was more powerful, it was chosen as the appropriate current for use in electrocutions. However, "compelling evidence suggests that the commission's ultimate recommendation of electrocution as the most humane method of effecting death was influenced heavily by the financial competition between Thomas Edison and George Westinghouse concerning whose current would dominate the electrical industry."[34] Alternating current's cost-effectiveness and its powerful ability to provide electricity to the city may have swayed the commission's decision.

A more significant reason Kemmler did not succeed in overturning his death sentence was the state judiciary's refusal to invalidate a state law. Kemmler lost his legal battle primarily because he failed to meet the stringent burden of proof that the Electrocution Act was unconstitutional. In his first appeal,

---

[32]Deborah W. Denno, *Is Electrocution an Unconstitutional Method of Execution? The Engineering of Death Over the Century*, 35 WM. & MARY L. REV. 551, 566 (1994).

[33]*Id.*

[34]Deborah W. Denno, *Lethally Humane? The Evolution of Execution Methods in the United States.* In James R. Acker, Robert M. Bohm, and Charles S. Lanier (eds.), AMERICA'S EXPERIMENT WITH CAPITAL PUNISHMENT: REFLECTIONS OF THE PAST, PRESENT, AND FUTURE OF THE ULTIMATE PENAL SANCTION (2003), pp. 693–762.

the county court was unconvinced that Kemmler had proven beyond a reasonable doubt that alternating current was a form of cruel and unusual punishment, and thus the court preserved the constitutionality of the Act. The Court further emphasized that:

> *(1) every legislative act is presumed to be constitutional; (2) in a doubtful case, no act should be annulled by the judiciary since mere conflict of interpretation between the legislative and judicial powers is not a sufficient basis for determining that the legislature had erred; and (3) a single judge should declare a law to be invalid on constitutional grounds only when his duty to do so is entirely clear.*[35]

The court also noted that the Eighth Amendment was not applicable to the states. In fact, it stated that "the Eighth Amendment did not refer to punishments provided in state courts for crimes against the State, but was addressed solely to the national government, as a constraint on its power."[36] The court further noted that "it had no duty to attempt to interpret any accurate and comprehensive definition"[37] of the cruel and unusual punishment clause of the Eighth Amendment. Thus, relying on the state's constitutional provision against cruel and unusual punishment as a guide, the court concluded that electrocution was not cruel or unusual and that "electricity would produce immediate and painless death, thereby preventing the unsightly and horrifying spectacles which now not infrequently attend executions by hanging."[38]

In a subsequent appeal to the New York Supreme Court, Kemmler faced similar obstacles. The court concluded that Kemmler had not met the burden of proving beyond a reasonable doubt that electrocution would be a cruel form of punishment. The court refrained from casting doubt on the constitutionality of the Electrocution Act, thus refusing to invalidate an act by the state legislature. The court said that "nothing in the Constitution or in the nature of things suggested that the court's judgment was superior to the legislature's in determining a mere question of fact involved in legislation."[39] Because the New York Court of Appeals affirmed the decision of the New York Supreme Court, Kemmler appealed to the United States Supreme Court, but the Court did not overturn his death sentence.

C *Louisiana ex rel. Francis v. Resweber:* **The Constitutionality of Being Executed Twice**

In 1947, the Court was presented with another case regarding the method of execution of a capital offender: Willie Francis.[40] Francis, who was convicted of murder and sentenced to death by electrocution in the state of Louisiana, was seated in the electric chair waiting to be executed. However, because of a mechanical malfunction, the electric current was not strong enough to cause his death. He was returned to prison and a new death warrant was issued by the governor. In his appeal to the Louisiana Supreme Court, Francis contended that a second attempt to execute him would violate the cruel and unusual punishment clause of the Eighth Amendment as well as the double jeopardy clause of the Fifth Amendment.

---

[35]Deborah W. Denno, *Is Electrocution an Unconstitutional Method of Execution? The Engineering of Death Over the Century*, 35 Wm. & Mary L. Rev. 551, 584 (1994).
[36]*Id.* at 581.
[37]*Id.* at 583.
[38]*Id.* at 582.
[39]*Id.* at 587.
[40]*Louisiana ex rel. Francis v. Resweber*, 329 U.S. 459 (1947).

The Louisiana Supreme Court denied his appeal, primarily holding that no current of sufficient intensity to cause death had passed through to Francis's body, and therefore no pain was inflicted.

On appeal, the Supreme Court was asked to determine whether the state of Louisiana could legally execute Francis after the electric chair had malfunctioned. The Court answered yes, saying that the second attempt to execute Francis would not violate the cruel and unusual punishment clause of the Eighth Amendment because "the fact that the petitioner has already been subjected to a current of electricity does not make his subsequent execution any more cruel in the constitutional sense than any other execution."[41] The Court also stated that the Eighth Amendment only prohibits the "infliction of unnecessary pain," not simply pain suffered as a result of an "unforeseeable accident."[42] The Fifth Amendment affirms that "no person shall be subject for the same offense to be twice put in jeopardy of life or limb," but the Court held that "when an accident, with no suggestion of malevolence, prevents the consummation of a sentence, the state's subsequent course in the administration of its criminal law is not affected on that account by any requirement of due process."[43]

The holding that a second attempt to execute Francis would not violate the Eighth or Fifth Amendments was supported by only four justices of the Court and therefore was a plurality decision. Justice Frankfurter, who wrote a concurring opinion, disagreed with the Court but only with respect to its use of the Eighth Amendment. Justice Frankfurter argued that when the Fourteenth Amendment was ratified, it was not meant to disrupt state criminal justice systems. Although the amendment prohibited states from infringing on the "privileges and immunities of citizens" and constrained them by affirming that no state "shall deprive any person of life, liberty, or property, without due process of law . . .," Justice Frankfurter opined that the amendment did not place any restraints upon the states in the formulation or administration of their criminal law. Thus, the states were "free to carry out their own notions of criminal justice . . . unless in doing so offends some principles of justice so rooted in the traditions and conscience of our people as to be ranked fundamental."[44] Justice Frankfurter concluded by saying that because the first attempt to execute Francis did not cause his death and because such accident was unforeseeable, there was no miscarriage of justice grave enough to violate the Eighth Amendment.

The four dissenting justices said that the Court should have barred the state of Louisiana from executing Francis and should have required the state to conduct an investigation of the electrical current and voltage that was used during the first failed attempt at electrocution. However, they also said that to allow Francis to be subjected to a second electrocution, regardless of whether the first attempt was an accident or due to mechanical failure, would violate the due process clause of the Fourteenth Amendment and the cruel and unusual clause of the Eighth Amendment. Thus, according to the dissent, the Eighth Amendment applied to the states regardless of the original applicability of the Bill of Rights, because subjecting a person to electric shocks in intervals of several days "shocks the most fundamental instincts of civilized man."[45] The justices added that it was the duty of state officials to ensure that the current used to electrocute capital offenders was of sufficient intensity to cause a painless and instantaneous death. Because such precautions were not taken, Francis's death sentence should have been overturned.

---

[41]*Id.* at 463.
[42]*Id.*
[43]*Id.*
[44]*Id.* at 469.
[45]*Id.* at 473.

D Additional Changes in the Death Penalty Prior to 1972

Before the ruling in *Francis*, the Court had criticized the imposition of the death penalty in the case of *Powell v. Alabama* (1932).[46] Although the case was mainly decided on the issue of ineffective counsel (Sixth Amendment), the Court overturned the death sentences of seven black youths who were charged with the rapes of two white girls. The youths, who became known as the "Scottsboro Boys" due to the location of their arrest, were poor and illiterate. Arraigned the same day as their arrest, the youths were never told of their right to have appointed or retained counsel for their defense and were eventually given counsel on the day of their separate trials. Because of such flagrant violations of the Sixth Amendment, the Court ruled that "a defendant should be afforded a fair opportunity to secure counsel of his own choice. Not only was that not done here, but such designation of counsel as was attempted was either so indefinite or so close upon trial as to amount to a denial of effective and substantial aid in that regard."[47]

In *Patton v. Mississippi* (1947),[48] the Court was asked to determine the constitutionality of eliminating capital jurors solely on the basis of their race. The Court ruled that it was unconstitutional to systematically exclude blacks from trial juries. Specifically, the Court stated, "when a jury selection plan, whatever it is, operates in such way as always to result in the complete and long-continued exclusion of any representative at all from a large group of negroes, or any other racial group, indictments and verdicts returned against them by juries thus selected cannot stand."[49] In 1968, the Court was presented with another issue regarding jurors in death penalty cases. In *Witherspoon v. Illinois* (1968),[50] William Witherspoon had been sentenced to death for the murder of a police officer. He appealed his conviction and subsequent death sentence, stating that an Illinois law that allowed the prosecution to exclude all jurors who were opposed to or had mere reservations about the death penalty violated his Sixth Amendment right to a fair trial. The Court agreed and ruled that when a state excluded "from the jury all who expressed conscientious or religious scruples against capital punishment and all who opposed it in principle, the state crossed the line of neutrality. In its quest for a jury capable of imposing death, the state produced a jury uncommonly willing to condemn a man to die."[51]

Five years prior to *Gregg v. Georgia* (1976),[52] the Court issued rulings with regard to capital jurors in two cases: *McGautha v. California* (1971)[53] and *Crampton v. Ohio* (1971).[54] In both cases, defendants petitioned the Court for a reversal of their death sentences on grounds that jurors were given absolute or unguided discretion in deciding whether to impose the death penalty or a life sentence and that such unguided discretion violated the due process clause of the Fourteenth Amendment. An additional issue was raised in *Crampton*—the use of unitary trial, in which jurors decided both guilt and punishment during the same criminal proceeding. In a 6-to-3 decision, the Court ruled that

---

[46]*Powell v. Alabama*, 287 U.S. 45 (1932).

[47]*Id.* at 53.

[48]*Patton v. Mississippi*, 332 U.S. 463 (1947).

[49]*Id.* at 469.

[50]*Witherspoon v. Illinois*, 391 U.S. 510 (1968).

[51]*Id.* at 521.

[52]*Gregg v. Georgia*, 428 U.S. 153 (1976).

[53]*McGautha v. California*, 402 U.S. 183 (1971).

[54]*Crampton v. Ohio*, 402 U.S. 183 (1971).

"the absence of standards to guide the jury's discretion on the punishment issue is constitutionally tolerable."[55] With respect to a unitary trial, the Court did not find it to be unconstitutional.

IV THE CURRENT STATUS OF THE DEATH PENALTY IN THE UNITED STATES
A Retentionist versus Abolitionist States

There are 32 states plus the federal government that retain the statutory right to impose a penalty of death, whereas 18 states have abolished this ultimate penalty.[56] Among the abolitionist states, five repealed their death penalty statutes in the past six years: New Jersey (in 2007), New Mexico (in 2009), Illinois (in 2011), Connecticut (in 2012), and Maryland (in 2013).[57] Additionally, the state of New York, whose appellate court ruled their death penalty statute unconstitutional, has not taken any action to revise and/or restore the death penalty. This has essentially established de facto abolition in the state. In recent years, there has also been more legislative activity with respect to repealing the death penalty. In 2012, California's Proposition 34 (also called The SAFE California Act), for instance, called for a repeal of the death penalty statute in favor of life imprisonment without the possibility of parole. By a narrow margin (52% voting against the repeal), voters opted to retain the death penalty. However, California has not executed an individual sentenced to death since 2006, primarily because the judicial branch, including a federal judge and several state judges, has ruled the three-drug lethal injection protocol cruel and unusual. With 736 inmates on death row, a state-wide moratorium, and a public that supports the death penalty, California is now exploring a single-drug option. The needed state-level approvals for a new drug protocol, however, coupled with drug manufacturers' reluctance to sell their pharmaceutical remedy for the purpose of a state-imposed execution, mean that California's moratorium will likely continue for some time.

California is not the only state rethinking the death penalty. In 2012, senators in 10 of the retentionist states proposed bills to abolish the death penalty while five senators in the abolitionist states put forward legislation to restore the penalty; none of these bills passed. Other states, such as South Carolina, recommended an expansion to their death penalty statutes for the inclusion of murder in the course of a home invasion. Yet in 2012 there were additional states, such as Ohio, Pennsylvania, and Kentucky, that considered bills to study the death penalty. Ohio, for instance, proposed to establish a blue-ribbon commission to review all aspects of the death penalty. The proposal for a blue-ribbon commission is not surprising in light of Ohio's troubles. The state has been under attack since 2007 when the American Bar Association (ABA) found serious deficiencies in its administration of the death penalty. Among some of the concerns cited by the ABA were instances of racial and geographic disparities in imposing the penalty. Ohio's predicament continues, and thus it has been exploring various avenues of reform. To guard against bias, the latest proposal would authorize a panel (consisting of former prosecutors) to decide whether to charge an individual with a capital offense. This would essentially disarm local prosecutors, restrict their discretion in death penalty cases, and empower an impartial panel to make

---

[55]*Id.* at 196.
[56]Death Penalty Information Center, *States With and Without the Death Penalty*, August 8, 2013. Available at: www.deathpenaltyinfo.org/states-and-without-death-penalty.
[57]Id.

a determination on whether to seek the death penalty. Several legal scholars also propose a similar scheme for all retentionist states whereby the state would empanel a group of prosecutors, defense attorneys, and judges who would be solely responsible for determining the appropriateness of imposing capital murder charges on a defendant.[58] They argue that this would curtail racial disparities and the disproportionate distribution of the death penalty among counties in one particular state. Texas, for instance, has 254 counties, yet only a fraction of those counties seek the death penalty.

In 2013, there were 13 state proposals to repeal the death penalty, including proposals in Arizona and Texas. Although unlikely to pass, the trend to propose legislation to abolish the death penalty continues. There is also a trend to study the death penalty, including the intersection between race, geography, and victim characteristics. A study conducted in Connecticut the same year it repealed the death penalty indicates that the sentence was overwhelmingly being invoked on minority offenders whose victims were white; "they were three times more likely to receive a death sentence than white defendants whose victims were white."[59] Additional studies in several states have documented similar findings. This has prompted some states to pass legislation, commonly known as Racial Justice Acts, allowing death row inmates the opportunity to appeal their sentence based on findings from studies revealing evidence of racial bias. However, one state (North Carolina) recently repealed its Racial Justice Act.

B A Decline in Death Sentences and Executions

Since the death penalty was reinstated in 1976, there has been a substantial decline in the number of death sentences imposed in the United States. As Figure 1.1 illustrates, death sentences peaked in 1994 (when 328 defendants were sentenced to death) and remained at similar levels for several years, then steadily declined over the last decade and a half. In 2011 and 2012, 76 and 77 death sentences, respectively, were issued across the country, marking the lowest number of new sentences since the reinstatement of the ultimate penalty.[60] Several notable states, such as North Carolina, South Carolina, Virginia, and Indiana, had no new death sentences in 2012. New death sentences were mainly issued in Florida, California, Texas, and Pennsylvania. In looking at individual state data, even the most death-prone counties, such as Harris County in Texas (which includes the city of Houston), had fewer sentences in 2011 and no new death sentences in 2012. Recent research reveals that there is now more pronounced evidence that the penalty of death is actually imposed by a minority of states and, further, by a minority of counties within those states.[61]

Executions have also declined (see Figure 1.2). Although the number of executions in the United States was the same in 2011 and 2012 (43), only 13 states and 12 states, respectively, carried out executions. In 2012, Texas, Oklahoma, Mississippi, and Arizona "were responsible for over three-quarters of the executions in the U.S."[62] When analyzing the data further, we find that 29 states have not held

---

[58]Adam M. Gershowitz, *Statewide Capital Punishment: The Case for Eliminating Counties' Role in the Death Penalty*, 63 VANDERBILT LAW REVIEW 307 (2010).
[59]Death Penalty Information Center, *The Death Penalty in 2012: Year End Report*, August 14, 2013. Available at: http://deathpenaltyinfo.org/YearEnd2012.
[60]Id.
[61]James S. Liebman and Peter Clarke, *Minority Practice, Majority's Burden: The Death Penalty Today*, OHIO STATE JOURNAL OF CRIMINAL LAW, 9 (2011).
[62]Death Penalty Information Center, *The Death Penalty in 2012: Year End Report*, August 14, 2013, pg. 2. Available at: http://deathpenaltyinfo.org/YearEnd2012.

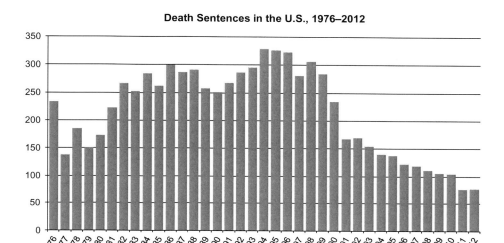

FIGURE 1.1

Trends in Death Sentences in the United States

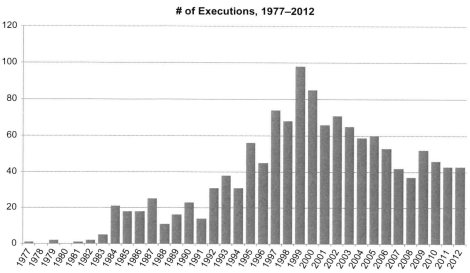

FIGURE 1.2

Trends in Executions in the United States

an execution in the past five years. Additionally, "fewer than 1% of all U.S. counties have carried out 30% of all executions since 1976."[63] As of mid-2013, there were fewer executions than at the same point in 2012.

Legal scholars posit that the decline has occurred for several reasons, including growing awareness of errors and wrongful convictions in capital cases and the increasing use of life sentences without the possibility of parole.[64] As more jurors are becoming cognizant of flaws in the administration of the death penalty, coupled with more awareness that life without the possibility of parole means that offenders would truly spend the rest of their natural lives behind prison walls, they may be less inclined to issue a death sentence. Others, however, argue that the death penalty is becoming a minority practice in the United States: "More than anything else, it is the practices, policies, habits, and political milieu of local prosecutors, jurors, and judges that dictate whether a given defendant in the United States— whatever his crime—will be charged, tried, convicted, and sentenced capitally and executed."[65] Researchers have thus surmised that there is a typology of death penalty states that includes four categories: (1) abolishing states, (2) states that have the death penalty but rarely invoke it, (3) states that frequently impose death sentences but rarely execute them, and (4) states that impose and execute fairly frequently. With more states falling under types 2 and 3 and as fewer counties within those states impose fewer sentences and carry out fewer executions, researchers conclude that the death penalty is a minority practice for which the burden (e.g., cost) is felt by the majority of citizens in a given state. Thus, "notwithstanding broad public and statutory support, the vast bulk of death sentences are imposed on behalf of a small minority of Americans."[66]

With respect to public opinion, which is more comprehensively discussed in Chapter 11, the 2012 American Values Survey captured an almost even split among the populace.[67] Respondents were almost evenly divided between support for the death penalty and support for life without the possibility of parole. A recent Gallup poll found that there was a significant decline in the percentage of individuals who found the death penalty morally acceptable.[68] Does this mean that the death penalty will be abolished? Not necessarily. It means that public perception is slowly changing with respect to the death penalty, but unless the trend of retentionist states repealing the death penalty continues in earnest, the penalty of death will continue to be invoked in the United States.

C Recent Supreme Court and Circuit Court Rulings

The Supreme Court has heard numerous cases related to the death penalty in recent years. Among the most frequent issues before the Court is ineffective assistance of counsel, usually reaching the court via a habeas corpus appeal also invoking the statute of limitations provision contained in the

---

[63]The National Coalition to Abolish the Death Penalty, *National Stats*, August 14, 2013. Available at: www.ncadp.org/map.
[64]William W. Berry, III, *Ending Death By Dangerousness: A Path to the De Facto Abolition of the DeathPenalty*, Arizona Law Review 52 (2010).
[65]James S. Liebman and Peter Clarke, *Minority Practice, Majority's Burden: The Death Penalty Today*, Ohio State Journal of Criminal Law, 9, 262 (2011).
[66]Id at 265.
[67]Death Penalty Information Center, *Public Opinion: American Values Survey Shows Even Split on Death Penalty, with More Catholics Opposed*, August 14, 2013. Available at: www.deathpenaltyinfo.org/public-opinion-american-values-survey-shows-even-split-death-penalty-more-catholics-opposed.
[68]Gallup, *Death Penalty*, August 15, 2013. Available at: www.gallup.com/poll/1606/death-penalty.aspx.

Antiterrorism and Effective Death Penalty Act (AEDPA). In addition to clarifying several provisions of the AEDPA, the Court is recurrently being asked for its opinion on cases related to mental illness/impairment. Although appellate courts hear these issues too, they have been inundated with cases regarding methods of execution. Legal scholars believe it is only a matter of time before the Court is again asked to give its judgment on the constitutionality of lethal injection.[69] While it did so most recently in *Baze v. Rees* (2008), the volume of appeals to circuit courts on this issue would seem to indicate a ruling in the near future. But predicting the Court's actions is difficult and perhaps unwise. Jurisprudence, meaning the course of decisions by the Supreme Court, is complicated and ever changing. Admittedly, changes in direction are attributable to the composition of the Court. In looking at the makeup of the Court today, Chief Justice John Roberts, together with Justices Antonin Scalia, Clarence Thomas, and Samuel Alito, are said to mostly take a conservative approach to issues, including the death penalty. Conversely, Justices Ruth Bader Ginsburg, Stephen Breyer, Sonia Sotomayor, and Elena Kagan are known for a more liberal ideological orientation. Justice Anthony Kennedy tends to serve as the swing vote.[70]

In the death penalty legal arena, the conservative versus more liberal ideological viewpoints of the justices generally translate into disagreement over states' rights to impose a particular sanction including the death penalty. The most conservative justices tend to provide deference to state decisions, whereas the more liberal justices might want to intervene, requiring alterations to the laws that govern the death penalty. But again, although past decisions of justices do give us some indication of their future opinions, it is difficult to predict with any accuracy the Court's future rulings on the death penalty. An overview of the Court's most recent cases appears to indicate that it has, in some areas, taken a hands-on and active approach in defining death penalty jurisprudence while *mostly* remaining respectful of state decisions and respectful of provisions such as the AEDPA. Although not a death penalty case, *Miller v. Alabama* (2012)[71] demonstrates the ideological division of the court. In this case involving a juvenile offender, Justice Kagan, writing the majority opinion and joined by Justices Kennedy, Ginsburg, Breyer, and Sotomayor, opined that imposing a life sentence without the possibility of parole on a juvenile offender would constitute cruel and unusual punishment in violation of the Eighth Amendment. Chief Justice Roberts, Justice Thomas, and Justice Alito formed the dissenting opinions, arguing that the Court should not interfere with a state's decision to impose such a sentence. The latter argued that 29 jurisdictions had this provision in their penal codes and the majority's decision would undermine states' rights to impose particular punishments. Justice Alito said, "When the majority of this Court countermands that democratic decision, what the majority is saying is that members of society must be exposed to the risk that these convicted murderers, if released from custody, will murder again."[72]

One can also attribute the Court's usual deference to state court decisions regarding the death penalty to the language of the AEDPA—restrictive legislation passed in 1996 that not only curtails the number of appeals filed by death row inmates but also instructs appellate courts to overturn state court

---

[69]John Bessler, *Tinkering Around the Edges: The Supreme Court's Death Penalty Jurisprudence*, AMERICAN LAW REVIEW, 2011–2012.

[70]Legal Information Institute, *Supreme Court 2011–2012 Term Highlights*, August 14, 2013. Available at: **www.law.cornell.edu/supct/cert/supreme_court_2011-2012_term_highlights**.

[71]132 S. Ct. 2455 (2012).

[72]Id at 62.

decisions only when there is an unreasonable application of federal law.[73] The AEDPA also sets limits on the time within which defendants can file appeals. However, the Court has recently elaborated on the parameters of the AEDPA and is willing to bend the one-year statute of limitations for filing appeals, but it is not willing to do so in certain situations. For instance, the Court in *Holland v. Florida* (2010)[74] held that extending the statute of limitations was reasonable if the defendant "was pursuing his rights diligently and some extraordinary circumstance stood in his way." Yet in *Tibbals v. Carter* (2012)[75] and *Ryan v. Gonzales* (2012)[76] —two cases involving mental competency during appeals processes— the Court was unwilling to place an indefinite hold on habeas corpus appeals, even when it is alleged that a defendant's mental state precludes him or her from fully communicating with defense attorneys during a habeas corpus appeal. These cases are further discussed in upcoming chapters, but it is important to note that there is incongruence among the federal appellate courts regarding the provisions of the AEDPA. For instance, when interpreting the AEDPA's condition that defendants should be barred from filing second and successive petitions on similar legal grounds, the First, Second, Third, Eighth, Ninth, and Tenth Circuit Courts have consistently rejected a literal interpretation of this rule and instead look at the defendant's intent for filing. Unless it is determined that a defendant is abusing a habeas corpus appeal, the circuit courts will not bar the petition.[77]

Though deconstructing the Court's opinions in recent cases is instructive and sheds light on the current status of the Court's death penalty jurisprudence, perhaps a better insight is gained from the Justices' personal viewpoints captured in public forums or interviews in news outlets. Justice Stephen Breyer, interviewed by a news outlet, indicated that it is not the function of the Supreme Court to decide the constitutionality of the death penalty itself. Rather, the decision regarding the future of the ultimate penalty rests with the states. Despite the fact that he said "only the legislature can abolish the death penalty,"[78] he encouraged state legislative and executive branches to reexamine their use of the death penalty. Justice Ruth Bader Ginsberg, during various speaking engagements, voiced her personal opinion in opposition of the death penalty. Though she admits feeling conflicted when deciding issues of life or death, she is committed to upholding her duties as a Supreme Court Justice.[79] Justice Antonin Scalia, while also committed to his service on the bench, takes a more conservative approach on death penalty issues and favors an original interpretation of the Constitution. He has said, "For me, therefore, the constitutionality of the death penalty is not a difficult, soul–wrenching question. It was clearly permitted when the Eighth Amendment was adopted (not merely for murder, by the way, but for all felonies— including, for example, horse–thieving, as anyone can verify by watching a western movie). And so it is clearly permitted today. There is plenty of room within this system for "evolving standards of decency," but the instrument of evolution (or, if you are more tolerant of the Court's approach, the herald that evolution has occurred) is not the nine lawyers who sit on the Supreme Court of the United States

---

[73]Bryan A. Stevenson, *The Politics of Fear and Death: Successive Problems in Capital Federal Habeas Corpus Cases*, 77 N.Y.U. L. Rev. 699 (2002).

[74]560 US 2549 (2010).

[75]132 S. Ct. 1738 (2012).

[76]133 S. Ct. 696 (2013).

[77]Mark Pavkov, *Does Second Mean Second?: Examining the Split Among Circuit Courts of Appeals in Interpreting AEDPA's Second or Successive Limitations on Habeas Corpus Petitions*, Case Western Reserve Law Review 57, 4, (2007).

[78]Death Penalty Information Center, *Statements on the Death Penalty by Supreme Court Justices*, August 12, 2013. Available at: www.deathpenaltyinfo.org/statements-death-penalty-supreme-court-justices.

[79]Id.

but rather the Congress of the United States and the legislatures of the 50 states, who may, within their own jurisdictions, restrict or abolish the death penalty as they wish.[80]

Thus, the authority to retain or abolish the death penalty currently rests with the states, and although justices may have personal views for or against the ultimate sanction, the Court maintains respect for both the U.S. Constitution and the wishes of state legislatures and state laws.

Federal circuit courts also tend to respect state laws. As the gatekeepers of the Supreme Court, federal circuit courts hear and decide on issues before they reach the highest court in the land. The appeals process is complex and can be quite lengthy for death row inmates, but circuit courts rule over a tremendous number of cases. One issue that has not reached the Supreme Court since *Baze v. Rees* (2008)[81] is the method used to execute capital offenders. However, this issue is widely brought to the attention of appellate courts. Ironically, the *Baze* case opened the door for more challenges to the lethal injection protocol, especially given Justice Stevens's (retired in 2010) concurring opinion. Not only did he question the constitutionality of the death penalty, but Justice Stevens also noted:

> *The question whether a similar three-drug protocol may be used in other States remains open, and may well be answered differently in a future case on the basis of a more complete record. Instead of ending the controversy, I am now convinced that this case will generate debate not only about the constitutionality of the three-drug protocol, and specifically about the justification for the use of the paralytic agent, pancuronium bromide, but also about the justification for the death penalty itself.[82]*

Challenges to lethal injection are varied in their target, ranging from the actual intravenous procedure to the administration of the drugs to monitoring of their effects, and more commonly to the three drugs used in the execution.[83] Until recently, all retentionist states used three drugs to execute capital offenders: an anesthetic, pancuronium bromide (a paralytic agent to prevent involuntary muscle movement), and potassium chloride to stop the inmate's heart.[84] Some death row inmates argue that the concoction would cause excessive pain because the anesthetic would not sedate them enough to buffer the pain of execution.[85] Recent challenges have also focused on the secrecy of some states that withhold information about the exact drugs or protocol used to extinguish life. In Georgia, for instance, the department of corrections did not disclose the drugs it would use to execute Warren Lee Hill. In an appeal, a Georgia Superior Court Judge said, "to be executed without being aware of basic information regarding the protocols the State will use to carry out such an execution is surely an irreparable harm." Louisiana[86] and Florida[87] are also facing challenges regarding the lack of transparency in their lethal injection protocol. In another twist in

---

[80]Id.

[81]553 U.S. 35 (2008).

[82]Id at 17 (dissenting opinion).

[83]Harvey Gee, *Eighth Amendment Challenges After Baze v. Rees: Lethal Injection, Civil Rights Lawsuits, and the Death Penalty*, Boston College Third World Law Journal 31 (2011).

[84]Death Penalty Information Center, Lethal Injection, August 14, 2013. Available at: www.deathpenaltyinfo.org/lethal-injection-moratorium-executions-ends-after-supreme-court-decision.

[85]Id.

[86]Della Hasselle, *State Must Reveal Details of Death-Penalty Practices, Federal Magistrate Rules*, The Lens. Available at: http://thelensnola.org/2013/06/05/state-must-reveal-details-of-death-penalty-practices-federal-judge-rules/.

[87]Death Penalty Information Center, *Lethal Injection: Shortage of Drugs Leaves Texas Unsure About Future Executions*, August 10, 2013. Available at: www.deathpenaltyinfo.org/lethal-injection-shortage-drugs-leaves-texas-unsure-about-future-executions.

the lethal injection debate, the U.S. Court of Appeals for the District of Columbia Circuit ruled that the Food and Drug Administration violated federal law when it allowed the importation of a foreign-made drug without proper inspection. Since some of the supply of lethal drugs is obtained from companies abroad, this ruling does not ease state concerns. Additionally, with states already frenzied over drug manufactures' unwillingness to sell their products for the purposes of a state-sanctioned death and having to find alternative means to execute offenders, this further complicates matters.[88]

V IN SUMMARY, WHAT DO THESE CASES SAY?

Because the death penalty was an acceptable form of punishment during colonial times, jurisprudence on its constitutionality was nonexistent until the late nineteenth century. When the Supreme Court finally entered the arena of debate about the death penalty in 1878, it merely affirmed the public's attitude on this issue. In the few early cases decided by the Court prior to 1972, constitutionality of the death penalty was never an issue. The only issues presented before the high court were methods of execution and the constitutionality of certain procedural rules, such as jury selection. There appeared to be an assumption that the death penalty itself was constitutional.

Of significance in these early cases was the Court's use of the Eighth Amendment's proscription against cruel and unusual punishment, despite the fact that this amendment was not held binding on the states until 1962. Although the states were not bound to follow the mandates of the Eighth Amendment, the Court nonetheless used this amendment to uphold the constitutionality of several methods of execution. For instance, in *Wilkerson*, the Court held that all capital punishments, even those imposed by territories of the United States, must be in accord with the Eighth Amendment. It also held that death by firing squad did not fall within the meaning of "cruelty" as prohibited by the Constitution. In *Kemmler*, the Court hesitated to use the Eighth Amendment and conceded that states were not bound by this federal constitutional amendment. The decision, however, did not prevent the Court from using the Eighth Amendment 57 years later in *Louisiana ex rel. Francis v. Resweber*, when it ruled on the constitutionality of being executed twice. In totality, these cases on the death penalty dealt with methods of execution and demonstrate the degree of respect given to state court decisions as well as to laws enacted by the states.

Prior to the Court's ruling in *Louisiana ex rel. Francis v. Resweber*, the Court issued a surprising ruling in *Powell v. Alabama*. The Court's ruling was unexpected because prior to 1932, the Court's customary position was merely to rubber-stamp capital sentences issued by the states. However, in *Powell* the Court overturned several death sentences on grounds that they violated the Sixth Amendment's right to counsel. In the late 1940s the Court took issue with the systematic and prejudicial exclusion of jurors in *Patton v. Mississippi* and ruled that such practice violated the Constitution. By the late 1960s, the Court resolved issues of unguided discretion, which it had previously supported, and ruled that such discretion violated the due process class of the Fourteenth Amendment. It also ruled that the absence of jury standards in death penalty cases violated the Constitution. These latter cases are significant because they set the stage for the most important rulings issued by the Supreme Court in the cases of *Furman v. Georgia* (1972) and *Gregg v. Georgia* (1976).

---

[88]Id.

Today the Court is active in interpreting issues surrounding the death penalty, but it is mindful of states' right. Although recent cases before the Court pertain to ineffective assistance of counsel, the AEDPA, and mental health issues, it has kept its distance on method of execution cases since its decision in *Baze v. Rees*. But with such a high volume of cases reaching the appellate court level regarding the latter issue, legal scholars believe that it is only a matter of time before we hear from the Court on this issue.

VI CONCLUSION

The history of the death penalty in the United States dates back to the early seventeenth century, a time when European settlers were beginning to establish the first permanent colonies in the New World. The cultural heritage of these first permanent settlers, coupled with the subsequent waves of immigrants from Europe during the 1600 s, influenced the administration of justice in the colonies, including the use of the death penalty. As was customary in Europe, the death penalty in colonial America was imposed for a variety of crimes. Analyses of early colonial criminal codes reveals that the death penalty was imposed for many crimes, including witchcraft, blasphemy, idolatry, poisoning, adultery, and murder. Furthermore, analyses of these early criminal codes reflect that religious doctrine, principally based on the Mosaic Code of the Old Testament, served as the primary justification for imposing the death penalty.

Although the cultural heritage of the first European settlers contributed to the virtual importation of the death penalty to colonial America, the Age of Enlightenment, which began in Europe during the seventeenth century, greatly influenced movements to abolish the death penalty. In addition to serving as the impetus for revolution and independence, the Age of Enlightenment swayed several states to abolish the death penalty for some crimes. It also influenced notable figures such as Thomas Jefferson and Benjamin Rush to advocate for the abolition of the death penalty for all crimes except treason and murder, and for solitary confinement as an alternative to the death penalty. Because of the Age of Enlightenment and the fervor of Rush and other death penalty abolitionists, significant changes in the use of this ultimate sanction occurred. From 1790 to 1950, several states modified their death penalty statutes to: (1) distinguish between first- and second-degree murder; (2) discontinue public executions; (3) eliminate mandatory death sentences; and (4) modify the methods used to execute offenders.

In 1791, when the Bill of Rights was adopted, the framers of the Constitution affirmed the use of the death penalty by establishing procedural safeguards in both the Fifth and Eighth Amendments. The Bill of Rights has not been found to prohibit the practice of executing offenders found guilty of capital offenses, except for a brief period from 1972 to 1976 as a result of the Court's decision in *Furman v. Georgia* (1972).[89] Accordingly, the constitutionality of the death penalty was not a legal matter that required the attention of the Court. In 1879, when the Court first entered the arena of debate about the death penalty, executions, particularly by firing squad, became a constitutionally justifiable form of punishment. The following year, the Court upheld executions by electric chair. In 1932, in *Powell v. Alabama*,[90] the Court was critical of the imposition of the death penalty for seven black youths and for the first time overturned their death sentences because the youths were denied the right

---

[89]*Furman v. Georgia*, 408 U.S. 153 (1972).
[90]*Powell v. Alabama*, 287 U.S. 45 (1932).

to effective counsel. However, the Court did not mandate the abolition of the death penalty. From 1947 to 1971, the Court issued several more rulings on the death penalty but again refrained from debating its constitutionality.

Since the Court's first ruling regarding the death penalty in 1879, the legal landscape of this ultimate penal sanction has changed dramatically. Until very recently, however, one legal aspect of the death penalty that had remained virtually unaltered was the constitutionality of the method used to execute capital offenders. Since *Louisiana ex rel. Francis v. Resweber* (1947),[91] the Court had not heard another case regarding the constitutionality of a method of execution, despite a steady flow of death penalty cases appealed on this basis. But in 2008 the Court considered the constitutionality of lethal injection in the case of *Baze v. Rees*.[92] The Court ruled, however, that the combination of drugs was not violative of the Eighth Amendment's ban on cruel and unusual punishment; thus, lethal injection remains an acceptable form of execution.

Because the Court has in the past refused to hear these types of cases, legal scholars contended that the Court had closed any further arguments regarding the constitutionality of methods of execution. Thus, they opined that it was highly unlikely that the Court would hold unconstitutional any of the existing methods used to execute offenders. Since *Baze v. Rees*, however, more appeals have come forth regarding the methods used to extinguish life. Justice Stevens, in his concurring opinion, predicted a flurry of challenges to lethal injection. Admittedly, he opened the door on the progression of challenges flooding appellate courts. In his opinion, Justice Stevens voiced concern about the justification for the continued use of the death penalty as well as concerns about the use of pancuronium bromide. To him, the paralytic agent served no "therapeutic purpose"[93] and masked the actual pain suffered by inmates. But, he also noted:

> *Although experience demonstrates that imposing that penalty constitutes the pointless and needless extinction of life with only negligible social or public returns, this conclusion does not justify a refusal to respect this Court's precedents upholding the death penalty and establishing a framework for evaluating the constitutionality of particular execution methods, under which petitioners' evidence fails to prove that Kentucky's protocol violates the Eighth Amendment.*[94]

One legal scholar surmises that in light of declining death sentences and executions, the Court will have to decide whether keeping the penalty constitutes cruel and unusual punishment in violation of the Eighth Amendment.[95] Generally, the Court relies on the language of the Eighth Amendment to protect inmates from harmful actions. Yet it has remained silent about abolishing the death penalty—a penalty that is slowly becoming a rarity in the United States. With an almost even split in some public opinion polls regarding the utility of the death penalty and with the increasing frequency of states repealing their death penalty statutes, the time for the Court to reexamine the death penalty may be coming.

---

[91]*Louisiana ex rel. Francis v. Resweber*, 329 U.S. 459 (1947).
[92]*Baze v. Rees*, 553 U.S. 35 (2008).
[93]Id at 3 (Justice Stevens, concurring opinion).
[94]Id at 17 (Justice Stevens, concurring opinion).
[95]John Bessler, *Tinkering Around the Edges: The Supreme Court's Death Penalty Jurisprudence*, 49 Am. Crim. L. Rev. 1913 (2012).

CASES BRIEFED IN CHAPTER 1

Case	Issue	Holding
Wilkerson v. Utah 99 U.S. 130 (1878)	Does the failure to include a specific method of execution prohibit the court from imposing death by firing squad?	The failure to include a specific provision concerning the method of execution does not forbid the court from imposing death by firing squad.
	Is the imposition of death by firing squad in violation of the Eighth Amendment?	The imposition of death by firing squad does not violate the Eighth Amendment.
In re Kemmler 136 U.S. 436 (1890)	Is the Electrocution Act of 1888, which authorizes electrocution as a method of execution, in violation of the due process clause of the Fourteenth Amendment?	Electrocution is not a punishment that is cruel and unusual within the meaning of the due process clause of the Fourteenth Amendment.
Louisiana ex rel. Francis 329 U.S. 459 (1947)	Is carrying out the execution of a criminal after a failed first attempt a violation of the Eight Amendment and the Fifth Amendment?	Carrying out a second execution after a failed first attempt due to mechanical malfunction does not violate the cruel and unusual clause or the double jeopardy clause of the Constitution.

CASE BRIEFS

WILKERSON v. UTAH 99 U.S. 130 (1878)

CAPSULE: The failure to include a specific method of execution in a Utah statute did not bar the court from imposing death by firing squad, nor was this method of execution a violation of the laws of Utah or the Eighth Amendment to the Constitution.

FACTS: Wallace Wilkerson, who was indicted by a grand jury in the territory of Utah for the willful, malicious, and premeditated murder of William Baxter, was tried and convicted of murder in the first degree. The trial judge ordered that Wilkerson be safely confined until December 14 and transferred to "some place within the district . . . to be publicly shot until . . . dead." Since 1851, prior to Utah becoming a state, the General Assembly of the territory of Utah decreed that capital offenders, who were found guilty of murder and sentenced to die, "shall suffer death by being shot, hung, or beheaded." Because Utah had repealed the section of its death penalty statute offering three methods of execution (firing squad, hanging, or beheading) in 1876, Wilkerson petitioned the court on grounds that his particular mode of execution violated the Eighth Amendment's proscription against cruel and unusual punishment.

ISSUES:
1. Does the failure to include a specific method of execution in a Utah statute bar the court from imposing death by firing squad? NO.
2. Is the imposition of death by firing squad a violation of the Eighth Amendment to the U.S. Constitution? NO.

HOLDING:
1. The failure to include a specific statutory provision regarding the mode of execution does not bar a court from imposing death by firing squad because the statute authorized the court to choose the method of execution most fitting for the crime committed.

Continued

WILKERSON v. UTAH 99 U.S. 130 (1878)—cont'd

2. The imposition of death by firing squad did not violate the Eighth Amendment because in the territory of Utah this method of execution was common practice and thus not unusual. Furthermore, death by firing squad is not considered cruel within the meaning of the Eighth Amendment.

REASON: "The law of Utah provided that whenever any person was convicted of a capital offense, he should suffer death by being shot, hanged or beheaded, as the court should direct. This law was repealed by the Code, which provided that every person guilty of murder should suffer death, but did not provide the mode of executing the sentence, but which devolved a duty upon the court authorized to pass sentence for the crimes declared the punishment therein, to determine and impose the punishment prescribed. Construed as that provision must be in connection with the enactment that every person guilty of murder in the first degree shall suffer death, and in view of the fact that the laws of the Territory contain no other specific regulation as to the mode of executing such a sentence, the court here is of the opinion that the assignment of error shows no legal ground for reversing the judgment of the court below."

"The Territories are invested with legislative power which extends to all rightful subjects of legislation not inconsistent with the Constitution and the laws of the United States. By virtue of that power the legislative branch of the Territory may define offenses and prescribe the punishment of offenders, subject to the prohibition of the Constitution that cruel and unusual punishment shall not be inflicted."

"Cruel and unusual punishments are forbidden by the Constitution, but . . . the punishment of shooting as a mode of executing the death penalty for the crime of murder in the first degree is not included in that category, within the meaning of the Eighth Amendment."

CASE SIGNIFICANCE: The significance of this case is twofold. First, this case marks the beginning of the Court's death penalty jurisprudence. Although the Court's decision was not surprising in light of the overwhelming support for the death penalty during the colonial period, this case ended almost a decade of silence by the Court regarding the constitutionality of any matter regarding the death penalty. Second, this case represents a unique judicial problem because at the time the Court issued its ruling, the Eighth Amendment had not yet been incorporated to the states (the Eighth Amendment was not incorporated to the states until 1962 in the case of *Robinson v. California*, 370 U.S. 666), much less to a territory of the United States (Utah did not become a state until 1896). Nonetheless, the Court used this amendment to uphold the constitutionality of death by firing squad. The Court held that although the legislative branch of the territory of Utah may prescribe the specific punishment for offenders, such punishment must be in accord with the mandate of the cruel and unusual punishment clause of the Eighth Amendment. However, because Utah had originally used death by firing squad, in addition to hanging and beheading, to execute capital offenders, the Court held that the imposition of death by firing squad was not an unusual form of punishment.

IN RE KEMMLER 136 U.S. 436 (1890)

CAPSULE: The Electrocution Act of 1888, which prescribed the use of electrical current (electric chair) to execute a capital offender, did not violate the due process clause of the Fourteenth Amendment.

FACTS: In 1889, William Kemmler was tried and convicted of the murder of his mistress in the state of New York. Rather than being sentenced to die by hanging, Kemmler was sentenced to die by electrocution—the prescribed method of execution under the recently enacted Electrocution Act of 1888. On appeal to the county court, Kemmler then petitioned to have his death sentence overturned on grounds that the method of execution violated the Eighth Amendment's proscription against cruel and unusual punishment and also violated New York law banning similar punishments. The county court, which held an evidentiary hearing to determine the constitutionality of the Electrocution Act, ruled that Kemmler failed to prove beyond a reasonable doubt that the act was unconstitutional.

IN RE KEMMLER 136 U.S. 436 (1890)—cont'd

Based on testimonial evidence that electrocution was a reliable method of execution as well as a method that would cause instantaneous and painless death, the court concluded that electrocution was not violative of state constitutional law barring cruel and unusual punishment. Because the Eighth Amendment was not applicable to the states, the court refrained from issuing a ruling in this regard.

Kemmler appealed to both the Supreme Court of New York and the New York Court of Appeals, but the appeals failed. Because the appellate courts had both ruled that the Electrocution Act did not violate either the cruel and unusual punishment clause of the Eighth Amendment or state law, Kemmler changed his legal strategy and filed a petition with the Court saying that the act violated the due process clause of the Fourteenth Amendment.

ISSUE: Does the Electrocution Act of 1888, which authorizes electrocution as a method of execution, violate the due process clause of the Fourteenth Amendment? NO.

HOLDING: Electrocution is not a punishment that is cruel and unusual within the meaning of the due process clause of the Fourteenth Amendment because it is neither inhumane nor barbarous, nor does it involve torture or lingering death. Electrocution does not "involve more than the mere extinguishment of life."

REASON: "Section 5 of article 1 of the Constitution of the State of New York provides that excessive bail shall not be required, nor excessive fines imposed, nor shall cruel and unusual punishments be inflicted, nor shall witnesses be unreasonably detained. The Eighth Amendment to the Federal Constitution reads: excessive bail shall not be required, nor excessive fines imposed, nor cruel and unusual punishments inflicted. By the Fourteenth Amendment it is provided that: all persons born or naturalized in the United States, and subject to the jurisdiction thereof, are citizens of the United States and of the State wherein they reside. No state shall make or enforce any law which shall abridge the privileges or immunities of citizens ... nor shall any state deprive any person of life, liberty or property without due process of law ... The enactment of this statute [the Electrocution Act] was in itself within the legitimate sphere of the legislative power of the state, and in the observance of those general rules prescribed by our systems of jurisprudence; and the legislature of New York determined that it did not inflict cruel and unusual punishment and its courts have sustained that determination. We cannot perceive that the state has thereby abridged the privileges or immunities of the petitioner, nor deprived him of due process of law."

"Punishments are cruel when they involve torture or lingering death; but the punishment of death is not cruel within the meaning of that word as used in the Constitution. It implies there is something inhumane and barbarous, something more than the mere extinguishment of life. Electrocution did not involve more than the mere extinguishment of life."

CASE SIGNIFICANCE: This case is significant for several reasons. First, unlike the ruling in *Wilkerson v. Utah*, the Court specifically stated that the cruel and unusual punishment clause of the Eighth Amendment was not applicable to the states. Second, and more important, this case is significant because it demonstrated the deference afforded to the legislative branch and subsequently to statutory laws. Every law is presumed to be constitutional on its face. Thus, petitioners challenging the constitutionality of any law, such as the Electrocution Act of 1888, must prove that the law is unconstitutional by presenting evidence to that effect. At the time of Kemmler's appeals, the required burden of proof was reasonable doubt. Therefore, Kemmler needed to prove beyond a reasonable doubt that the Act was unconstitutional. However, because the state of New York passed the Electrocution Act specifically to end torturous deaths and cruelty, Kemmler had a difficult time proving that the act was unconstitutional. In addition, Kemmler faced a difficult burden because there was overwhelming support for the notion that electrocution was a more humane form of punishment. As noted by the Supreme Court of New York, "It is within easy reach of electrical science at this day to so generate and apply to the person of the convict a current of electricity of such known and sufficient force as certainly to produce instantaneous, and therefore painless death." This sentiment was echoed by every court that heard Kemmler's appeal, including the Supreme Court, which held that unless a punishment involves torture or lingering death, it will not be deemed a violation of the Constitution. Electrocution as a method of execution remained unchallenged for 56 years, despite the fact that Kemmler's death was not instantaneous.

LOUISIANA ex rel. FRANCIS v. RESWEBER 329 U.S. 459 (1947)

CAPSULE: Carrying out a second execution after a failed first attempt due to mechanical malfunction does not violate the cruel and unusual punishment clause or the double jeopardy clause of the Constitution.

FACTS: Francis was convicted of murder and in 1945 was sentenced to death. Pursuant to a proper death warrant, Francis was placed in the official electric chair of the State of Louisiana and received through his body a current of electricity intended to cause death. The execution attempt failed due to a mechanical defect in the electric chair. Francis was removed from the chair and returned to prison. A new death warrant was issued.

ISSUE: Is carrying out the execution of a criminal after a failed first attempt a violation of the Eighth and Fifth Amendments to the Constitution? NO.

HOLDING: Carrying out a second execution of a convicted person after the first execution attempt failed because of a mechanical defect in the electric chair does not constitute double jeopardy, nor does it constitute cruel and unusual punishment, and therefore is not forbidden by the Constitution.

REASON: "Petitioner's suggestion is that because he once underwent the psychological strain of preparation for electrocution, now to require him to undergo this preparation again subjects him to lingering or cruel and unusual punishment. Even the fact that petitioner has already been subjected to a current of electricity does not make his subsequent execution any more cruel in the constitutional sense than any other execution. The cruelty against which the Constitution protects a convicted man is cruelty inherent in the method of punishment, not necessary suffering involved in any method employed to extinguish life humanely. The fact that an unforeseeable accident prevented the prompt consummation of the sentence cannot, it seems to us, add an element of cruelty to a subsequent execution.

"We cannot agree that the hardship imposed upon the petitioner rises to that level of hardship denounced as denial of due process because of cruelty."

CASE SIGNIFICANCE: In this case, the defendant was placed in the electric chair and received a current of electricity intended to cause death, but due to a mechanical defect in the electric chair, death did not occur. He was returned to prison and given a new execution date. The defendant claimed that carrying out a second execution after a failed first attempt violated his constitutional protection from double jeopardy and cruel and unusual punishment.

The Court rejected both objections, holding that "when an accident, with no suggestion of malevolence, prevents the consummation of a sentence, the state's subsequent course in the administration of its criminal law is not affected on that account by any requirement of due process . . ." As for the allegation of cruel and unusual punishment, the Court did not find the second attempt at execution as constituting a violation of this constitutional protection, saying that "even the fact that the petitioner has already been subjected to a current of electricity does not make his subsequent execution any more cruel in the constitutional sense than any other execution." The Court added that "the cruelty against which the Constitution protects a convicted man is cruelty inherent in the method of punishment, not the necessary suffering involved in any method employed to extinguish life humanely." In sum, the Court said that the taking of life itself does not constitute cruel and unusual punishment; what is prohibited instead is the method of punishment, which may be cruel and unusual.

Key Terms

The Age of Enlightenment
Benjamin Rush

Cesare Beccaria
Electrocution Act
firing squad
In re Kemmler
lethal injection
John Locke
Louisiana ex rel. Francis v. Resweber
mandatory death sentences
moratorium
Pennsylvania Quakers
public executions
Thomas Jefferson
Wilkerson v. Utah

CRITICAL THINKING QUESTIONS

1. From 1790–1950, significant changes to the death penalty occurred, such as discontinuing the practices of holding executions at public venues. Explain the rationale behind this move and whether removing executions from the public eye has lessened the penalty's general deterrent effect.

2. In *Wilkerson v. Utah*, the Supreme Court ruled that death by firing squad was constitutional. Do you think that Utah's failure to include specific language in its statute regarding methods of execution should have halted the use of the firing squad? Also, do you think the Court should have relied on the Eighth Amendment, especially since this amendment was not applicable to the states at the time?

3. In *In re Kemmler*, why did the Court rely on the Fourteenth Amendment instead of the Eighth Amendment in making its decision? Also, why did Kemmler face so many difficulties in challenging the constitutionality of the Electrocution Act?

4. Explain some of the reasons for the decline in death sentences and executions.

Internet Resources

History of the Death Penalty
http://news.nationalpost.com/2013/07/19/graphic-a-short-history-of-u-s-capital-punishment/
www.deathpenaltyinfo.org/history-death-penalty
www.pbs.org/wgbh/pages/frontline/shows/execution/readings/history.html
http://justice.uaa.alaska.edu/death/history.html

Death Penalty in the United States
www.deathpenaltyinfo.org/category/categories/facts/us-supreme-court
www.amnestyusa.org/our-work/issues/death-penalty/us-death-penalty-facts

The Foundation Cases: *Furman v. Georgia* and *Gregg v. Georgia*

CHAPTER OUTLINE

I INTRODUCTION

Most legal scholars agree that the two most significant and widely known cases regarding the death penalty are *Furman v. Georgia* (1972) and *Gregg v. Georgia* (1976). These cases have laid the foundation for most court decisions involving the death penalty, and their impacts are felt to this day. Both cases made headlines when decided, but their after-effects are different. *Furman*, decided June 29, 1972, is significant because it stopped executions during the four years and three days when it was the law of the land. That came to an end on July 2, 1976, when the decision was repudiated in *Gregg v. Georgia*. *Gregg* held that the death penalty could be constitutional in some instances. *Furman* was hailed by abolitionists for bringing about the long-delayed demise of executions by the state; *Gregg* was cheered by retentionists for restoring the death penalty but also for ushering in a new era of executions that are deemed fairer and more humane. *Furman* did not spawn many decisions during the four years it was law, because the decision itself was categorical: The death penalty was unconstitutional. By contrast, *Gregg* resulted in a spate of cases that have reached the Court for almost four decades now. These cases have sought to further clarify the meaning of *Gregg* and extend or contract some of its legal boundaries.

II *FURMAN v. GEORGIA* (1972): THE DEATH PENALTY IS UNCONSTITUTIONAL

A The Background

The Supreme Court had decided a number of cases on the death penalty prior to *Furman v. Georgia*. Prior cases, however, dealt with the procedure for execution and did not raise the issue of constitutionality of the penalty itself, the prevailing assumption being that this ultimate form of punishment was constitutional. There were good reasons to assume this—the penalty was used in England even before the Pilgrims came to America and it was used in the Colonies as a form of punishment. In *Furman*, the sole issue before the Court was: "Does the imposition and carrying out of the death penalty constitute cruel and unusual punishment in violation of the Eighth and Fourteenth Amendments?" For the first time, substance and not only process was at issue. *Furman* produced an almost unprecedented flurry of opinions from the Court, each opinion with its own nuanced reasoning. Decided on a five-to-four vote, it featured a total of nine different opinions—five for the majority and four for the dissent. The opinions are summarized in this chapter because they are the same arguments used by abolitionists and retentionists in the debate over the death penalty today. They are as current and controversial today as they were when first written.

  Furman was the lead case of the three cases appealed to the Court that raised the same issue—the constitutionality of the death penalty. The other two cases were *Jackson v. Georgia* (a black man, 21 years old, convicted of the rape of a white woman in Georgia and sentenced to death) and *Branch v. Texas* (a black man convicted of rape in Texas and also given the sentence of death). *Furman* just happened to be the lead case in the group and therefore received all the publicity and attention. *Jackson v. Georgia* and *Branch v. Texas* have been virtually forgotten. All three defendants had this in common: They were poor, powerless, black, and charged with serious crimes.

B The Facts

The facts in *Furman* are uncomplicated. Furman, a black man, tried to enter a home at night and shot the victim through a closed door. He was 26 years old and had a sixth-grade education. His court-appointed attorney entered a defense of insanity during trial. The staff in the facility where Furman was committed pending trial recommended that "this patient should retain his present diagnosis of Mental Deficiency, Mild to Moderate, with Psychotic Episodes associated with Convulsive Disorder." The superintendent agreed with his staff's finding but concluded that Furman was "not psychotic at present, knows right from wrong and is able to cooperate with his counsel in preparing his defense." Furman was charged with, tried for, and found guilty of murder. He was sentenced to death and appealed his conviction to the U.S. Supreme Court.

C The Majority Opinions

The Court voted five to four, declaring the death penalty unconstitutional but for different reasons. In an opinion written by Justice William O. Douglas, three of the five justices agreed that the death penalty is "unusual" if it discriminates by reason of "race, religion, wealth, social position, or class, or if it is imposed under a procedure that gives room for the play of such prejudices." Justice Douglas's opinion is interesting because it blended the two constitutional provisions asserted by the defendants, saying, "there is increasing recognition of the fact that the basic theme of equal protection is implicit in 'cruel and unusual punishments.'" Justice Douglas concluded by saying that "the high service rendered by the 'cruel and unusual punishment' clause of the Eighth Amendment is to require legislatures to write penal laws that are evenhanded, nonselective, and non-arbitrary, and to require judges to see to it that general laws are not applied sparsely, selectively, and spottily to unpopular groups." Thus, although the opinion is anchored on the Eighth Amendment's Cruel and Unusual Punishment Clause, its substance rests on the Equal Protection Clause of the Fourteenth Amendment, which prohibits discrimination.

Justice William J. Brennan, siding with the majority, was more vehement in his denunciation of the death penalty. His lengthy opinion is remembered for having popularized a phrase that has since become even more contentious in death penalty cases. He said: "We know 'that the words of the [Cruel and Unusual Punishment Clause] are not precise, and that their scope is not static.' We know, therefore, that the clause 'must draw its meaning from the *evolving standards of decency that mark the progress of a maturing society*'" (italics added). That phrase is not original; it is in fact quoted from the majority opinion in *Trop v. Dulles* (1958), but hardly anyone had heard of that phrase before its use in *Furman*. It has since become the center of the debate in death penalty cases, a mantra for abolitionists and a catalyst for examinations of public support for the death penalty and trends in its use.

Justice Potter Stewart, in a majority concurring opinion, is remembered for concluding his opinion thus: "I simply conclude that the Eighth and Fourteenth Amendments cannot tolerate the infliction of a sentence of death under legal systems that permit this unique penalty to be *so wantonly and so freakishly imposed*" (italics added). He admitted that cruel and unusual punishment is implicated in the death penalty but said that he did not want to base his opinion on the Eighth Amendment, saying that death sentences "are cruel and unusual in the same way that being struck by lightning is cruel and unusual," meaning that there is no design or malice to it; rather that its cruel and unusual nature is remote and accidental. Since *Furman*, the phrase "wanton and freakish manner" has become the catchall phrase for abolitionists who maintain that the death penalty is inherently discriminatory.

Justice Byron White, concurring with the majority, based his opinion primarily on the concept that "the penalty is so infrequently imposed that the threat of execution is too attenuated to be of substantial service to criminal justice." Given this, the death penalty fails to achieve the "social ends it was deemed to serve," meaning crime deterrence. Because of the infrequency of executions for even the most atrocious of crimes, Justice White concluded that "there is no meaningful basis for distinguishing the few cases in which it is imposed from the many cases in which it is not." His opinion is based on the Equal Protection Clause (only a few of the many who are convicted are executed) of the Fourteenth Amendment rather than on the Eighth Amendment's prohibition of cruel and unusual punishment.

Justice Thurgood Marshall, also concurring, wrote a lengthy and exhaustive opinion. He is remembered for saying that "American citizens know almost nothing about capital punishment" and that if the public knew more about the death penalty, it would consider the punishment cruel and unusual. He said: "Assuming knowledge of all the facts presently available regarding capital punishment, the average citizen would, in my opinion, find it shocking to his conscience and sense of justice." This came to be known as the *Marshall hypothesis*, spurring much research testing its veracity. He said that six purposes are conceivably served by the death penalty: "retribution, deterrence, prevention of repetitive criminal acts, encouragement of guilty pleas and confessions, eugenics, and economy." He then proceeded to discuss each of these purposes and concluded that none of them was served by capital punishment. He ended his lengthy prohibitionist discourse with these words:

> At a time in our history when the streets of the Nation's cities inspire fear and despair, rather than pride and hope, it is difficult to maintain objectivity and concern for our fellow citizens. But, the measure of a country's greatness is its ability to retain compassion in time of crisis. No nation in the recorded history of man has a greater tradition of revering justice and fair treatment for all its citizens in times of turmoil, confusion, and tension than ours. This is a country which stands tallest in troubled times, a country that clings to fundamental principles, cherishes its constitutional heritage, and rejects simple solutions that compromise the values that lie at the roots of our democratic system.

Justice Marshall's concluding words were: "We achieve 'a major milestone in the long road up from barbarism' and join the approximately 70 other jurisdictions in the world which celebrate their regard for civilization and humanity by shunning capital punishment."

The five majority opinions had one common theme: The death penalty is unconstitutional. Each opinion was a variation of that common theme; but importantly, the basis for the opinions differed. Nonetheless, it achieved the purpose of suspending executions in the United States for four years.

D The Dissenting Opinions

The four dissenters in *Furman* wrote four separate opinions, although not quite with the same vehemence as the majority opinions.

Justice Warren E. Burger, the Chief Justice at the time, opined that the Constitution does not prohibit the imposition of the death penalty. Even the lawyers for the defendants, he said, "properly concede that capital punishment was not impermissibly cruel at the time of the adoption of the Eighth Amendment" and that "in the 181 years since the enactment of the Eighth Amendment, not a single decision of this Court has cast the slightest shadow of a doubt on the constitutionality of capital punishment." He then added that "twentieth century modes of execution surely involve no greater physical suffering than the means employed at the time of the Eighth Amendment's adoption." In the absence of proof that "the mode of punishment authorized by a domestic legislature was so cruel as to be fundamentally at odds with our basic notions of decency," he concluded that "the primacy of the legislative role narrowly confines the scope of judicial inquiry." In sum, Justice Burger opined that in the absence of proof that the death penalty is prohibited by the Constitution or is clearly cruel and unusual, respect must be given by the Court to the judgment made by state legislatures to impose death as the ultimate punishment.

Justice Harry Blackmun started his dissent with what amounts to a personal testimonial, saying "I yield to no one in the depth of my distaste, antipathy, and, indeed, abhorrence, for the death penalty, with all its aspects of physical distress and fear and of moral judgment exercised by finite minds. That distaste is buttressed by a belief that capital punishment serves no useful purpose that can be demonstrated. For me, it violates childhood's training and life experiences, and is not compatible with the philosophical convictions I have been able to develop." He then added: "Were I a legislator, I would vote against the death penalty for the policy reasons argued by counsel for the respective petitioners and expressed and adopted in the several opinions filed by the Justices who vote to reverse these judgments." Having said all that, however, he then concludes: "Although personally I may rejoice at the Court's result, I find it difficult to accept or to justify as a matter of history, of law, or of constitutional pronouncement. I fear the Court has overstepped. It has sought and has achieved an end." The words of Justice Blackmun are significant because years later, just before he retired from the Court, he announced that were he to sit in judgment on death penalty cases again, he would vote against it. He had changed his mind.

The dissenting opinion by Justice Lewis F. Powell, Jr., is also long and exhaustive, refuting the arguments presented by the majority opinions on wide-ranging issues—from the purposes of punishment to the state of public opinion on the issue of the death penalty. His main argument, however, focused on the relationship between the judiciary and the legislature, agreeing with then-Chief Justice Burger and Justice Blackmun that respect must be given to laws passed by state legislatures in the absence of clear evidence that the death penalty violates the Constitution. He urged judicial restraint, particularly because the issue involved punishment for crimes, an issue that is historically a legislative concern because of the legislature's duty to protect the public.

Justice William Rehnquist, who also sided with the dissenters, started by saying: "The Court's judgments today strike down a penalty that our Nation's legislators have thought necessary since our country was founded. My Brothers Douglas, Brennan, and Marshall would at one fell swoop invalidate laws enacted by Congress and 40 of the 50 state legislatures . . ." He discussed the history of the relationship between the judicial and legislative branches of government from the time of the framing of the Constitution. He observed that constitutional jurisprudence proves that judicial restraint was implied, if not expressed, by the framers of the Constitution as a condition of the grant of authority for judicial review. He then concluded that the majority decision in this case completely disregarded the limits of the doctrine of judicial review.

In sum, the majority opinions in *Furman* declaring the death penalty unconstitutional were based on two grounds: Three of the justices (Douglas, Stewart, and White) said it violated the Equal Protection Clause of the Fourteenth Amendment; two of the justices (Brennan and Marshall) said it was a violation of the Eighth Amendment prohibition against cruel and unusual punishment. The four dissenting opinions were based on one main ground: respect for laws passed by state legislatures in the absence of proof that the death penalty is clearly unconstitutional in both its history and its application.

III *GREGG v. GEORGIA* (1976): THE DEATH PENALTY IS CONSTITUTIONAL IN SOME CASES

A The Background

After the decision in *Furman v. Georgia*, 35 states and the federal government revised their death penalty laws to avoid equal protection problems. Had all five of the justices in *Furman* based their decision on the prohibition against cruel and unusual punishment, the issue would have been settled in 1972. But three of the five justices who voted with the majority based their vote on the Equal Protection Clause of the Fourteenth Amendment, thus leaving the door open for the issue to be revisited. The death penalty states knew that if their laws and systems could be made less discriminatory, their statutes would be deemed constitutional and executions could resume. After *Furman*, states revised their laws in an attempt to make them acceptable to the other members of the Court.

In revising their statutes, states took two different approaches: mandatory death penalty statutes and guided discretion statutes. Mandatory death penalty statutes made the death penalty automatic for anyone convicted of a particular crime (e.g., first-degree murder). Guided discretion statutes, on the other hand, retained jury discretion in deciding in which particular cases the death penalty would be applied. Though mandatory death penalty statutes successfully removed arbitrariness by removing any discretion over who, among convicted capital murderers, gets the death penalty, in *Woodson v. North Carolina* (1976) and *Roberts v. Louisiana* (1976) the Supreme Court rejected them on the grounds that they did not sufficiently narrow the use of the death penalty for only the "worst of the worst," or those truly deserving this most severe punishment. The other legislative approach resulted in what came to be known as "guided discretion" statutes. These provided both procedural safeguards to avoid arbitrariness and discriminatory application as well as processes for reserving the death penalty only for the "worst of the worst" among murderers. This was represented to the Supreme Court in Georgia's new death penalty statute. So, four years after *Furman v. Georgia* (1972) came *Gregg v. Georgia* (1976). This time the Georgia law that was declared unconstitutional in *Furman* had been revised by the Georgia legislature and was vastly different. Would it fare better than the earlier law? Yes.

B The Facts

Troy Gregg was charged under the new Georgia law with armed robbery and murder. He and a traveling companion were hitchhiking in Florida and were picked up by Fred Simmons and Bob Moore. While still in Florida, they picked up another hitchhiker; all of them rode together to Atlanta. The men later interrupted their trip at a rest stop along the highway. The following day, the bodies of Simmons and Moore were discovered in a ditch nearby. Both had died from bullet wounds. Gregg later admitted that he shot Simmons and Moore but claimed that he had acted in self-defense, saying they had attacked him. Gregg was charged with and convicted of two counts of armed robbery and two counts of murder. The jury imposed the death penalty.

Gregg challenged the constitutionality of Georgia's death penalty statute, his appeal ultimately reaching the U.S. Supreme Court. The Court was faced with two questions: (1) Is the death penalty constitutional as a form of punishment? and (2) If it is, does the Georgia law contain sufficient safeguards against arbitrary and capricious imposition?

Gregg was decided by a 7-to-2 vote and had a total of five opinions. In sum, it held that "the death penalty is not a form of punishment that may never be imposed, regardless of the circumstances of the offense, regardless of the character of the offender, and regardless of the procedure followed in reaching the decision to impose it." In short, it is constitutional provided that states impose proper safeguards. Eight of the nine justices who decided *Furman* were still on the Court and cast votes in *Gregg*. Only Justice Douglas was gone; his place on the Court was taken by Justice John Paul Stevens. The final vote was predictable. The dissent in *Furman* would now become the majority if the objectionable provisions were removed from the various state laws. Four years later, the tide had turned and *Furman* was history.

C The Majority Opinions

The main majority opinion in *Gregg* was written by Justice Stewart. Four years earlier he had opined in *Furman* that the death penalty was unconstitutional because it violated the Equal Protection Clause of the Constitution. Justice Stewart addressed the two issues raised on appeal and came to a different conclusion than he had in *Furman,* because the law in Georgia had changed. On the first issue, Justice Stewart concluded that the death penalty did not violate the prohibition against cruel and unusual punishment, saying that the history of the death penalty clearly indicated that its use has traditionally been accepted in the United States. He looked at previous cases and said that judicial precedents supported the constitutionality of the penalty. Conceding that the meaning of cruel and unusual punishment must be drawn from the "evolving standards of decency that mark the progress of a maturing society," he nonetheless said that "the public perceptions of standards of decency with respect to criminal sanctions are not conclusive." In the absence of a clear showing that the public is against the death penalty, judges must give deference to the wishes of legislators, saying, "we may not act as judges as we might as legislators."

Having concluded on the first issue that the death penalty was not in itself unconstitutional, Justice Stewart then addressed the second issue—whether the revised Georgia law was constitutional. He started by saying: *"Furman* mandates that where discretion is afforded a sentencing body on a matter so grave as the determination of whether a human life should be taken or spared, that *discretion must be suitably directed and limited so as to minimize the risk of wholly arbitrary and capricious action"* (italics added). He concluded with these words: "The new Georgia sentencing procedures . . . focus the jury's attention on the particularized nature of the crime and the particularized characteristics of the circumstances, it must find and identify at least one statutory aggravating factor before it may impose a penalty of death. In this way the jury's discretion is channeled. No longer can a jury wantonly and freakishly impose the death sentence; it is always circumscribed by the legislative guidelines."

These statements are key to understanding the change of vote by Justices Stewart and White, both of whom voted with the majority in *Furman*. It highlighted the overriding concern that the Court has had in all death penalty cases since *Gregg*: that discretion must be "suitably directed and limited so as to minimize the risk of wholly arbitrary and capricious action." That said, the question remained: Who determines that, and how? The answer is the Supreme Court, on a case-by-case basis. This explains why there is a never-ending stream of cases that reach the Court each year seeking a determination of whether state laws and practices comport with or violate that standard. The guidelines given by the Court in *Gregg* have not been always clear or authoritative, as the cases in this book show. This is perhaps inevitable because the terms *arbitrary* and *capricious* are inherently subjective and elude precise definition.

The majority decision in *Gregg v. Georgia* is best understood in the context of the Georgia law under which Gregg was prosecuted. Box 2.1 presents the important features of that law and should be read to know better what the Court looks for in state death penalty laws. These carefully crafted provisions ensured constitutionality for the Georgia statute and serve as a template for other state laws on the death penalty.

Justice White also voted in *Furman* to declare the death penalty unconstitutional. He wrote a concurring opinion that called attention to the procedures under the new Georgia law and concluded that the law was constitutional because of procedural safeguards. Among the safeguards that made a difference were: (1) a listing of the 10 aggravating circumstances that could increase the penalty to death; (2) a unanimous finding by the jury beyond a reasonable doubt that at least one statutorily defined aggravating circumstance existed; (3) provision for prompt review by the Georgia Supreme Court; (4) a questionnaire provided to the Georgia Supreme Court during review, which asked six questions designed to disclose whether race played a role in the case, and (5) a set of questions the Georgia Supreme Court must answer to determine whether the sentence of death was influenced by passion or prejudice and whether the sentence was excessive or disproportionate to the offense committed. Taken together, Justice White concluded that, unlike the statute in *Furman*, arbitrariness and capriciousness were now purged from the Georgia death penalty process.

BOX 2.1 FEATURES OF THE REVISED GEORGIA LAW (1976)

The following were the features of the new Georgia law, revised after *Furman v. Georgia* was decided, that led the U.S. Supreme Court to declare the law constitutional because they removed arbitrariness and capriciousness in the imposition of the death penalty.

- It imposed the death penalty for six categories of crime: murder, kidnapping for ransom or where the victim is harmed, armed robbery, rape, treason, and aircraft hijacking.
- Guilt or innocence is determined either by a trial judge or a jury in the first stage of a bifurcated trial.
- "If trial is by a jury, the trial judge is required to charge lesser included offenses when they are supported by any view of the evidence."
- The law lists 10 aggravating circumstances. The sentence of death may be imposed "only if the jury or judge finds one of the statutory aggravating circumstances beyond a reasonable doubt and then elects to impose that sentence."
- The law provides for an expedited direct review of all death penalty sentences by the Supreme Court of Georgia. The expedited review aims at determining the appropriateness of imposing the death sentence in a particular case. In conducting the review, the court must determine:
  (1) "Whether the sentence of death was imposed under the influence of passion, prejudice, or any other arbitrary factor, and
  (2) "Whether, in cases other than treason or aircraft hijacking, the evidence supports the jury's or judge's finding of a statutory aggravating circumstance, and
  (3) "Whether the sentence of death is excessive or disproportionate to the penalty imposed in similar cases, considering both the crime and the defendant."
- "A transcript and complete record of the trial, as well as a separate report by the trial judge, are transmitted to the court for its use in reviewing the sentence." This report is in the form of a "6½ page questionnaire, designed to elicit information about the defendant, the crime, and the circumstances of the trial.... Included in the report are responses to detailed questions concerning the quality of the defendant's representation, whether race played a role in the trial, and whether, in the trial court's judgment, there is any doubt about the defendant's guilt or the appropriateness of the sentence."

Justice Burger, the Chief Justice at that time, wrote a one-sentence concurring opinion, saying: "We [with Justice Rehnquist] concur in the judgment and join the opinion . . . agreeing with its analysis that Georgia's system of capital punishment comports with the Court's holding in *Furman v. Georgia*." He had written a lengthy dissent in *Furman*; he simply wanted to reiterate those arguments in *Gregg*, but now he was on the winning side of the issue.

D The Dissenting Opinions

As expected, Justices Brennan and Marshall dissented. They voted for unconstitutionality in *Furman*, saying that the death penalty itself constituted cruel and unusual punishment. They held steadfast to that view but, as discussed in *Furman*, for different reasons.

Justice Brennan reaffirmed that the Cruel and Unusual Punishment Clause "must draw its meaning from the evolving standards of decency that mark the progress of a maturing society." After quoting some of the arguments he used in *Furman*, he then said that "the punishment of death, like punishments on the rack, the screw, and the wheel, is no longer morally tolerable in our civilized society." Then, using caustic language, he said: "The fatal constitutional infirmity in the punishment of death is that it treats members of the human race as nonhumans, as objects to be toyed with and discarded. It is thus inconsistent with the fundamental premise of the Clause that even the vilest criminal remains a human being possessed of common human dignity."

Justice Marshall was just as vehement in his dissent in *Gregg* as he was in his majority opinion in *Furman*. Saying that he had no intention of repeating the long and tedious journey that led to his conclusion in *Furman*, he stated: "In *Furman* I concluded that the death penalty is constitutionally invalid for two reasons. First, the death penalty is excessive. And second, the American people, fully informed as to the purposes of the death penalty and its liabilities, would in my view reject it as morally acceptable." He again said that "the American people are largely unaware of the information critical to a judgment on the morality of the death penalty" and that "if they were better informed they would consider it shocking, unjust, and unacceptable." He added that the death penalty is excessive and serves no penological purpose, be it deterrence or retribution.

IV IN SUMMARY, WHAT DO THESE CASES SAY?

Taken together, the *Furman* and *Gregg* cases hold that the death penalty does not constitute cruel and unusual punishment and is not in itself unconstitutional. *Gregg* makes it clear that the death penalty may be imposed if state laws are carefully crafted to avoid the twin vices of arbitrariness and capriciousness. In short, the Court said: Remove arbitrariness and capriciousness from your laws and you can go ahead with executions. Additionally, by rejecting mandatory death penalty statutes, the Court also said that jury discretion should be retained in such cases but should be guided in a way that avoids discriminatory and arbitrary decision making. It also reinforced the importance of the consideration of individual case circumstances in the application of the death penalty, thereby asserting the notion that "death is different" and should be reserved only for those most deserving of such a severe and irrevocable punishment.

Other constitutional issues have been raised in death penalty cases (such as the right to counsel and the right to due process), but they have not occupied as much of the Court's attention as have the Eighth Amendment's prohibition of cruel and unusual punishment and the Equal Protection Clause of the Fourteenth Amendment. The debate over whether society has evolved to a point where the death penalty violates "standards of decency" and is thus cruel and unusual punishment is ongoing, reemerging every time states repeal, revise, or enact death penalty legislation. And discrimination in the enforcement of the death penalty will continue to be one of the main issues as long as state laws differ and differential weights are given to aggravating and mitigating circumstances that make death penalty decisions subjective and human.

V CONCLUSION

The *Furman* and *Gregg* cases deserve extensive discussion because they are landmarks and are arguably the most significant and widely known cases on death penalty law. The opinions expressed by the justices of the Court in these decisions generate as much controversy today as they did when they were decided. *Furman* suspended the imposition of the death penalty for four years, but *Gregg* is doubtless the more significant case because it restored the death penalty and is the "mother" of most death penalty cases decided since 1976. Many of the cases appealed by defendants to the Court claim that a state's death penalty law is arbitrary and capricious—descriptive words that were first used in *Furman* and given substance and meaning in *Gregg*. Since then, the efforts to remove provisions that create arbitrariness and capriciousness have been a recurring theme in legislative enactments and Court decisions. The search for a wand that draws a magical bright line between what is constitutional and what is not will likely continue as long as the death penalty is imposed. The cases in the other chapters in this book show that the search for death penalty laws and practices that are totally cleansed of legal impurities in this most severe and final of punishments is indeed long and tedious and may never end as long as the death penalty itself exists.

CASES BRIEFED IN CHAPTER 2

Case	Issue	Holding
Furman v. Georgia 408 U.S. 238 (1972)	Is the death penalty constitutional?	The death penalty is unconstitutional because it violates the Equal Protection Clause of the Fourteenth Amendment and the prohibition against cruel and unusual punishment.
Gregg v. Georgia 428 U.S. 153 (1976)	Is the death penalty constitutional? If yes, does the Georgia law contain sufficient safeguards against arbitrary and capricious imposition?	The death penalty is constitutional as a form of punishment. The Georgia law contains sufficient safeguards against arbitrary and capricious imposition.

CASE BRIEFS

FURMAN v. GEORGIA 408 U.S. 238 (1972)

CAPSULE: The death penalty is unconstitutional because it violates the Equal Protection Clause of the Fourteenth Amendment and the prohibition against cruel and unusual punishment.

FACTS: Furman attempted to enter a private home at night. He shot and killed the homeowner through a closed door. He was 26 years old and had a sixth-grade education. Prior to trial, Furman was committed to the Georgia Central State Hospital for a psychiatric examination on his plea of insanity. The hospital superintendent reported that the staff diagnosis concluded that "this patient should retain his present diagnosis of Mental Deficiency, Mild to Moderate, with Psychotic Episodes associated with Convulsive Disorder." The physicians added that although Furman was not psychotic at present, he was not capable of cooperating with his counsel in the preparation of his criminal defense, and they believed he needed further treatment. The superintendent later amended the report by stating that Furman knew right from wrong and was capable of cooperating with counsel. Furman was tried and found guilty of the murder of the homeowner. A jury sentenced him to death.

ISSUE: Is the death penalty constitutional? NO.

HOLDING: The death penalty is unconstitutional because it violates the Equal Protection Clause of the Fourteenth Amendment and the Eighth Amendment prohibition against cruel and unusual punishment.

Continued

FURMAN v. GEORGIA 408 U.S. 238 (1972)—cont'd

REASON: "There are, then, four principles by which we may determine whether a particular punishment is 'cruel and unusual.' The primary principle, which I believe supplies the essential predicate for the application of the others, is that a punishment must not by its severity be degrading to human dignity. The paradigm violation of this principle would be the infliction of a tortuous punishment of the type that the Clause has always prohibited. Yet '[i]t is unlikely that any State at this moment in history,' *Robinson v. California*, 370 U.S., at 666, would pass a law providing for the infliction of such a punishment. Indeed, no such punishment has ever been before this Court. The same may be said of the other principles. It is unlikely that this Court will confront a severe punishment that is obviously inflicted in wholly arbitrary fashion; no State would engage in a reign of blind terror. Nor is it likely that this Court will be called upon to review a severe punishment that is clearly and totally rejected throughout society; no legislature would be able even to authorize the infliction of such a punishment. Nor, finally, is it likely that this Court will have to consider a severe punishment that is patently unnecessary; no State today would inflict a severe punishment knowing that there is no reason whatever for doing so. In short, we are unlikely to have occasion to determine that a punishment is fatally offensive under any one principle.

"In sum, the punishment of death is inconsistent with all four principles: Death is an unusually severe and degrading punishment; there is a strong probability that it is inflicted arbitrarily; its rejection by contemporary society is virtually total; and there is no reason to believe that it serves any penal purpose more effectively than the less severe punishment of imprisonment. The function of these principles is to enable a court to determine whether a punishment comports with human dignity. Death, quite simply, does not."

CASE SIGNIFICANCE: For the first time, the Supreme Court in *Furman v. Georgia* declared the death penalty unconstitutional, based on two constitutional provisions: the Equal Protection Clause and the prohibition against cruel and unusual punishment. Had all the five justices based their decision solely on a violation of the Cruel and Unusual Punishment Clause, the death penalty could not have been imposed for a long time after 1972 unless the Court changed its mind. Only two justices (Brennan and Marshall), however, used this provision, whereas the three others based their decision on the manner in which death sentences were being carried out. Their objection was not to the death penalty itself but to the way it discriminated against the poor, minorities, and the powerless, thus violating the Equal Protection Clause.

After the *Furman* decision, 35 states and the federal government revised their capital punishment laws to eliminate equal protection problems. Every state statute that carried the death penalty had to undergo review by the U.S. Supreme Court, if appealed, to determine whether the revision removed equal protection problems. The stage was therefore set for *Gregg v. Georgia*, decided in 1976, in which the Court held that the death penalty was not in itself cruel and unusual punishment and could be imposed if there were safeguards against arbitrary and capricious imposition.

GREGG v. GEORGIA 428 U.S. 153 (1976)

CAPSULE: Death penalty laws that have sufficient safeguards against arbitrary and capricious imposition are constitutional.

FACTS: While hitchhiking in Florida, Gregg and a companion were picked up by two motorists. The bodies of the two motorists were later found beside a road near Atlanta, Georgia. The next day Gregg and his companion were arrested. A .25 caliber pistol was found in Gregg's possession and subsequently identified as the murder weapon. Gregg confessed to the robberies and murders but claimed self-defense. He was found guilty of all four counts and was sentenced to death.

Continued

GREGG v. GEORGIA 428 U.S. 153 (1976)—cont'd

The Georgia death penalty statute had the following features: (1) a bifurcated trial; (2) instructions from the judge to the jury on what penalties they could recommend; (3) consideration of mitigating and aggravating factors, of which they must agree that at least one aggravating factor exists if they wish to recommend death; and (4) an automatic appeal to the Georgia Supreme Court. Moreover, the Georgia Supreme Court was required to review each death sentence for evidence of passion, prejudice, or any other arbitrary factor; whether the evidence supports the finding of an aggravating circumstance; and whether the death penalty "is excessive or disproportionate to the penalty imposed in similar cases, considering both the crime and the defendant."

ISSUES:
1. Is the death penalty constitutional as a form of punishment? YES.
2. If the death penalty is constitutional, does the Georgia statute have sufficient safeguards against arbitrary and capricious imposition? YES.

HOLDING:
1. The death penalty is constitutional as a form of punishment.
2. The Georgia law is constitutional because it contains sufficient safeguards against arbitrary and capricious imposition.

REASON: "Four years ago, the petitioners in *Furman* and its companion cases predicated their argument primarily upon the asserted proposition that standards of decency had evolved to the point where capital punishment no longer could be tolerated. The petitioners in those cases said, in effect, that the evolutionary process had come to an end, and that standards of decency required that the Eighth Amendment be construed finally as prohibiting capital punishment for any crime regardless of its depravity and impact on society. This view was accepted by two Justices. Three other Justices were unwilling to go so far; focusing on the procedures by which convicted defendants were selected for the death penalty rather than on the actual punishment inflicted, they joined in the conclusion that the statutes before the Court were constitutionally invalid.

"While *Furman* did not hold that the infliction of the death penalty per se violates the Constitution's ban on cruel and unusual punishments, it did recognize that the penalty of death is different in kind from any other punishment imposed under our system of criminal justice. Because of the uniqueness of the death penalty, *Furman* held that it could not be imposed under sentencing procedures that created a substantial risk that it would be inflicted in an arbitrary and capricious manner.

"The basic concerns of *Furman* centered on those defendants who were condemned to death capriciously and arbitrarily. Under the procedures before the Court in that case, sentencing authorities were not directed to give attention to the nature of the circumstances of the crime committed or the character or record of the defendant. Left unguided, juries imposed the death sentence in a way that could only be called freakish. The new Georgia sentencing procedures, by contrast, focus the jury's attention on the particularized nature of the crime and the particularized characteristics of the individual defendant. While the jury is permitted to consider any aggravating or mitigating circumstances, it must find and identify at least one statutory aggravating factor before it may impose a penalty of death. In this way the jury's discretion is channeled. No longer can a jury wantonly and freakishly impose the death sentence; it is always circumscribed by the legislative guidelines. In addition, the review function of the Supreme Court of Georgia affords additional assurance that the concerns that prompted our decision in *Furman* are not present to any significant degree in the Georgia procedure applied here."

CASE SIGNIFICANCE: *Gregg v. Georgia*, decided four years after *Furman v. Georgia*, is the most important case ever decided by the Court on the death penalty. The Court said that the death penalty is not in itself unconstitutional and may therefore be imposed as long as there are safeguards against arbitrariness and capriciousness. *Gregg v. Georgia* overruled *Furman v. Georgia*. This did not mean, however, that the statutes in the various states were automatically declared constitutional and that executions could resume. What it meant was that the Court could now

Continued

> ### *GREGG v. GEORGIA* 428 U.S. 153 (1976)—cont'd
>
> examine each state law in an appropriate case to determine whether its provisions contain sufficient guarantees against arbitrariness and capriciousness in its imposition.
>
> In the years since *Gregg*, the Court has decided many cases upholding the constitutionality of various state statutes. As a result, executions have taken place in a number of states. But although there are many prisoners on death row in the United States (3,146 at the end of 2012), only a small number (a total of 43 in 2012, and all men) were executed. The explanation may be twofold. First, there is hesitation by the public to carry out the death penalty, despite its availability. It is easy to leave that ultimate penalty in our penal codes; it is difficult to implement it. With an increasing number of prisoners on death row being found innocent and evidence that innocent people may have been executed, the public has become increasingly wary of the death penalty. Second, numerous appeals are available to capital offenders. This frustrates the public, which believes that justice is not served by repeated delays. There is no simple solution to the problem except to realize that the wheels of justice usually turn slowly in a civilized and constitutional society, particularly when a life-and-death decision is involved.

Key Terms

arbitrary and capricious
cruel and unusual punishment
"death is different"
Eighth Amendment
Equal Protection Clause
evolving standards of decency
Fourteenth Amendment
Furman v. Georgia
Gregg v. Georgia
guided discretion statutes
judicial review
mandatory death penalty statutes
Marshall hypothesis
procedural safeguards

CRITICAL THINKING QUESTIONS

1. In *Furman v. Georgia*, each Supreme Court Justice wrote a separate opinion. This was a particularly important factor in terms of the majority. Characterize the various majority opinions in *Furman v. Georgia* and explain the ultimate holding of the Court and how it was important to the future of the death penalty in the United States.

2. In reinstating the death penalty in *Gregg v. Georgia*, the Supreme Court established particular procedural safeguards necessary to ensure its constitutionality. What are these procedural safeguards? Why are they important in terms of the constitutionality of the death penalty?

3. When reinstating the death penalty in 1976, the Supreme Court considered two types of death penalty statutes: mandatory death penalty statutes and guided discretion statutes. What is the difference between these, and why did the Supreme Court choose the guided discretion approach?

Internet Resources

Furman **Revisited: The Nexus Between Race and the Death Penalty**
www.youtube.com/watch?v=eEEFkFAP8a8

40 Years After *Furman*, **the U.S. Death Penalty Is In Disarray**
www.huffingtonpost.com/david-a-love/abolish-death-penalty-_b_1629359.html

Court Eliminates Mandatory Death Sentence
www.nytimes.com/1987/06/23/us/court-eliminates-mandatory-death-sentence.html

The History and Structure of Capital Punishment
http://deathpenaltycurriculum.org/student/c/about/history/history-5.htm

Struck by Lightning: The Continuing Arbitrariness of the Death Penalty Thirty-Five Years After Its Reinstatement in 1976
www.deathpenaltyinfo.org/documents/StruckByLightning.pdf

Race and the Death Penalty

I INTRODUCTION

Race plays a significant historical role in the use of the death penalty and in death penalty jurisprudence. In the early periods of executions, the death penalty was often tied to lynching and the control of slaves; racial disparities were pervasive and pronounced during that time.[1] Today racial disparities continue but often to a lesser degree and in a more nuanced manner. A contemporary understanding of the role of race in the modern death penalty is most prominently grounded in the research of David Baldus and colleagues, which exposed widespread racial disparities in the death penalty system.[2] Baldus's work was the focus of the landmark 1987 case of *McCleskey v. Kemp* in which the

---

[1]David Garland, PECULIAR INSTITUTION: AMERICA'S DEATH PENALTY IN AN AGE OF ABOLITION (2010).
[2]See, for example, David C. Baldus, Charles Pulaski, and George Woodworth, *Arbitrariness and Discrimination in the Administration of the Death Penalty: A Challenge to State Supreme Courts,* 15 STETSON L. REV. 133 (1986), and David C. Baldus, et al., *Racial Discrimination and the Death Penalty in the Post-Furman Era: An Empirical and Legal Overview, with Recent Findings from Philadelphia,* 83 CORNELL L. REV. 1638 (1998).

United States Supreme Court declared that findings of racial disparity don't necessarily imply unconstitutional racial discrimination.

To be sure, claims of, and concerns about, racial disparities and discrimination are present throughout every facet of the criminal justice system and have been throughout history. There is evidence that racial minorities historically have been more likely to be apprehended and arrested, and punished more severely when they are. Laws have been attacked for targeting certain races over others.[3] Racial profiling conducted by police officers continues to be a concern of the courts and the legislatures, today manifested in controversial "stop and frisk" policies.[4]

In death penalty cases, however, issues of and concerns about possible racial disparities and discrimination come into even sharper relief. Given the grave nature of the death penalty and the Supreme Court's declaration that "death is different," the possibility of racial discrimination warrants heightened scrutiny. Are prosecutors striking minorities from capital juries due to the color of their skin? Does race play a role in prosecutors' decisions about whether to pursue the death penalty? Does race impact the decision making of capital jurors? Do the races of the perpetrator and victim affect the likelihood of a death sentence? This chapter explores these questions and examines the legal issues surrounding racial disparities and discrimination in relation to the death penalty.

‖ BIAS IN DEATH PENALTY CASES AND JURY SELECTION IN CAPITAL PROCEEDINGS

There was little legal examination of racial bias in administration of the death penalty prior to 1972. The states were left to enact their own capital statutes and carry out death sentences with little or no federal intervention or oversight. In 1972, the landmark case of *Furman v. Georgia*[5] halted capital punishment due to the arbitrary manner in which death sentences were being carried out in the state of Georgia. The five-to-four decision was controversial because three of the justices who were in the majority did not oppose the death penalty as such but were opposed to the manner in which Georgia enforced and imposed it. The statute in *Furman* was struck down because it gave judges and juries power to exercise discretion in a capricious and arbitrary manner. Two justices in the *Furman* decision believed that the Georgia death penalty statute was "pregnant with discrimination." Justice Douglas believed that "the death sentence [was] disproportionately imposed and carried out on the poor, the Negro, and the members of the unpopular groups."[6] Two dissenting justices in *Furman* also noted racial discrimination as a salient issue. The Supreme Court chose not to set standards to stop or prevent racial disparity in the death penalty but left the states to amend their death penalty statutes.

Although *Furman v. Georgia* is an important starting point in gaining insight into racial issues in the death penalty, *McCleskey v. Kemp*[7] is the most prominent Supreme Court decision concerning racial

---

[3]Michelle Alexander, The New Jim Crow: Mass Incarceration in the Age of Colorblindness (2010).

[4]Joseph Goldstein, *Judge Rejects New York's Stop and Frisk Policy*, New York Times (Aug. 13, 2013). Accessed on Sept. 9, 2013, at www.nytimes.com/2013/08/13/nyregion/stop-and-frisk-practice-violated-rights-judge-rules.html?pagewanted=all&_r=0.

[5]*Furman v. Georgia*, 408 U.S. 238 (1972).

[6]408 U.S. at 257 (Douglas, J., dissenting).

[7]*McCleskey v. Kemp*, 481 U.S. 279 (1987).

disparity and the death penalty.[8] McCleskey was a young black male who was convicted of robbing a furniture store and killing a white police officer in Georgia. McCleskey was sentenced to death by a jury comprising 11 whites and one black. On appeal, McCleskey pointed to the statistics in the studies conducted by University of Iowa Professor David C. Baldus in which he examined the race of the defendant and the race of the victim and their effect on capital sentencing in Georgia. Baldus's research indicated that discrepancies in capital sentencing were, in part, explained by race (particularly race of the victim).[9] McCleskey argued that in light of this evidence, his race and the race of the victim played a significant role in the decision of the jury, and his death sentence should be overturned because it was a violation of the Fourteenth Amendment's equal protection clause.

The Court did not dispute the validity of the statistical evidence presented by McCleskey regarding the impact that race of the victim had on death sentences in Georgia. But the Supreme Court, in a six-to-three decision, held that this evidence was insufficient to support a claim of discrimination under the equal protection clause of the Fourteenth Amendment. McCleskey did not prove that the Georgia legislature enacted the state's death penalty statute with the intent to discriminate. While the Baldus studies suggested that race was a factor in capital sentencing, they did not prove discriminatory intent. The Court believed that the legislature in Georgia did not enact the statute to further a racially motivated agenda. While the Court said that a risk of racial prejudice was involved in a jury's decision, it held that the level of risk was insufficient to establish a violation of a constitutional right. The Supreme Court was reluctant to limit the discretion of juries because "it is the jury's function to make the difficult and uniquely human judgments that defy codification and that build discretion, equity, and flexibility into a legal system."[10] The majority was also concerned with the possibility that a favorable ruling in *McCleskey* would cause a flood of claims of discrimination in other types of criminal proceedings. The Court claimed that if McCleskey's arguments were accepted, statistical analysis would be used to show discrepancies in gender of victim or the race of the trial attorneys or judges.[11] The precedent in *McCleskey* still stands, but the Supreme Court has since decided other cases that relate to the racial composition of juries and federal and state legislatures have begun to take up the mantle of protecting against racial discrimination in capital cases.

III LEGISLATIVE RESPONSES TO DISCRIMINATION IN CAPITAL PROCEEDINGS

A Federal Response: The Proposed Racial Justice Act and Its Failure

In response to the decision in *McCleskey v. Kemp* (1987), federal legislation was drafted in 1988 by Senator Edward Kennedy and Representative John Conyers. The legislation, known as the Racial Justice Act, created a federal statutory right to be free from discrimination in capital cases. The act

---

[8]*McCleskey v. Zant*, 580 F. Supp 338 (N.D. Ga. 1984).
[9]David C. Baldus, Charles Pulaski, and George Woodworth, *Comparative Review of Death Sentences: An Empirical Study of the Georgia Experience.* 74 J. CRIM. L. & CRIMINOLOGY, 661–753 (1983).
[10]*McCleskey v. Kemp* (quoting H. KALVEN AND H. ZIESAL, THE AMERICAN JURY 498, 1966).
[11]*Id.* at 46.

provided a way to circumvent the Supreme Court by providing a constitutional guarantee to be free from state-sponsored racial discrimination during sentencing.[12]

Had it been passed, the Act would have allowed statistical evidence to establish discriminatory practices and patterns in applying death sentences. "The rationale behind the Racial Justice Act . . . is that since the Supreme Court has allowed the use of statistics to prove racial discrimination under Title VII [of the Civil Rights Act of 1964], statistics should also be allowed to prove racial discrimination in death penalty cases."[13] Despite repeated attempts, the Racial Justice Act drew a lot of criticism and has never been approved by Congress. Critics have argued, as did the U.S. Supreme Court, that the human element in determining and dispensing American justice is essential and historically based. Statistics often do not account for differences in offender background and demeanor as well as the nature and quality of offenders' actions. Statistical correlations and evidence of disparity, critics say, do not necessarily indicate racial discrimination on the part of juries. While federal attempts at legislation have failed, legislation at the state level has had mixed success.

B State Responses: Racial Justice Acts and Examination of Statistical Disparities

In 1998 Kentucky became the first state to enact legislation similar to the federal Racial Justice Act. A study conducted in 1996 showed the existence of racial disparities in the administration of Kentucky's capital sentencing. Not one inmate on Kentucky's death row was convicted of murdering a black person, whereas 100 percent of the death row inmates were responsible for killing white victims.[14] Other research supported the claims of widespread racial bias in Kentucky's implementation of the death penalty,[15] grabbing the attention of the state's legislature and culminating in the passage of the first Racial Justice Act.[16] The passage of this Act encouraged other states to reexamine their policies and practices in administering the death penalty, though it would take a lot of time before another state enacted a Racial Justice Act of its own.

In 2009, North Carolina became the second state to enact a racial justice act. The act provided the means for a defendant to present relevant evidence to establish that race was a significant factor in seeking or imposing the death penalty. After defendants had been sentenced to death, they could present evidence that race influenced decisions to exercise peremptory challenges during jury selection. These racial justice acts did not require evidence of intentional discrimination, only whether race played a significant role in the outcome in a case. It was incumbent upon the defendant to establish and articulate how race played this role.

The enactment of racial justice acts, rare though they might be, represents an important legal shift in the scrutiny of race and racial disparity in capital cases. Allowing challenges to death sentences based on racial discrimination or disparity *without* proof of intent on the part of prosecutors or other legal

---

[12]Monica Wiley, McCleskey v. Kemp: *Race-conscious Decision Making in Reforming Capital Decision Making*, 3 Howard Scroll: The Social Justice Review 81 (1995).

[13]*Id.* at 96.

[14]Richard C. Deiter, *Death Penalty in Black and White: Who Lives, Who Dies, Who Decides* (1998). Accessed Aug. 25, 2013, at www.deathpenaltyinfo.org/death-penalty-black-and-white-who-lives-who-dies-who-decides.

[15]T.J. Keil and G.F. Vito, *Capriciousness or Fairness? Race and Prosecutorial Decisions to Seek the Death Penalty in Kentucky*, 4 J. of Ethnicity in CJ 27 (2006).

[16]G.F. Vito, *The Racial Justice Act in Kentucky*, 37 N. Ky. L. Rev. 273 (2010).

actors had the potential to change the legal landscape in terms of the role of race in not only the death penalty but throughout the criminal justice system.

In 2012, a North Carolina judge, invoking the state's Racial Justice Act, commuted the death sentences of three death row inmates to life in prison. He cited evidence of racial bias in the selection of jurors and statistical evidence of racial disparities throughout the state's death penalty system.[17] Though for some this represented a victory for the trailblazing Racial Justice Act, for others it only exposed the Act as contributing to a flawed justice system. Opponents of the Act argued that the legislation had backlogged the courts and was denying justice for victims.[18] That year, a bill to repeal the Racial Justice Act was passed by the state legislature, only to be vetoed by the governor. The following year (2013), with a new governor having taken office, North Carolina's Racial Justice Act was repealed. With North Carolina's repeal of its law and other states declining to pass their own racial justice acts, the future of such legislation is in question. However, states are taking other steps to address racial bias in capital cases, including broader examination of statistical disparities, implementation of moratoria on the death penalty, and even repeal of the death penalty altogether.

While New Jersey has no legislation similar to Kentucky's or North Carolina's Racial Justice Acts, its state Supreme Court did commission researchers to examine its death-eligible cases to explore concerns about racial discrimination in the implementation of the death penalty. The commissioned researchers were David Baldus and his colleagues, who were made famous by their national study of racial disparities used in the *McCleskey* case. In examining New Jersey's death penalty, Baldus and his research team set out to answer the following questions:

1. Is racial discrimination in death sentencing inevitable, or can legal procedures be adopted by legislators, prosecutors, or courts to prevent it?
2. Can such racial discrimination be validly detected: (a) in subgroups of cases within the system, and (b) in individual cases?
3. Can racial discrimination be corrected by subgroups of cases and in individual cases without the de facto abolition of capital punishment or the use of quotas?

In the 1992 case of *State v. Marshall*,[19] based on these questions New Jersey sought to find out whether the system of capital sentencing in New Jersey was unconstitutionally discriminatory. In spite of Baldus' answers to these questions suggesting an inevitability of racial discrimination in capital cases, the court did not find evidence of unconstitutional discrimination. However, it was willing to take corrective measures if necessary, through judicial oversight or more detailed standards to guide prosecutorial discretion.[20] In the end, however, New Jersey, along with other states, came to believe that legislation would not rectify the problem, opting instead to repeal the death penalty completely. Other states with high numbers of executions such as Virginia, Texas, Florida, and Oklahoma opted

---

[17]Bryan Mims, *Judge: Race a Factor in Picking Juries for Death Penalty Cases*, WRAL.com (Dec. 13, 2012). Accessed on Aug. 24, 2103, at www.wral.com/judge-race-a-factor-in-picking-juries-for-death-penalty-cases/11875278/.
[18]Kim Severson, *North Carolina Repeals Law Allowing Racial Bias Claim in Death Penalty Challenges,* NEW YORK TIMES (June 5, 2013). Retrieved on Aug. 20, 2013, at www.nytimes.com/2013/06/06/us/racial-justice-act-repealed-in-north-caro lina.html?_r=2&.
[19]*State v. Marshall*, 613 A.2d 1059 (N.J. 1992).
[20]David Baldus, George Woodworth, and Charles Pulaski, *Reflections on the Inevitability of Racial Discrimination in Capital Sentencing and the Impossibility of its Prevention, Detection, and Correction*, 51 WASH. & LEE L. REV. 359 (1994).

instead to deny the possibility that racial prejudice exists within their death penalty statutes, thus asserting that a legislative response to the death penalty is unnecessary.[21]

In May 2002, the governor of Maryland imposed a moratorium on executions because of racial bias in the state's death penalty system. A January 2003 study released by the University of Maryland concluded that race and geography are major factors in death penalty decisions. Specifically, prosecutors are more likely to seek a death sentence when the victim is white and are less likely to seek a death sentence when the victim is black.[22] Maryland has since repealed the death penalty (in 2013), in part due to the state's determination that it could not be administered free of racial bias.[23]

Generally, studies have found that race of the victim plays more of a role than race of the offender in whether to seek the death penalty, even if states contest the findings. A 2007 study conducted by a professor at Yale University reviewed 207 Connecticut murder cases dating back to the early 1970s that were eligible for death penalty prosecution and found the following:

- Black defendants receive death sentences at three times the rate of white defendants in cases where the victims were white.
- When it comes time to decide the charges, killers of white victims are treated more severely than people who kill minorities.
- Minorities who kill whites receive death sentences at higher rates than minorities who kill minorities.[24]

The study, similar to the study presented in *McCleskey*, was used in a suit brought by death row inmates in the state challenging the constitutionality of the manner in which the death penalty was being applied.

The American Bar Association (ABA) has conducted a series of reviews of states' use of the death penalty, including concerns about racial bias and fairness in its application. Based on their analyses, the ABA has provided several recommendations for states to ensure a fair and equitable death penalty process. Box 3.1 presents the ABA recommendations for two states: Pennsylvania and Ohio. In its review of Ohio's death penalty, the ABA found that serious flaws persisted in Ohio's capital punishment system—so serious that it was recommended that the death penalty be suspended until the state could conduct a thorough analysis of the system's fairness and consistency. The consequent study was conducted by a 10-member panel of Ohio attorneys and legal experts who concluded that the state's death penalty was inherently flawed in terms of racial and geographic bias and disparities. Of the 93 ABA recommendations to ensure a fair capital punishment system, Ohio was found to only meet four of them.[25]

---

[21]Amnesty International, United States of America: Death by Discrimination: The Continuing Role of Race in Capital Cases (2003). Accessed on Sept. 6, 2013, at www.amnesty.org/en/library/info/AMR51/046/2003.

[22]*Id.*

[23]Joe Sutton, Maryland governor signs death penalty repeal (May 2, 2013). Retrieved on Aug. 24, 2013, at www.cnn.com/2013/05/02/us/maryland-death-penalty.

[24]Dave Collins, Yale Study: Racial Bias, Randomness Mar Conn. Death Penalty Cases, Associated Press, Dec. 12, 2007.

[25]American Bar Association, Evaluating Fairness and Accuracy in State Death Penalty Systems: The Ohio Death Penalty Assessment Report (Sept. 2007). Accessed on Aug. 25, 2013, at www.americanbar.org/content/dam/aba/migrated/moratorium/assessmentproject/ohio/finalreport.authcheckdam.pdf.

BOX 3.1 THE AMERICAN BAR ASSOCIATION'S RECOMMENDATIONS FOR PENNSYLVANIA'S AND OHIO'S DEATH PENALTY

ABA recommendations: Pennsylvania

- **Pennsylvania should ensure that it provides adequate opportunities for death row inmates to prove their innocence.** The state should require the preservation of biological evidence for as long as the defendant remains incarcerated and should require crime labs and law enforcement agencies to be certified by nationally recognized certification organizations. It should also require audio- or videotaping of all interrogations in potential capital cases and implement lineup procedures that protect against incorrect eyewitness identifications.
- **Pennsylvania should ensure that all capital defendants and death row inmates who are poor receive competent lawyers.** The assessment team found that the state fails to guarantee the appointment of two attorneys at all stages of capital cases and that attorneys often are provided insufficient access to experts and investigators or to information in discovery. The panel also noted that Pennsylvania lacks a statewide independent appointing authority responsible for training, selecting, and monitoring capital defense attorneys.
- **Pennsylvania should provide state funding for capital indigent defense services.** The group found that the state currently has no funding for indigent defense services but instead relies on county-funded systems. As a result, the quality of Pennsylvania's capital indigent defense system varies widely among counties and fails to afford uniform, quality representation to many capital defendants.
- **Pennsylvania should eliminate racial and geographic bias from its death penalty system.** The assessment team found that Pennsylvania is "second only to Louisiana in the percentage of blacks on death row" and that black defendants in Philadelphia County were sentenced at a "significantly higher rate" than similarly situated nonblack defendants. The review concluded that one-third of black death row inmates in Philadelphia County would have received sentences of life imprisonment if they had not been black.
- **Pennsylvania should collect and make available data on death-eligible cases.** Without a statewide entity that collects data on all death-eligible cases in the state, Pennsylvania cannot ensure that its system guarantees proportionality in charging or sentencing nor determine the extent of racial or geographic bias in its capital system.
- **Pennsylvania should ensure that all death row inmates receive meaningful review in state post-conviction proceedings.** State law imposes several restrictions on state post-conviction proceedings that seriously impede the adequate development and judicial consideration of a death row inmate's claims, including a 60-day time limitation for filing a successive post-conviction petition.
- **Pennsylvania should ensure that capital jurors understand their roles and responsibilities.** The group revealed that the overwhelming majority of Pennsylvania capital jurors fail to understand their roles and responsibilities when deciding whether to impose a death sentence. More than 98% of these jurors failed to understand "at least some" portion of the jury instructions, and of those questioned, about 82% did not believe "that a life sentence really meant life in prison." The ABA urged the state to redraft its capital jury instructions with the objective of preventing common juror misconceptions and to provide a clearer understanding of the definition of life in prison without parole.

ABA recommendations: Ohio

- **Ohio should ensure that it provides adequate opportunities for death row inmates to prove their innocence.** This includes improved preservation of biological evidence while inmates are incarcerated, creation of nationally certified crime laboratories, videotaping of all interrogations in potential capital cases, and implementation of lineup procedures that protect against incorrect eyewitness identification. In addition, the report recommends that Ohio Governor Ted Strickland supplement the state's current clemency process by appointing a commission to conduct investigations, hold hearings, and test evidence to review cases of factual innocence in capital cases.
- **Ohio should ensure that all capital defendants and death row inmates who are poor receive competent lawyers.** The panel noted that Ohio does not have safeguards in place to ensure competent representation in all cases. It urged compliance with the ABA Guidelines for the Appointment and Performance of Defense Counsel in Death Penalty Cases. It also urged lawmakers to better compensate defense attorneys to ensure high-quality representation and to provide defense teams with sufficient funds for access to experts and investigators.

Continued

BOX 3.1 THE AMERICAN BAR ASSOCIATION'S RECOMMENDATIONS FOR PENNSYLVANIA'S AND OHIO'S DEATH PENALTY—cont'd

- **Ohio should exempt people with severe mental disabilities from the death penalty.** The panel found that while Ohio does protect those with mental retardation from facing the death penalty, it does not extend this protection to those with other types of serious mental disorders.
- **Ohio should eliminate racial and geographic bias from its death penalty system.** As part of its assessment, the ABA conducted a racial and geographic disparity study that examined death sentences in Ohio between 1981 and 2000. The review found that those who kill white victims are 3.8 times more likely to receive a death sentence than those who kill black victims. It also found that the chances of receiving a death sentence in Hamilton County are 2.7 times higher than in the rest of the state, 3.7 times higher than in Cuyahoga County, and 6.2 times higher than in Franklin County.
- **Ohio should provide increased discovery in state post-conviction appeals.** The panel noted that Ohio denies petitioners access to discovery procedures necessary to develop post-conviction claims. The ABA criticized an existing policy that allows reporters and other members of the public to use the public records law to obtain materials in support of post-conviction claims but prohibits a petitioner from using this law to obtain these same documents.

Sources:

American Bar Association, Evaluating Fairness and Accuracy in State Death Penalty Systems: The Pennsylvania Death Penalty Assessment Report (Oct. 2007). Accessed on Aug. 25, 2013, at www.americanbar.org/content/dam/aba/migrated/moratorium/assessmentproject/pennsylvania/finalreport.authcheckdam.pdf.

American Bar Association, Evaluating Fairness and Accuracy in State Death Penalty Systems: The Ohio Death Penalty Assessment Report (Sept. 2007). Accessed on Aug. 25, 2013, at www.americanbar.org/content/dam/aba/migrated/moratorium/assessmentproject/ohio/finalreport.authcheckdam.pdf.

A recent study conducted by a professor at the University of Maryland reviewed 500 murder cases in Harris County, Texas, historically the leading county in death sentences. The study found that the District Attorney's Office of Harris County was 3.5 times more likely to seek the death penalty when the defendant is African-American than when the defendant is white. When the cases were submitted to Harris County juries, the net result was a greater proportion of death sentences for African-American defendants than for white defendants. In one case, an expert for the prosecution stated outright that he believed the defendant was more of a risk to society because he was black.[26] In another study, conducted in 2012, it was found that compared to other groups, blacks convicted of killing whites were not only more likely to receive a death sentence, but they were also more likely to be executed.[27] Additionally, if the victim was a white female, an African-American was five times as likely to receive a death sentence. Tables 3.1 and 3.2 illustrate these realities. The message that many take away from the research is that the U.S. criminal justice system places more value on white lives.[28] When it comes to the death penalty, racial disparities and bias seem to be magnified in terms of both their apparent pervasiveness and the graveness of their consequences.

---

[26]Ray Paternoster, Racial Disparity in the Case of Duane Edward Buck (unpublished paper, 2012). Accessed on Sept. 6, 2013, at www.naacpldf.org/files/case_issue/Duane%20Buck-FINAL%20Signed%20Paternoster%20Report%20%2800032221%29.pdf.

[27]S. Phillips, *Continued Racial Disparities in the Capital of Capital Punishment: The Rosenthal Era,* 50 HOUSTON LAW REVIEW, 2012.

[28]*Id.*

State	Race of Victim Disparities	Race of Defendant Disparities	State	Race of Victim Disparities	Race of Defendant Disparities
Alabama	v	v	Nevada		
Arizona	v		New Hampshire**		
California	v		New Jersey	v	v
Colorado	v		New Mexico*		
Connecticut	v		New York**		
Delaware	v		North Carolina	v	
Florida	v	v	Ohio	v	
Georgia	v		Oklahoma	v	v
Idaho*			Oregon*		
Illinois	v		Pennsylvania	v	v
Indiana	v	v	South Carolina	v	v
Kansas**			South Dakota*		
Kentucky	v	v	Tennessee	v	v
Louisiana	v		Texas	v	v
Maryland	v	v	Utah*		
Mississippi	v	v	Virginia	v	
Missouri	v		Washington	v	v
Montana*			Wyoming		
Nebraska	v				

Table 3.1 Racial Disparities in Death Penalty States, 1998

*States for which no death penalty race data are available.
**States in which no death sentences imposed as of January 1, 1998.
Source: Richard C. Dieter, The Death Penalty in Black and White: Who Lives, Who Dies, Who Decides. *Death Penalty Information Center (June 1998).*

IV THE LEGAL COMMUNITY: AN ASSESSMENT OF PROSECUTORS AND DEFENSE ATTORNEYS

A District Attorneys

The vast majority of chief district attorneys in counties that gave death sentences are white; a 1998 study put the percentage at 98%.[29] The decision to pursue or not to pursue a death sentence rests with the prosecutor, and there are no standards that govern whether a death sentence should be sought. Some prosecutors frequently seek capital convictions, while other district attorneys choose not to seek the death penalty at all.[30] Prosecutorial discretion plays a decisive role in how, when, and why capital murder

---

[29]Richard C. Deiter, *Death Penalty in Black and White: Who Lives, Who Dies, Who Decides* (1998). Accessed Aug. 25, 2013, at www.deathpenaltyinfo.org/death-penalty-black-and-white-who-lives-who-dies-who-decides.
[30]Stephen S. Bright, *Discrimination, Death and Denial: The Tolerance of Racial Discrimination in Infliction of the Death Penalty*, 35 SANTA CLARA L. REV. 433 (1995).

Table 3.2 Death Row Populations by Race, Winter 2013

State	Total	Black	White	Latino	Native American	Asian
Alabama	198	100 (50.5%)	94 (47.5%)	3 (1.5%)	0 (0.0%)	1 (0.5%)
Arizona	127	15 (11.8%)	82 (64.6%)	25 (19.7%)	3 (2.4%)	2 (1.5%)
Arkansas	38	24 (63.2%)	14 (36.8%)	0 (0.0%)	0 (0.0%)	0 (0.0%)
California	727	264 (36.3%)	256 (35.2%)	170 (23.4%)	12 (1.7%)	25 (3.4%)
Colorado	4	3 (75.0%)	0 (0.0%)	1 (25.0%)	0 (0.0%)	0 (0.0%)
Connecticut	11	6 (54.5%)	4 (36.4%)	1 (9.1%)	0 (0.0%)	0 (0.0%)
Delaware	18	11 (61.1%)	4 (22.2%)	3 (16.7%)	0 (0.0%)	0 (0.0%)
Florida	413	151 (36.6%)	223 (54.0%)	36 (8.7%)	1 (0.2%)	2 (0.5%)
Georgia	97	47 (48.5%)	46 (47.4%)	4 (4.1%)	0 (0.0%)	0 (0.0%)
Idaho	13	0 (0.0%)	13 (100.0%)	0 (0.0%)	0 (0.0%)	0 (0.0%)
Indiana	12	3 (25.0%)	9 (75.0%)	0 (0.0%)	0 (0.0%)	0 (0.0%)
Kansas	10	4 (40.0%)	6 (60.0%)	0 (0.0%)	0 (0.0%)	0 (0.0%)
Kentucky	34	5 (14.7%)	29 (85.3%)	0 (0.0%)	0 (0.0%)	0 (0.0%)
Louisiana	88	58 (65.9%)	26 (29.6%)	3 (3.4%)	0 (0.0%)	1 (1.1%)
Maryland	5	4 (80.0%)	1 (20.0%)	0 (0.0%)	0 (0.0%)	0 (0.0%)
Mississippi	48	27 (56.3%)	20 (41.7%)	0 (0.0%)	0 (0.0%)	1 (2.1%)
Missouri	48	21 (43.8%)	27 (56.2%)	0 (0.0%)	0 (0.0%)	0 (0.0%)
Montana	2	0 (0.0%)	2 (100.0%)	0 (0.0%)	0 (0.0%)	0 (0.0%)
Nebraska	11	2 (18.2%)	4 (36.4%)	5 (45.4%)	0 (0.0%)	0 (0.0%)
Nevada	79	30 (38.0%)	40 (50.6%)	8 (10.1%)	0 (0.0%)	1 (1.3%)
New Hampshire	1	1 (100.0%)	0 (0.0%)	0 (0.0%)	0 (0.0%)	0 (0.0%)
New Mexico	2	0 (0.0%)	2 (100.0%)	0 (0.0%)	0 (0.0%)	0 (0.0%)
North Carolina	161	83 (51.5%)	65 (40.4%)	4 (2.5%)	8 (5.0%)	1 (0.6%)
Ohio	147	76 (51.7%)	65 (44.2%)	3 (2.0%)	1 (0.7%)	2 (1.4%)
Oklahoma	60	25 (41.7%)	29 (48.3%)	3 (5.0%)	4 (7.0%)	0 (0.0%)
Oregon	36	4 (11.1%)	28 (77.8%)	3 (8.3%)	1 (2.8%)	0 (0.0%)
Pennsylvania	202	116 (57.4%)	67 (33.2%)	17 (8.4%)	0 (0.0%)	2 (1.0%)
South Carolina	53	29 (54.7%)	22 (41.5%)	2 (3.8%)	0 (0.0%)	0 (0.0%)
South Dakota	3	0 (0.0%)	3 (100.0%)	0 (0.0%)	0 (0.0%)	0 (0.0%)
Tennessee	87	37 (42.6%)	45 (51.7%)	1 (1.1%)	2 (2.3%)	2 (2.3%)
Texas	300	121 (40.3%)	87 (29.0%)	88 (29.3%)	0 (0.0%)	4 (1.4%)
Utah	9	1 (11.1%)	5 (55.6%)	2 (22.2%)	1 (11.1%)	0 (0.0%)

Table 3.2 Death Row Populations by Race, Winter 2013—cont'd

State	Total	Black	White	Latino	Native American	Asian
Virginia	11	4 (36.4%)	6 (54.5%)	1 (9.1%)	0 (0.0%)	0 (0.0%)
Washington	8	4 (50.0%)	4 (50.0%)	0 (0.0%)	0 (0.0%)	0 (0.0%)
Wyoming	1	0 (0.0%)	1 (100.0%)	0 (0.0%)	0 (0.0%)	0 (0.0%)
U.S. Government	61	30 (49.2%)	24 (39.3%)	6 (9.8%)	1 (1.7%)	0 (0.0%)
U.S. Military	5	3 (60.0%)	2 (40.0%)	0 (0.0%)	0 (0.0%)	0 (0.0%)

charges are brought. Some district attorney's offices virtually admitted bias in practice, as was the case in *Miller-El v. Dretke* (2005).[31] In this case, the prosecutor's office circulated a memo calling for automatic dismissal of minority jurors through peremptory strikes, regardless of education or socioeconomic status. For an example of such a "memorandum," see Box 3.2, which exhibits an excerpt from a prosecutor's manual on jury selection in a criminal case that was leaked from the Dallas County, Texas, prosecutor's office to *The Texas Observer* in 1973.

BOX 3.2 EXCERPT FROM: PROSECUTOR'S MANUAL ON JURY SELECTION IN A CRIMINAL CASE (1973)

- You are not looking for a fair juror but rather a strong, biased, and sometimes hypocritical individual who believes that defendants are different from them in kind rather than in degree. You are not looking for any member of a minority group which may subject him to oppression—they almost always empathize with the accused. You are not looking for free thinkers or flower children.
- Observation is worthwhile . . . look for physical afflictions. These people usually sympathize with the accused.
- I don't like women jurors because I can't trust them. They do, however, make the best jurors in cases involving crimes against children.
- Extremely overweight people, especially women and young men, indicate a lack of self-discipline and oftentimes instability. I like the lean and hungry look.
- If the veniremen have not lived in the county long, ask where they were born and reared. People from small town and rural areas generally make good state's jurors. People from the east and west coasts often make bad jurors.
- Intellectuals such as teachers etc. generally are too liberal and contemplative to make good State's jurors.
- Ask veniremen their religious preference. Jewish veniremen generally make poor State's jurors. Jews have a history of oppression and generally empathize with the accused. Lutherans and Church of Christ veniremen usually make good State's jurors.

Source. The *Texas Observer*, May 11, 1973: p. 9.

Though there is rarely a "smoking gun" memorandum similar to that presented in Box 3.2, many prosecutors utilize the same reservations during voir dire, believing that minority jurors are less willing to sentence someone to death, particularly if the defendant is of the same race. Another practice used by

---

[31]*Miller-El v. Dretke*, 545 U.S. 231 (2005).

prosecutors to exclude minorities is jury shuffling. This process allows the parties to rearrange the order in which the potential jurors are questioned during voir dire. The only information available on the juror cards is juror appearance. In the *Miller-El* case,[32] the prosecutors used jury shuffling to move blacks that were at the front of the potential jury panel to the back of the potential jury panel, which would lessen their chances of being selected. In the trial of Albert Jefferson in Alabama, for instance, the prosecutor used discretionary challenges against 24 of the 26 prospective jurors who were black. The result was an all-white jury. Long after the trial had concluded, counsel for Jefferson discovered that the district attorney had applied the following juror ranking system: (a) Strong, (b) Medium, (c) Weak, and the least desirable category, (d) Black. Even in the wake of this discovery, the Alabama court refused to grant Jefferson relief based on the blatant discrimination based on race (he did, however, obtain relief on another issue).[33]

Information given to prosecutors by the police may also influence prosecutorial decisions when pursuing a death sentence. The amount of hard evidence may be different because police and sheriff's departments often pursue criminal activity in white neighborhoods more aggressively than crime in black or minority neighborhoods. Discrimination or racial bias on the part of law enforcement may have a significant and direct impact on the prosecutor's ability to pursue the death penalty. There have been few, if any, limitations on prosecutorial discretion, even in light of the "death is different" position of the Supreme Court. The following examples in *The Color of Justice*[34] show some cases of prosecutorial appeals to bias:

- An Alabama prosecutor declared, "Unless you hang this Negro, our white people living out in the country won't be safe."[35]
- A prosecutor in North Carolina dismissed an implausible claim of three black men that the white women they were accused of raping had consented to sex with them. The prosecutor stated that "the average white woman abhors anything of this type in nature that had to do with a black man."[36]
- A prosecutor in a rape case involving a black man and a white woman asked the jurors, "Gentlemen, do you believe that she would have had intercourse with this black brute?"[37]
- A prosecutor in a case involving the alleged kidnapping of a white man by two black men said in his closing argument that "not one white witness has been produced" to rebut the victim's testimony.[38]
- A prosecutor stated during the penalty phase of a capital case involving Walter J. Blair, a black man charged with murdering a white woman, "Can you imagine [the victim's] state of mind when she woke up at 6 o'clock that morning staring into the muzzle of a gun held by this black man?"[39]

---

[32]Id.

[33]Bryan A. Stevenson and Ruth E. Friedman, *Deliberate Indifference: Judicial Tolerance of Racial Bias in Criminal Justice*, 51 WASH. & LEE L. REV. 509, 520, 527 n.45 (1994).

[34]Samuel Walker, Cassia Spohn, and Miriam DeLone, THE COLOR OF JUSTICE: RACE, ETHNICITY, AND CRIME IN AMERICA, 5th ed., 2012.

[35]*Moulton v. State*, 199 Ala. 411 (1917).

[36]*Miller v. North Carolina*, 583 F.2d 701 (4th Cir. 1978).

[37]*State v. Washington*, 67 So. 930 (La. Sup. Ct. 1915).

[38]*Withers v. United States*, 602 F.2d 124 (6th Cir. 1976).

[39]*Blair v. Armontrout*, 916 F.2d 1310 (8th Cir. 1990).

The judiciary rarely reviews prosecutorial decisions due to separation-of-powers concerns, the desire to enhance the efficiency of the criminal justice system, and the potential chilling effect on law enforcement and because the prosecutors' decisions reflect their expertise. Deferring to the expertise and discretion of prosecutors, the Supreme Court typically resists calls to review prosecutorial decisions, instead deferring to prosecutors' expertise and discretion and presuming that the duties of the district attorney are being carried out correctly. This was most prominently displayed in the decision in *United States v. Bass* (2002).[40] In a per curiam opinion, the Supreme Court ruled that a defendant must establish that the prosecutors were motivated by intentions to discriminate and that the actions of the prosecutor had a discriminatory impact on the defendant. Some legal scholars argue that this decision is misguided and places a different burden on defendants.[41] The Court in *Bass* relied on *United States v. Armstrong* (1993),[42] which created the general standard for selective prosecution claims in which the defendant must show evidence that individuals with similar sets of circumstances could have faced prosecution but did not. The Court did not want to intrude on the executive branch's power to enforce laws. It is not inconceivable that this decision might give prosecutors even more power to decide whom to send to a capital trial.

The case of *Snyder v. Louisiana*[43] (2008) is one in which the prosecutor's use of peremptory challenges to strike prospective black jurors has been decided by the Supreme Court. Justice Breyer commented during oral arguments that he believed if district attorneys could not learn to use peremptory challenges in a race-neutral way, then peremptory challenges should be done away with altogether. While it is unlikely that the Supreme Court would resort to such lengths in the wake of *Snyder*, the decision handed down by the Supreme Court could further restrict the ability of prosecutors to offer "racially neutral" explanations that are weak or unfeasible.

B Defense Attorneys

Many issues surround the effectiveness of counsel for capital defendants. The ABA, after an exhaustive study of the issues, found that "the inadequacy and inadequate compensation of counsel at trial" was one of the "principal failings of the capital punishment systems in the states today."[44] Another extensive study of death penalty cases in six Southern states revealed that capital trials are "more like a random flip of the coin than a delicate balancing of the scales" because defense attorneys are too often "ill-trained, unprepared . . . and grossly underpaid."[45] A recent report by the ACLU concluded the following about the problems inherent in legal representation in capital cases:

> *While capital cases are among the most complex, time-intensive, and financially draining cases to try, indigent capital defendants often are appointed attorneys who are overworked, underpaid, lacking critical resources, incompetent, or inexperienced in trying death penalty cases. Incompetent*

---

[40]*United States v. Bass*, 536 U.S.862 (2002).
[41]Jessie Larson, Unequal Justice: *The Supreme Court's Failure to Curtail Selective Prosecution for the Death Penalty*, 93 J. Crim. L. & Criminology 1009 (2003).
[42]992 F.2d 171 (8th Cir. 1993).
[43]*Snyder v. Louisiana*, 552 U.S. 472 (2008).
[44]American Bar Association, *Toward a More Just and Effective System of Review in State Death Penalty Cases*, 40 Am. U. L. Rev. 1, 79–92 (1990).
[45]Marcia Coyle et al., *Fatal Defense: Trial and Error in the Nation's Death Belt*, Nat. L.J., June 11, 1990, at 30.

defense attorneys fail to investigate cases thoroughly, fail to present compelling mitigating evidence, and fail to call witnesses that would aid in the defense. In addition, enormous caseloads, caps on defender fees, and a critical lack of resources for investigation and expert assistance are barriers to the presentation of an adequate and effective defense. The problem of inadequate counsel is not isolated to a few bad attorneys; it is a widespread and systematic failure to ensure access to justice for defendants facing capital charges and those convicted of capital crimes.[46]

A poor person facing the death penalty has little choice but to accept representation by an attorney who has little or no experience working on capital or other serious criminal cases. Moreover, appointed counsel in capital cases may be reluctant or resistant to representing the defendant, likely has little or no empathy or understanding of the accused or his particular plight, lacks appropriate knowledge of criminal or capital punishment law, and is unaware of the need to document and present mitigating circumstances.[47] These appointed attorneys typically have other cases and no vested interest in representing the defendant. One attorney explained his dilemma:

I could not take days at a time out of my office to do essentially non-legal work. And investigation is necessary, certainly, to prepare a case, but it is non-legal. . . . You're actually pounding the pavement, trying to come up with the same information that a person who is paid substantially less per hour could take care of, I mean, whether it be the investigator for the Sheriff's Department or the District Attorney's office or the FBI, or the U.S. Attorney's office. You don't find the U.S. Attorney pounding the pavement, trying to investigate facts. . . . And it just creates a terrible situation when you have to do everything for yourself.[48]

It is difficult to ensure effectiveness of counsel due to lack of funding and overburdened public defenders, but it is of greater concern if the lawyer shows racial prejudice. In order for an adequate defense to be raised, lawyers must research a defendant's social history and meet with friends and family members to prepare for trial. A lawyer who has feelings of racial superiority cannot adequately fill the role of advocate for the defendant. Melvin Wade was assigned such an attorney. During the trial, Wade's attorney used racial slurs to refer to Wade and failed to present Wade's childhood abuse as a mitigating factor. The lawyer also told the jury during closing arguments that he believed his client should receive the death penalty.[49] In a declaration to the Ninth Circuit Court of Appeals in California, Kim Taylor summarized how counsel's racial bias influenced his trial performance: "From the evidence before me, it seems clear that race played a significant and insidious role in Mr. Wade's trial . . . he was represented by a man who viewed blacks with contempt, and this evidence is supported by the manner in which he carried himself at trial."[50]

Another case in which the court-appointed attorney showed racial bias was the case of Wilburn Dobbs. His lawyer referred to Dobbs as "colored" and stated before the trial that he was in a better position to prosecute the case than defend it. During a federal court hearing on Dobbs's appeal, the

---

[46]ACLU, Slamming the Courthouse Doors: Denial of Access to Justice and Remedy in America (Dec. 2010). Accessed on Aug. 25, 2013, at www.aclu.org/files/assets/HRP_UPRsubmission_annex.pdf.

[47]Stephen Bright, *Counsel for the Poor: The Death Sentence Not for The Worst Crime but for the Worst Lawyer*, 103 YALE L. J. 1835 (1994).

[48]*Id.*

[49]*Wade v. Calderon*, 29 F.3d 1342 (1994).

[50]*Id.*

lawyer testified that he believed blacks were uneducated and less intelligent than whites. He also admitted he used the word "nigger" in a joking context.[51]

Obviously, not all public defenders or court-appointed attorneys are so blatant about their prejudices. Would a conscientious and neutral counsel have helped Wade or Dobbs avoid a death sentence? The federal court that heard Dobbs's appeal did not believe so, ruling that neither the attitudes of the trial judge nor defense attorney, nor the racial prejudice of the jury, required that Dobbs's death sentence be set aside, because none of the jurors "viewed blacks as more prone to violence than whites or as morally inferior to whites."[52] Their logic might leave the impression that racial prejudice that is not tolerated in other facets of American society might still be tolerated in some U.S. courts. While such blatant bias likely exists, it does not characterize the proceedings in most U.S. courts.

V THE JURY: A BIASED BUNCH OR VICTIMS OF MISINFORMATION?

Juries are an American tradition, and the right to a trial by jury is constitutionally guaranteed. Recently the Supreme Court decided in *Ring v. Arizona* (2002)[53] that death sentences must be determined by juries, not judges alone. In Arizona prior to the *Ring* decision and following a jury's finding of guilt in capital cases, the trial judge, sitting alone, determined the presence of aggravating factors required by Arizona law for imposition of the death penalty. The *Ring* decision changed this and emphasized the importance and central fact-finding role of juries in criminal trials (and particularly in capital trials).

In the earlier case of *Walton v. Arizona* (1990),[54] the Supreme Court had upheld Arizona's law allowing judges to make the determination of aggravating factors and thus placing in their hands alone the decision of whether to sentence a defendant to death. Justice Stevens, writing for the dissent, criticized the Court's decision, arguing that the jury's critical role existed at the time the Bill of Rights was adopted. He stated that "by that time,"

> [T]he English jury's role in determining critical facts in homicide cases was entrenched. As fact-finder, the jury had the power to determine not only whether the defendant was guilty of homicide but also the degree of the offense. Moreover, the jury's role in finding facts that would determine a homicide defendant's eligibility for capital punishment was particularly well established. Throughout its history, the jury determined which homicide defendants would be subject to capital punishment by making factual determinations, many of which related to difficult assessments of the defendant's state of mind. By the time the Bill of Rights was adopted, the jury's right to make these determinations was unquestioned.[55]

---

[51]*Dobbs v. Zant*, 963 F.2d at 1407 (1991).
[52]*Id.*
[53]*Ring v. Arizona*, 536 U.S. 584 (2002).
[54]*Walton v. Arizona*, 497 U.S. 639 (1990).
[55]Id. at 710–711, quoting White, *Fact-Finding and the Death Penalty: The Scope of a Capital Defendant's Right to Jury Trial*, 65 Notre Dame L. Rev. 1, 10–11 (1989).

Ten years later, in *Apprendi v. New Jersey* (2000),[56] the Supreme Court said that judges alone may not determine a finding of facts that increases the level of punishment for the defendant. It held that this was a violation of the right to a trial by jury. Justice Scalia, in a concurring opinion, wrote the following:

> *[Such an approach might be] an admirably fair and efficient scheme of criminal justice designed for a society that is prepared to leave criminal justice to the State . . . The founders of the American Republic were not prepared to leave it to the State, which is why the jury-trial guarantee was one of the least controversial provisions of the Bill of Rights. It has never been efficient: but it has always been free.[57]*

In *Ring* the Supreme Court agreed with this argument and applied it to the sentencing phase of capital cases, reemphasizing the importance of juries in the death penalty process.

A Jury Selection

In 1880 the Supreme Court decided *Strauder v. West Virginia*[58] and stated that a West Virginia law restricting jury service to white males violated the equal protection clause of the Fourteenth Amendment. The Court concluded that it was harmful to blacks and states could no longer create laws that banned blacks from juries. Therefore, some states, particularly those in the southern United States, developed techniques to ensure that minorities were excluded from jury service. One such example existed in Delaware:

> *In Delaware, for example, local jurisdictions used lists of taxpayers to select "sober and judicious" persons for jury service. Under this system, African American taxpayers were eligible for jury service, but were seldom, if ever, selected for the jury pool. The state explained this result by noting that few of the African Americans in Delaware were intelligent, experienced, or moral enough to serve as jurors. As the chief justice of the Delaware Supreme Court concluded: "That none but white men were selected is in nowise remarkable in view of the fact—too notorious to be ignored—that the great body of black men residing in this State are utterly unqualified by want of intelligence, experience, or moral integrity."[59]*

Since that time the states and the Supreme Court have argued about issues of racial prejudice in jury selection. While the Court has made it increasingly difficult to discriminate on the basis of race, procedures for jury selection may not always be racially neutral.

Some states use lists of potential jurors from property tax rolls, automobile registrations, and voter registration lists. While the practice seems objective on its face, in many counties or areas minorities are less likely than whites to register to vote or own a vehicle or property.[60] In his book, *No Equal Justice*, David Cole notes that many minorities are less likely to report for jury service due to a variety of reasons, including fear of alienation, loss of wages at work, and skepticism about the criminal justice

---

[56]*Apprendi v. New Jersey,* 530 U. S. 466 (2000).
[57]Id. at 498.
[58]100 U.S. 303 (1880).
[59]Samuel Walker, Cassia Spohn, and Miriam DeLone, THE COLOR OF JUSTICE (5 ed. 2011).
[60]Id.

system. Cole also points to the irony of American jury selection, stating, "[t]hree facts about jury discriminations are largely undisputed. First, the all-white jury has been a staple of the American criminal justice system for most of our history. Second, the Supreme Court has long condemned discrimination in jury selection. And third, race discrimination in jury selection remains a pervasive feature of our justice system to this day. The interesting question is how all of these facts can be true at the same time."[61]

Batson v. Kentucky[62] changed the precedent that required the defendant to prove that the jurisdiction had engaged in a pattern of racial discrimination that was well established.[63] During Batson's trial the prosecution struck all four black venire members from the jury pool. The defense attorney argued that this exclusion of minority jury members violated the Sixth and Fourteenth Amendments. The Supreme Court believed that the burden of proof should not rest with the defendant; instead, it should be the prosecution's burden to explain the exclusion of the jurors. The dissent in *Batson* was concerned that this ruling puts an additional burden on the historical tradition of peremptory challenges.

In 1995, nine years after the *Batson* decision, the Court reinterpreted *Batson v. Kentucky* in *Purkett v. Elem*[64] (1995). In *Purkett*, a prosecutor offered an explanation for striking two black men from the jury pool:

> *I struck number twenty-two because of his long hair. He had long curly hair. He had the longest hair of anybody on the panel by far. He appeared not to be a good juror for that fact, the fact that he had long hair hanging down to shoulder length, curly, unkempt hair. Also, he had a moustache and goatee type beard. And juror number twenty-four also had a moustache and a goatee type beard. Those are the only two people on the jury . . . with the mustache and goatee type beard . . . And I don't like the way they looked, with the way the hair is cut, both of them. And the mustache and the beards looked suspicious to me.*[65]

The Supreme Court held only that a racially neutral explanation had to be given but did not have to be reasonable. The face validity of the explanation offered was the key component, regardless of whether it appeared to be frivolous or based on superstition. Opponents of the *Purkett* holding argue that it allows for circumvention of the requirement that a race-neutral explanation be related to the case that was being tried. In his dissent in *Purkett*, Justice Stevens cautioned as follows: "Today without argument, the Court replaces the *Batson* standard with the surprising announcement that any neutral explanation, no matter 'how implausible or fantastic,' even if it is silly or superstitious, is sufficient to rebut a prima facie case of discrimination."[66]

It has been argued that in order for people to be willing to serve on a jury, the incentive to serve must be better than a few dollars a day and a take-out lunch. Some jurisdictions offer an increase in pay, bus vouchers to and from the courthouse, and money for childcare expenses.[67] Others eschew these

---

[61]David Cole, No EQUAL JUSTICE: RACE AND CLASS IN THE AMERICAN CRIMINAL JUSTICE SYSTEM (1999) at 103.
[62]476 U.S. 79 (1986).
[63]Swain v. Alabama, 380 U.S. 202 (1965).
[64]514 U.S. 765 (1995).
[65]*Purkett v. Elem*, 514 U.S. 765 (1995).
[66]*Purkett v. Elem*, 514 U.S. 765 (1995) (Stevens, J., dissenting).
[67]Michael Higgins, *Few Are Chosen*, A.B.A.J. 50 (1999).

measures, saying that jury service should not require large financial compensation. At the core of the American judicial system is the concept that citizens in the community should do their civic duty regardless of race or ethnicity.

Another, even more controversial, method of selecting jurors known as "race-conscious jury selection" has been advocated. This process could be described as affirmative action for the jury system. This is done by saving seats for minority jurors, sending disproportionate numbers of jury summonses to areas with more minority citizens, or eliminating prospective white jurors until the jury pool matches the minority proportion in the population.[68] The arguments against race-conscious juries are similar to the arguments against affirmative action. Members who are selected because of their minority status might feel as though they are "token" jurors or may feel pressured to act as representatives of their race rather than as neutral jurors. The Sixth Circuit Court of Appeals in *United States v. Ovalle* (1998)[69] held that subtracting whites from jury pools to reach racial proportionality violated the equal protection clause. The debate will certainly continue as proponents believe it is a simple and effective way to create a jury that truly consists of peers in any given community.

B Peremptory Challenges

The Supreme Court has ruled that individuals may not be excluded from jury pools based on their race, but it has not been as stringent in its requirements for jury selection. Thus, peremptory challenges, which are challenges that need no cause or explanation, can and have been used in a discriminatory way toward minorities.

Prosecutors might be under the impression that minorities will side with minority defendants. Conversely, defense attorneys might believe that minority jurors will be more likely to convict white defendants. In Philadelphia a district attorney advised fellow prosecutors that young black women have "resentment for law enforcement. There is resentment for authority and as a result you don't want these people on your jury."[70] The Supreme Court was recently asked to decide whether a set of different questions used for different races was unconstitutional. In *Miller-El v. Dretke* (2005),[71] Dallas County prosecutors used peremptory strikes to exclude 10 of 11 eligible blacks to serve on a capital jury. The petitioner moved that the jury be struck down on the grounds that the exclusion violated the equal protection clause. Although the petitioner presented evidence supporting his motion at a pretrial hearing, he was denied relief by the trial judge. The trial judge found no evidence, under then-controlling *Swain v. Alabama* (1965),[72] that a systematic exclusion of blacks had occurred. The jury found Miller-El guilty and sentenced him to death.

Blacks were excluded from Miller-El's jury at a significantly higher ratio than whites. Twenty blacks were initially previewed by the prosecution and defense out of a possible 108. Nine of the 20 were excused by agreement or cause. All but one of the remaining black jurors were excluded

---

[68]*Supra* note 30 at 1840.
[69]136 F.3d 1092 (1998).
[70]*Former Philadelphia Prosecutor Accused of Racial Bias in Election Year*, NEW YORK TIMES (April 3, 1997:B19).
[71]545 U.S. 231 (U.S. 2005).
[72]380 U.S. 202 (1965).

by prosecution peremptory strikes (91%), while only four out of 31 (13%) nonblack jurors were stricken from the jury by the prosecution. The prosecution questioned potential jurors about their views on the death penalty and their willingness to serve on a capital jury. Responses that showed reluctance or hesitation to impose the death penalty were used as a justification for peremptory strikes (*Wainwright v. Witt*, 1985).[73] The members of the jury were given different sets of questions, by race, that attributed the varying degrees of responses. Black prospective jurors were read a description of what would happen to Miller-El in the execution chamber and then asked whether they could sentence someone to death. The majority of white jurors were asked how they felt about capital punishment and whether they could serve on a capital jury. An even greater disparity occurred in the way in which the prosecution questioned members of the venire about their willingness to impose the minimum sentence for murder. White jurors were asked if they could give a person five years if the case was justified. In *Huffman v. State*,[74] an unwillingness to do so was justified for removal from a case. All but one of the black jurors was asked what they thought a minimum sentence should be.

The prosecution in *Miller-El* also utilized jury shuffling. Under this Texas criminal procedure practice, parties are permitted to rearrange the order in which the potential jurors are questioned. The only information known is juror appearance and the order of juror cards. The cards are shuffled into a new order. Jurors shuffled to the back of the panel are far less likely to be questioned or to serve, since jurors not questioned during voir dire are excused at the end of the week. The prosecution on at least two occasions shuffled the jury when a large number of blacks were at the beginning of the panel. The petitioner also presented evidence in which the Dallas County prosecutor's office had a formalized policy to exclude minorities from juries. A circular created by the district attorney's office in 1963 instructed prosecutors to exercise their peremptory strikes against minorities regardless of wealth or education. A manual had been distributed to prosecutors that included the reasons for minority exclusion from jury service. The manual had been available to a prosecutor in Miller-El's trial. Although the state claimed that these practices had been discontinued, the state, by its own admission, had requested a jury shuffle to reduce the number of blacks on the jury panel.

The state's defense at the trial relied on *Swain*, which did not require a judge to analyze the credibility of prosecution explanations. The *Batson* hearing was held two years after voir dire, where distortion is not uncommon due to the passage of time. The prosecution claimed that it excused black jurors in view of the fact that they showed ambivalence about the death penalty and hesitated to execute those capable of rehabilitation. White jurors who were selected for the jury also showed ambivalence and unwillingness to give a death sentence. The Court in *Batson* thought that proof of discriminatory impact "may for all practical purposes demonstrate unconstitutionality because in various circumstances the discrimination is very difficult to explain on nonracial grounds."[75] The state's use and delay of jury shuffling also shows a desire to dismiss minority jurors. The Dallas County District Attorney's Office had admitted using jury shuffling to exclude minorities. Blacks had historically been excluded from jury service. In *Minnesota v. McRae* (1992),[76] the prosecutor questioned and struck down the

---

[73]469 U.S. 412 (1985).
[74]450 S.W.2d 858 (Tex. Crim. App. 1970).
[75]*Batson v. Kentucky*, 476 U.S. at 93.
[76]494 N.W.2d 252 (1992).

only black member of the venire. She was struck down due to her views that the judicial system had been historically unfair to minorities. The Minnesota Supreme Court found this to be a *Batson* violation because the race of the juror was given relevant consideration. Should jurors be excluded purely on their belief that the system has been unfair to minorities? This question may soon be before the Supreme Court. Recently, in *Rico v. Leftridge-Byrd* (2003),[77] the Third Circuit Court of Appeals ruled that *Batson* applied to Italian-Americans. Jurors in the case were stricken from the jury due to their Italian surnames.[78] To extend *Batson* beyond the scope of blacks could prove to be difficult because ethnicity can be difficult to define.[79] Although the Court decided in *United States v. Martinez-Salazar*[80] that a peremptory challenge to remove a juror solely on the basis of gender, ethnic group, or race was unconstitutional, confusion as to what is a valid race-neutral argument still exists in the courts today.[81]

Snyder v. Louisiana[82] is the most recent case that tackles the issue of peremptory challenges, the striking of jurors, and the offering of "racially neutral" explanations. The prosecutor in this case, whose self-proclaimed specialty was securing the death penalty for murderers, told reporters that this was his "O.J. Simpson case."[83] Even more of an issue is that he did not limit these comments to reporters but commented to the all-white jury that they should not let this defendant "get away with it" like O.J. This, when coupled with the fact that the prosecutor struck all prospective black jurors, was enough to raise the question of whether the prosecutor was purposely discriminatory.

One example given by Snyder's defense attorney during oral arguments before the Supreme Court concerned a black college student. The student was in the middle of student teaching and concerned that the trial would interfere with him completing his teaching duties. The court clerk contacted the dean, who said that serving on the jury would not be a problem. The student said he was "OK" with the dean's comments and would be fine with serving on the jury. A white juror expressed concern that as a contractor he would not be able to finish promised work and that his wife, who had just had surgery, would need help at home with their two children. The prosecutor moved successfully to strike the black juror but raised no objections to the white contractor. The defense attorney for Snyder believed that when a black juror's circumstances are almost identical to a white juror's circumstances and only the black juror is excluded, it is difficult to rule out race as a motivation.[84] The decision by the Supreme Court in *Snyder v. Louisiana*[85] focused mainly on the prosecutor's decision to strike this particular black college student, Mr. Brooks. He was one of 50 individuals who expressed concern about missing work and then expressed willingness to serve once permission or exception was granted by a superior. The Supreme Court also examined the prosecutor's explanation that Mr. Brooks appeared "nervous." Because the trial judge did not make note of Brooks' demeanor, the Court could not assume that

---

[77]340 F.3d 178 (3d Cir. 2003).

[78]Shannon Duffy, *Extension of* Batson *Valid Approach*, 229 THE LEGAL INTELLIGENCER 1 (2003).

[79]*Id.* at 2.

[80]528 U.S. 304 (2000).

[81]Shannon Duffy, *Extension of* Batson *to Whites Is Valid*, NEW JERSEY L.J. (August 15, 2003).

[82]*Snyder v. Louisiana*, 552 U.S. 472 (2008).

[83]Robert Barnes, *Blacks Were Improperly Kept Off La. Jury.* THE WASHINGTON POST, Thursday, March 20, 2008:A3.

[84]Lyle Denniston, *Commentary: Trial Judges on Trial?* Tues., Dec. 4, 2007. Accessed Feb. 4, 2008, at www.scotusblog.com/wp/uncategorized/commentary-trial-judges-on-trial.

[85]Snyder v. Louisiana, *supra.*

Mr. Brooks was any more nervous than most prospective jurors. The decision by the Supreme Court reaffirms the importance of *Batson v. Kentucky*[86] and the role that race might play in jury selection.

Peremptory challenges carry a great potential for misuse.[87] The judicial system should take every precaution to ensure that they are carried out within the boundaries set forth by the Constitution.[88] The vast corruption in the jury process makes systematic changes necessary.[89] The cliché "If it looks like a duck and walks like a duck and talks like a duck . . . then it must be a duck" would apply to racial discrimination in jury selection. The judicial system is so deeply saturated with procedural issues that it fails to examine unfairness that is obvious even to laypeople. The decisions by the Supreme Court have undoubtedly played a role in America's response to racial discrimination and its effect on the death penalty.

The inappropriate use of peremptory challenges was commented on in *Batson v. Kentucky* by Justice Marshall, who stated, "misuse of the peremptory challenge to exclude black jurors has become both common and flagrant."[90] *Batson v. Kentucky* (1986) provided that prosecutors must prove that their exclusions were not racially motivated. *Purkett v. Elem* allowed for a racially neutral explanation to stand regardless of its frivolity. Would changes to the use of peremptory challenges help alleviate claims of racial prejudice? It might be possible to limit the number of strikes allowed to each side. Because the demise of the peremptory challenge is unlikely, the role of racial bias in jury selection will continue to be an issue.

VI IN SUMMARY, WHAT DO THESE CASES SAY?

The Supreme Court began examining racial bias in the death penalty with *Furman v. Georgia* (1972),[91] in which they found the Georgia statute to be biased against racial minorities, particularly blacks. In *Furman*, the Court declared the death penalty unconstitutional but believed that it could be reinstated if the statutes were changed to ensure safeguards that would protect defendants from racial prejudice.

After the death penalty's reinstatement in 1976, the Court once again wrestled with issues of racial discrimination in *McCleskey v. Kemp* (1987).[92] McCleskey sought to use statistics to prove that racial discrimination existed in Georgia's administration of the death penalty. The Court said that general statistics could not show discrimination in particular cases and that defendants must prove that prosecutors and jurors acted discriminatorily, specifically in their case. Just one year before *McCleskey v. Kemp* was decided, the Court decided in *Turner v. Murray* (1986)[93] that defendants had the right to tell jurors in the jury pool the race of their victims to see whether this would prejudice the veniremen against the defendant. Death penalty opponents were struck another blow when the Supreme

---

[86]*Batson v. Kentucky*, 476 US 79 (1986).
[87]Cherie Song, *A Twist on the* Batson *Jury Rule*, Nat'l L.J. Vol. 25, No. 44:7 (2003).
[88]28 U.S.C.A. § 1411.
[89]*Supra* note 12.
[90]*Batson v. Kentucky*, 476 U.S. 79 (1986) (Marshall, J., concurring).
[91]*Furman v. Georgia*, 408 U.S. 238 (1972).
[92]*McCleskey v. Kemp*, 481 U.S. 279 (1987).
[93]*Turner v. Murray*, 476 U.S. 28 (1986).

Court decided *Purkett v. Elem* (1995).[94] In *Purkett*, the Court concluded that if prosecutors offered race-neutral explanations for minority juror exclusion, prosecutors could not be considered as acting in a racially discriminatory manner. This was problematic because any racially neutral explanation could be offered, regardless of its credibility or truth.

The most recent developments in racial discrimination jurisprudence have come in the decisions in *Miller-El v. Dretke* (2005),[95] in which the Supreme Court decided that racially disparate questioning and jury shuffling could not be used to exclude minority jurors and that a Certificate of Eligibility (COE) should have been granted and in *Snyder v. Louisiana* (2008)[96] in which the Court held that striking all black jurors with no substantiated race-neutral explanation violates the Equal Protection Clause. In the latter, the Louisiana Supreme Court upheld the lower court's ruling that the peremptory challenges made by the prosecutor did not constitute racial discrimination. The Supreme Court reversed the state supreme court's decision finding that the prosecutor in the case did engage in purposeful discrimination. This decision potentially reclarifies for prosecutors and defendants alike the necessary protections against racial discrimination in jury selection in light of *Batson* and *Miller-El*.

These cases paint an erratic picture. The Supreme Court, while making decisions to disallow racial discrimination, has also seemingly made it easy for prosecutors and other players in the court process to discriminate as long as it is explained.

VII CONCLUSION

Literature is a way in which one can express views that may not be popular at the time but become accepted as philosophies and societies evolve. In the novel *To Kill a Mockingbird*, author Harper Lee declared, "In our courts, when it's a white man's word against a black man's the white man always wins. They're ugly but those are the facts of life. The one place where a man ought to get a square deal is a courtroom, be he any color of the rainbow, but people have a way of carrying their resentments right into a jury box."[97] As noted in the court cases we've discussed, racial discrimination and bias still exist in decisions about the death penalty, whether subtly or blatantly. *Turner v. Murray* (1986) gave defendants the right to bring the issue of potential bias to the jury on the issue of the victim's race. One year later, death penalty opponents were dealt a major setback when the Supreme Court ruled in *McCleskey v. Kemp*[98] that general statistics do not in themselves establish unconstitutional discrimination in individual cases. There is still no definitive answer as to how racial bias can be eradicated in capital proceedings. With human beings involved in every phase of the criminal justice system, it is perhaps naïve to think that discrimination can be eliminated in death penalty cases, where bias-free proceedings should be the constitutional norm.

---

[94]514 U.S. 765 (1995).
[95]545 U.S. 231 (2005).
[96]552 U.S. 472 (2008).
[97]Harper Lee, To Kill a Mockingbird (1960) at 220.
[98]481 U.S. 279 (1987).

CASES BRIEFED IN CHAPTER 3

Case	Issue	Holding
Batson v. Kentucky 476 US 79 (1986)	Does the equal protection clause forbid the use of peremptory challenges based solely on race?	It is unconstitutional to use peremptory challenges on the basis of race.
McClesky v. Kemp 481 U.S. 279 (1987)	Does a statistical study showing racial disparity in death penalty cases establish an individual's claim of racial bias as a violation of the Eighth and Fourteenth Amendments to the Constitution?	Statistical studies that show racial prejudice in capital proceedings do not indicate constitutional violations, because they fail to prove that the decision makers in a particular case acted with racial prejudice.
Turner v. Murray 476 US 28 (1986)	Does a defendant have the right to inform the jury that he or she is accused of an interracial capital crime and to question jurors on their racial bias?	A defendant accused of an interracial capital crime is entitled to have prospective jurors informed of the victim's race and questioned on the issue of racial bias.
Miller-El v. Dretke 545 U.S. 231 (2005)	Is the use of racially disparate questioning in jury selection a violation of the Equal Protection Clause of the Fourteenth Amendment?	It is a violation of the Constitution to use racially disparate questioning to exclude prospective jurors in a capital proceeding.
Snyder v. Louisiana 552 U.S. 472 (2008)	Did the state's exclusion of all black prospective jurors through the use of peremptory challenges, coupled with the prosecutor's reference to the O.J. Simpson case, constitute a violation of the Equal Protection Clause of the Fourteenth Amendment?	It is a violation of the Equal Protection Clause to strike all black jurors if no substantiated racially neutral explanations are offered.

CASE BRIEFS

BATSON v. KENTUCKY 476 U.S. 79 (1986)

CAPSULE: Excluding members of the defendant's race from a jury solely on racial grounds violates the equal protection rights of both the defendant and the excluded jurors.

FACTS: Batson was brought to trial on charges of second-degree burglary and receipt of stolen goods. During voir dire the prosecutor utilized peremptory strikes to exclude all four black individuals in the jury pool. The jury that was selected comprised only white individuals. Counsel for the defendant moved to strike the jury before it was sworn in because the removal of all of the black veniremen was a violation of the defendant's Sixth Amendment right to a jury of one's peers and a Fourteenth Amendment violation of equal protection. The trial judge ruled that peremptory challenges could be utilized to "strike anybody they wanted to," reasoning that the cross-section of the community component of the Sixth Amendment only applied to the venire and not the actual jury itself.

Continued

BATSON v. KENTUCKY 476 U.S. 79 (1986)—cont'd

ISSUE: Does the equal protection clause forbid the use of peremptory challenges based solely on race? YES.

HOLDING: It is unconstitutional to use peremptory challenges to exclude potential jurors on the basis of race.

REASON: "A defendant has no right to a petit jury composed in whole or in part of persons of his own race. *Strauder v. West Virginia*, 100 U.S. 303, 305. However, the Equal Protection Clause guarantees the defendant that the State will not exclude members of his race from the jury venire on account of race, or on the false assumption that members of his race as a group are not qualified to serve as jurors. By denying a person participation in jury service on account of his race, the State also unconstitutionally discriminates against the excluded juror. Moreover, selection procedures that purposefully exclude black persons from juries undermine public confidence in the fairness of our system of justice."

"The same equal protection principles as are applied to determine whether there is discrimination in selecting the venire also govern the State's use of peremptory challenges to strike individual jurors from the petit jury. Although a prosecutor ordinarily is entitled to exercise peremptory challenges for any reason, as long as that reason is related to his view concerning the outcome of the case to be tried, the Equal Protection Clause forbids the prosecutor to challenge potential jurors solely on account of their race or on the assumption that black jurors as a group will be unable impartially to consider the State's case against a black defendant."

"A defendant may establish a prima facie case of purposeful discrimination solely on evidence concerning the prosecutor's exercise of peremptory challenges at the defendant's trial. The defendant first must show that he is a member of a cognizable racial group, and that the prosecutor has exercised peremptory challenges to remove from the venire members of the defendant's race. The defendant may also rely on the fact that peremptory challenges constitute a jury selection practice that permits those to discriminate who are of a mind to discriminate. Finally, the defendant must show that such facts and any other relevant circumstances raise an inference that the prosecutor used peremptory challenges to exclude the veniremen from the petit jury on account of their race. Once the defendant makes a prima facie showing, the burden shifts to the State to come forward with a neutral explanation for challenging black jurors. The prosecutor may not rebut a prima facie showing by stating that he challenged the jurors on the assumption that they would be partial to the defendant because of their shared race or by affirming his good faith in individual selections."

CASE SIGNIFICANCE: *Batson v. Kentucky* reestablished the principle that peremptory strikes cannot be based solely upon the race or racial assumptions. The Court extended the *Swain v. Alabama* (1965)[99] decision in that once the prima facie case of racial discrimination has been made, the burden of proof is no longer on the defendant to establish that the elimination of blacks was part of an established pattern of discrimination. The Court, however, in *Purkett v. Elem* (1995)[100] noted that *Batson* required only that the prosecutor provide a race-neutral justification for the exclusion, not that the justification is plausible. In *Batson* the Court outlined three steps that courts must follow in resolving cases of peremptory jury disqualification based on race:

1. The side making the allegations must establish a prima facie (at first sight) case of discrimination based on race or other forbidden grounds.
2. If step 1 is established, then the burden shifts to the side that made the peremptory strike to come up with a race-neutral explanation for the strike.
3. The trial court is then required to decide whether the side opposing the peremptory challenges has proved purposeful discrimination.

---

[99]*Swain v. Alabama*, 380 U.S. 202 (1965).
[100]*Purkett v. Elem*, 514 U.S. 765 (1995).

McCLESKEY v. KEMP 481 U.S. 279 (1987)

CAPSULE: Statistical studies that indicate racial bias in capital sentencing do not violate the Eighth and Fourteenth Amendments. What is needed is proof of racial bias in that defendant's case.

FACTS: McCleskey, who was black, was sentenced to death for the murder of a white police officer that occurred during the commission of a robbery. McCleskey challenged the death sentence as a violation of the Equal Protection Clause of the Fourteenth Amendment and claimed that it was a cruel and unusual sentence under the Eighth Amendment. McCleskey used the Baldus study, which claimed to show that racial disparity existed in the imposition of death sentences in Georgia. The study shows that black defendants who are accused of killing white victims have the highest likelihood of receiving the death penalty.

ISSUE: Does a statistical study showing racial disparity in death penalty cases establish an individual's claim of racial bias as a violation of the Eighth and Fourteenth Amendments to the Constitution? NO.

HOLDING: Statistical studies that show racial prejudice in capital proceedings do not indicate constitutional violations because they fail to prove that the decision makers in a particular case acted with racial prejudice.

REASON: "McCleskey's first claim is that the Georgia capital punishment statute violates the Equal Protection Clause of the Fourteenth Amendment. He argues that race has infected the administration of Georgia's statute in two ways: persons who murder whites are more likely to be sentenced to death than persons who murder blacks, and black murderers are more likely to be sentenced to death than white murderers. As a black defendant who killed a white victim, McCleskey claims that the Baldus study demonstrates that he was discriminated against because of his race and because of the race of his victim. In its broadest form, McCleskey's claim of discrimination extends to every actor in the Georgia capital sentencing process, from the prosecutor who sought the death penalty and the jury that imposed the sentence, to the State itself that enacted the capital punishment statute and allows it to remain in effect despite its allegedly discriminatory application. We agree with the Court of Appeals, and every other court that has considered such a challenge, that this claim must fail."

"McCleskey also suggests that the Baldus study proves that the State as a whole has acted with a discriminatory purpose. He appears to argue that the State has violated the Equal Protection Clause by adopting the capital punishment statute and allowing it to remain in force despite its allegedly discriminatory application. But "'[discriminatory purpose' . . . implies more than intent as volition or intent as awareness of consequences. It implies that the decisionmaker, in this case a state legislature, selected or reaffirmed a particular course of action at least in part 'because of,' not merely 'in spite of,' its adverse effects upon an identifiable group." To evaluate McCleskey's challenge, we must examine exactly what the Baldus study may show. Even Professor Baldus does not contend that his statistics prove that race enters into any capital sentencing decisions or that race was a factor in McCleskey's particular case. Statistics at most may show only a likelihood that a particular factor entered into some decisions. There is, of course, some risk of racial prejudice influencing a jury's decision in a criminal case. There are similar risks that other kinds of prejudice will influence other criminal trials. See *infra*, at 315–318. The question "is at what point that risk becomes constitutionally unacceptable," *Turner v. Murray*, 476 U.S. 28, 36 (1986). McCleskey asks us to accept the likelihood allegedly shown by the Baldus study as the constitutional measure of an unacceptable risk of racial prejudice influencing capital sentencing decisions. This we decline to do."

"Because of the risk that the factor of race may enter the criminal justice process, we have engaged in 'unceasing efforts' to eradicate racial prejudice from our criminal justice system. *Batson v. Kentucky*, 476 U.S. 79, 85 (1986). Our efforts have been guided by our recognition that "the inestimable privilege of trial by jury . . . is a vital principle, underlying the whole administration of criminal justice.""

CASE SIGNIFICANCE: "This case declares that in death penalty cases, statistical studies showing discrimination in the imposition of the penalty do not in themselves prove that the state has violated the equal protection clause of the Constitution. In order for a claim of discrimination to succeed, 'petitioner must prove that decision makers in

Continued

McCLESKEY v. KEMP 481 U.S. 279 (1987)—cont'd

his case acted with discriminatory purpose.' It is not enough to allege and prove through statistical study that a particular race has been discriminated against (as established by the Baldus study); the person alleging discrimination must prove that there was discrimination in his or her particular case."[101]

The Court said that discretion is essential in criminal justice and that "exceptionally clear proof is required before this Court will infer that the discretion has been abused." That was not proved in this case. All that the defendant proved was that there was discrimination against blacks in the imposition of the death penalty in Georgia, not that discretion was clearly abused. The Court added that the defendant's claim, taken to its logical conclusion, "throws into serious question the principles that underlie the entire criminal justice system." Were the defendants to prevail, his claim could be extended "to apply to other types of penalties and to claims based on unexplained discrepancies correlating to membership in other minority groups and even to gender." Absolute equality in sentences is not required by the Constitution. What the Constitution prohibits is abuse of discretion that amounts to a violation of the Equal Protection Clause.[102]

TURNER v. MURRAY 476 U.S. 28 (1986)

CAPSULE: A defendant accused of an interracial capital crime is entitled to have prospective jurors informed of the victim's race and questioned on the issue of racial bias.

FACTS: Turner, who was black, shot and killed a white jewelry store proprietor with a sawed-off shotgun during the robbery of the jewelry store. During voir dire of the jury, Turner's counsel requested that the prospective jurors be told that Turner was black and that his victim was white and be asked if this would prejudice them against Turner. This request was denied by the judge. The jury, which consisted of eight whites and four blacks, sentenced Turner to death.

ISSUE: Does a defendant have the right to inform the jury that he or she is accused of an interracial capital crime and to question jurors on their racial bias? YES.

HOLDING: A defendant accused of an interracial capital crime is entitled to have prospective jurors informed of the victim's race and questioned on the issue of racial bias.

REASON: "Because of the range of discretion entrusted to a jury in a capital sentencing hearing, there is a unique opportunity for racial prejudice to operate but remain undetected. On the facts of this case, a juror who believes that blacks are violence prone or morally inferior might well be influenced by that belief in deciding whether petitioner's crime involved the aggravating factors specified under Virginia law. Such a juror might also be less favorably inclined toward petitioner's evidence of mental disturbance as a mitigating circumstance. More subtle, less consciously held racial attitudes could also influence a juror's decision in this case. Fear of blacks, which could easily be stirred up by the violent facts of petitioner's crime, might incline a juror to favor the death penalty."

"The risk of racial prejudice infecting a capital sentencing proceeding is especially serious in light of the complete finality of the death sentence. "The Court, as well as the separate opinions of a majority of the individual Justices, has recognized that the qualitative difference of death from all other punishments requires a correspondingly greater degree of scrutiny of the capital sentencing determination." *California v. Ramos*, 463 U.S. 992, 998–999 (1983). We have struck down capital sentences when we found that the circumstances under which they were imposed "created an

Continued

---

[101]Rolando V. Del Carmen, Susan E. Ritter, and Betsy A. Witt, Briefs of Leading Cases in Corrections (5th ed. 2008) at 219-20.
[102]*Id.*

TURNER v. MURRAY 476 U.S. 28 (1986)—cont'd

unacceptable risk that 'the death penalty [may have been] meted out arbitrarily or capriciously' or through 'whim . . . or mistake.'" *Caldwell, supra*, at 343 (O'Connor, J., concurring in part and concurring in judgment) (citation omitted). In the present case, we find the risk that racial prejudice may have infected petitioner's capital sentencing unacceptable in light of the ease with which that risk could have been minimized. By refusing to question prospective jurors on racial prejudice, the trial judge failed to adequately protect petitioner's constitutional right to an impartial jury."

"The inadequacy of voir dire in this case requires that petitioner's death sentence be vacated. It is not necessary, however, that he be retried on the issue of guilt. Our judgment in this case is that there was an unacceptable risk of racial prejudice infecting the capital sentencing proceeding. This judgment is based on a conjunction of three factors: the fact that the crime charged involved interracial violence, the broad discretion given the jury at the death-penalty hearing, and the special seriousness of the risk of improper sentencing in a capital case."

CASE SIGNIFICANCE: Race affects the thinking of nearly everyone in society. For some, this is neither conscious nor malicious. Justice White explained that three factors—the interracially violent crime, the broad discretion given the jury at the death penalty hearing, and the special seriousness of the risk of improper sentencing in a capital case—make the risk of racial prejudice unacceptable in capital sentencing proceedings. Mock jury studies examining the effects of the defendant's race on jurors' decisions, however, show that the defendant's race affects guilt determinations more often than it affects sentences; it is the subtle, unconscious alteration of judgment, not the conscious desire to injure, that most threatens the fair administration of the criminal justice system. A meta-analysis of experimental studies on racial bias in criminal sentencing found that both the race of the defendant and that of the victim influenced white mock jurors' sentencing decisions across a range of cases, resulting in a pattern that most negatively affects black defendants whose victims are white.[103]

MILLER-EL v. DRETKE 545 U.S. 231 (2005)

CAPSULE: Prosecutors cannot use racially disparate questioning or jury shuffling to exclude minorities from jury service.

FACTS: Dallas County prosecutors used peremptory strikes to exclude 10 of 11 eligible blacks to serve on a capital jury. The petitioner moved that the jury be struck down on the ground that the exclusion violated the Equal Protection Clause. Although the petitioner presented evidence supporting his motion at a pretrial hearing, he was denied relief by the trial judge. The trial judge found no evidence, as required by the controlling precedent in *Swain v. Alabama* (1965),[104] that a systematic exclusion of blacks had occurred. The jury found Miller-El guilty and sentenced him to death. While his appeal was pending, the Supreme Court established a three-part process for evaluating equal protection claims like that of the petitioner in *Batson v. Kentucky* (1986).[105] The Texas Court of Criminal Appeals remanded the case in light of *Batson* and the original trial court reheard the evidence. The trial court believed that the petitioner failed to meet the first step outlined in *Batson* because the evidence did not infer racial motivation by the state's peremptory challenges. The three-step process outlined in *Batson* is:

1. The side making the allegations must establish a prima facie (at first sight) case of discrimination based on race or other forbidden grounds.

Continued

---

[103]Laura T. Sweeney and Craig Haney, *The Influence of Race on Sentencing: A Meta-Analytic Review of Experimental Studies*, 10 Behav. Sci. & L. 179 (1992).
[104]Swain v. Alabama, 380 U.S. 202 (1965).
[105]Batson v. Kentucky, 476 U.S. 79 (1986).

MILLER-EL v. DRETKE 545 U.S. 231 (2005)—cont'd

---

2. If step 1 is established, then the burden shifts to the side that made the peremptory strike to come up with a race-neutral explanation for the strike.
3. The trial court is then required to decide whether the side opposing the peremptory challenges has proved purposeful discrimination.

The court also believed that the state did not violate steps 2 or 3 because the prosecutors had reasonable race-neutral explanations for excluding the blacks. Miller-El then filed a federal habeas petition after appeals and state habeas petitions were denied.

ISSUE: Is the use of racially disparate questioning in jury selection a violation of the Equal Protection Clause of the Fourteenth Amendment? YES.

HOLDING: It is a violation of the Constitution to use racially disparate questioning to exclude prospective jurors from a capital proceeding.

REASON: "A comparative analysis of the venire members demonstrates that African-Americans were excluded from petitioner's jury in a ratio significantly higher than Caucasians were. Of the 108 possible jurors reviewed by the prosecution and defense, 20 were African-American. Nine of them were excused for cause or by agreement of the parties. Of the 11 African-American jurors remaining, however, all but one were excluded by peremptory strikes exercised by the prosecutors. On this basis, 91% of the eligible black jurors were removed by peremptory strikes. In contrast, the prosecutors used their peremptory strikes against just 13% (4 out of 31) of the eligible non-black prospective jurors qualified to serve on petitioner's jury. These numbers, while relevant, are not petitioner's whole case. During voir dire, the prosecution questioned venire members as to their views concerning the death penalty and their willingness to serve on a capital case. Responses that disclosed reluctance or hesitation to impose capital punishment were cited as a justification for striking a potential juror for cause or by peremptory challenge. *Wainwright v. Witt*, 469 U.S. 412 (1985). The evidence suggests, however, that the manner in which members of the venire were questioned varied by race. To the extent a divergence in responses can be attributed to the racially disparate mode of examination, it is relevant to our inquiry."

"In this case, three of the State's proffered race-neutral rationales for striking African-American jurors pertained just as well to some white jurors who were not challenged and who did serve on the jury. The prosecutors explained that their peremptory challenges against six African-American potential jurors were based on ambivalence about the death penalty; hesitancy to vote to execute defendants capable of being rehabilitated; and the jurors' own family history of criminality. In rebuttal of the prosecution's explanation, petitioner identified two empaneled white jurors who expressed ambivalence about the death penalty in a manner similar to their African-American counterparts who were the subject of prosecutorial peremptory challenges. One indicated that capital punishment was not appropriate for a first offense, and another stated that it would be 'difficult' to impose a death sentence. Similarly, two white jurors expressed hesitation in sentencing to death a defendant who might be rehabilitated; and four white jurors had family members with criminal histories. As a consequence, even though the prosecution's reasons for striking African-American members of the venire appear race-neutral, the application of these rationales to the venire might have been selective and based on racial considerations. Whether a comparative juror analysis would demonstrate the prosecutors' rationales to have been pretexts for discrimination is an unnecessary determination at this stage, but the evidence does make debatable the District Court's conclusion that no purposeful discrimination occurred."

CASE SIGNIFICANCE: Race seemed to be a historical motivator in the Dallas County prosecutor's office and continued in the *Miller-El* case. In *Brown v. State* (2002),[106] a prosecutor who offered justifications for excluding a particular black individual on its face seemed plausible, but upon further inspection the Georgia Court of

Continued

---

[106]*Brown v. State*, 568 S.E.2d 62 (Ga. App. 2002).

MILLER-EL v. DRETKE 545 U.S. 231 (2005)—cont'd

Appeals found that the explanations were not race-neutral and constituted a *Batson* violation. In *Batson*, the Court held that to exclude members of the defendant's race from a jury solely on racial grounds violates the equal protection rights of both the defendant and the excluded jurors. In *Hernandez* and *Purkett*, even after the prosecutor offers a race-neutral explanation, the trial court may find a *Batson* violation if the explanation is pretextual. In *Minnesota v. McRae* (1992),[107] the prosecutor questioned and struck down the only black member of the venire. She was struck down due to her views that the judicial system had been historically unfair to minorities. The Minnesota Supreme Court found this to be a *Batson* violation because the race of the juror was given relevant consideration. Should jurors be excluded purely on their belief that the system has been unfair to minorities? This question may soon be before the Court. Recently, in *Rico v. Leftridge-Byrd* (2003),[108] the Third Circuit Court of Appeals ruled that *Batson* applies to Italian-Americans. Jurors in the case were stricken from the jury due to their Italian surnames. To extend *Batson* beyond the scope of blacks could prove to be difficult, as ethnicity is difficult to define. The Court decided in *United States v. Martinez-Salazar* (2000)[109] that a peremptory challenge to remove a juror solely on the basis of gender, ethnic group, or race was unconstitutional. The Supreme Court stated that obvious racial prejudice in jury selection through ostensibly "racially neutral" means was still in fact racial discrimination.

SNYDER v. LOUISIANA 552 U.S. 472 (2008)

CAPSULE: It is a violation of the Equal Protection Clause of the Fourteenth Amendment to strike black jurors without substantiated racially neutral reasons that apply equally to jurors of all races.

FACTS: In 1996, Snyder was indicted in Jefferson Parish for first-degree murder of his estranged wife's companion, Howard Wilson, in which he inflicted nine knife wounds. During voir dire, the prosecution used peremptory challenges to eliminate all five black prospective jurors. The defendant charged that the State had exercised its peremptory challenges against black jurors in a racially discriminatory manner violating *Batson v. Kentucky* (1986). In his closing argument, the prosecutor, having struck from the panel all the potential black jurors, compared the defendant, a black man charged with stabbing his wife to death, to O.J. Simpson and told the all-white jury that Mr. Simpson, acquitted of murder 10 months earlier, had "got away with it." Snyder's *Batson* claim was denied by the trial court, and the defendant, who was black, was tried by an all-white jury and sentenced to death. The decision of the trial court was affirmed by the Louisiana Supreme Court, stating that the trial court had not abused its discretion or erred in denying Snyder's *Batson* claim. Snyder filed a writ of certiorari to the Supreme Court in which they vacated the judgment of the Louisiana Supreme Court and remanded the case for further consideration in light of the decision in *Miller-El v. Dretke* (2005). The Louisiana Supreme Court again upheld the conviction of Snyder, holding that the trial court did not err in denying Snyder's *Batson* claim. The Supreme Court agreed to hear the case.

ISSUE: Did the state's exclusion of all black prospective jurors through the use of peremptory challenges, coupled with the prosecutor's reference to the O.J. Simpson case, constitute a violation of the Equal Protection Clause of the Fourteenth Amendment? YES.

HOLDING: It is a violation of the Equal Protection Clause to strike all black jurors if no substantiated racially neutral explanations are offered.

Continued

[107]*Minnesota v. McRae*, 494 N.W.2d 252 (1992).
[108]*Rico v. Leftridge-Byrd*, 340 F.3d 178 (3d Cir. 2003).
[109]*United States v. Martinez-Salazar*, 528 U.S. 304 (2000).

SNYDER v. LOUISIANA 552 U.S. 472 (2008)—cont'd

REASON: The Supreme Court held that both of the two arguments for challenging prospective juror Brooks, a black college student, were not racially neutral when taken in light of the white jurors who were not challenged. The prosecutor contended that Mr. Brooks was "nervous," although there was no record of the trial judge believing him to be overly nervous. Because the trial judge gave no reason for upholding the prosecutor's challenge of Mr. Brooks, the Supreme Court believed they could not presume that the trial judge perceived him as more nervous or uncharacteristically nervous. The prosecutor also stated that he believed Mr. Brooks would be motivated to have a quick trial so as not to miss his student teaching obligations and therefore would be easily swayed by the majority in order to obtain a quick verdict. The Supreme Court noted that the prosecutor himself believed that the trial would be brief. The Supreme Court found the prosecutor's argument to be faulty, especially considering that Mr. Brooks appeared more than willing to serve once his dean assured him he would be able to make up his student teaching. Peremptory strikes that are shown to have been motivated by discrimination should not and must not be sustained.

CASE SIGNIFICANCE: The case reiterates the confusion over the issue of race and peremptory challenges. The Louisiana Supreme Court relied heavily on the three-part *Batson* test outlined by the Supreme Court:

> A defendant's Batson *challenge to a peremptory strike requires a three-step inquiry. First, the trial court must determine whether the defendant has made a prima facie showing that the prosecutor exercised a peremptory challenge on the basis of race. Second, if the showing is made, the burden shifts to the prosecutor to present a race-neutral explanation for striking the juror in question. Although the prosecutor must present a comprehensible reason, the second step of this process does not demand an explanation that is persuasive, or even plausible; so long as the reason is not inherently discriminatory, it suffices. Third, the court must then determine whether the defendant has carried his burden of proving purposeful discrimination. This final step involves evaluating the persuasiveness of the justification proffered by the prosecutor, but the ultimate burden of persuasion regarding racial motivation rests with, and never shifts from, the opponent of the strike. [Internal quotations and citations omitted.]*

The Supreme Court found that the trial court was in error in denying Snyder's *Batson* claim and should not have sustained the peremptory challenges of the prosecutor.

Key Terms

Baldus study
Batson v. Kentucky
Contract system
McCleskey v. Kemp
Miller-El v. Dretke
Peremptory challenges
Prosecutorial discretion
Public defenders
Racial bias
Racial discrimination
Racial disparity
Racial Justice Act
Racially neutral explanations
Snyder v. Louisiana
Turner v. Murray
Voir dire

CRITICAL THINKING QUESTIONS

1. Race has historically been a significant factor in the death penalty and death penalty jurisprudence. Explain how race played a role in the landmark *Furman* and *Gregg* cases. Then explain the Court's decision in *McClesky v. Kemp* and what it meant for legal challenges based on racial disparity or discrimination.

2. Explain current Racial Justice Act legislation at the federal and state levels. What are the pros and cons of such legislation? Propose some ways in which these laws could be improved.

3. Jurors play an important role in capital proceedings. What are some ways to ensure that capital juries are fair and impartial during trial and sentencing? Is there any way to eliminate or reduce possible racial bias in jury decision making?

4. Explain the difference between racial *disparity* and racial *discrimination*. Discuss how these factors differ in terms of legal ramifications in capital cases.

Internet Resources

The Death Penalty in Black and White: Who Lives, Who Dies, Who Decides?
www.deathpenaltyinfo.org/death-penalty-black-and-white-who-lives-who-dies-who-decides

North Carolina's Racial Justice Act
www.deathpenaltyinfo.org/north-carolina-racial-justice-act-ruling-summary#Interp

ACLU: Race and the Death Penalty
https://www.aclu.org/capital-punishment/race-and-death-penalty

NCADP: Racial Bias in the Death Penalty
www.ncadp.org/index.cfm?content=19

Explaining Death Row's Population and Race
www.amnestyusa.org/our-work/issues/death-penalty/us-death-penalty-facts/death-penalty-and-race

The Mentally Impaired and the Death Penalty

CHAPTER OUTLINE

I INTRODUCTION

The Supreme Court of the United States has struggled with issues surrounding who should be eligible for the death penalty since the penalty's reinstatement in 1976. Laws of various states provide that some offenders should receive special treatment due to special circumstances, including considerations such as age at the time of offense and a lack of mental capacity to understand and comprehend the crime that was committed and/or the punishment that is being served. This special treatment poses legal questions: Do certain classes or categories of persons deserve to be treated differently when considering the death penalty as punishment? Should those with particular mental impairments such as developmental or intellectual disabilities be exempted from death as punishment, and if so, what tests should be used to determine whether an individual is so mentally impaired? Should those who suffer from psychiatric disorders or mental illness also be treated differently? This chapter examines these issues and the significant cases that address mental impairment in relation to the death penalty in the United States.

II SUPREME COURT CASES: PAST AND PRESENT

A A Starting Point: *Penry v. Lynaugh* (1989)

In *Penry v. Lynaugh,* the Supreme Court was asked to decide whether the execution of the mentally retarded[1] was a violation of the Eighth Amendment's ban on cruel and unusual punishment. The Court concluded that it was not a violation of the Eighth Amendment, because at the time there was no national consensus against executing mentally retarded individuals. The majority believed that if more state legislatures banned the execution of the mentally retarded, it might offend the "evolving standards of decency," making the execution of mentally retarded individuals unconstitutional. In *Penry*[2] the Court stated that mental retardation was an issue that should be raised as a mitigating factor but should not automatically exclude someone from facing a death sentence. Mitigating factors are those presented by the defendant to show a lessened state of culpability or harmful intent. The Court noted in *Penry* that juries should consider the testimony of experts about mental retardation as a crucial component to a "reasoned moral response" about whether to impose the death penalty.[3]

At the time of the *Penry* decision, the American Association of Mental Retardation (AAMR) concluded that mentally retarded individuals have deficits in cognition and moral reasoning that prevented them from having the level of blame (or *culpability*) needed in order for courts to impose capital punishment.[4] In 2002, the Supreme Court overturned its decision in *Penry*, concluding that it is unconstitutional to execute the mentally retarded. What made the Court change its mind? This is explained in the Court's decision in *Atkins v. Virginia* (2002).[5]

B Executing the Mentally Retarded Is Unconstitutional: *Atkins v. Virginia*

More than a decade after *Penry*, the Court agreed to hear the *Atkins* case and thus reexamine the *Penry* decision. After 1989, many state legislatures debated the issue and passed statutes prohibiting the execution of mentally retarded offenders. The Court thought it was time to revisit the issue and determine whether times had indeed changed. The Court concluded that they had, and it reversed the *Penry* decision. Voting five to four, the Court said: "Our independent evaluation of the issue reveals no reason to disagree with the judgment of 'the legislatures that have recently addressed the matter' and concluded that death is not a suitable punishment for a mentally retarded criminal. We are not persuaded that the execution of mentally retarded criminals will measurably advance the deterrent or the retributive

---

[1] Though the term *mentally retarded* has fallen out of favor and may be considered offensive, we use it here because it was the *legal* term used by the Supreme Court at the time.

[2] *Penry v. Lynaugh*, 492 U.S. 302 (1989).

[3] *Id.* at 322.

[4] *Id.* at 336.

[5] *Atkins v. Virginia*, 534 U.S. 1122 (2002).

purpose of the death penalty. Construing and applying the Eighth Amendment in the light of our 'evolving standards of decency,' we therefore conclude that such punishment is excessive and that the Constitution 'places a substantive restriction on the State's power to take the life' of a mentally retarded offender."[6]

Daryl Atkins was convicted of capital murder and related crimes by a Virginia jury and sentenced to death. Affirming, the Virginia Supreme Court relied on *Penry* in rejecting Atkins's contention that he could not be sentenced to death because he is mentally retarded. The Court decision in *Atkins* is not surprising when examined against the backdrop of "evolving standards of decency," first enunciated in *Trop v. Dulles* (1958).[7] The Court concluded that the national consensus against the death penalty for the mentally retarded that was absent in *Penry* in 1989 had in fact become a reality in 2002.

Retribution is something done to an offender as payback or vengeance for a crime or act that he or she has committed, a form of balancing the scales in response to wrongdoing (often referred to as "just deserts"). The Court concluded that retribution is not served when imposing capital punishment on the mentally retarded, adding that if the offender is not fully aware of the severity of the offense, the purposes of retribution would not be served.[8] The Court also observed that the execution of the mentally retarded did not serve as a deterrent to further offenses because a mentally retarded offender is not capable of the level of logical reasoning assumed in deterrence theory. Moreover, exempting the mentally retarded offender from capital punishment does not lessen the potential of capital punishment to deter offenders who are fully able to understand the seriousness of their criminal behavior.

The decision in *Atkins* left many questions unanswered. Because it was now unconstitutional to execute mentally retarded offenders, what definition of mental retardation was to be used? Should all offenders who suffer from mental retardation be exempted, regardless of the degree or severity of the retardation? Would those inmates deemed mentally retarded have their sentences commuted to life in prison? Would the courts be flooded with petitions from defendants claiming mental retardation? Would "expert" testimony on mental retardation have limitations, and what qualifications will be used to classify someone as an expert qualified to diagnose mental retardation? A decade after the *Atkins* decision, these questions to a large degree remain open. They are addressed in a later portion of this chapter.

C Cases After *Atkins*

Several key cases have emerged since the ruling on *Atkins* in 2002. In 2003, the Eighth Circuit ruled in *Singleton v. Norris*[9] that it was not a violation of the Eighth Amendment to execute an individual who became incompetent while on death row and was rendered competent through forced medication. The case points to state interests and whether or not a state is willing to forcefully medicate solely for the purpose of rendering the offender competent to be executed. The Eighth Circuit relied on a rationale that states would have more important reasons to forcefully medicate an inmate beyond that of restoring competency for an impending execution. If the state deemed the forced medication to be in the inmate's best medical interests, additional motives (even *ulterior* motives), including execution, are not

---

[6]*Atkins v. Virginia*, 122 S. Ct. at 2252.
[7]356 U.S. 86 (1958).
[8]Slobogin, Christopher, *What* Atkins *Could Mean for People with Mental Illness*, 33 N.M. L. Rev. 293 (2003).
[9]*Singleton v. Norris,* 319 F.3d 1018 (2003).

important. Of particular interest in the *Singleton* decision is the fact that Singleton was diagnosed with schizophrenia while on death row. This distinction is important when coupled with the decision made in *Panetti v. Quarterman* in 2007 (discussed below).

In 2004, *Tennard v. Dretke*[10] was decided, in which it was concluded that jurors must be allowed to consider mental retardation as a mitigating factor, particularly when life and death are at stake. Jurors in the case were not asked to consider this at sentencing and were instead asked the two "special issue" questions that were in current use in Texas to determine whether someone was deserving of a death sentence. These questions were:

1. Was the conduct of the defendant that caused the death of the deceased committed deliberately and with reasonable expectation that death of the deceased or another would result? (This is known as the "deliberateness special issue.")
2. Is there a probability that the defendant would commit criminal acts of violence that would constitute a continuing threat to society? (This is known as the "future dangerousness special issue.")

The jury answered "yes" to both of these questions, and Tennard received a death sentence. At issue in the case was Tennard's IQ of 67, which was evidence of significantly impaired mental functioning. The Court believed that such impaired functioning warranted consideration by a jury and might also be a basis for a sentence less than death. The decision in *Tennard* once again points to the unwillingness of courts to instruct jurors to consider mental impairment as a mitigating factor in the sentencing phase of capital trials. The Court's decision reaffirms the importance of weighing mental and developmental disabilities in capital proceedings, upholding the tradition that "death is different."

Mental competence was again considered by the Court in *Panetti v. Quarterman* (2007).[11] At issue in *Panetti* was the difference between an inmate being "aware" of a state's rationale for execution and the inmate "understanding" that rationale. Panetti was convicted of capital murder and sentenced to death in Texas. He had a long documented history of mental illness. According to Panetti's lawyers, Panetti knew that Texas was seeking to execute him for the murder of his in-laws but believed that Texas had conspired against him and sentenced him to death so that he would stop "preaching." The Court held that the Fifth Circuit's formal and narrow test of competence to be executed was "too restrictive," not allowing for any consideration of an inmate's rational awareness and understanding of an impending execution. However, the Court also acknowledged that what constitutes a "rational understanding" is difficult to determine. The Court failed to set down a rule for competency hearings and remanded the case, requiring the district court to try to formulate and apply a better standard. If the Court is unwilling to define "rational awareness," it is not surprising that jurors, lawyers, judges, and circuit courts are unsure of or unwilling to establish a standard. The decision in *Panetti* points to the confusion about terms such as "competence" and "developmental disability" and how these terms should be defined for consideration in death penalty proceedings.

In 2009, the Supreme Court decided the case of *Bobby v. Bies*.[12] In 1992, Michael Bies was convicted of murder, rape, and kidnapping and was sentenced to death in Ohio. Bies argued that he was mentally retarded and that this should have served as a mitigating factor in the penalty phase of his trial. The court sentenced

---

[10]*Tennard v. Dretke*, 542 U.S. 274 (2004).
[11]*Panetti v. Quarterman*, 448 F.3d 815 (2007).
[12]*Bobby v. Bies,* 556 U.S. 825 (2009).

him to death and this sentence was affirmed twice, though the court sided with Bies, stating that his mental retardation should serve as a mitigating factor. In 2003, in light of the *Atkins* decision, Bies filed a habeas corpus petition stating that he could not be executed, because he was mentally retarded. The state argued that he was, in fact, *not* mentally retarded, and thus the *Atkins* decision did not apply in his case. Bies argued that, since the state had previously concluded that he was mentally retarded, the double jeopardy clause banned the state from reconsidering this fact. In a unanimous decision, the Court found that the Ohio courts were not prevented by the double jeopardy clause from conducting a rehearing in regard to Bies's mental retardation. The Court argued that Ohio was not putting Bies in jeopardy of being convicted twice, since he was not acquitted in his original trial.[13]

Recently, the Court heard and consolidated two cases that dealt with the issue of mental competency and habeas corpus petitions. In *Ryan v. Gonzales*,[14] Gonzales filed a habeas corpus petition after being given a death sentence in 1996. One of his claims involved whether or not he was competent and able to communicate with his court-appointed attorneys in a meaningful and helpful manner during the habeas corpus process. The federal district court denied Gonzales's motion for a competency hearing, and Gonzales appealed to the Ninth Circuit, which disagreed with the lower court and held that Gonzales should be granted a stay of execution pending a determination of competency. In the case of *Tibbals v. Carter*, Carter was found incompetent to assist his attorneys after his capital conviction. The federal district court granted Carter a stay on his habeas proceedings and the appellate court affirmed this decision. The U.S. Supreme Court granted certiorari to answer the same question posed in *Ryan v. Gonzales*, consolidating the two cases.[15] In a unanimous decision, the Court reversed the judgment of both the Sixth and Ninth Circuits and held that there is no constitutional or statutory right to a competency hearing during federal habeas corpus proceedings. Interestingly, the Court noted that an attorney can handle the petition on his own and that even if competency was necessary, the district court should only grant a stay if a defendant is likely to become competent in the near future. It contended that granting a stay otherwise would place unnecessary burdens on the judicial system.

III ISSUES WITH MENTAL IMPAIRMENT IN CAPITAL CASES
A Definition of Mental Retardation/Development Disability

The Supreme Court in *Atkins* did not define what constitutes "mental retardation," leaving it instead to the discretion of the states. An article by Douglas Mossman, M.D., stated that the diagnosis of mental retardation is an "entirely abstract construct" and that the line that separates persons who are given this diagnosis and those who are "just below average" is changing and arbitrary.[16] The AAMR had updated its definition of mental retardation 10 times in the past century. Until 2007, the AAMR defined mental retardation as "a disability characterized by significant limitations both in intellectual functioning and adaptive behavior as expressed in conceptual, social, and practical adaptive skills. This disability originates before the age of 18."[17] Of great importance to the debate about "mental retardation" is even in the name itself. In February 2007, the AAMR became the American Association of Individuals with

---

[13]*Id.*

[14]*Ryan v. Gonzales*, 568 U.S. ___ (2013).

[15]*Id.*

[16]Mossman, Douglas, M.D., Atkins v. Virginia: *A Psychiatric Can of Worms*, 33 N.M. L. Rᴇᴠ. 255 (2003).

[17]American Association of Mental Retardation, AAMR homepage. Available at www.aamr.org (accessed June 6, 2004).

Developmental Disabilities (AAIDD). The AAIDD changed the term "mental retardation" and its organizational title by using what was perceived to be a less stigmatizing term, "intellectual disability." The change in wording also reflects the association's attempt to broaden the scope to include developmental disorders, such as autism. According to the AAIDD the definition of intellectual disability is as follows:

Intellectual Functioning
Intellectual functioning—*also called intelligence—refers to general mental capacity, such as learning, reasoning, problem solving, and so on.*
One way to measure intellectual functioning is an IQ test. Generally, an IQ test score of around 70 or as high as 75 indicates a limitation in intellectual functioning.

Adaptive Behavior
Adaptive behavior *is the collection of conceptional, social, and practical skills that are learned and performed by people in their everyday lives.*

- Conceptual skills—language and literacy; money, time, and number concepts; and self-direction.
- Social skills—interpersonal skills, social responsibility, self-esteem, gullibility, naïveté (i.e., wariness), social problem solving, and the ability to follow rules/obey laws and to avoid being victimized.
- Practical skills—activities of daily living (personal care), occupational skills, healthcare, travel/transportation, schedules/routines, safety, use of money, use of the telephone.

Standardized tests can also determine limitations in adaptive behavior.

Age of Onset
This condition is one of several developmental disabilities—that is, there is evidence of the disability during the developmental period, which in the U.S. is operationalized as before the age of 18.

Additional Considerations
But in defining and assessing intellectual disability, the AAIDD stresses that additional factors must be taken into account, such as the community environment typical of the individual's peers and culture. Professionals should also consider linguistic diversity and cultural differences in the way people communicate, move, and behave.

Finally, assessments must also assume that limitations in individuals often coexist with strengths, and that a person's level of life functioning will improve if appropriate personalized supports are provided over a sustained period.

Only on the basis of such many-sided evaluations can professionals determine whether an individual has intellectual disability and tailor individualized support plans.[18]

In an article published in the *AAIDD Journal*, it was noted that the term "intellectual disability" covers the same population of individuals who were diagnosed previously with mental retardation in number, kind, level, type, and duration of the disability, and the need of people with this disability for individualized services and support. Furthermore, every individual who is or was eligible for a diagnosis of mental retardation is eligible for a diagnosis of intellectual disability.[19]

---

[18]AAIDD, Definition of Intellectual Disability, found Sept. 10, 2013, at http://aaidd.org/intellectual-disability/definition#.UjNcJq_9U8U.

[19]Schalock, Robert L., et al., *The Renaming of* Mental Retardation: *Understanding the Change to the Term* Intellectual Disability. INTELLECTUAL AND DEVELOPMENTAL DISABILITIES 45, 2: 116–124, 2007.

The former version of the Diagnostic and Statistical Manual (DSM-IV-TR) of the American Psychiatric Association characterized mental retardation as "significantly sub average general intellectual functioning accompanied by significant limitations in adaptive functioning in at least two of the following skill areas: communication, self-care, home living, social/interpersonal skills, use of community resources, self-direction, functional academic skills, work, leisure, health, and safety. The onset must occur before age 18 years."[20] Although the AAMR and the American Psychiatric Association have similar definitions, there are some important differences. In 2013, the DSM-5 replaced the term "mental retardation" with the more appropriate "intellectual disability." It provided the following definition of intellectual disability:

Intellectual disability involves impairments of general mental abilities that impact adaptive functioning in three domains, or areas. These domains determine how well an individual copes with everyday tasks:

- *The conceptual domain includes skills in language, reading, writing, math, reasoning, knowledge, and memory.*
- *The social domain refers to empathy, social judgment, interpersonal communication skills, the ability to make and retain friendships, and similar capacities.*
- *The practical domain centers on self-management in areas such as personal care, job responsibilities, money management, recreation, and organizing school and work tasks.*

While intellectual disability does not have a specific age requirement, an individual's symptoms must begin during the developmental period and are diagnosed based on the severity of deficits in adaptive functioning. The disorder is considered chronic and often co-occurs with other mental conditions like depression, attention-deficit/hyperactivity disorder, and autism spectrum disorder.[21]

The AAIDD, by contrast, examined patterns of limitations as a means of categorization and used support needed as a means of classification, such as: intermittent, limited, extensive, pervasive, or completely necessary.[22]

It is important to note that the term "mentally retarded" remains in use as a legal term associated with key cases determining the constitutionality of the death penalty. Regardless of semantics, the question remains: How shall mental retardation, intellectual disability, or developmental disability be determined for purposes of capital punishment? As previously mentioned, the Court left this responsibility to the states. As a result, states have varied widely in the way they define mental retardation or intellectual disability and in the process by which it is to be determined. At a fundamental level, most states have set 70 as the minimum IQ score for death penalty consideration. States also consider the level of impairment in adaptive behavior in qualifying an individual as mentally retarded, but there is significant variation in what this level is and how it should be determined. Table 4.1 presents the statutory definitions of mental retardation for states that altered their statutes to comply with the Supreme Court's decision in *Atkins v. Virginia.*

---

[20]American Psychiatric Association, Diagnostic and Statistical Manual for Mental Disorders (4th ed. 2000).
[21]American Psychiatric Association, Diagnostic and Statistical Manual for Mental Disorders (5th ed. 2013).
[22]*Supra* note 18.

Table 4.1 Post-*Atkins* Statutory Definitions of Mental Retardation

State	Statute Citation	Definition of Mental Retardation	Qualified Examiners	Determined
California	Penal Code 1376	Significantly subaverage general intellectual functioning existing concurrently with deficits in adaptive behavior and manifested before the age of 18.	None stated. Burden of proof is on the defense.	In a pre-trial hearing by a judge or jury.
Delaware	11-4209	"Seriously mentally retarded" or "serious mental retardation" means that an individual has significantly subaverage intellectual functioning that exists concurrently with substantial deficits in adaptive behavior, and both the significantly subaverage intellectual functioning and the deficits in adaptive behavior were manifested before the individual became 18 years of age. "Significantly subaverage intellectual functioning" means an intelligence quotient of 70 or below obtained by assessment with one or more of the standardized, individually administered general intelligence tests developed for the purpose of assessing intellectual functioning. "Adaptive behavior" means the effectiveness or degree to which the individual meets the standards of personal independence expected of the individual's age group, sociocultural background, and community setting, as evidenced by significant limitations in not less than two of the following adaptive skill areas: communication, self-care, home living, social skills, use of community resources, self-direction, functional academic skills, work, leisure, health, or safety.	None stated. Burden of proof is on the defense.	Before trial by a judge.

Continued

Table 4.1 Post-*Atkins* Statutory Definitions of Mental Retardation—cont'd

State	Statute Citation	Definition of Mental Retardation	Qualified Examiners	Determined
Idaho	19-2515A	"Mentally retarded" means significantly subaverage general intellectual functioning that is accompanied by significant limitations in adaptive functioning in at least two (2) of the following skill areas: communication, self-care, home living, social or interpersonal skills, use of community resources, self-direction, functional academic skills, work, leisure, health, and safety. The onset of significant subaverage general intelligence functioning and significant limitations in adaptive functioning must occur before age 18. "Significantly subaverage general intellectual functioning" means an intelligence quotient of 70 or below.	No specific qualifications. Refers only to "expert witness" for either side.	Before trial by a judge.
Louisiana	2003 LA Acts 698, Code of Criminal Procedure Article 905.5.1	A disability characterized by significant limitations in both intellectual functioning and adaptive behavior as expressed in conceptual, social, and practical adaptive skills. Onset must have occurred before age 18.	When a defendant makes a claim under this article, the state has the right to an independent psychological and psychiatric examination of the defendant. Must be licensed by Louisiana state board of examiners of psychologists.	Before trial (if the prosecutor agrees) by the judge, or during sentencing by the jury.
Nevada	NRS 174	Significant subaverage general intellectual functioning that exists concurrently with deficits in adaptive behavior and manifested during the developmental period.	None stated. Only reference to examiners is that they are to be selected by the prosecution.	Before trial.
Utah	77-15a-101	Significant subaverage general intellectual functioning that results in and exists concurrently with significant	The court shall order the Department of Human Services to appoint at least two	Before trial.

Continued

Table 4.1 Post-*Atkins* Statutory Definitions of Mental Retardation—cont'd

State	Statute Citation	Definition of Mental Retardation	Qualified Examiners	Determined
		deficiencies in adaptive functioning that exist primarily in the areas of reasoning or impulse control, or in both of these areas; and the subaverage general intellectual functioning and the significant deficiencies in adaptive functioning under Subsection (1) are both manifested prior to age 22.	mental health experts to examine the defendant and report to the court. The experts: (i) may not be involved in the current treatment of the defendant; and (ii) shall have expertise in mental retardation assessment.	
Virginia	§ 19.2-264.3	"Mentally retarded" means a disability, originating before the age of 18 years, characterized concurrently by (i) significantly subaverage intellectual functioning as demonstrated by performance on a standardized measure of intellectual functioning administered in conformity with accepted professional practice, that is at least two standard deviations below the mean, and (ii) significant limitations in adaptive behavior as expressed in conceptual, social, and practical adaptive skills.	A psychiatrist, a clinical psychologist, or an individual with a doctorate degree in clinical psychology, (b) skilled in the administration, scoring and interpretation of intelligence tests and measures of adaptive behavior, and (c) qualified by experience and by specialized training, approved by the Commissioner of Mental Health, Mental Retardation, and Substance Abuse Services, to perform forensic evaluations. The defendant shall not be entitled to a mental health expert of the defendant's own choosing or to funds to employ such expert.	By the jury (or the judge in nonjury trials) during the sentencing phase.

Source: www.deathpenaltyinfo.org/states-have-changed-their-statutes-comply-supreme-courts-decision-atkins-v-virginia.

States also vary on the issue of whether the deficits in adaptive functioning must occur before a certain age. In North Carolina and Tennessee, the deficit must be reached before the age of 18, whereas Washington and Nebraska have no set age limit.[23] Arizona and Arkansas have set the minimum IQ at 65, although their definitions of developmental disability differ, as do their procedures for establishing developmental disability. An important question is whether those administering IQ tests will be able to remain objective when point assessments may mean the possibility of life or death. If point systems are used, a person who has an IQ of 72 could possibly be given the death penalty, whereas a person with an IQ of 69 might not. Does this small three-point distinction really indicate a meaningful differentiation in culpability?

The American Psychiatric Association indicates three important Standard Error of Measurement (SEM) considerations in discussing IQ point assessments:

1. Instruments vary in SEM; example: the Wechsler scale of 70 represents the range of scores 65–75.
2. No MR diagnosis if individual IQ score below 70 without significant deficits in adaptive functioning.
3. Possible to diagnose MR in an individual with IQ score 70–75 who presents with significant deficits in adaptive functioning. Otherwise will receive diagnosis of borderline intellectual functioning.[24]

One should also note three other important considerations in a diagnosis of a mental retardation or developmental disability:

1. IQ score is considered a more stable construct, whereas adaptive functioning can improve with "support."
2. Comorbid disorders in individuals with MR are estimated to be 3–4 times more likely than in the general population. Most common disorders include attention deficit hyperactive disorder (ADHD), mood disorders, pervasive developmental disorders (PDD), stereotypic movement disorders, and mental disorders due to a medical condition—for example, dementia due to head trauma.
3. "MR often accompanies PDD."

Precise IQ cutoffs may create the impression that a one- or two-point difference in IQ score shows a substantial difference in criminal intent. This is why some states have taken IQ scores out of their definition of developmental disability. This falls in line with AAIDD and DSM-5 definitions of intellectual disability and reinforces that IQ is only one piece of a larger puzzle regarding what constitutes a developmental disability. The statutory definitions range from the general requirement of subaverage intelligence and shortfalls in adaptive functioning to the definition in Kansas, which requires an inability to appreciate the criminality of one's conduct. There is no uniform definition as to what constitutes developmental disability. As noted previously, individuals in some states will be spared execution if they have an IQ of 67, but if they test four points higher they could face execution. This is particularly problematic when we consider the margin of error in IQ testing.

Scholars are debating whether states should be bound by the language and strict definition of developmental disability in considering who should face capital punishment when individuals who

---

[23]Dowling, Alexis Krulish, *Post-Atkins Problems with Enforcing the Supreme Court's Ban on Executing the Mentally Retarded*, 33 Seton Hall L. Rev. 773 (2003).

[24]V62.89: This category can be used when the focus of clinical attention is associated with borderline intellectual functioning—that is, an IQ in the 71–84 range. Differential diagnosis between borderline intellectual functioning and mental retardation (an IQ of 70 or below) is especially difficult when the coexistence of certain mental disorders (e.g., schizophrenia) is involved.

demonstrate the same vulnerabilities as persons who are "developmentally disabled" are not given the same considerations. Baroff (2003)[25] and Kanaya et al. (2002)[26] argue that more flexibility in defining developmental disability is necessary due to issues in evaluating IQ across tests and over time. Should IQ tests be given less consideration than adaptive functioning tests? Kanaya et al. (2002) state that:

> *Some borderline death row inmates or capital murder defendants who were not classified as mentally retarded in childhood because they took an older version of an IQ test might have qualified as retarded if they had taken a more recent test . . . Our results imply that the year that a capital murder defendant was tested can determine whether she or he is sentenced to death as opposed to life imprisonment. This raises concerns regarding inmates on death row who tested above the 70–75 cutoff on a test that was near the end of its normal cycling—when scores are highly inflated as well as an inmate who tested in the mental retardation range during the earliest years of a new norm—when the test is the hardest.*[27]

No standard definition exists in the legal community as to what constitutes intellectual or developmental disability. Cooperation between psychologists, psychiatrists, other mental health professionals, and criminal justice agents could potentially bridge the gap in understanding that surrounds defining and diagnosing "developmental disabilities."

B The Fear of Faking

The evidence suggests that mental retardation is difficult to effectively fake because it has its roots in childhood. Historically, the U.S. legal system has had a fear of "feigned insanity" (or malingering) and is skeptical of expert testimony about mental illness and insanity.[28] The *Atkins* decision and other subsequent cases decided by the Court may in fact only serve to make members of the legal and criminal justice community more apprehensive. A defendant who is diagnosed as mentally retarded may never be executed, regardless of the severity or nature of the crimes. In his dissenting opinion in *Atkins*, Justice Antonin Scalia expressed serious concerns about what he considers to be the new capital trial "game." He argued that, at the time, many of the AAMR and DSM-IV symptoms could be feigned, with nothing to lose. It would appear that of key concern in the process is the role that mental health professionals play in effective diagnosis of developmental disability. Malingering, or faking mental illness, is addressed by the American Psychiatric Association, which lists four conditions that in combination may show malingering. These four conditions are:

1. Medico-legal context of presentation (i.e., referral from an attorney for diagnosis);
2. Discrepancy between the person's apparent disability or stress and objective findings;
3. Lack of cooperation during the diagnostic evaluation or in complying with treatment programs; and
4. The presence of antisocial personality disorder.[29]

[25]Baroff, G.S. (2003). *Establishing Mental Retardation in Capital Cases: An Update.* MENTAL RETARDATION, 41, 198–202.
[26]Kanaya, Y., M. Scullin, and S. Ceci (2002). *The Flynn Effect and U.S. Policies: The Impact of Rising IQ Scores on American Society via Mental Retardation Diagnosis.* AMERICAN PSYCHOLOGIST, 58, 778–779.
[27]*Id.* at 788–789.
[28]PERLIN, MICHAEL L., THE HIDDEN PREJUDICE: MENTAL DISABILITY ON TRIAL 236 (2000).
[29]*Supra* note 20 at 739.

Mental health clinicians are now able to use tests that can identify faked psychological symptoms. These tests include the Test of Memory Malingnancy (TOMM), the Structured Interview of Repeated Symptoms (SIRS), and portions of the Minnesota Multiphasic Personality Inventory (MMPI).

Mental health professionals must remain unbiased and base their evaluations on actual behavior and assessment tools, rather than gut feelings. The American Psychological Association (APA) Ethical Principles of Psychologists and Code of Conduct provide standards of professional conduct for psychologists. This code is commonly applied by state boards and courts to those practicing in the field of psychology.[30] The APA ethics code states that evaluations for courts must be based solely "on information that is sufficient to appropriate substantiation for their findings."[31] The APA has also provided a set of guidelines for psychologists who are experts in the legal system. These "specialty guidelines" require the psychologist to conduct an adequate examination utilizing the most up-to-date tests and measures and to avoid providing testimony "about the psychological characteristics of particular individuals when they have not had an opportunity to conduct an examination of the individual adequate to the scope of the statements, opinions, or conclusions."[32] Psychiatrists may have a more unique dilemma because they take the Hippocratic Oath, which requires that the physician's first consideration be the benefit of the patient and imposes a duty that the doctor do no harm and take no life.

C Mental Retardation versus Mental Illness

Mental illness is different from mental retardation in significant ways. The diagnosis of mental illness relies more heavily on subjective diagnoses, whereas mental retardation is most often found through objective tests of intellectual and adaptive functioning. The DSM-5 alludes to the fact that it may be difficult to distinguish between a strongly held idea and a delusion, and "bizarreness" of delusions may be difficult to judge, particularly across varying cultures.[33] Mental illness is typically more treatable than mental retardation, which could essentially make the mentally ill more responsible. For example, if a mentally ill person chooses not to take medication, knowing the consequences of doing so, should that person not be held liable for his or her actions? It could also be argued that a mentally ill offender has a higher mental competence to understand the rules and laws that govern society and a stronger capacity to understand right from wrong.

Atkins focused on the issue of mental retardation, which is different from mental illness. Courts and legislatures agree that mental retardation is a mitigating circumstance. Mental illness has also been used to mitigate punishments in death penalty offenses. But the Court has not decided whether people with other mental impairments or mental illness should receive the protections against execution afforded to those with mental retardation. Mental illness is a broad term that has a variety of diagnoses. As such, the decisions regarding whether people with mental illness (or particular mental illnesses) should, like those with mental retardation, be immune from the death penalty are much more complex.

---

[30]American Psychological Association, *Ethical Principles of Psychologists and Code of Conduct*. In DONALD BERSOFF (ED.), ETHICAL CONFLICTS IN PSYCHOLOGY 6 (1995).
[31]*Id.*
[32]Committee on Ethical Guidelines for Forensic Psychologists, *Specialty Guidelines for Forensic Psychologists*. In DONALD BERSOFF (ED.), ETHICAL CONFLICTS IN PSYCHOLOGY 441 (1995).
[33]*Supra* note 21 at 307.

Some individuals with mental illnesses suffer from the same limitations that diminish blame in the case of the mentally retarded. Recent studies suggest that as many as 20 percent of death row offenders have a mental disorder that is accompanied by impaired reasoning and cognition.[34] The language in *Atkins* could be applied to mental illness in such cases because those mentally ill offenders have a "diminished capacity to understand and process information, to communicate, to abstract from mistakes and learn from experience, to engage in logical reasoning to control impulses, and to understand the reaction of others."[35] An individual suffering from schizophrenia, for example, might be described in this way. There are other mental impairments that raise similar questions of culpability in death penalty cases. In 2013, a California inmate challenged his death penalty conviction claiming to be autistic and therefore deserving of the legal protection given to those who are protected under *Atkins*. As this case works its way through the judicial system, it could be a true test of the scope of intellectual disabilities covered by the *Atkins* decision and how this will apply to capital proceedings.

IV INSANITY AND THE DEATH PENALTY
A Insanity: Different from Other Mental Impairments

It is important to separate insanity from mental retardation and mental illness. Sanity is a legal term, not a medical or psychiatric term. Psychiatrists and mental health clinicians examine individuals and present their findings to the court, but it is ultimately judges and juries who determine whether a defendant is "sane" or "insane." Though mental illness is obviously a part of the legal distinction of sanity, it is not the same as insanity; a person can be mentally ill but not legally insane.

Insanity plays a significant role in eligibility for the death penalty, but compared to the issue of sanity at the time of offense, which is a broader concern related to the culpability of all criminal defendants, capital or not, the concern as it relates to the death penalty is with insanity at the time of execution. The Court, in *Ford v. Wainwright* (1986),[36] held that it is unconstitutional to execute a person who is insane at the time of the scheduled execution because it would constitute cruel and unusual punishment. Prior to the *Ford* decision the Court had not addressed the execution of the insane under the Eighth Amendment. The Supreme Court took into account in *Ford* "objective evidence of contemporary values before determining whether a particular punishment comports with the fundamental human dignity that the Eighth Amendment protects."[37] From this emerged the issue of competency to be executed. What is a reasonable standard for determining competency for execution? The American Bar Association suggests the following:

> *A condemned individual must have sufficient mental capacity to understand the nature of the proceedings against him, for what he was tried, the purpose of the punishment, and his impending fate. Furthermore, he must exhibit sufficient understanding to recognize and comprehend any existing fact*

---

[34]Cunningham, Mark D., and Mark P. Vigen, *Death Row Inmate Characteristics, Adjustment and Confinement: A Critical Review of the Literature*, 20 BEHAV. SOC. LAW 191 (2002).
[35]536 U.S. at 318.
[36]*Ford v. Wainwright*, 477 U.S. 399 (1986).
[37]*Id.* at 406 (1986).

which might render his punishment unjust or unlawful, and he must have the intelligence necessary to convey such information to his attorney or the court. The offender must comprehend the rationale behind society's moral outrage concerning his actions and must have an affective knowledge of facts regarding both his crime and his punishment. If this knowledge and understanding is not present then the offender can be characterized as insane.[38]

B Reasons for Not Executing the Insane

The U.S. Supreme Court drew a clear line in *Ford v. Wainwright*,[39] deciding that it violates the Eighth Amendment to execute an insane person. It based its decision on two reasons. First, for centuries insane persons were not executed in this country. States were unwilling to do so even though the constitutional question had never been addressed. Second, the Court believed that the justifications for the death penalty were not met by executing a mentally incompetent person—that doing so failed to achieve the penological goals of this ultimate punishment. The Court also referenced theological and humanitarian reasons for barring the execution of individuals who are insane.

1 Failure to Achieve Penological Goals
a Deterrence
Because an insane individual does not fully understand the consequences of his or her behavior, it is difficult to believe that the execution of an insane individual would deter other people from committing crimes, particularly because the U.S. criminal justice system seeks not only to deter crime but also to incapacitate and rehabilitate criminal wrongdoers. Deterrence is divided into two categories. The first is *general deterrence*, in which punishment is meant to discourage all people from engaging in criminal activity. *Specific deterrence* is meant to prevent a particular individual from engaging in future criminal behaviors. Executing the mentally insane would not deter society as a whole, because the vast majority of people are not mentally incompetent and generally do not have the same patterns of thinking as insane persons. In seeking specific deterrence, the death penalty for the insane is not altogether necessary, because insane offenders will be isolated from society at a mental health facility or institution, and therefore the commission of further harm or violence is no longer a fear.

b Retribution
Retribution is the attempt to "pay back" or deliver "just deserts" upon a person who has violated the rights of others. It embodies the "eye for an eye and a tooth for a tooth" approach to criminal sanctions. The severity of the sanction generally attempts to fit the severity of the crime. If individuals do not have the capacity to understand whether and how their behavior harms society, they will not understand why they might be punished. There is no moral equivalence between the sanction and the offense. There will be no appropriate suffering or anguish because the person does not fully appreciate the sanction that is being imposed on them (in death penalty cases, that he or she will be put to death) due to criminal actions; therefore, retribution is not achieved.

---

[38]AMERICAN BAR ASSOCIATION, CRIMINAL JUSTICE MENTAL HEALTH STANDARDS 7–5.6 (b) (1989).
[39]*Ford v. Wainwright, supra.*

2 Theological

The Court in *Ford* said that it is cruel and unusual to end a person's life without first affording him the opportunity to prepare himself spiritually for the journey into the afterlife.[40] An insane person does not have the mental capacity for the type of preparation that is necessary to secure peace for him or herself. Whereas this religious argument has been supported by some groups, the approach has been understandably controversial in both legal and religious communities.

3 Humanity

Another premise that underlies some arguments against the execution of the insane is that "madness itself is its own punishment."[41] Inmates who are deemed "insane" typically spend their lives in institutions and are not exonerated. For an inmate to have no concept of his surroundings or not to live freely in society is considered punishment enough.

The above discussion offers insight into why the Supreme Court found the execution of the insane to be in violation of the Eighth Amendment. However, it should be noted that although it is unconstitutional to execute an inmate deemed mentally ill or insane at the time of execution, this does not completely exempt them from being executed. If restored to sanity or mental health, the execution may then be carried out. Psychiatric treatment, including the use of medication, may be used to restore an inmate to competency for execution.[42]

C Mental Competence and the Death Penalty

The decision in *Ford v. Wainright* clearly banned the execution of the insane, but this applied only to those who were determined to be insane at the time of execution, or, in other words, mentally incompetent for execution. How, then, was a defendant to be declared incompetent? Justice Lewis F. Powell provided some guidance, offering the fundamental notion that inmates must be "unaware of the punishment they are about to suffer and why they are to suffer it."[43] It should be noted that most mental illnesses would not qualify an inmate as incompetent for execution. Rather, insanity for the purpose of execution refers to:

> . . . the psychoses. These mental disorders—which include schizophrenia, bipolar disorders, and some organic mental disorders—are most likely to affect a person's ability to interpret reality, usually as a result of delusions, hallucinations, and tangential and confused thinking.[44]

The Court and mental health professionals alike clearly specify mental competency in terms of mental deficiencies that render the individual unable to understand his current surroundings or circumstances and actions occurring in the moment. Box 4.1 further illustrates standards for mental competency in relation to the death penalty, as currently defined by the ABA.

The fact that a person is deemed insane and thus not competent to be executed does not mean that he may *never* be executed. Many psychoses are treatable with medication, and if an inmate can be treated to the point that he understands the circumstances and reality of his punishment, he may be found

---

[40]*Id.* at 407.

[41]*Id.*

[42]Miller, Kent S., and Michael L. Radelet, Executing the Mentally Ill: the Criminal Justice System and the Case of Alvin Ford (1993).

[43]*Ford v. Wainwright*, 477 U.S. 399, 422 (1986).

[44]Slobogin, Christopher, *Mental Illness and the Death Penalty*, 24 Mental & Physical Disability L. Rep. 667 (2000).

BOX 4.1 ABA STANDARDS FOR COMPETENCY AND THE DEATH PENALTY

Standard d 7-5.6. Currently incompetent condemned convicts; stay of execution

(a) Convicts who have been sentenced to death should not be executed if they are currently mentally incompetent. If it is determined that a condemned convict is currently mentally incompetent, execution should be stayed.

(b) A convict is incompetent to be executed if, as a result of mental illness or mental retardation, the convict cannot understand the nature of the pending proceedings, what he or she was tried for, the reason for the punishment, or the nature of the punishment. A convict is also incompetent if, as a result of mental illness or mental retardation, the convict lacks sufficient capacity to recognize or understand any fact which might exist which would make the punishment unjust or unlawful, or lacks the ability to convey such information to counsel or the court.

Standard 7-5.7. Evaluation and adjudication of competence to be executed; stay of execution; restoration of competence

(a) Whenever a correctional official, other state official, the prosecution, or counsel for the convict have reason to believe that a convict who has been sentenced to death may be currently incompetent, such person should petition the court for an order requiring an evaluation of the convict's current mental condition. If the court concludes that the information in the petition indicates reasonable cause to believe that the convict may be incompetent, it should order an evaluation. Unless counsel for the defendant is the petitioner, counsel should be notified that such an evaluation is to be conducted. If the convict is not represented by counsel, the court should appoint counsel at the same time it orders the evaluation.

(b) Any interested person who has reason to believe that the convict may be currently incompetent may petition the court for an order requiring an evaluation of the convict's current mental condition. If the court concludes that the information in the petition indicates reasonable cause to believe that the convict may be incompetent, it should order an evaluation, and, if the convict is not represented by counsel, appoint counsel for the convict.

(c) In the absence of a petition, if the court obtains information that indicates reasonable cause to believe that the convict may be incompetent, it should order an evaluation *sua sponte*. If the convict is not represented by counsel, the court should appoint counsel at the same time it orders the evaluation.

(d) All evaluations of a convict's current mental condition for purpose of determining the issue of competence to be executed should be conducted by mental health and/or mental retardation professionals whose qualifications meet the requirements of Standards 7-3.10 and 7-3.12(c)(ii). The convict should be entitled to an evaluation by a qualified professional or professionals who should present the results of their evaluation to the convict's counsel. If the convict is indigent, the court should appoint an appropriate professional evaluator or evaluators for the convict, and such evaluators should be compensated at public expense. The state should be permitted to have its own qualified professional or professionals conduct an evaluation as well.

(e) If, after receiving the reports of the evaluation or evaluations, counsel for the convict believes that the convict is currently incompetent, counsel should move for a hearing on the issue of competence. Upon receiving such a motion, the court should order a hearing.

(f) Following the hearing, if the court finds, by a preponderance of the evidence, that the convict is currently incompetent, it should stay the order of execution for the duration of the convict's incompetence. The court's finding on the issue of competence should be considered a final, appealable order.

(g) If evaluations or proceedings under this standard cannot be accomplished before the scheduled date of the convict's execution, the court should order a stay of execution until the proceedings on the issue of competence are completed.

(h) In the absence of good faith doubt about the convict's current competence, it is improper for an attorney to move for an evaluation pursuant to paragraph (a) or (b) of this Standard. It is improper to use proceedings on the issue of current mental condition solely for the purpose of delay.

(i) When the appropriate state official has reason to believe that a condemned convict who has been found incompetent pursuant to paragraph (f) of this Standard has been restored to competence, the official may petition the court for an order recognizing the restoration to competence and lifting the stay of execution. Upon receipt of such a petition, the court should order the convict's current mental condition reevaluated under the provisions of paragraph (d) of this Standard. Counsel for the defendant should be notified that such an evaluation is to be conducted. Following the reevaluation, the court should hold a hearing on the convict's current mental condition. The convict should be represented by counsel at the hearing. Following the hearing, the court should lift the stay of execution if it finds, by a preponderance of the evidence, that the convict is no longer incompetent. The court's finding on the issue of competence should be considered a final, appealable order.

Source: www.americanbar.org/publications/criminal_justice_section_archive/ crimjust_standards_mentalhealth_tocold.html.

competent and execution may proceed. *Singleton v. Norris*[45] reinforced this notion, holding that states could execute individuals who were made competent through medication, further asserting that such competence could be gained through forced medication. States only had to maintain that the medicine was not solely for the purposes of execution but also for other medical benefits. Ulterior motives behind the medication were irrelevant as long as the state had a legitimate claim that the medication would be medically beneficial to the inmate. Obviously, medical ethical issues inevitably arise from this process.

The most recent Supreme Court decision pertaining to mental competence and the death penalty is *Panetti v. Quarterman.*[46] Panetti had a long history of severe mental illness, including documented chronic schizophrenia and schizoaffective disorder. At his initial trial, Panetti was taking his medication; however, his attorney reported that he had not had a meaningful conversation with his client. In spite of his attorney's attempts to challenge Panetti's competence to stand trial, Panetti was found competent by a Texas jury. As noted previously, jurors are reluctant to declare a defendant mentally incompetent, fearing that the defendant may be "putting one over" on them. Even if Panetti was initially found competent to stand trial, it was up to the court to reassess his competency based on his behavior and condition. Panetti, while at trial, was no longer taking his medication and chose to represent himself. The judge in the case,, without reevaluating Panetti's mental competency, ruled that Panetti was competent to represent himself. According to the trial record, Panetti often wore cowboy garb to trial and attempted to call more than 200 witnesses, including John F. Kennedy and Jesus Christ. A psychiatrist who had treated Panetti for a period of six years prior to trial noted that his courtroom behavior pointed to his severe mental illness.[47] If the judge believed that Panetti was not actually mentally ill, it is not surprising that the jury in Panetti's case found him guilty and sentenced him to death.

Following his conviction and death sentence, Panetti filed a *Ford* petition claiming he was not competent to be executed. Panetti's competence hinged on medication, or in his case, forced medication. The Court refrained from making a decision in the *Panetti* case that would determine or clarify exactly what constitutes a "rational understanding" for the sake of execution, thus leaving open the question of what standards should apply in determining competence to be executed. Controversy and debate continue to brew over this question. Moreover, given that states continue to be allowed to execute offenders who are deemed competent when taking medication, whether voluntarily or involuntarily, there is much debate about whether it is ethical or moral to make an ill person well only for the purpose of carrying out an execution. The issues brought to the surface in *Panetti* embody these struggles that are always present when competence of a capital defendant is in question.

V IN SUMMARY, WHAT DO THESE CASES SAY?

The Supreme Court established in *Ford v. Wainwright*[48] (1986) that it is unconstitutional to execute a person who is insane at the time of execution because doing so constitutes cruel and unusual punishment. Three years later, however, the Court concluded in *Penry v. Lynaugh* (1989)[49] that it was not a

---

[45]*Singleton v. Norris*, 319 F.3d 10184 (2003).
[46]*Panetti v. Quarterman*, 551 U.S. 930 (2007).
[47]Joint Appendix, *Panetti v. Quarterman*, 127 S. Ct. 2842 at 29.
[48]*Ford v. Wainwright*, 477 U.S. 399 (1986).
[49]*Penry v. Lynaugh*, 492 U.S. 302 (1989).

violation of the Eighth Amendment to execute a mentally retarded individual. Mental retardation could and should be a mitigating factor but should not necessarily preclude someone from being executed, particularly because there was no national consensus against the death penalty for the mentally retarded. But in 2002, the Court revisited the issue of whether it was unconstitutional to execute the mentally retarded and came to a conclusion divergent from that in *Penry*. The reason for this change in *Atkins v. Virginia* (2002)[50] was due to "evolving standards of decency." The Court found that most states and countries believed that it was cruel and unusual to execute people who are mentally retarded and, in following suit, declared the practice unconstitutional. *Tennard v. Dretke* (2004)[51] pointed to, and reinforced, the need for jurors to consider serious mental impairment as a mitigating factor in making sentencing decisions in capital cases. The cases of *Singleton v. Norris* (2003)[52] and *Panetti v. Quarterman* (2007)[53] highlight the confusion and challenge in applying competency standards to individuals on death row. A clear and definitive set of standards in establishing competence to be executed continues to elude the legal community. The more recent cases of *Bobby v. Bies* (2009)[54] and *Ryan v. Gonzales* (2013)[55] further highlight the facts that mental competence and establishing intellectual disability are issues that continue to evolve in death penalty jurisprudence and that continue to play a central role of import to the constitutional implementation of the death penalty.

VI **CONCLUSION**

Questions surrounding the role mental impairment should play in eligibility for the death penalty have plagued the Supreme Court since the reemergence of the death penalty after *Gregg*. The Court has declared that some mental impairments reduce the culpability of individuals and thus give them immunity from punishment. It has also asserted that inmates must have a certain level of rational understanding of their circumstances and punishment for the death penalty to serve its penological goals. The execution of insane individuals was determined not to meet these objectives, and thus inmates can be executed only if they are deemed sane at the time of execution. The execution of the mentally retarded is unconstitutional because it violates the Eighth Amendment ban on cruel and unusual punishment. Both of these prohibitions have come with controversy and complex legal maneuvering by the states. The Supreme Court in *Atkins* only addressed the question of whether mentally retarded individuals can be executed, leaving it to the states to determine how to define and measure mental retardation for the purposes of execution. In *Ford*, the Court only addressed the question of whether a person who is insane at the time of execution could be executed, creating the notion of competency to be executed. Recent cases have highlighted the confusion that exists in defining and applying competence labels to individuals facing the death penalty and/or executions. The Court has failed to set a standard definition of mental competency to be executed, leaving states to decide what it means to have "rational understanding" and to be "rationally aware." However, the Court has allowed inmates to be involuntarily medicated so that they become competent to be executed. Is it moral to execute individuals who

---

[50]*Atkins v. Virginia*, 536 U.S. 304 (2002).
[51]*Tennard v. Dretke*, 542 US 274 (2004).
[52]*Singleton v. Norris*, 319 F.3d 10184 (2003).
[53]*Panetti v. Quarterman*, 551 U.S. 930 (2007).
[54]*Bobby v. Bies*, 556 U.S. 825 (2009).
[55]*Ryan v. Gonzales*, 568 U.S. ___ (2013).

are forced into competency in their "best interest," only to be executed as a result of medication they neither desired nor chose to take? Is forced competency really competency at all? It is likely that the Court will continue to be faced with these and other issues involving mental competency and impairment for some time to come.

CASES BRIEFED IN CHAPTER 4

Case	Issue	Holding
Ford v. Wainwright 477 U.S. 399 (1986)	1. Does it violate the Eighth Amendment to execute a prisoner who is insane at the time of his scheduled execution? 2. Were the Florida procedures to determine sanity of a person to be executed sufficient?	1. It is a violation of the Eighth Amendment to put to death a prisoner who is insane at the time of execution. 2. An evidentiary hearing to determine competency must be granted to determine if a person who has received a death sentence is insane.
Penry v. Lynaugh 492 U.S. 302 (1989)	1. Does the execution of a mentally retarded offender violate the Eighth Amendment prohibition against cruel and unusual punishment? 2. When requested, should a jury be instructed by the judge to consider mental retardation as a mitigating factor at the sentencing portion of a capital trial?	1. It is constitutional to impose the death penalty on a mentally retarded defendant who has the ability to reason. 2. If the defense requests jury instructions concerning mental retardation as a mitigating factor, such requests must be granted.
Atkins v. Virginia 536 U.S. 304 (2002)	Is it a violation of the Eighth Amendment to execute a mentally retarded offender?	It is a violation of the Eighth Amendment to put to death an offender who is mentally retarded.
Singleton v. Norris 319 F.3d 10184 (2003)	Is it a violation of due process and the Eighth Amendment to forcefully medicate an inmate to render him competent to be executed?	It is not a violation of the Constitution to execute an inmate who is being involuntarily medicated to obtain competency, as long as it is not the sole purpose for the medication.
Tennard v. Dretke 524 U.S. 274 (2004)	Should mental retardation be considered as a mitigating factor, even if that mental retardation is not shown to be related to the crime?	Evidence of mental retardation should be considered as possible mitigation by a capital jury, even if the defendant's crime is not directly attributable to such intellectual or cognitive impairment.
Panetti v. Quarterman 551 U.S. 930 (2007)	1. Is it a violation of the Eighth Amendment to execute an inmate who, because of mental illness, lacks a rational understanding of the State's rationale for the execution but has a factual awareness of that rationale?	1. The Supreme Court refused to make a determinative statement regarding standards for what constitutes a "rational understanding" of the State's rationale for execution.

Continued

Case	Issue	Holding
	2. Is it a violation of the Constitution to fail to provide adequate measures to challenge an execution based on claims of mental incompetency?	2. It is a violation of the Constitution to fail to provide adequate measures for a defendant to challenge an execution based on claims of incompetency to be executed.
Bobby v. Bies 556 U.S. 825 (2009)	Is it a violation of the double jeopardy clause to re-litigate a defendant's claim of mental retardation?	It is not a violation of the double jeopardy clause for a state to determine if a defendant is mentally retarded or developmentally disabled, even if another, earlier determination has been made.
Ryan v. Gonzalez/ Tibbals v. Carter 568 U.S. ___ 2013	Does a death row inmate have a right to suspend federal habeas proceedings based on a claim of incompetence to assist counsel?	A death row inmate does not have a constitutional or statutory right to competence during federal habeas corpus proceedings.

CASE BRIEFS

FORD v. WAINWRIGHT 477 U.S. 399 (1986)

CAPSULE: A prisoner who is insane may not be executed.

FACTS: In 1974, Ford was convicted of murder in Florida and sentenced to death. Ford was not considered incompetent at the time of the offense, at trial, or at sentencing. After sentencing, Ford began to manifest changes in behavior, indicating a mental disorder that rendered him incapable of communication. Ford had separate examinations by two psychiatrists at his counsel's request, one of whom concluded that he was not competent to suffer execution because he had a severe mental disease that resembled paranoid schizophrenia. This diagnosis would limit Ford's ability to assist in his defense. The governor appointed three psychiatrists to ascertain whether Ford had the mental capacity to understand his death sentence. The psychiatrists interviewed Ford together for a total of 30 minutes. Each psychiatrist filed a separate report with the governor, to whom the statute delegates the final decision. The reports all concluded that Ford had a mental disorder, but all three agreed that petitioner was competent. The governor subsequently signed a death warrant without explanation or statement based solely upon the accounts of the three state-appointed psychiatrists.

ISSUES:
1. Does it violate the Eighth Amendment to execute a prisoner who is insane at the time of his scheduled execution? YES.
2. Were the Florida procedures used to determine a person's competence to be executed sufficient? NO.

HOLDING:
1. It is a violation of the Eighth Amendment to put to death a prisoner who is insane at the time of execution.
2. An evidentiary hearing to determine competency must be granted to determine whether a person who has received a death sentence is insane.

Continued

FORD v. WAINWRIGHT 477 U.S. 399 (1986)—cont'd

REASON: "The Eighth Amendment prohibits the State from inflicting the penalty of death upon a prisoner who is insane. Petitioner's allegation of insanity in his habeas corpus petition, if proved, therefore, would bar his execution. The question before us is whether the District Court was under an obligation to hold an evidentiary hearing on the question of Ford's sanity. In answering that question, we bear in mind that, while the underlying social values encompassed by the Eighth Amendment are rooted in historical traditions, the manner in which our judicial system protects those values is purely a matter of contemporary law. Once a substantive right or restriction is recognized in the Constitution, therefore, its enforcement is in no way confined to the rudimentary process deemed adequate in ages past."

"Having identified various failings of the Florida scheme, we must conclude that the State's procedures for determining sanity are inadequate to preclude federal redetermination of the constitutional issue. We do not here suggest that only a full trial on the issue of sanity will suffice to protect the federal interests; we leave to the State the task of developing appropriate ways to enforce the constitutional restriction upon its execution of sentences. It may be that some high threshold showing on behalf of the prisoner will be found a necessary means to control the number of nonmeritorious or repetitive claims of insanity. Other legitimate pragmatic considerations may also supply the boundaries of the procedural safeguards that feasibly can be provided."

CASE SIGNIFICANCE: The Court decided that an insane person could not be executed, because such would be a violation of the Eighth Amendment ban on cruel and unusual punishment. The case was a departure from traditional insanity cases in that Ford was sane at the time of his trial and conviction but became insane while awaiting execution. If Ford had been insane at the time of his trial, he could not have been tried, because competency is required for a defendant to stand trial. The issue here, however, was different from whether a person who was insane at the time the offense was committed could be given the death penalty.

PENRY v. LYNAUGH 492 U.S. 302 (1989)

CAPSULE: It is constitutional to impose the death penalty on a mentally retarded defendant who has the ability to reason.

FACTS: Penry, who was 22 years old when the crime was committed, was convicted of capital murder. Penry raised the insanity defense at trial. The insanity defense failed, but psychiatric testimony during the trial described him as mentally retarded with an IQ of 54 and a mental age of six years. The jury found Penry competent to stand trial, and he was found guilty of capital murder. At that time, during the penalty phase of a capital trial, Texas law provided that the jury consider three "special issues":

1. Whether the conduct of the defendant that caused the death of the deceased was committed deliberately and with the reasonable expectation that death would result;
2. Whether the defendant would constitute a continuing threat to society; and
3. Was the killing an unreasonable response to provocation, if any, by the victim?

Penry requested that the jury receive specific instructions defining terms in the special issues and that mercy be considered on the basis of mitigating circumstances. The jury sentenced Penry to death.

ISSUES:
1. Does the execution of a mentally retarded offender violate the Eighth Amendment prohibition against cruel and unusual punishment? NO.
2. When requested, should a jury be instructed by the judge to consider mental retardation as a mitigating factor at the sentencing portion of a capital trial? YES.

Continued

PENRY v. LYNAUGH 492 U.S. 302 (1989)—cont'd

HOLDING:
1. It is constitutional to impose the death penalty on a mentally retarded defendant who has the ability to reason.
2. If the defense requests jury instructions concerning mental retardation as a mitigating factor, such requests must be granted.

REASON: "Since the common law prohibited the punishment of 'idiots'—which term was generally used to describe persons totally lacking in reason, understanding, or the ability to distinguish between good and evil—it may indeed be 'cruel and unusual punishment' to execute persons who are profoundly or severely retarded and wholly lacking in the capacity to appreciate the wrongfulness of their actions. Such persons, however, are not likely to be convicted or face the prospect of punishment today, since the modern insanity defense generally includes 'mental defect' as part of the legal definition of insanity, and since *Ford v. Wainwright*, *supra*, prohibits the execution of persons who are unaware of their punishment and why they must suffer it. Moreover, petitioner is not such a person, since the jury (1) found him competent to stand trial and therefore to have a rational as well as factual understanding of the proceedings; and (2) rejected his insanity defense, thereby reflecting the conclusion that he knew his conduct was wrong and was capable of conforming it to the requirements of law. Nor is there sufficient objective evidence today of a national consensus against executing mentally retarded capital murderers, since petitioner has cited only one state statute that explicitly bans that practice and has offered no evidence of the general behavior of juries in this regard. Opinion surveys indicating strong public opposition to such executions do not establish a societal consensus, absent some legislative reflection of the sentiment expressed therein."

"To be sure, retardation has long been regarded as a factor that may diminish culpability, and, in its most severe form, may result in complete exculpation . . . Mentally retarded persons, however, are individuals whose abilities and behavioral deficits can vary greatly depending on the degree of their retardation, their life experience, and the ameliorative effects of education and habilitation. On the present record, it cannot be said that all mentally retarded people of petitioner's ability—by virtue of their mental retardation alone, and apart from any individualized consideration of their personal responsibility—inevitably lack the cognitive, volitional, and moral capacity to act with the degree of culpability associated with the death penalty."

CASE SIGNIFICANCE: The Court affirmed that a state could sentence a mentally retarded offender to death, stating that, "the Eighth Amendment does not categorically prohibit the execution of mentally retarded capital murderers of petitioner's reasoning ability." The decision was controversial because it gave a "go ahead" signal for the execution of mentally retarded defendants. The Court used the concept of "evolving standards of decency" to determine whether this practice is constitutional or not, adding that there was no national consensus at that time against such penalties. Thirteen years later, the Court changed its mind in *Atkins v. Virginia* (2002)[56] and overturned the *Penry* decision. In *Atkins*, the Court held that the "evolving standards of decency" had reached a point where it was deemed unconstitutional to execute a mentally retarded offender. The decision in the case is no longer binding or significant. It is included here primarily for historical purposes.

ATKINS v. VIRGINIA 536 U.S. 304 (2002)

CAPSULE: Executing a mentally retarded offender violates the Eighth Amendment prohibition against cruel and unusual punishment.

FACTS: Atkins was convicted of abduction, armed robbery, and capital murder and sentenced to death. In the penalty phase, the defense relied on one witness, Dr. Evan Nelson, a forensic psychologist who had evaluated Atkins before trial and concluded that he was "mildly mentally retarded." His conclusion was based on interviews with people who knew Atkins, a review of school and court records, and the administration of a standard intelligence test, which

Continued

---

[56]*Id.*

ATKINS v. VIRGINIA 536 U.S. 304 (2002)—cont'd

indicated that Atkins had an IQ of 59. The jury sentenced Atkins to death, but the Virginia Supreme Court ordered a second sentencing hearing because the trial court had used a misleading verdict form. At the resentencing, Dr. Nelson again testified. The state presented an expert rebuttal witness, Dr. Stanton Samenow, who testified that Atkins was not mentally retarded but rather was of "average intelligence, at least" and had antisocial personality disorder. The jury again sentenced Atkins to death. The decision was affirmed by the Virginia Supreme Court, relying on the precedent set in *Penry v. Lynaugh* (1989).[57]

ISSUES: Is it a violation of the Eighth Amendment to execute a mentally retarded offender? YES.

HOLDING: It is a violation of the Eighth Amendment to put to death an offender who is mentally retarded.

REASON: "As Chief Justice Warren explained in his opinion in *Trop v. Dulles*, 356 U.S. 86 (1958): "The basic concept underlying the Eighth Amendment is nothing less than the dignity of man . . . The Amendment must draw its meaning from the evolving standards of decency that mark the progress of a maturing society." *Id.*, at 100–101. Proportionality review under those evolving standards should be informed by 'objective factors to the maximum possible extent' . . . This consensus unquestionably reflects widespread judgment about the relative culpability of mentally retarded offenders, and the relationship between mental retardation and the penological purposes served by the death penalty. Additionally, it suggests that some characteristics of mental retardation undermine the strength of the procedural protections that our capital jurisprudence steadfastly guards.

"In light of these deficiencies, our death penalty jurisprudence provides two reasons consistent with the legislative consensus that the mentally retarded should be categorically excluded from execution. First, there is a serious question as to whether either justification that we have recognized as a basis for the death penalty applies to mentally retarded offenders. *Gregg v. Georgia*, 428 U.S. 153, 183 (1976), identified "retribution and deterrence of capital crimes by prospective offenders" as the social purposes served by the death penalty. Unless the imposition of the death penalty on a mentally retarded person, 'measurably contributes to one or both of these goals, it is nothing more than the purposeless and needless imposition of pain and suffering,' and hence an unconstitutional punishment. The reduced capacity of mentally retarded offenders provides a second justification for a categorical rule making such offenders ineligible for the death penalty."

The risk "that the death penalty will be imposed in spite of factors which may call for a less severe penalty," *Lockett v. Ohio*, 438 U.S. 586, 605 (1978), is enhanced, not only by the possibility of false confessions but also by the lesser ability of mentally retarded defendants to make a persuasive showing of mitigation in the face of prosecutorial evidence of one or more aggravating factors. Mentally retarded defendants may be less able to give meaningful assistance to their counsel and are typically poor witnesses, and their demeanor may create an unwarranted impression of lack of remorse for their crimes. As *Penry* demonstrated, moreover, reliance on mental retardation as a mitigating factor can be a two-edged sword that may enhance the likelihood that the aggravating factor of future dangerousness will be found by the jury. 492 U.S., at 323–325. Mentally retarded defendants in the aggregate face a special risk of wrongful execution.

CASE SIGNIFICANCE: This case is important because it puts an end to the execution of mentally retarded offenders. The Supreme Court had decided the controversial *Penry* case differently more than a decade prior to *Atkins*. This case reverses *Penry*.

The Court said that the states must create suitable methods to enforce the *Atkins* decision. The Court did not, however, provide any guidance as to what constitutes mental retardation and how to assess and diagnose mental

Continued

---

[57]*Penry v. Lynaugh*, 492 U.S. 302 (1989).

ATKINS v. VIRGINIA 536 U.S. 304 (2002)—cont'd

retardation. Thus, although the *Atkins* case prohibits the execution of the mentally retarded, it has left many questions unanswered. These issues will likely be considered by the Court in future cases. For now, however, the issue of the constitutionality of executing the mentally retarded is settled. It is unconstitutional.

SINGLETON v. NORRIS 319 F.3D 1018 (8TH CIR. 2003)

CAPSULE: It is not a violation of the Eighth Amendment to execute a prisoner who became mentally incompetent while on death row but regained competency through forced medication.

FACTS: Charles Singleton murdered a woman, Mary Lou York, on June 1, 1979. York died from two stab wounds inflicted in her neck. Singleton was convicted of capital murder and sentenced to death in June 1982. Many years of appeals followed. During Singleton's federal habeus corpus petition, Singleton conceded in his appeal that through voluntary taking of antipsychotic medication he was competent for execution. In 1997, after a period in which Singleton failed to take medication, a review panel decreed that Singleton should be given involuntary medication as he was a danger to himself and/or others. Singleton then filed another habeus corpus petition arguing that the state could not forcefully medicate him solely to make him competent to be executed, because it violated his due process and Eighth Amendment rights. The district court dismissed the case, stating that it believed the state was not forcefully medicating him solely for the purpose of carrying out his execution. The Eighth Circuit upheld the decision. The Supreme Court denied certiorari.

ISSUE: If there are medically necessary purposes for the medication, is it a violation of due process and the Eighth Amendment to forcefully medicate an inmate to render him competent to be executed? NO.

HOLDING: It is not a violation of the constitution to execute an inmate who is being involuntarily medicated to obtain competency as long as it is not the sole purpose for the medication.

REASON: The Eighth Circuit held that "the mandatory medication regime, valid under the pendancy of a stay of execution, does not become unconstitutional under *Harper* when an execution date is set." The court adopted the same rule that had been applied in *United States v. Sell*, 539 U.S. 166 (2003). The Eighth Circuit noted that in order to justify the forcible medication of an inmate when the medication rendered the inmate competent for execution, three conditions must be met:

1. Present an essential state interest that outweighs the individual's interest in remaining medication free.
2. Prove that there is no less intrusive way to fulfill the essential interest.
3. Prove by clear and convincing evidence that the medication is medically appropriate.[58]

Medication is appropriate and in the best medical interest of the inmate when the medication renders the inmate competent and when the severity of the side effects of the medication does not surpass its benefits. The Eighth Circuit held that when a state executes an inmate who lost competency while on death row but regains competency due to medical care, including forced medication, it is not a violation of a prisoner's Eighth Amendment rights. If the state has an obligation to administer medication in the prisoner's best medical interest, any additional motives, if they are present, are immaterial.

CASE SIGNIFICANCE: The decision in this case allows for states to execute offenders who, without medication, would be considered to be incompetent but with medication are declared competent, regardless of Eighth Circuit also allows states to forcefully medicate an inmate if it is in their "medical best interest," even if they have an ulterior motive of carrying out a death sentence.

---

[58]Citing *United States v. Sell*, 282 F.3d 560, 567 (2002).

TENNARD v. DRETKE 542 U.S. 274 (2004)

CAPSULE: Mental retardation has applicable mitigating effect beyond its relationship to the crime and the defendant's ability to act deliberately.

FACTS: In 1986 the petitioner was convicted of capital murder in which Tennard and two accomplices killed two of his neighbors while robbing their home. Tennard had stabbed one of the victims. During the penalty phase of the trial, defense counsel called Tennard's parole officer as the only witness who testified that Tennard's IQ was 67 when tested at age 17. The parole officer had obtained the information from Tennard's prison record. Tennard had been convicted of rape at age 16, in which his victim had escaped when she was allowed to use the bathroom on the promise that she would not run away. During deliberation, jurors were asked two "special issue" questions used at the time in Texas to determine whether a life or death sentence would be imposed:

1. Was the conduct of the defendant, which caused the death of the deceased, committed deliberately and with reasonable expectation that death of the deceased or another would result? (This became known as the "deliberateness special issue.")
2. Is there a probability that the defendant would commit criminal acts of violence that would constitute a continuing threat to society? (This became known as the "future dangerousness special issue.")

The jury answered "yes" to both questions, and Tennard was subsequently sentenced to death. Tennard, on appeal, argued that his death sentence was in violation of *Penry* in that the jury instructions were not sufficient for the jury to consider mental retardation as a mitigating factor. The Texas Court of Criminal Appeals rejected Tennard's *Penry* claim, citing that Tennard failed to meet the standard of mental retardation in Texas. The District Court denied his habeus corpus petition, and the Court of Appeals for the Fifth Circuit denied his request for a Certificate of Appealability (COA) on the grounds that even if Tennard was determined to be mentally retarded, he had failed to show that his crime was in any way attributable to such mental retardation.

ISSUE: Should mental retardation be considered as a mitigating factor, even if that mental retardation is not shown to be related to the crime? YES.

HOLDING: Evidence of mental retardation should be considered as possible mitigation by a capital jury, even if the defendant's crime is not directly attributable to such intellectual or cognitive impairment.

REASON: "Reasonable jurists could conclude that the low IQ evidence Tennard presented was relevant mitigating evidence. Evidence of significantly impaired intellectual functioning is obviously evidence that 'might serve as a basis for a sentence less than death.'"

"Reasonable jurists also could conclude that the Texas Court of Criminal Appeals' application of Penry to the facts of Tennard's case was unreasonable. The relationship between the special issues and Tennard's low IQ evidence has the same essential features as the relationship between the special issues and Penry's mental retardation evidence. Impaired intellectual functioning has mitigating dimension beyond the impact it has on the individual's ability to act deliberately. A reasonable jurist could conclude that the jury might well have given Tennard's low IQ evidence aggravating effect in considering his future dangerousness, not only as a matter of probable inference from the evidence but also because the prosecutor told them to do so: '[W]hether he has a low IQ or not is not really the issue. Because the legislature, in asking you to address that question, the reasons why he became a danger are not really relevant. The fact that he is a danger, that the evidence shows he's a danger, is the criteria to use in answering that question.' Indeed, the prosecutor's comments pressed exactly the most problematic interpretation of the special issues, suggesting that Tennard's low IQ was irrelevant in mitigation, but relevant to the question whether he posed a future danger."

CASE SIGNIFICANCE: The definition of mental retardation is still an issue in states that have the death penalty. The Fifth Circuit denied a COA based upon whether Tennard's mental retardation was "uniquely severe" and a "nexus" to the crime. The Supreme Court held that this was not in line with the standard set in *Penry* and that members of a jury must be able to fully consider a capital defendant's mitigating circumstances. The decision in *Tennard* reaffirms the notion that impaired intellectual functioning is a relevant mitigating factor to be considered by capital juries in sentencing decisions.

PANETTI v. QUARTERMAN 551 U.S. 930 (2007)

CAPSULE: A prisoner's awareness of a state's rationale for an execution is not the same as a rational understanding of it.

FACTS: The petitioner was convicted of capital murder in a Texas state court and sentenced to death, even in light of a well-documented history of mental illness. Panetti was denied relief on direct appeal, and his habeas corpus petition was denied by the district court and the Fifth Circuit. At no point in his initial appeal did the petitioner argue that he was mentally incompetent to stand trial. Once an execution date was set, the petitioner, for the first time, filed a motion that he was not competent to be executed due to his mental illness. Panetti had a well-documented history of severe mental illness, including at least 12 involuntary commitments in Wisconsin and Texas. The psychiatrist who found him competent to stand trial noted his "chronic delusions and occasional hallucinations . . ." The trial judge denied the motion without a hearing, and the Texas Criminal Court of Appeals dismissed the appeal for lack of jurisdiction. Panetti then filed a second habeas petition in which the District Court stayed his execution so that the state trial court could consider his current mental state. Without ruling on the outstanding motions, the judge found the petitioner competent and closed the case. Petitioner then returned to the Federal District Court, seeking a resolution of his pending habeus petition. The District Court concluded that the state-court competency proceedings failed to comply with Texas law and were constitutionally inadequate in light of the procedural requirements mandated by *Ford* v. *Wainwright*, 477 U.S. 399. Although the court therefore reviewed petitioner's incompetency claim without deferring to the state court's finding of competency, it nevertheless granted no relief, finding that petitioner had not demonstrated that he met the standard for incompetency. Under Fifth Circuit precedent, the court explained, petitioner was competent to be executed as long as he knew the fact of his impending execution and the factual predicate for it. The Fifth Circuit affirmed.

ISSUES:
1. Is it a violation of the Eighth Amendment to execute an inmate who, because of mental illness, lacks a rational understanding of the state's rationale for the execution but has a factual awareness of that rationale? UNANSWERED.
2. Is it a violation of the Constitution to fail to provide adequate measures to challenge an execution based on claims of mental incompetency? YES.

HOLDINGS:
1. The Supreme Court refused to make a determinative statement regarding standards for what constitutes a "rational understanding" of the state's rationale for execution.
2. It is a violation of the Constitution to fail to provide adequate measures for a defendant to challenge an execution based on claims of incompetency to be executed.

REASON: "The state court failed to provide the procedures to which petitioner was entitled under the Constitution. *Ford* identifies the measures a State must provide when a prisoner alleges incompetency to be executed. As Justice Powell elaborated, once a prisoner seeking a stay of execution has made 'a substantial threshold showing of insanity,' 477 U.S., at 424, the Eighth and Fourteenth Amendments entitle him to a fair hearing including an opportunity to submit 'expert psychiatric evidence that may differ from the State's own psychiatric examination,' *id.*, at 427. The procedures the state court provided petitioner were ruled so deficient that they cannot be reconciled with any reasonable interpretation of the *Ford* rule. It is uncontested that petitioner made a substantial showing of incompetency. It is also evident from the record, however, that the state court reached its competency determination without holding a hearing or providing petitioner with an adequate opportunity to provide his own expert evidence. Moreover, there is a strong argument that the court violated state law by failing to provide a competency hearing. If so, the violation undermines any reliance the State might now place on Justice Powell's assertion that 'the States should have substantial leeway to determine what process best balances the various interests at stake.' *Id.*, at 427. Having determined that the state court unreasonably applied *Ford* when it accorded petitioner the procedures in question, the Court then considered petitioner's claim on the merits without deferring to the state court's competency finding."

"Although the Court rejects the Fifth Circuit's standard, it does not attempt to set down a rule governing all competency determinations. The record is not as informative as it might be because it was developed by the District Court under the rejected standard, and, thus, this Court finds it difficult to amplify its conclusions or to make them

Continued

PANETTI v. QUARTERMAN 551 U.S. 930 (2007)—cont'd

more precise. It is proper to allow the court charged with overseeing the development of the evidentiary record the initial opportunity to resolve petitioner's constitutional claim."

CASE SIGNIFICANCE: The case affirms the belief that "death is different" and that the protection of the severely mentally ill sentenced to death is still an issue in American death penalty jurisprudence. Whereas the decision in *Atkins v. Virginia* instituted a ban on the execution of the mentally retarded, there is no universal ban on capital punishment for the mentally ill. The case highlights the notion that states are still struggling with the standard set out in *Ford* and how incompetence to stand trial is defined. Panetti had a history of severe mental illness and yet was still found to be competent by a Texas jury (after his first jury deadlocked and a mistrial was declared). This case also confirms the continued belief by many in the criminal justice system that mental illness is an "excuse" or a "way to get off easy." Jurors, even when faced with substantial evidence of schizophrenic delusions and acute psychiatric disorders, are skeptical at best and may be even less likely to show sympathy if they believe the defendant is "pretending." The Supreme Court in *Panetti* has reaffirmed that mentally ill defendants in capital proceedings must be afforded protection in establishing competency to be executed.

BOBBY v. BIES 556 U.S. 825 (2009)

CAPSULE: It is not a violation of the double jeopardy clause for a state to reassess the nature of a defendant's mental capacity in order to determine his or her eligibility for the death penalty.

FACTS: In 1992, Michael Bies was convicted of rape, kidnapping, and murder and sentenced to death in Ohio. Bies filed an appeal in the state appellate court and ultimately the supreme court of Ohio. The defense for Bies argued that he was mentally retarded and that this fact should mitigate his capital conviction. Both the lower and appellate courts affirmed his conviction and sentence but also agreed that he was mentally retarded. While the defendant proceeded with his post-conviction appeals, the Supreme Court rendered its decision in *Atkins,* stating that "death is not a suitable punishment for mentally retarded people." Bies then subsequently filed a petition for habeas corpus relief in an Ohio federal district court, relying on *Atkins*. The state then contended that Bies was not mentally retarded. Bies argued that the double jeopardy clause barred the state from relitigating the claim of his mental retardation. The district court agreed and granted Bies's petition for habeas corpus relief and ordered that he be resentenced. The Sixth Circuit affirmed, agreeing that the double jeopardy clause did in fact prevent the Supreme Court of Ohio from determining whether Bies was or was not mentally retarded.

ISSUES: Is it a violation of the double jeopardy clause to relitigate a defendant's claim of mental retardation? NO.

HOLDING: It is not a violation of the double jeopardy clause for a state to determine whether a defendant is mentally retarded or developmentally disabled, even if another, earlier determination by the state has been made.

REASON: "The Sixth Circuit, in common with the District Court, fundamentally misperceived the application of the Double Jeopardy Clause and its issue preclusion (collateral estoppel) component. First, Bies was not 'twice put in jeopardy.' He was sentenced to death, and Ohio sought no further prosecution or punishment. Instead of 'serial prosecutions by the government, this case involves serial efforts by the defendant to vacate his capital sentence.' Further, mental retardation for purposes of *Atkins*, and mental retardation as one mitigator to be weighed against aggravators, are discrete issues. Most grave among the Sixth Circuit's misunderstandings, issue preclusion is a plea available to prevailing parties. The doctrine bars relitigation of determinations necessary to the ultimate outcome of a prior proceeding. The Ohio courts' recognition of Bies' mental state as a mitigating factor was hardly essential to the death sentence he received. On the contrary, the retardation evidence cut against the final judgment. Issue preclusion, in short, does not transform final judgment losers, in civil or criminal proceedings, into partially prevailing parties."

Continued

BOBBY v. BIES 556 U.S. 825 (2009)—cont'd

CASE SIGNIFICANCE: The Court decided that the state has a salient interest in determining whether a defendant is mentally retarded, and a determination of this fact after conviction is not a violation of the double jeopardy clause. The decision allows for states to, in essence, reassess a defendant's claim of mental retardation and to redetermine whether the defendant should or should not face execution as a result.

RYAN v. GONZALES/TIBBALS v. CARTER 568 U.S. ___(2013)

CAPSULE: A death row inmate does not have the right to suspend federal habeas corpus proceedings when the inmate is found incompetent to assist counsel in appellate processes.

FACTS: In 1991, an Arizona jury convicted Ernest Valencia Gonzales of first-degree murder and sentenced him to death. After exhausting his state court appeals, Gonzales initiated federal habeas corpus proceedings in 1999. Gonzales began to display signs of delusion and paranoia in the subsequent years after his federal habeas petitions and refused visits from his attorney. The district court denied his attorney's motion to stay the habeas proceedings pending a competency determination. The Ninth Circuit eventually granted mandamus relief, holding that the capital inmate's right to counsel in federal habeas proceedings under 18 U.S.C. § 3599(a)(2) implicitly includes a right to be competent to assist one's counsel. The director of the Arizona Department of Corrections, Charles Ryan, appealed the Ninth Circuit's decision, arguing that the circuit court misread the law to include a "right to competency" in assisting counsel. Ryan asserts that such a right would allow for indefinite stays of habeas proceedings based on incompetency that contravene Congress's intent in the Antiterrorism and Effective Death Penalty Act (AEDPA). Gonzales countered that district courts have discretion to issue stays and that such stays are appropriate where incompetency would deprive the offender of a "meaningful" right to counsel.

In *Tibbals v. Carter*, Sean Carter was convicted of aggravated murder, aggravated robbery, and rape and was given a capital conviction. His counsel filed a federal habeas corpus petition challenging his conviction and requested a pre-petition competency hearing to determine whether Carter was competent to participate in the federal habeas proceeding. The federal district court granted both the petition and the request. Two years later, the district court determined that Carter was incompetent and dismissed his federal habeas petition. The Ohio Department of Rehabilitation and Correction challenged the district court's decision, and the Sixth Circuit determined that even though the district court was justified in finding Carter incompetent, the proper course of action was to stay, rather than dismiss, the habeas proceedings until Carter was competent.

ISSUES: Do death row inmates possess a "right to competence" in federal habeas proceedings? NO.

HOLDING: There is no statutory or constitutional right to competence during a federal habeas corpus proceeding.

REASON: "Section 3599(a)(2) guarantees federal habeas petitioners on death row the right to federally funded counsel. The statute provides that petitioners who are 'financially unable to obtain adequate representation . . . shall be entitled to the appointment of one or more attorneys.' Appointed attorneys are required to have experience in death penalty litigation, §§3599(b)–(d), and, once appointed, are directed to 'represent the defendant throughout every subsequent stage of available judicial proceedings,' §3599(e). The statute also gives district courts the power to authorize funding for 'investigative, expert, or other services' as are 'reasonably necessary for the representation of the defendant.' §3599(f). But §3599 does not direct district courts to stay proceedings when habeas petitioners are found incompetent. 'In any postconviction proceeding under [28 U. S. C. §2254 or§2255], seeking to vacate or set aside a death sentence, any defendant who is or becomes financially unable to obtain adequate representation or investigative, expert, or other reasonably necessary services shall be entitled to the appointment of one or more attorneys and the furnishing of such other services in accordance with subsections

Continued

RYAN v. GONZALES/TIBBALS v. CARTER 568 U.S. ___(2013)—cont'd

(b) through (f).' 18 U. S. C. §3599(a)(2). In fact, §3599(e), which contains the section's sole reference to 'competency,' cuts against the Ninth Circuit's conclusion."

"In addition to lacking any basis in the statutory text, the assertion that the right to counsel implies a right to competence is difficult to square with our constitutional precedents. The right to counsel is located in the Sixth Amendment. ('In all criminal prosecutions, the accused shall enjoy the right . . . to have the Assistance of Counsel for his defence.') If the right to counsel carried with it an implied right to competence, the right to competence at trial would flow from the Sixth Amendment. But '[w]e have repeatedly and consistently recognized that 'the criminal trial of an incompetent defendant violates *due process*,' not the Sixth Amendment. *Cooper* v. *Oklahoma*, 517 U. S. 348, 354 (1996) (quoting *Medina* v. *California*, 505 U. S. 437, 453 (1992); emphasis added)."

CASE SIGNIFICANCE: These two cases establish that an individual does not need to be competent to file or have heard a federal habeas corpus petition. These Supreme Court decisions represent an important addition to capital punishment jurisprudence related to mental health and mental competency. An individual who is insane or mentally retarded may not be executed, but this does not preclude such a person from, through their attorney, bringing valid appellate motions or habeas corpus petitions. The mental competence right afforded to those facing criminal trial (i.e. "competence to stand trial") does not necessarily extend to post-conviction processes such as habeas corpus petitions. In other words, being unable to assist one's attorney in these efforts and processes does not equate to a violation of the right to counsel in capital cases.

Key Terms

AAIDD
Atkins v. Virginia
Bobby v. Bies
competency to be executed
DSM-5
Ford v. Wainwright
Insanity
intellectual disability
intelligence quotient (IQ)
malingering
mental health
mental illness
mental retardation
Panetti v. Quarterman
Penry v. Lynaugh
Ryan v. Gonzalez
Singleton v. Norris
Tennard v. Dretke
Tibbals v. Carter

CRITICAL THINKING QUESTIONS

1. In *Penry v. Lynaugh*, the Supreme Court held that, though mental retardation may be a mitigating factor, it did not warrant automatic exclusion from execution. In *Atkins v. Virginia*, the Court overturned this, asserting that it was unconstitutional to execute a mentally retarded offender. What happened between *Penry* and *Atkins* to bring about this change?

2. Identify and discuss the typical criteria for determining that an offender is mentally retarded (intellectually/developmentally disabled). Who do you think should make these determinations, and when should they be made in respect to death penalty cases?

3. In *Atkins v. Virginia*, the Supreme Court prohibited the use of the death penalty on offenders who are deemed mentally retarded. Explain the reasoning for this prohibition.

4. In *Ford v. Wainwright*, the Supreme Court held that it is a violation of the Eighth Amendment to execute someone who is insane at the time of execution. In the context of the purpose of criminal sanctions, what is the reasoning behind this decision?

5. Though people who are insane at the time of execution may not be executed, they can be treated and restored to competency to be executed. Consider and discuss how this might be controversial.

Internet Resources

Intellectual Disability and the Death Penalty
www.deathpenaltyinfo.org/intellectual-disability-and-death-penalty

Juries and Their Knowledge of Mental Health
www.deathpenalty.org/article.php?id=621

ACLU-Mental Illness and the Death Penalty
https://www.aclu.org/capital-punishment/mental-illness-and-death-penalty-0

Recent Developments on Intellectual Disability and the Death Penalty
www.ncadp.org/blog/c/intellectual-disability

The Death Penalty for Juveniles

CHAPTER OUTLINE

I INTRODUCTION

The death penalty for juveniles has undergone jurisprudential evolution with a 180-degree twist. Common law practice was to punish offenders without considering their age.[1] The first recorded execution

---

[1] *Dendy v. Wilson*, 142 Tex. 460, 464 (1944).

in the United States of a juvenile happened in Plymouth Colony, Massachusetts.[2] The juvenile, Thomas Graunger, was convicted of bestiality and subsequently put to death at age 16. At that time, the death penalty could be imposed for a variety of crimes committed by children; however, records indicate that between the years of 1806 and 1882 there were only two children under the age of 14 put to death in the United States.[3] From 1973 to 2005, there were 227 death sentences imposed on juveniles; however, only 22 resulted in executions.[4]

The Supreme Court interprets limitations on the death penalty based on "evolving standards that mark the progress of a maturing society."[5] Sharp disagreement prevails among Supreme Court Justices as to the factors that determine evolving standards of decency. Conservatives maintain that the interpretation of evolving standards should be strictly based on objective factors such as the acts of state legislatures and the sentencing practices of juries. In contrast, liberals advocate a broader interpretation. Their view considers objective factors and the social purposes of the death penalty. These include factors such as moral proportionality, penal goals, and the views of relevant groups on the juvenile death penalty. Although the Court predominantly uses contemporary standards of decency based on state legislation and other legal markers to evaluate the death penalty for juveniles, Justices' ongoing debate involves broader concerns regarding the appropriate age for executing juveniles.

This chapter reviews U.S. Supreme Court decisions on the juvenile death penalty. It begins with an analysis of three major Supreme Court cases: *Thompson v. Oklahoma* (1988),[6] *Stanford v. Kentucky* (1989),[7] and *Atkins v. Virginia* (2002).[8] It then devotes extended coverage to *Roper v. Simmons* (2005),[9] the most recent, and ostensibly last, word from the Court on the execution of juveniles. The chapter closes with an examination of the Court's interpretations of evolving standards of decency in the context of the juvenile death penalty and its recent decisions on the constitutionality of life without parole for juveniles.

II *THOMPSON v. OKLAHOMA*: EXECUTING JUVENILES AGE 15 AND YOUNGER IS UNCONSTITUTIONAL

A Facts

William Wayne Thompson, along with three accomplices, actively participated in the murder of his former brother-in-law during the early hours of January 23, 1983. The victim was shot two times and sustained multiple knife wounds to his throat, chest, and abdomen. Thompson and his accomplices threw the body into a river, where it was undiscovered for approximately four weeks.

---

[2]Streib, Victor L., *Moratorium on the Death Penalty for Juveniles*, 61 LAW & CONTEMP. PROBS. 55, n.1 (1998).
[3]Platt, Anthony, and Bernard Diamond, *The Origins of the "Right and Wrong" Test of Criminal Responsibility and Its Subsequent Development in the United States: An Historical Survey*, 54 CAL. L. REV. 1227, 1233–34 (1966).
[4]Martin, Carrie, *Spare the Death Penalty, Spoil the Child: How the Execution of Juveniles Violates the Eighth Amendment's Ban on Cruel and Unusual Punishment in 2005*, 46 S. TEX L. REV. 695 (2005).
[5]*Trop v. Dulles*, 356 U.S. 86 (1958).
[6]*Thompson v. Oklahoma*, 487 U.S. 815 (1988).
[7]*Stanford v. Kentucky*, 492 U.S. 361 (1989).
[8]*Atkins v. Virginia*, 536 U.S. 304 (2002).
[9]*Roper v. Simmons*, 543 U.S. 551 (2005).

Although Thompson was considered a child according to Oklahoma law, he was certified to stand trial as an adult and was subsequently convicted. During the penalty phase, the prosecutor sought the death penalty. The prosecutor asked the jury to find that aggravating circumstances existed, namely: (1) that the murder was particularly heinous and cruel, and (2) that there was a reasonable probability that the defendant would present a continuing threat to society if set free. The jury found that the first aggravating circumstance existed and Thompson was given the death penalty.

The Supreme Court granted certiorari in *Thompson* to decide whether the death penalty was constitutional for juveniles who committed their crime at the age of 15. At the time *Thompson* was decided, the Supreme Court had not established a minimum age for executing juveniles. States had the power to set their own minimum age for imposing the death penalty.

B The Court's Holding

The Court held that the execution of juveniles who committed the crime at age 15 constitutes cruel and unusual punishment. The Court said that the interpretation of evolving standards should be based on "relevant legislative enactments, jury determinations and explaining why a young person is not capable of acting with the degree of culpability that can justify the ultimate penalty."[10] Four of the Supreme Court Justices shared this view. A separate concurring opinion was written by Justice Sandra Day O'Connor. In her concurring opinion, Justice O'Connor agreed with the plurality's decision but claimed that when a state has not established a minimum age for execution, the Court cannot assume that the state intended such executions to take place. Because the majority of state legislatures did not set a minimum age for execution, she concluded that the execution of 15-year-olds was unconstitutional.

C Reasoning

The Court first examined the acts of state legislatures in order to determine whether a national consensus existed against the execution of juveniles who committed their crime before reaching the age of 16. In its analysis of state laws, the Court distinguished between the rights of minors and the rights of adults. Because most states, including Oklahoma, prohibited 15-year-olds from serving as jurors, voting, or using alcohol or cigarettes, the Court concluded that adult and juvenile rights were different.[11] The Court said that different rights for adults and juveniles meant that "society assumes that minors do not act as adults do, and thus [society] acts in their interest by restricting certain choices that they are not yet ready to make with the full benefit of the costs and benefits attending to such decisions."[12]

At the time *Thompson* was decided, most states did not statutorily define their minimum age for execution. In states with no minimum age for execution, judges and prosecutors were required to certify juveniles in order for them to be eligible for the death penalty. However, a total of 18 states set their legal age at 16.[13] The Court inferred that these 18 states constituted a national consensus against the death penalty for juveniles because no states set their minimum age for execution below the age of 16.

---

[10]*Thompson*, 487 U.S. at 821–823.
[11]*Id.*
[12]*Id.* at 825.
[13]*Id.* at 826–829.

The Court then looked at the sentencing patterns of juries and concluded that society did not believe that the death penalty should be constitutional for juveniles 15 and younger, because most juries did not sentence these individuals to death. As evidence of then-contemporary sentencing patterns, the Court noted that between the years 1982 and 1986, only five of about 1,400 capital offenders were under the age of 16.[14] The Court was also influenced by the fact that only 18 to 20 juveniles age 15 and younger were put to death during the twentieth century, all of which occurred before 1948.[15] These factors, taken together, led the Court to conclude that executing juvenile offenders 15 years of age and younger was unconstitutional. But what about juveniles who were 16 or 17 years of age? It did not take long for the Court to resolve the issue left unanswered in *Thompson*. The Court addressed that issue in *Stanford v. Kentucky* the following year.

III *STANFORD v. KENTUCKY*: EXECUTING JUVENILES AGES 16 TO 17 IS CONSTITUTIONAL

A Facts

Kevin Stanford was 17 years old when he brutally murdered Barbel Poore in Jefferson County, Kentucky. On January 7, 1981, Stanford and his accomplice repeatedly raped and sodomized Poore, who worked as a gas station attendant. The perpetrators then drove their victim to a removed area, where Stanford shot her twice in the head. Stanford and his accomplice obtained 300 cartons of cigarettes, a couple of gallons of gas, and a nominal amount of cash. A corrections officer testified that Stanford explained the crime in this manner: "He said, I had to shoot her, [she] lived next door to me and she would recognize me.... I guess we could have tied her up or something or beat [her up]... and tell her if she tells, we would kill her... Then after he said that he started laughing."[16]

Because Stanford was charged with a Class A felony or capital crime and was over 16 years of age at the time of his crime, the juvenile court waived jurisdiction. Given Stanford's past record of juvenile delinquency, the juvenile court certified Stanford to stand trial as an adult. He was convicted of numerous crimes, including murder, and sentenced to death plus 45 years. On appeal, Stanford argued that the death penalty was cruel and unusual punishment for offenders who committed their crime at the age of 16 or 17.

B The Court's Holding

In *Stanford*, the Court addressed the same issue raised in a companion case, *Wilkins v. Missouri* (1989).[17] Wilkins and Stanford were 16 and 17 years old, respectively. Although the two cases are separate and involved different facts, the cases are often referred to as the *Stanford* case because they involved the same rule. The *Stanford* Court addressed the issue of whether the death penalty was cruel and unusual punishment for juveniles 16 or 17 years old at the time of the crime. As in *Thompson*, the Court used "evolving standards of decency"[18] to determine whether a national consensus against the

---

[14]*Id.* at 832–833.
[15]*Id.*
[16]734 S.W.2d 781, 788 (Ky. 1987).
[17]492 U.S. 361 (1989).
[18]*Id.* at 369.

death penalty for juveniles under the age of 18 had emerged. In a five-to-four decision, the Court held that the death penalty was not cruel and unusual punishment for juveniles aged 16 or 17 at the time the crime was committed.

C Reasoning

The *Stanford* Court took a narrow approach to analyzing the evolving standards doctrine. Justice Antonin Scalia, writing for the majority, said that evolving standards of decency must be evaluated according to "statutes passed by society's elected representatives"[19] and also the sentencing practices of state juries. The Court said that a categorical rule prohibiting the death penalty for juveniles ages 16 or 17 would unnecessarily restrict states from exercising their legislative authority to establish minimum ages for execution. Justice Scalia claimed that the views of professional, religious, and international groups on the execution of 16- or 17-year-olds should not be considered influential when evaluating evolving standards.

At the time *Stanford* was decided, 37 states had the death penalty.[20] After noting the number of states authorizing the death penalty, the Court focused on states allowing the death penalty for 16- and 17-year-olds. According to then-existing law, the Court found that 15 states rejected the death penalty for juveniles who committed their crimes prior to reaching the age of 16. It also determined that 12 states refused to impose the death penalty on individuals who committed their crimes when younger than 17.[21] The Court then concluded that the number of states permitting the death penalty for 16- or 17-year-olds was sufficient to establish a national consensus in favor of the juvenile death penalty.

The *Stanford* Court conceded that the number of state juries sentencing juveniles to death was far fewer than that for adults. The Court acknowledged that only about 2 percent of offenders executed during the years 1642 to 1986 were under the age of 18 at the time of their crimes.[22] However, the Court considered the statistics unimportant because it was "not only possible, but overwhelmingly probable, that the very considerations which induce petitioners and prosecutors and juries to believe that death should never be imposed on offenders under 18 cause prosecutors and juries to believe that it should rarely be imposed."[23] The Court held that the death penalty was not cruel and unusual punishment for 16- or 17-year-olds.

IV *ATKINS v. VIRGINIA*: A CASE INVOLVING THE MENTALLY RETARDED, BUT A PRELUDE TO THE ABOLITION OF THE JUVENILE DEATH PENALTY

A The Issue and Holding

In *Atkins v. Virginia* (2002),[24] the Court addressed the question of whether the death penalty was cruel and unusual punishment for mentally retarded offenders. The *Atkins* Court held that imposing the death penalty on mentally retarded defendants violates the Eighth and Fourteenth Amendments. In *Atkins*, the

---

[19]*Id.* at 370–374.
[20]*Id.* at 370.
[21]*Id.*
[22]*Id.* at 373–374.
[23]*Id.* at 374.
[24]*Atkins, Supra.*

Court overruled its earlier decision in *Penry v. Lynaugh* (1989),[25] in which the Court held that the execution of mentally retarded defendants was not cruel and unusual punishment. The Court returned to the "evolving standards of decency" test, focusing on state legislation, sentencing practices, and the diminished culpability of mentally retarded defendants.

The Court first examined the number of state laws that changed between 1989 and 2002.[26] The Court considered important the fact that 18 states legislatively banned the practice of executing mentally retarded offenders during these years, noting "the consistency and direction of change"[27] of state legislation, which was a critical component of the holding. In addition, the Court said that since *Penry*, juries were less likely to impose death as punishment for mentally retarded defendants. The Court took into account the opinions of the professional, social, religious, and international communities on the execution of mentally retarded defendants. It concluded that "although these factors are by no means dispositive, their consistency with the legislative evidence lends further support to our conclusion that there is a consensus among those who have addressed the issue."[28]

The Court assessed the policy implications served by executing the mentally retarded offenders, saying that mentally retarded offenders "have diminished capacities to understand and process information, to communicate, to abstract from mistakes and learn from experience."[29] The Court then concluded that the deterrent and retributive value of the death penalty was undermined by allowing further executions of the mentally retarded.

B Significance of *Atkins* for the Juvenile Death Penalty: The Missouri Supreme Court's Decision in *Simmons v. Roper*

The *Atkins* case is important because of its impact on the death penalty for juveniles. One year after *Atkins*, the Missouri Supreme Court decided *Simmons v. Roper*.[30] In that case, the Missouri Supreme Court held that the Eighth and Fourteenth Amendments prohibited the execution of juveniles who committed their crimes before reaching the age of 18. Most of the state court's opinion rested on the logic used in *Atkins*. In *Atkins*, the U.S. Supreme Court cited changes in state legislation since *Penry* on the execution of the mentally retarded, as well as trends in sentencing practices by juries and the policy implications behind the death penalty. Holding that current standards of decency now prohibit the execution of the mentally retarded, the Missouri Supreme Court then found that a national consensus against the execution of juveniles had emerged since the Supreme Court decided *Stanford*.

The Missouri Supreme Court compared the number of states opposing the death penalty for the mentally retarded in *Penry* (2) to the number in *Atkins* (18). While only six states had raised their minimum statutory age between the time *Stanford* and *Simmons* were decided, the "consistency and direction of change"[31] of state legislation was the most critical factor.

---

[25]*Penry v. Lynaugh*, 492 U.S. 302 (1989).
[26]*Atkins, Supra.* at 314–315.
[27]*Id.*
[28]*Id.* at 316.
[29]*Id.* at 318.
[30]*Simmons v. Roper*, 112 S.W.3d 397 (Mo. 2003).
[31]*Id.* at 408.

Based on the analysis adopted in *Atkins*, the Missouri Supreme Court said that juveniles, as well as the mentally retarded, are less likely to receive death sentences by state juries. The Missouri Supreme Court noted that of the 22 states allowing the death penalty for juveniles, only six states had executed juvenile defendants since *Stanford*. It indicated that only three of these six states—Texas, Virginia, and Oklahoma—had imposed the death penalty on a juvenile since 1993.[32] The Missouri Supreme Court said that the international, professional, social, and religious communities opposed the death penalty for juveniles in the same manner as they did for mentally retarded defendants. It noted that although the U.S. Supreme Court had taken different approaches to interpreting evolving standards of decency in the past, "*Atkins* clearly demonstrated a shift back to reliance on such evidence."[33]

The Missouri Supreme Court declared the execution of juveniles unconstitutional, which made it difficult for the U.S. Supreme Court to dodge the issue. The Missouri high court said the execution of juveniles was cruel and unusual based on contemporary standards of decency: In effect, it boldly overruled what the Supreme Court held in *Stanford*.

V *ROPER v. SIMMONS*[34]: THE SUPREME COURT DECLARES THE EXECUTION OF JUVENILES UNCONSTITUTIONAL

A Facts

Christopher Simmons was 17 years old when he committed a brutal murder. Before committing the crime, Simmons stated that he wanted to kill someone, and he discussed with friends his plan to commit the act. On the night of the crime, Simmons and his accomplice entered the home of Shirley Crook through an open window and awakened her. Simmons later stated that he intended to kill Mrs. Crook because of their mutual involvement in a previous car accident.

Simmons and his accomplice used duct tape to cover the victim's eyes, mouth, and hands. They used the victim's van to drive her to a nearby state park. After walking to the top of a bridge, they covered her face with a towel, tied her feet and hands together with wire, and threw her into the Meramec River. The victim was later discovered by fisherman; she had drowned.

During police interrogation, Simmons confessed to the crime. He was charged with burglary, kidnapping, stealing, and murder in the first degree. Because Simmons was 17 at the time of his crime, he was not considered a juvenile under Missouri law. In seeking the death penalty, the state submitted aggravating factors to the jury. The defense also offered mitigating evidence in Simmons' behalf, including the fact that he had no prior convictions and that he cared for his family. The trial court convicted Simmons and sentenced him to death.

After the decision in *Atkins*, Simmons subsequently filed a habeas corpus claim on the grounds that the Eighth and Fourteenth Amendments prohibited the execution of a juvenile who committed the crime while under the age of 18. The Missouri Supreme Court agreed.

---

[32]*Id.* at 409.
[33]*Id.* at 411.
[34]*Roper v. Simmons*, 543 U.S. 551 (2005).

B The Holding

After the Missouri Supreme Court decided *Simmons*, the defendant's death sentence was set aside and he was given life imprisonment without eligibility for probation, parole, or release except by act of the governor. The U.S. Supreme Court granted certiorari in order to determine whether the death penalty for 16- or 17-year-olds violated the Eighth and Fourteenth Amendments to the Constitution. Using the evolving standards test, the U.S. Supreme Court, in a five-to-four vote, held that the Eighth and Fourteenth Amendments prohibited the imposition of the death penalty for offenders who commit their crimes prior to reaching the age of 18, thus overturning the *Stanford* ruling that allowed execution of juveniles who were over the age of 15.

C Majority Opinion

The majority opinion in *Simmons* was written by Justice Anthony Kennedy and joined by Justices John Paul Stevens, David Souter, Ruth Bader Ginsburg, and Stephen Breyer. This section analyzes the majority opinion.

The *Simmons* Court used the same approach taken in *Thompson* and *Atkins* to assess whether the death penalty for 16- or 17-year-olds violates the Eighth and Fourteenth Amendments. The Court first examined trends in state legislation and the sentencing practices of juries during the years since the decision in *Stanford*. The Court used the evolving standards test to determine whether the death penalty for juveniles was "so disproportionate as to be cruel and unusual."[35] Relying on *Atkins*, the Court compared the number of states prohibiting the execution of 16- and 17-year-olds to those that maintained it for adults. The Court indicated that 18 states prohibited the execution of the mentally retarded but retained it for other adults. Next, the Court said that since *Stanford*, only six states had executed juveniles ages 16 or 17. Similarly, five states had executed mentally retarded defendants since *Penry* (when the Court held that the death penalty for the mentally retarded was not unconstitutional). The Court said, "[t]he evidence of national consensus against the death penalty for juveniles is similar, and in some respects parallel, to the evidence *Atkins* held sufficient to demonstrate a national consensus against the death penalty for the mentally retarded."[36] However, the Court noted a key difference between the decisions in *Penry* and *Atkins* on the one hand and those of *Stanford* and *Simmons*. The Court said that the rate of change was greater in the cases dealing with the mentally retarded—16 states banned the death penalty for the mentally retarded since *Penry*, making a total of 18 states opposing executions at the time of *Atkins*. Conversely, only five states banned the death penalty for 16- or 17-year-olds between *Stanford* and *Simmons*, a much smaller number. The *Simmons* Court stressed that it was not only the number of states changing legislation but the "consistency and the direction of change"[37] of that legislation. The *Simmons* Court stressed the idea that a national consensus against the execution of 16- or 17-year-olds gained stronger support earlier rather than later because 12 states opposed the death penalty for 16- or 17-year-olds at the time of *Stanford*. This resulted in a total of 17 states that legislatively prohibited the execution of juveniles at the time of the *Simmons* decision, only one less than prohibited the execution of the mentally retarded at the time of *Atkins*.

---

[35]*Id.* at 11.
[36]*Id.*
[37]*Atkins*, 536 U.S. 315–316.

In part two of its opinion, the Court used its own "independent judgment to demonstrate that the death penalty is a disproportionate punishment for juveniles."[38] It relied heavily on the logic developed in *Atkins*, claiming that juveniles are "categorically less culpable than the average criminal."[39]

The Court indicated that there are three significant differences between juveniles and adults that make juveniles undeserving of the death penalty:

1. Juveniles lack the intellectual and emotional maturity of adults. The Court said that a juvenile's lack of maturity is more likely to result in unreasoned, spontaneous action. States have passed forms of legislation prohibiting juveniles from serving on juries, voting, or marrying without their parents' consent based on this premise.
2. Juveniles are more vulnerable to peer pressure. The Court cited recent studies saying that juveniles were more likely to engage in dangerous behavior and therefore have less control over their environment.
3. Juveniles have less developed personality traits. The Court indicated that the relationship between a juvenile's underdeveloped personality traits and his or her actions makes a juvenile more prone to act irrationally.

These general differences, the Court said, mean that juveniles do not belong to the worst class of offenders; therefore, they should not be executed. Using current research on juvenile behavior, the Court reasoned that juveniles were not deserving of the death penalty, because "only a relatively small proportion of adolescents who experiment with risky or illegal activities develop entrenched patterns of problem behavior that persist into adulthood."[40]

Addressing the policy objectives behind the juvenile death penalty, the Court indicated that the social purposes of the death penalty—retribution and deterrence—could not be accomplished by allowing juveniles to be executed. Juveniles, like the mentally retarded, do not have the same culpability as typical murderers, let alone the worst murderers. Because *Atkins* acknowledged that average murderers were not worthy of the death penalty, the *Simmons* Court similarly concluded that the death penalty for juveniles is cruel and unusual punishment.

The Court said the Eighth Amendment requires more than individualized consideration of aggravating and mitigating factors in juvenile death penalty cases. It claimed that it is too risky to allow juries and judges to decide whether the death penalty is an appropriate form of punishment for juveniles, because trained psychiatrists and psychologists frequently disagree on the subject. Instead, the Court said that one's youth constitutes an automatic exception to the death penalty because "an unacceptable likelihood exists that the brutality or cold-blooded nature of any particular crime would overpower mitigating arguments based on youth as a matter of course."[41]

The Court found that most foreign nations viewed the death penalty for juveniles as a form of disproportionate punishment; therefore, the practice must be abolished. The majority said the laws of foreign nations were "instructive for interpretation of the Eighth Amendment's prohibition of cruel and unusual punishments."[42] It indicated that Article 37 of the United Nations Convention on the Rights of the Child, a form of international legislation rejecting the death penalty for juveniles, was ratified by

---

[38]*Id.* at 13.
[39]*Id.*
[40]*Id.* at 15.
[41]*Id.* at 16.
[42]*Id.* at 18.

every country in the world except the United States and Somalia.[43] The Court was influenced by this fact and by the reality that almost every other country in the world opposes the juvenile death penalty. Although the Court acknowledged that the views of the international community should not control evolving standards, it concluded that it is clear for now that international laws play an important role in the understanding of what is truly cruel and unusual punishment.

D Dissenting Opinions

Justices O'Connor and Scalia wrote separate dissenting opinions. This section discusses Justice O'Connor's opinion, followed by that of Justice Scalia.

The important points in Justice O'Connor's dissenting opinion are as follows:

1. The Court's moral proportionality analysis does not account for the fact that some juveniles, like adults, can commit crimes that are equally heinous.

   She acknowledged the Court had a "constitutional obligation"[44] to determine whether a certain type of punishment was appropriate for a given group of offenders. Although the majority believed that a categorical exemption for juveniles was appropriate given their diminished culpability, Justice O'Connor said that the proportionality of punishment must be considered in terms of the amount of harm inflicted on the victim, in addition to the defendant's culpability. She recalled her earlier opinion in *Thompson*, in which she stated, "[I]t does not necessarily follow that all 15-year-olds are incapable of the moral culpability that would justify the imposition of capital punishment."[45]

   Next, Justice O'Connor differentiated between categorical rules for juveniles and the mentally retarded. She said that in *Atkins*, the Court concluded that mentally retarded defendants were so different from average adults that "these deficits called into serious doubt whether the execution of mentally retarded offenders would measurably contribute to the principal penological goals that capital punishment is intended to serve—retribution and deterrence."[46]

2. There is a lack of objective evidence establishing a national consensus against the death penalty for juveniles.

Justice O'Connor criticized the majority for affirming the decision of the Missouri Supreme Court without so much as a "slap on the hand."[47] She said that only the Supreme Court has the power to overrule one of its own precedents; furthermore, the Missouri Supreme Court abused its authority when it, in effect, overruled the *Stanford* decision. She concluded that the majority's affirmation of the lower court's decision "threatens to invite frequent and disruptive reassessments of our Eighth Amendment precedents."[48]

After pointing out the majority's failure to address this error, Justice O'Connor explained why a national consensus against the death penalty for juveniles had not been established. She said that

---

[43]*Id.*
[44]*Id.* at 68.
[45]*Thompson*, at 853.
[46]*Atkins*, at 319–321.
[47]*Simmons*, at 71.
[48]*Id.*

although the number of states opposing the death penalty for juveniles and the mentally retarded were identical (18), the consensus was stronger in *Atkins*. She concluded that because eight states still permitted the death penalty for juveniles, there was no consensus among legislatures on the death penalty for 16- and 17-year-olds.

Justice O'Connor criticized the majority's determination of a national consensus against the death penalty for juveniles on other grounds. She said that the Court did not present clear evidence demonstrating that juveniles, unlike adults, are incapable of committing crimes that are just as bad. Justice O'Connor said that the majority was wrong for not considering cases on a factual basis. The majority was wrong, she said, because it did not show that juries were incapable of determining when the death penalty is appropriate; it simply concluded this without a valid explanation.

Justice Scalia wrote a separate dissenting opinion in *Simmons*. He was joined by the Chief Justice and Justice Clarence Thomas. His dissenting opinion consisted of four main arguments, which are:

1. The fact that less than 50 percent of states oppose the juvenile death penalty does not establish a national consensus.

    Justice Scalia said "words have no meaning if the views of less than 50 percent of the death penalty States can constitute a national consensus."[49] There must be significant opposition to a given punishment in order for there to be a national consensus. Justice Scalia cited *Coker v. Georgia* (1977),[50] in which the Court held that the Eighth Amendment prohibited a state from imposing the death penalty on an offender who committed rape when only one state allowed rape offenders to be executed. Justice Scalia said *Simmons* was drastically different from *Coker* due to the fact that "twelve States favoring no executions says something about consensus against the death penalty, but nothing—absolutely nothing—about consensus that offenders under 18 deserve special immunity from such a penalty."[51]

2. The real factor driving the majority opinion in this case is not the actions of state legislators but their own subjective judgment that juveniles can never be deserving of the death penalty, regardless of the circumstances.

    Justice Scalia said that the majority was wrong for returning to the approach used in *Thompson*, when the Court acknowledged that its own subjective opinion about the morality of executing juveniles should be the decisive factor when determining the propriety of a particular punishment. He claimed that the Court should only interpret evidence of evolving standards rather than form its own opinion about what society believes is truly moral.

3. The views of the international community should not be considered when determining the constitutionality of the juvenile death penalty.

    Justice Scalia claimed that the majority was mistaken when it concluded that the laws of the international community should influence the Court's decision. He said that the United States' reluctance to ratify the International Covenant on Civil and Political Rights was not evidence of a national ban against the execution of juveniles but rather legislative evidence that the practice is acceptable in this country. He indicated that the majority failed to consider the fact that the laws of the United States and many foreign nations differ in many respects. For example, he cited laws

---

[49]*Id.* at 81.
[50]*Coker v. Georgia*, 433 U.S. 584, 595–596 (1977).
[51]*Simmons*, at 82.

regarding religion in other countries, where foreign governments do not require the laws separating church and state. In Justice Scalia's opinion, these laws conflict with the provision of the First Amendment that "Congress shall make no law respecting an establishment of religion."[52]

4. The Missouri Supreme Court does not have the authority to overrule *Stanford*, which it obviously did when it decided *Roper v. Simmons* and disregarded United States Supreme Court precedent.

Justice Scalia chastised the majority for not reprimanding the Missouri Supreme Court when it disregarded the Supreme Court's decision in *Stanford* (which held the execution of 16- and 17-year-olds constitutional). He noted that the majority "silently approved"[53] the Missouri Supreme Court's decision by choosing not to address the issue. In Justice Scalia's view, this is "no way to run a legal system."[54]

VI EVOLVING STANDARDS AND FUTURE ISSUES CONCERNING THE SENTENCING OF JUVENILES

The U.S. Supreme Court has always interpreted the Eighth Amendment's cruel and unusual punishment clause according to "evolving standards of decency that mark the progress of a maturing society."[55] It has acknowledged that what constitutes cruel and unusual punishment is not static and must be reevaluated according to society's changing views. In *Thompson*, the Court first interpreted evolving standards in the context of the juvenile death penalty. The Court said that executing juveniles who commit their crimes before reaching the age of 16 violates the Eighth and Fourteenth Amendments. One year later, the *Stanford* Court revisited the issue of whether the death penalty was cruel and unusual punishment for defendants who commit their crimes when they are 16 or 17 years old. After the Court held that the imposition of the death penalty for 16- and 17-year-olds was constitutional, the states had a national standard to follow. For the next 14 years the law as interpreted by the Supreme Court did not change. States had the authority to set their minimum age for execution. In *Simmons*, the Court reevaluated the same issue that was raised in *Stanford*. The *Simmons* Court said that the evolving standards of decency prohibited the execution of juveniles who commit their crimes before reaching the age of 18.

Supreme Court Justices have disagreed on the appropriate test for interpreting evolving standards of decency. Justices William Rehnquist, Scalia, and Thomas (the conservatives) firmly believed that the death penalty for juveniles should be interpreted according to objective factors, such as trends in state legislation and jury practices. Justices Ginsburg, Souter, Stevens, and Breyer (the liberals) viewed measures of evolving standards to include analyses of penal goals and proportionality. Each of these three cases dealing with the juvenile death penalty was decided by a five-to-four decision.

However, in the last several years the compositional make-up of the Supreme Court has changed. The new Chief Justice, John Roberts, as well as Justices Samuel Alito, Sonia Sotomayor, and Elena Kagan, have been appointed to the Court since the *Simmons* case was decided. Although it may be

---

[52]*Id.* at 90.
[53]*Id.* at 92.
[54]*Id.* at 93.
[55]*Trop*, 356 U.S. 86, 100–101 (1958).

too early to describe Kagan or Sotomayor as liberal or conservative, a handful of cases provide some insight into their respective ideologies. Justice Sotomayor, a former prosecutor, came to the Supreme Court having served as a federal trial and appellate court judge, and some progressive critics believe this experience may cause her to vote more frequently in favor of the government.[56] Justice Kagan, on the other hand, came to the Court with no prior judicial experience. Both Justices have tended to vote against the government in a number of death penalty cases.[57] On the other end of the continuum, Chief Justice Roberts and Justice Alito are considered conservatives, often joining Justices Thomas and Scalia in support of the government. Thus, it remains to be seen how the new composition of the Court may affect decisions regarding punishment issues for juveniles.

In *Graham v. Florida* (2010)[58] the Court took up the issue of whether it is constitutional to sentence juveniles who commit nonhomicide offenses to life sentences without the possibility of parole. Writing for the majority, Justice Kennedy once again represented the critical swing vote on an issue pertaining to cruel and unusual punishment.[59] The majority held that the sentencing of juveniles to a sentence of life without parole (LWOP) for a nonhomicide crime violates the Eighth Amendment to the U.S. Constitution. The Court reasoned that although the vast majority of U.S. jurisdictions permitted a LWOP sentence for juveniles who commit nonhomicide offenses, 77 of the 123 juveniles serving their sentences were in Florida. Therefore, the Court concluded that these sentences were very rare and that a national consensus did not support the sentence of LWOP in cases where a juvenile does not commit murder. The *Graham* Court acknowledged that LWOP is similar to the death penalty because it "alters the offender's life by a forfeiture that is irrevocable" (p. 18), effectively making the sanction "our other death penalty."[60] The impact of *Graham* continued with the recent expansion of its holding in *Miller v. Alabama* (2012).[61]

In *Miller*, the Court held that a sentencing scheme mandating the possibility of life without parole, without allowing for individualized case considerations, violates for juveniles Eighth Amendment's ban on cruel and unusual punishment. The decision forbids states from imposing *mandatory* death sentences for youth who commit murder without taking into consideration mitigating factors such as age, background of the offender, and offense characteristics. However, the Court's narrow holding leaves open the possibility for the imposition of LWOP for juvenile murderers as long as they are given individualized consideration of these factors at sentencing. Given the developmental factors that distinguish adults from juveniles as noted in the *Simmons* and *Graham* decisions, the provision that sentencing bodies give attention to the individual histories of juvenile defendants is a significant development.

---

[56]See Linda Greenhouse, Commentary, *The Roberts Court*, Version 4.0, N.Y. TIMES, Oct. 2, 2010, available at http://opinionator.blogs.nytimes.com/2010/10/02/the-roberts-court-version-4-0/ (discussing the four different natural court periods during the Roberts Court era).

[57]See, for instance, votes in *Alabama v. Miller,* 183 L. Ed. 2d 407 (2012), *Cullen v. Pinholster,* 179 L. Ed. 2d 557 (2011), *Trevino v. Thaler,* 185 L. Ed. 2d 1044 (2013), *Maples v. Thomas,* 181 L. Ed. 2d 807 (2012).

[58]*Graham v. Florida,* 176 L. Ed. 2d 825 (2010).

[59]See, for instance, Kennedy's votes in *Atkins v. Virginia,* 536 U.S. 304 (2002); *Roper v. Simmons,* 543 U.S. 551 (2005); *Smith v. Texas,* 550 U.S. 297 (2007); Brewer v. *Quarterman,* 550 U.S. 233 (2007); *Abdul-Kabir v. Quarterman,* 127 S. Ct. 1654 (2007); and *Kennedy v. Louisiana,* 128 S. Ct. 2641 (2008).

[60]Johnson, Robert, and Sonia Tabriz, *Sentencing Children to Death by Incarceration: A Deadly Denial of Social Responsibility,* 91 THE PRISON JOURNAL, 198 (2011).

[61]*Miller v. Alabama,* 183 L. Ed. 2d 407 (2012).

History has indicated, however, that the Court's individualized consideration requirement at sentencing has not favored outcomes for youth sentenced to death. Prior to the Court's decision in *Simmons*, it had long required states to give individual consideration before imposing a death sentence on a juvenile capital defendant. Further, it remains to be seen whether the individualized consideration requirement significantly affects the sentencing patterns of juries in cases that involve the possibility of LWOP for juvenile murderers—a factor the Court has traditionally given heavy weight in Eighth Amendment cases.

Justice Kagan's opinion in *Miller* emphasizes the growing influence of recent scientific advancements in brain imaging research on youth sentencing policies. Scientists have debated the probative value of neuroscience as a legal defense for juveniles who engage in violent crime. On one hand, there is evidence indicating that adolescents' intelligence and ability to reason is similar to that of adults by the age of 16—what scientists refer to as "cold cognition."[62] On the other hand, extant research also shows that adolescents lack the ability to reason and effectively weigh the consequences of their actions.[63] Research also shows that juveniles are much more likely to exercise poor judgment as a result of peer pressure or when facing stressful situations, also known as "hot cognition."[64] Some argue that this research is enough to compel changes in the legal system and cause lawmakers to acknowledge the detrimental effects of sentencing policies that treat juveniles as they do adults. Although research is still in its infancy, there is ample evidence indicating that juveniles' brains have not developed to the level of their adult counterparts and that development continues well beyond the point of legal adulthood.

VII IN SUMMARY, WHAT DO THESE CASES SAY?

The legal perspective on the juvenile death penalty has evolved a great deal over time. Table 5.1 exhibits a comparison of the three key cases involving the death penalty for juveniles illustrating this evolution. The *Thompson* Court first declared the juvenile death penalty unconstitutional for offenders who committed their crimes before the age of 15. However, the *Thompson* Court did not say whether the execution of juveniles ages 16 or 17 at the time of the crime was constitutional. One year later, the Court decided *Stanford*, which held that the death penalty was constitutional for juveniles who commit their crime at the ages of 16 or 17. Thus, within a two-year period the Court gave the states a definitive age cutoff for imposing the death penalty. The Court's debate about what constitutes evolving standards can generally be discussed based on a two-part analysis. The framework for this analysis consists of: (1) trends in state legislation and the sentencing practices of juries, and (2) measures of proportionality, which include the views of the professional, social, and international communities.

---

[62]Dolcos, Florin, and Gregory McCarthy, *Brain Systems Mediating Cognitive Interference by Emotional Distraction*, 26 J. NEUROSCIENCE 2072 (2006).

[63]Steinberg, Laurence, et al., *Age Differences in Future Orientation and Delay Discounting*, 80 CHILD DEVELOPMENT 28 (2009).

[64]Dolcos, *Supra* note 25.

Table 5.1 A Comparison of *Thompson*, *Stanford*, and *Simmons*

Issue	Thompson v. Oklahoma	Stanford v. Kentucky	Roper v. Simmons
Is the death penalty cruel and unusual punishment for juveniles who commit their crimes while 16 or 17 years old?	Not answered because it was not an issue	No	Yes
Majority Justices	Justices Stevens, Brennan, Marshall, Blackmun, O'Connor	Justices Scalia, Kennedy, O'Connor, White, Chief Justice Rehnquist	Justices Kennedy, Souter, Stevens, Ginsburg, Breyer
Dissenting Justices	Justices Scalia, Rehnquist, White	Justices Brennan, Stevens, Blackmun, Marshall	Justices Scalia, Thomas, Chief Justice Rehnquist, O'Connor
Court used objective factors (trends in state legislatures and sentencing practices of juries)	Yes	Yes	Yes
Number of states authorizing the death penalty in general but prohibiting it for juveniles	32 states with no minimum age; 18 states set the minimum age at 16	15 states set the minimum age at 17; 12 states set it at age 18	18 states set the minimum age at 18
Court used subjective factors (penal goals analysis and measures of proportionality)	Yes	No	Yes
Should the views of the international community be considered when interpreting "evolving standards"?	Yes	No	Yes
Has the concept of stare decisis (let the decision stand) been undermined by *Simmons*?	Not a factor	Not a factor	Majority did not address this; dissent said yes
Are defendants who commit their crimes between the ages of 15 and 18 equally deserving of the death penalty?	No	Yes	No

In *Atkins*, the Supreme Court held that the execution of mentally retarded offenders is cruel and unusual punishment. *Atkins* is significant because it reaffirmed the analysis used to evaluate evolving standards by the *Thompson* Court. *Atkins* said that measures of proportionality and penal goals should be included when interpreting evolving standards. This set the stage in *Roper v. Simmons* to strike down the juvenile death penalty.

At the state level, the Missouri Supreme Court held in *Simmons* that the juvenile death penalty violates evolving standards of decency because such standards have evolved since *Stanford*. Although controlling precedent was established by the U.S. Supreme Court, the Missouri Supreme Court disregarded *Stanford* and ruled the practice of executing juveniles to be unconstitutional. It virtually urged the nation's highest court to change its mind about juvenile executions.

On appeal, the U.S. Supreme Court affirmed the decision of the Missouri Supreme Court and indeed changed its mind. Because of its reach, *Roper v. Simmons* has become the most important case thus far in juvenile death penalty jurisprudence. The Court in *Simmons* held that the Eighth and Fourteenth Amendments prohibit the death penalty for offenders who committed their crimes when they were under the age of 18. *Simmons* said the evolving standards of decency prohibited the execution of juveniles for two reasons:

1. The number of states (17) prohibiting the death penalty for juveniles is virtually the same as the number of states deemed sufficient to establish the objective standard held in *Atkins*. It is sufficient to establish a national consensus against executing juvenile offenders.
2. Juveniles are categorically less culpable than average criminals. Therefore, the social goals of the death penalty—retribution and deterrence—are not served.

VIII CONCLUSION

After *Stanford*, the debate about the juvenile death penalty accelerated. The "evolving standards of decency that mark the progress of a maturing society"[65] has been the test for determining whether a particular type of punishment is cruel and unusual. Traditionally, states have been given the legislative power to decide what age is appropriate for executing juveniles, as long as they do not set the age below 16. At the time the Court decided *Simmons*, 30 states and the federal government banned the juvenile death penalty for offenders who were less than 18 years old at the time of their crimes. Twelve of these states, however, do not allow the death penalty at all.

The *Simmons* case is significant because it revived the two-part analysis originally used in *Thompson*. This analysis includes: (1) a consideration of penal goals and measures of proportionality, and (2) the sentencing behavior of juries and trends in state legislation. The *Simmons* Court rejected the *Stanford* approach because it does not account for subjective factors that must be considered when analyzing the Eighth Amendment. The *Simmons* Court instead returned to the approach used in *Thompson* and affirmed that the evolving standards of decency should be based solely on the sentencing practices of juries and patterns in state legislation.

Simmons is also significant because in that decision the majority declared that the views of foreign nations may be taken into account when determining "evolving standards of decency," a view rejected by the dissenting justices. *Simmons* reaffirms that evolving standards of decency are shaped not only by legislative action and the sentencing patterns of juries but also by such other factors as the subjective views of the Supreme Court justices on measures of proportionality and penal goals, as well as by the views and practices of foreign countries. It is clear that standards of decency continue to evolve. In assessing the evolution of these standards, a distinction between juveniles and adults has been reiterated by the majority in *Simmons* and now in *Graham* and *Miller*. Whether dealing with the death penalty or sentences of life without parole, special considerations are given to juveniles in terms of the severity of punishment that is constitutionally allowed.

---

[65]*Trop*, 356 U.S. 86, 101 (1958).

CASES BRIEFED IN CHAPTER 5

Case	Issue	Holding
Thompson v. Oklahoma 487 U.S. 815 (1988)	Is the death penalty cruel and unusual punishment for a crime committed by an offender under the age of 16?	The execution of a person under the age of 16 at the time of offense is prohibited by the Eighth and Fourteenth Amendments.
Stanford v. Kentucky 492 U.S. 361 (1989)	Does the imposition of the death penalty for a crime committed at the age of 16 or 17 constitute cruel and unusual punishment?	The death penalty for juveniles who are older than 15 at the time of the crime does not violate the Eighth Amendment's prohibition of cruel and unusual punishment.
Roper v. Simmons 543 U.S. 551 (2005)	Does the imposition of the death penalty for offenders under the age of 18 violate the Eighth Amendment's ban on cruel and unusual punishment?	The Eighth Amendment prohibits the death penalty for individuals who are under the age of 18 at the time of the offense.

CASE BRIEFS

THOMPSON v. OKLAHOMA 487 U.S. 815 (1988)

CAPSULE: It is cruel and unusual punishment to impose the death penalty on an individual who commits their crime at the age of 15 or younger.

FACTS: Thompson, along with three accomplices, actively participated in the murder of his former brother-in-law during the early hours of January 23, 1983. The victim had been shot two times and his throat, chest, and his abdomen had been sliced. Once these injuries were inflicted on the victim, Thompson and his accomplices threw the body into a river, where it remained for approximately four weeks.

Although Thompson was considered a child according to Oklahoma law, he was certified to stand trial as an adult. He subsequently was convicted. During the penalty phase, the prosecutor sought the death penalty. The prosecutor asked the jury to find that aggravating circumstances existed, namely: (1) that the murder was particularly heinous and cruel, and (2) that there was a reasonable probability that the defendant would present a continuing threat to society if set free. The jury found that the first aggravating circumstance was present but rejected the second. Thompson was given the death penalty.

ISSUE: Is the death penalty cruel and unusual punishment for a crime committed by a 15-year-old? YES.

HOLDING: The Eighth and Fourteenth Amendments prohibit the imposition of the death penalty for offenders 16 or 17 years old at the time of their crimes.

REASON: "In determining whether the categorical Eighth Amendment prohibition applies, this Court must be guided by the 'evolving standards of decency that mark the progress of a maturing society,' *Trop v. Dulles*, 356 U.S. 86, 101,

Continued

THOMPSON v. OKLAHOMA 487 U.S. 815 (1988)—cont'd

and in doing so must review relevant legislative enactments and jury determinations and consider the reasons why a civilized society may accept or reject the death penalty for a person less than 16 years old at the time of the crime.

"Relevant state statutes—particularly those of the 18 states that have expressly considered the question of a minimum age for imposition of the death penalty, and have uniformly required that the defendant have attained at least the age of 16 at the time of the capital offense—support the conclusion that it would offend civilized standards of decency to execute a person who was less than 16 years old at the time his or her offense was committed.

"The juvenile's reduced culpability, and the fact that the application of the death penalty to this class of offenders does not measurably contribute to the essential purposes underlying the penalty, also support the conclusion that the imposition of the death penalty on persons under the age of 16 constitutes unconstitutional punishment."

CASE SIGNIFICANCE: In this case, the Court said that juveniles under the age of 16 at the time of their crimes could not be given the death penalty. Interpreting the Eighth Amendment, the Court claimed that "it would offend civilized standards of decency to execute a person who was less than 16 years old at the time of his or her offense." This case marked the first time the Court established a bright-line rule for states to follow when imposing the death penalty for juveniles. At the time *Thompson* was decided, there were 18 states with legislation prohibiting the execution of individuals who committed their crimes prior to reaching the age of 16. According to the Court, 18 states represented sufficient evidence that legislatures opposed the death penalty for individuals who were less than 16 at the time of their offenses. The Court also said that the sentencing practices of juries were important in considering whether the death penalty violates evolving standards. The Court indicated that juries rarely imposed death as punishment for individuals under the age of 16.

The *Thompson* Court said that the death penalty for juveniles was unconstitutional because "adolescents as a class are less mature and responsible than adults." The Court reasoned that the death penalty would be cruel and unusual punishment for juveniles because they inherently fail to evaluate the costs and benefits of their actions. Because juveniles have diminished culpability, the Court said the death penalty would not serve the social purposes of the death penalty—retribution and deterrence.

What this decision did not say was whether juveniles could be executed at all. Is 15 the minimum age, or would juvenile status be a better determinant of whether the offender should be executed? Opponents of the Oklahoma law wanted the Court to declare any execution of a juvenile to be unconstitutional. The Court did not go that far; however, one year later the Court said it was not cruel and unusual punishment to execute 16- or 17-year-olds in *Stanford v. Kentucky*, 492 U.S. 361 (1989).

STANFORD v. KENTUCKY 492 U.S. 361 (1989)

CAPSULE: The cruel and unusual punishment clause of the Eighth Amendment does not prohibit the death penalty for juveniles who commit their crime at the age of 16 or 17.

FACTS: Kevin Stanford was 17 years old when he brutally murdered Barbel Poore in Jefferson County, Kentucky. On January 7, 1981, Stanford and his accomplice repeatedly raped and sodomized Poore, who worked as a gas station attendant. The perpetrators then drove their victim to a remote area, where Stanford shot the victim twice in the head. Stanford and his accomplice obtained 300 cartons of cigarettes, a couple of gallons of gas, and a nominal amount of cash. A corrections officer later testified that Stanford explained the crime in this manner: "He said, I had to shoot her, [she] lived next door to me and she would recognize me.... I guess we could have tied her up or something or beat [her up]... and tell her if she tells, we would kill her... Then after he said that he started laughing."

Continued

STANFORD v. KENTUCKY 492 U.S. 361 (1989)—cont'd

Because Stanford had been charged with a Class A felony, or capital crime, and was over 16 years of age at the time of his crime, the juvenile court waived jurisdiction. Given Stanford's past record of juvenile delinquency, the juvenile court certified Stanford to stand trial as an adult. He was convicted of numerous crimes, including murder, and sentenced to death plus 45 years.

ISSUE: Does sentencing an offender to the death penalty for a crime they committed at the age of 16 or 17 constitute cruel and unusual punishment? NO.

HOLDING: The Eighth and Fourteenth Amendments do not prohibit the death penalty for juveniles who were 16 or 17 years old at the time of their crime.

REASONING: "Whether a particular punishment violates the Eighth Amendment depends on whether it constitutes one of 'those modes or acts of punishment... considered cruel and unusual at the time that the Bill of Rights was adopted,' *Ford v. Wainwright*, 477 U.S. 399, 405, or is contrary to the 'evolving standards of decency that mark the progress of a maturing society,' *Trop v. Dulles*, 356 U.S. 86, 101. Petitioners have not alleged that their sentences would have been considered cruel and unusual in the eighteenth century, and could not support such a contention, since, at that time, the common law set the rebuttable presumption of incapacity to commit felonies (which were punishable by death) at the age of 14.

"In determining whether a punishment violates evolving standards of decency, this Court looks not to its own subjective conceptions, but, rather, to the conceptions of modern American society as reflected by objective evidence, e.g., *Coker v. Georgia*, 433 U.S. 584, 592. The primary and most reliable evidence of national consensus—the pattern of federal and state laws—fails to meet petitioners' heavy burden of proving a settled consensus against the execution of 16- and 17-year-old offenders."

CASE SIGNIFICANCE: This case is a sequel to *Thompson v. Oklahoma*, 487 U.S. 815 (1988), in which the Court held that the death penalty was unconstitutional for juveniles who commit their crime prior to reaching the age of 16. The Court stated that "the imposition of capital punishment on an individual for a crime committed at 16 or 17 years of age does not constitute cruel and unusual punishment under the Eighth Amendment." The *Stanford* Court answered the question left open in *Thompson*, which was whether juveniles over the age of 15 at the time of their crime could be given the death penalty.

The *Stanford* Court based its interpretation of the Eighth Amendment solely on the acts of state legislatures and the sentencing practices of juries. The Court rejected the penal goals and proportionality arguments used by the *Thompson* Court. Justice Scalia, writing for the majority, said, "[I]t is not only possible, but overwhelmingly probable, that the very considerations which induce petitioners and their supporters to believe that death should never be imposed on offenders under the age of eighteen cause prosecutors and juries to believe that it should rarely be imposed."

The *Stanford* Court said that history as well as then-contemporary standards of decency did not prohibit the death penalty for individuals who commit their crimes before reaching the age of 18. By establishing the minimum age at 16, the Court gave states the power to set their minimum age for execution by statute at 16, 17, or 18 years of age.

ROPER v. SIMMONS 543 U.S. 551 (2005)

CAPSULE: The Eighth and Fourteenth Amendments prohibit the death penalty for juveniles who commit their crimes before the age of 18.

FACTS: When Christopher Simmons was 17 years old he committed a brutal murder. Before committing the crime, Simmons stated that he wanted to kill someone, even going to the extent of discussing with his friends his plan to

Continued

ROPER v. *SIMMONS* 543 U.S. 551 (2005)—cont'd

commit the act. On the night of the crime, at about 2:00 A.M., Simmons and his accomplice entered the home of Shirley Crook through an open window and awakened the victim. Simmons later stated that he intended to kill Mrs. Crook because of their mutual involvement in a previous car accident.

Simmons and his accomplice used duct tape to cover the victim's eyes, mouth, and hands. They then used the victim's van to drive her to a nearby state park. After walking to the top of a bridge, they covered her face with a towel, tied her feet and hands together with wire, and threw her into the Meramec River. The victim drowned and was later discovered by fishermen.

During police interrogation, Simmons confessed to the brutal crime. Simmons was then charged with burglary, kidnapping, stealing, and murder in the first degree. Because Simmons was 17 at the time of his crime, he was not considered a juvenile by the state of Missouri. In seeking the death penalty, the state submitted aggravating factors to the jury. The defense also offered mitigating evidence in Simmons's behalf, including the fact that he had no prior convictions and that he cared for his family. After weighing the evidence, the trial court convicted Simmons and sentenced him to death.

ISSUE: Is it cruel and unusual punishment to impose the death penalty on offenders who commit crimes before reaching the age of 18? YES.

HOLDING: The Eighth and Fourteenth Amendments prohibit the imposition of the death penalty on offenders who commit their crimes before reaching the age of 18.

REASONING: "Both objective indicia of consensus, as expressed in particular by the enactments of legislatures that have addressed the question, and the Court's own determination in the exercise of its independent judgment, demonstrate that the death penalty is a disproportionate punishment for juveniles."

"As in *Atkins*, the objective indicia of national consensus here—the rejection of the juvenile death penalty in the majority of States; the infrequency of its use even where it remains on the books; and the consistency in the trend toward abolition of the practice—provide sufficient evidence that today society views juveniles, in the words *Atkins* used respecting the mentally retarded, as "categorically less culpable than the average criminal."

"Rejection of the imposition of the death penalty on juvenile offenders under 18 is required by the Eighth Amendment. Capital punishment must be limited to those offenders who commit 'a narrow category of the most serious crimes' and whose extreme culpability makes them 'the most deserving of execution.' Three general differences between juveniles under 18 and adults demonstrate that juvenile offenders cannot with reliability be classified among the worst offenders. Juveniles' susceptibility to immature and irresponsible behavior means their irresponsible conduct is not as morally reprehensible as that of an adult. Their own vulnerability and comparative lack of control over their immediate surroundings mean juveniles have a greater claim than adults to be forgiven for failing to escape negative influences in their whole environment. The reality that juveniles still struggle to define their identity means it is less supportable to conclude that even a heinous crime committed by a juvenile is evidence of irretrievably depraved character. The *Thompson* plurality recognized the import of these characteristics with respect to juveniles under 16. The same reasoning applies to all juvenile offenders under 18. Once juveniles' diminished culpability is recognized, it is evident that neither of the two penological justifications for the death penalty—retribution and deterrence of capital crimes by prospective offenders—provides adequate justification for imposing that penalty on juveniles."

CASE SIGNIFICANCE: This case is arguably the most important case decided thus far on the issue of the constitutionality of the death penalty for juveniles. It holds that the death penalty constitutes cruel and unusual punishment for offenders who commit their crime before reaching the age of 18. The Court, in *Thompson v. Oklahoma* (1988) held that executing offenders who were 15 years old or younger at the time of the commission of

Continued

> ### *ROPER v. SIMMONS* 543 U.S. 551 (2005)—cont'd
>
> the offense is unconstitutional. *Simmons* extends that rule to include 16- and 17-year-olds and therefore overturns its earlier decision in *Stanford v. Kentucky.*
>
> This case puts an end to the execution of juveniles in the United States—for now. The Court can always change its mind, reverse this decision, and declare the execution of juveniles constitutional again. This case was decided on a five-to-four vote. A change in the composition of the U.S. Supreme Court can lead to a change of vote in a proper case. For now, however, juveniles in the United States cannot be executed, regardless of the seriousness of their crimes. This decision renders unconstitutional all laws (state and federal) that allow juveniles to be executed. Legislatures can repeal those laws or allow them to stay on the books, but they cannot now be enforced.

Key Terms

cold cognition
culpability
cruel and unusual punishment
deterrence
Eighth Amendment
evolving standards of decency
Graham v. Florida
hot cognition
international community
Miller v. Alabama
national consensus
neuroscience
retribution
Roper v. Simmons
Stanford v. Kentucky
Thompson v. Oklahoma

CRITICAL THINKING QUESTIONS

1. In *Simmons v. Roper* (2003), the Missouri Supreme Court declared the juvenile death penalty unconstitutional. Explain the significance of this ruling vis-à-vis the Supreme Court's ruling just two years later in *Roper v. Simmons* (2005).

2. Explain how the Supreme Court interprets evolving standards of decency with respect to punishment for juveniles. Are factors weighed differently for deciding the constitutionality of a death sentence versus LWOP?

3. The Supreme Court held in *Atkins v. Virginia* (2003) that the execution of mentally retarded offenders violates the Eighth Amendment. How did the Supreme Court's reasoning in *Atkins* compare to that in *Simmons*?

Internet Resources

Death Penalty Information Center: Juveniles and the Death Penalty
www.deathpenaltyinfo.org/juveniles-and-death-penalty

Human Rights Watch
www.hrw.org/news/2010/10/09/iran-saudi-arabia-sudan-end-juvenile-death-penalty

International Juvenile Justice Observatory
www.oijj.org/en

National Institute of Mental Health
www.nimh.nih.gov/health/publications/the-teen-brain-still-under-construction/index.shtml

Juries, Jurors, and the Death Penalty

6

CHAPTER OUTLINE

I INTRODUCTION

The United States Constitution gives U.S. citizens the right to a trial by jury. The Sixth Amendment further states that citizens have the right to "a speedy and public trial, by an impartial jury..." Moreover, all states incorporated this right in their constitutions upon entering the union.[1] This is perhaps the most sacred of all rights pertaining to the judicial process and one that places the greatest duty on citizens. The Supreme Court recently reinforced and strengthened this right in the case of *Apprendi v. New Jersey* (2000),[2] in which the Court said that "the jury tradition... is an indispensable part of our criminal justice system."[3]

By granting citizens the right to a jury trial, the criminal justice system also requires a great deal from citizens who serve on juries. This burden is particularly demanding on juries in capital cases. Since the *Furman* and *Gregg* decisions in the 1970s, juries have played multiple and increasingly crucial roles in capital cases. In *Gregg*, several procedural safeguards were required by the Court in order to ensure fair and consistent application of the death penalty. Among them was the bifurcated trial (a trial that is split into separate guilt and penalty phases) and the requirement of "guided discretion,"

---

[1]*Duncan v. Louisiana*, 391 U.S. 145, 153 (1968).

[2]*Apprendi v. New Jersey*, 530 U.S. 466, 490 (2000).

[3]*Id.* at 497.

which includes adequate consideration of aggravating and mitigating circumstances in determining the appropriate sentence. In the 2002 case of *Ring v. Arizona*,[4] the Supreme Court, citing *Apprendi*, held that juries, not judges, must make any determination of fact that leads to an elevated or more severe punishment. In capital cases, this generally means that the jury must make the decisive determination that leads to a death sentence. In the years since the Supreme Court handed down its decision, most states have altered their statutes to reflect the *Ring* ruling. However, several states either maintained their original statute (as is the case with Montana) or have attempted to construct hybrids that retain some of the judge's role in the sentencing decision. We are yet to see these statutes fully tested in relation to the ruling in *Ring*; thus there is uncertainty about its exact parameters. The full effect of the Supreme Court's decision in *Ring* is not yet known.[5]

The Supreme Court has consistently reinforced the centrality and importance of jury discretion in capital cases. As sacred as the jury is to a capital trial, however, this institution has not been without controversy. Jury discretion and decision making in capital cases are scrutinized more carefully by the Supreme Court. Thus, much of the Supreme Court's time and energy in the last few decades have been spent considering the appropriate role, makeup, and guidance of capital juries. This chapter discusses each of these issues and what the Supreme Court has had to say about them. Three primary areas of Supreme Court decisions will be examined: (1) the role of capital juries in sentencing, (2) jury selection and "death qualified" juries, and (3) jury instructions. Key Supreme Court cases are considered in each area, and current issues are discussed.

∥ THE ULTIMATE RESPONSIBILITY: BIFURCATED TRIALS AND THE ROLE OF CAPITAL JURIES

In *Gregg v. Georgia* (1976), when the Supreme Court reinstated the death penalty, state death penalty statutes under consideration were deemed constitutional contingent upon the presence of certain procedural safeguards. Primary among these safeguards was the bifurcated trial. A bifurcated trial is a trial separated into two phases: a guilt phase and a sentencing phase. In most cases the same jury sits for both phases and determines both guilt and the appropriate sentence. Upon a jury finding a defendant guilty, a separate hearing is held to decide the punishment. Usually the options are limited to life in prison (in some cases without the possibility of parole) or death. During this phase, the jury hears both aggravating and mitigating circumstances (discussed in greater detail in Chapter 9) and decides whether these circumstances warrant the death penalty (based on aggravating factors) or mercy via a life sentence (based on mitigating factors). In some states judges have traditionally had either the sole authority to impose the sentence or the authority to override the sentence imposed by the jury. Nevertheless, the Supreme Court has consistently reiterated the importance and centrality of juries in capital trials, making its strongest recent statement in *Ring v. Arizona* (2002),[6] holding that the factual determination of aggravating factors that elevates a punishment to death must be made by a jury and not a judge. This case severely called into question the role of judges in capital sentencing, and most states have already

---

[4]*Ring v. Arizona*, 536 U.S. 584 (2002).
[5]Taylor, Darian B., *Capital Sentencing in Arizona: A "Weighing State" in Name Only*, 42 AZ ATTORNEY 20 (2006); Radha Iyengar, *Who's the Fairest in the Land? Analysis of Judge and Jury Death Penalty Decisions*, 54 J. LAW & ECON. 693, 698 (2011).
[6]*Ring v. Arizona, supra.*

revised their statutes to conform to the Court's decision. However, the full effects of the *Ring* decision are yet to be fully realized.[7] But what is certain is that states allowing judges to override a jury and impose a harsher punishment (i.e., death over a life sentence) violate the Court's decision in *Ring*.

A Jury Override: Judges Trumping Juries

In most states, both phases of capital trials have always relied on juries for the final decisions. Juries decided both a defendant's guilt and punishment. However, in several states, death penalty statutes in the past have granted judges a substantial role in the sentencing of capital defendants. As shown in Table 6.1, some state statutes (Arizona, Colorado, Idaho, Montana, and Nebraska) have historically placed sole discretion for capital sentencing in the trial judge's hands. Others (Alabama, Delaware, Indiana, and Florida) enacted hybrid sentencing schemes in which the jury made a sentencing recommendation but the trial judge was responsible for making the final determination and imposition of sentence—in effect, the trial judge had the authority to override the conclusion of the jury.[8]

Table 6.1 States' Pre-*Ring* Capital Sentencing Schemes

Jury Sentencing States		Judicial Sentencing States	Hybrid States
Arkansas	New York	Arizona	Alabama
California	North Carolina	Colorado	Delaware
Connecticut	Ohio	Idaho	Florida
Georgia	Oklahoma	Montana	Indiana
Illinois	Oregon	Nebraska	
Kansas	Pennsylvania		
Kentucky	South Carolina		
Louisiana	South Dakota		
Maryland	Tennessee		
Mississippi	Texas		
Missouri	Utah		
Nevada	Virginia		
New Hampshire	Washington		
New Jersey	Wyoming		
New Mexico			

In *Spaziano v. Florida* (1984),[9] the Supreme Court first addressed the constitutionality of statutes allowing judges to override a jury's recommendation in a capital case. Although a majority of jurors recommended a life sentence for Spaziano, the trial judge, upon his own assessment of aggravating and mitigating circumstances, sentenced him to death. Florida's hybrid sentencing scheme was challenged on appeal as being in violation of the Eighth Amendment's prohibition of cruel and unusual punishment. Although accepting that "the jury is in the best position to decide whether a particular crime is so

---

[7]Taylor, *supra;* Iyengar, *supra.*

[8]Shapiro, Marc R., *Re-evaluating the Role of the Jury in Capital Cases after* Ring v. Arizona, 59 N.Y.U. ANN. SURV. AM. L. 633, 633 (2004).

[9]*Spaziano v. Florida*, 468 U.S. 447 (1984).

heinous that the community's response must be death,"[10] the Court upheld Florida's statute and thus the trial judge's authority to override sentencing recommendations of capital juries.

In *Walton v. Arizona* (1990),[11] the Supreme Court further strengthened the trial judge's authority to determine the sentence in capital cases by upholding Arizona's statute in which judges have full authority over the sentencing of capital defendants. In Arizona and other states with judicial sentencing schemes, judges are solely responsible for determining the presence of aggravating and mitigating circumstances based on testimony and evidence presented during the sentencing phase of trial. Based on their discretion in weighing these factors, they decide whether a death sentence is appropriate. Under those death penalty statutes, the jury's role in capital trials is restricted to the guilt phase.

Although the Supreme Court has historically allowed states to make their own determination as to whether a judge or jury imposes the sentence in capital trials, it has consistently emphasized the importance and value of the jury in criminal cases.[12] In *Duncan v. Louisiana* (1968),[13] the Supreme Court held that the right to a jury trial in serious criminal cases applies to the states as a fundamental protection against unfettered judicial and prosecutorial discretion. The Court stated that "[t]he guarantees of jury trial in the Federal and State Constitutions reflect a profound judgment about the way in which law should be enforced and justice administered."[14] More than 30 years later, in *Apprendi v. New Jersey* (2000),[15] the Court struck down a hate-crime statute that allowed a judge to make a determination of facts that led to an increase in a defendant's sentence. The Court held that only a jury can make an "assessment of facts that increase the prescribed range of penalties to which a criminal defendant is exposed" and that "[o]ther than the fact of a prior conviction, any fact that increases the penalty for a crime beyond the prescribed statutory maximum must be submitted to a jury, and proved beyond a reasonable doubt."[16] The Court's message was clear: The ultimate fate of criminal defendants is best left in the hands of a jury, not a judge.

B *Ring v. Arizona:* The End of Judicial Sentencing in Capital Cases?

Following *Apprendi*, the Supreme Court in *Ring v. Arizona* (2002)[17] placed strict limitations on the capacity for judges to override a jury's decision or determine the sentence in capital cases. The Court held that, based on the decision in *Apprendi v. New Jersey* (2000),[18] it was unconstitutional for judges to make determinations of aggravating factors that effectively elevate the crime to one warranting an increase in punishment—in capital cases, from life in prison to death. Because the jury failed to conclude that the death penalty was warranted in Ring's case, the judge, as authorized by statute, weighed the aggravating and mitigating circumstances and overrode the jury's conclusion and sentenced Ring to death. The Supreme Court held that this violated Ring's Sixth Amendment right to a jury trial in that the judge's finding regarding aggravating circumstances was "the functional equivalent of an element of a

[10]*Id.* at 461.
[11]*Walton v. Arizona*, 497 U.S. 639 (1990).
[12]*Shapiro, supra.*
[13]*Duncan v. Louisiana*, 391 U.S. 145 (1968).
[14]Cited in *Shapiro, supra* at 643.
[15]*Apprendi v. New Jersey*, 530 U.S. 466 (2000).
[16]*Id.* at 490.
[17]*Ring v. Arizona, supra.*
[18]*Apprendi v. New Jersey, supra.*

greater offense than the one covered by the jury's guilty verdict."[19] Importantly, the Court, in *Schriro v. Summerlin* (2004),[20] declared the holding in *Ring* not to be retroactive. Citing *Teague v. Lane* (1989),[21] the Court noted that *Ring* did not create a "watershed rule of criminal procedure" and thus did not warrant a retroactive application to previously concluded cases.[22] Thus, death row inmates who, prior to *Ring*, had been sentenced under schemes in which the judge made the ultimate sentencing decision were not spared by the Court's decision.

The effect of the *Ring* decision has been dramatic, leading to a virtual elimination of statutes that granted judges the authority to override juries in the application of a death sentence. Table 6.2 shows the states that were impacted by *Ring* and the changes to their statutes that followed the Supreme Court's decision. Arizona, the state whose statute was at issue in *Ring*, changed its statute to require that a jury unanimously agree to recommend death for the sentence of death to be imposed. In the event that a jury cannot reach unanimity, the judge has the choice to either impanel a new jury and retry the sentencing phase of the trial or sentence the defendant to life in prison without parole. This was most recently illustrated in the Jodi Arias trial, in which the original jury failed to reach unanimous agreement on whether Arias should receive a death sentence. As of this writing, prosecutors have proceeded with a retrial of the sentencing phase of the trial, and the defense has requested a delay in this hearing until January 2014.[23]

The Supreme Courts of Idaho and Colorado immediately reconsidered death sentences imposed under the old sentencing schemes,[24] and both states eventually altered their statutes in the wake of *Ring*.[25] Alabama, Indiana, and Florida, three of the four states that previously had hybrid sentencing schemes, also came around to require juries to make the ultimate determination of a death sentence (i.e., to disallow judge overrides in sentencing a defendant to death).[26] Delaware, Nebraska, and Montana, taking a more narrow interpretation of the *Ring* holding, require the jury to make a unanimous determination, beyond a reasonable doubt, on the presence of at least one aggravating circumstance and thus declare the defendant eligible for the death penalty but leave the final sentencing decision in the judge's hands.[27] The latter statutes maintain some sentencing authority for judges but attempt to avoid violating the *Ring* ruling by requiring that a jury, not a judge, make the key determination of fact allowing a death sentence to be applied. It is yet to be seen whether these statutes granting judges the final authority in imposing death sentences will stand up, given the requirements of *Ring,* or whether they will be struck down by the U.S. Supreme Court. Because the Supreme Court has so far resisted taking cases in which this question is raised, it has been left to federal circuit courts to determine the validity of death sentences in these states.[28]

---

[19]*Id.* at 605.

[20]*Schriro v. Summerlin*, 542 U.S. 348 (2004).

[21]*Teague v. Lane*, 489 U.S. 288 (1989).

[22]*Ring v. Arizona, supra.*

[23]Skoloff, Brian, *Jodi Arias Attorneys Seek Delay of Second Penalty Phase*, Huffington Post. Retrieved on July 30, 2013, at www.huffingtonpost.com/2013/06/13/jodi-arias-trial-delay_n_3438439.html.

[24]*Shapiro, supra.*

[25]Iyengar, *Supra* at 698.

[26]*Id.*

[27]*Id.*

[28]See, for example, *Summerlin v. Stewart*, 341 F.3d 1082 (9th Cir. 2003).

Table 6.2 States' Post-*Ring* Changes to Death Penalty Sentencing Statutes

State	Statutory Changes After *Ring*
Alabama	Jury determines presence of aggravating factors and whether the death penalty will be imposed.
Arizona	Jury must unanimously recommend a death sentence. If the jury fails to reach unanimity, the judge may choose to impanel a new jury for sentencing or sentence the defendant to life.
Colorado	Jury must unanimously decide to impose death sentence.
Delaware	Jury must unanimously determine death eligibility.
Florida	Jury must, by majority, determine the presence of aggravating factors and recommend the death penalty for it to be imposed.
Idaho	Jury is solely responsible for imposing death sentences.
Indiana	Unanimous jury decisions of life or death are binding. If a jury fails to reach a unanimous decision, a judge may determine the sentence but only if the jury previously found, beyond a reasonable doubt, the presence of aggravating factors.
Missouri	Jury decides the sentence, but if they fail to reach a unanimous decision, a judge may decide the sentence.*
Montana	Has not altered its statute.
Nebraska	Jury must find, beyond a reasonable doubt, the presence of at least one of the nine statutorily defined aggravating factors for a death sentence to be imposed.
Nevada	Jury determines sentence. If jury fails to unanimously decide on death sentence, a judge may either impanel a new jury or sentence the defendant to life without parole.
New Jersey**	Jury determines sentence.
New Mexico**	A special sentencing jury separate from the trial jury determines sentence.

*The Missouri Supreme Court has rejected death sentences handed down by judges in such cases.
**These states have subsequently repealed the death penalty completely.

‖ JURY INSTRUCTIONS: GUIDED DISCRETION IN CAPITAL CASES

When the Supreme Court, in 1976, reinstated the death penalty in *Gregg v. Georgia*[29] (along with *Proffitt v. Florida*[30] and *Jurek v. Texas*[31]), it approved only statutes that provided "guided discretion" for juries. In an effort to alleviate the "arbitrary," "capricious," and "wanton" nature of capital sentencing cited in *Furman*, the Court required in *Gregg* that juries' decisions be guided by judges. This guidance would consist of instructions about appropriate sentencing options and factors to be considered in weighing those options. As part of their role in the penalty phase, juries are called upon to consider extralegal factors submitted as aggravating (factors that make the crime especially heinous or worthy of the sentence of death) and mitigating (factors that mitigate either the defendant's culpability or the necessity of the penalty of death) circumstances (see Chapter 9 for further discussion of these issues).

[29]*Gregg v. Georgia*, 428 U.S. 153 (1976).
[30]*Proffitt v. Florida*, 428 U.S. 242 (1976).
[31]*Jurek v. Texas*, 428 U.S. 262 (1976).

When it approved the Georgia death penalty statute in *Gregg*, the Court also issued separate decisions striking down statutes providing for mandatory death sentences (*Woodson v. North Carolina*, 1976[32]; *Roberts v. Louisiana*, 1976[33]). Although mandatory death sentences for particular crimes resolved the problems associated with discriminatory and "arbitrary and capricious" results of unfettered jury discretion, it did not allow for the individualized case considerations necessary to ensure appropriate and proportional application of this most severe of penalties. The Court opted for "guided discretion" death penalty statutes and thus placed in the hands of juries the life and death fate of capital offenders. The Court spent much time and effort in the following decades determining the appropriate guidance that juries needed in the way of instructions in capital cases.

This guidance comes in both phases of the trial and in the appropriate composition and limitations regarding jury instructions. Both concerns have been dealt with repeatedly by the Supreme Court since *Gregg*. In the guilt phase, the Court has primarily considered instructions guiding the jury's consideration of lesser included (noncapital) offenses. The sentencing phase requires more guidance where much attention has revolved around the critical issue of future dangerousness. The major cases addressing the issues surrounding jury instructions at both these stages of trial are discussed in this section.

A Guilt Phase: Lesser Included Offenses

The primary issue the Supreme Court has addressed regarding jury instructions during the guilt phase of capital trials is whether juries should be given special instructions about lesser (noncapital) included offenses. Lesser included offenses are those that the jury can, as an alternative to that asserted by the prosecution, consider in their determination of guilt. The Supreme Court first confronted this issue in *Beck v. Alabama* (1980).[34] Alabama's death penalty statute at the time restricted a jury's decision to either conviction of a capital crime, and thus imposition of the death penalty, or outright acquittal. The Court, acknowledging the risks inherent in such a forced decision between two extremes, held that the statute violated due process and said that capital juries must be allowed to consider lesser (noncapital) offenses in the guilt phase of the trial and must be instructed regarding these options. In effect, the Court required that capital juries have the "third option" of convicting defendants without imposing the death penalty by default.

The Court has further clarified the *Beck* decision. In *Hopper v. Evans* (1982),[35] the Court held that *Beck* applies only when evidence supports a lesser included offense. Evans had appealed his capital conviction and death sentence in light of the *Beck* decision, claiming that the jury was not instructed as to lesser included offenses and thus his due process rights had been violated. The Supreme Court determined that because the defendant's own testimony made it clear (the defendant testified during trial that he had killed the victim and "had 'no intention whatsoever of ever reforming in any way' and would return to a life of crime if released"[36]) that he committed the capital offense with which he was charged, the jury need not be instructed about lesser included offenses. In 1998, the Supreme Court, in *Hopkins v. Reeves* (1998),[37] revisited *Beck*. The Court held that juries need not be instructed to consider options that are not

---

[32]*Woodson v. North Carolina*, 428 U.S. 280 (1976).
[33]*Roberts v. Louisiana*, 428 U.S. 325 (1976).
[34]*Beck v. Alabama*, 447 U.S. 625 (1980).
[35]*Hopper v. Evans*, 456 U.S. 605 (1982).
[36]*Id.* at 607.
[37]*Hopkins v. Reeves*, 524 U.S. 88 (1998).

provided by state law (in this case, Nebraska) as possible lesser included offenses for the crime charged. The issue was whether the jury should be instructed to consider second-degree murder and manslaughter in lieu of felony murder—an option not legally allowed under Nebraska law. The Court noted that the jury should be instructed regarding the lesser included offenses that were allowed by law and that this case differed from *Beck* in that "the trial court did not create an 'artificial barrier' for the jury; nor did it treat capital cases differently from noncapital cases."[38] Though requirements for jury instructions regarding lesser included offenses have not been further addressed by the Supreme Court, they continue to emerge as issues at the state level, particularly in regard to the evidence warranting such instructions. Of particular debate is whether a defendant must produce compelling evidence supporting a lesser offense and/or whether he/she must contest the facts of the capital murder in order to have the jury instructed about the option to convict the defendant of a statutorily defined, lesser included offense.[39]

B Penalty Phase: Future Dangerousness and Parole Eligibility

The fact that juries not only decide guilt but also decide the sentence in capital cases is unique in criminal trials. Leaving this decision, which has historically been reserved for judges with the education, experience, and training for making such decisions, in the hands of a jury requires that special attention be given to ensuring the jury's adequate understanding of the factors that determine whether a defendant should live or die. These are issues that have stirred much academic debate and have repeatedly reached the docket of the Supreme Court. The issues have mainly revolved around the appropriate consideration of aggravating and mitigating circumstances, and a more complete discussion of Supreme Court cases related to them is reserved for Chapter 9. However, one of the most prominent aggravating factors presented in capital cases—future dangerousness—has given rise to some issues about jury instructions that are worthy of consideration here. The Court recently decided a series of cases pertaining to jury instructions regarding the likelihood that the defendant is a potential danger to the public— an issue that weighs heavily on the minds of jurors.

There are two aspects to the issue of future dangerousness in capital trials: (1) the defendant's predisposition toward violence or likelihood of continuing to be a violent or dangerous person, and (2) the likelihood that the defendant will be a physical threat (i.e., will be free to potentially engage in future violent acts against other people). The first aspect is often determined by forensic psychologists or other mental health professionals who provide their expert testimony during the sentencing phase of capital trials. This aspect is discussed further in Chapter 9. It is the second aspect that is of interest here.

One of the questions that weigh most heavily on the minds of jurors is whether the defendant, if not executed, will ever be released and thus have the potential to commit murder or other serious violence again.[40] In *California v. Ramos* (1983),[41] the Supreme Court upheld a California law requiring that capital juries be instructed that a sentence of life without parole may be commuted to a sentence with the possibility of parole. The Court, citing *Jurek v. Texas* (1976), concluded that "[w]hat is essential is that the jury have before it all possible relevant information about the individual defendant whose fate it

---

[38]*Id.* at 96.

[39]Hoffheimer, Michael H., *The Future of Constitutionally Required Lesser Included Offenses*, 67 U. Pitt. L. Rev. 585 (2006).

[40]Blume, J.H., S.P. Garvey, and S.L. Johnson, *Future Dangerousness in Capital Cases: Always "At Issue,"* 86 Cornell L. Rev. 397 (2001).

[41]*California v. Ramos*, 463 U.S. 992 (1983).

must determine."[42] In this case, the Court determined that the possibility of eventual release from prison was important in a jury's consideration of the future danger to society that the defendant may present. More than a decade later, a string of cases revolving around South Carolina's capital trial procedure would bring this issue to greater light.

In South Carolina, trial courts had a history of, in one legal scholar's words, "determined and malign efforts to deprive juries in capital cases of information relevant to their decisions on whether to sentence defendants to life imprisonment or to impose the death penalty."[43] Although these words may be a bit strong, South Carolina had consistently refused to allow capital juries to be instructed about parole ineligibility when prosecutors argued that the defendant would be a future danger if sentenced to life in prison. It should be added that, in South Carolina, upon a finding of any aggravating factor, a life sentence does not carry the possibility of parole. However, absent an instruction to this effect, capital jurors may not be aware of this fact. In fact, research shows that jurors have a very poor understanding of the meaning and concept of life imprisonment and often misperceive that defendants will be released on parole even if the only option available is life without parole.[44] In *Simmons v. South Carolina* (1994),[45] the Supreme Court held that, as a matter of due process, the defense must be allowed to have the jury instructed about parole ineligibility when the prosecution has argued future dangerousness and the only sentencing options are death and life without parole.

More recently, the Court has again been confronted with South Carolina's refusal to instruct capital juries about parole eligibility in response to claims of future dangerousness. The first case to test the *Simmons* holding was *Shafer v. South Carolina* (2001).[46] The South Carolina Supreme Court upheld a death sentence in which the trial court refused to instruct the jury about parole eligibility, arguing that life with parole was an available sentence. The U.S. Supreme Court overruled, pointing out that, in fact, upon the jury's finding of aggravating factors, any sentence other than life without parole or death was removed, leaving just the two options. Although the Court reaffirmed its holding in *Simmons*, the question of what constitutes argument of future dangerousness, as required under *Simmons* in order to justify a jury instruction about parole eligibility, was left open. The Court maintained that such determinations should be "left open for the state court's attention and disposition."[47]

A year later, the Supreme Court was forced to address this question and clarify the vague statement in *Simmons* that future dangerousness must be "at issue" in order to justify a jury instruction about parole eligibility. In *Kelly v. South Carolina* (2002),[48] the Court said that in order for future dangerousness to be "at issue," it does not necessarily have to be explicitly argued by the prosecution. Rather, "evidence of future dangerousness under *Simmons* is evidence with a tendency to prove dangerousness in the future."[49] Evidence presented by the prosecution implying future dangerousness suffices to

---

[42]*Id.* at 1003 (citing *Jurek v. Texas, supra* at 276).

[43]Bradley, Craig M., *South Carolina's Death Penalty Odyssey Continues*, TRIAL, Apr. 2002, at 68.

[44]See, for example, William J. Bowers and Benjamin D. Steiner, *Death by Default: An Empirical Demonstration of False and Forced Choices in Capital Sentencing*, 77 TEX. L. REV. 605 (1998), and Benjamin D. Steiner, *Folk Knowledge as Legal Action: Death Penalty Judgments and the Tenet of Early Release in a Culture of Mistrust and Punitiveness*, 33 L. & SOC. REV. 461 (1999).

[45]*Simmons v. South Carolina*, 512 U.S. 154 (1994).

[46]*Shafer v. South Carolina*, 532 U.S. 36 (2001).

[47]*Id.* at 55.

[48]*Kelly v. South Carolina*, 534 U.S. 246 (2002).

[49]*Id.* at 254.

warrant a jury instruction about parole eligibility in capital cases. Some judges and scholars have suggested that this standard broadens the application of *Simmons* to virtually all capital cases.[50] This may be true. The Supreme Court, in *Kelly*, has reaffirmed its commitment to heightened due process, guided discretion, and fully informed juries in capital cases, a posture that goes back to the Court's reinstatement of the death penalty in *Gregg v. Georgia* (1976), *Jurek v. Texas* (1976), and its earliest decision regarding jury instructions in *California v. Ramos* (1983).

IV JURY SELECTION IN CAPITAL CASES: DEATH QUALIFICATION

Once the sentencing decision was placed in the hands of the jury, the jury selection process became more complex; it now requires that jurors be screened in regard to their ability to both dispassionately and objectively determine guilt and appropriate sentence. Courts use a process of voir dire to select jurors for criminal trials from a venire. The venire is a pool of potential jurors from which actual jurors will be selected upon determining that they are qualified to serve on the jury in an unbiased and objective manner. Voir dire is the process of screening jurors to ensure these qualifications. Prospective jurors during voir dire may be excluded from the venire as a result of one of two challenges: (1) a judge may remove a prospective juror from the venire "for cause," or based on statutorily defined criteria; or (2) attorneys in the case may exclude prospective jurors via peremptory challenges, in which case they need not give any explanation or specific reason for their challenge. In capital cases, voir dire must take into account potential jurors' ability to appropriately determine both guilt and the sentence. Although the voir dire process in the guilt phase of capital trials is generally the same as in other criminal trials, the sentencing phase demands something different. Specifically, prospective jurors are questioned about their views on the death penalty and whether they have moral or religious scruples that may prevent them from imposing the death penalty. Historically, those expressing any opposition to the death penalty were excluded from capital juries "for cause." This process has come to be known as "death qualification."

Prior to 1968, prospective jurors who expressed any opposition to the death penalty were generally excluded from capital juries for cause. The exclusion of such prospective jurors was based on the idea that those expressing opposition to the death penalty would not be able to make a fair determination of sentence in capital trials—meaning they would not be able to sentence the defendant to death. In 1968, this process was challenged in *Witherspoon v. Illinois* (1968)[51] and would undergo several transformations through Supreme Court decisions in the following decades.

In *Witherspoon*, the death qualification process was challenged as a violation of the Sixth Amendment right to an impartial jury. It was specifically challenged on two grounds: (1) it biased the jury toward a guilty verdict, and (2) it biased the jury toward a death sentence. The Supreme Court agreed with the second claim and held that excusing jurors simply because they opposed the death penalty was unconstitutional. However, the Court noted that its decision did "not involve the right of the prosecution to challenge for cause those prospective jurors who state that their reservations about capital punishment would prevent them from making an impartial decision as to the defendant's guilt. Nor does it involve the State's assertion of a right to exclude from the jury in a capital case those who say that they could never

---

[50]Vollum, Scott, Rolando V. del Carmen, and Dennis R. Longmire, *Should Jurors Be Informed About Parole Eligibility in Death Penalty Cases? An Analysis of* Kelly v. South Carolina, 84 THE PRISON JOURNAL 395 (2004).
[51]*Witherspoon v. Illinois*, 391 U.S. 510 (1968).

vote to impose the death penalty or that they would refuse even to consider its imposition in the case before them."[52] So, although it placed restrictions on the blanket exclusions common to death qualification prior to 1968, the Court did not eliminate the death qualification process itself.

The Supreme Court revisited *Witherspoon* and the death qualification issue three times in the 1980s. In *Adams v. Texas* (1980),[53] the Court qualified the ruling in *Witherspoon*, holding that jurors can be removed for cause if their views on the death penalty would preclude them from obeying their oath or conforming their decision to the law. The Court reaffirmed *Adams* in *Wainwright v. Witt* (1985),[54] adding that exclusion of a juror should occur in the same manner as in any other case. It was determined that if a juror's views would bias his or her ability to impose the death penalty, then that juror should be excluded. The Supreme Court's final word on death qualification came the following year, in *Lockhart v. McCree* (1986).[55] The Court held that, in spite of research suggesting that death-qualified juries are "conviction-prone" in comparison to noncapital juries, death qualification does not violate the Sixth Amendment right to a fair and impartial jury. The justices concluded that prospective jurors whose attitudes about capital punishment would preclude them from sentencing a defendant to death in any case or set of circumstances can be excluded. An interesting twist on the death qualification process arose in the 1992 case of *Morgan v. Illinois* (1992)[56]—a case that would come to be known as the "reverse-*Witherspoon*" case. In *Morgan* the Court held that prospective jurors who would automatically vote for the death penalty upon conviction of the defendant, regardless of the specific circumstances of the case, can be excluded from the jury for cause.

The process of death qualification again took center stage in 2007 in the case of *Uttecht v. Brown*.[57] This case involved the exclusion of a juror who had expressed, and presented a general demeanor suggesting, reluctance to impose the death penalty. Although unable to imagine a situation in which he would impose the death penalty as opposed to a true life sentence, the juror assured the trial judge that he could consider the sentence of death in compliance with state law. The juror was excluded by the trial judge and the defendant (Brown) was ultimately sentenced to death. The Supreme Court upheld the sentence, stating that: (1) the trial transcript indicated that the juror seemed confused about whether and in what instances he would be able to impose the death penalty, and (2) the trial court is in the best position to judge the demeanor of prospective jurors and thus is entitled to deference.[58] The Court noted that the trial court found that the juror was "substantially impaired in his ability to impose the death penalty" and thus exercised its due discretion in determining the juror to be excludable under *Witherspoon* and *Lockhart* standards.[59] Some argue that this case broadens the process of death qualification by reverting back to pre-*Witherspoon* standards, making excludable even those who simply have qualms about imposing the death penalty.[60] Critics further assert that this fact further removes the death-qualified jury from any semblance of a representative cross-section of the American

---

[52]*Id.* at 513–514.
[53]*Adams v. Texas*, 448 U.S. 38 (1980).
[54]*Wainwright v. Witt*, 469 U.S. 412 (1985).
[55]*Lockhart v. McCree*, 476 U.S. 162 (1986).
[56]*Morgan v. Illinois*, 504 U.S. 719 (1992).
[57]*Uttecht v. Brown*, 551 U.S. 1 (2007).
[58]*Id.*
[59]*Id.* at 3.
[60]Death Penalty Information Center, "Supreme Court Decision Allows Broader Exclusion of Jurors, But May Further Isolate the Death Penalty." Accessed July 30, 2013, at www.deathpenaltyinfo.org/article.php?did=2367&scid=64.

population.[61] Whether *Uttecht v. Brown* predicates these shifts is debatable, but what is certain is that the process of death qualification continues to raise constitutional questions and concerns.

The controversy over the death qualification process and its potential biasing effects are much researched and discussed in academic and legal circles. Research has shown that the death qualification process leads to a conviction-prone and death sentence-prone jury. Both the composition of a death-qualified jury (meaning only those who do not oppose the death penalty) and the questioning process by which jurors are selected (in which guilt is presumed) have been cited as factors biasing the capital jury toward guilt.[62] This research supports the claims of the dissenting justices in *Lockhart* who argued that not only does death qualification produce juries that are conviction-prone, but it also creates an unfair imbalance in favor of the prosecution and thus violates the defendant's Sixth Amendment right to a fair trial. Other scholars have found that death qualification perpetuates racial disparities in the application of the death penalty in violation of the Fourteenth Amendment's equal protection clause.[63] In his dissenting opinion in *Lockhart*, Justice Thurgood Marshall expressed the following concern: "[t]he true impact of death qualification on the fairness of a trial is likely even more devastating than the studies show."[64] The research that has been conducted since the *Lockhart* decision seems to support Justice Marshall's statement. Nevertheless, the death qualification process continues to be used in capital cases in virtually all jurisdictions in the United States.

V IN SUMMARY, WHAT DO THESE CASES SAY?

In the wake of *Gregg v. Georgia* (1976),[65] the capital jury has been a focus of the Supreme Court's death penalty jurisprudence. Three primary issues regarding capital juries have caught the Court's attention: (1) the role juries play in capital trials, (2) the instructions given to juries in capital trials, and (3) the jury selection process in capital trials. In each area, the Court has upheld the importance and autonomy of juries in death penalty cases.

The crucial and central role of the jury in capital trials was most recently reemphasized in *Ring v. Arizona* (2002),[66] in which the Court held that juries, not judges, must make the ultimate determination of whether a defendant receives the death sentence. In *Gregg*, the Court granted capital juries the unique responsibility of making both the guilt and sentencing decisions, separated into two distinct

---

[61]Swafford, Alec T., *Qualified Support: Death Qualification, Equal Protection, and Race*, 39 Am. J. Crim. L. 147 (2011).
[62]See, for example, William J. Bowers, Marla Sandys, and Benjamin D. Steiner, *Foreclosed Impartiality in Capital Sentencing: Jurors' Predispositions, Guilt-Trial Experience, and Premature Decision Making*, 83 CORNELL L. REV. 1476 (1998); Craig Haney, DEATH BY DESIGN: CAPITAL PUNISHMENT AS A SOCIAL PSYCHOLOGICAL SYSTEM (2005); and Craig Haney, Lorelei Sontag, and Sally Costanzo, *Deciding to Take a Life: Capital Juries, Sentencing Instructions, and the Jurisprudence of Death*, 50 J. SOC. ISSUES 149 (1994). For thorough reviews and analyses of the extant research on death qualification, see the following meta-analyses: M. Allen, E. Mabry, and D. McKelton, *Impact of Juror Attitudes about the Death Penalty on Juror Evaluations of Guilt and Punishment: A Meta-Analysis*, 22 L. & HUM. BEHAV. 715 (1998); J.W. Filkins, C.M. Smith, and R.S. Tindale, *An Evaluation of the Biasing Effects of Death Qualification: A Meta-Analytic/Computer Simulation Approach*, in R.S. Tindale, L. Heath, J. Edwards, E.J. Posavac, F.B. Bryant, Y. Suarez-Balcazar, E. Henderson-King, and J. Myers (EDS.), THEORY AND RESEARCH ON SMALL GROUPS, 153–175 (1998); M.T. Nietzel, D.M. McCarthy, and M.J. Kern, *Juries: The Current State of the Empirical Literature*, in R. Roesch, S.D. Hart, and J.R.P. Ogloff, (EDS.), PSYCHOLOGY AND LAW: THE STATE OF THE DISCIPLINE, 23–50 (1999).
[63]*Swafford, Supra.*
[64]*Lockhart v. McCree, supra* at 190.
[65]*Gregg v. Georgia, supra.*
[66]*Ring v. Arizona, supra.*

stages of the trial—the guilt stage and the penalty stage. This bifurcated trial structure, while allowing for heightened scrutiny of the circumstances to ensure that the death penalty is only imposed in the most severe cases, also places an additional burden on the jury. Nevertheless, the Supreme Court for years allowed the practice of judicial override, in which judges had the authority to override the jury's sentencing decision, thus nullifying the jury's otherwise authoritative role. Although the full extent is not yet clear, it appears that the Court's decision in *Ring* has brought this practice to an end, more solidly placing the sentencing decision in the hands of the capital jury.

The Supreme Court has held that the jury must be instructed about lesser included offenses for which they can convict a defendant. However, these lesser included offenses must be provided for in the state's statute and supported by evidence to warrant an instruction to the jury. The Court has also said that juries must be instructed about parole eligibility or ineligibility and the real meaning of life without parole when evidence of future dangerousness is used by the prosecution.

Issues surrounding the instructions that juries receive have occupied a significant amount of the Court's time over the past few decades as well. Of particular interest are jury instructions surrounding the defendant's parole eligibility. The Supreme Court has determined that when the prosecution argues (or even suggests) that the defendant poses a future danger, the defense, if it so requests, is entitled to jury instructions regarding the defendant's parole eligibility or ineligibility. This is based on the due process right to attempt to refute evidence with counter-evidence (future dangerousness with the reality that the defendant will receive life without parole if not sentenced to death).

Jury composition and selection attracted much early attention by the Supreme Court, ultimately leading to the concept now known as "death qualification" of juries. This refers to the practice that no one unequivocally opposed to the death penalty can be included on a jury. Many, including scholars, researchers, and legal professionals, have argued that such a practice is unduly biasing and prejudicial in both the guilt and sentencing phase of capital trials. However, the Court has determined that in order for a juror to fulfill her duties, she must be free of a bias that comes with strict opposition to the death penalty. These issues reemerged in the 2007 case of *Uttecht v. Brown*, in which the Court seemed to be slightly loosening the restrictions on what makes a juror excludable in the death qualification process. Though the death qualification process continues to draw controversy and challenges from scholars and critics of the death penalty, the Court has remained silent on the practice in recent years, and death qualification remains a hallmark of capital trials and the death penalty in the United States.

VI CONCLUSION

The jury is one of the most sacred institutions in the U.S. criminal justice system. The very idea of a trial by jury—that one has the right to be judged by his or her fellow citizens and not simply by an official agent of the government—is at the heart of the judicial process and the notions of due process and fundamental fairness. So it is not a surprise that capital juries, to whom we entrust decisions of the greatest gravity—those involving life and death—have occupied much of the Supreme Court's attention since the reinstatement of the death penalty in 1976.

The Supreme Court, since reinstating the death penalty in *Gregg*, has mandated "guided discretion" as the cornerstone of death penalty law and procedure. Having rejected mandatory death penalty statutes, the Court opted for guided discretion statutes in which the jury is required to consider the many facts and circumstances of the individual case and use its discretion in sentencing the defendant to either death or life in prison based on those facts and circumstances. In line with the principle of guided discretion, the Court has generally held that the jury should be given sufficiently clear and thorough instructions from the judge as a form of guidance.

The Supreme Court's 2002 decision in *Ring v. Arizona* makes probably the strongest statement regarding the critical role of juries in capital trials. The Court held in *Ring v. Arizona* that only juries, not judges, should be given the authority to determine when a sentence as severe as death is warranted. Capital juries are granted the power to determine whether a defendant will live or die. With this power comes a great burden but also a heightened scrutiny of juries and the criminal justice processes surrounding them. The Supreme Court has consistently reinforced the importance of capital juries and held them up as a cornerstone of the U.S. justice system. Since the reinstatement of the death penalty in *Gregg v. Georgia*, the Supreme Court has repeatedly been called upon to consider the appropriate role, guidance, and composition of capital juries. Although these issues are constantly fine-tuned and the message often changes, the centrality and importance of juries to death penalty jurisprudence never wanes.

CASES BRIEFED IN CHAPTER 6

Case	Issue	Holding
Witherspoon v. Illinois 391 U.S. 510 (1968)	Is it constitutional to remove prospective jurors for cause merely because they generally oppose capital punishment?	The removal of prospective jurors for cause based only on the fact that they express conscientious scruples against the death penalty violates the rights to due process and an impartial jury.
Beck v. Alabama 447 U.S. 625 (1980)	Does the Constitution allow the death penalty to be imposed when the jury was not allowed to consider a lesser included noncapital offense?	Alabama's prohibition of the consideration of lesser included noncapital offenses, where evidence would support the lesser included offense, violates due process rights.
Lockhart v. McCree 476 U.S. 162 (1986)	Is it constitutional to remove prospective jurors whose opposition to the death penalty would impair their ability to perform their duties in the sentencing phase of a capital trial?	A prospective juror whose opposition to the death penalty is so strong as to impair their ability to perform their duties at the sentencing phase of trial (i.e., would preclude them from ever imposing a death sentence) may be removed for cause.
Mills v. Maryland 486 U.S. 367 (1988)	Must a jury unanimously agree that a mitigating factor exists for that mitigating factor to be considered by any juror in their sentencing decision?	Capital jurors may not be prohibited from considering mitigating factors simply because the jury does not unanimously agree on their presence. Sentencing instructions giving the impression that unanimity is required violate a defendant's due process rights.
Morgan v. Illinois 504 U.S. 719 (1992)	Does a trial court's refusal to ask prospective jurors whether they would automatically impose the death penalty upon defendant's conviction violate due process?	The due process clause of the Fourteenth Amendment requires that, if requested by the defendant, prospective jurors must be questioned regarding whether they would automatically impose the death penalty if they find the defendant guilty.

Continued

Case	Issue	Holding
Simmons v. South Carolina 512 U.S. 154 (1994)	Does the refusal to instruct a capital jury about parole ineligibility when the prosecution has argued future dangerousness violate due process?	In a case in which a defendant's future dangerousness is argued by the prosecution and in which state law prohibits parole, the defendant has a right to have the jury instructed about defendant's parole ineligibility.
Weeks v. Angelone 528 U.S. 225 (2000)	Is it a violation of due process for a trial judge to refuse to clarify sentencing requirements beyond what is indicated in the original jury instructions?	A trial judge is not required, even if requested by the jury, to clarify the sentencing requirements in a capital case beyond the words provided in the original jury instructions.
Ring v. Arizona 536 U.S. 584 (2002)	Does the Sixth Amendment require that a jury, not a judge, must make the determination of the presence of an aggravating circumstance that elevates a punishment to death?	A judge may not alone make a determination of aggravating circumstances that elevate a punishment to death. Such aggravating circumstances are "the functional equivalent of an element of a greater offense" and therefore must be determined by a jury, as required by the Sixth Amendment.
Uttecht v. Brown 551 U.S. 1 (2007)	Is a trial court judge's determination that a juror is substantially impaired in his or her ability to consider the sentence of death sufficient to remove that juror?	Trial courts should be given deference in their ability to ascertain whether a prospective juror is substantially impaired in his or her ability to follow the law and consider the death penalty in the sentencing phase of capital trials.

CASE BRIEFS

WITHERSPOON v. ILLINOIS 391 U.S. 510 (1968)

CAPSULE: Prospective jurors may not be excluded from capital juries merely because they have general scruples against the death penalty.

FACTS: At the trial of Witherspoon, charged with capital murder, the prosecution eliminated all prospective jurors who expressed general scruples against or objections to the death penalty. Illinois law allowed for challenges of any member of the venire who had reservations about the use of capital punishment. Under the authority of this law, the prosecution had nearly half of the venire removed, most of whom were never questioned to find out whether their scruples would preclude them from imposing a death sentence regardless of the specific circumstances of the case and responsibilities as a capital juror. Witherspoon was convicted and sentenced to death.

ISSUE: Is it constitutional to remove prospective jurors for cause merely because they generally oppose capital punishment? NO.

HOLDING: The removal of prospective jurors for cause based only on the fact that they express conscientious scruples against the death penalty and without questioning them about whether these scruples would cause them to automatically vote against the imposition of the death penalty regardless of the specific facts of the case violates the rights to due process and an impartial jury.

Continued

WITHERSPOON v. ILLINOIS 391 U.S. 510 (1968)—cont'd

REASON: "A man who opposes the death penalty, no less than one who favors it, can make the discretionary choice of punishment entrusted to him by the State and can thus obey the oath he takes as a juror; but in a nation where so many have come to oppose capital punishment, a jury from which all such people have been excluded cannot perform the task demanded of it—that of expressing the conscience of the community on the ultimate question of life or death.

"Just as a State may not entrust the determination of whether a man is innocent or guilty to a tribunal organized to convict, so it may not entrust the determination of whether a man should live or die to a tribunal organized to return a verdict of death; and no sentence of death can be carried out, regardless of when it was imposed, if the voir dire testimony indicates that the jury that imposed or recommended that sentence was chosen by excluding veniremen for cause simply because they voiced general objections to capital punishment or expressed conscientious or religious scruples against its infliction."

CASE SIGNIFICANCE: *Witherspoon v. Illinois* was the first case to consider the process of "death qualification," or the elimination of jurors based on their opposition to the death penalty. The Supreme Court's decision substantially limited the practice of death qualification by declaring it unconstitutional to exclude jurors simply because they have scruples or views in opposition to the death penalty. The Court ruled that prospective capital jurors may be removed for cause only if their opposition meant that they would automatically refuse to sentence a defendant to death if he or she were convicted. Importantly, the Court only applied this to exclusion from the sentencing phase of trial. This restrictive standard for excusing such jurors remained intact for only a short time and was eventually replaced by the standard set in *Lockhart v. McCree* (1986).[67] This case, however, represented the Supreme Court's first pronouncement on death qualification.

BECK v. ALABAMA 447 U.S. 625 (1980)

CAPSULE: Capital juries must be allowed to consider a guilty verdict on lesser included offenses.

FACTS: Alabama law provides for felony murder as a lesser included offense of robbery-intentional killing, a capital crime. In contrast, Alabama capital punishment law prohibits the trial judge from granting this option to the jury. Rather, the jury must decide whether to convict on the capital charge and sentence the defendant to death or acquit him altogether. At trial, Beck admitted participating in the robbery but denied any role in the killing of the victim. He was convicted of robbery-intentional killing and sentenced to death. The state appellate courts rejected Beck's claim that the conviction and death sentence were unconstitutional due to the statutory preclusion on lesser included offense instructions. The conviction and death sentence were upheld.

ISSUE: Does the Constitution allow the death penalty to be imposed when the jury was not allowed to consider a guilty verdict on a lesser included noncapital offense that was supported by evidence? NO.

HOLDING: Alabama's prohibition of the consideration of lesser included noncapital offenses at the guilt phase of trial, where evidence would support the lesser included offense, violates due process rights.

REASON: "Providing the jury with the 'third option' of convicting on a lesser included offense ensures that the jury will accord the defendant the full benefit of the reasonable-doubt standard. This procedural safeguard is especially important in cases such as this one. For when the evidence establishes that the defendant is guilty of a serious,

Continued

---

[67]*Lockhart v. McCree, supra.*

BECK v. ALABAMA 447 U.S. 625 (1980)—cont'd

violent offense but leaves some doubt as to an element justifying conviction of a capital offense, the failure to give the jury such a 'third option' inevitably enhances the risk of an unwarranted conviction. Such a risk cannot be tolerated in a case in which the defendant's life is at stake.

"The jury's 'option' of refusing to return any verdict at all, thus causing a mistrial, is not an adequate substitute for proper instructions on lesser included offenses. Nor does the fact that the trial judge has the ultimate sentencing power compensate for the risk that the jury may return an improper verdict because of the unavailability of the 'third option.' If the jury finds the defendant guilty only of a lesser included offense, the judge would not have the opportunity to impose the death sentence. Moreover, the jury's verdict must have a tendency to motivate the judge to impose the same sentence that the jury did. Under these circumstances, it cannot be presumed that a post-trial hearing will always correct whatever mistakes occurred in the performance of the jury's factfinding function."

CASE SIGNIFICANCE: This was the first case following the reinstatement of the death penalty to test the requirements of "heightened standards of reliability," set forth in *Gregg*, as they apply to capital juries. This case set a standard that juries should be given all opportunities to consider options other than the death penalty. The issue here was whether the jury must be given the option of considering conviction on lesser included offenses as provided by state statute. The state law allowing a jury to consider the lesser included offense of felony murder (which did not carry a death sentence) in lieu of robbery-intentional killing (which carried a death sentence) was in conflict with Alabama's death penalty law, which only allowed the jury the option of either convicting on the capital offense of robbery-intentional killing or acquitting the defendant. The Court concluded that this was not a realistic option for the jury if it determined that the defendant's role in the crime did not warrant the death penalty. Being faced with the only other option of acquittal and release, the jury may be compelled to convict on the capital charge and send the defendant to his death, even if the jury does not think the penalty is warranted. Noting the gravity of capital cases, the Court held that the jury must be allowed to consider the lesser included offenses, thus supporting the notion that a capital jury's hands should not be tied when making decisions that could cost the defendant his or her life.

LOCKHART v. McCREE 476 U.S. 162 (1986)

CAPSULE: Prospective jurors may be removed for cause if they oppose the death penalty.

FACTS: McCree was charged with capital felony murder after being pursued while driving a car that matched an eyewitness's description of the getaway vehicle seen leaving a gas station where the owner was robbed and murdered. McCree admitted to being at the store at the time of the robbery and murder but claimed that "a tall black stranger wearing an overcoat" had taken McCree's gun from his car and killed the store owner. McCree further stated that the stranger rode in his car with him, eventually getting out and walking away with the gun. Two eyewitnesses who saw McCree in his car during the time between the murder and the time McCree reported the stranger exiting his car contradicted his story by reporting that only one person, McCree, was in the car.

During voir dire, the judge removed, for cause, all prospective jurors who stated that they could not vote for the death penalty under any circumstances. McCree was convicted of capital felony murder but was sentenced by the jury to life imprisonment without parole. McCree filed a federal habeas corpus petition challenging the conviction and claiming that the process of "death qualification" violated his Sixth Amendment right to an impartial jury representing a cross-section of the community.

ISSUE: Is it constitutional to remove prospective jurors whose opposition to the death penalty would substantially impair their ability to perform their duties in the sentencing phase of a capital trial? YES.

Continued

LOCKHART v. McCREE 476 U.S. 162 (1986)—cont'd

HOLDING: A prospective juror whose opposition to the death penalty is so strong as to impair his or her ability to perform his or her duties at the sentencing phase of trial (i.e., would preclude them from ever imposing a death sentence) may be removed for cause.

REASON: "'Death qualification' of a jury does not violate the fair-cross-section requirement of the Sixth Amendment, which applies to jury panels or venires but does not require that petit juries actually chosen reflect the composition of the community at large. Even if the requirement were extended to petit juries, the essence of a fair-cross-section claim is the systematic exclusion of a 'distinctive group' in the community—such as blacks, women, and Mexican-Americans—for reasons completely unrelated to the ability of members of the group to serve as jurors in a particular case. Groups defined solely in terms of shared attitudes that would prevent or substantially impair members of the group from performing one of their duties as jurors, such as the '*Witherspoon*-excludables' at issue here, are not 'distinctive groups' for fair-cross-section purposes. 'Death qualification' is carefully designed to serve the State's legitimate interest in obtaining a single jury that can properly and impartially apply the law to the facts of the case at both the guilt and sentencing phases of a capital trial."

CASE SIGNIFICANCE: States that impose the death penalty usually use a two-step procedure: a guilt stage and a sentencing stage. In an earlier case, *Witherspoon v. Illinois* (1968),[68] the Supreme Court said that in choosing juries for sentencing defendants (as opposed to determining guilt) in capital cases, prosecutors may exclude for cause potential jurors who say they are unwilling to vote for a death sentence under any circumstance. This means that a juror who says he or she is unwilling to vote for the death sentence could not be excluded from the guilt stage but could be excluded from the sentencing stage. This case goes further by saying that prospective jurors whose opposition to capital punishment is so strong as to lead them to say that they would never vote for imposing the death penalty may now be excluded from the guilt stage as well as from the sentencing stage. Note, however, that prospective jurors cannot be rejected from either stage merely because they are opposed to the death penalty. To be disqualified, these jurors must indicate that they would automatically vote against the death penalty irrespective of the facts of the case.[69]

MILLS v. MARYLAND 486 U.S. 367 (1988)

CAPSULE: Jury instructions that suggest that unanimity is required for a jury to find mitigating circumstances are unconstitutional.

FACTS: Mills was tried and convicted for the murder of his cellmate while serving time in a Maryland prison. The jury, during the sentencing phase, agreed that the murder was aggravated because it was committed while the defendant was confined to a correctional institution. Further, they answered "no" in regard to whether they had reached a unanimous decision on the presence of each mitigating circumstance indicated on the verdict form. The death penalty was imposed. Mills challenged the sentence, claiming that it was unconstitutionally mandated by the manner in which the jury was instructed and the implementation of the verdict form. He argued that, in effect, the instructions and verdict form indicated that the death penalty was mandatory if the jury unanimously agreed to the presence of the aggravating factor and failed to unanimously agree to the presence of any mitigating factor.

ISSUE: Must a jury unanimously agree that a mitigating factor exists in order for that mitigating factor to be considered by any juror in their sentencing decision? NO.

Continued

---

[68]*Witherspoon v. Illinois, supra.*

[69]Adapted from ROLANDO V. DEL CARMEN, SUSAN E. RITTER, AND BETSY A. WITT, BRIEFS OF LEADING CASES IN CORRECTIONS (5th ed. 2008).

MILLS v. MARYLAND 486 U.S. 367 (1988)—cont'd

HOLDING: Capital jurors may not be prohibited from considering mitigating factors simply because the jury is not unanimous in its determination of the presence of those mitigating factors. Maryland's sentencing instructions gave the impression that unanimity was required and thus violated the defendant's due process rights.

REASON: "With respect to findings of guilt, a jury's verdict must be set aside if it can be supported on one ground but not on another, and the reviewing court is uncertain which of the two grounds was relied upon by the jury in reaching the verdict. Review of death sentences demands even greater certainty that the jury's conclusions rested on proper grounds.

"While the Court of Appeals' construction of the jury instructions and verdict form is plausible, it cannot be concluded, with any degree of certainty, that the jury did not adopt petitioner's interpretation instead. Nothing in the verdict form or the judge's instructions even arguably is construable as suggesting that the jury could leave an answer blank and proceed to the next step in its deliberations. A jury following the instructions set out in the verdict form could be precluded from considering mitigating evidence if only a single juror adhered to the view that such evidence should not be so considered.

"There is no extrinsic evidence of what the jury in this case actually thought, but the portions of the record relating to the verdict form and the judge's instructions indicate that there is at least a substantial risk that the jury was misinformed. Moreover, since the time when this case was decided below, the Court of Appeals has promulgated a new verdict form expressly covering the situation where there is a lack of unanimity as to the existence or nonexistence of a particular mitigating factor, and providing for the consideration of all mitigating evidence in determining the sentence. This shows at least some concern on that court's part that juries could misunderstand the previous instructions as to unanimity and the consideration of mitigating evidence by individual jurors."

CASE SIGNIFICANCE: This was the first case to address requirements surrounding jurors' consideration of mitigating circumstances in the sentencing phase of a capital trial. The issue here revolved around sentencing instructions given to the jury that could easily be perceived as requiring that the jury be unanimous in finding mitigating circumstances in order for those circumstances to be factors in the sentencing decision. Believing that unanimity was required, according to the jury instructions and the instructions on the verdict form, the jury (which could not unanimously agree on the presence of mitigating factors) sentenced the defendant to death. The Court ruled that the instructions gave the impression that unanimity was required and were thus unconstitutional. More important, the Court said that unanimity in findings of mitigating circumstances is not required in order for such factors to weigh in the sentencing decision. In the years to come the Court continued to emphasize that jurors must individually be allowed to consider whatever mitigating factors they believe are relevant to their decision whether to impose the death penalty.

MORGAN v. ILLINOIS 504 U.S. 719 (1992)

CAPSULE: Refusal by the court, upon defendant's request, to inquire whether prospective jurors would automatically impose the death sentence upon conviction of the defendant is a violation of due process.

FACTS: Morgan was hired to kill a narcotics dealer for $4,000. He lured the victim, a friend, into an empty apartment and shot him in the head six times. Morgan was convicted of first-degree murder and sentenced to death. Voir dire was conducted, in accordance with state law, by the trial court. The state pursued the death penalty and accordingly requested that prospective jurors, per *Witherspoon*, be questioned about whether they opposed the death penalty and would thus refuse to impose it upon conviction under any circumstances. The court allowed such inquiry and 17 potential jurors were removed. In response, the defendant requested that prospective jurors also be asked the following question: "If you found Derrick Morgan guilty, would you automatically vote to impose the death penalty no matter what the facts are?" The court refused to present the question. The Illinois Supreme Court affirmed the lower court's decision.

Continued

MORGAN v. ILLINOIS 504 U.S. 719 (1992)—cont'd

ISSUE: Does a trial court's refusal, upon defendant's request, to ask prospective jurors whether they would automatically impose the death penalty upon defendant's conviction violate due process? YES.

HOLDING: The due process clause of the Fourteenth Amendment requires that, if requested by the defendant, prospective jurors be questioned in voir dire regarding whether they would automatically impose the sentence of death if they find the defendant guilty.

REASON: "On voir dire a trial court must, at a defendant's request, inquire into the prospective jurors' views on capital punishment. Part of the guarantee of a defendant's right to an impartial jury is an adequate voir dire to identify unqualified jurors. Morgan could not exercise intelligently his challenge for cause against prospective jurors who would unwaveringly impose death after a finding of guilt unless he was given the opportunity to identify such persons by questioning them at voir dire about their views on the death penalty. Absent that opportunity, his right not to be tried by those who would always impose death would be rendered as nugatory and meaningless as the State's right, in the absence of questioning, to strike those who never do so.

"A juror to whom mitigating evidence is irrelevant is plainly saying that such evidence is not worth consideration, a view which has long been rejected by this Court and which finds no basis in Illinois statutory or decisional law. Here, the instruction accords with the State's death penalty statute, which requires that the jury be instructed to consider any relevant aggravating and mitigating factors, lists certain relevant mitigating factors, and directs the jury to consider whether the mitigating factors are "sufficient to preclude" the death penalty's imposition. Since the statute plainly indicates that a lesser sentence is available in every case where mitigating evidence exists, a juror who would invariably impose the death penalty would not give the mitigating evidence the consideration the statute contemplates."

CASE SIGNIFICANCE: In *Witherspoon v. Illinois* (1968)[70] and *Lockhart v. McCree* (1986),[71] the Supreme Court held that jurors may be removed for cause from serving on capital juries if their views about the death penalty would prohibit them from ever imposing a death sentence regardless of circumstances. In this case, often referred to as the "reverse-*Witherspoon*" case, the converse was addressed: whether jurors may be removed if their views meant that they would automatically vote for a death sentence upon conviction of the defendant. The Court held that the defense should have the opportunity to question prospective jurors on this point and that those who, like the *Witherspoon* excludables, would never be able to consider both options of life sentence and death sentence may be excluded from capital juries. This levels the playing field for the defense and the prosecution in the selection of jurors based on their views about the death penalty.

SIMMONS v. SOUTH CAROLINA 512 U.S. 154 (1994)

CAPSULE: When future dangerousness is at issue in a capital trial and parole is prohibited if a life sentence is imposed, the jury must be informed about the defendant's parole ineligibility.

FACTS: In 1990, Simmons beat and killed an elderly woman in her home. Before the capital trial for this murder began, Simmons also pled guilty to two counts of sexual assault on two other elderly women and to first-degree burglary. His guilty pleas and convictions on the violent offenses rendered Simmons ineligible for parole if convicted on the capital murder charge.

Prior to jury selection, the prosecution requested that any mention of parole be barred throughout the trial. Despite the objection of the defense, this request was granted by the trial court. The defense was barred from mentioning parole or even questioning jurors regarding their understanding of the meaning of a "life" sentence.

Continued

---

[70]*Witherspoon v. Illinois, supra.*
[71]*Lockhart v. McCree, supra.*

SIMMONS v. SOUTH CAROLINA 512 U.S. 154 (1994)—cont'd

In the closing arguments, the prosecution argued that Simmons was a future danger to society, adding that "[y] our verdict will be an act of self-defense." The defense, in an attempt to rebut this argument, requested that the jury be instructed about the true meaning of "life imprisonment" in this case, which would include the fact that Simmons would never be eligible for parole. The trial court refused. During deliberations, the jury sent a note asking the judge this question: "Does the imposition of a life sentence carry with it the possibility of parole?" The judge responded that the jury was not to consider parole or parole eligibility in reaching their verdict and that the terms life imprisonment and death sentence were to be understood in their plain and ordinary meaning. Simmons's appeal that the judge's refusal to instruct the jury about his parole eligibility violated the Eighth Amendment and his due process rights under the Fourteenth Amendment. The South Carolina Supreme Court rejected his appeal.

ISSUE: Does the refusal to instruct a capital jury about parole ineligibility when the prosecution has argued future dangerousness violate due process? YES.

HOLDING: Due process requires that a defendant have the right to rebut evidence presented against him. In a case in which a defendant's future dangerousness is argued by the prosecution and in which state law prohibits parole, the defendant has a right to have the jury instructed about the defendant's parole ineligibility.

REASON: "In assessing future dangerousness, the actual duration of the defendant's prison sentence is indisputably relevant. Holding all other factors constant, it is entirely reasonable for a sentencing jury to view a defendant who is eligible for parole as a greater threat to society than a defendant who is not. Indeed, there may be no greater assurance of a defendant's future nondangerousness to the public than the fact that he never will be released on parole. The trial court's refusal to apprise the jury of information so crucial to its sentencing determination, particularly when the prosecution alluded to the defendant's future dangerousness in its argument to the jury, cannot be reconciled with our well-established precedents interpreting the Due Process Clause."

"The Due Process Clause does not allow the execution of a person 'on the basis of information which he had no opportunity to deny or explain.' *Gardner v. Florida*, 430 U.S. 349, 362 (1977). In this case, the jury reasonably may have believed that petitioner could be released on parole if he were not executed. To the extent this misunderstanding pervaded the jury's deliberations, it had the effect of creating a false choice between sentencing petitioner to death and sentencing him to a limited period of incarceration. This grievous misperception was encouraged by the trial court's refusal to provide the jury with accurate information regarding petitioner's parole ineligibility, and by the State's repeated suggestion that petitioner would pose a future danger to society if he were not executed. Three times petitioner asked to inform the jury that in fact he was ineligible for parole under state law; three times his request was denied. The State thus succeeded in securing a death sentence on the ground, at least in part, of petitioner's future dangerousness, while at the same time concealing from the sentencing jury the true meaning of its noncapital sentencing alternative, namely, that life imprisonment meant life without parole. We think it is clear that the State denied petitioner due process."

CASE SIGNIFICANCE: This case deals with an issue raised by an increasing number of state laws that prohibit release on parole for certain heinous offenses. South Carolina law provided that for the type of offense committed by the defendant in this case, imprisonment for life meant that the defendant could not be released on parole. This is important because jurors might not impose the death penalty and could opt for life imprisonment if they are informed that life imprisonment for some defendants means that these defendants will never be released from prison. The assumption is that if life imprisonment can mean parole, jurors would rather impose the death penalty so that society may be protected from dangerous parolees. However, if jurors know that life imprisonment means that the defendant will never be released, then future danger to society does not become a consideration in imposing the penalty. The Court said that due process requires that the information on "life without parole" as an alternative to the death penalty in certain states be made known to the jury when determining the sentence to be imposed. It could make a difference in the punishment the jury ultimately imposes.[72]

---

[72]This case significance is taken from Rolando V. Del Carmen, Susan E. Ritter, and Betsy A. Witt, Briefs of Leading Cases in Corrections (5th ed. 2008).

WEEKS v. ANGELONE 528 U.S. 225 (2000)

CAPSULE: Even if a jury requests clarification, judges in capital cases are not required to further clarify sentencing requirements beyond reference to the actual words of the jury instructions.

FACTS: Lonnie Weeks Jr. was a passenger in a car he had stolen but that his uncle, Lewis Dukes, was driving. They were pursued by a state trooper and eventually stopped near an exit ramp. Upon the trooper's request, Dukes exited and stood near the rear of the car. The trooper then asked that Weeks do the same. As Weeks exited the car, he brandished a handgun loaded with hollow-point bullets and fired six shots at the trooper, killing him.

Weeks was arrested the next day and confessed to the murder of the police officer. A jury found him guilty of capital murder. During the sentencing phase of the trial, the prosecution presented evidence and testimony that he "would constitute a continuing threat to society" and that his crime was "outrageously or wantonly vile, horrible or inhuman, in that it involved depravity of mind."

During deliberations, the jurors asked the judge a series of questions. First, they asked about whether a life sentence would carry the possibility of parole, to which the judge responded that they were to make their decision within the instructions given and not concern themselves with what may happen after their decision. The jury then asked the following:

> If we believe that Lonnie Weeks, Jr. is guilty of at least 1 of the alternatives, then is it our duty as a jury to issue the death penalty? Or must we decide (even though he is guilty of one of the alternatives) whether or not to issue the death penalty, or one of the life sentences? What is the Rule? Please clarify?

The judge responded by simply referring the jury to the original instructions. The defense requested that the judge instruct the jury that even if they find the presence of aggravating factors, they may still choose to impose a life sentence. The judge refused and Weeks was sentenced to death.

ISSUE: Is it a violation of due process for a trial judge to refuse to clarify sentencing requirements beyond what is indicated in the original jury instructions? NO.

HOLDING: A trial judge is not required, even if requested by the jury, to clarify the sentencing requirements in a capital case beyond the words provided in the original jury instructions.

REASON: "A jury is presumed to follow its instructions. *Richardson v. Marsh*, 481 U.S. 200, (1987). Similarly, a jury is presumed to understand a judge's answer to its question. Weeks' jury did not inform the court that after reading the relevant paragraph of the instruction, it still did not understand its role. ('Had the jury desired further information, they might, and probably would, have signified their desire to the court. The utmost willingness was manifested to gratify them, and it may fairly be presumed that they had nothing further to ask'). To presume otherwise would require reversal every time a jury inquires about a matter of constitutional significance, regardless of the judge's answer."

"Given that petitioner's jury was adequately instructed, and given that the trial judge responded to the jury's question by directing its attention to the precise paragraph of the constitutionally adequate instruction that answers its inquiry, the question becomes whether the Constitution requires anything more. We hold that it does not."

CASE SIGNIFICANCE: This case is significant in that it marks a turning point in the degree of guidance a jury is afforded in capital cases. The jurors clearly indicated that they were confused about the meaning of the instructions they were given. They did not know: (1) the meaning of life imprisonment, (2) whether upon finding an aggravating factor, they were required to impose the death penalty, or (3) whether they were allowed to consider mitigating circumstances and potentially sentence the defendant to life as opposed to death. In response to their inquiries, the only guidance they received was the judge directing them to the written instructions they had been provided

Continued

WEEKS v. ANGELONE 528 U.S. 225 (2000)—cont'd

and that had confused them in the first place. Until this case, the Supreme Court had generally maintained that jurors should be given all possible guidance when considering aggravating and mitigating factors and how those factors are to weigh in their sentencing decision. In spite of the obvious confusion on the part of the jury, the Court in *Weeks* held that the written instructions were sufficient guidance and that no further instructions from the judge were needed.

RING v. ARIZONA 536 U.S. 584 (2002)

CAPSULE: A judge may not alone make a determination of aggravating circumstances and then elevate the punishment to death.

FACTS: Timothy Ring and two accomplices stole an armored bank truck from in front of a mall in Glendale, Arizona, killing the driver and stealing $562,000 in cash and $271,000 in checks. Acting on the tip of an informant, Glendale police began investigating Ring and one of his accomplices, James Greenham, for their role in the robbery and murder. Their investigation revealed that each had made expensive purchases shortly after the robbery. They subsequently placed wiretaps on the telephones of Ring and Greenham and another suspected accomplice, William Ferguson. Recorded conversations implicated each of the men in the robbery and murder. A search of Ring's house revealed a duffel bag containing more than $271,000 in cash and notes indicating planned "splits" among the three suspects.

At trial, the jury failed to find Ring guilty of premeditated murder but convicted him of felony murder in the course of armed robbery. Arizona law required further findings of aggravation in order for him to be eligible for the death penalty. Arizona law requires that a sentencing hearing be conducted in which aggravating and mitigating circumstances are considered and that the judge determine whether such circumstances are present and thus whether the defendant should receive the death penalty. The judge, having heard further testimony from Ring's accomplice Greenham that Ring had premeditated and been the one to actually kill the driver, and having found the presence of aggravating circumstances, entered a "Special Verdict" sentencing Ring to death.

ISSUE: Does the Sixth Amendment require that a jury, not a judge, make the determination of the presence of an aggravating circumstance that elevates a punishment to death? YES.

HOLDING: The decision of whether to execute a defendant must be made by a jury. A judge may not alone make a determination of aggravating circumstances that elevate a punishment to death. Such aggravating circumstances are "the functional equivalent of an element of a greater offense" and therefore must be determined by a jury as required by the Sixth Amendment.

REASON: "In various settings, the Court has interpreted the Constitution to require the addition of an element or elements to the definition of a crime in order to narrow its scope. If a legislature responded to such a decision by adding the element the Court held constitutionally required, surely the Sixth Amendment guarantee would apply to that element. There is no reason to differentiate capital crimes from all others in this regard. Arizona's suggestion that judicial authority over the finding of aggravating factors may be a better way to guarantee against the arbitrary imposition of the death penalty is unpersuasive. The Sixth Amendment jury trial right does not turn on the relative rationality, fairness, or efficiency of potential factfinders. In any event, the superiority of judicial factfinding in capital cases is far from evident, given that the great majority of states responded to this Court's Eighth Amendment decisions requiring the presence of aggravating circumstances in capital cases by entrusting those determinations to the jury. Although stare decisis is of fundamental importance to the rule of law, this Court has overruled prior decisions where, as here, the necessity and propriety of doing so has been established."

Continued

RING v. ARIZONA 536 U.S. 584 (2002)—cont'd

"If a State makes an increase in a defendant's authorized punishment contingent on the finding of a fact, that fact—no matter how the State labels it—must be found by a jury beyond a reasonable doubt. A defendant may not be exposed to a penalty exceeding the maximum he would receive if punished according to the facts reflected in the jury verdict alone.... Based solely on the jury's verdict finding Ring guilty of first-degree felony murder, the maximum punishment he could have received was life imprisonment."

CASE SIGNIFICANCE: This is one of the most significant recent Supreme Court cases on the death penalty. It has the potential to be of great impact on states where judges are given the responsibility for making the final sentencing decision. Several state death penalty statutes give judges the authority to override the jury's sentencing "recommendation." In *Ring*, the Court held that, in accordance with *Apprendi v. New Jersey* (2000),[73] a jury must be the authority that makes the determination of the presence of aggravating factors that would elevate the sentence to death. For a judge to do so, as in *Ring*'s case, violates due process and the Sixth Amendment right to a jury trial. In effect, the judge made an independent finding that raised the level of the offense to one in which the death penalty was appropriate.

This decision invalidated all statutes giving judges sole discretion in the sentencing of convicted capital defendants. But the full impact of this decision on states in which judges play a partial role is not yet known. Nor is it known whether the decision will be retroactive, resulting in the invalidation of existing death sentences across the United States. Several states with sentencing schemes allowing judges a role in sentencing decisions have already begun to revise their statutes to comport with the *Ring* decision.

UTTECHT v. BROWN 551 U.S. 1 (2007)

CAPSULE: A trial court judge's determination that a juror's views on the death penalty would substantially impair his or her ability to consider a death sentence is sufficient to exclude the juror.

FACTS: Brown robbed, raped, and stabbed to death a Washington woman, then two days later robbed, raped, and attempted to murder a second woman in California. When apprehended, Brown confessed to these crimes and pleaded guilty to the crimes in California, for which he received a life sentence. He was subsequently tried for capital murder in Washington for the rape, robbery, and murder of the first victim. Brown was sentenced to death in the state of Washington.

The capital jury was selected over a period of several weeks, during which much time was devoted to the process of "death qualification." One juror (referred to as "Juror Z") was questioned extensively about his views on the death penalty and his perceived ability to fairly apply the law in deciding whether to impose the death penalty. Juror Z was excused for cause based on his general reluctance to consider the death penalty except in cases in which the defendant would likely re-offend if released from prison. Although Juror Z had answered that he could follow the law and impose the death penalty if warranted, the trial court judge determined that Juror Z was confused about the law and that his views and demeanor indicated that he was "substantially impaired" in his ability to do so. Brown's conviction and sentence were upheld by the Washington State Supreme Court. Brown filed a habeas corpus petition, which was denied by the U.S. District Court. The U.S. Court of Appeals for the Ninth Circuit rejected the federal district court's denial and reversed the lower court's sentence of death, holding that the exclusion of Juror Z was a violation of Brown's Sixth and Fourteenth Amendment rights.

ISSUE: Is a trial court judge's determination that a juror is substantially impaired in his or her ability to consider the sentence of death sufficient to remove that juror? YES.

Continued

---

[73]*Apprendi v. New Jersey, supra.*

UTTECHT v. BROWN 551 U.S. 1 (2007)—cont'd

HOLDING: Trial courts should be given deference in their ability to ascertain whether a prospective juror is substantially impaired in his or her ability to follow the law and consider the death penalty in the sentencing phase of capital trials.

REASON: "Juror Z's answers on their face could have led the trial court to believe that Juror Z would be substantially impaired in his ability to impose the death penalty in the absence of the possibility that Brown would be released and would reoffend. And the trial court, furthermore, is entitled to deference because it had an opportunity to observe the demeanor of Juror Z. We do not know anything about his demeanor, in part because a transcript cannot fully reflect that information but also because the defense did not object to Juror Z's removal. Nevertheless, the State's challenge, Brown's waiver of an objection, and the trial court's excusal of Juror Z support the conclusion that the interested parties present in the courtroom all felt that removing Juror Z was appropriate under the *Witherspoon-Witt* rule."

"Juror Z's assurances that he would consider imposing the death penalty and would follow the law do not overcome the reasonable inference from his other statements that in fact he would be substantially impaired in this case because there was no possibility of release. His assurances did not require the trial court to deny the State's motion to excuse Juror Z. The defense itself had told the trial court that any juror would make similar guarantees and that they were worth little; instead, defense counsel explained, the court should listen to arguments concerning the substance of the juror's answers. The trial court in part relied, as diligent judges often must, upon both parties' counsel to explain why a challenged juror's problematic beliefs about the death penalty would not rise to the level of substantial impairment. Brown's counsel offered no defense of Juror Z. In light of the deference owed to the trial court the position Brown now maintains does not convince us the decision to excuse Juror Z was unreasonable."

"Deference to the trial court is appropriate because it is in a position to assess the demeanor of the venire, and of the individuals who compose it, a factor of the critical importance in assessing the attitude and qualifications of potential jurors."

CASE SIGNIFICANCE: This case is significant in that it grants increased discretion to trial court judges in making the decision to exclude a juror for cause in the process of death qualification. It also relaxes the criteria for death qualification by setting the standard that a prospective juror's views about the death penalty may simply be perceived to "substantially limit" his or her ability to impose the death penalty if warranted. The Court notes that deference should be given to the trial court judge in that he or she is in the best position to gauge the attitude and demeanor of the prospective juror. The Court's decision represents a possible return to pre-*Witherspoon* standards in which prospective capital jurors could be excluded for expressing general qualms about or scruples against the death penalty. Dissenting justices and critics alike argue that this decision opens the door for arbitrariness and increases potential bias in capital juries.

Key Terms

Beck v. Alabama
death qualification
future dangerousness
guided discretion
jury instructions
jury override
jury selection
lesser included offenses
life without parole

Lockhart v. McCree
Mills v. Maryland
Morgan v. Illinois
Ring v. Arizona
Simmons v. South Carolina
Uttecht v. Brown
Weeks v. Angelone
Witherspoon v. Illinois

CRITICAL THINKING QUESTIONS

1. Consider the Supreme Court's notion that "death is different" and briefly list the ways in which this notion plays out in terms of capital juries. What Supreme Court decisions concerning capital juries seem to reinforce this notion? How?

2. Why, in your opinion, might it be important that a jury, rather than a judge, make the decision about whether or not to sentence someone to death? Are there advantages and disadvantages to each approach? What are they?

3. Imagine you are on a capital jury and must decide whether or not to sentence a defendant to death. What role would evidence of future dangerousness play in your decision? What role would information about parole eligibility play? Consider how you might weigh these factors in making your decision.

4. What is the legal reasoning for allowing the practice of "death qualification" in capital trials? What are potential problems with it?

Internet Resources

Capital Jury Project
www.albany.edu/scj/13192.php

Death Qualification
www.capitalpunishmentincontext.org/resources/deathqualification

Capital Jury Bibliography
www.kentlaw.iit.edu/institutes-centers/jury-center/selected-annotated-bibliography/capital-juries

Jury Instructions: Jurors' Understandings and Misunderstandings
www.capitalpunishmentincontext.org/issues/juryinstruct

Would You Be Chosen to Serve on a Jury?
http://deathpenaltycurriculum.org/student/c/courtroom/jury/question.htm

The Right to Effective Assistance of Counsel and the Death Penalty

7

CHAPTER OUTLINE

I INTRODUCTION

The Sixth Amendment to the United States Constitution states that "in all criminal prosecutions, the accused shall enjoy the right to have the assistance of counsel for his defense."[1] The Supreme Court has said that "of all the rights that an accused person has, the right to be represented by counsel is by far the most pervasive, for it affects his ability to assert any other rights he may have," *United States v. Cronic* (1984).[2] However, the right did not originally apply to all criminal defendants. Initially the Bill of Rights, which included the first 10 amendments, only applied to the actions of the federal government. However, the Supreme Court decided in *Powell v. Alabama* (1932)[3] that the right to effective assistance of counsel existed for indigent, capital defendants. It was not until about 30 years later, when the Court decided in *Gideon v. Wainright* (1963),[4] that this right automatically applied to all state defendants through the due process clause.

---

[1] U.S. CONST., AMEND. VI.
[2] *United States v. Cronic*, 466 U.S. 654 (1984).
[3] *Powell v. Alabama*, 287 U.S. 45 (1932).
[4] *Gideon v. Wainright*, 372 U.S. 335 (1963).

After *Gideon*, lower courts were only required to meet the minimum expectation that a criminal defendant be represented by counsel. The assumption, however, was that counsel was competent in every case. This fundamental protection was challenged in *McMann v. Richardson* (1970).[5] In *McMann*, the Court resolved the issue of whether the guilty pleas that had been made by three defendants were valid. In *McMann*, the Court took its first step toward acknowledging the difference between mere representation and effective assistance of counsel. The Court said that "if the right to counsel guaranteed by the Constitution is to serve its purpose, defendants cannot be left to the mercies of incompetent counsel."[6] The Court concluded that the claims made by the defendants were without merit because the attorneys had given them advice that was reasonably competent. The Court, however, did little to clarify this legal standard for the benefit of the lower courts. Throughout the 1970s and early 1980s, state courts were faced with making their own interpretations of "effective counsel" in light of *McMann*. This caused widespread disagreement among courts as to the meaning of the decision.

The Court has since made great strides toward clarifying the meaning of "effective counsel" under the Sixth Amendment. This chapter discusses the decisions of the Court dealing with a capital defendant's right to effective assistance of counsel. The landmark decision that clarified what is now known as "effective assistance of counsel" came in *Strickland v. Washington* (1984).[7] Developing a two-part test for making a determination of whether a capital defendant was provided ineffective assistance of counsel, the Court in *Strickland* said that such a claim was valid only if: (1) the counsel's performance was objectively unreasonable, and (2) there was a reasonable likelihood that the trial would have had a different outcome because of such performance. Using this approach, the Court has maintained that defendants bear a significant burden in proving that their counsel was ineffective. Several recent decisions reflect the Court's growing concern regarding access to counsel during post-conviction proceedings. In addition, the Court has provided more guidance regarding the standard for attorney incompetence in mitigation investigations. Indeed, the high volume of cases decided on right-to-counsel issues in 2011 and 2012 suggests that it merits the epithet "right-to-counsel" term.

II *STRICKLAND*: A TWO-PART TEST FOR DECIDING INEFFECTIVE ASSISTANCE CLAIMS

Prior to 1984, the Court did not have a definitive test for assessing ineffective assistance of counsel claims. Instead, the Court deferred authority to state and lower federal courts to decide matters arising from ineffectiveness of counsel. *Strickland* (1984) established a clear test for analyzing a defendant's Sixth Amendment claim of ineffective assistance of counsel. In *Strickland*, the defendant committed a series of stabbing murders. He was convicted and given the death penalty. Strickland's habeas corpus claim alleged that his trial counsel failed to present character witnesses or psychiatric testimony as mitigating evidence for him during his sentencing. Instead, his counsel chose not to present such evidence "in order to prevent the state from cross-examining Washington about his background or putting forth psychiatric testimony."[8] Defense counsel also feared that any character testimony given during sentencing could have harsh consequences for his client, a judgment call by the attorney.

---

[5]*McMann v. Richardson*, 397 U.S. 759 (1970).
[6]*Id.*, at 771.
[7]*Strickland v. Washington*, 466 U.S. 668 (1984).
[8]Gross, David, *Supreme Court Review: Sixth Amendment—Defendant's Dual Burden in Claims of Ineffective Assistance of Counsel:* Strickland v. Washington, 75 Crim. L. & Criminology 755 (1984).

On appeal, the Court held that a claim for ineffective assistance of counsel must demonstrate the following: (1) counsel's performance was deficient, and (2) such deficiency prejudiced the defendant's case. This means that there must be a reasonable probability that the attorney's errors caused the wrong decision. The Court said that in the practice of law there is a presumption that an attorney's performance, knowledge, and decisions are to be considered reasonable. Recognizing the fact that an attorney's legal tactics may vary depending on the circumstances, the Court refused to adopt a more rigid standard for determining what constitutes "unreasonable" representation.

Instead of developing concrete guidelines for lower courts to follow, the *Strickland* Court gave the states the authority to define the meaning of "unreasonable" representation. The Court, however, went no further than to say that the failure to present character witnesses or psychiatric testimony as mitigating factors during sentencing did not, in itself, constitute ineffective assistance of counsel in violation of the Sixth Amendment.

III INEFFECTIVE ASSISTANCE OF COUNSEL AND THE AEDPA

Capital defendants making ineffective assistance of counsel claims were dramatically impacted by the passage of the Antiterrorism and Effective Death Penalty Act (AEDPA) of 1996. This law significantly affects death penalty defendants because it restricts their ability to file habeas corpus claims in federal courts.

Traditionally, habeas corpus is a way in which state and federal prisoners may challenge their conviction by demanding new trials, even while they are incarcerated. Having its heritage in English common law, the writ evolved to become one of America's most sacred legal avenues for criminal defendants, particularly capital defendants.[9] Originally, the writ applied only to federal prisoners. However, in 1867 Congress passed the Habeas Corpus Act,[10] which extended the authority of habeas corpus petitions to state prisoners. Specifically, the Act held that any federal court could issue the writ in "cases where any person may be restrained of his or her liberty in violation of the Constitution."[11]

Today, federal courts draw their authority to issue habeas writs from the Constitution. Federal habeas procedure is codified at 28 U.S.C. §§ 2241–2255.[12] Section 2254 of that title specifically deals with the authority of the federal courts to hear federal challenges by state inmates. As the federal courts became inundated with cases arising from state challenges, the federal government decided that habeas corpus writs needed to be streamlined so that only the meritorious cases reached the federal bench. In 1996, President Bill Clinton signed the AEDPA, which has since served this purpose. The passage of the AEDPA and the amendment of § 2254(d) had the most substantial impact on death penalty defendants. The law mandates that federal judges consider state rulings regarding death penalty cases to be correct; however, there are instances in which capital defendants can succeed in a legitimate claim.

---

[9]Walker, Stuart, *"What We Meant Was . . ."* : *The Supreme Court Clarifies Two Ineffective Assistance Cases in* Bell v. Cone, 54 MERCER L. REV. 1271 (2003).
[10]14 STAT. at 385 (1867).
[11]*Id.*
[12]Walker, *supra* note 9, at 3.

The AEDPA prohibits a capital defendant from making a successful claim unless the state proceeding "resulted in a decision that was contrary to, or involved an unreasonable application of, clearly established federal law, as determined by the Supreme Court of the United States."[13] Section 2254 (d)(1) reads:

> *(d) A determination . . . made by a State court . . . of competent jurisdiction . . . shall be presumed to be correct, unless the applicant shall establish or it shall otherwise appear . . .*
> *(1) that the merits of the factual dispute were not resolved in the State court hearing.*

One important case that involved the right to counsel and this specific provision of the AEDPA came before the Court in *Williams v. Taylor* (2000).[14] Williams had been convicted of capital murder and filed a habeas corpus petition alleging that he had been held unconstitutionally. Williams asserted that his attorney had failed to make an adequate investigation and thus was unable to present important mitigating evidence on his behalf during sentencing. In deciding *Williams*, the Court expanded on a previous habeas corpus case—*Teague v. Lane* (1989).[15] In *Teague*, the Court restricted habeas relief for capital defendants by ruling that an individual using a collateral attack may not rely on a federal law that was not in existence at the time of initial conviction. For capital defendants, this meant that any court ruling or federal law established after the conviction could not be the basis of a successful habeas claim. The *Williams* Court, in relying on *Teague*, claimed that state courts do not violate the "unreasonable application" phrase codified in § 2254 of the AEDPA when they choose the correct rule of law but apply it incorrectly. Because the Supreme Court was only permitted to settle issues of law rather than fact, the Court said that "federal courts were not permitted to disturb the judgment of state courts for merely applying the law incorrectly."[16] Although Williams's claim prevailed in the Supreme Court, the decision effectively promoted the goal of the AEDPA by significantly limiting a capital defendant's chances of sustaining a habeas corpus claim.

Lower courts have traditionally used two approaches to deciding issues of ineffective assistance of counsel in death penalty cases—one based on performance and the other on the principle of agency.[17] The latter approach is much narrower in scope, and the Supreme Court has made clear that simple negligence on the part of an attorney is not enough to overcome a procedural default that occurs in habeas proceedings. Procedural errors that take place in state court proceedings, such as failing to raise claims or meet filing deadlines, can prohibit a petitioner from pursuing those claims further in federal court; this is known as "procedural default." In recent years the Supreme Court has decided a number of cases involving this issue and the application of the AEDPA to claims of ineffective assistance of counsel. The following group of cases illustrates the Court's use of the performance model (*Strickland*) to decide claims of attorney incompetence: *Holland v. Florida* (2010),[18] *Martel v. Clair* (2012),[19] and *Martinez v. Ryan* (2012).[20] In *Maples v. Thomas* (2012),[21] on the other hand, the Court applied the

---

[13]28 U.S.C. § 2254 (d)(1).
[14]*Williams v. Taylor*, 529 U.S. 362 (2000).
[15]*Teague v. Lane*, 490 U.S. 1031 (1989).
[16]Walker, *supra* note 9, at 4.
[17]Zupac, Wendy, *Mere Negligence or Abandonment? Evaluating Claims of Attorney Misconduct After* Maples v. Thomas, 122 Yale L.J. 1328 (2013).
[18]*Holland v. Florida*, 560 U.S. 2549 (2010).
[19]*Martel v. Clair*, 182 L. Ed. 2d 135.
[20]*Martinez v. Ryan*, 182 L. Ed. 2d 272.
[21]*Maples v. Thomas*, 181 L. Ed. 2d 807.

agency or relationship model to decide the outcome of the case. *Trevino v. Thaler* (2013)[22] also involved the application of the AEDPA but focused on the state's appellate procedure governing ineffective assistance of counsel claims.

Albert Holland was represented by Collins, a state-appointed attorney, in state and federal habeas proceedings. While his petition was under review in state court, Holland "wrote Collins letters asking him to make certain that all of his claims would be preserved for any subsequent federal habeas corpus review."[23] Holland became dismayed by the lack of communication from Collins and attempted to petition the Florida Supreme Court for substitution of counsel. However, Holland was prohibited from communicating directly with the Court because he was represented by counsel. Five weeks after the deadline had passed to file his federal habeas petition, Holland submitted his own pro se petition to the federal district court, which was dismissed for failing to meet the deadline.

The Supreme Court held that a prisoner is entitled to equitable tolling of filing procedures if he can demonstrate (1) "that he has been pursuing his rights diligently, and (2) that some extraordinary circumstance stood in his way' and prevented timely filing."[24] The Court concluded that the attorney's failure to communicate and satisfy professional standards of care were extraordinary circumstances justifying an exception to the normal filing procedures. The Court further delineated between simple negligence and "egregious" conduct that warrants equitable tolling of the statute. The Court's opinion was supported by an amicus brief filed by legal ethics scholars who contended that Collins had "violated fundamental canons of professional responsibility" set forth in case law, the Restatements of Agency, and the American Bar Association's Model Rules of Professional Conduct.[25]

The Court's decision in *Holland* applied to an egregious set of circumstances. The Court also used the performance-based model to evaluate defense counsel's effectiveness in *Martel v. Clair* (2012), although the outcome of the case was different. In this case, the Court addressed whether a death penalty defendant is allowed to replace his court-appointed attorney with another court-appointed attorney because he is dissatisfied and claims his attorney failed to investigate evidence that was potentially valuable. Clair had written a letter to the court requesting substitution of counsel, and the court made inquiry to Clair's counsel of record, who informed the Court that he had spoken with his client and that Clair was willing to allow the attorney to represent him for the time being. On the eve of denying the writ of habeas corpus, the federal court clerk received a letter from a private investigator who informed the court of potentially important physical evidence that had not been tested. Clair claimed his attorney of record knew that this evidence existed. The federal court denied the petition and the Ninth Circuit reversed. In delivering the opinion of the Court, Justice Elena Kagan held that the "interest of justice" standard guides decisions regarding the substitution of counsel in death penalty cases. However, the majority reasoned that at the time the request for substitution came to the district court's attention, "counsel could do nothing more in the proceedings and any conflict with counsel no longer mattered."[26]

To understand the implications of these cases, it is first necessary to realize that in *Coleman v. Thompson* (1991)[27] the Court held there is no constitutional right to effective assistance of counsel

---

[22]*Trevino v. Thaler*, 133 S. Ct. 1911 (2013).

[23]*Holland,* at 2555.

[24]*Holland,* at 2564 (quoting *Pace v. DiGuglielmo*, 544 U.S. 408, 418 (2005)).

[25]*Holland,* at 2564 (citing Brief for Legal Ethics Professors et al. as Amici Curiae). Support of Petitioner, *Holland*, 130 S. Ct. 2549 (No. 09-5327), 2009 WL 5177143).

[26]*Clair,* at 1288.

[27]501 U.S. 722 (1991).

in state post-conviction proceedings. However, in that case the Court did not resolve the issue of whether errors committed by trial counsel could be litigated in state post-conviction proceedings when such is the first opportunity to address issues of ineffective assistance of counsel. Although not a death penalty case, this was the issue in *Martinez v. Ryan*.[28]

Arizona law prohibited Martinez from raising a claim of ineffective assistance of counsel on direct appeal. Claims of this nature could only be litigated in the first instance on collateral relief. Martinez's state-appointed counsel filed a petition for state post-conviction review but did not raise an ineffective assistance of counsel claim in the petition; his petition was dismissed. New pro bono counsel for Martinez filed a second petition for post-conviction relief, on this occasion citing numerous claims of attorney incompetence. The state courts, however, found these claims to be procedurally defaulted because they were not, but could have been, raised in the initial post-conviction proceeding.

Martinez argued that his initial appellate attorney's omission constituted "cause" to forgive the procedural default. However, his claim was barred by *Thompson*, at least according to the lower federal courts. In delivering its opinion of the Supreme Court, Justice Anthony Kennedy held that ineffective assistance of post-conviction counsel resulting in a procedural default does not preclude a petitioner from raising that claim in federal court, at least for states that require the claim to be raised post-conviction.

In contrast to cases taking a performance-based approach, the Court's decision in *Maples v. Thomas* (2012) is an example of an agency, or relationship-based, approach. The issue in this case was whether the appellate court correctly held that no "cause" existed to excuse a procedural default when the state and not the petitioner was to blame for the default and counsel had abandoned the petitioner at the time of the default. In granting habeas review, the Supreme *Maples* Court held that the current facts were quite different from those in *Coleman*, the latter of which held that "the ineffectiveness of post-conviction appellate counsel could not qualify as cause."[29] The *Maples* Court concluded that in this situation counsel had severed the attorney-client relationship and thus the agency principles that normally excuse an attorney's conduct did not apply. Therefore, when a prisoner is "disarmed by extraordinary circumstances quite beyond his control,"[30] he has established sufficient cause to overcome a procedural default.

In 2013, the *Martinez* decision was again the central focus of a death penalty case involving AEDPA procedures, although this time the issue was more about procedure than the conduct of defense counsel. In *Trevino v. Thaler* (2013)[31] the Court addressed the issue of whether a procedural default prevents an ineffective assistance of counsel claim when the state's procedure makes it virtually impossible for appellate counsel to make an ineffective assistance claim on direct review. Trevino was convicted of capital murder in Texas and sentenced to death. There was no attempt by his attorneys in direct appeal or on collateral review to raise the issue that his trial counsel had failed to conduct an adequate investigation and present mitigating factors on his behalf at sentencing. The Texas procedure did not present counsel with a meaningful opportunity to make a colorable claim, because of time constraints related to filing deadlines, motions, and the availability of trial transcripts. The normal practice called for ineffective assistance claims to be raised during state collateral review. Because Trevino did not

---

[28]*Martinez v. Ryan*, 566 U.S. ____ (2012).
[29]*Maples*, at 921, Quoting *Coleman v. Thompson*, 501 U.S. 722 (1991).
[30]*Id.*, at 923.
[31]*Trevino v. Thaler*, 133 S. Ct. 1911 (2013).

raise the issue on initial collateral review, the state court found his claim defaulted. The federal district court concluded that the state procedural default barred federal habeas review because it was not raised on initial collateral review. The Fifth Circuit affirmed.

On writ of certiorari to the Fifth Circuit, the Supreme Court held that the rule adopted in *Martinez* applies where a state's procedural framework makes it extremely difficult to make a meaningful claim of ineffective assistance of trial counsel claim. *Thaler* is significant because it expands the holding in *Martinez* to states that have procedures that create unfairness and are not in harmony with AEDPA requirements.

The Court has historically employed two analytical approaches to analyze claims of ineffective assistance of counsel. In *Holland, Clair,* and *Martinez*, the Court adopted a performance-based approach, but in *Maples* it employed a relationship approach. *Thaler* does not fit neatly within either framework—it represents the Court's general concern that the procedures used in some states are unfair and make it difficult for habeas petitioners to successfully raise claims of ineffective assistance of counsel. The use of different approaches to decide ineffective assistance of counsel claims is not unique to the Supreme Court. Before these cases were decided, circuit courts used different models to decide whether counsel's ineffectiveness was sufficient to excuse the restrictions imposed by the AEDPA. In each of these cases the Supreme Court loosened the restrictions on AEDPA procedures enabling death penalty petitioners to obtain habeas relief in the federal courts.

IV REPRESENTATION FOR INDIGENT CAPITAL DEFENDANTS

Following the Supreme Court's decision in *Gideon v. Wainright* (1963),[32] research began to reveal the poor quality of representation afforded to indigent capital defendants.[33] This research has shown the impact of poor funding at the local level and the perverse problems associated with "incompetent or inexperienced" attorneys; long delays in securing representation for death penalty defendants; a lack of a coherent system for training, staffing, and appointing defense counsel, and unmanageable caseloads.[34] Budget reductions at the local, state, and federal level are primary sources of these problems. In 2011 the Justice Policy Institute indicated that "public defense has been historically underfunded and overburdened since *Gideon*; however, the recent economic downturn and fiscal/budget crises have made it worse."[35] It is estimated that about 80% of criminal defendants are indigent.[36] Furthermore, given the current fiscal climate, the ability to provide adequate defense to capital defendants is significantly more difficult because death penalty trials are so much more expensive than typical criminal prosecutions. Although the body of law defining ineffective assistance of counsel has evolved quite dramatically over the years, the performance of defense counsel is ultimately contingent on resources that are needed to provide effective assistance.

---

[32]*Gideon v. Wainright,* 372 U.S. 335 (1963).

[33]The Constitution Project, Nat'l Right to Counsel Comm., *Justice Denied: America's Continuing Neglect of Our Constitutional Right to Counsel* 50 (2009).

[34]Lucas, Lauren S., *Reclaiming Equality to Reframe Indigent Defense Reform*, 97 MINN. L. REV. 1197 (2013).

[35]Justice Policy Inst., *System Overload: The Costs of Under-Resourcing Public Defense* 8 (2011).

[36]Cohen, Thomas H., *Who's Better at Defending Criminals? Does Type of Defense Attorney Matter in Terms of Producing Favorable Case Outcomes*, BUREAU OF JUSTICE STATISTICS 14 (2011), http://papers.ssrn.com/sol3/papers.cfm?abstract_id=1876474&download=yes.

The issue of whether federal funding should be provided for federally appointed counsel in state clemency hearings was the focus of the Supreme Court's decision in *Harbison v. Bell* (2009).[37] In that case, petitioner Harbison argued that the Terrorist Death Penalty Enhancement Act of 2005 authorizes funding for state prisoners in clemency proceedings. The Court held that Section 3599 of that law authorizes federally appointed counsel to represent defendants in state clemency proceedings and that they shall be compensated for their representation. The Court decision expands the right to counsel for indigent defendants in state clemency proceedings—an issue that has drawn different interpretations from circuit courts.

As discussed previously, the Court has refused to extend the right to effective counsel during post-conviction review, where mistakes can be disastrous.[38] However, the recent decisions in *Maples, Martinez,* and *Clair* indicate the Court's acknowledgment of the need for effective assistance of counsel in post-conviction proceedings. Although the Court refused to extend the right to effective assistance during post-conviction review, these decisions are important, given the limited availability of resources for indigent criminal defense across the states.

Some examples illustrate the impact of reduced funding and downsizing of public defender units across the country. The Supreme Court of Washington recently implemented limits to public defender caseloads due to the extraordinarily high number of cases each attorney was handling on a yearly basis.[39] Another case involving extreme action taken in response to budget cuts occurred in New Orleans, where approximately 10% of the attorney staff was cut, in addition to the amount of funding reduced for appointed counsel in death penalty cases. At the federal level, one public defender in Pennsylvania declined to represent death penalty defendant Jessie Con-Ui, who is alleged to have murdered a federal correctional guard in Waymart.[40] The impact of mandatory furlough requirements and fewer resources available to public defender units across the nation has also been felt with respect to mitigation work—another topic that has received extensive attention from courts as well as organizations such as the American Bar Association.

V DEFENSE COUNSEL'S DUTY TO INVESTIGATE AND DEFEND

Since the decision in *Strickland*, the Court has not granted many writs of habeas corpus for claims of ineffective assistance of counsel. However, following the Court's decision in *Wiggins v. Smith* (2003),[41] the Supreme Court became much more attuned to claims involving attorney incompetence, particularly with regard to the quality of mitigation work at sentencing. In large part this increased attention is reflective of funding problems at the local level as well as an overall lack of knowledge on the part of defense attorneys on how to adequately investigate the social backgrounds of their clients. The American Bar Association's standards provided some support in this regard, but recent cases

---

[37]*Harbison v. Bell*, 556 U.S. 180 (2009).

[38]Durocher, Christopher, *Are We Closer to Fulfilling Gideon's Promise? The Effects of the Supreme Court's "Right to Counsel Term,"* AMERICAN CONSTITUTION FOR LAW AND POLICY, January 2013.

[39]Johnson, Gene, *Wash. Cities Grapple with New Public Defense Rules,* ASSOCIATED PRESS, June 25, 2012, http://seattletimes.com/html/localnews/2018528020_apwapublicdefense.html.

[40]Morgan-Besecker, Terrie, *Budget Cuts Decimating Public Defender Offices,* THE TIMES-TRIBUNE, http://thetimes-tribune.com/news/budget-cuts-decimating-federal-public-defender-offices-1.1527554.

[41]*Wiggins v. Smith*, 539 U.S. 510 (2003).

illustrate the Court's struggle to establish clear guidelines for lower courts to follow when deciding whether defense counsel's performance is considered unconstitutional within the meaning of *Strickland*. In the *Wiggins* decision, the Court gave new substance to protections under the Sixth Amendment and opened the door for what would become one of the overriding death penalty issues that would occupy the Supreme Court's time in the coming years.

In 1989, Kevin Wiggins was convicted of first-degree murder, robbery, and two counts of larceny. He was subsequently sentenced to death for committing a capital offense. Wiggins filed a habeas corpus case based on ineffective assistance of counsel. At his original trial, Wiggins was represented by two public defenders who allegedly performed an inadequate investigation by failing to uncover his "dysfunctional background."[42]

His new counsel later found that Wiggins had been the victim of physical and sexual abuse as a child and a young adolescent. This, however, was never raised as a mitigating factor during his original sentencing. At his habeas proceeding, the original public defenders testified that they chose not to investigate the dysfunctional background of Wiggins because their focus was to dispute his actual culpability for the murder. Furthermore, the attorneys claimed that this was simply a tactical decision, not an act of negligence.

On appeal, the Supreme Court held that the Maryland Supreme Court unreasonably applied the two-pronged test set forth in *Strickland*. The Court said that the performance of the attorneys "fell short of professional norms"[43] because they failed to adequately investigate the mitigating evidence that existed, which prejudiced Wiggins' defense. The Court claimed that it was routine practice in Maryland at that time to conduct a background investigation of a capital defendant's history prior to sentencing. The Supreme Court also referred to standards developed by the American Bar Association, which call for an adequate investigation into potential mitigating evidence that could be presented at a defendant's sentencing hearing. Because the public defenders had acquired only "rudimentary knowledge"[44] of Wiggins's social history, the Court viewed their performance to be constitutionally deficient. The Supreme Court differentiated *Wiggins* from previous cases in which defense counsel failed to present mitigating evidence for the defendant. The Supreme Court cited *Burger v. Kemp* (1987),[45] in which the court found that a limited investigation was reasonable because the majority of the evidence that could potentially have been presented would have had a harmful outcome on the defendant's case, and *Darden v. Wainwright* (1986),[46] in which the Court said that the defense attorney's decision not to present mitigating evidence was reasonable because it would have revealed damaging testimony that would have harmed the defendant's case.

In *Rompilla v. Beard* (2005),[47] the Court revisited the importance of counsel's responsibility to develop and present adequate mitigating evidence for capital defendants during sentencing. The Supreme Court held that defense counsel's failure to investigate Rompilla's prior charge for rape and assault constituted ineffective assistance of counsel in violation of the Sixth Amendment. Applying *Strickland*'s two-part test, the Court ruled that counsel's duty was more than common sense, but that, at minimum, the

---

[42]*Wiggins v. Smith*, 123 S. Ct. at 2532.
[43]*Id.*, at 2542–44.
[44]*Id.*, at 2537.
[45]*Burger v. Kemp*, 483 U.S. 776 (1987).
[46]*Darden v. Wainright*, 477 U.S. 168 (1986).
[47]*Rompilla v. Beard*, 545 U.S. 374 (2005).

American Bar Association required defense attorneys to examine the prosecutor's case file for possible mitigating leads. Finding that counsel's performance was constitutionally deficient, the Court then had to decide whether counsel's errors biased the defendant's case. The Court cited numerous factors supporting the argument that trial counsel failed to build an adequate mitigating case, such as the omission of school, medical, and imprisonment records indicating a long history of antisocial and mentally unstable behavior. The Court noted post-conviction counsel's link between this evidence and Rompilla's abusive childhood, which bore "no relation to the few naked pleas for mercy actually put before the jury."[48] However, trial counsel never explored these issues in depth. Taking these issues into consideration, the Court decided that the evidence "might well have influenced the jury's appraisal of culpability."[49]

The Court has traditionally granted defense attorneys considerable latitude in preparing the best legal strategy for their clients. Reiterating this stance, Justice Kennedy, arguing for the dissent, claimed the Court was wrong to conclude that defense counsel's investigation of mitigating evidence was incompetent. Relying on *Strickland*, Justice Kennedy cited the need to avoid "the temptations of analysis through hindsight."[50] Justice Kennedy opined that trial counsel's strategy was reasonable because evidence of Rompilla's upbringing and mental condition was best substantiated through testimony from the three mental health professionals, Rompilla himself, and his family. Since all of these sources were tapped during his original trial, counsel had no duty to review the prosecutor's conviction file, and therefore counsel's performance was adequate. The dissent went on to say that even assuming trial counsel's performance was deficient, Rompilla was not entitled to habeas relief because the conviction record was found in an initial transfer petition, which was an obscure document located in the prosecutor's file. As a result, Justice Kennedy concluded that the majority imposed an inflexible standard on defense attorneys, defying wisdom and existing case law.

A ABA Guidelines: A New Model for Conducting Mitigation Investigations

Shortly after the Court's decision in *Williams* indicating that death penalty counsel is required to conduct an investigation into the defendant's background and social history, the American Bar Association started to revise its *Guidelines for the Appointment and Performance of Defense Counsel in Death Penalty Cases* ("ABA Guidelines").[51] Although the previous version of the Guidelines suggested that investigations into mitigating factors "should comprise efforts to discover all reasonably available mitigating evidence and evidence to rebut any aggravating evidence that may be introduced by the prosecutor,"[52] the new version was much more specific about the nature and scope of the investigation. Moreover, the more detailed guidelines were implemented to provide more clarity to defense counsel who continued to conduct less than adequate mitigation investigations, despite the Court's decision in *Williams*.[53] Although capital attorneys were aware of the impact of mitigation evidence at sentencing, they just "did not know how to do it properly."[54]

---

[48]*Id.*

[49]*Id.*, at 2469.

[50]*Id.*, at 2478.

[51]Guidelines for the Appointment & Performance of Def. Counsel in Death Penalty Cases (rev. ed. 2003).

[52]Guidelines for the Appointment & Performance of Def. Counsel in Death Penalty Cases guideline 11.4.1(C) (1989).

[53]Haugh, Todd, *Can the CEO Learn From the Condemned? The Application of Capital Mitigation Strategies to White-Collar Cases*, 62 Am. U.L. Rev. 1 (2012).

[54]Maher, Robin M., *The ABA and the Supplementary Guidelines for the Mitigation Function of Defense Teams in Death Penalty Cases*, 36 Hofstra L. Rev. 763, 770 (2008).

The revised guidelines gave defense counsel detailed instructions on how to construct a mitigation case. To begin, they were required to increase and reorganize their defense teams. Staff now had to include an individual qualified to diagnose mental disorders, a mitigation "specialist," an investigator, and a minimum of two defense counsel. In addition, investigations into mitigating factors were required, even when the client failed to provide support. And last, the new rules acknowledged that a proper mitigation investigation required a thorough canvass of the defendant's background and social history "from the moment of conception." Although the Court had provided guidance to capital defense counsel on the types of mitigating evidence considered most crucial, the ABA rules established an informal policy for the defense team to follow. The new recommendations marked a turning point for capital defense as courts approved and enforced their rules.

In 2008, the ABA provided further guidance in developing mitigation cases when it published the *Supplementary Guidelines for the Mitigation Function of Defense Teams in Death Penalty Cases* ("Supplemental Guidelines").[55] Among other things, the Supplementary Guidelines provided capital defense counsel with a detailed list of factors for mitigation specialists to investigate:

> *Mitigation evidence includes, but is not limited to, compassionate factors stemming from the diverse frailties of humankind, the ability to make a positive adjustment to incarceration, the realities of incarceration and the actual meaning of a life sentence, capacity for redemption, remorse, execution impact, vulnerabilities related to mental health, explanations of patterns of behavior, negation of aggravating evidence regardless of its designation as an aggravating factor, positive acts or qualities, responsible conduct in other areas of life (e.g. employment, education, military service, as a family member), any evidence bearing on the degree of moral culpability, and any other reason for a sentence less than death.[56]*

To add to this list of factors, the Supplemental Guidelines suggested that the mitigation specialist develop this information through "in-person, face-to-face, one-on-one interviews." Documentation of the evidence was to come from multiple sources (witness statements, interviews, school records, etc.) and present a complete profile of the defendant's social history. Collectively, the new directives were intended to ensure that capital defendants received an adequate defense by taking the sole responsibility of developing a mitigation case from one person and allowing multiple experts to collect the information. Although these guidelines are not binding on attorneys, they do provide guidance for those representing capital defendants.

B Recent Cases Challenging the Adequacy of Mitigation Defense Work

Several cases regarding the efficacy of mitigation investigations have been decided since the 2009 Supplemental Guidelines were implemented. In several cases—*Wood v. Allen* (2010),[57] *Bobby v. Van Hook* (2009),[58] *Wong v. Belmontes* (2009), *Smith v. Spisak* (2010),[59] and *Cullen v. Pinholster* (2011)[60]—the Court held that the investigation was adequate or, if inadequate, did not justify reversing a death sentence.

---

[55]*Supplementary Guidelines for the Mitigation Function of Defense Teams in Death Penalty Cases*, 36 Hofstra L. Rev. 677 (2008).
[56]*Supra Note*, at 679.
[57]*Wood v. Allen*, 130 S. Ct. 841 (2010).
[58]*Bobby v. Van Hook*, 130 S. Ct. 13 (2009).
[59]*Smith v. Spisak*, 130 S. Ct. 676 (2010).
[60]*Cullen v. Pinholster*, 131 S.Ct. 1388 (2011).

In contrast, *Sears v. Upton* (2010),[61] *Porter v. McCollum* (2009),[62] and *Jefferson v. Upton* (2010)[63] reflect the Court's interpretations of inadequacy and bias associated with mitigation investigations. This section discusses the implications of these cases and highlights the challenges the Court faces in resolving the complexities of mitigation work.

In *Wood v. Allen* (2010), petitioner Wood entered his former girlfriend's house and killed her while she was asleep in bed. The least experienced attorney on Wood's trial team, who "had been admitted to the bar five months before the time he was appointed,"[64] was assigned to run the penalty phase of the trial. Wood was eventually convicted and sentenced to death. The central issue in Wood's federal habeas case was whether his attorney's decision not to present evidence of Wood's mental retardation to the jury was considered "strategic." The state court found that the decision was in fact strategic, but the federal district court disagreed. On habeas review, the Supreme Court ruled that although it may have been "debatable" that defense counsel's decision was strategic, the state did not make "an unreasonable determination of the facts in light of the evidence presented in the state-court proceedings."[65]

Like *Wood*, the *Van Hook* Court determined that it was not unreasonable for the lower court to conclude that the defense attorney's decision not to present certain mitigating evidence was reasonable. Van Hook murdered his victim after he went to a bar that "catered to homosexual men, hoping to find someone to rob."[66] His defense attorney called eight witnesses to testify on Van Hook's behalf. In comparing the attorney's performance in this case to that in *Wiggins* and *Rompilla*, the Court concluded "this is not a case in which the defendant's attorneys failed to act while potentially powerful mitigating evidence stared them in the face."[67] The Court further reasoned that the attorney's performance was compatible with prevailing professional norms that were in place at the time of Van Hook's trial. The Court criticized the Sixth Circuit for relying on ethical standards that were published 18 years after the petitioner's trial. It cautioned that "'American Bar Association standards and the like' are 'only guides' to what reasonableness means, not its definition."[68]

Although the Court's analysis of *Wood* and *Van Hook* centered on the competency of the mitigation investigation, *Wong v. Belmontes* (2009) involved a debate among the lower courts on whether the incomplete investigation biased the petitioner's case. During the commission of a burglary, Belmontes killed the victim by "striking her in the head 15 to 20 times with a steel dumbbell bar."[69] After committing the murder, Belmontes and his accomplices stole a stereo from the victim, "sold it for $100, and used the money to buy beer and drugs for the night."[70] On habeas review, petitioner Belmontes claimed that his attorney's failure to present certain mitigating evidence at sentencing unconstitutionally prejudiced his case. The defense attorney chose not to present testimony indicating Belmontes's lack of propensity toward violence, because that would have opened the door for the defense attorney to introduce rebuttal evidence indicating his involvement in a prior murder case. Instead, defense called nine

---

[61]*Sears v. Upton*, 130 S. Ct. 3259 (2010).
[62]*Porter v. McCollum,* 130 S. Ct. 447 (2009).
[63]*Jefferson v. Upton*, 130 S. Ct. 2217 (2010).
[64]*Wood*, at 854.
[65]*Id.,* at 845.
[66]*Bobby v. Van Hook*, 130 S.Ct. at 15.
[67]*Id.,* at 19.
[68]*Id.,* at 17.
[69]*Wong*, at 384.
[70]*Id.*

witnesses to testify regarding the petitioner's troubled childhood and religious conversion in prison. The Court held that although defense counsel's performance was deficient, it was unlikely that the sentence would have been different had all the aggravating and mitigating evidence been introduced at his sentencing.

Smith v. Spisak (2010)[71] involved another claim of constitutionally ineffective counsel at sentencing. Spisak was convicted of murdering four people at Cleveland State University in 1983. He entered a plea of not guilty by reason of insanity, at one point claiming to be a disciple of Adolf Hitler. During closing arguments, Spisak's attorney elaborated about the gruesome nature of the murders and downplayed his client's mental illness as a mitigating factor. On habeas review, the federal district court viewed the strategy as "an appropriate part of trial counsel's strategy to confront the heinousness of the murders before the prosecution had the opportunity to do so."[72]

On appeal to the Supreme Court, the Ohio attorney general maintained that the attorney's strategy was "reasonable when viewed from counsel's perspective at the time."[73] In an amicus curiae brief, a group of well-known law professors argued that Spisak's closing strategy exacerbated the risk of a death sentence for his client and was "below any reasonable measure of professional competence."[74] They further opined that to conclude that counsel's strategy was anything but deficient "would teach generations of future lawyers incorrect lessons about how to present a case"[75] and would undermine the purpose of the Sixth Amendment.

Despite the arguments chastising Spisak's performance, the Court found no Sixth Amendment violation. Justice Stephen Breyer reasoned that, in light of the fact that Spisak had admitted to the killings and intended to "create terror" by using racial profiling to target victims, there was no "reasonable probability" that an argument without these deficiencies would have resulted in a better outcome for Spisak.

In *Cullen v. Pinholster* (2011),[76] the issue before the Supreme Court was whether a federal habeas court may consider evidence unavailable to a state court when deciding whether an attorney's performance is constitutionally deficient. Pinholster sought habeas relief after having been convicted of two counts of murder. At sentencing, the state presented eight witnesses who testified regarding Pinholster's previous criminal history and disciplinary actions in prison. Pinholster's attorney requested and obtained an evaluation from a psychiatrist who diagnosed Pinholster with antisocial personality disorder. The psychiatrist determined that Pinholster was not affected by any significant "emotional disturbance" at the time the crimes occurred. Moreover, the only mitigating evidence offered by Pinholster's attorney was testimony from his mother.

On state habeas review, Pinholster argued that his attorney's performance was ineffective because the mitigation investigation was inadequate. At this proceeding he presented more extensive information as mitigating evidence to include legal, medical, and school records. In addition, habeas counsel obtained a second evaluation from Pinholster that diagnosed him with bipolar mood disorder as well as seizure disorders. After hearing this evidence, the California Supreme Court denied relief.

---

[71]*Smith v. Spisak*, 130 S. Ct. 676 (2010).
[72]*Spisak v. Hudson,* 512 F.3d 852 (2008).
[73]Brief of Petitioner at 36, *Smith v. Spisak*, 130 S. Ct. 676 (2010).
[74]Brief of Stephen Lubet et al. as Amici Curiae in Support of Respondent at 2–3, *Smith v. Spisak*, 130 S. Ct. 676 (2010).
[75]*Id.*
[76]131 S.Ct. 1388 (2011).

During federal habeas proceedings, counsel for Pinholster presented a declaration from the first psychiatrist indicating that, based on the new information available in the medical and school records, he would have diagnosed Pinholster as having brain damage. After having the claim denied again by the state court, Pinholster was granted an evidentiary hearing, where he presented further evidence of mental abnormalities. The District Court granted relief, and the Ninth circuit affirmed. However, the Supreme Court held that review by a federal court is limited to the record before the state court that adjudicated the claim, and any new evidence that comes to light during an evidentiary hearing cannot be considered. Thus, Pinholster's habeas claim failed.

In addition to those cases not resulting in successful ineffective assistance of counsel claims, three additional cases illustrate the Court's interpretation of incompetent mitigation investigations. *Sears v. Upton* (2010)[77] involved a murder that took place during the course of an armed robbery and kidnapping. At sentencing, Sears's defense attorney presented mitigating evidence "describing his childhood as stable, loving, and essentially without incident."[78] The attorney's strategy backfired when the prosecutor maintained during closing arguments that Sears had "rejected every opportunity that was afforded him"[79] and thus did not deserve sympathy for his actions. The question before the Supreme Court in this case was whether the state's post-conviction court had used the correct prejudice inquiry in determining the adequacy of defense counsel's mitigation case.

The Court held that the state court failed to apply the proper prejudice inquiry, observing that "we have never limited the prejudice inquiry under *Strickland* to cases in which there was only little or no mitigation evidence presented."[80] The fact that defense counsel had presented mitigating evidence indicating the positive attributes of his childhood did not preclude an inquiry into whether the scope of that information was adequate to satisfy the prejudice prong of *Strickland*. The Court concluded that the state's inquiry prejudiced Sears because information was not presented by the defense attorney at his trial, including evidence showing "significant frontal lobe abnormalities . . . [and] several serious head injuries he suffered as a child as well as drug and alcohol abuse."[81] A similar issue occurred in *Jefferson v. Upton* (2010).[82] After Jefferson was convicted of killing a coworker while fishing, he was sentenced to death. The question before the Supreme Court was whether the Sixth Circuit erred when it ruled that the adoption of a prosecutor's finding of fact unconstitutionally prejudiced Jefferson when the state court failed to consider the full range of exceptions that may justify setting aside such a finding. At the center of the debate was the accuracy of the prosecutor's interpretation of the significance of a head injury Jefferson had suffered in his childhood. The Court vacated and remanded the decision to the Eleventh Circuit to decide "whether the state court's factual findings warrant a presumption of correctness, and to conduct any further proceedings as may be appropriate in light of their resolution of that issue."[83]

To elaborate on the flawed reasoning of the lower court, the *Sears* Court compared the facts to *Porter v. McCollum* (2009)—another case involving the constitutionality of a mitigation investigation.

[77]130 S.Ct. 3259 (2010).
[78]*Id.*, at 3262.
[79]*Id.*
[80]*Id.*, at 3266.
[81]*Id.*, at 3262.
[82]130 S. Ct. 2217 (2010).
[83]*Id.*, at 2222.

After Porter was convicted of committing a double homicide, a jury sentenced him to death. Porter's defense counsel instructed the jury that he was not "mentally healthy" but failed to explain the exact nature of his mental condition. On initial habeas review, the state court determined that Porter was not prejudiced by his trial attorney's failure to present to the jury evidence of the fact that he was a decorated veteran with serious mental health difficulties. The Court concluded that the state court had erred, because it had unreasonably discounted the significance of Porter's heroic military service and history of child abuse.

In summary, the Court's decisions on the adequacy of mitigation investigations has likely been a response to conflicting interpretations among the lower courts on what constitutes constitutional performance by defense counsel.[84] The Court's attention to this issue also highlights the difficulties courts face when deciding cases that are highly fact-intensive but have profound implications for the destiny of death penalty defendants.

VI **ATTORNEY-CLIENT NEGOTIATIONS**

Since 1986, the Court has made significant changes to the *Strickland* rule that have clarified the meaning of "ineffective assistance" in terms of the Sixth Amendment. These changes have ultimately made the habeas appeal process much more difficult for capital defendants. The remainder of this chapter focuses on key case decisions in which the Supreme Court has clarified, refined, and elaborated on the concept of ineffective assistance of counsel.

In *Bell v. Cone* (2002),[85] the Court reconciled two competing tests that the Court used to assess ineffective assistance claims. In *United States v. Cronic* (1984),[86] the Court held that a defense counsel's performance was deficient only when the entire proceeding failed to subject the prosecution to meaningful adversarial testing. In *Cronic*, the Court considered five factors that would constitute a presumption of prejudice among defense counsel and therefore eliminate the need for the *Strickland* test. Those factors included: (1) the amount of time defense counsel had to prepare for trial, (2) the experience level of the attorney, (3) the gravity of the charge, (4) the complexity of the case, and (5) the accessibility of witnesses. In *Bell*, the Court considered the attorney's lack of time to prepare for trial but found that counsel was given adequate time, considering the type of question at issue—rebuttal of evidence showing intent to defraud. The Court concluded that because defense counsel had a reasonable amount of time to prepare—approximately three weeks—and the Court found the other factors to be unpersuasive, there was no ineffective assistance of counsel. This test was challenged in *Bell* when the petitioner alleged that the entire proceeding at his trial was prejudiced because his counsel's performance was deficient.

In this case, Cone had exhausted the appeals process in state and federal court. He then filed a writ of habeas corpus challenging the constitutionality of his incarceration based on an unreasonable application of clearly established law. Cone alleged that because his counsel did not present mitigating evidence or make a final argument at the sentencing stage of his trial, his legal representation was ineffective. The Supreme Court relied on the interpretation of *Cronic* in which the Court ruled that

---

[84]Hughes, Emily, *Arbitrary Death: An Empirical Study of Mitigation*, 89 Wash. U. L. Rev. 581 (2012).
[85]*Bell v. Cone*, 535 U.S. 685 (2002).
[86]*United States v. Cronic*, 466 U.S. 654 (1984).

defendants were entitled to a presumption of prejudice in certain circumstances, such as the require-ment that defense counsel engage in "meaningful adversarial testing."[87] The Court had to clarify the competing standards developed in *Strickland* and *Cronic*. The Court focused on the decisions of defense counsel using the objectivity test and found that an attorney was entitled to considerable leeway in making such decisions.

The Court further stated that Cone's attorney had reasons for not introducing evidence that Cone believed to be compelling. It examined the credibility of Cone's mother as a witness and concluded that the attorney's failure to allow her testimony was simply a strategic decision to prevent the prosecution from cross-examining her. Because Cone's mother was not believed to be a good witness, his lawyer did not put her on the stand. Also, Cone claimed that his defense counsel was ineffective because counsel did not make a final argument on Cone's behalf or plead for his life. The Court analyzed the consequences of not making a final argument and found that the attorney could have reasonably believed that to do so would have put his client at a higher risk for receiving the death penalty. Because the prosecutor did not reiterate the horrific nature of Cone's crimes, the defense counsel simply elected to avoid the prosecutor's opportunity for rebuttal.

The Court held that the *Cronic* standard did not apply to situations in which a defense counsel's performance was deficient at certain points. Instead, the Court said that in order for an ineffective assis-tance claim to succeed, the "entire proceeding" must be prejudiced. Justice William Rehnquist, writing for the majority, claimed that prejudicial errors must be evaluated in terms of degree, which means that even though Cone's attorney chose not to present certain witnesses or make a final argument on his behalf during sentencing, Cone was effectively represented.

In summary, the Supreme Court's decision in *Bell v. Cone* means that future defendants claiming ineffective assistance of counsel must show that their attorney's performance was objectively unrea-sonable. This, according to the Court, was the correct interpretation of the prejudice requirement in *Strickland*. If defendants do not make this showing in state court, their claims are unlikely to succeed on habeas review. For now, the Supreme Court has maintained that the *Cronic* decision applies to sit-uations in which the defense counsel's performance was a "complete failure."[88] Because the *Cronic* Court held that a defendant does not have to satisfy the prejudice prong of *Strickland* when an attorney completely fails to subject the prosecution's case to "meaningful adversarial testing," there is some hope for future challengers alleging ineffective assistance. However, unless his or her representation is systematically deficient, success in federal court on habeas review is unlikely.

At about the same time the Court decided *Bell*, the Court also ruled in another important case that a trial court's failure to investigate an uncontested conflict of interest between defense counsel and her client, even though such conflict was made known to the trial judge, did not constitute a valid ineffec-tive assistance of counsel claim. In *Mickens v. Taylor* (2002),[89] the Court said that such conflicts of interest did not constitute prejudice unless the defendant demonstrated that she was adversely affected by the existing conflict. As in *Cone*, the *Mickens* Court sent a message to state prisoners who challenged their incarceration based on a claim of ineffective assistance of counsel. The Court's ruling "lessened the day-to-day workload of a trial judges by removing any duty to inquire into counsel's conflicts of

---

[87]*United States v. Cronic*, 466 U.S. at 659.
[88]*Bell v. Cone*, 535 U.S. 685 (2002).
[89]*Mickens v. Taylor*, 535 U.S. 162 (2002).

interest that may potentially adversely affect a criminal defendant . . .”[90] The Court refrained from passing on the burden of logistical problems to state judges, because to fashion such a rule for trial judges would require them to investigate possible conflicts of interest in every criminal case. To illustrate this dilemma more completely, a discussion of the *Mickens* case follows.

Walter Mickens was indicted for the sodomy and murder of Timothy Hall. After he was found guilty of capital murder in state court, he filed a writ of habeas corpus in the Eastern District of Virginia, declaring ineffective assistance of counsel at his trial. At his habeas corpus proceeding, the attorney discovered that Bryan Saunders, Mickens's former counsel, had previously represented Hall in an unrelated case. The attorney also discovered that the presiding judge in that case and the case involving Hall and Mickens were the same; however, Mickens was never informed by Saunders or the presiding judge about the pre-existing conflict.

Justice Antonin Scalia, writing for the majority, held that "in order to demonstrate a Sixth Amendment violation where the trial court failed to inquire into a potential conflict of interest about which it knew or should have reasonably known, the defendant must establish that the conflict of interest adversely affected counsel's performance."[91] The Court first applied one of its *pre-Strickland* rulings, *Wood v. Georgia* (1981),[92] to the facts. Justice Scalia claimed that actual conflicts and possible conflicts of interest are not governed by the same rule of law. Furthermore, because *Wood* required a reviewing court to automatically reverse a conviction where an actual conflict occurred, the same rule did not apply to Mickens. This was because Mickens did not demonstrate the occurrence of an actual conflict. Justice Scalia stated that to require an appellate court to automatically reverse a conviction without first making an inquiry as to whether a conflict in fact occurred would not "make good policy sense."[93] This meant that defendants claiming ineffective assistance of counsel based on an alleged conflict of interest between their attorney and a third party, such as a witness or victim, must demonstrate that this conflict adversely affected their case. In most cases, therefore, capital defendants face a substantial burden when seeking a reversal of their conviction on habeas corpus review.

Although no other case dealt specifically with an ineffective assistance claim based on successive prosecutions, lower courts have generally held that trial courts do not have a duty to conduct inquiries into a possible conflict of interest unless they know that there is an obvious conflict among two or more parties. In the interest of maintaining legal ethics, however, at least one legal scholar has suggested that lawyers should "avoid conflicting representations and to advise the court promptly when a conflict of interest arises during the course of trial."[94]

During the last 30 years, the Supreme Court has seldom deviated from the *Strickland* standard when deciding cases regarding ineffective assistance of counsel. In *Nixon*, the Court struck down a decision by the Florida Supreme Court by relying on this legal rule, which has guided state and federal courts for some time. The *Nixon* Court ruled that death penalty defendants do not have to give their attorney express consent to waive arguments at the trial stage, when such a strategic decision is made to preserve

---

[90]Glassman, Jeffrey, *Mickens v. Taylor: The Court's New Don't Ask, Don't Tell Policy for Attorneys Faced With a Conflict of Interest*, 18 St. John's J.L. Comm. 919 (2004).
[91]Capone, John, *Supreme Court Review: Facilitating Fairness: The Judge's Role in the Sixth Amendment Right to Counsel*, 93 J. Crim. L. & Criminology 881 (2003).
[92]*Wood v. Georgia*, 450 U.S. 261 (1981).
[93]*Mickens v. Taylor*, 535 U.S. at 172 (2002).
[94]*Glassman, supra* note 29, at 6.

the credibility of the defense's arguments at sentencing. This case clarified two important concepts dealing with ineffective assistance of counsel cases. First, it affirmed the fact that the Court is focused on minimizing legal loopholes that can easily be taken advantage of by death penalty defendants in state and federal courts. Second, it explained the extent to which the *Cronic* rule applies, while the majority of cases can likely be resolved by the two-part rule adopted in *Strickland*.

The *Nixon* Court unanimously agreed that the Florida Supreme Court had erred in its decision. The Court first differentiated the facts in *Nixon* from the facts in *Brookhart v. Janis*.[95] In *Brookhart*, the defense had agreed to a "prima facie" trial, which meant the prosecution did not have to show evidence of guilt beyond a reasonable doubt. The *Nixon* Court, however, differentiated the facts in this case from those in *Brookhart* by explaining that "while the 'prima facie' case in *Brookhart* was fairly characterized as the equivalent of a guilty plea, the full presentation to the jury in Nixon's case does not resemble that severely abbreviated proceeding."[96] Further, the Court emphasized that Nixon retained all of his constitutional rights in this case, unlike the defendant in *Brookhart*. By focusing on these issues, the Court clearly rejected the idea of adopting an automatic rule requiring the defendant's express consent to a strategy of conceding guilt, particularly when the possibility of a death sentence is imminent.

The Supreme Court also differentiated the applicability of the *Cronic* rule to ineffective assistance of counsel claims. The Court has previously reserved that rule for the most extreme circumstances, such as when the defense fails to test the merits of the adversarial process as a whole. In *Nixon*, the Court concluded that the Florida Supreme Court used the *Cronic* rule, which was incorrect given the factual circumstances. Because the Florida Supreme Court first presumed that the performance of defense counsel was deficient, it was led to apply the wrong legal test. The Court said that the *Strickland* rule was the correct legal principle because defense counsel's performance was objectively reasonable; thus, if it used *Strickland* rather than *Cronic*, it would have reached the opposite result. The Court distinguished *Cronic* from *Nixon* by stating that defense counsel's "concession of guilt does not rank as a failure to function in any meaningful sense as the government's adversary."[97] The Court emphasized the fact that defense counsel had conducted two evidentiary hearings on behalf of his client, which clearly demonstrated that he had fully informed his client of his proposed trial strategy and its costs and benefits. The justices also emphasized that the gravity of the sentencing stage in death penalty cases is much higher than in "run-of-the-mine"[98] cases; therefore, the Court concluded that the attorney's strategic decision was realistic and may have been the best tactical choice given the facts.

Capital defendants are not always remorseful or supportive, even during sentencing proceedings indicative of their punishment. Occasionally capital defendants refuse to assist their attorneys with the investigation of mitigating evidence, or they directly impede efforts during the sentencing phase. In 2007 the Supreme Court addressed this particular issue in *Schriro v. Landrigan*. In a five-to-four decision written by Justice Clarence Thomas, the Court held that a defendant's repeated demands that his attorney not introduce mitigating evidence during the punishment phase provided sufficient cause to deny his habeas petition. Applying the *Strickland* rule for ineffective assistance of counsel claims, the Court ruled defense counsel's performance did not bias the defendant's case. At sentencing,

---

[95]*Brookhart v. Janis*, 384 U.S. 1 (1966).
[96]*Florida v. Nixon*, 543 U.S. 175 (2004).
[97]*Id.*
[98]*Id.*

Landrigan instructed his ex-wife and mother not to testify on his behalf, which would have likely revealed evidence of mental health problems, such as possible brain disorder, exposure to alcohol and other drugs, and an abusive family history. Instead, at his sentencing proceeding he told the judge to "bring [the death penalty] right on. I'm ready for it."[99] During habeas proceedings, Landrigan claimed that his objections were directed specifically toward the presentation of witness testimony from his ex-wife and mother, not *all* relevant mitigating evidence. The Ninth Circuit agreed, concluding that counsel's "last-minute decision regarding presentation could not excuse his [counsel's] failure to conduct an adequate investigation prior to sentencing."[100] However, the Supreme Court reversed, finding that counsel's performance was reasonable given Landrigan's repeated objections. The Court further ruled that the Anti-Effective Death Penalty Act of 1996 did not require federal courts to grant evidentiary hearings unless Landrigan could demonstrate a colorable Sixth Amendment claim on the basis of the facts. Finding that the evidence did not support the need for an evidentiary hearing, the Supreme Court reversed and remanded.

In his dissenting opinion, Justice Stevens argued that the Ninth Circuit's opinion should have been affirmed. He indicated that all reviewing courts had acknowledged that counsel's performance was ineffective, given that counsel failed to seek advice from mental health experts or investigate Landrigan's history of substance abuse. The dissent further opined that *Wiggins v. Smith* (2003)[101] required an adequate investigation of the defendant's background, which trial counsel neglected to do. Because Landrigan had no knowledge of important neurological evidence discovered later by post-conviction counsel, the dissent argued that "he could not have made a knowing, intelligent, and voluntary waiver of the right to adduce mitigating evidence."[102] Therefore, the dissent concluded that trial counsel's performance was deficient and that counsel's errors established prejudice under *Strickland*.

The *Landrigan* case is important for several reasons. First, it highlights the assumption that capital defendants are capable of aiding in their own defense, despite the inherent connection between mental illness and violent behavior. Capital defendants, and violent offenders in general, routinely flaunt the callous nature of their crimes and their lack of guilt while portraying the image they are not afraid to be put to death.[103] Nevertheless, courts must be alert to the fact that this conduct may be associated with psychological illness, family violence, or substance abuse, which necessitates a thorough investigation of mitigating evidence. Second, this decision raises the question as to the appropriate standard for deciding a valid, intelligent, and knowing waiver of the right to counsel and presentation of mitigating evidence. Long-standing Supreme Court precedent suggests that a rigid standard for waiver determinations is required, especially in capital cases.[104]

Landrigan expressly objected to the presentation of witness testimony from his ex-wife and mother, but the Court interpreted this action as an intent to waive the presentation of *all* relevant mitigating evidence. *Landrigan* highlights the importance of the need for juries to give an individualized

---

[99]*Schriro v. Landrigan*, 127 S. Ct. 1938 (2007).

[100]*Landrigan v. Schriro*, 441 F.3d at 647 (9th Cir. 2006).

[101]*Wiggins v. Smith*, 593 U.S. 510 (2003).

[102]*Schriro v. Landrigan*, 127 S. Ct. 1947 (2007).

[103]Harvard Law Review Association, *The Supreme Court, 2006 Term: Leading Case-Ineffective Assistance of Counsel*, 121 HARV. L. REV. 255 (2007).

[104]See *Rees v. Peyton*, 384 U.S. 312, 314 (1966); *Johnston v. Zerbst*, 304 U.S. 458, 464 (1938); *Schneckloth v. Bustamonte*, 412 U.S. 218, 237–38 (1973).

consideration of all mitigating factors before sentencing. This is particularly important given that research shows the significant influence of mitigating evidence on jury decisions about life or death.[105] However, the Court's opinion in this case and its decision in *Abdul-Kabir v. Quarterman* (2007) that "sentencing juries must be able to give meaningful consideration and effect to all mitigating evidence"[106] appear somewhat contradictory. For now, the Court has said that a defendant has no viable Sixth Amendment claim of ineffective assistance of counsel when incompetence is due to interference.

VII IN SUMMARY, WHAT DO THESE CASES SAY?

The *Strickland* test remains authoritative in assessing ineffective assistance claims. Since the *Strickland* decision, the Supreme Court has consistently applied its two-pronged approach to virtually every capital case dealing with a Sixth Amendment violation based on ineffective assistance of counsel. *Strickland* held that in order for a defendant's claim to prevail in state court, the defendant must show that: (1) the defense counsel's performance was "objectively unreasonable," and (2) the performance led to a reasonable probability that the outcome of the trial would have been different. The decision is important because it defines the standard for future capital cases involving ineffective assistance of counsel.

Since 1996, the Court has based its decisions on ineffective assistance claims in accordance with the restrictions set by the AEDPA. In order for a defendant to prevail under these guidelines, he or she must show that: (1) the state court unreasonably applied the law to the set of facts, or (2) the decision was contrary to clearly established law as determined by the Supreme Court. What this means is that capital defendants alleging ineffective assistance of counsel claims must prove that the state court's decision was "objectively unreasonable" and that the decision prejudiced the defense.

In 2000, the Court broke new ground in *Williams*, in which Justice Sandra Day O'Connor held that state courts do not violate the "unreasonable application" phrase of the AEDPA when they choose the correct rule of law but apply it incorrectly. The Court said that a defendant's "failure to develop a claim's factual basis in state court proceedings is not established unless there is lack of diligence, or some greater fault, attributable to the prisoner or his counsel."[107] The Court ruled that "the statute does not bar the evidentiary hearing petitioner seeks on his juror bias and prosecutorial misconduct claims, but bars a hearing on his *Brady* claim because he 'failed to develop' that claim's factual basis in state court and concedes his inability to satisfy the statute's further stringent conditions for excusing the deficiency."[108] In this case, the Court found for the first time since *Strickland* that a defendant had a bona fide claim for ineffective assistance of counsel that could withstand the AEDPA's stringent requirements.

One of the most significant legal obstacles habeas petitioners face is that they are often procedurally barred from pursuing significant constitutional claims in federal court if those claims were not also filed in state court. Courts have taken two different approaches in reconciling claims of ineffective

---

[105]Barnett et al., Michelle E., *When Mitigation Evidence Makes a Difference: Effects of Psychological Mitigating Evidence on Sentencing Decisions in Capital Trials*, 22 BEHAV. SCI. & L. 751, 764–66. (2004).

[106]*Abdul-Kabir v. Quarterman*, 127 S. Ct. 1654, 1664 (2007).

[107]*Williams*, 529 U.S. 362 (2000).

[108]*Id.*

assistance of counsel. Under the relationship approach, the Court has said that "a petitioner is bound by his attorney's failure to meet a filing deadline and cannot rely on that failure to establish cause."[109] The decision in *Maples v. Thomas* illustrates the development of the "abandonment" principle in death penalty cases and holds that a state petitioner may overcome a state post-conviction default in federal habeas proceedings when the attorney-client relationship is severed. The Court's decisions in *Holland*, *Martel*, and *Martinez* show that the Court takes a performance-based approach as long as defense counsel remains engaged with his client; therefore, the *Strickland* rule determines whether counsel's performance is constitutionally deficient.

On the basis of *Wiggins* and its progeny, it is clear that the Court will consider the reasonableness of the defendant's trial tactics as a means for determining whether the decision to present mitigating evidence in a capital defendant's trial was appropriate. For example, the *Rompilla* Court held that defense counsel's failure to review and obtain documented evidence of a prior conviction constitutes ineffective assistance of counsel. Recent decisions in *Sears* and *Porter* also show that defense counsel's failure to present unique information about the defendant, such as military recognition or evidence of severe mental abnormalities, is sufficient to trigger a *Strickland* violation. In contrast, the Court has held that a defense attorney is not in violation of *Strickland* when his client impedes his ability to present mitigating evidence at sentencing or when existing aggravating evidence outweighs the mitigating evidence that defense counsel fails to present on his client's behalf.

This is not to say that the Court will scrutinize every judgment made by defense counsel in the form of trial tactics. The Court has, in the past, given great deference to a defense lawyer in deciding how best to represent a client's case. But the Court's attention to the adequacy of mitigation investigations has sent a message to lower courts that defense counsel's failure to perform according to prevailing professional norms will likely result in a viable claim of ineffective assistance of counsel.

In future cases, the Court will likely continue to provide defense attorneys with a great deal of tactical discretion in determining the best legal strategies for their clients. Defense attorneys will continue to use such strategies in order to preserve defendants' credibility during sentencing, as long as counsel does not discount available mitigating evidence that may warrant a punishment less than death.

VIII CONCLUSION

It is arguable that the Supreme Court has maintained a consistent perspective toward ineffective assistance of counsel claims since the decision in *Strickland*. The Court has made it clear that when a defense attorney makes "strategic decisions" regarding the presentation of mitigating evidence, those decisions must be based on careful considerations about benefits and consequences. Whereas in the past the Court refused to grant writs based on ineffective assistance, saying that lawyers should be entitled to exercise discretion, that principle is now being scrutinized more carefully.

In light of *Wiggins*, defendants have to show that, because their attorney failed to present mitigating evidence on their behalf, the attorney's decision was objectively unreasonable and that the decision prejudiced the defendant. Because the Court has increasingly focused on the issue of mitigating evidence, it is likely that this will compel defense attorneys to continue to place great value on the use of

---

[109]*Maples*, at 753.

mitigation experts during sentencing. The ABA Guidelines advocate the use of multiple experts who can collectively assess a defendant's social history and aid a defendant at his sentencing by presenting the maximum potential of all mitigating evidence.

The Court also continues to focus heavily on the quality of mitigation defense work in capital cases. This is likely a result of the fact that mitigating investigations are inherently complex and require substantial resources in order to perform them properly. However, the Court has said that although defense counsels owe a duty to their clients to build a comprehensive mitigation case, the aggravating and mitigating factors must be considered in context according to *Strickland*.

Although the Court has curtailed the ability of a defendant to succeed under the limiting provisions of the AEDPA, the federal courts will likely continue in the near future to hear and decide cases involving ineffective assistance of counsel claims. Recent decisions from the Court in *Holland v. Florida*, *Martel v. Clair*, and *Maples v. Thomas* illustrate the Court's concern with attorney incompetence given the strict guidelines of the AEDPA. When an attorney severs the attorney-client relationship by abandoning his client and no substitute counsel is obtained, the Court has said that such egregiousness constitutes ineffective assistance of counsel. However, absent a clear break in the relationship, mere negligence by defense counsel to follow through on investigative leads or file documents in a timely manner likely will not be deemed a constitutional violation.

CASES BRIEFED IN CHAPTER 7

Case	Issue	Holding
Strickland v. Washington 466 U.S. 688 (1984)	Do defendants claiming ineffective assistance of counsel have to show that, were it not for counsel's errors, there was a reasonable probability that the result of the sentencing decision would have been different?	To demonstrate ineffective assistance of counsel, the following conditions must be met: (1) there must be objectively unreasonable deficiency in counsel's performance, and (2) this deficiency must have led to a reasonable probability that the result would have been different.
Lockhart v. Fretwell 506 U.S. 364 (1993)	Does the failure to object to "double-counting" constitute ineffective assistance of counsel when the precedent in question was subsequently overruled prior to habeas review?	"Double-counting" is not a violation of the *Strickland* rule; thus no ineffective assistance of counsel is present.
Mickens v. Taylor 535 U.S. 162 (2002)	Does a trial court's failure to inquire into an alleged attorney conflict of interest require an automatic reversal of conviction?	An alleged conflict of interest involving a defense attorney must adversely impact the defendant in order to be considered ineffective assistance of counsel.
Bell v. Cone 535 U.S. 685 (2002)	Do strategic decisions not to present closing arguments or witness statements in mitigation entitle a capital defendant to a presumption of prejudice? Did the state court reasonably apply the *Strickland* rule to this case?	Failure to present mitigating evidence, such as testimony from select witnesses, or to make final arguments does not constitute ineffective assistance if viewed as strategic decisions.

Continued

Case	Issue	Holding
Wiggins v. Smith 539 U.S. 510 (2003)	Does the failure by a defense lawyer to investigate a capital defendant's childhood history and discover evidence of a "dysfunctional background" violate the Sixth Amendment?	Failure to conduct a reasonable investigation into a defendant's childhood history and "dysfunctional background" constitutes ineffective counsel.
Florida v. Nixon 543 U.S. 175 (2004)	Does a trial strategy of conceding guilt without express consent from a capital defendant constitute ineffective assistance of counsel according to the *Strickland* rule?	No ineffective assistance of counsel exists when defense lawyers do not obtain express consent from their clients as to a trial strategy of conceding guilt.
Rompilla v. Beard 545 U.S. 374 (2005)	Does counsel's failure to make a reasonable effort to review and obtain documented evidence that counsel knows the prosecution will use to support a death sentence constitute ineffective assistance of counsel?	A defense attorney must make a reasonable effort to review and obtain documented evidence retained by the prosecutor, such as a prior conviction, that counsel knows the prosecution will likely rely on during sentencing to support a death sentence.
Schriro v. Landrigan 550 U.S. 465 (2007)	(1) Does a district court's failure to grant an evidentiary hearing when a defendant cannot demonstrate a colorable ineffective assistance of counsel claim violate the Sixth Amendment? (2) Does a defense attorney's failure to present mitigating evidence such as testimony of a disadvantaged background at sentencing constitute ineffective assistance of counsel when the defendant objects to counsel's strategy?	The AEDPA does not require courts to grant evidentiary hearings when defendants cannot make colorable ineffective assistance-of-counsel claims. Further, a defense attorney's failure to present mitigating evidence when a defendant interferes with his counsel's strategy does not constitute ineffective assistance of counsel.
Wood v. Allen 558 U.S. 290 (2010)	Is it unreasonable for a state court to conclude that an inexperienced attorney's decision not to present evidence of a client's mental retardation at sentencing was strategic, given the presentation of other mitigating evidence supporting a life sentence? NO. Did the Eleventh Circuit neglect to exercise its judicial review authority when it failed to decide whether the state court's determination was reasonable, given the evidence contained in the state record? UNANSWERED.	A state court's conclusion that counsel made a strategic choice not to present evidence indicating capital defendant's mental abnormalities is not unreasonable, given the entirety of the evidence presented during the state court proceedings. Further, a state court's determination of the facts is not unreasonable simply because a different conclusion would have been reached by a federal habeas court.
Maples v. Thomas 656 U.S. ____ (2012)	Did the appellate court correctly rule that no "cause" existed to excuse a procedural default when the State, and not the petitioner, was to blame for the default and the petitioner's attorneys had abandoned him at the time of the default? NO.	Counsel's failure to meet a filing deadline constitutes sufficient "cause" to excuse the petitioner's default in state habeas proceeding; thus the petitioner was entitled to federal habeas review.

CASE BRIEFS

STRICKLAND v. WASHINGTON 466 U.S. 688 (1984)

CAPSULE: In order for an ineffective assistance-of-counsel claim to succeed, the defendant must prove that the defense counsel's errors were objectively unreasonable and that this deficiency led to a reasonable probability that the sentencing outcome would have been different.

FACTS: The defendant, David Leroy Washington, was convicted in state trial court of committing three stabbing murders in 1976. Washington's attorney did not present any character witnesses or request a psychiatric evaluation of his client prior to sentencing. According to defense counsel, these were "strategic decisions" aimed at preventing the prosecution from rebuttal during cross-examination. The defense counsel claimed that Washington had no criminal history and that something had "gone badly wrong during extremely stressful circumstances." Washington was convicted. He later filed a habeas corpus petition in state trial court alleging ineffective assistance of counsel in violation of the Sixth Amendment.

ISSUE: Do defendants claiming ineffective assistance of counsel have to show that, but for defense counsel's errors, there was a reasonable probability that the result of the sentencing decision would have been different? YES.

HOLDING: Two criteria must be met in order to succeed on an ineffective assistance of counsel claim: (1) the petitioner must prove that defense counsel's performance was objectively unreasonable and (2) this deficiency led to a reasonable probability that the sentencing decision would have been different.

REASON: "The proper standard for judging attorney performance is that of reasonably effective assistance, considering all the circumstances. When a convicted defendant complains of the ineffectiveness of counsel's assistance, the defendant must show that counsel's representation fell below an objective standard of reasonableness. Judicial scrutiny of counsel's performance must be highly deferential, and a fair assessment of attorney performance requires that every effort be made to eliminate the distorting effects of hindsight, to reconstruct the circumstances of counsel's challenged conduct, and to evaluate the conduct from counsel's perspective at the time. A court must indulge a strong presumption that counsel's conduct falls within the wide range of reasonable professional assistance. These standards require no special amplification in order to define counsel's duty to investigate, the duty at issue in this case."

"With regard to the required showing of prejudice, the proper standard requires the defendant to show that there is a reasonable probability that, but for counsel's unprofessional errors, the result of the proceeding would have been different. A reasonable probability is a probability sufficient to undermine confidence in the outcome. A court hearing an ineffectiveness claim must consider the totality of the evidence before the judge or jury."

CASE SIGNIFICANCE: The *Strickland* decision established a definitive test for analyzing ineffective assistance of counsel claims raised by capital defendants. Prior to this ruling, the Supreme Court had not answered the question as to what standard a defense attorney's performance should be judged against when a claim of ineffective assistance of counsel is made. Lower courts were left to interpret the broad language of *McMann*, which left most of the discretion to state trial courts. However, trial courts had no guidance from appellate courts for judging ineffective assistance of counsel claims. The *Strickland* Court required lower courts to analyze ineffective assistance of counsel according to a two-part legal standard. The rule states that an ineffective assistance of counsel claim can succeed if the petitioner proves that: (1) his defense counsel's performance was objectively unreasonable, and (2) there is a reasonable probability that the deficiency would have led to a different sentencing decision.

LOCKHART v. FRETWELL 506 U.S. 364 (1993)

CAPSULE: No ineffective assistance of counsel claim existed when a defense attorney failed to object to a "double-counting" technique that was based on then-existing Eighth Circuit law and subsequently overruled prior to habeas review.

FACTS: Fretwell was convicted of the capital murder of Sherman Sullins. During the sentencing phase of his trial, the jury weighed aggravating and mitigating factors. One of the aggravating factors considered by the trial court was that Fretwell had committed the crime for pecuniary gain, which also happened to be an element of the crime—capital murder. After considering the evidence, the jury sentenced Fretwell to death. According to Eighth Circuit law at the time, this so-called "double-counting" technique was unconstitutional in light of *Collins v. Lockhart*.

ISSUE: Does the failure to object to "double-counting" constitute ineffective assistance of counsel when the precedent case in question was subsequently overruled prior to habeas review? NO.

HOLDING: Defense attorneys who fail to object to an unconstitutional sentencing practice, such as "double-counting," do not give rise to an ineffective assistance claim when the law on which the claim was based has since been overruled.

REASON: "Counsel's failure to make the *Collins* objection during the sentencing proceeding did not constitute prejudice within the meaning of *Strickland*. To show prejudice under *Strickland*, a defendant must demonstrate that counsel's errors are so serious as to deprive him of a trial whose result is unfair or unreliable, not merely that the outcome would have been different. Unfairness or unreliability does not result unless counsel's ineffectiveness deprives the defendant of a substantive or procedural right to which the law entitles him. The sentencing proceeding's result in the present case was neither unfair nor unreliable, because the Court of Appeals, which had decided *Collins* in 1985, overruled it in *Perry v. Lockhart*, 871 F.2d 1384 (1989), four years later. Thus, respondent suffered no prejudice from his counsel's deficient performance. Contrary to Fretwell's argument, prejudice is not determined under the laws existing at the time of trial. Although contemporary assessment of counsel's conduct is used when determining the deficient performance component of the *Strickland* test, the prejudice component, with its focus on fairness and reliability, does not implicate the same concerns that motivated the former component's adoption: that a more rigid requirement could dampen the ardor and impair the independence of defense counsel, discourage the acceptance of assigned cases, and undermine the trust between attorney and client. The instant holding is not inconsistent with the retroactivity rule announced in *Teague v. Lane*. The circumstances that gave rise to that rule do not apply to claims raised by a federal habeas petitioner, who has no interest in the finality of the state-court judgment under which he was incarcerated and, unlike the States, ordinarily has no claim of reliance on past judicial precedent as a basis for his actions."

CASE SIGNIFICANCE: This case exemplifies the Court's unwillingness to consider serious, although individual, misjudgments by defense attorneys. The Court held that a Sixth Amendment violation would occur only when the overall fundamental fairness and reliability of the proceeding had been compromised. This means that future defendants alleging ineffective assistance of counsel cannot rely on an individual misjudgment by defense counsel as a basis for their habeas petition, even when that error would have led to a reasonable probability that a life sentence would have been imposed. By the time this case was decided, the Court had held in *Teague v. Lane* (1989) that a defendant could not prevail on habeas corpus review by relying on new rules of constitutional law because the "principle of finality in criminal convictions otherwise would be seriously undermined." This case said that the *Teague* rule could not benefit a capital defendant alleging ineffective assistance of counsel because that rule was intended to promote the interests of the state, not the defendant.

MICKENS v. TAYLOR 535 U.S. 162 (2002)

CAPSULE: Defendant must establish that a conflict of interest adversely impacted his attorney's performance; furthermore, simply demonstrating that an inquiry into such a conflict of interest was due is insufficient to sustain a claim based on ineffective assistance of counsel.

FACTS: Mickens was convicted of the premeditated murder and sodomy of Timothy Hall. He was subsequently sentenced to death after a jury found that aggravating circumstances existed. Prior to his trial, Mickens was not aware that his attorney, Brian Saunders, had represented Hall in an unrelated case. In addition, the same judge who had presided over Hall's case in juvenile court appointed Saunders to represent Mickens in this case. At no time did Saunders disclose to the court or his client the fact that he had previously represented Hall. Mickens filed a writ of habeas corpus in district court, alleging ineffective assistance of counsel based on the conflict of interest, but he was denied relief. He then filed a writ of habeas corpus in federal district court, where he was again denied relief.

ISSUE: Does a trial court's failure to inquire into an alleged conflict of interest require an automatic reversal of the conviction? NO.

HOLDING: Ineffective assistance claims based on an alleged conflict of interest do not rise to the level of a Sixth Amendment claim. A conflict must adversely affect the defense's performance in order for a violation to be established.

REASON: "A defendant alleging ineffective assistance generally must demonstrate a reasonable probability that, but for counsel's unprofessional errors, the result of the proceeding would have been different. *Strickland v. Washington*, 466 U.S. 668, 694, (1986). An exception to this general rule presumes a probable effect upon the outcome where assistance of counsel has been denied entirely or during a critical stage of the proceeding. The Court has held in several cases that 'circumstances of that magnitude,' *United States v. Cronic*, 466 U.S. 648, 659, (1984) may also arise when the defendant's attorney actively represented conflicting interests."

"This Court rejects petitioner's argument that the remand instruction in *Wood*, directing the trial court to grant a new hearing if it determined that 'an actual conflict of interest existed,' established that where the trial judge neglects a duty to inquire into a potential conflict the defendant, to obtain reversal, need only show that his lawyer was subject to a conflict of interest, not that the conflict adversely affected counsel's performance."

CASE SIGNIFICANCE: In this case, the Court answered the following question: Does a trial court's failure to inquire into a conflict of interest require an automatic reversal of a conviction? The Court said no. The Court was careful to avoid making a new rule of law that required trial courts to inquire into any possible conflict between parties in a case. The Court recognized the logistical problems that would ensue if trial courts were required to make such inquiries. Instead, the Court relied on *Wood* and *Sullivan* to explain that defendants alleging ineffective assistance of counsel must demonstrate some connection between their counsel's performance and the actual conflict. Absent that, the conviction stands.

This case is also significant because it was one of the few cases in which the Court did not use the *Strickland* case as the basis for its ruling. Because the Court was dealing with circumstances that could not be adequately tested by the *Strickland* standard, the Court used previous case law instead to determine whether prejudice was shown.

BELL v. CONE 535 U.S. 685 (2002)

CAPSULE: Strategic decisions, such as the choice not to present mitigating evidence, which could be considered harmful if subjected to cross-examination, do not establish a valid claim of ineffective assistance of counsel.

FACTS: In August 1980, Cone robbed a jewelry store and then led police on a high-speed pursuit through the city of Memphis, Tennessee. He subsequently killed two elderly individuals after breaking into their residence. Cone was convicted of first-degree murder and intent to commit robbery by use of deadly force and was given the death penalty. Although Cone appealed his case on numerous procedural grounds to the Tennessee Supreme Court, his sentence was affirmed.

ISSUES:
1. Do strategic decisions to not present closing arguments or witness statements in mitigation entitle a capital defendant to a presumption of prejudice? NO.
2. Did the state court reasonably apply the *Strickland* standard to the facts in this case? YES.

HOLDING: Defense counsel's failure to present mitigating evidence, such as witness testimony or making final arguments at sentencing, do not, in themselves, constitute a valid ineffective assistance claim.

REASONING: "Section 2254(d)(1)'s 'contrary to' and 'unreasonable application' clauses have independent meaning. A federal habeas court may grant relief under the former clause if the state court applies a rule different from the governing law set forth in this Court's cases, or if it decides a case differently than this Court has done on a set of materially indistinguishable facts. *Williams v. Taylor*, 529 U.S. 362, 405–406, (2000). The federal court may grant relief under the latter clause if the state court correctly identifies the governing legal principle from this Court's decisions but unreasonably applies it in the particular case. Such application must be objectively unreasonable, which is different from incorrect. To satisfy *Strickland*'s two-part test for evaluating claims that counsel performed so incompetently that a defendant's sentence or conviction should be reversed, the defendant must prove that counsel's representation fell below an objective reasonableness standard and that there is a reasonable probability that, but for counsel's unprofessional error, the proceeding's result would have been different."

"The challenged aspects of counsel's performance—failing to adduce mitigating evidence and waiving closing argument—are plainly of the same ilk as other specific attorney errors subject to *Strickland*'s performance and prejudice components. See, e.g., *Darden v. Wainwright*, 477 U.S. 168, 184 (1986). Because the state court correctly identified *Strickland*'s principles as those governing the analysis of respondent's claim, there is no merit in his contention that the state court's adjudication was contrary to this Court's clearly established law."

CASE SIGNIFICANCE: This case demonstrates the difficulty capital defendants face when making an ineffective assistance of counsel claim. For capital defendants it is the prejudice prong of *Strickland* that causes the most difficulty on habeas review. In order for a defendant's ineffective assistance of counsel claim to be valid according to *Strickland*, the defendant must show that: (1) the defense attorney's performance was objectively unreasonable, and (2) that such deficiency led to a reasonable probability that the sentencing decision would have been different. During the years since *Strickland*, the Court has increasingly limited the ability of defendants to obtain a writ of habeas corpus based on an ineffective assistance claim. This strict standard is largely the result of the respect given by the Supreme Court to tactical or strategic decisions made by trial attorneys in court.

Potential harm to capital defendants is heightened in cases in which defense attorneys make strategic decisions that are detrimental. However, the Court is reluctant to set specific guidelines or rules that define the meaning of a "reasonable probability" leading to a particular sentencing decision. On this prong, the Court has not given much guidance as to what factors will lead to an ineffective assistance of counsel claim.

WIGGINS v. SMITH 539 U.S. 510 (2003)

CAPSULE: Failure to conduct a reasonable investigation into a defendant's "dysfunctional background" for use as mitigating evidence for a capital defendant constitutes ineffective assistance of counsel.

FACTS: Kevin Wiggins was indicted in October 1988 for the first-degree murder of Florence Lacs. Wiggins was represented by two public defenders. After conviction, the defense attorneys chose to bifurcate the sentencing proceedings. Throughout Wiggins's trial, the attorneys maintained that their client was innocent of the crimes; therefore, the sentencing proceeding was separated in order to make final arguments contesting his innocence and to present mitigating evidence on his behalf. However, the trial judge denied the motion for bifurcation, and Wiggins was sentenced to death. Wiggins filed a writ of habeas corpus, arguing that he had ineffective assistance of counsel because his attorneys failed to present evidence of his "dysfunctional background." Wiggins alleged that his attorneys should have investigated his background more thoroughly. The attorneys said that they had chosen to contest Wiggins's actual responsibility for the crime rather than to pursue a case of mitigation by investigating his childhood history. The trial judge held that the decision by the public defenders not to investigate his childhood history was simply a matter of trial tactics, which did not rise to the level of a constitutional violation.

ISSUE: Does the failure to investigate a capital defendant's childhood history and discover evidence of a "dysfunctional background" violate the Sixth Amendment? YES.

HOLDING: Ineffective assistance of counsel claims based on the defense attorney's failure to conduct a reasonable investigation into a defendant's "dysfunctional background" and childhood history constitutes ineffective assistance of counsel.

REASONING: "Here, as in *Strickland*, counsel claim that their limited investigation into petitioner's background reflected a tactical judgment not to present mitigating evidence and to pursue an alternative strategy instead. In evaluating petitioner's claim, this Court's principal concern is not whether counsel should have presented a mitigation case, but whether the investigation supporting their decision not to introduce mitigating evidence of Wiggins' background was itself reasonable. The Court thus conducts an objective review of their performance, measured for reasonableness under prevailing professional norms, including a context-dependent consideration of the challenged conduct as seen from counsel's perspective at the time of that conduct."

"Counsel's failures prejudiced Wiggins' defense. To establish prejudice, a defendant must show that there is a reasonable probability that, but for counsel's unprofessional errors, the proceeding's result would have been different. This Court assesses prejudice by reweighing the aggravating evidence against the totality of the mitigating evidence adduced both at trial and in the habeas proceedings. The mitigating evidence counsel failed to discover and present here is powerful."

CASE SIGNIFICANCE: This case is important because it is one of only two cases since the decision in *Strickland* in which the Court has ruled in favor of a capital defendant when alleging a claim based upon ineffective assistance of counsel. However, this decision is also important for two other reasons. First, the Court has made it clear that the restrictions imposed by the Antiterrorism and Effective Death Penalty Act of 1996 on capital defendants do not result in a process whereby federal courts automatically uphold state court decisions. The Court has also signaled that attorney competence in capital cases should be more closely examined by reviewing courts, particularly if it is associated with finding mitigating evidence for use during the sentencing phase of a capital trial.

FLORIDA v. NIXON 543 U.S. 175 (2004)

CAPSULE: A defense attorney's failure to obtain consent from a death penalty defendant as to a strategy of conceding guilt does not automatically result in a Sixth Amendment violation of ineffective assistance of counsel.

FACTS: After overwhelming evidence of his guilt was gathered by the state, Nixon was indicted on charges of first-degree murder. The public defender representing Nixon, Mr. Corin, initially filed a plea of not guilty in the case but later changed that plea to guilty after reviewing all of the evidence pointing to his client's guilt. Prosecutors refused plea negotiations, intent on seeking the death penalty for Nixon. Corin decided to launch a trial strategy of conceding guilt, which was an effort to establish credibility during the sentencing phase of the trial, when he would argue that his client was unsuitable for the death penalty. Nixon, nevertheless, was unresponsive to Corin's trial strategy and did not approve or disapprove of it. Corin proceeded to deliver to the court the mitigating evidence he had compiled in his client's favor, including witness testimony indicating his client's history of emotional instability and psychiatric care, low IQ, his youth, and his erratic behavior prior to committing the murder. The trial court, however, convicted Nixon and sentenced him to death. The Florida Supreme Court eventually reversed that decision, concluding that Corin's failure to obtain express consent from his client amounted to ineffective assistance of counsel under the test established in *United States v. Cronic*, 466 U.S. 648.

ISSUE: Does the failure to obtain a defendant's consent to a trial strategy of conceding guilt constitute ineffective assistance of counsel? NO.

HOLDING: A defense attorney's failure to obtain consent from a defendant as to a strategy of conceding guilt does not fall below an objective standard of reasonableness, thus it does not automatically result in ineffective assistance of counsel.

REASONING: "The Florida Supreme Court erred in requiring Nixon's affirmative, explicit acceptance of Corin's strategy because it mistakenly deemed Corin's statements to the jury the functional equivalent of a guilty plea. Despite Corin's concession of Nixon's guilt, Nixon retained the rights accorded a defendant in a criminal trial. The State was obliged to present during the guilt phase competent, admissible evidence establishing the essential elements of the crimes with which Nixon was charged. That aggressive evidence would thus be separated from the penalty phase, enabling the defense to concentrate that portion of the trial on mitigating factors."

"Counsel's effectiveness should not be evaluated under the *Cronic* standard, but under the standard prescribed in *Strickland*: Did counsel's representation "fall below an objective standard of reasonableness?" The Florida Supreme Court's erroneous equation of Corin's concession strategy to a guilty plea led it to apply the wrong standard. The court first presumed deficient performance, then applied the presumption of prejudice that *Cronic* reserved for situations in which counsel has entirely failed to function as the client's advocate. Corin's concession of Nixon's guilt does not rank as such a failure. Although a concession of guilt in a run-of-the-mine trial might present a closer question, the gravity of the potential sentence in a capital trial and the proceeding's two-phase structure vitally affect counsel's strategic calculus. Attorneys representing capital defendants face daunting challenges in developing trial strategies: Prosecutors are more likely to seek the death penalty, and to refuse to accept a plea to a life sentence, when the evidence is overwhelming and the crime heinous. Counsel therefore may reasonably decide to focus on the trial's penalty phase, at which time counsel's mission is to persuade the trier that his client's life should be spared."

CASE SIGNIFICANCE: This case has had a substantial effect on the way defense lawyers develop trial strategies, particularly in cases in which their client's guilt is obvious. In *Nixon*, the Court held that a trial lawyer may concede the guilt of his or her client when that person has neither agreed nor disagreed to such a strategy. In this case, the Court emphasized the fact that the defense attorney's statements to the jury were not the same as a guilty plea. This was because Nixon still maintained all the constitutional rights available to him in a criminal trial. The Court found

Continued

FLORIDA v. NIXON 543 U.S. 175 (2004)—cont'd

that the defense attorney's strategic decision to avoid arguing for his client's innocence was reasonable, given the gravity associated with the possibility of his client facing the death penalty during the sentencing phase.

The Court found that the Florida Supreme Court had mistakenly used the wrong legal test to determine whether the defense attorney's performance was unreasonable. The Court concluded that the test established in *United States v. Cronic* was inappropriate because that test was reserved for "circumstances that are so likely to prejudice the accused that the cost of litigating their effect in a particular case is unjustified."[51] Justice Ginsburg, writing for the majority, found that the defense attorney's concession did not fail to subject the government's case to meaningful adversary testing. Therefore, the *Cronic* test was improperly used by the Florida Supreme Court. The Court determined that the *Strickland* test was the appropriate rule to use given the circumstances; furthermore, the defense attorney's performance did not violate that standard because it was not objectively unreasonable.

The Court has settled another important Sixth Amendment issue in *Nixon* regarding ineffective assistance of counsel. Allowing defendants to challenge the constitutionality of their death sentence simply because they did not approve or disapprove of their attorney's strategy of conceding guilt would lead to an endless number of cases flooding the federal court dockets. The Court has justifiably limited the ability of defendants to raise ineffective assistance claims and ensured that they will remain accountable for their actions once they have been convicted in state court.

ROMPILLA v. BEARD 545 U.S. 374 (2005)

CAPSULE: A defense counsel's failure to make a reasonable effort to investigate documented mitigating evidence such as a prior conviction, which is likely to be disclosed by the prosecution at sentencing, constitutes ineffective assistance of counsel.

FACTS: Rompilla was convicted of first-degree murder for the brutal killing of James Scanlon. The only mitigating evidence presented by defense counsel at sentencing was the testimony of Rompilla's family members, who pled with the jury to spare his life. After finding that aggravating factors outweighed the evidence in mitigation, the Pennsylvania jury sentenced Rompilla to death. The Pennsylvania Supreme Court affirmed. In state habeas corpus proceedings, Rompilla argued that his right to effective assistance of counsel had been violated because the trial attorney failed to present documented mitigating evidence, such as a prior conviction for rape and assault. Although the prosecutor alerted defense counsel of the prior conviction, defense counsel failed to investigate the prosecutor's file. Contained in the file was significant mitigating evidence about Rompilla's troubled childhood, mental illness, and alcohol use. However, the state courts found that trial counsel had built a significant mitigation case and denied Rompilla habeas relief.

On federal habeas appeal, the District Court held that trial counsel's performance was deficient because they failed to investigate documented evidence of the defendant's troubled upbringing, mental illness, and criminal history. The Third Circuit reversed, finding that trial counsel's performance was reasonable given their efforts to investigate mitigating evidence from Rompilla himself, his family members, and mental health professionals. The court held that although trial counsel's investigation was limited, there was no reason for the attorneys to believe that further investigation would reveal useful information. The Supreme Court of the United States granted certiorari to determine whether trial counsel's performance was constitutionally deficient according to the standard enunciated in *Strickland v. Washington* (1984).

ISSUE: Does counsel's failure to make a reasonable effort to review and obtain documented evidence that counsel knows the prosecution will use to support a death sentence constitute ineffective assistance of counsel? YES.

Continued

ROMPILLA v. BEARD 545 U.S. 374 (2005)—cont'd

HOLDING: A defense attorney must make a reasonable effort to review and obtain documented evidence retained by the prosecutor, such as a prior conviction, that counsel knows the prosecution will likely rely on during sentencing to support a death sentence.

REASON: "Here, the lawyers were deficient in failing to examine the court file on Rompilla's prior rape and assault conviction. They knew that the Commonwealth intended to seek the death penalty by proving that Rompilla had a significant history of felony convictions indicating the use or threat of violence, that it would attempt to establish this history by proving the prior conviction, and that it would emphasize his violent character by introducing a transcript of the rape victim's trial testimony. Although the prior conviction file was a public record, readily available at the courthouse where Rompilla was to be tried, counsel looked at no part of it until warned by the prosecution a second time, and even then did not examine the entire file. With every effort to view the facts as a defense lawyer would have at the time, it is difficult to see how counsel could have failed to realize that not examining the file would seriously compromise their opportunity to respond to an aggravation case. Their duty to make all reasonable efforts to learn what they could about the offense the prosecution was going to use certainly included obtaining the Commonwealth's own readily available file to learn what it knew about the crime, to discover any mitigating evidence it would downplay, and to anticipate the details it would emphasize. The obligation to examine the file was particularly pressing here because the violent prior offense was similar to the crime charged and because Rompilla's sentencing strategy stressed residual doubt. This obligation is not just common sense, but is also described in the American Bar Association Standards for Criminal Justice, which are 'guides to determining what is reasonable.' The state court's conclusion that defense counsel's efforts to find mitigating evidence by other means were enough to free them from further enquiry fails to answer the considerations set out here, to the point of being objectively unreasonable. No reasonable lawyer would forgo examination of the file thinking he could do as well by asking the defendant or family relations what they recalled. Nor would a reasonable lawyer compare possible searches for school reports, juvenile records, and evidence of drinking habits to the opportunity to take a look at a file disclosing what the prosecutor knows and plans to read from in his case."

CASE SIGNIFICANCE: This case is significant because it clarifies the scope and importance of building an adequate mitigation case for capital defendants. In *Rompilla*, the Supreme Court faced the issue of whether defense counsel's failure to examine the prosecutor's file, which contained important mitigating evidence, constituted a Sixth Amendment violation. In delivering the opinion of the Court, Justice David Souter claimed that "it flouts prudence to deny that a defense lawyer should try to look at a file he knows the prosecution will cull for aggravating evidence, let alone when the file is sitting in the trial courthouse, open for the asking." After applying the two-part test established in *Strickland*, the majority held that defense counsel's performance was deficient and that this deficiency led to a reasonable probability that the result of the trial would have been different.

Relying on the American Bar Association Standards of Criminal Justice for guidance, the Court found that trial counsel had committed a constitutional error because the prosecution's conviction file also contained a number of other untapped leads. The file included evidence of schizophrenia and mental retardation, as well as the fact that Rompilla had dropped out of school at the age of 16 and had been in and out of jail as a youth. Although the majority conceded that defense counsel was not constitutionally obligated to pursue every lead of mitigating possibilities, there were a number of avenues left unexplored by defense counsel.

The presumption in the practice of law is that an attorney's performance is reasonable, that hindsight should be discounted, and that deference should be given to counsel's judgments. In judging ineffective assistance of counsel claims, the Court has historically taken a case-by-case approach. The *Strickland* test has proven to be a workable framework for assessing the reasonableness of counsel's actions and omissions, given the infinite number of scenarios that may render counsel's performance constitutionally deficient. Although some degree of precision and standardization may be sacrificed, intuition is sometimes more realistic where questions of fundamental fairness are at issue.

SCHRIRO v. LANDRIGAN 550 U.S. 465 (2007)

CAPSULE: A defense attorney's failure to present mitigating evidence such as testimony of a disadvantaged background at sentencing when the defendant objects to counsel's strategy does not constitute ineffective assistance of counsel.

FACTS: Landrigan was convicted of first-degree murder. At sentencing, Landrigan's lawyer attempted to present mitigating evidence on his behalf, including witnesses that could testify to his disadvantaged childhood and good character. He also objected when his lawyer tried to present additional mitigating evidence and told the Arizona trial judge to "bring on" the death penalty. Subsequently, the state court sentenced him to death and the sentence was affirmed. The state post-conviction court concluded that Landrigan had no colorable claim of ineffective assistance of counsel, holding that he had directed his lawyer not to present any mitigating evidence on his behalf. In response to Landrigan's federal habeas petition, the District Court denied his motion for an evidentiary hearing, finding that his claim was without merit. The Ninth Circuit reversed, holding that defense counsel's performance was deficient according to *Strickland v. Washington* (1984). Landrigan argued that his counsel was ineffective because he failed to present mitigating evidence during sentencing and that he should be entitled to an evidentiary hearing of the facts.

ISSUES:
1. Does a district court's failure to grant an evidentiary hearing when a defendant cannot demonstrate a colorable ineffective assistance of counsel claim violate the Sixth Amendment? NO.
2. Does a defense attorney's failure to present mitigating evidence such as testimony of a disadvantaged background at sentencing constitute ineffective assistance of counsel when the defendant objects to counsel's strategy? NO.

HOLDING: The AEDPA does not require courts to grant evidentiary hearings when defendants cannot make colorable ineffective assistance of counsel claims. Further, a defense attorney's failure to present mitigating evidence when a defendant interferes with his counsel's strategy does not constitute ineffective assistance of counsel.

REASONING: "The Antiterrorism and Effective Death Penalty Act of 1996 (AEDPA) has not changed the basic rule that the decision to grant an evidentiary hearing is left to the district court's sound discretion, but it has changed the standards for granting federal habeas relief by prohibiting such relief unless a state court's adjudication 'resulted in a decision that was contrary to, or involved an unreasonable application of, clearly established Federal law, as determined by [this Court],' § 2254(d)(1), or 'was based on an unreasonable determination of the facts in light of the evidence presented in the State court proceeding,' § 2254(d)(2). Because § 2254's deferential standards control whether to grant habeas relief, a federal court must take into account those standards in deciding whether an evidentiary hearing is appropriate. In deciding whether to grant an evidentiary hearing, a federal court must consider whether the hearing could enable an applicant to prove the petition's factual allegations, which, if true, would entitle the applicant to federal habeas relief. It follows that if the record refutes the applicant's factual allegations or otherwise precludes habeas relief, a district court is not required to hold an evidentiary hearing.

"The Ninth Circuit also erred in rejecting the District Court's finding that the poor quality of Landrigan's alleged mitigating evidence prevented him from making a colorable prejudice claim. Because most of the evidence that Landrigan now wishes to offer would have been offered by this birth mother and ex-wife had he allowed them to testify, and because the sentencing court had much of the evidence before it by way of counsel's proffer, the District Court could reasonably conclude that any additional evidence would have made no difference in the sentencing. Even assuming the truth of all the facts Landrigan sought to prove at an evidentiary hearing, he still could not be granted federal habeas relief because the state courts' factual determination that he would not have allowed counsel to present any mitigating evidence at sentencing is not an unreasonable determination of the facts under § 2254(d) (2) and the mitigating evidence he seeks to introduce would not have changed the result."

CASE SIGNIFICANCE: This case has had a significant effect in terms of defense counsel's capacity to submit mitigating evidence on behalf of capital defendants, particularly in cases where a client's mental competency is in question. In

Continued

SCHRIRO v. LANDRIGAN 550 U.S. 465 (2007)—cont'd

Landrigan, the Court held that federal district courts retain sound discretion on the issue of granting evidentiary hearings under the guidelines established in the Antiterrorism and Effective Death Penalty Act of 1996 (AEDPA). The Court also found that the Sixth Amendment is not violated when defense counsel fails to present mitigating evidence because the defendant interferes with his lawyer's legal strategy. In this case, the Court emphasized the fact that even if an evidentiary hearing had been granted, Landrigan would have been unable to demonstrate a colorable ineffective assistance of counsel claim because he advised his lawyer not to present *any* mitigating evidence on his behalf. For this reason, the District Court was within its discretion to deny habeas relief according to AEDPA guidelines.

The Court also determined that the Ninth Circuit erred when it found that the defendant's "last-minute decision" to block testimony did not obviate defense counsel's duty to perform an adequate investigation of the mitigating evidence, as required in *Wiggins v. Smith* (2003). The Court stressed the fact that it had never decided a case where a capital defendant objected to the introduction of mitigating evidence at sentencing. Therefore, it was not objectively unreasonable for the Arizona post-conviction court to hold that counsel's performance was constitutionally deficient according to the guidelines established in *Strickland v. Washington* (1984). The Court also rejected the Ninth Circuit's requirement that a defendant's decision to block the introduction of mitigating evidence must be "informed and knowing." Opining that Landrigan had received adequate notice from his attorney as to the importance of mitigating evidence in death penalty cases, the Court held that Landrigan had been fully informed of the potential consequences of his actions.

The Court also disagreed with the Ninth Circuit when it determined that Landrigan would have been able to demonstrate a colorable ineffective assistance of counsel claim had the District Court granted the evidentiary hearing. Rejecting this argument, the Court averred that most of Landrigan's new evidence would have been proffered by his ex-wife and birth mother had he allowed them to testify at sentencing. Moreover, the District Court could have reasonably concluded that all of the available mitigating evidence was available at Landrigan's sentencing and that the introduction of additional evidence would not have changed the outcome of the case.

An important issue in this case is the assumption that potentially incompetent capital defendants can assist their attorneys in the development of an effective defense strategy. In his dissenting opinion, Justice John Paul Stevens criticized the majority's view that Landrigan's evidence was weak and insubstantial, opining that the defendant may suffer from an undiagnosed brain disorder—fetal alcohol syndrome. Justice Stevens further maintained that if a brain disorder were diagnosed, this would result in powerful mitigating evidence that would likely render him ineligible for the death penalty. The argument here is that there is a logical connection between mental deficiency and belligerent behavior in the courtroom and that adequate psychological testing should be conducted to determine whether a mental disorder exists prior to sentencing.

WOOD v. ALLEN 558 U.S. 290 (2010)

CAPSULE: Failure to present evidence of a petitioner's mental retardation at sentencing while emphasizing other mitigating factors is strategic and does not constitute ineffective assistance of counsel.

FACTS: Petitioner Holly Wood was convicted in 1994 for shooting his ex-girlfriend in the head while she was asleep in her bedroom. Of the three attorneys that were appointed to represent Wood at his trial, one had recently passed the bar exam only five months prior to his appointment. The attorneys with more experience assigned the lesser experienced attorney to handle the penalty phase of the trial. After the court sentenced Wood to death, he argued that his defense attorney failed to provide important mitigating evidence at his sentencing, which included a history of mental disabilities. The state court relied solely on the Alabama Attorney General's conclusions of fact and denied Wood's petition for habeas relief. The federal district court rejected the state court's finding that counsel's decision

Continued

WOOD v. ALLEN 558 U.S. 290 (2010)—cont'd

not to present the mitigating evidence was strategic and concluded that the attorney's performance unconstitutionally prejudiced Wood. The district court concluded that the evidence supporting his mental retardation should have been introduced during sentencing. The Eleventh Circuit reversed the decision, concluding that the attorney's performance was in fact strategic and thus Wood was not entitled to relief. The Court's decision in this case better clarifies the importance of state factual determinations in federal habeas proceedings.

ISSUES:
1. Is it unreasonable for a state court to conclude that an inexperienced attorney's decision not to present evidence of a client's mental retardation at sentencing was strategic, given the presentation of other mitigating evidence supporting a life sentence? NO.
2. Did the Eleventh Circuit neglect to exercise its judicial review authority when it failed to decide whether the state court's determination was reasonable, given the evidence contained in the state record? UNANSWERED.

HOLDING: A state court's conclusion that counsel made a strategic choice not to present evidence indicating a death penalty defendant's mental abnormalities is not unreasonable, given the entirety of the evidence presented during the state court proceedings. Further, a state court's determination of the facts is not unreasonable simply because a different conclusion would have been reached by a federal habeas court.

REASONING: "Even under Wood's reading of §2254(d)(2), the state court's conclusion that his counsel made a strategic decision not to pursue or present evidence of his mental deficiencies was not an unreasonable determination of the facts in light of the evidence presented in the state-court proceedings. This Court need not reach the question whether §2254(e)(1) applies in every case presenting a challenge under §2254(d)(2), because its view of the state court's factual determination here does not depend on an interpretative difference regarding the relationship between those provisions. While '[t]he term "unreasonable" is ... difficult to define,' it suffices to say that a state-court factual determination is not unreasonable merely because the federal habeas court would have reached a different conclusion in the first instance. Here, the state-court record shows that all of Wood's counsel read the Kirkland report. Trotter testified that Dozier told him that nothing in the report merited further investigation, a recollection supported by the attorneys' contemporaneous letters; and Trotter told the sentencing judge that counsel did not intend to introduce the report to the jury. This evidence can fairly be read to support the Rule 32 court's factual determination that counsel's failure to pursue or present evidence of Wood's mental deficiencies was not mere oversight or neglect but the result of a deliberate decision to focus on other defenses. Most of the contrary evidence Wood highlights—e.g., that Dozier and Ralph put the inexperienced Trotter in charge of the penalty phase proceedings—speaks not to whether counsel made a strategic decision, but to whether counsel's judgment was reasonable, a question not before this Court. Any evidence plausibly inconsistent with the strategic-decision finding does not suffice to show that the finding was unreasonable."

CASE SIGNIFICANCE: This case is unique because it involved conflicting interpretations of two provisions dealing with state court factual determinations under the AEDPA and fails to resolve a complicated area of death penalty law. Section 2254(d)(2) states that a federal habeas court may grant relief when a state's finding "was based on an unreasonable determination of the facts in light of the evidence presented in the State court proceeding." Similarly, section 2254(e)(1) articulates that "a determination of a factual issue made by a State court shall be presumed to be correct" except when clear and convincing evidence supports a rebuttal of the presumption.

The question whether section (e)(1) governs claims filed under (d)(2) was not answered by the Court. Moreover, do capital defendants have to prove by clear and convincing evidence in federal habeas proceedings that a state court's presumption of the evidence was correct in addition to demonstrating that it was unreasonable?

Although the court did not resolve this issue, it concluded that the petitioner's claim did not prevail according to either provision of the AEDPA. Viewing the interpretation most favorable to Wood, the Court concluded that his claim failed because the attorney's performance was reasonable given the totality of mitigating evidence involved in the case.

MAPLES v. THOMAS 565 U.S. ____ (2012)

CAPSULE: Counsel's failure to meet a filing deadline amounts to ineffective assistance of counsel when the petitioner is not to blame for the error and the attorneys of record are no longer acting in the petitioner's interests.

FACTS: The state of Alabama convicted Cory Maples of murder and sentenced him to death. During post-conviction proceedings, Maples alleged that his trial attorneys were ineffective because they were underpaid and lacked experience. Two pro bono attorneys from the New York law firm of Sullivan and Cromwell, Jaasai Munanka and Clara Ingen-Housz, filed Maples's post-conviction petition. The pro bono attorneys subsequently left the firm and failed to notify their firm or the client; thus no one from the firm sought substitution of counsel for Maples. Further, when the Alabama post-conviction court rejected Maples's claim, it notified the firm. The letter was subsequently returned to the Alabama clerk's office marked "return to sender," and no other action was taken. After the period to file an appeal expired, Maples's claim became procedurally defaulted. Maples was made aware of the procedural default when the Alabama State Attorney General's Office notified him of the missed deadline for appeal and of his impending deadline to file an appeal in federal court. Maples called his mother, who notified the law firm. Maples was eventually able to reinstate the 42-day appellate period, but the trial court denied his motion. After failing to obtain state post-conviction relief, he sought federal habeas relief, but both the district court and the Eleventh Circuit denied his request based on his procedural default in state court. The Supreme Court granted review to decide whether the Eleventh Circuit correctly ruled that no "cause" existed to exempt a procedural default when the petitioner's attorneys of record were to blame for the error.

ISSUE:

1. Did the appellate court correctly rule that no "cause" existed to excuse a procedural default when the state, and not the petitioner, was to blame for the default and the petitioner's attorneys had abandoned him at the time of the default? NO.

HOLDING: Counsel's failure to meet a filing deadline constitutes sufficient "cause" to excuse the petitioner's default in state habeas proceeding, thus the petitioner is entitled to federal habeas review.

REASON: "'Cause for a procedural default exists where 'something external to the petitioner, something that cannot fairly be attributed to him[,] . . . impeded [his] efforts to comply with the State's procedural rule.' A prisoner's postconviction attorney's negligence does not qualify as 'cause,' ibid., because the attorney is the prisoner's agent, and under 'well-settled' agency law, the principal bears the risk of his agent's negligent conduct. Thus, a petitioner is bound by his attorney's failure to meet a filing deadline and cannot rely on that failure to establish cause.

"A markedly different situation arises, however, when an attorney abandons his client without notice, and thereby occasions the default. In such cases, the principal-agent relationship is severed and the attorney's acts or omissions 'cannot fairly be attributed to [the client].' Nor can the client be faulted for failing to act on his own behalf when he lacks reason to believe his attorneys of record, in fact, are not representing him.

"Not only was Maples left without any functioning attorney of record; the very listing of Munanka, Ingen-Housz, and Butler as his representatives meant that he had no right personally to receive notice. He in fact received none within the 42 days allowed for commencing an appeal. Given no reason to suspect that he lacked counsel able and willing to represent him, Maples surely was blocked from complying with the State's procedural rule.

"The cause and prejudice requirement shows due regard for States' finality and comity interests while ensuring that 'fundamental fairness [remains] the central concern of the writ of habeas corpus.' In the unusual circumstances of this case, agency law principles and fundamental fairness point to the same conclusion: there was indeed cause to excuse Maples' procedural default. Through no fault of his own, he lacked the assistance of any authorized attorney during the 42-day appeal period. And he had no reason to suspect that, in reality, he had been reduced to pro se status."

Continued

MAPLES v. THOMAS 565 U.S. _____ (2012)—cont'd

CASE SIGNIFICANCE: One of the most significant legal obstacles habeas petitioners face is being procedurally barred from pursuing significant constitutional claims in federal court if those claims were not also filed in state court. This case illustrates the development of the "abandonment" principle in death penalty cases and holds that a state petitioner may overcome a state post-conviction default in federal habeas proceedings.

The Supreme Court has used two distinct approaches to evaluate ineffective assistance of counsel claims. The broader of the two—the performance based model—focuses on the level and quality of representation the attorney has provided to a client. The more narrow approach is the relationship model, which evaluates the nature of the relationship between the attorney and the client. Although the Court found that "under agency principles, a client cannot be held responsible for the acts or omissions of an attorney who abandons him," the Court's decision does not alter the general rule that the client assumes the risk of an attorney's conduct unless the attorney effectively abandons him, resulting in dissolution of the principal-agent relationship.

Further, *Maples* presents state post-conviction clients with an "out" when counsel ceases to operate in their client's interest. More broadly, it makes a statement regarding the Court's willingness to find avenues for relief when states have failed to provide appointed counsel or other systems for reliable representation. *Maples* sends a message to the states that post-conviction counsel have a significant role to play in litigating federal constitutional claims in their courts.

Key Terms

ABA guidelines
adversarial testing
AEDPA
Bell v. Cone
clemency
collateral relief
direct appeal
equitable tolling
Florida v. Nixon
habeas corpus
interest of justice
Maples v. Thomas
Mickens v. Taylor
mitigation investigation
prevailing professional norms
procedural default
post-conviction review
Rompilla v. Beard
Sixth Amendment
Strickland v. Washington
Wiggins v. Smith
Wood v. Allen
writ of certiorari

CRITICAL THINKING QUESTIONS

1.   The Supreme Court has defined what constitutes an incompetent mitigation investigation. Provide two examples of incompetent mitigation investigations and two examples of incompetent investigations by defense counsel and explain their significance.

2.   Lower courts have traditionally used two approaches to deciding issues of ineffective assistance of counsel in death penalty cases—one based on performance and the other the principle of agency. Provide two examples of cases using each approach and explain their significance.

3.   How has the Court responded to challenges involving conflicts of interest between death penalty defendants and their attorneys? Have these cases made it easier or more difficult for defendants to prevail during post-conviction review? Why?

Internet Resources

The Innocence Project
www.innocenceproject.org/understand/Bad-Lawyering.php

Capital Defense Project
www.capdefnet.org

Justice Denied
www.justicedenied.org

The Constitution Project
www.constitutionproject.org

The American Bar Association
www.americanbar.org/aba.html

Due Process and the Death Penalty

8

CHAPTER OUTLINE

I INTRODUCTION

The death penalty requires that special attention be given to the legal rights of capital defendants. Whether in criminal prosecutions or on habeas corpus review, courts must give maximum attention to Eighth and Fourteenth Amendment principles in death penalty cases. The U.S. Supreme Court mandates that courts make decisions that adhere to societal standards of decency in capital cases, elevated to what is often referred to as "super due process." As such, capital cases repeatedly raise questions about procedural fairness for death penalty defendants.

In general, the Supreme Court has interpreted the due process clause as that which "guarantees more than fairness... [it] provides heightened protection against government interference with certain fundamental rights and liberty interests."[1] In death penalty cases, the due process clause grants capital

---

[1]Bird, Daniel, *Life on the Line: Pondering the Fate of a Due Process Challenge to the Death Penalty*, 40 Am. Crim. L. Rev. 1329.

defendants fundamental fairness on the basis of rights that go beyond those explicitly stated in the Constitution.

This chapter presents an analysis of due process issues in death penalty cases. Particular attention is devoted to three key areas of death penalty law. The first section examines the concept of guided discretion in jury decision making, which has historically had its roots in due process protections. For example, due process was clearly at issue in *Holmes v. South Carolina* (2006),[2] where the Court reconciled South Carolina's third-party guilt statute with Holmes's ability to present an alternative perpetrator defense. The second section analyzes cases involving due process and the admissibility of psychiatric examinations. The Court's decision in *Estelle v. Smith* (1981)[3] is the seminal case in this area, but the Court's recent decision to grant certiorari in *Kansas v. Cheever* (2012)[4] reveals the difficulty in interpreting state law defenses such as voluntary intoxication within the bounds of *Smith*. Finally, the chapter closes with a discussion of due process and the prosecution's duty to disclose exculpatory evidence to the defense. Recent Supreme Court cases *Connick v. Thompson* (2011) and *Smith v. Cain* (2012) reveal the different approaches the Court has used to sanction prosecutorial misconduct and the remedies that are available to capital litigants.

II GUIDED DISCRETION, JURIES, AND DUE PROCESS

After the landmark decision in *Gregg*, the Supreme Court sought to prevent juries and judges from making decisions that were arbitrary or capricious. The *Gregg* Court compelled states to enact statutory guidelines for sentencing bodies to follow when deciding whether to impose the death penalty on a capital defendant. The Court extended the concept of due process in subsequent cases, such as those involving (1) consideration of mitigating evidence during sentencing, (2) the defendant's opportunity to deny or refute the state's evidence, (3) evidence of future dangerousness, and (4) the process of jury decision making.

A Due Process Requires Consideration of Mitigating Evidence

In *Woodson v. North Carolina* (1976)[5] the Court examined a North Carolina statute that mandated the death penalty for defendants convicted of first-degree murder despite the presence of mitigating circumstances. Because the Court in *Furman v. Georgia* (1972)[6] ruled that unguided discretion on the part of the jury was unconstitutional, the legislature responded by enacting laws that were more restrictive and therefore less discriminatory. The *Woodson* Court concluded that the North Carolina statute violated the "evolving standards of decency" test that was established in *Trop v. Dulles* (1958)[7] and reiterated in *Gregg*. Through the due process clause of the Fourteenth Amendment, the Court struck down the statute because it did not consider mitigating evidence for the defendant. Specifically, the Court

---

[2]*Holmes*, 547 U.S. 319 (2006).
[3]451 U.S. 454 (1981).
[4]295 Kan. 229 (2012).
[5]428 U.S. 280 (1976).
[6]*Furman v. Georgia*, 408 U.S. 238 (1972).
[7]*Trop v. Dulles*, 356 U.S. 86 (1958).

stated that factors concerning his character or criminal background or any circumstances surrounding the offense that could potentially lead to a sentence less severe than death should have been taken into account during sentencing. Citing the need to ensure individualized sentencing in capital trials, the Court claimed that the finality associated with the death sentence requires heightened reliability to ensure that the penalty is applied fairly. The Court ruled that individualized sentencing is needed to ensure that state courts are sufficiently guided when deciding the appropriate punishment for a capital defendant. Although the Court held in *Woodson* that sentencing bodies should consider certain types of mitigating evidence before issuing a sentence, it also maintained that discretion must be limited.

In *Lockett v. Ohio* (1978),[8] the Court expanded the application of the Eighth and Fourteenth Amendments by invalidating an Ohio capital sentencing statute. The law under review by the Court did not mandate that the state trial judge consider individual mitigating factors, such as criminal history, offense characteristics, or age of the defendant, when deciding the appropriate sentence. In this case, the trial judge interpreted the defendant's age as the only relevant mitigating factor, but the Supreme Court disagreed, holding that the statute was unconstitutional because the Eighth and Fourteenth Amendments required consideration of any mitigating evidence offered by the defendant that supported a sentence less than death.

Prior to this case, the Court had not decided the issue as to the type of evidence to be considered in mitigating a death sentence. Citing the need for courts to make individualized determinations regarding each mitigating factor, the Court reinforced its command in *Lockett* by holding that all mitigating evidence must be weighed before a death sentence can be imposed.

In a later case, *Eddings v. Oklahoma* (1982),[9] the Supreme Court held that a sentencing body may not refuse to consider a pertinent mitigating fact, even when that fact has been deemed insignificant. In *Eddings*, the trial judge instructed the jury to disregard certain mitigating evidence presented by the defense. On appeal, the Court rejected the lower court's decision to exclude mitigating evidence altogether by ruling that the due process clause required that evidence be weighed independently in the context of all other aggravating and mitigating factors. The Court held that the Oklahoma trial and appellate courts should have allowed certain mitigating evidence to be introduced to the jury "that might indicate a sentence lesser than death."[10] Therefore, while the *Lockett* Court required that all mitigating evidence be introduced during sentencing, the *Eddings* Court gave sentencing juries more discretionary power by allowing them to make individual determinations as to whether a particular fact should be considered as mitigating evidence. In an effort to achieve the goals sought in *Gregg* while also being cognizant of the fears raised after *Woodson* and *Lockett*, the *Eddings* Court struck a middle ground by acknowledging the importance of individual differences among capital defendants.

B **Due Process Requires Opportunity to Rebut State's Evidence**

Whereas the initial cases involving individual sentencing guidelines dealt with both the Eighth and Fourteenth Amendments, the Court deviated from this approach in *Gardner v. Florida* (1977).[11] In this case, the Court invalidated a trial court's decision by exclusively relying on the concept of due process

---

[8]*Lockett v. Ohio*, 438 U.S. 586 (1978).
[9]*Eddings v. Oklahoma*, 455 U.S. 104 (1982)
[10]Richardson, Eric W., *Due Process Requirements of Jury Charges in Capital Cases*, 64 U. Cin. L. Rev. 755 (1996).
[11]*Gardner v. Florida*, 430 U.S. 349 (1977).

as basis for its holding. Whereas the *Eddings* and *Lockett* Courts held that juries must be able to consider any type of mitigating factor during sentencing, the *Gardner* Court found that the due process clause precluded a court from sentencing a defendant to death when he "had no opportunity to deny or explain the evidence against him."[12] In this case, the Court held that the due process clause prohibited a trial court from sentencing a defendant to death on the basis of confidential information found in a presentence report that was not initially available for consideration by the jury during sentencing.

The facts in *Gardner* presented a different problem for the Court compared to previous cases. The trial court originally imposed a life sentence after convicting the defendant of first-degree murder. After reviewing the separate confidential presentence report, however, the trial judge found that the aggravating factors outweighed the mitigating circumstances presented by the defense and changed the sentence from life imprisonment to death. On appeal, the Supreme Court of Florida affirmed the trial court's decision. The U.S. Supreme Court reversed, finding that the defendant's right to due process was violated when the trial judge withheld confidential information from the jury during sentencing.

The Court acknowledged the significance of giving the defense the chance to rebut evidence held in a confidential presentence report, especially in death penalty cases. The Court explained that sentencing Gardner to death on the basis of confidential information that had never been made available to him at his trial, which led to his death sentence, was unconstitutional. This case is important because it recognizes that the due process clause protects a defendant from arbitrary sentencing procedures that can potentially take place in death penalty cases.

The Court distinguished the facts of *Gardner* to the circumstances in *Netherland v. Gray* (1996).[13] In that case, the Court held that Gray's due process rights were not violated when the prosecutor announced, one day before sentencing, that he planned to use evidence from an unrelated murder case during the penalty phase of the trial. Chief Justice William Rehnquist, writing for the majority, said that Gray's claim was different because he "had the opportunity to hear the testimony of the witnesses and to cross-examine them."[14] Because Gray had the opportunity to request a continuance, he was not deprived of adequate notice; thus, there was no due process violation.

C Future Dangerousness and the Right to Due Process

Capital juries often must decide whether a defendant's conduct represents a future danger to society before they impose a death sentence. The Supreme Court has consistently relied on the due process clause to decide issues about the types of evidence that can be used to demonstrate future dangerousness. As states began to include provisions in their statutory schemes for assessing future dangerousness, the Court shifted its attention to the defendant's right to rebut the state's evidence in support of this theory.

The Court first used the due process clause to decide issues on future dangerousness in *Skipper v. South Carolina* (1986).[15] In *Skipper*, the Court decided that the defendant's Eighth and Fourteenth Amendment rights were violated when the trial court denied the defendant the opportunity to introduce

---

[12]*Id.*
[13]*Netherland v. Gray*, 519 U.S. 1301 (1996).
[14]*Id.* at 1307.
[15]*Skipper v. South Carolina*, 476 U.S. 1 (1986).

evidence of his good behavior in jail as a mitigating factor at his sentencing. Therefore, the Court found that his constitutional rights had been violated, because the *Lockett* decision mandated that a sentencing body make an individualized determination of aggravating and mitigating factors when the prosecutor alleges future dangerousness. In addition, the petitioner's right to due process was violated because he was unable to deny or explain the evidence used against him as specified by the *Gardner* Court.

In *California v. Ramos* (1983),[16] the Court held that a jury instruction regarding the possibility of a commuted life sentence did not violate the Eighth Amendment or due process clause of the Fourteenth Amendment. In this case, the Court considered whether such an instruction interfered with the jury's ability to make a reliable determination regarding individual mitigating elements. The Court held that the instruction was not unconstitutional because it merely afforded the jury an opportunity to consider each of the defendant's characteristics individually. After *Ramos*, the Court began to examine future dangerousness and sentencing standards predominantly in the context of the due process clause.

Due process is the constitutional mechanism for ensuring that state sentencing schemes are fundamentally fair. In addition to issues pertaining to the introduction of mitigating evidence, the Court has also relied on due process to evaluate the constitutionality of state laws and sentencing practices that limit the discretion of juries when deciding guilt or innocence. The following section discusses these issues in more depth.

D Due Process and Third-Party Guilt

In *Holmes v. South Carolina* (2006),[17] the overarching issue before the Court was federalism, specifically the power of states to enact their own rules of evidence for criminal proceedings.[18] The South Carolina law the Court addressed in *Holmes* posited that if the state has strong forensic evidence, a defendant cannot raise an "alternative perpetrator defense."[19] States have devised these rules to prevent juror confusion and to prevent the introduction of misleading stories by additional parties.[20] Writing for a unanimous majority opinion, Justice Samuel Alito held that the South Carolina law violated the Sixth and Fourteenth Amendments. The case is significant because the Court's reasoning can be similarly applied to all criminal cases, not just capital cases. However, given the variety of evidentiary standards that exist among the states, it is possible that the Court's holding may have caused more confusion in the lower courts than what was intended.

The Court stated that South Carolina's evidence rule was unconstitutional for three main reasons. First, in *State v. Gay* (2001),[21] the South Carolina Supreme Court barred defendants from invoking the "alternative perpetrator" defense in some instances, which prevented the defendant from successfully challenging the state's case. If the judge, not the jury, determined that the prosecutor's evidence was "strong," then the defendant could not proffer evidence suggestive of third-party guilt. The state's law precluded Holmes from suggesting that the state's evidence was flawed, staged, or tainted. Further, Justice Alito claimed that

---

[16]*California v. Ramos*, 463 U.S. 992 (1983).
[17]*Holmes*, 547 U.S. 319 (2006).
[18]Klein, Richard, *Eighteenth Annual Supreme Court Review: Death Penalty and Right to Counsel Decisions in the October 2005 Term*, 22 Touro L. Rev. 1003 (2007).
[19]*Supra* note 5.
[20]Seigel, Andrew, *A Tale of 2 Terms: A Transitional Year for the United States Supreme Court*, 18 S. Carolina Lawyer 30 (2006).
[21]541 S.E.2d 541 (S.C. 2001).

the South Carolina procedure was arbitrary, meaning that it did not further the interests of typical third-party guilt rules. Next, the Court stated that the standard set in *Gay* was deficient because it did not allow juries to determine the credibility of witnesses and thus whether this evidence was considered "strong." To emphasize the prejudicial effect of the state's rule, the Court suggested that it is as irrational as its opposite: "a rule barring the prosecution from introducing evidence of a defendant's guilt if the defendant is able to proffer, at a pretrial hearing, evidence that, if believed, strongly supports a verdict of not guilty."[22] The Court concluded that without requiring jury consideration of the evidence, the law was illogical. And last, the Court reasoned that a defendant must be given a meaningful opportunity to present a thorough defense. Without allowing a defendant to advance an alternative theory for the crime solely on the thrust of the prosecution's evidence, the rule fails to serve a legitimate purpose that related rules are intended to promote.

At present, state and federal courts use a mixture of standards to evaluate the admissibility of evidence.[23] Generally speaking, there are two main approaches. Under the first scheme, 17 states, including South Carolina, require defendants to present evidence indicating a "direct link" between a particular third party and the offense. Although this is the most common approach, other states use variations of this model. A second category of states relies on Federal Rule of Evidence 401 to determine evidence admissibility. Under this Federal Rule, the evidence is admissible if it significantly contributes to reasonable doubt of the defendant's guilt. This is a more flexible approach than requiring that defendants establish that there is a direct connection linking the third party to the crime. So, whereas the South Carolina rule focuses on the relevance of the evidence indicating the culpability of a third party, the federal test is concerned with how the evidence relates to the defendant's culpability.

Regardless of which approach a state adopts, courts frequently use characteristics of both when relating the law to a given set of facts.[24] Given the many variations of these rules within the states, it is likely that the U.S. Supreme Court and lower appellate courts will confront similar challenges to state evidentiary standards in capital cases in the future.

E Due Process and the Issue of Shackling

Courts have traditionally recognized, as a product of state or constitutional law, a defendant's right to appear in court free of obvious restraints. The basis for this reasoning lies in the defendant's right to due process and the presumption of innocence until proven guilty beyond a reasonable doubt. However, the Supreme Court had never addressed this issue until 2005 in the case of *Deck v. Missouri*.[25] In a seven-to-two vote written by Justice Stephen Breyer, the majority held that, absent an overwhelming state interest such as courtroom security, the practice of shackling capital defendants is inherently biasing and fundamentally unfair, therefore violating a defendant's right to due process of law.

The Court began its opinion addressing the practice of shackling in the context of its prior holdings in *Estelle v. Williams* (1976), *Illinois v. Allen* (1970), and *Holbrook v. Flynn* (1986). In each of these cases the Court noted that the practice of shackling was always used as a last resort. In Flynn, for example, the Court distinguished the presence of additional security personnel in the courtroom from the practice of shackling,

---

[22]547 U.S. 327.

[23]Blume, J.H., S.L. Johnson, and E.C. Paavola, *Every Juror Wants a Story: Narrative Relevance, Third-Party Guilt, and the Right to Present a Defense*, 44 AM. CRIM. L. REV. 1069 (2007).

[24]*Supra* note 8.

[25]*Deck v. Missouri*, 544 U.S. 622 (2005).

calling the latter inherently prejudicial. In general, the Court's ruling was based on three central criticisms: (1) that shackling may lead to biased juror perceptions undermining the presumption of innocence; (2) that shackling is likely to interfere with a defendant's capacity to assist in his own defense; and (3) that shackling may undercut key principles characterizing this nation's courtrooms—dignity, fairness, and justice.

Using this framework of analysis, the Court opined that the concerns about guilt-phase shackling also apply to the sentencing phase of capital trials. The Court reasoned that, although the issue of guilt or innocence is moot during the penalty phase, the jury is still deliberating between life or death, a decision of equal significance for capital defendants. The issue of juror bias was of particular concern to the Court because shackling implies that the defendant represents a future danger to society, which many states consider to be an aggravating factor supporting a death sentence. Shackling, according to the majority's view, undermines the presumption of innocence and insinuates that a defendant needs to be separated from the rest of society. The Court next explained that the practice of shackling generally interferes with a defendant's right to counsel and to communicate or participate normally with defense counsel. As an example, the Court pointed to a 1696 King's Bench case illustrating a criminal defendant's decision to avoid taking the witness stand because he was in shackles and could not move about freely. The Court's third justification for supporting a general prohibition on the practice of shackling focused on the maintenance of dignity, equality, and justice, principles essential to the courtroom. The Court proffered that the atmosphere of the Nation's courts "reflect a seriousness of purpose that helps to explain the judicial system's power to inspire the confidence and to affect the behavior of a general public whose demands for justice our courts seek to serve."

In his dissenting opinion, Justice Clarence Thomas argued that the majority's conception of the history of shackling was misplaced. He opined that common law restrictions on shackling were traditionally applied for the welfare of defendants, not the principles outlined by the majority. Justice Thomas distinguished modern restraints from the types of shackles used at common law, noting that irons of that period were heavy and extremely painful. To counter the majority's opinion, Justice Thomas noted that most states had not addressed the issue of shackling, at least as defined by modern practice, until the end of the twentieth century. To further his argument, Justice Thomas reasoned that state opinions on the issue were contradictory, with many opinions resting heavily on the discretion of trial judges. In response to the three fundamental legal tenets that the majority outlined, the dissent claimed that Deck had never asserted that his right to counsel had been impaired; thus he had no legitimate claim. Second, Justice Thomas stated that the right to dignity and decorum in the courtroom was not an essential part of due process and that the practice only minimally affected courtroom security. He conceded that shackling raised concerns during the guilt phase but reasoned that the same concerns did not exist during the penalty phase. Justice Thomas opined that the presumption of innocence was negated at this stage and therefore no constitutional violation existed.

F Due Process and the Importance of the Jury Verdict

Until recently, there has been no answer as to whether a life sentence imposed by a court constitutes a form of acquittal and bars a retrial for a harsher sentence. In *Sattazahn v. Pennsylvania* (2003),[26] the Court resolved this issue by relying on the concept of due process and the Fifth Amendment's double

---

[26]*Sattazahn v. Pennsylvania*, 537 U.S. 101 (2003).

jeopardy clause. The *Sattazahn* case raised questions regarding the consequences associated with the appeals process, especially in capital punishment cases. In this case, the Court held that, because the jury made no findings with respect to the alleged aggravating circumstance, Sattazahn was not acquitted of death in the first trial. Therefore, he was not legally entitled to his life sentence and could be retried without being put twice in jeopardy. Although the Pennsylvania statute obligated the trial judge to impose a life sentence when the jury failed to unanimously agree on the sentence, Justice Antonin Scalia, writing for the majority, disagreed with the dissent's position that the ruling by the trial judge "had the hallmarks of guilt or innocence."[27] The Court claimed that when Sattazahn opted for a retrial, he invoked a separate "process"; therefore the Fourteenth Amendment did not render immutable any "life or liberty" interest given by Pennsylvania law. Likewise, no due process violation occurred.

After *Sattazahn*, criminal defendants who have not technically been acquitted will be confronted with a momentous choice: They must accept the original verdict as final in an effort to avoid the death penalty or take the chance of receiving a more severe penalty when attempting to obtain an acquittal from the jury on retrial. Although placing criminal defendants in this position was not found by the Court to be unconstitutional, in future cases claimants will likely fear the possibility that they may receive a more severe punishment after a second trial. Overall, the Court has carved an exception to previous case law on the double jeopardy clause as it applies to capital murder cases.

III ADMISSIBILITY OF PSYCHIATRIC EXAMINATIONS

The Court began to extend the application of due process to other legal areas following the *Gardner* and *Eddings* decisions. In *Estelle v. Smith* (1981),[28] the Court held that testimony from a psychiatrist based on a court-ordered psychiatric examination violated the Fifth, Sixth, and Fourteenth Amendments when the defendant was not advised of his constitutional rights. By using the Fourteenth Amendment, which was made applicable to the states through the due process clause, the Court claimed that Smith's Fifth and Sixth Amendment rights were violated, because due process ensures that these protections apply to the sentencing as well as the guilt determination stage of a capital trial.

Prior to Smith's trial, the judge ordered that he undergo a psychiatric examination by the state's psychiatrist. The competency examination was performed, and the psychiatrist concluded that Smith was competent to stand trial. After the defendant was found guilty of capital murder, the psychiatrist testified at the sentencing stage that Smith represented a future danger to society because he was a severe sociopath. Finding that the privilege against self-incrimination applied equally to the guilt as well as the sentencing stage of a capital trial, the Supreme Court stated that the introduction of such evidence was prohibited "unless the defendant was warned prior to questioning that his statements could be introduced against him at the sentencing stage."[29] However, the Court cautioned that such a defense might not succeed in some cases, such as when the state's psychiatrist was testifying to rebut evidence proffered by a defense psychiatrist.

The *Smith* Court also found that the government had violated the defendant's right to counsel when he was denied the opportunity to consult with his lawyer concerning the psychiatrist's testimony. When

[27]*Id.*
[28]*Estelle v. Smith*, 451 U.S. 454 (1981).
[29]White, Welsh, Government, *Psychiatric Examinations and the Death Penalty*, 37 Ariz. L. Rev. 869 (1995).

the state failed to notify Smith's attorney that such testimony would address their client's future dangerousness to society, the state also violated his Sixth Amendment right to counsel. The Court stated that in order for the psychiatrist's testimony to be admissible, Smith would have to have been told that he had a right to remain silent prior to the psychiatrist's examination.

Since the decision in *Smith*, the Court has not directly addressed the issue of pretrial examinations and the capital defendant's rights in these situations. However, the Supreme Court clarified the Smith ruling in *Buchanan v. Kentucky* (1987).[30] In this case, the Court held that government psychiatric testimony could be used to rebut capital defense testimony by a psychiatrist concerning the emotional background of the defendant. Speaking for the Court, Justice Harry Blackmun claimed that when a capital defendant presents evidence of "extreme emotional disturbance,"[31] the government could, in turn, impugn the defense psychiatrist's testimony on the grounds that it was unreliable. This issue of emotional stability raises several implications for the prosecution as well as the defense during the rebuttal process.

Since 1987, the Court has not considered individual factors beyond "extreme emotional stability" that can determine when a prosecutor's right to rebuttal is invoked. One scholar has claimed that a plausible solution to this problem would be to allow a defense psychiatrist to testify regarding the defendant's emotional stability at the time of the crime without accounting for prior criminal history.[32] One benefit to this defense is that the prosecution would be precluded from introducing evidence regarding the defendant's uncharged conduct. By the same token, if testimony by a defense psychiatrist is perceived to be biased, the prosecutor can argue that his or her evaluation is unreliable. Whether a court considers a particular psychological evaluation to be valid or invalid, the defendant is protected by two legal interests: (1) the right to limit the range of the state psychiatrist's examination, and (2) an interest in not being compelled to reveal information about his or her prior criminal history. A frequent response by the government is to provide use immunity for capital defendants in these situations. This legal tactic prohibits the state's psychiatrist from using prior criminal history as a determinative factor of emotional stability, which can be used as a mitigating factor during the sentencing stage.

In December, 2013, the Supreme Court announced its decision in *Kansas v. Cheever* (2013)[33]. At issue in this case was whether a state violates a defendant's Fifth Amendment right against self-incrimination and due process when it introduces evidence obtained from a court-ordered mental health evaluation to rebut testimony proffered by the defense that the defendant suffered from prolonged methamphetamine use and therefore lacked the necessary culpability to commit capital murder. The Kansas Supreme Court held that the State violated the defendant's Fifth Amendment right because Cheever did not waive his right against compulsory self-incrimination during that examination, which occurred as part of a separate federal case against him. The Court was not able to conclude beyond a reasonable doubt that the State's expert evaluation did not influence the outcome of his trial, and therefore the error could not be considered harmless. As a result, Cheever's convictions were reversed and the case was remanded for a new trial. In a unanimous opinion written by Justice Sotomayor, the Court reversed the Kansas Supreme Court's opinion and held that the state did not violate Cheever's right to due process and protection against self-incrimination. The Court reasoned that to deny the prosecution

---

[30]*Buchanan v. Kentucky*, 483 U.S. 402 (1987).
[31]White, *supra* note 16 at 4.
[32]White, *supra* note 16 at 5.
[33]*Kansas v. Cheever*, 187 L. Ed. 2d 519, (2013).

the opportunity to rebut testimony proffered by the defense would undermine the adversarial process. Because Cheever used psychiatric testimony to show he lacked the ability to contemplate the murder, The Court held that the prosecution must be afforded the opportunity to counter that evidence. However, the Court did not answer the question whether the defense of "voluntary intoxication" is tantamount to a "mental status" defense. The Supreme Court ultimately remanded the case to the Kansas Supreme Court to decide whether the scope of the prosecution's expert testimony went beyond the parameters of Kansas law.

IV THE *BRADY* RULE AND THE RIGHT TO DUE PROCESS

The preceding sections have discussed the application of due process in various phases of capital litigation. The Court has also decided a number of cases involving a defendant's due process right to discovery of exculpatory evidence the state possesses.

In *Brady v. Maryland* (1963),[34] the Supreme Court held that "the suppression by prosecution of evidence favorable to an accused upon request violates due process where the evidence is material either to guilt or to punishment, irrespective of the good faith or bad faith of the prosecution."[35] For all intents and purposes, the implications of the *Brady* rule extend beyond the case itself. It encompasses the domain of criminal procedure applicable to the prosecutor's duty to disclose favorable or exculpatory evidence to the accused. Most important, the *Brady* Court articulated the standard of proof required to demonstrate a due process violation warranting relief resulting from nondisclosure of evidence subject to the disclosure rule. Further, defendants are only required to show that a reasonable probability exists that a more favorable outcome would have occurred had the exculpatory evidence been made available. Defendants are not required to demonstrate that they would have actually been acquitted—a much higher burden of proof to establish. In *Smith v. Cain* (2012),[36] the Supreme Court recently emphasized this standard when it opined: "A reasonable probability does not mean that the defendant 'would more likely than not have received a different verdict with the evidence,' only that the likelihood of a different result is great enough to 'undermine confidence in the outcome of the trial.'"[37]

Much debate exists over whether the *Brady* rule is grounded in procedural or substantive due process. One scholar claims it is "a free-standing due process right."[38] In a substantive sense, the *Brady* rule is concerned with preserving innocence. Further, it is universally applicable to all types of criminal prosecutions. Therefore, *Brady* and its progeny govern procedures that are similarly applicable in non-death penalty cases. The prosecution has the same constitutional duty to disclose favorable evidence in a death penalty case as it does in any other criminal prosecution.

Notwithstanding the universal application of the *Brady* rule to criminal cases, the Supreme Court has decided several important death penalty cases involving the *Brady* rule. The following sections

---

[34]*Brady v. Maryland*, 373 U.S. 83 (1963).
[35]*Id.* at 373 U.S. 83, 87 (1963).
[36]*Smith v. Caine,* 132 S.Ct. 627 (2012).
[37]*Id.* at 630 (quoting *Kyles v. Whitley*, 514 U.S. 419, 434 (1995)).
[38]See Jerold H. Israel, *Free-Standing Due Process and Criminal Procedure: The Supreme Court's Search for Interpretative Guidelines*, 45 St. Louis U. L.J. 303, 390-91 & n.498 (2001).

present an overview of case law interpreting the *Brady* rule and highlight recent issues the Court has resolved in death penalty litigation.

A The Disclosure Duty

In a line of post-*Brady* decisions, the Court resolved several key issues regarding the prosecution's duty to disclose favorable evidence as required by the due process clause. In *United States v. Agurs* (1976),[39] a nondeath penalty case, the Court established that disclosure was required even when defense counsel did not specifically request disclosure of the evidence. Some years later, the Court expanded the scope of the *Brady* rule to include not only exculpatory evidence but also evidence of impeachment.[40] Following the Court's decision in *Bagley*, the Court ruled in *Strickler v. Greene* (1999)[41] that inaccuracies or "significant" omissions in the prosecutor's file constitute a *Brady* violation, even when the prosecutor has an open file policy allowing defense attorneys to inspect the state's evidence.

However, the Court's decision in a key death penalty case—*Kyles v. Whitley* (1995)[42]—provided more clarity for lower courts on the scope of *Brady* and the prosecution's duty to disclose. The *Kyles* Court indicated that the prosecutor has a duty to disclose all favorable evidence to the defense that develops through the state's investigation. This includes police investigation details and agents connected with the prosecution's team. In other words, the failure on behalf of the police to disclose pertinent, exculpatory evidence to the prosecutor may result in a *Brady* violation. *Kyles* also held that a *Brady* violation is triggered by the totality of the nondisclosed evidence that is favorable to the accused. This makes it less burdensome for defendants to establish a due process violation, because facts are examined cumulatively instead of independently. Finally, the Court's holding establishes that the prosecutor has the ultimate responsibility in determining whether the evidence is important to the defense and therefore governed by the disclosure rule. This is a rather subjective determination because it may not always be obvious to prosecutors what evidence may be favorable to the accused.[43]

B Recent Brady Challenges in Death Penalty Cases

According to *Brady* and subsequent cases, the defense must only show that a reasonable probability exists that the result of the trial may have been different in order to demonstrate a violation, regardless of good or bad intent on the part of the prosecution. The Court has recently decided a series of cases involving the failure of the prosecution to disclose *Brady* evidence to defense counsel. Collectively, these cases signal the Court's increasing sensitivity to misconduct on the part of prosecutors, particularly when violations are egregious.

Cone v. Bell (2009)[44] involved an underlying *Brady* violation with the central issues being (1) whether habeas claims that are presented twice in state courts are procedurally defaulted in federal

---

[39]427 U.S. 97, 106 (1976).
[40]*United States v. Bagley*, 473 U.S. 667, 676 (1985).
[41]527 U.S. 263, 276 (1999).
[42]514 U.S. 419 (1995).
[43]Sullivan, J. Thomas, *Brady, Arkansas Rule 17.1, and Disclosure of Scientific Evidence and Expert Opinion*, 35 U. Ark. Little Rock L. Rev. 245 (2013).
[44]556 U.S. 449 (2009).

court, and (2) whether a federal habeas court has the authority to decide if a state court incorrectly held that state law bars review of a habeas case. A Tennessee trial court convicted Gary Cone of murdering Shipley O. Todd and Cleopatra Todd in their homes in August 1980. Cone's initial appeal and state post-conviction petitions failed, but in a second petition for habeas relief in the state courts he maintained that the state withheld potentially exculpatory evidence, including police reports and witness statements, which would have bolstered his defense of insanity and mitigation in the case. After the state courts denied relief, Cone filed a federal habeas petition in District Court. But because Cone failed to raise the claim in his initial petition, the District Court concluded that he had defaulted. The District Court further opined that even if Cone's claim was not procedurally defaulted, it would have failed because there was no reasonable likelihood that the result of the trial would have been different given the totality of the evidence. On certiorari to the Sixth Circuit, the Supreme Court held that the state court's denial of habeas relief was incorrect and that Cone was entitled to post-conviction review of his *Brady* claim. The Court determined that the lower courts failed to adequately consider the relevance of undisclosed documents to Cone's sentencing. The Court further determined that there was no reasonable probability that the undisclosed evidence, if admitted properly, would have resulted in a different outcome for Cone on his insanity defense. But in terms of his death sentence, the Court held that the suppressed evidence was "material to the jury's assessment of the proper punishment, [and] a full review of that evidence and its effect on the sentencing verdict"[45] was warranted.

By way of *Cone v. Bell* (2009), the Court reminds us that the *Brady* rule encompasses evidence that may not reduce a defendant's culpability but nevertheless mitigates punishment. Importantly, the Court noted that while "[e]vidence that is material to guilt will often be material for sentencing purposes as well, the converse is not always true."[46] Despite the fact that the suppressed witness accounts, police documents, and interview transcripts were not sufficient to mount a successful insanity defense for Cone, the Court believed the jury should have had the opportunity to consider that evidence at sentencing.

The consequences associated with a *Brady* violation were originally limited to the possibility of a reversal of the conviction or a remand to consider any evidence that was not disclosed to defense counsel at trial. But recently, the Court has vacillated somewhat between mechanisms of accountability for failing to disclose *Brady* evidence. For example, the Supreme Court's decision in *Van de Kamp v. Goldstein* (2009)[47] further insulated governmental entities from liability when district attorneys fail to properly train and supervise their staffs. In *Connick v. Thompson* (2011),[48] the Court ultimately refused to provide relief to Thompson because the New Orleans District Attorney's office did not commit a pattern of *related* Brady violations that would have put the agency on notice that training was constitutionally required.

Much attention has surrounded the Court's decision in *Connick*, primarily because of its unique circumstances. The New Orleans District Attorney's office acknowledged it had committed a *Brady* violation when it failed to disclose a crime lab report that indicated Thompson was not guilty of committing murder. Thompson chose not to testify at his murder trial because his prior robbery conviction could be used against him by the prosecution. Nevertheless, the trial court convicted

---

[45]*Id.* at 472.
[46]*Id.* at 474.
[47]129 S. Ct. 855 (2009).
[48]131 S. Ct. 1350 (2011).

Thompson and sentenced him to death. In 1994, Deegan, one of the prosecutors originally assigned to Thompson's case, became terminally ill. Deegan admitted to another prosecutor, Riehlmann, he had not provided blood evidence to Thompson's defense attorney as required by *Brady*. Riehlmann also chose not to come forward with the information. But shortly before Thompson was scheduled to be executed, his private investigator discovered the exculpatory evidence. Connick was found not guilty of committing murder after a reviewing court vacated his convictions. As a matter of recourse, Thompson filed a Section 1983 civil lawsuit against the New Orleans District Attorney's office alleging that it had been deliberately indifferent, failing to provide training for prosecutors on ways to improve disclosure procedures. The trial court held that Thompson did not have to establish that a pattern of similar *Brady* violations had occurred but only that there was a clear need for training. Thompson was awarded a $14 million judgment for having been wrongfully incarcerated and sentenced to death.

On certiorari to the Fifth Circuit, the Supreme Court held that a single *Brady* violation is insufficient to establish Section 1983 liability on the part of a prosecutor's office for failing to provide training on *Brady* disclosure to its staff. The Court's decision ultimately vacated Thompson's judgment and provided him no remedy for the state's error.

One commentator has referred to *Connick* as "one of the meanest Supreme Court decisions ever."[49] Ultimately, the *Connick* decision weakens the deterrent function of *Brady* because most violations are never discovered. The Court's decision to provide immunity for the state in this case is likely a reflection of its concern that prosecutors may be less willing to vigorously prosecute cases if they also risk being held monetarily liable for failing to disclose favorable evidence to the defense. But those advocating for more transparency in the disclosure process disagree.

Ultimately, they believe *Connick* "sends a deeply unfortunate message about both the government's duty to prevent prosecutorial misconduct and the Court's duty to acknowledge, remedy, and prevent egregious harms."[50]

Ironically, the Court's decision in *Connick* occurred during the same time period during which it accepted review of Juan Smith's case. After Smith was convicted in state court for murdering five people during an armed robbery, a jury sentenced him to life in prison. Chief Justice John Roberts's opinion focused exclusively on eyewitness statements made by Boatner, the lone witness implicating Smith's involvement in the crime. Writing for the majority in *Smith v. Cain* (2012),[51] the Chief Justice concluded that the statements made by Boatner to the New Orleans investigator were clearly *Brady* material because the detective's notes indicated that at one point he was unable to identify any suspects connected with the crime. Justice Thomas issued a lengthy dissent opining that "When, as in this case, the Court departs from its usual practice of declining to review alleged misapplications of settled law to particular facts . . . the Court should at least consider all of the facts."[52]

Although the Court did not break new ground with its decision in *Smith*, its opinion appears inconsistent with its holding in *Thompson* that the New Orleans prosecutor's office lacked a track record of unprofessionalism. The recent decisions in *Cone*, *Thompson*, and *Smith* illustrate the Court's continued

---

[49]Lithwick, Dahlia, *Cruel But Not Unusual*, SLATE (Apr. 1, 2011, 7:43 A.M.), www.slate.com/id/2290036/.

[50]Bandes, Susan A., *The Lone Miscreant, the Self-Training Prosecutor, and Other Fictions: A Comment on* Connick v. Thompson, 80 FORDHAM L. REV. 715, 716 (2011).

[51]*Smith v. Cain*, 132 S.Ct. 627 (2012).

[52]*Id.* at 640.

concern with prosecutorial misconduct but that it is unwilling to impose deeper monetary sanctions on local governments for occasional malfeasance on the part of the state. Absent a chronic pattern of *Brady* violations committed by a prosecutorial entity, there is little recourse available to defendants who may be wrongfully convicted and incarcerated.

V IN SUMMARY, WHAT DO THESE CASES SAY?

The Court has relied on the due process clause to evaluate many aspects of death penalty litigation, ranging from the plea bargaining stage to sentencing. The decisions in *Woodson*, *Lockett*, and *Eddings* were three of the Court's earliest cases expressing a need for juries to be able to consider mitigating evidence proffered by the defendant that could potentially lead to a sentence less than death. The need to ensure individualized sentencing and heightened reliability in future capital cases was initially based on the Eighth Amendment's cruel and unusual punishment clause during this era. As additional cases were decided, the Court began to use the right to due process of law instead of the Eighth Amendment as a basis for invalidating state capital sentencing procedures. In *Gardner v. Florida* (1977), the Court found that a capital defendant's right to due process precluded a trial court from sentencing a defendant to death when he or she "had no opportunity to deny or explain the evidence against him." Recognizing that a defendant must have a constitutional right to rebut evidence used during the trial stage, the Court has observed that more cases on state capital sentencing law are based on due process protections rather than individualization in sentencing standards.

In *Sattazahn*, the Court invalidated another state law that mandated a life sentence on retrial when the defendant was given the death penalty in the first trial. Choosing the due process rationale as a basis for its holding, the Court asserted that Sattazahn's rights had not been violated when he invoked a separate process at his own discretion; therefore, he had forfeited his claim to a punishment of life imprisonment after he was sentenced to death on retrial.

The Court's decisions in *Deck* and *Holmes* suggest that due process is a key safeguard that transcends many aspects of death penalty law. The *Deck* Court settled the issue on the practice of shackling in both the guilt and penalty phases, declaring it unconstitutional. The *Holmes* Court addressed an area of death penalty law that typically does not receive much attention—the viability of state evidentiary rules. *Holmes* declared the South Carolina evidentiary rule as violative of the Sixth and Fourteenth Amendments. It is clear that the right to due process can be found in most challenges on capital punishment, whether they involve the trial process, evidentiary standards, or jury deliberations.

Not only has the Court used the due process clause to evaluate trial and sentencing procedures; the *Brady* rule clearly indicates that the right to fundamental fairness applies during the discovery phase as well. The Court's recent decisions in *Cone*, *Connick*, and *Bell* reflect the Court's concern regarding the grave potential for prosecutors to sidestep their constitutional obligation to release evidence in their possession that may be exculpatory or otherwise favorable to the defense. However, the Court has set a high standard for plaintiffs wishing to sue the government for prosecutorial misconduct. The consequence is that those who have been wrongfully convicted and have suffered long periods of incarceration will have no remedy unless prosecutors engage in a pattern of similar *Brady* violations.

VI CONCLUSION

The aim of this chapter was to present a cross-section of Supreme Court cases dealing with a capital defendant's right to due process in capital sentencing procedures. As discussed, the right to due process is often combined by the Court with other fundamental rights, such as those included in the Fifth, Sixth, and Eighth Amendments. These rights begin to apply to defendants well before trial and remain in effect throughout the appeals process. For example, the Court has said that prosecutors have a duty to disclose favorable evidence to the defense prior to trial. At the other end of the spectrum, the Court has indicated that due process must be taken into consideration when the state seeks the death penalty on retrial after the defendant chooses to appeal his original conviction.

The trend of the Supreme Court has recently been to use the due process clause as a justification for granting or limiting rights for death penalty defendants. Because due process is applicable to any stage of a criminal proceeding, it is therefore interwoven with many other constitutional rights. And because the Court has said that "death is different," the right to due process becomes particularly critical for death penalty defendants, warranting what many have termed "super due process." Moreover, as the recent exposure of widespread incidents of wrongful conviction in capital cases continues, failures of due process become more apparent and pressures to ensure these rights, especially in death penalty cases, grow.

CASES BRIEFED IN CHAPTER 8

Case	Issue	Holding
Gardner v. Florida 430 U.S. 349 (1977)	Is a capital defendant deprived of the right to refute or explain testimony or evidence such as a confidential presentence report at sentencing if such information was not made available to him?	The right to deny or explain evidence used for prosecution must be given to capital defendants at sentencing.
Estelle v. Smith 451 U.S. 454 (1981)	Does the failure to advise a capital defendant of his Fifth and Sixth Amendment rights during a pretrial psychiatric examination constitute constitutional error, thus barring statements made regarding his future dangerousness to society?	Fifth, Sixth, and Fourteenth Amendment rights apply to capital defendants during pretrial psychiatric examinations.
Eddings v. Oklahoma 455 U.S. 104 (1982)	Must a trial court consider individualized mitigating factors, such as evidence of a difficult family history and emotional disturbance, when deciding death penalty cases?	Trial courts must consider character evidence such as that which indicates a difficult family history or emotional disturbance.
Gray v. Netherland 518 U.S. 152 (1996)	Does the failure to provide defendants with adequate notice of incriminating evidence at sentencing constitute a violation of due process?	Due process is not violated when the state fails to give adequate notice regarding evidence used at the sentencing to show future dangerousness.

Continued

Case	Issue	Holding
Sattazahn v. Pennsylvania 537 U.S. 101 (2003)	Does the due process clause prohibit a state from seeking the death penalty upon retrial if the state mandates a life sentence when the jury is unable to reach a verdict?	No due process violation occurs if states seek the death penalty upon retrial after the imposition of a life sentence based on state statute.
Deck v. Missouri 544 U.S. 622 (2005)	Does shackling a death penalty defendant during the sentencing stage of a capital case violate the due process clauses of the Fifth and Fourteenth Amendments?	The shackling of a capital defendant during the penalty phase violates the Fifth and Fourteenth Amendments to the Constitution unless it is justified by an overwhelming, essential state interest such as courtroom security.
Holmes v. South Carolina 547 U.S. 319 (2006)	Does an evidence rule restricting the introduction of third-party guilt evidence violate a capital defendant's right to due process, compulsory process, or confrontation of witnesses?	An evidence rule that bars the introduction of third-party guilt evidence if a prosecutor produces strong forensic evidence of guilt violates a capital defendant's constitutional right to due process, compulsory process, and confrontation of witnesses.
Cone v. Bell 556 U.S. 449 (2009)	When a federal habeas claim is presented twice at the state court level, is it considered "procedurally defaulted?" Does a federal court have the authority to review a claim that the state violated the *Brady* standard by suppressing material evidence?	Because petitioner's habeas claim was never properly reviewed by the state court, it was not procedurally defaulted. Further, the suppressed evidence should have been considered by the jury during sentencing; thus it was considered *Brady* material.
Connick v. Thompson 563 U.S. ___ (2011)	Absent a pattern of constitutional violations, may a prosecutor's office be held liable for failure to train its employees?	A single *Brady* violation is insufficient to establish liability of a prosecutor's office for failure to train its employees.

CASE BRIEFS

GARDNER v. FLORIDA 430 U.S. 349 (1977)

CAPSULE: A capital defendant must be given the opportunity to deny or explain testimony or evidence used by the state during sentencing. The prosecutor's reliance on a confidential presentence report, which was not made available to defense counsel, violates the defendant's Eighth and Fourteenth Amendment rights.

FACTS: Gardner was found guilty by a jury of first-degree murder in the Circuit Court of Citrus County, Florida. At sentencing, the jury recommended a sentence of life in prison because the relative mitigating circumstances outweighed the aggravating factors. Based on his reliance on a confidential presentence report that was not made available to the jury, the trial judge replaced the jury's verdict and entered a death sentence for Gardner. Furthermore, the trial judge differed with the jury on the weight of aggravating factors associated with the case, calling the crime "heinous, atrocious and cruel." Although the judge claimed that a copy of the confidential report was given to the defendant's counsel, he did not comment on the contents of the confidential portion as it related to Gardner's crime.

Continued

GARDNER v. FLORIDA 430 U.S. 349 (1977)—cont'd

ISSUE: Is a capital defendant deprived of the right to refute or explain testimony or evidence, such as a confidential presentence report, at sentencing if such information was not made available to him? NO.

HOLDING: The prosecutor's reliance on a confidential presentence report, which was not made available to defense counsel, violates the defendant's Eighth and Fourteenth Amendment rights.

REASON: "Even if it were permissible upon finding good cause to withhold a portion of a presentence report from the defendant, and even from defense counsel, nevertheless the full report must be made a part of the record to be reviewed on appeal. Since the State must administer its capital-sentencing procedures with an even hand, that record must disclose to the reviewing court the considerations motivating the death sentence in every case in which it is imposed, since otherwise the capital-sentencing procedure would be subject to the defects that resulted in the holding of unconstitutionality in *Furman v. Georgia*, 408 U.S. 238 (1972)."

"Here defense counsel's failure to request access to the full presentence report cannot justify the submission of a less complete record to the reviewing court than the record on which the trial judge based his decision to sentence petitioner to death, nor does such omission by counsel constitute an effective waiver of the constitutional error."

CASE SIGNIFICANCE: Before *Gardner*, the Supreme Court had not specifically relied on the due process clause as the sole basis for declaring unconstitutional state capital sentencing practices. Because Gardner had no opportunity to deny or explain the evidence that was used against him, which was contained in the presentence report, his constitutional right to due process was violated. The Court claimed that the defense had no opportunity to defend itself from the adverse impact of the confidential presentence document.

By relying on the due process clause, the Court generated controversy from legal critics regarding the impact of the Eighth and Fourteenth Amendments. Some have argued that the sentencing procedures at issue did not allow the sentencing body to make a reliable sentencing determination; therefore, the Eighth Amendment was a more effective means for banning such practices. Since *Gardner*, however, the Court has increasingly used the due process clause of the Fourteenth Amendment rather than the Eighth Amendment's cruel and unusual punishment clause, as a reason for striking down capital sentencing procedures.

ESTELLE v. SMITH 451 U.S. 454 (1981)

CAPSULE: Testimony of a psychiatrist based on court-ordered psychiatric evaluation, if the defendant was not advised of his constitutional rights, violates the Fifth, Sixth, and Fourteenth Amendments; therefore, testimony from the evaluation is not admissible during sentencing.

FACTS: After being indicted for murder in Texas, Smith was evaluated for competency to stand trial by a state psychiatrist as prescribed by the trial court. Without being advised of his Fifth Amendment right to be protected from self-incrimination, the psychiatrist obtained information that would later be used to demonstrate Smith's future dangerousness. Smith was subsequently convicted of capital murder. At the sentencing stage, the psychiatrist testified that Smith would pose a continuing threat to society; therefore, he was sentenced to death.

ISSUE: Does the failure to advise a capital defendant of his Fifth and Sixth Amendment rights during a pretrial psychiatric examination result in constitutional error, which bars the resulting testimony from being introduced at sentencing to establish future dangerousness? YES.

Continued

ESTELLE v. SMITH 451 U.S. 454 (1981)—cont'd

HOLDING: Testimony of a psychiatrist based on a court-ordered psychiatric evaluation when the defendant was not advised of his constitutional rights violates the Fifth, Sixth, and Fourteenth Amendments; therefore, evidence presented during the sentencing phase is rendered inadmissible.

REASON: "The admission of the doctor's testimony at the penalty phase violated respondent's Fifth Amendment privilege against compelled self-incrimination, because he was not advised before the pretrial psychiatric examination that he had a right to remain silent and that any statement he made could be used against him at a capital sentencing proceeding."

"Respondent's Sixth Amendment right to the assistance of counsel also was violated by the State's introduction of the doctor's testimony at the penalty phase. Such right already had attached when the doctor examined respondent in jail, and that interview proved to be a 'critical stage' of the aggregate proceedings against respondent. Defense counsel was not notified in advance that the psychiatric examination would encompass the issue of their client's future dangerousness, and respondent was denied the assistance of his counsel in making the significant decision of whether to submit to the examination and to what end the psychiatrist's findings could be employed."

CASE SIGNIFICANCE: In this case, the Supreme Court used the due process clause as a means of extending Fifth and Sixth Amendment rights to capital defendants during the penalty phase of a capital trial. It was one of the Court's original cases using the due process clause as a way to apply other constitutional rights to capital defendants. In this case, the Court held that the state psychiatrist's evaluation of a capital defendant prior to trial may be protected by the Fifth Amendment's self-incrimination clause in some cases. The Court said that because the defendant never raised the insanity defense, the government could not impugn the testimony of the defense psychiatrist by providing testimony from its own psychiatric expert. However, Buchanan acknowledged that when a capital defendant presents evidence of "extreme emotional disturbance," the defendant waives her Fifth Amendment protection against self-incrimination. Therefore, the evidence obtained during the evaluation can be used. Since *Smith* was decided, lower courts interpret the Court's holding to mean that any type of mental defense raised by the defendant opens the door for state prosecutors to rebut evidence by using a government psychiatrist's testimony.

Another significant issue that was raised in the *Smith* case was the defendant's right to be notified that a state psychiatrist's testimony would be used against him as proof of his future dangerousness to society. Because Smith was interviewed by the government psychiatrist in the absence of his lawyer, the state violated his right to counsel. In this case, the Court said that there was no difference between the type of protections provided by the Fifth Amendment during the guilt or sentencing stages of a capital trial. Because a defendant's exposure to punishment is the same, a person cannot be denied Fifth or Sixth Amendment rights in either stage of the trial.

EDDINGS v. OKLAHOMA 455 U.S. 104 (1982)

CAPSULE: Mitigating circumstances, including age and relevant social history, must be considered in juvenile capital cases.

FACTS: Eddings was a 16-year-old offender who was tried and convicted as an adult of the capital murder of a police officer. At the time of the trial, the state of Oklahoma had a statute prescribing that "any mitigating circumstances," as well as any of the designated aggravating factors, could be considered by a sentencing body. The state presented certain aggravating factors to the jury for consideration; however, Eddings proffered extensive evidence describing his exposure to a traumatic family history, including child abuse and emotional distress. The trial judge found that each of the three alleged aggravating factors had been proven by the state. However, the judge did not consider the evidence presented in mitigation to be persuasive, such as the offender's youth and traumatic background, and therefore he was sentenced to death.

Continued

EDDINGS v. OKLAHOMA 455 U.S. 104 (1982)—cont'd

ISSUE: Must mitigating circumstances, such as social history, be considered in the sentencing phase of a juvenile capital case? YES.

HOLDING: The court must consider any and all mitigating factors in determining the sentence in a juvenile capital case. The weight and relevance of such factors are discretionary, but total exclusion of a mitigating factor is improper.

REASON: "The Eighth and Fourteenth Amendments require that the sentencer... not be precluded from considering, as a mitigating factor, any aspect of a defendant's character or record and any of the circumstances of the offense that the defendant proffers as a basis for a sentence less than death. This rule follows from the requirement that capital punishment be imposed fairly and with reasonable consistency or not at all, and recognizes that a consistency produced by ignoring individual differences is a false consistency."

"The limitation placed by the courts below upon the mitigating evidence they would consider violated the above rule. Just as the State may not by statute preclude the sentencer from considering any mitigating factor, neither may the sentencer refuse to consider, as a matter of law, any relevant mitigating evidence. The sentencer and the reviewing court may determine the weight to be given relevant mitigating evidence but cannot totally exclude it from their consideration. Here, the evidence of a difficult family history and of emotional disturbance petitioner offered at the sentencing hearing should have been duly considered in sentencing."

CASE SIGNIFICANCE: In this case, the Supreme Court held that all reasonably relevant mitigating factors must be considered in a juvenile capital offense sentencing determination. This includes social history factors that may or may not have an impact on the behavior that resulted in the current charge of murder in the first degree. The Court did not say what weight should be given to specific evidence, choosing instead to leave such decisions up to the judge in whose court the case is tried. It required, however, that there be proof in the record of the case that all relevant mitigating evidence was considered by the court prior to sentencing.

The Court ruled that age is a relevant mitigating factor to consider. It also held that, in cases involving juveniles, all social history mitigating factors must be seriously considered by the court prior to sentencing. Although a judge usually enjoys discretion in determining which mitigating factors are to be considered during sentencing, that discretion is narrowed in capital cases involving juveniles.

GRAY v. NETHERLAND 518 U.S. 152 (1996)

CAPSULE: Due process is not violated when the state fails to give notice regarding evidence used at the sentencing stage to show future dangerousness.

FACTS: At the beginning of petitioner's trial, the prosecutor announced that, if the trial should reach the sentencing stage, the state would submit evidence to the jury indicating that Gray admitted to inmates that he had murdered Lisa Sorrell and her daughter. Once Gray was convicted of capital murder, Gray's case was submitted to the jury for sentencing. The prosecutor proceeded to introduce evidence, which included testimony from the investigating officer assigned to the Sorrell case as well as crime scene photographs, all of which incriminated Gray in the Sorrell murders. Defense counsel objected to the prosecutor's introduction of evidence for an unrelated crime because he did not have adequate notice to rebut the state's case. The motion to exclude was denied by the trial judge, and Gray was sentenced to death. Gray filed a habeas corpus petition in federal district court alleging that his due process rights had been violated when the state sought to introduce evidence at sentencing without giving him adequate notice of it and that the prosecutor failed to produce exculpatory evidence in his favor, which tended to misrepresent his case.

Continued

GRAY v. NETHERLAND 518 U.S. 152 (1996)—cont'd

ISSUE: At a capital murder trial, does the failure to provide a defendant with adequate notice of incriminating evidence at sentencing constitute a violation of the due process clause? NO.

HOLDING: On habeas corpus review, a capital defendant's right to due process is not violated when the state fails to give adequate notice regarding evidence used at the sentencing stage to show future dangerousness.

REASON: "A petitioner does not satisfy the exhaustion requirement by presenting the state courts only with the facts necessary to state a claim for relief. Nor is it enough to make a general appeal to a constitutional guarantee as broad as due process to present the 'substance' of such a claim to a state court."

"Petitioner contends that he was deprived of adequate notice when he received only one day's notice of the additional evidence, but, rather than seeking a continuance, he sought to have all such evidence excluded. For him to prevail, he must establish that due process requires that he receive more than a day's notice of the Commonwealth's evidence. He must also show that due process required a continuance whether or not he sought one, or that, if he chose not to seek a continuance, exclusion was the only appropriate remedy. Only the adoption of a new constitutional rule could establish these propositions. A defendant has the right to notice of the charges against which he must defend. However, he does not have a constitutional right to notice of the evidence which the state plans to use to prove the charges, and *Brady*, which addressed only exculpatory evidence, did not create one. Even if notice were required, exclusion of evidence is not the sole remedy for a violation of such a right, since a continuance could minimize prejudice. Petitioner made no such request here, and in view of his insistence on exclusion, the trial court might well have felt that it would have been interfering with counsel's tactical decision to order a continuance on its own motion."

CASE SIGNIFICANCE: In this case, the Supreme Court said that there was a difference between being provided the opportunity to refute or deny evidence used by the prosecution and being denied that opportunity. In *Gardner*, the Court held that the defendant's right to due process was violated because confidential information included in a presentence report was not made available to the defense but was relied on by the court during sentencing. The Court said that the factual circumstances in this case were different. Because Gray had the opportunity to request a continuance but failed to do so, his due process right was not violated. The Court claimed that, in order for Gray to show that such a right had been violated, he would have to establish that due process required a continuance, even though he did not request one, or that it required more than one day's notice for preparation. The court found that due process did not entitle the petitioner to an exclusion of the evidence in this case. In the Court's opinion, the petitioner could not be granted habeas relief, because it would give him the benefit of a new rule of federal constitutional law, in violation of *Teague v. Lane*, 489 U.S. 288 (1989).

SATTAZAHN v. PENNSYLVANIA 537 U.S. 101 (2003)

CAPSULE: A life sentence imposed by state law when a jury is unable to reach a unanimous verdict at the penalty stage does not constitute an "acquittal" and therefore does not bar the imposition of the death penalty upon retrial following a reversal of the defendant's conviction on appeal.

FACTS: At Sattazahn's original death penalty trial, the jury reported to the trial judge that it was hopelessly deadlocked nine-to-three for life imprisonment. The jury was unable to reach a unanimous decision regarding the presence of certain aggravating or mitigating factors, which determine whether life in prison or the death penalty should be imposed. In this case, the trial judge was required to enter, as a matter of Pennsylvania law, a default judgment of life imprisonment for Sattazahn. On appeal, Sattazahn alleged that the trial court erred in its instructions given to the jury, and the Pennsylvania Supreme Court reversed the lower court's decision in favor of the petitioner and remanded the case. At retrial, the state of Pennsylvania announced that it would be seeking the death penalty once again; however, this time the jury imposed the death penalty. The second time around, the Supreme Court of Pennsylvania affirmed the

Continued

SATTAZAHN v. PENNSYLVANIA 537 U.S. 101 (2003)—cont'd

decision of the trial court, holding that neither the Fifth Amendment's double jeopardy clause nor the Fourteenth Amendment's due process clause precluded the state of Pennsylvania from seeking the death penalty on retrial.

ISSUE: Does the Fifth Amendment's double jeopardy clause or the Fourteenth Amendment's due process clause preclude a state from seeking the death penalty upon retrial if state law mandates a life sentence in cases in which the jury is unable to reach a unanimous decision? NO.

HOLDING: No due process violation occurs if states seek the death penalty on retrial after the imposition of the death penalty based on statutory law; furthermore, the failure to reach a unanimous verdict at the penalty stage does not constitute an "acquittal" nor trigger double jeopardy protections.

REASON: "Double-jeopardy protections were not triggered when the jury deadlocked at petitioner's first sentencing proceeding and the court prescribed a life sentence pursuant to Pennsylvania law. The jury in that first proceeding was deadlocked and made no findings with respect to the alleged aggravating circumstance. That result, or nonresult, cannot fairly be called an acquittal, based on findings sufficient to establish legal entitlement to a life sentence. Neither was the entry of a life sentence by the judge an 'acquittal.' Under Pennsylvania's scheme, a judge has no discretion to fashion a sentence once he finds the jury is deadlocked, and he makes no findings and resolves no factual matters. The Pennsylvania Supreme Court also made no finding that the Pennsylvania Legislature intended the statutorily required entry of a life sentence to create an 'entitlement' even without an 'acquittal.'

"The Due Process Clause also did not bar Pennsylvania from seeking the death penalty at the retrial. Nothing in § 1 of the Fourteenth Amendment indicates that any 'life' or 'liberty' interest that Pennsylvania law may have given petitioner in the first proceeding's life sentence was somehow immutable, and he was "deprived" of any such interest only by operation of the "process" he invoked to invalidate the underlying first-degree murder conviction. This Court declines to hold that the Due Process Clause provides greater double-jeopardy protection than does the Double Jeopardy Clause."

CASE SIGNIFICANCE: In this case, the Court had not addressed the issue as to whether a life sentence imposed by a court constitutes an acquittal and bars a retrial for a harsher sentence. Sattazahn resolved this issue but raised questions regarding the consequences associated with the appeals process. When Sattazahn was given life imprisonment, Pennsylvania law provided that the judge had to impose the penalty of life imprisonment rather than death if the jury could not unanimously agree that an aggravating circumstance existed. Sattazahn received a life sentence during the first trial, not because he was acquitted of the death penalty charge but because of the automatic operation of state law. His new trial constituted a new proceeding in which he could be given the death penalty. The problem with this case is that this precedent may discourage a defendant who has escaped the death penalty during the first trial from appealing a conviction for fear that a second trial will result in a death sentence.

DECK v. MISSOURI 544 U.S. 622 (2005)

CAPSULE: The Fifth and Fourteenth Amendments forbid the use of visible shackles during a capital trial's penalty phase, as it does during the guilt phase, unless that use is justified by an overwhelming state interest, such as courtroom security.

FACTS: In July 1996, petitioner Deck robbed and murdered an elderly couple. The state required Deck to wear leg braces that were allegedly invisible to the jury. Deck was convicted of the crimes, but an en banc panel of the state supreme court set aside the sentence. The state then conducted a new sentencing proceeding. In the new proceeding, Deck was shackled with leg irons, handcuffs, and a belly chain. Although Deck's counsel repeatedly objected to the use of shackles, the judge overruled counsel's objections. At sentencing, Deck was again required to be placed in shackles. He was sentenced to death. Deck appealed the state's decisions, claiming that his shackling violated both Missouri law and the Federal Constitution. However, the Missouri Supreme Court disagreed, stating

DECK v. MISSOURI 544 U.S. 622 (2005)—cont'd

that: (1) the jury was not aware of the restraints; (2) there was no proof that the restraints prevented Deck from participating in his trial; and (3) there was evidence to support the claim that Deck may have been a flight risk because he was a repeat offender. Further, the State Supreme Court held that Deck had not established that the use of shackles had prejudiced the outcome of his trial at any stage of his trial. The Court reaffirmed his death sentence.

ISSUE: Does shackling a death penalty defendant during the sentencing stage of a capital case violate the due process clauses of the Fifth and Fourteenth Amendments? YES.

HOLDING: The shackling of a capital defendant during the penalty phase violates the Fifth and Fourteenth Amendments to the Constitution, unless it is justified by an overwhelming, essential state interest such as courtroom security.

REASON: "The law has long forbidden routine use of visible shackles during a capital trial's guilt phase, permitting shackling only in the presence of a special need. In light of *Holbrook*, early English cases, and lower court shackling doctrine dating back to the nineteenth century, it is now clear that this is a basic element of due process protected by the Federal Constitution. Thus, the Fifth and Fourteenth Amendments prohibit using physical restraints visible to the jury absent a trial court determination, in the exercise of its discretion, that restraints are justified by a state interest specific to the particular defendant on trial.

"If the reasons motivating the guilt phase constitutional rule—the presumption of innocence, securing a meaningful defense, and maintaining dignified proceedings—apply with like force at the penalty phase, the same rule will apply there. The latter two considerations obviously apply. As for the first, while the defendant's conviction means that the presumption of innocence no longer applies, shackles at the penalty phase threaten related concerns. The jury, though no longer deciding between guilt and innocence, is deciding between life and death, which, given the sanction's severity and finality, is no less important. Nor is accuracy in making that decision any less critical. Yet the offender's appearance in shackles almost inevitably implies to a jury that court authorities consider him a danger to the community (which is often a statutory aggravator and always a relevant factor); almost inevitably affects adversely the jury's perception of the defendant's character; and thereby inevitably undermines the jury's ability to weigh accurately all relevant considerations when determining whether the defendant deserves death. The constitutional rule that courts cannot routinely place defendants in shackles or other restraints visible to the jury during the penalty phase is not absolute. In the judge's discretion, account may be taken of special circumstances in the case at hand, including security concerns, that may call for shackling in order to accommodate the important need to protect the courtroom and its occupants."

CASE SIGNIFICANCE: In *Deck*, the United States Supreme Court decided that the due process clause prohibits capital defendants from appearing before juries in shackles in either the guilt or penalty phase of a capital proceeding unless a state interest specific to the defendant, such as courtroom safety, exists. The Court began its examination of the constitutionality of visible shackling by noting that most states prohibited the practice at the guilt stage. The Court relied on three of its previous holdings—*Illinois v. Allen*, *Holbrook v. Flynn*, and *Estelle v. Williams*—all of which established the constitutional rule reflecting an early common law ban against the use of visible restraints at trial. The Court's opinion hinged on three main tenets supporting the sentencing phase shackling rule: the presumption of innocence, the right to counsel, and the maintenance of the order and stateliness of the nation's courtrooms. In applying this approach, the Court ruled that the use of visible restraints during the sentencing stage of a capital trial violates due process and is therefore unconstitutional. However, the Court acknowledged that judges are authorized to make exceptions to this rule, such as in cases where courtroom security is at issue.

HOLMES v. SOUTH CAROLINA 547 U.S. 319 (2006)

CAPSULE: A capital defendant's constitutional rights are violated by an evidence rule prohibiting the introduction of third-party guilt evidence when the prosecutor has produced forensic evidence strongly supporting a guilty verdict.

FACTS: Eighty-six-year-old Mary Stewart was beaten, raped, and murdered in her home on the morning of December 31, 1989. At Holmes's trial, the prosecutor relied heavily on forensic evidence linking him to the crimes. As a counter-strategy, Holmes sought the introduction of expert witness testimony indicating that the forensic evidence was tainted and that the police had intended to frame him. Additionally, Holmes alleged that another suspect, White, was in the neighborhood at the time the crimes occurred and had ostensibly incriminated himself in regard to the crimes. However, White later denied making the alleged statements and produced an alibi. Petitioner Holmes was convicted and sentenced to death. Relying on the *Gregory* rule that third-party guilt evidence must be more than bare suspicion but raise a reasonable inference of innocence, the trial court excluded petitioner's evidence. The state supreme court affirmed, citing its earlier decisions in *Gregory* and *Gay* regarding restrictions on the introduction of third-party guilt evidence. The state supreme court held that when the prosecutor produces strong forensic evidence of the defendant's guilt, a defendant cannot raise a reasonable inference as to actual innocence. Therefore, the court held that Holmes could not rebut the forensic evidence against him.

ISSUE: Does an evidence rule restricting the introduction of third-party guilt evidence violate a capital defendant's right to due process, compulsory process, or confrontation of witnesses? YES.

HOLDING: An evidence rule that bars the introduction of third-party guilt evidence if a prosecutor produces strong forensic evidence of guilt violates a capital defendant's constitutional right to due process, compulsory process, and confrontation of witnesses.

REASON: "State and federal rulemakers have broad latitude under the Constitution to establish rules excluding evidence from criminal trials. This latitude, however, has limits. Whether rooted directly in the Due Process Clause of the Fourteenth Amendment or in the Compulsory Process or Confrontation clauses of the Sixth Amendment, the Constitution guarantees criminal defendants 'a meaningful opportunity to present a complete defense.' This right is abridged by evidence rules that 'infringe upon a weighty interest of the accused' and are 'arbitrary' or 'disproportionate to the purposes they are designed to serve.'"

"Interpreted in this way, the rule applied by the State Supreme Court does not rationally serve the end that the *Gregory* rule and its analogues in other jurisdictions were designed to promote, i.e., to focus the trial on the central issues by excluding evidence that has only a very weak logical connection to the central issues. The rule applied in this case appears to be based on the following logic: Where (1) it is clear that only one person was involved in the commission of a particular crime and (2) there is strong evidence that the defendant was the perpetrator, it follows that evidence of third-party guilt must be weak. But this logic depends on an accurate evaluation of the prosecution's proof, and the true strength of the prosecution's proof cannot be assessed without considering challenges to the reliability of the prosecution's evidence. Just because the prosecution's evidence, if credited, would provide strong support for a guilty verdict, it does not follow that evidence of third-party guilt has only a weak logical connection to the central issues in the case. And where the credibility of the prosecution's witnesses or the reliability of its evidence is not conceded, the strength of the prosecution's case cannot be assessed without making the sort of factual findings that have traditionally been reserved for the trier of fact and that the South Carolina courts did not purport to make in this case."

CASE SIGNIFICANCE: In Justice Alito's first Supreme Court opinion, a unanimous Court invalidated South Carolina's rule prohibiting the introduction of third-party guilt evidence as a means to rebut strong forensic evidence, as a means of suggesting the defendant's actual innocence. States have formed these doctrines to limit prejudice, potential confusion, and probativeness. Most states have similar restrictions regarding the admissibility of evidence, but South Carolina defense attorneys had long claimed that their rules were far more rigid than schemes used in other states. The Supreme Court found that South Carolina's rule was unconstitutional for several reasons. First, the state's

Continued

HOLMES v. SOUTH CAROLINA 547 U.S. 319 (2006)—cont'd

rule in *Gay* prevented the defense, to some degree, from successfully challenging the state's case. Second, the Court determined that determinations regarding the credibility of witnesses should be left to the jury, particularly the witnesses who claimed White was the person who committed the murder. And third, the Court said that the constitution requires that a defendant be given the chance to present an adequate defense.

The significance of this case goes well beyond South Carolina's "third-party perpetrator" evidence rule. The fact that this was a capital case may have prompted Supreme Court review; however, the decision has implications for all state rules restricting the admissibility of evidence in certain instances. The Court has signaled that it is willing to consider the constitutionality of these rules in the context of due process, confrontation, and compulsory process. Further, the Court's opinion is particularly important because its reasoning is equally applicable to all criminal cases.

CONE v. BELL 556 U.S. 449 (2009)

CAPSULE: A habeas claim is not barred from review by a federal court when the state's decision is not based on an independent and adequate state ground; thus a defendant is entitled to proper review of his *Brady* claim by a federal court.

FACTS: A Tennessee trial court convicted Gary Cone of murdering Shipley O. Todd and Cleopatra Todd in their homes in August 1980. Cone's initial appeal and state post-conviction petitions failed, but in a second petition for habeas relief in the state courts he maintained that the state withheld potential exculpatory evidence, including police reports and witness statements, which would have bolstered his defense of insanity and his mitigation case. After the state courts denied relief, Cone filed a federal habeas petition in District Court. But because Cone failed to raise the claim in his initial petition, the District Court concluded that he had defaulted. The District Court further opined that even if Cone's claim was not procedurally defaulted, it would have failed because there was no reasonable likelihood the result of the trial would have been different given the totality of the evidence.

ISSUES:
1. When a federal habeas claim is presented twice at the state court level, is it considered "procedurally defaulted?" NO.
2. Does a federal court have the authority to review a claim that the state violated the *Brady* standard by suppressing material evidence? YES.

HOLDING: Because petitioner's habeas claim was never properly reviewed by the state court, it was not procedurally defaulted. Further, the suppressed evidence should have been considered by the jury during sentencing; thus it was considered *Brady* material.

REASONING: "The lower federal courts failed to adequately consider whether the withheld documents were material to Cone's sentence. Both the quantity and quality of the suppressed evidence lend support to Cone's trial position that he habitually used excessive amounts of drugs, that his addiction affected his behavior during the murders, and that the State's contrary arguments were false and misleading. Nevertheless, even when viewed in the light most favorable to Cone, the evidence does not sustain his insanity defense: His behavior before, during, and after the crimes was inconsistent with the contention that he lacked substantial capacity either to appreciate the wrongfulness of his conduct or to conform it to the requirements of law. Because the likelihood that the suppressed evidence would have affected the jury's verdict on the insanity issue is remote, the Sixth Circuit did not err by denying habeas relief

Continued

CONE v. BELL 556 U.S. 449 (2009)—cont'd

on the ground that such evidence was immaterial to the jury's guilt finding. The same cannot be said of that court's summary treatment of Cone's claim that the suppressed evidence would have influenced the jury's sentencing recommendation. Because the suppressed evidence might have been material to the jury's assessment of the proper punishment, a full review of that evidence and its effect on the sentencing verdict is warranted."

SIGNIFICANCE: This case reminds us that the *Brady* rule applies to the outcome of the trial as well as sentencing disposition. To establish a successful *Brady* claim, a defendant must only show that there is a reasonable probability that the result of the trial would have been different. Subsequent cases expanded the original interpretation of *Brady* to include the sentencing outcome as well as guilt or innocence. Second, although this standard may not appear burdensome for defendants, the Court has always said suppressed evidence must be examined within the context of all of the remaining aggravating and mitigating evidence. Therefore, a defendant must show that, relative to the other evidence, there was a reasonable probability that a different result would have occurred. The *Cone* Court also clarified the scope of authority that federal courts have to review state habeas claims. That is, federal habeas courts have authority to review state court determinations about whether claims are considered procedurally defaulted.

CONNICK v. THOMPSON 563 U.S. _____ (2011)

CAPSULE: In order to establish deliberate indifference for failure to train on the part of a prosecutor's office, a defendant must show that a pattern of similar constitutional violations by untrained employees has occurred.

FACTS: The New Orleans District Attorney's office acknowledged it had committed a *Brady* violation when it failed to disclose a crime lab report that suggested Thompson was not guilty of committing murder. Thompson chose not to testify at his murder trial because his prior robbery conviction could be used against him by the prosecution. Nevertheless, the trial court convicted Thompson and sentenced him to death. In 1994, Deegan, one of the prosecutors originally assigned to Thompson's case, became terminally ill. Deegan admitted to another prosecutor, Riehlmann, he had not provided blood evidence to Thompson's defense attorney as required by *Brady*. Riehlmann also chose not to come forward with the information. However, shortly before Thompson was scheduled to be executed, his private investigator discovered the exculpatory evidence. Thompson was found not guilty of committing murder after a reviewing court vacated his convictions. As a matter of recourse, Thompson filed a Section 1983 civil lawsuit against the New Orleans District Attorney's office, alleging that it had been deliberately indifferent in failing to provide training for prosecutors on ways to improve disclosure procedures. The trial court held that Thompson did not have to establish that a pattern of similar *Brady* violations had occurred, only that there was a clear need for training. Thompson was awarded a $14 million judgment for having been wrongfully incarcerated and sentenced to death ($1 million for each year spent on death row).

ISSUE: Absent a pattern of constitutional violations, may a prosecutor's office be held liable for failure to train its employees? NO.

HOLDING: A single *Brady* violation is insufficient to establish liability of a prosecutor's office for failure to train its employees.

REASONING: "A pattern of similar constitutional violations by untrained employees is 'ordinarily necessary' to demonstrate deliberate indifference. Without notice that a course of training is deficient, decisionmakers can hardly be said to have deliberately chosen a training program that will cause violations of constitutional rights. Thompson

Continued

CONNICK v. THOMPSON 563 U.S. ____ (2011)—cont'd

does not contend that he proved a pattern of similar *Brady* violations, and four reversals by Louisiana courts for dissimilar *Brady* violations in the 10 years before the robbery trial could not have put the district attorney's office on notice of the need for specific training."

SIGNIFICANCE: In *Connick*, the Supreme Court restricted the available avenues for recourse when prosecutors violate their constitutional duty under *Brady v. Maryland*. In *Van de Kamp* (2009), the Supreme Court had already established that a prosecutorial entity is not liable under Section 1983 unless the constitutional violations are related to administrative procedures, not decisions that require legal knowledge or discretion. Because Connick's employees did not engage in a pattern of related constitutional violations, the agency could not assume that they had been put on notice that their conduct was in violation.

The decision would not likely have received the attention it did had it not been for the fact that it resulted in the reversal of a $14 million judgment for Thompson, who spent 18 years in prison for a crime he did not commit (14 of them on death row). The discovery of the blood evidence by Thompson's investigator shortly before his execution added to the drama, as prosecutors within the New Orleans Parish District Attorney's office engaged in a systematic scheme to cover up the *Brady* violation, nearly sending an innocent man to his death.

Key Terms

alternative perpetrator defense
acquittal
Brady rule
Cone v. Bell
Connick v. Thompson
Deck v. Missouri
deliberate indifference
double jeopardy
due process
Eddings v. Oklahoma
Estelle v. Smith
fundamental fairness
Gardner v. Florida
Gray v. Netherland
guided discretion
Holmes v. South Carolina
individualized sentencing
mitigating factors
procedural default
rebuttal evidence
Sattazahn v. Pennsylvania
super due process
third-party guilt statute

CRITICAL THINKING QUESTIONS

1. Explain the scope of the *Brady* rule. What is the standard that courts use to evaluate whether a constitutional violation has occurred, and what are the challenges that defendants face in establishing that violation?

2. In what circumstances has the Supreme Court held that a defendant may be tried twice for a capital offense and sentenced to death? Explain.

3. Explain the Court's rule on the presentation of mitigating evidence at sentencing. Under what circumstances does the presentation of mitigating evidence violate due process?

Internet Resources

Cornell Law School, *Chronicle Online*: "Supreme Court Unanimously Backs Cornell Law Professor John Blume's Argument in Death Penalty Case"
www.news.cornell.edu/stories/May06/Blume.Supreme.win.lbm.html

Death Penalty Information Center, The Federal Death Penalty
http://deathpenaltyinfo.org/article.php?scid=29&did=147

Historic Brady Rule Doesn't Always Hold Up
www.innocenceproject.org/Content/Historic_Brady_Rule_Doesnt_Always_Hold_Up.php

ACLU: Fairness and the Death Penalty
www.aclu.org/capital/general/10441pub19971231.html#unfair

PBS: The Death Penalty, Pro and Con
www.pbs.org/wgbh/pages/frontline/angel/procon/deathissue.html

Aggravating and Mitigating Factors in Death Penalty Cases

CHAPTER OUTLINE

I INTRODUCTION

In *Gregg v. Georgia* (1976),[1] the Supreme Court noted that "death is different." The Court approved death penalty statutes with adequate procedural safeguards to ensure that only the most serious cases receive the ultimate punishment. A major requirement of statutes in the wake of *Gregg* is that they narrow the range of cases for which the death penalty could be an option. The death penalty is to be reserved for only the most extreme acts of violence. Moreover, the Court requires individualized consideration in the application of the death penalty; each case and defendant is to be considered separately in deciding whether death is an appropriate punishment. The Court therefore struck down mandatory death penalty statutes in Louisiana (*Roberts v. Louisiana*, 1976)[2] and North Carolina (*Woodson v. North Carolina*, 1976),[3] which, although potentially narrowing the death-eligible crimes, did not

---

[1]*Gregg v. Georgia*, 428 U.S. 153 (1976).
[2]*Roberts v. Louisiana*, 431 U.S. 633 (1977).
[3]*Woodson v. North Carolina*, 428 U.S. 280 (1976).

allow individual consideration in the penalty decision. The central features of both the narrowing and individualization features of death penalty statutes consist of aggravating and mitigating factors.[4]

This chapter focuses on procedural issues inherent in the consideration of aggravating and mitigating factors required in capital cases. The Supreme Court has had much to say about these special factors since it approved them in *Gregg v. Georgia* in 1976. The nature of capital trials (particularly the penalty phase) is to a great degree shaped by aggravating and mitigating factors and the Supreme Court's many decisions surrounding them. In the sections that follow, the Supreme Court's decisions are analyzed to determine how they have shaped death penalty law and capital trial procedure. Further, the many constitutional issues that have arisen in the context of "special" factors and what the Supreme Court has said about them are considered. But first, death penalty statutes and the role of aggravating and mitigating factors in capital punishment schemes are addressed.

‖ *GREGG v. GEORGIA* AND THE EMERGING IMPORTANCE OF AGGRAVATING AND MITIGATING FACTORS

Prior to the abolition of the death penalty in *Furman v. Georgia* (1972),[5] death penalty statutes varied widely by state in regard to the consideration of "special" factors or circumstances calling for death or mercy. Juries were given very little, if any, guidance when considering such factors, if presented. Rather, the decision of whether to sentence a defendant to death was left to the "judgment, conscience, and absolute discretion of the jury."[6] The lack of consistent and formal standards in the structure of death penalty statutes and the "unfettered discretion" that resulted were, in part, the bases for the Supreme Court's decision in *Furman* declaring the death penalty, as administered at the time, unconstitutional. When the death penalty was reinstated in *Gregg v. Georgia* (1976), a new approach to capital cases emerged—one that requires the consideration of special factors in determining whether a defendant should be sentenced to death or life in prison. These factors are referred to as aggravating and mitigating factors.

Aggravating factors are those that make the offense or the offender particularly "worthy" of a penalty as extreme as death. This narrowed the range of murders for which the penalty of death is appropriate. These aggravating factors may come into play at multiple points in the capital trial process and generally revolve around three factors: (1) characteristics of the offense, (2) characteristics of the offender, and (3) characteristics of the victim.[7] The two primary functions of aggravating factors are: (1) restricting eligibility for the death penalty (the eligibility function); and (2) guiding the selection of those for whom the death penalty is appropriate (the individualization function). The eligibility function primarily exists prior to the sentencing phase of capital trials and acts as a filter ensuring that

---

[4]Although the term "circumstances" is often used, it is somewhat limiting in its connotation. The term "factors" is used here because it more broadly applies to all forms of aggravating circumstances and evidence, whether that pertains to the circumstances of the crime or other factors or characteristics of the defendant or victim.

[5]*Furman v. Georgia*, 408 U.S. 238 (1972).

[6]*McGautha v. California*, 402 U.S. 183, 190 (1971).

[7]Acker, James R., and Charles S. Lanier, *Beyond Human Ability? The Rise and Fall of Death Penalty Legislation*. In James R. Acker, Robert M. Bohm, and Charles S. Lanier (Eds.) , America's Experiment With Capital Punishment: Reflections on the Past, Present, and Future of the Ultimate Penal Sanction, 77 (1998).

the death penalty is available in only the most extreme cases. Virginia's death penalty statute, for example, lists 15 "aggravated" offenses that constitute capital murder.[8] Some examples that are typical of death penalty statutes are murder during a kidnapping, murder during the commission of a felony, murder of a police officer, and multiple murders. Aggravating factors also play a significant role in the sentencing phase of capital trials and thus perform that second function of guiding the selection of defendants for the death penalty. Aggravating factors may be explicitly listed in the statute for the jury to consider, or they may be nonstatutory factors presented by the prosecution for the jury's consideration in determining the appropriate punishment. Some examples of aggravating factors serving this individual selection function are whether the murder was particularly brutal or "heinous," whether the offender has a history of violence, and whether the offender is likely to be a danger to society in the future.

Mitigating factors are those that provide some level of explanation or justification (but not excuse or defense of the act) for a murder and are reserved for the sentencing phase of capital trials. Common mitigating factors are cognitive deficits or a history of the defendant's own violent victimization. As with aggravating factors, mitigating factors can be statutory (meaning they are specifically listed in a state's death penalty statute) or nonstatutory. Mitigating factors may also come in the form of refutations to common aggravating factors. For example, factors such as a lack of criminal or violent history or good adjustment to institutional life in jail or prison may be presented to indicate a lack of what would otherwise be potentially aggravating factors in the minds of capital jurors.

Consideration of both aggravating and mitigating factors was approved as a necessary procedural safeguard when the Court upheld the "guided discretion" statutes of Florida, Georgia, and Texas in 1976. (Box 9.1 presents the text of each of these states' current statutes.) Each of these statutes, however, provided a different framework for the consideration of these factors in the sentencing phase of capital trials. As a result, there are various ways in which states institute aggravating and mitigating factors into their death penalty law and capital trial procedure. The Supreme Court, although strictly requiring the inclusion of aggravating and mitigating factors, left up to the states the specific structure and framework within which such considerations would occur. Bohm, using the Florida, Georgia, and Texas statutes (the three statutes the Supreme Court originally approved in *Gregg v. Georgia*) as examples, identifies three types of guided discretion statutes pertaining to their treatment of aggravating and mitigating circumstances: (1) aggravating versus mitigating, (2) aggravating only, and (3) structured discretion.[9]

Aggravating versus mitigating death penalty statutes are those that require the jury to first consider whether any aggravating factors exist. Upon finding the presence of at least one aggravating factor, the jury then considers both statutory and nonstatutory mitigating factors and weighs the aggravating factors against the mitigating factors. If, in the minds of the jurors, mitigating factors do not outweigh aggravating factors, then the appropriate sentence is death. It is important to note that this is not simply a call to enumerate the aggravating and mitigating factors and base the sentence on which set of factors is greatest. Rather, it is up to the jurors to apply what they believe to be appropriate weights to each particular factor. Florida's death penalty statute is an example of the aggravating versus mitigating scheme (see Box 9.1).

---

[8]VA. CODE ANN. § 18.2–31
[9]Bohm, Robert M., DEATHQUEST: AN INTRODUCTION TO THE THEORY AND PRACTICE OF CAPITAL PUNISHMENT IN THE UNITED STATES (4th ED. 2012).

BOX 9.1 FLORIDA, GEORGIA, AND TEXAS DEATH PENALTY STATUTES

Florida

Florida Statutes
§ 921.141. Sentence of death or life imprisonment for capital felonies; further proceedings to determine sentence

(1) SEPARATE PROCEEDINGS ON ISSUE OF PENALTY.—Upon conviction or adjudication of guilt of a defendant of a capital felony, the court shall conduct a separate sentencing proceeding to determine whether the defendant should be sentenced to death or life imprisonment as authorized by s. 775.082. The proceeding shall be conducted by the trial judge before the trial jury as soon as practicable. If, through impossibility or inability, the trial jury is unable to reconvene for a hearing on the issue of penalty, having determined the guilt of the accused, the trial judge may summon a special juror or jurors as provided in chapter 913 to determine the issue of the imposition of the penalty. If the trial jury has been waived, or if the defendant pleaded guilty, the sentencing proceeding shall be conducted before a jury impaneled for that purpose, unless waived by the defendant. In the proceeding, evidence may be presented as to any matter that the court deems relevant to the nature of the crime and the character of the defendant and shall include matters relating to any of the aggravating or mitigating circumstances enumerated in subsections (5) and (6). Any such evidence which the court deems to have probative value may be received, regardless of its admissibility under the exclusionary rules of evidence, provided the defendant is accorded a fair opportunity to rebut any hearsay statements. However, this subsection shall not be construed to authorize the introduction of any evidence secured in violation of the Constitution of the United States or the Constitution of the State of Florida. The state and the defendant or the defendant's counsel shall be permitted to present argument for or against sentence of death.

(2) ADVISORY SENTENCE BY THE JURY.—After hearing all the evidence, the jury shall deliberate and render an advisory sentence to the court, based upon the following matters:
  (a) Whether sufficient aggravating circumstances exist as enumerated in subsection (5);
  (b) Whether sufficient mitigating circumstances exist which outweigh the aggravating circumstances found to exist; and
  (c) Based on these considerations, whether the defendant should be sentenced to life imprisonment or death.

(3) FINDINGS IN SUPPORT OF SENTENCE OF DEATH.—Notwithstanding the recommendation of a majority of the jury, the court, after weighing the aggravating and mitigating circumstances, shall enter a sentence of life imprisonment or death, but if the court imposes a sentence of death, it shall set forth in writing its findings upon which the sentence of death is based as to the facts:
  (a) That sufficient aggravating circumstances exist as enumerated in subsection (5), and
  (b) That there are insufficient mitigating circumstances to outweigh the aggravating circumstances.

In each case in which the court imposes the death sentence, the determination of the court shall be supported by specific written findings of fact based upon the circumstances in subsections (5) and (6) and upon the records of the trial and the sentencing proceedings. If the court does not make the findings requiring the death sentence within 30 days after the rendition of the judgment and sentence, the court shall impose sentence of life imprisonment in accordance with s. 775.082.

(4) REVIEW OF JUDGMENT AND SENTENCE.—The judgment of conviction and sentence of death shall be subject to automatic review by the Supreme Court of Florida and disposition rendered within 2 years after the filing of a notice of appeal. Such review by the Supreme Court shall have priority over all other cases and shall be heard in accordance with rules promulgated by the Supreme Court.

(5) AGGRAVATING CIRCUMSTANCES.—Aggravating circumstances shall be limited to the following:
  (a) The capital felony was committed by a person previously convicted of a felony and under sentence of imprisonment or placed on community control or on felony probation.
  (b) The defendant was previously convicted of another capital felony or of a felony involving the use or threat of violence to the person.
  (c) The defendant knowingly created a great risk of death to many persons.
  (d) The capital felony was committed while the defendant was engaged, or was an accomplice, in the commission of, or an attempt to commit, or flight after committing or attempting to commit, any: robbery;

Continued

BOX 9.1 **FLORIDA, GEORGIA, AND TEXAS DEATH PENALTY STATUTES—cont'd**

---

sexual battery; aggravated child abuse; abuse of an elderly person or disabled adult resulting in great bodily harm, permanent disability, or permanent disfigurement; arson; burglary; kidnapping; aircraft piracy; or unlawful throwing, placing, or discharging of a destructive device or bomb.

(e) The capital felony was committed for the purpose of avoiding or preventing a lawful arrest or effecting an escape from custody.

(f) The capital felony was committed for pecuniary gain.

(g) The capital felony was committed to disrupt or hinder the lawful exercise of any governmental function or the enforcement of laws.

(h) The capital felony was especially heinous, atrocious, or cruel.

(i) The capital felony was a homicide and was committed in a cold, calculated, and premeditated manner without any pretense of moral or legal justification.

(j) The victim of the capital felony was a law enforcement officer engaged in the performance of his or her official duties.

(k) The victim of the capital felony was an elected or appointed public official engaged in the performance of his or her official duties if the motive for the capital felony was related, in whole or in part, to the victim's official capacity.

(l) The victim of the capital felony was a person less than 12 years of age.

(m) The victim of the capital felony was particularly vulnerable due to advanced age or disability, or because the defendant stood in a position of familial or custodial authority over the victim.

(n) The capital felony was committed by a criminal street gang member, as defined in s. 874.03.

(o) The capital felony was committed by a person designated as a sexual predator pursuant to s. 775.21 or a person previously designated as a sexual predator who had the sexual predator designation removed.

(6) MITIGATING CIRCUMSTANCES.—Mitigating circumstances shall be the following:

(a) The defendant has no significant history of prior criminal activity.

(b) The capital felony was committed while the defendant was under the influence of extreme mental or emotional disturbance.

(c) The victim was a participant in the defendant's conduct or consented to the act.

(d) The defendant was an accomplice in the capital felony committed by another person and his or her participation was relatively minor.

(e) The defendant acted under extreme duress or under the substantial domination of another person.

(f) The capacity of the defendant to appreciate the criminality of his or her conduct or to conform his or her conduct to the requirements of law was substantially impaired.

(g) The age of the defendant at the time of the crime.

(h) The existence of any other factors in the defendant's background that would mitigate against imposition of the death penalty.

(7) VICTIM IMPACT EVIDENCE.—Once the prosecution has provided evidence of the existence of one or more aggravating circumstances as described in subsection (5), the prosecution may introduce, and subsequently argue, victim impact evidence. Such evidence shall be designed to demonstrate the victim's uniqueness as an individual human being and the resultant loss to the community's members by the victim's death. Characterizations and opinions about the crime, the defendant, and the appropriate sentence shall not be permitted as a part of victim impact evidence.

(8) APPLICABILITY.—This section does not apply to a person convicted or adjudicated guilty of a capital drug trafficking felony under s. 893.135.

Georgia

Code of Georgia

§ 17-10-30. Procedure for imposition of death penalty generally.

(b) In all cases of other offenses for which the death penalty may be authorized, the judge shall consider, or he shall include in his instructions to the jury for it to consider, any mitigating circumstances or aggravating circumstances otherwise authorized by law and any of the following statutory aggravating circumstances which may be supported by the evidence:

Continued

BOX 9.1 FLORIDA, GEORGIA, AND TEXAS DEATH PENALTY STATUTES—cont'd

(1) The offense of murder, rape, armed robbery, or kidnapping was committed by a person with a prior record of conviction for a capital felony;

(2) The offense of murder, rape, armed robbery, or kidnapping was committed while the offender was engaged in the commission of another capital felony or aggravated battery, or the offense of murder was committed while the offender was engaged in the commission of burglary or arson in the first degree;

(3) The offender, by his act of murder, armed robbery, or kidnapping, knowingly created a great risk of death to more than one person in a public place by means of a weapon or device which would normally be hazardous to the lives of more than one person;

(4) The offender committed the offense of murder for himself or another, for the purpose of receiving money or any other thing of monetary value;

(5) The murder of a judicial officer, former judicial officer, district attorney or solicitor-general, or former district attorney, solicitor, or solicitor-general was committed during or because of the exercise of his or her official duties;

(6) The offender caused or directed another to commit murder or committed murder as an agent or employee of another person;

(7) The offense of murder, rape, armed robbery, or kidnapping was outrageously or wantonly vile, horrible, or inhuman in that it involved torture, depravity of mind, or an aggravated battery to the victim;

(8) The offense of murder was committed against any peace officer, corrections employee, or firefighter while engaged in the performance of his official duties;

(9) The offense of murder was committed by a person in, or who has escaped from, the lawful custody of a peace officer or place of lawful confinement;

(10) The murder was committed for the purpose of avoiding, interfering with, or preventing a lawful arrest or custody in a place of lawful confinement, of himself or another; or

(11) The offense of murder, rape, or kidnapping was committed by a person previously convicted of rape, aggravated sodomy, aggravated child molestation, or aggravated sexual battery.

(c) The statutory instructions as determined by the trial judge to be warranted by the evidence shall be given in charge and in writing to the jury for its deliberation. The jury, if its verdict is a recommendation of death, shall designate in writing, signed by the foreman of the jury, the aggravating circumstance or circumstances which it found beyond a reasonable doubt. In nonjury cases the judge shall make such designation. Except in cases of treason or aircraft hijacking, unless at least one of the statutory aggravating circumstances enumerated in subsection (b) of this Code section is so found, the death penalty shall not be imposed.

Texas

Texas Code of Criminal Procedure
Art. 37.071. PROCEDURE IN CAPITAL CASE

Sec. 1. If a defendant is found guilty in a capital felony case in which the state does not seek the death penalty, the judge shall sentence the defendant to life imprisonment without parole.

Sec. 2. (a)(1) If a defendant is tried for a capital offense in which the state seeks the death penalty, on a finding that the defendant is guilty of a capital offense, the court shall conduct a separate sentencing proceeding to determine whether the defendant shall be sentenced to death or life imprisonment without parole. The proceeding shall be conducted in the trial court and, except as provided by Article 44.29(c) of this code, before the trial jury as soon as practicable. In the proceeding, evidence may be presented by the state and the defendant or the defendant's counsel as to any matter that the court deems relevant to sentence, including evidence of the defendant's background or character or the circumstances of the offense that mitigates against the imposition of the death penalty. This subdivision shall not be construed to authorize the introduction of any evidence secured in violation of the Constitution of the United States or of the State of Texas. The state and the defendant or the defendant's counsel shall be permitted to present argument for or against sentence of death. The introduction of evidence of extraneous conduct is governed by the notice requirements of Section 3(g), Article 37.07. The court, the attorney representing the state, the defendant, or the defendant's counsel may not inform a juror or a prospective juror of the effect of a failure of a jury to agree on issues submitted under Subsection (c) or (e).

Continued

BOX 9.1 FLORIDA, GEORGIA, AND TEXAS DEATH PENALTY STATUTES—cont'd

(2) Notwithstanding Subdivision (1), evidence may not be offered by the state to establish that the race or ethnicity of the defendant makes it likely that the defendant will engage in future criminal conduct.

  (b) On conclusion of the presentation of the evidence, the court shall submit the following issues to the jury:

  (1) whether there is a probability that the defendant would commit criminal acts of violence that would constitute a continuing threat to society; and

  (2) in cases in which the jury charge at the guilt or innocence stage permitted the jury to find the defendant guilty as a party under Sections 7.01 and 7.02, Penal Code, whether the defendant actually caused the death of the deceased or did not actually cause the death of the deceased but intended to kill the deceased or another or anticipated that a human life would be taken.

  (c) The state must prove each issue submitted under Subsection (b) of this article beyond a reasonable doubt, and the jury shall return a special verdict of "yes" or "no" on each issue submitted under Subsection (b) of this Article.

  (d) The court shall charge the jury that:

  (1) in deliberating on the issues submitted under Subsection (b) of this article, it shall consider all evidence admitted at the guilt or innocence stage and the punishment stage, including evidence of the defendant's background or character or the circumstances of the offense that militates for or mitigates against the imposition of the death penalty;

  (2) it may not answer any issue submitted under Subsection (b) of this article "yes" unless it agrees unanimously and it may not answer any issue "no" unless 10 or more jurors agree; and

  (3) members of the jury need not agree on what particular evidence supports a negative answer to any issue submitted under Subsection (b) of this article.

  (e) (1) The court shall instruct the jury that if the jury returns an affirmative finding to each issue submitted under Subsection (b), it shall answer the following issue:

  Whether, taking into consideration all of the evidence, including the circumstances of the offense, the defendant's character and background, and the personal moral culpability of the defendant, there is a sufficient mitigating circumstance or circumstances to warrant that a sentence of life imprisonment without parole rather than a death sentence be imposed.

  (2) The court shall:

  (A) instruct the jury that if the jury answers that a circumstance or circumstances warrant that a sentence of life imprisonment without parole rather than a death sentence be imposed, the court will sentence the defendant to imprisonment in the Texas Department of Criminal Justice for life without parole; and

  (B) charge the jury that a defendant sentenced to confinement for life without parole under this article is ineligible for release from the department on parole.

  (f) The court shall charge the jury that in answering the issue submitted under Subsection (e) of this article, the jury:

  (1) shall answer the issue "yes" or "no";

  (2) may not answer the issue "no" unless it agrees unanimously and may not answer the issue "yes" unless 10 or more jurors agree;

  (3) need not agree on what particular evidence supports an affirmative finding on the issue; and

  (4) shall consider mitigating evidence to be evidence that a juror might regard as reducing the defendant's moral blameworthiness.

  (g) If the jury returns an affirmative finding on each issue submitted under Subsection (b) and a negative finding on an issue submitted under Subsection (e)(1), the court shall sentence the defendant to death. If the jury returns a negative finding on any issue submitted under Subsection (b) or an affirmative finding on an issue submitted under Subsection (e)(1) or is unable to answer any issue submitted under Subsection (b) or (e), the court shall sentence the defendant to confinement in the Texas Department of Criminal Justice for life imprisonment without parole.

  (h) The judgment of conviction and sentence of death shall be subject to automatic review by the Court of Criminal Appeals.

  (i) This article applies to the sentencing procedure in a capital case for an offense that is committed on or after September 1, 1991. For the purposes of this section, an offense is committed on or after September 1, 1991, if any element of that offense occurs on or after that date.

Aggravating-only statutes require a jury to consider statutory aggravating factors and then decide whether those factors warrant the death penalty. In contrast to the aggravating versus mitigating form of statute, the jury is not required to consider mitigating factors and may decide to impose either a death sentence or life imprisonment based solely on their consideration of aggravating factors. Mitigating factors are generally not listed in the statute but may be considered by the jury prior to sentencing. Georgia's death penalty statute is an example of the aggravating-only form of statute (see Box 9.1).

Structured discretion statutes, the rarest form of death penalty statute, call upon a jury to answer specific questions after hearing all relevant evidence presented as either aggravating factors or mitigating factors during the sentencing phase of the trial. The answers to these questions determine the sentence. In Texas, for example (see Box 9.1), the jury is asked to answer "yes" or "no" to two questions: one pertaining to the likelihood of the defendant presenting a future danger to society and the other pertaining to whether the defendant directly committed the murder in question. If the jury unanimously answers "yes" to both questions, it is then asked a third question regarding whether there are sufficient mitigating factors to warrant mercy in the case and thus a lesser sentence of life in prison. If all 12 jurors answer "no" to this question, a death sentence is imposed.[10] The Texas statute has recently drawn attention by the U.S. Supreme Court. In two Texas cases, *Brewer v. Quarterman* and *Abdul-Kabir v. Quarterman* (2007)[11], the Court held that capital sentencing statutes cannot restrict a jury from giving, and being instructed to give, full consideration to all relevant mitigating evidence. Juries must be instructed, beyond a simple verbatim reading of the statutory special issues, to consider all mitigating evidence presented during the sentencing hearing.

The U.S. Supreme Court has generally deferred to states in the way they set up their capital sentencing schemes as long as the state statute allows for due consideration of both aggravating and mitigating factors. This fact is illuminated in the case of *Kansas v. Marsh* (2006).[12] In *Kansas v. Marsh*, the Court considered the Kansas capital sentencing statute, which requires the imposition of the death penalty when a unanimous jury finds that aggravating and mitigating factors are in equipoise (i.e., are, in the minds of the jurors, equal in weight). This was the first time the Court was faced with this issue, because the weighing function has generally been concerned with whether there are more or fewer aggravating factors in comparison to mitigating factors. The Supreme Court decided that the Kansas statute is constitutional. In spite of arguments that such a sentencing scheme creates a presumption in favor of death, the Court held that it is constitutional to impose the death penalty as long as mitigating factors do not outweigh aggravating factors, even if that means that they are at equivalent levels.[13]

Although aggravating and mitigating factors have been included in death penalty procedures in the United States since they were established in *Gregg v. Georgia* (1976), serious issues have been raised regarding their implementation. Many capital cases heard by the Supreme Court have revolved around procedural and statutory issues involving aggravating and mitigating circumstances. These cases and what the Supreme Court has said over the years regarding aggravating and mitigating circumstances are discussed in the following two sections.

---

[10]For an answer of "no" to the first two questions to be valid, 10 of the 12 jurors must answer "no"; for an answer of "yes" to the mitigation question to be valid, 10 of 12 jurors must answer "yes."

[11]*Brewer v. Quarterman*, 550 U.S. 286 (2007); *Abdul-Kabir v. Quarterman*, 550 U.S. 233 (2007).

[12]*Kansas v. Marsh*, 548 U.S. 163 (2006).

[13]*Id.*

III AGGRAVATING FACTORS

A General Procedural Requirements

In *Gregg v. Georgia* (1976),[14] the Supreme Court required that statutes adequately narrow the range of cases in which the death penalty may be imposed and that the jury's sentencing discretion be sufficiently guided by the consideration of aggravating factors. The Court also maintained that these aggravating factors must be stated and defined in a manner that is not overly vague or broad so as to adequately inform the jury of the specific factors guiding their decision. Although the Supreme Court, in *Gregg v. Georgia*, laid down these broad requirements pertaining to aggravating factors and their role in capital trials, specific processes for implementing these requirements were not prescribed by the Court. In the years that followed, the Supreme Court elaborated on and clarified these requirements.

Early on in the years following *Gregg*, the Supreme Court reaffirmed the requirement of aggravating circumstances. In *Presnell v. Georgia* (1978),[15] the Court held that at least one statutory aggravating circumstance must be found to exist beyond a reasonable doubt in order for the death penalty to be imposed. Furthermore, unanimity is generally required in a jury's determination of aggravating factors. The ultimate sentencing decision is not limited only to those unanimously found to be aggravating circumstances listed in the state's statute, however. In *Barclay v. Florida* (1983),[16] the Supreme Court established that when at least one statutory aggravating circumstance is found beyond a reasonable doubt, any aggravating factor, statutory and nonstatutory, can be considered in sentencing a capital defendant.

Although a statutory aggravating factor is required for the imposition of the death penalty, it does not mandate that the death penalty be imposed. A jury may find aggravating circumstances in a trial but still decide against the death penalty. As we will see later in the chapter, one reason for not imposing the death penalty may be a jury finding that mitigating factors are present. But even where jurors find no mitigating circumstances, their determination that aggravating factors are present usually does not preclude them from giving a sentence less than death. However, in *Blystone v. Pennsylvania* (1990),[17] the Supreme Court upheld Pennsylvania's statute mandating a death sentence when at least one aggravating factor and no mitigating factors are found. Although seemingly contradicting its previously strong stance against any form of mandatory death penalty,[18] the Supreme Court concluded that sufficient individualization in the sentencing decision exists under such statutes. As seen in the next section, however, even in cases in which such mandates do not exist, jurors are often left to believe that they must impose the death penalty in such circumstances.

B Vagueness and Guided (or Unguided) Discretion

The cases that came later to the Supreme Court dealt more with the substance and clarity of aggravating factors. A central concern of the Court in *Gregg* was that aggravating factors not be overly broad or vague so as to apply to virtually all murder cases and leave the jury with unbridled discretion and a lack

---

[14]*Gregg v. Georgia, supra.*
[15]*Presnell v. Georgia*, 439 U.S. 14 (1978).
[16]*Barclay v. Florida*, 463 U.S. 939 (1983).
[17]*Blystone v. Pennsylvania*, 494 U.S. 299 (1990).
[18]*Roberts v. Louisiana, supra; Woodson v. North Carolina, supra.*

of real guidance. Georgia's statute provided the following aggravating factor: "[if the murder was] outrageously wanton or vile, horrible or inhuman in that it involved torture, depravity of mind or an aggravated battery to the victim."[19] Although the Court upheld Georgia's death penalty statute, it warned that such aggravating factors and the language used were too broad and vague but left it to Georgia and other states to adequately specify aggravating factors that would appropriately narrow death penalty eligibility and guide capital juries' decisions. The Court again warned against vague language in *Godfrey v. Georgia* (1980),[20] holding that the meaning of statutory aggravating circumstances must be adequately clarified and applied independently to the facts of the particular case. Nevertheless, concerns were raised about vague and overly broad wording in aggravating factors and the fact that juries were not being given adequate guidance when considering aggravating factors in capital cases. Many death penalty statutes include some variation of the Georgia statute's wording, about which the Supreme Court expressed such concern. The Supreme Court has decided numerous cases addressing claims of overly broad and vague aggravating factors, but these decisions have not been all that clear or consistent.

In spite of the Supreme Court's rejection of overly broad and vague aggravating factors and its call for sentencing schemes that "suitably direct and limit" sentencing discretion to minimize the arbitrariness and capriciousness of the application of the death sentence, its later decisions exhibited what many consider a loosening of such standards. In *Lewis v. Jeffers* (1990),[21] the Court held that the phrase "especially heinous, cruel or depraved manner" was not unconstitutionally vague and sufficiently guided the sentencing authority. In spite of extant research raising concerns about juror confusion[22] and the proclaimed need for guidance in capital cases, the Supreme Court went on to approve increasingly vague descriptions of aggravating factors and refused to require increased clarification in the process of capital trials. In *Arave v. Creech* (1993),[23] the Court held that the phrase "utter disregard for human life" used as a statutory aggravating factor sufficiently limited sentencing discretion and therefore was deemed not to be in violation of Eighth and Fourteenth Amendment rights. The Court further upheld, in *Tuilaepa v. California* (1994),[24] factors such as the circumstances of the crime, the defendant's history of violent crime, and the defendant's age as not overly broad or vague and therefore constitutional as factors considered in the sentencing phase of a capital trial.

The Court has increasingly approved the inclusion of more and more aggravating factors in the sentencing phase of capital trials, many of which may be characterized as vague. However, the guidance a jury receives in considering aggravating factors, a notion emphasized in *Gregg v. Georgia*, has been the most recent casualty of the Supreme Court's jurisprudence on aggravating factors in capital cases. In *Tuilaepa v. California* (1994),[25] the Court held that capital juries need not be given instructions on how to weigh the various sentencing factors presented. In *Weeks v. Angelone* (2000)[26]

---

[19]O.C.G.A. § 17-10-30(b)(7).
[20]*Godfrey v. Georgia*, 446 U.S. 420 (1980).
[21]*Lewis v. Jeffers*, 497 U.S. 764 (1990).
[22]Lynch, Mona, and Craig Haney, *Capital Jury Deliberation: Effects on Death Sentencing, Comprehension, and Discrimination,* 33 Law Hum. Behav. 481 (2009); Ursula Bentele and William J. Bowers, *How Jurors Decide on Death: Guilt Is Overwhelming; Aggravation Requires Death; and Mitigation Is No Excuse,* 66 Brooklyn L. Rev. 1011 (2001).
[23]*Arave v. Creech*, 507 U.S. 463 (1993).
[24]*Tuilaepa v. California*, 512 U.S. 967 (1994).
[25]*Id.*
[26]*Weeks v. Angelone*, 528 U.S. 225 (2000).

the Court determined that upon request by the jury, the judge is not required to further clarify sentencing requirements beyond reference to the actual words of the jury instructions. (The actual instructions used had previously been approved by the Supreme Court in *Buchanan v. Angelone*, 1998.[27]) In *Weeks* the jury mistakenly believed that the presence of one of two aggravating circumstances required the jury to impose a death sentence, when in fact the law stated that the presence of such a factor only indicated that the death penalty was appropriate. After indicating their confusion to the judge and the fact that they were basing their decision on misunderstood instructions, the jurors received only a rereading of the instructions about which they were confused. Research has shown that such confusion and misperception on the part of capital jurors are not isolated occurrences.[28] Nevertheless, the Supreme Court has consistently supported states' refusals to clarify the actual law so that jurors adequately understand their duties and responsibilities in capital sentencing.

C The Special Case of Victim Impact Evidence

The role of victims in capital cases has changed significantly in the past few decades. Traditionally, victims were virtually absent from capital trials. Their role was often relegated to that of observers in court, and in some instances they were allowed to prepare a written victim impact statement that would be presented to the judge along with a presentencing report. Because in a majority of capital cases juries decided the sentence, the voice of victims often went unheard and had no impact on sentencing. The Supreme Court played a direct role in keeping it this way. In the late 1980s, the Supreme Court decided two cases regarding victim impact statements, condemning their use in both. In *Booth v. Maryland* (1987),[29] the Court declared that the introduction of victim impact statements violated the defendant's Eighth Amendment protections from cruel and unusual punishment. In *South Carolina v. Gathers* (1989),[30] the Court was more specific and held that the prosecution's reading of a prayer found in the victim's possession and statements regarding personal characteristics of the victim violated the Eighth Amendment.

This all changed with the Supreme Court's landmark decision in *Payne v. Tennessee* (1991).[31] Overruling, in part, both the *Booth* and *Gathers* decisions, the Court held that the admission of victim impact statements in the sentencing phase of a capital trial does not constitute an Eighth Amendment violation as long as the information presented does not violate principles of fundamental fairness for the defendant. The Court qualified its decision, stating that only statements regarding characteristics of the victim and the emotional impact of the crime on the victim's family are permissible during the sentencing phase of capital trials. Statements characterizing the crime or the defendant would not be allowed.

The *Payne* decision caused extensive controversy about the appropriate role of victim impact evidence in capital trials. Although some applaud it for bringing the victims' voices into the capital sentencing process and as a step toward victim-focused justice, many have criticized it as further inflaming jurors and thus leading to death sentences based on emotional reactions as opposed to neutral and

---

[27]*Buchanan v. Angelone*, 522 U.S. 269 (1998).
[28]*Bentele and Bowers, supra.*
[29]*Booth v. Maryland*, 482 U.S. 496 (1987).
[30]*South Carolina v. Gathers*, 490 U.S. 805 (1989).
[31]*Payne v. Tennessee*, 501 U.S. 808 (1991).

objective reasoning.[32] In 2008, these issues were considered in the case of *Kelly v. California*[33] in which the U.S. Supreme Court was being asked to limit the application of victim impact evidence to curtail its prejudicial impact. Though the Court denied certiorari in the case, three justices expressed concerns about the presence and effect of victim impact evidence in capital cases. Justice John Paul Stevens, in his comments in dissent from the denial of certiorari, encapsulates the concerns about victim impact evidence and its current application in death penalty cases:

> *In the years since* Payne *was decided, this Court has left state and federal courts unguided in their efforts to police the hazy boundaries between permissible victim impact evidence and its impermissible, 'unduly prejudicial' forms . . . Having decided to tolerate the introduction of evidence that puts a heavy thumb on the prosecutor's side of the scale in death cases, the Court has a duty to consider what reasonable limits should be placed on its use.*[34]

Others, like Justice Stevens, have argued that clearer and more stringent standards are needed for what victim impact evidence is permissible.[35] Whether or not the Court will take up this issue in a future case and thus set clearer parameters governing victim impact evidence in capital cases is unknown.

Opponents of the inclusion of victim impact statements in capital cases are not insensitive to the needs of victims of such horrible crimes, however, and do not wish them to be removed from the criminal justice process altogether. On the contrary, many have noted that victim impact statements and other victim impact evidence do not, in fact, serve the interests of victims and victims' survivors well. One legal scholar argues that "[a]lthough such testimony invariably serves the prosecution's goal of procuring a death sentence, the opportunity to testify does not address most of the needs of the survivors of murder that could be met by the criminal justice process."[36]

D The Special Case of Future Dangerousness

A final issue, and one that plays a central role in many capital cases, relates to the future dangerousness of the defendant or the likelihood that he or she will pose a violent threat to the public in the future. Although research has shown that the ability of psychiatrists and psychologists to predict future dangerousness is generally no better than chance,[37] death sentences often hinge on such "expert" determinations of this aggravating factor. In fact, in Texas and Oregon, the key question on which the jury's

---

[32]Paternoster, Ray, and Jerome Deise, *A Heavy Thumb on the Scale: The Effect of Victim Impact Evidence on Capital Decision Making*, 49 CRIMINOLOGY 129 (2011); Laura Walker, *Victim Impact Evidence in Death Penalty Sentencing Proceedings: Advocating for a Higher Relevancy Standard*, 22 GEO. MASON U. CIV. RTS. L.J. 89 (2011); John H. Blume, *Ten Years of Payne: Victim Impact Evidence in Capital Cases*, 88 CORNELL L. REV. 257 (2003); Austin Sarat, WHEN THE STATE KILLS: CAPITAL PUNISHMENT AND THE AMERICAN CONDITION (2001).

[33]*Kelly v. California*, 555 U.S. 1020 (2008).

[34]*Id.* at 1024; 1026.

[35]*Walker, Supra.*

[36]Burr, Richard, *Litigating with Victim Impact Testimony: The Serendipity That Has Come from* Payne v. Tennessee, 88 CORNELL L. REV. 517 (2003).

[37]Campbell, Mary Ann, Sheila French, and Paul Gendreau, *The Prediction of Violence in Adult Offenders: A Meta-Analytic Comparison of Instruments and Methods of Assessment*, 36 CRIM. J & BEHAV. 567 (2009); John Monahan, PREDICTING VIOLENT BEHAVIOR: AN ASSESSMENT OF CLINICAL TECHNIQUES (1981); Christopher Slobogin, *Dangerousness and Expertise*, 133 U. PA. L. REV. 97 (1984); Randy K. Otto, *On the Ability of Mental Health Professionals to Predict Dangerousness: A Commentary on Interpretations of the Dangerousness Literature*, 18 L. & PSYCHOLOG. REV. 43 (1994).

sentencing decision relies is whether the defendant is likely to present a future danger to society.[38] It was a Texas case that brought the issue of future dangerousness to the forefront of the jurisprudential landscape.

In *Barefoot v. Estelle* (1983), the Supreme Court addressed Texas's sentencing scheme, which required a jury to unanimously answer "yes" to a question asking "whether there is a probability that the defendant would commit criminal acts of violence that would constitute a continuing threat to society."[39] The case centered around the role of psychiatric and psychological experts in making these determinations and the admissibility of the associated evidence of future dangerousness. In spite of research findings,[40] amicus briefs filed by the American Psychiatric Association contesting the accuracy of such predictions, and the Court's own admission that "[p]sychiatrists simply have no expertise in predicting long-term future dangerousness,"[41] the Supreme Court held that psychiatric evidence on the prediction of future dangerousness is admissible at the sentencing phase of a capital case.

Barefoot v. Estelle has proved to be the final word on the admissibility of testimony about future dangerousness. To this day, death sentences are often determined primarily based on testimony regarding, and jurors' perceptions of, the future dangerousness of the defendant.[42] Some scholars have pointed out that whether explicitly provided by statute or simply argued by the prosecution, future dangerousness is "always at issue" in capital cases.[43] The role of experts in determining and testifying to future dangerousness has become increasingly central to a state's ability to evoke death sentences. In Texas, for example, one psychiatrist, Dr. Grigson, came to be known as "Dr. Death" because he testified for the state in more than 100 capital cases in which he pronounced the defendant a future threat to society, often declaring with 100 percent (and in some cases, 1,000 percent!) certainty that the defendant would kill again. In 1995, Dr. Grigson was expelled from the American Psychiatric Association for arriving at these conclusions without actually examining the defendants.[44]

IV MITIGATING FACTORS

In addition to the presence of aggravating factors, jurors' decisions in capital cases are guided further by consideration of mitigating circumstances or factors that may warrant mercy or leniency in the determination of whether the defendant will receive the death penalty. The inclusion of mitigating factors in capital sentencing furthers the goal set forth in *Gregg* of guiding capital juries' discretion and narrowing the use of the death penalty on only those deemed most deserving. Mitigating factors in

---

[38]Edens, John F., John Petrila, and Jacqueline Buffington-Vollum, *Psychopathy and the Death Penalty: Can the Psychopathy Checklist-Revised Identify Offenders Who Represent "A Continuing Threat to Society"?* 29 J. Psychiatry & L. 433 (2001).
[39]*Barefoot v. Estelle*, 463 U.S. 880, 884 (1983).
[40]Campbell et al., *Supra.*; Mitzi Dorland and Daniel Krauss, *The Danger of Dangerousness in Capital Sentencing: Exacerbating the Problem of Arbitrary and Capricious Decision-Making,* 29 Law & Psychol. Rev. 63 (2005).
[41]Dorland and Krauss, *Id.* at 921.
[42]Cunningham, Mark D., Jon R. Sorensen, Mark P. Vigen, and S.O. Woods, *Life and Death in the Lone Star State: Three Decades of Violence Predictions by Capital Juries,* 29 Behav. Sci. Law 1 (2011); Mark D. Cunningham and Thomas J. Reidy, *Integrating Base Rate Data in Violence Risk Assessments at Capital Sentencing,* 16 Behav. Sci. Law 71 (1998).
[43]Blume, John H., Stephen P. Garvey and Sheri Lynn Johnson, *Future Dangerousness in Capital Cases: Always "At Issue,"* 86 Cornell L. Rev. 397 (2001).
[44]Texas Defender Service, A State of Denial: Texas Justice and The Death Penalty (2000).

capital trials exist solely in the sentencing phase, with specific focus on the defendant and whether he or she should receive the death penalty. These factors often revolve around personal history, such as whether the defendant experienced abuse as a child or experienced other trauma as a result of an adverse environment. Specific characteristics may also come into play; age, cognitive deficits, and mental illness are common mitigating factors. Finally, predictions of the future are also often presented as mitigating factors. The defendant's ability to adapt to institutional life and lack of threat of future violence may be raised in mitigation. As with aggravating factors, the Supreme Court has spent a great deal of time considering the appropriate procedural requirements and substance of mitigating factors in capital trials.

A General Procedural Requirements

Although the Supreme Court in *Gregg* said that the sentencing authority in capital cases must consider mitigating factors before determining the sentence, little guidance was given as to specific requirements. In a pair of Ohio cases (*Lockett v. Ohio*, 1978[45]; *Bell v. Ohio*, 1978[46]) decided two years after *Gregg*, the Supreme Court declared that both statutory and non-statutory mitigating circumstances may be presented by the defense and all presented mitigating factors must be considered in the sentencing phase of trial. This was an important advance from the general provision of mitigating factors indicated in *Gregg*. In *Hitchcock v. Dugger* (1987),[47] the Supreme Court reaffirmed *Lockett* and *Bell*, stating that jurors may not refuse to consider any relevant mitigating evidence—they must consider all statutory and nonstatutory mitigating circumstances appropriately presented. In *Parker v. Dugger* (1991),[48] the Court extended this to judges who either make the final sentencing decision or override a jury's recommendation of a sentence less than death. It was held that all sentencing authorities (judges or panels of judges in addition to juries) must consider all statutory and nonstatutory mitigating evidence previously presented.

A decade later, in *Mills v. Maryland* (1988)[49] and *McKoy v. North Carolina* (1990),[50] the Court held that the jury does not need to be unanimous in determining the presence of mitigating circumstances and that sentencing instructions requiring unanimity on the presence of a mitigating circumstance are unconstitutional. Although such unanimity is not required for individual jurors to consider particular mitigating circumstances in weighing factors toward their decision, states are allowed to require some level of agreement among jurors regarding the presence of mitigating factors. For example, Texas law requires that 10 of the 12 jurors agree that mitigating factors warrant a life sentence rather than a sentence of death.[51]

---

[45]*Lockett v. Ohio*, 438 U.S. 586 (1978).
[46]*Bell v. Ohio*, 438 U.S. 637 (1978).
[47]*Hitchcock v. Dugger*, 481 U.S. 393 (1987).
[48]*Parker v. Dugger*, 498 U.S. 308 (1991).
[49]*Mills v. Maryland*, 486 U.S. 367 (1988).
[50]*McKoy v. North Carolina*, 494 U.S. 433 (1990).
[51]Tex. Code Crim. Proc., Art. 37.071 § 2g(2).

B Evidence Allowed

The Supreme Court has generally held that just about any relevant mitigating factors must be allowed to be presented and accordingly considered by the sentencing authority (usually the jury). The Court has periodically been confronted by statutes and trial procedures that deny this right. In *Eddings v. Oklahoma* (1982),[52] the Court held that refusal to allow family history as a mitigating factor in the sentencing phase of a capital trial is unconstitutional. This watershed case opened the door to a wide array of information and evidence that could be presented as mitigating evidence in capital trials. History of abuse, neglect, and childhood trauma are now mainstays of mitigation in the sentencing phase of capital trials. In *Penry v. Lynaugh* (1989),[53] the Court further specified that a defendant's mental retardation and child abuse victimization must be considered, if presented, as mitigating factors and that a trial court's refusal to instruct the jury to this effect is unconstitutional.

In *Skipper v. South Carolina* (1986),[54] the Court addressed a different form of mitigating evidence—that relating to current and future circumstances. As mentioned previously, future dangerousness is a key element in many capital cases, usually presented as an aggravating factor that justifies imposing the death penalty. In *Skipper*, however, the Court considered whether evidence that the defendant had adjusted well to incarceration (i.e., was not violent or likely to be violent in jail or prison) was admissible as a mitigating factor in the sentencing phase of a capital trial. In line with its general inclination to allow all relevant mitigating factors, the Court proclaimed that, in accordance with *Lockett* (1978), it was admissible. This presented a potential counterpoint to the commonly used aggravating factor of future dangerousness, the argument being that if the interest of public safety is just as well served by incarceration, then the death penalty for that individual is unnecessary.

In recent years, the Court has been a bit more reluctant to take the "anything goes" perspective on what mitigating evidence may be allowed during the sentencing phase of capital trials. In *Oregon v. Guzek* (2006)[55] the Supreme Court addressed the specific issue of whether evidence of innocence can be presented as mitigating evidence during the sentencing phase of a capital trial. Guzek had been found guilty and sentenced to death initially and then again after the state supreme court overturned his original sentence. The question before the Court concerned whether Guzek could present evidence of innocence (specifically, an alibi) that was not presented during the original trial. Oregon law restricts the presentation of innocence-related evidence during sentencing or resentencing hearings to that presented at the original guilt phase of the capital trial. The U.S. Supreme Court held that Oregon's requirement does not violate the Constitution and thus the defendant does not have a right to present new evidence of innocence at a sentencing or resentencing hearing in capital cases.[56] This is one of the few restrictions on allowable mitigating evidence that has been deemed acceptable by the Supreme Court. This is also one of several recent cases that seem to indicate an increasing deference to states by the Court.

---

[52]*Eddings v. Oklahoma*, 455 U.S. 104 (1982).
[53]*Penry v. Lynaugh*, 492 U.S. 302 (1989).
[54]*Skipper v. South Carolina*, 476 U.S. 1 (1986).
[55]*Oregon v. Guzek*, 546 U.S. 517 (2006).
[56]*Id.*

C Jury Instructions

Another major issue that arose as the Supreme Court fine-tuned its decisions on mitigating factors in capital cases was that of jury instructions. Although issues regarding jury instructions were presented in Chapter 6, they warrant attention here as they relate to mitigating factors. Jury instructions are central to the role of mitigating factors in capital trials. One of the primary concerns in *Gregg* (1976) was that juries be adequately guided in their sentencing decision. For this guidance to be effective, jury instructions must be clear and informative enough to provide the jury with adequate understanding of the meaning and function of mitigating factors in the capital sentencing process.

Although the Court has generally held that most relevant mitigating factors must be allowed at the sentencing phase of capital trials, it has been more equivocal about the associated jury instructions. Again, in spite of research indicating that capital jurors are often confused about the meaning and applicability of mitigating circumstances in their sentencing decision,[57] the Supreme Court has, over the years, consistently resisted imposing specific requirements on state trial courts regarding jury instructions about mitigating factors. In 1993, the Supreme Court handed down two decisions pertaining to jury instructions about mitigating factors in capital cases. In *Johnson v. Texas* (1993),[58] the Court held that specific instructions to consider the defendant's youth as a mitigating factor were not required, and in *Delo v. Lashley* (1993),[59] it proclaimed that courts are not required to instruct juries to consider mitigating circumstances when supporting evidence has not been adequately presented (in this case, lack of prior criminal history). In 1998, the Court declared its broadest decision related to jury instructions about mitigating factors.

In *Buchanan v. Angelone* (1998),[60] it held that the failure to instruct a jury as to the specific meaning of the mitigating circumstances it is to consider, or to give explicit guidance in regard to such mitigating circumstances, was not a violation of the Eighth or Fourteenth Amendments. The Court contended that the judge's instruction to consider "all the evidence" was sufficient. The Court continued its approval of seemingly ambiguous instructions regarding mitigating factors in the case of *Ayers v. Belmontes* (2006).[61] In this case, the California trial judge had instructed the jury to consider 11 mitigating factors (factors *a* through *k*). Included among these was a catch-all factor ("factor k") telling jurors to consider "[a]ny other circumstances which extenuate the gravity of the crime even though it is not a legal excuse for the crime."[62] Belmontes appealed his death sentence on the grounds that this factor was ambiguous and led to possible confusion over whether the jury should or should not consider mitigating factors not related to the crime. The Court upheld the factor k instruction, holding that it was sufficient to inform the jury that they must consider all relevant mitigating factors, including noncrime-related factors.

Some of the Supreme Court's most recent decisions, however, give some indication of a new direction in the requirements for jury instructions about mitigating factors in capital cases. A series of Texas cases has presented the Court with ample opportunity to define appropriate guidance regarding jury

---

[57]Lynch & Haney, *supra.* Craig Haney, Lorelei Sontag, and Sally Costanzo, *Deciding to Take a Life: Capital Juries, Sentencing Instructions, and the Jurisprudence of Death,* 50 J. Soc. Issues 149 (1994).
[58]*Johnson v. Texas,* 509 U.S. 350 (1993).
[59]*Delo v. Lashley,* 507 U.S. 272 (1993).
[60]*Buchanan v. Angelone, supra.*
[61]*Ayers v. Belmontes,* 549 U.S. 7 (2006).
[62]*Id.*

instructions about mitigating evidence. In *Smith v. Texas* (2004),[63] the Court held that Texas's failure to instruct juries about the appropriate consideration of mitigating factors (in this case, low IQ, a troubled family background, and a history of learning disabilities) violated the Eighth Amendment. Neverthe-less, the Texas Court of Criminal Appeals resentenced Smith to death, contending that the error made in the jury instructions did not constitute "egregious harm" in the original sentencing of Smith.[64] In the follow-up case (*Smith v. Texas*, 2007[65]), the U.S. Supreme Court rejected Texas's resentencing of Smith, holding that the Texas court's standard of requiring Smith to show "egregious harm" was invalid and that corrective instructions were not sufficient to undo the original error.[66]

The pair of *Smith* cases was followed by another pair of 2007 Texas cases (consolidated as com-panion cases): *Abdul-Kabir v. Quarterman* (2007)[67] and *Brewer v. Quarterman* (2007).[68] In these cases, the Texas capital sentencing statute was challenged in that it was being used to disallow jury instructions directing jurors to consider all mitigating evidence presented during the sentencing hear-ing. Instead, the trial judge instructed the jury to only consider the two special issues stated explicitly in the statute: that the defendant caused the death of the victim and that the defendant presented a con-tinuing threat of violence to society. The U.S. Supreme Court decided that jury instructions limited to Texas's two special issues were not sufficient to give full consideration and effect to mitigating factors in a capital trial. Juries must be informed about their duty to consider all relevant mitigating evidence. Although the decisions suggest a change toward stricter requirements and detail in instructing juries about the consideration of mitigating factors in capital cases, it remains to be seen what the broader impact of these decisions will be.

V IN SUMMARY, WHAT DO THESE CASES SAY?

In *Gregg v. Georgia* (1976)[69] the Supreme Court not only reinstated the death penalty, it also set the standards for modern-day death penalty procedure. Central to this procedure was the consideration of aggravating and mitigating factors at the sentencing stage of capital trials. The Court maintained that in order to ensure that the death penalty is reserved for only the most serious and severe cases and that individual factors and circumstances are thoroughly considered, factors about the crime, defendant, and victim may be presented and considered prior to sentencing. Aggravating factors are those that elevate a crime to death penalty status, usually referring to factors that make the death penalty particularly appropriate. These factors are often about the particularly heinous nature of the offense, the future dan-ger the defendant poses, and even the impact of the crime on the victim's family. Mitigating factors, on the other hand, are those that may warrant the mercy of the jury. Often these factors focus on charac-teristics of the defendant, such as diminished mental capacity or a history of child abuse, or circum-stances of the offense that might attenuate culpability. By considering and weighing these factors, capital juries must come to a decision about whether a defendant deserves to live or die.

---

[63]*Smith v. Texas*, 543 U.S. 37 (2004).
[64]*Smith v. Texas*, 550 U.S. 297 (2007).
[65]*Id.*
[66]*Id.*
[67]*Abdul-Kabir v. Quarterman*, 550 U.S. 233 (2007).
[68]*Brewer v. Quarterman*, 550 U.S. 286 (2007).
[69]*Gregg v. Georgia, supra.*

Although approving varying state approaches to the consideration of aggravating and mitigating factors in capital cases, the Supreme Court has established some relatively clear guidelines. First, a jury must be unanimous in its determination of the presence of an aggravating factor in order for that factor to weigh in its decision. On the other hand, unanimity is not required for a mitigating factor to be considered. Second, at least one statutory aggravating circumstance must be found in order for the death penalty to be imposed. States may or may not specifically provide statutory mitigating factors in their death penalty statutes, but the Supreme Court has generally held that any mitigating factors supported by evidence must be allowed to be considered by the jury and that jury instructions must provide sufficient guidance in this regard. Where the Court has been less willing to intervene is in the *nature* of jury instructions regarding the consideration of mitigating factors.

Some of the most significant Supreme Court decisions on aggravating and mitigating circumstances are about specific forms of testimony and evidence. In *Barefoot v. Estelle* (1983),[70] the Court upheld psychiatric testimony about the future dangerousness of the defendant as an aggravating factor justifying the sentence of death. To this day, such testimony plays an important role in securing death sentences in many states. On the other hand, in *Skipper v. South Carolina* (1986),[71] the Court held that evidence suggesting that a defendant is not a future danger was admissible as a mitigating factor in the sentencing phase of capital trials. In *Payne v. Tennessee* (1991),[72] the Court said that testimony about the victim and the impact of the crime on the victim's family is admissible as an aggravating factor in capital cases. Through these and other related decisions, the Supreme Court has molded the intricate workings of death penalty procedure and ensured that all relevant factors are considered in the implementation of this most extreme form of punishment.

VI CONCLUSION

The Supreme Court has proclaimed that "this most irrevocable of sanctions should be reserved for a small number of extreme cases."[73] The Court has called for a complex set of requirements revolving around aggravating and mitigating factors in death penalty cases. Aggravating factors serve to narrow the range of offenses eligible for the death penalty and guide individualized consideration in capital cases. Mitigating factors ensure that juries have the option to show mercy to particular defendants.

The Supreme Court has been clear on the requirements for aggravating circumstances in capital cases. At least one aggravating circumstance must be unanimously found by the jury in order for the death penalty to be considered. Aggravating factors must be guided by the court to ensure that they are not overly broad or vague. However, in recent cases the Court has loosely interpreted the standards for such guidance and clarification. Once an aggravating factor is found to be present, almost any other aggravating factors can be presented by the prosecutor. There are some restrictions, however. Although the Supreme Court decided that victim impact statements are admissible in the sentencing phase of a

---

[70]*Barefoot v. Estelle, supra.*
[71]*Skipper v. South Carolina, supra.*
[72]*Payne v. Tennessee, supra.*
[73]*Id.* at 182.

capital trial, it limited this to statements about the character of the victim and the emotional impact of the crime. The Court prohibits victim impact statements characterizing the offender or the offense. Finally, statutory aggravating factors must be adequately clarified and appropriately applied to the facts of the case in the judge's instructions to the jury.

The Supreme Court requires that all relevant mitigating circumstances presented by the defense be considered in the sentencing phase of a capital case. The Court has applied this requirement to both statutory and nonstatutory mitigating factors. The Court has generally held that virtually anything can be admitted as a mitigating factor and that such factors must be considered by the sentencing authority at any stage of the process. It has also held that juries must be given adequate guidance via jury instructions pertaining to their duty to consider all relevant mitigating evidence. The Court has been less willing, however, to infringe on *how* states choose to inform juries about their consideration of these mitigating factors. Jury unanimity in regard to specific mitigating circumstances is not required; however, mitigating circumstances must be supported by evidence.

The decisions in *Furman* and *Gregg* ushered in a new era. In line with the notion that "death is different," statutes must now ensure that the specific circumstances of a case are thoroughly considered before a decision is made to impose death. The Supreme Court has consistently required that this extreme and irrevocable punishment be characterized by rigorous scrutiny to ensure that it is used only for extreme cases. Consideration of aggravating and mitigating factors in the capital sentencing process is the mechanism by which this is accomplished.

CASES BRIEFED IN CHAPTER 9

Case	Issue	Holding
Woodson v. North Carolina 428 U.S. 280 (1976)	Do mandatory death penalty statutes violate Eighth and Fourteenth Amendment rights?	Statutes making death sentences mandatory violate the Eighth and Fourteenth Amendments because they fail to take into consideration the individual aspects of the criminal and crime and the particular circumstances of the case.
Lockett v. Ohio 438 U.S. 586 (1978)	Must mitigating factors be considered in the sentencing of capital defendants?	Death penalty statutes must allow for consideration of mitigating factors regarding the character or history of a defendant as well as the circumstances of the offense.
Presnell v. Georgia 439 U.S. 14 (1978)	Is it constitutional to sentence a defendant to death in the absence of any aggravating circumstances?	It is a violation of due process to sentence a defendant to death if no aggravating circumstances required for a death sentence are found by the jury to be present.

Continued

Case	Issue	Holding
Barefoot v. Estelle 463 U.S. 880 (1983)	Does the Constitution prohibit psychiatric testimony offering predictions of future dangerousness in capital trials?	Psychiatric testimony regarding future dangerousness is admissible during the sentencing phase of capital trials.
Lewis v. Jeffers 497 U.S. 764 (1990)	Is the aggravating circumstance that a crime is "especially heinous, cruel or depraved" unconstitutionally vague or overly broad?	The aggravating circumstance that the crime was "especially heinous, cruel or depraved" is not unconstitutionally vague or overly broad.
McKoy v. North Carolina 494 U.S. 433 (1990)	Does a statute requiring a unanimous finding by the jury for a mitigating circumstance to be considered during sentencing violate the standard set in *Mills v. Maryland* (1988)?	North Carolina's death penalty statute requiring unanimity among capital jurors regarding mitigating factors violates the U.S. Supreme Court's prior decision in *Mills v. Maryland*.
Payne v. Tennessee 501 U.S. 808 (1991)	Does the Eighth Amendment prohibit victim impact statements from being presented at the sentencing phase of a capital trial?	Victim impact statements pertaining to characteristics of the victim and the emotional impact of the crime on the victim's family do not violate the Eighth Amendment and are admissible in the sentencing phase of trial.
Kansas v. Marsh 548 U.S. 163 (2006)	Is it constitutional to impose the death penalty when aggravating and mitigating factors are unanimously found to be equal?	It is constitutional to impose the death penalty when a unanimous jury finds aggravating and mitigating factors to be equal.
Brewer v. Quarterman 550 U.S. 286 (2007)	Can a state's capital sentencing statute prevent a jury from giving, or being instructed to give, meaningful consideration to constitutionally relevant mitigating factors and evidence?	It is unconstitutional for a state's capital sentencing statute to restrict the jury's consideration of relevant mitigating evidence. Such statutes must allow for the full consideration of mitigating factors by the jury, and jury instructions should reflect this.

CASE BRIEFS

WOODSON v. NORTH CAROLINA 428 U.S. 280 (1976)

CAPSULE: Mandatory death penalty statutes are unconstitutional.

FACTS: Woodson and three accomplices were convicted of armed robbery of a convenience store in which a cashier was killed and a customer was seriously wounded. Two of Woodson's accomplices made plea agreements, testifying against Woodson in exchange for pleading guilty to lesser offenses. Woodson maintained that he was coerced by accomplices and therefore innocent. He was found guilty on all charges and, in accordance with North Carolina law,

Continued

WOODSON v. NORTH CAROLINA 428 U.S. 280 (1976)—cont'd

was automatically sentenced to death upon conviction of felony murder. The state Supreme Court affirmed the verdict. The U.S. Supreme Court granted certiorari to consider whether North Carolina's death penalty statute mandating automatic imposition of the sentence of death upon conviction of first-degree murder was constitutional.

ISSUE: Do mandatory death penalty statutes violate Eighth and Fourteenth Amendment rights? YES.

HOLDING: Statutes making death sentences mandatory violate the Eighth and Fourteenth Amendments because they fail to take into consideration the individual aspects of the criminal and crime and the particular circumstances of the case.

REASON: "The North Carolina statute fails to provide a constitutionally tolerable response to Furman's rejection of unbridled jury discretion in the imposition of capital sentences. Central to the limited holding in that case was the conviction that vesting a jury with standardless sentencing power violated the Eighth and Fourteenth Amendments, yet that constitutional deficiency is not eliminated by the mere formal removal of all sentencing power from juries in capital cases. In view of the historic record, it may reasonably be assumed that many juries under mandatory statutes will continue to consider the grave consequences of a conviction in reaching a verdict. But the North Carolina statute provides no standards to guide the jury in determining which murderers shall live and which shall die.

"The respect for human dignity underlying the Eighth Amendment requires consideration of aspects of the character of the individual offender and the circumstances of the particular offense as a constitutionally indispensable part of the process of imposing the ultimate punishment of death. The North Carolina statute impermissibly treats all persons convicted of a designated offense not as uniquely individual human beings, but as members of a faceless, undifferentiated mass to be subjected to the blind infliction of the death penalty."

CASE SIGNIFICANCE: In *Gregg v. Georgia*, 428 U.S. 153 (1976), the Supreme Court reinstated the death penalty. But the Court also declared the form that death penalty statutes must take in order to be constitutional. The Court approved "guided discretion" statutes, or statutes that allowed the sentencing authority to consider individual case circumstances in determining the appropriate sentence. At the same time as the decision in *Gregg*, the Supreme Court also considered a different form of death penalty statute: those making the death penalty mandatory upon conviction of capital murder. In this case, the Court declared such statutes unconstitutional and thus added to the emphasis made in *Gregg* on individual case consideration. Although mandatory death penalty statutes certainly avoid the arbitrary, discriminatory, and disproportionate application of the death penalty, such statutes do not allow for the individual consideration needed in death penalty cases. As the Supreme Court has stated, "death is different." The Court's decision in *Woodson* reinforced this notion and stressed that statutes not providing adequate procedural safeguards and individualized consideration of the circumstances are unacceptable.

PRESNELL v. GEORGIA 439 U.S. 14 (1978)

CAPSULE: The death penalty cannot be imposed unless at least one aggravating circumstance is found to be present by the jury.

FACTS: Presnell was indicted for three capital offenses: rape, kidnapping with bodily injury, and murder with malice aforethought. The jury convicted him of all three offenses. Georgia law provides that a jury may sentence a defendant to death if at least one of 10 aggravating circumstances is present. One of the aggravating factors enumerated in Georgia's statute was that an offender could be sentenced to death if the capital offense was committed during the commission of another capital felony. The jury concluded that each offense was committed during the commission of other capital offenses and sentenced Presnell to three death sentences.

Continued

PRESNELL v. GEORGIA 439 U.S. 14 (1978)—cont'd

The Georgia Supreme Court overruled the death sentences for the rape and kidnapping charges because it determined that both sentences depended upon Presnell having committed forcible rape. The jury had not established this because the jury actually only convicted Presnell of statutory rape, not forcible rape. Because the kidnapping with bodily injury depended upon the act of sodomy associated with forcible rape, this conviction was also thrown out. In spite of establishing that neither of the other capital felonies was valid and that the death sentence for murder depended upon the aggravating factor of being committed during the commission of another capital offense, the Georgia Supreme Court nonetheless upheld the third death penalty.

ISSUE: Is it constitutional to sentence a defendant to death in the absence of any aggravating circumstances? NO.

HOLDING: It is a violation of due process to sentence a defendant to death if no aggravating circumstances required for a death sentence are found by the jury to be present.

REASON: "Under due process principles of procedural fairness, a state-court, jury-imposed death sentence for murder with malice aforethought—based on the aggravating circumstance that the offense was committed while the defendant was engaged in the commission of 'kidnapping with bodily injury, aggravated sodomy'—cannot stand, where (1) the state's highest court had vacated the defendant's conviction on another count for rape, along with death penalties on counts involving the rape, on the ground that the jury had not properly convicted the defendant of 'forcible' rape (required for a death sentence), because the jury had been instructed both on forcible and statutory rape but had not specified in its verdict which offense it had found [and] (2) the state's highest court had also held that the state could not rely upon sodomy as constituting the bodily injury associated with the kidnapping..."

CASE SIGNIFICANCE: In one of the earliest cases to follow the landmark decision in *Gregg v. Georgia* (1976),[74] the Court made the first of many decisions regarding the specific requirements of the procedural safeguards. In *Gregg*, the Court stated that the death penalty should be reserved only for those cases that are extreme or "aggravated" in some way. The Court left it to the states to determine what is sufficiently aggravating to elevate an offense to death sentence eligibility. But the Court made it clear that such aggravating circumstances were necessary for the death penalty to be imposed. In this case, the defendant was originally convicted of three felonies, thus triggering the aggravating factor of having committed murder in the act of other felonies. However, two of the felonies were found to be unsubstantiated and were thus removed by the trial court. Nevertheless, the trial court imposed the previously applied death penalty. The Court ruled the death penalty invalid in this case due to the absence of any remaining aggravating factors upon which a death sentence must rest. This is an important decision because it underscored the need for aggravating circumstances in sentencing a defendant to death. It also stresses the Court's requirement that the death penalty be reserved only for the most extreme cases.

LOCKETT v. OHIO 438 U.S. 586 (1978)

CAPSULE: Death penalty statutes must allow for the consideration of mitigating factors.

FACTS: Lockett was convicted of aggravated murder after taking part in the planning and carrying out of the robbery of a pawnshop in which the shop owner was killed. Although she had not entered the pawnshop with her accomplices and did not have a direct role in the murder of the owner, Lockett was found guilty by the jury for her role in the crime. Upon conviction, the Ohio death penalty statute required the judge to impose a death sentence unless he or she found the presence of any of three factors that mitigated the defendant's culpability: (1) whether the victim induced or facilitated the offense; (2) whether the defendant committed the offense under duress, coercion, or strong

Continued

---

[74]*Gregg v. Georgia, supra.*

LOCKETT v. OHIO 438 U.S. 586 (1978)—cont'd

provocation; and (3) whether the offense was a result of the defendant's psychosis or mental deficiency. The judge concluded that the offense was not a result of mental deficiency or psychosis and, without specifically addressing the other two statutory mitigating factors, sentenced Lockett to death.

ISSUE: Must mitigating factors be considered in the sentencing of capital defendants? YES.

HOLDING: Death penalty statutes must allow for consideration of mitigating factors regarding the character or history of a defendant as well as the circumstances of the offense.

REASON: "The Eighth and Fourteenth Amendments require that the sentencer, in all but the rarest kind of capital case, not be precluded from considering as a mitigating factor, any aspect of a defendant's character or record and any of the circumstances of the offense that the defendant proffers as a basis for a sentence less than death.

"The need for treating each defendant in a capital case with the degree of respect due the uniqueness of the individual is far more important than in noncapital cases, particularly in view of the unavailability with respect to an executed capital sentence of such post-conviction mechanisms in noncapital cases as probation, parole, and work furloughs.

"A statute that prevents the sentencer in capital cases from giving independent mitigating weight to aspects of the defendant's character and record and to the circumstances of the offense proffered in mitigation creates the risk that the death penalty will be imposed in spite of factors that may call for a less severe penalty, and when the choice is between life and death, such risk is unacceptable and incompatible with the commands of the Eighth and Fourteenth Amendments."

CASE SIGNIFICANCE: In *Presnell v. Georgia* (1978),[75] the Supreme Court held that aggravating circumstances must be present for the death penalty to be imposed. In this case, the Court reinforced that other side to the "guided discretion" set forth in *Gregg v. Georgia*, 428 U.S. 153 (1976)[76]: mitigating circumstances. The consideration of aggravating and mitigating circumstances has become almost sacred in death penalty cases. This case said that mitigating circumstances must be adequately considered in the sentencing phase of the trial. Moreover, the Court said that consideration of mitigating circumstances should not be overly limited and should include factors about the defendant's character and history and the circumstances of the crime. This set a broad standard of what mitigating circumstances may be considered in the sentencing phase of capital trials. There are very few restrictions placed on the mitigating factors the sentencing authority is allowed to consider in deciding whether to impose the death penalty.

BAREFOOT v. ESTELLE 463 U.S. 880 (1983)

CAPSULE: Testimony regarding a defendant's future dangerousness is admissible during the sentencing phase of capital trials.

FACTS: Barefoot was convicted of capital murder for the killing of a police officer in Bell County, Texas. During the sentencing phase of the trial, the jury, under Texas law, was asked two questions: (1) whether the defendant deliberately killed the victim or acted with "reasonable expectation that the death of the deceased or another would result," and (2) whether "there is a probability that the defendant would commit criminal acts of violence that would constitute a continuing threat to society." Texas law required that the death penalty be imposed if a jury answered "yes" to both questions. In pursuit of the latter question, the prosecution called two psychiatrists who testified that Barefoot "would probably commit further acts of violence and represent a continuing threat to society." Barefoot

Continued

---

[75]*Presnell v. Georgia, supra.*
[76]*Gregg v. Georgia, supra.*

BAREFOOT v. ESTELLE 463 U.S. 880 (1983)—cont'd

contended, on appeal, that the psychiatrists' testimony regarding future dangerousness was unconstitutional due to their inability to accurately predict future dangerousness and the fact that both had made their conclusions without actually examining the defendant. The Texas Court of Criminal Appeals rejected his arguments and affirmed the conviction and death sentence.

ISSUE: Does the Constitution prohibit psychiatric testimony offering predictions of future dangerousness in capital trials? NO.

HOLDING: Psychiatric testimony regarding future dangerousness is admissible during the sentencing phase of capital trials. A psychiatrist need not actually interview or examine a defendant in person in order for his or her testimony and predictions to be admissible.

REASON: "There is no merit to petitioner's argument that psychiatrists, individually and as a group, are incompetent to predict with an acceptable degree of reliability that a particular criminal will commit other crimes in the future and so represent a danger to the community. To accept such an argument would call into question predictions of future behavior that are constantly made in other contexts. Moreover, under the generally applicable rules of evidence covering the admission and weight of unprivileged evidence, psychiatric testimony predicting dangerousness may be countered not only as erroneous in a particular case but also as generally so unreliable that it should be ignored. Nor, despite the view of the American Psychiatric Association supporting petitioner's view, is there any convincing evidence that such testimony is almost entirely unreliable and that the factfinder and the adversary system will not be competent to uncover, recognize, and take due account of its shortcomings."

CASE SIGNIFICANCE: Future dangerousness is a common aggravating circumstance in death penalty statutes and is explicitly required in Texas and Oregon. This case centered on the admissibility of psychiatric predictions of future dangerousness. In spite of protest from the American Psychiatric Association and research indicating that psychiatrists' predictions of future dangerousness are inherently unreliable, the Court concluded that such testimony is allowed as aggravating evidence in the sentencing phase of capital trials. Playing on the fears of jurors that the defendant will likely be a violent threat in the future, evidence of future dangerousness is powerful and has arguably been responsible for a substantial number of death sentences. The Court in this case said that such testimony would be admissible and that standard remains intact to this day. Interestingly, expert testimony that the defendant is not a future danger is becoming increasingly used as mitigation in capital trials. In spite of serious questions regarding the reliability of such predictions and conclusions, future dangerousness remains a central consideration in death penalty sentencing.

LEWIS v. JEFFERS 497 U.S. 764 (1990)

CAPSULE: The aggravating circumstance that the crime was "especially heinous, cruel, or depraved" is not unconstitutionally vague or overly broad.

FACTS: In May 1976, Jeffers and his girlfriend, Penelope Cheney, were arrested on charges of possession of narcotics and receipt of stolen property. Jeffers posted bond for Cheney but was unable to do the same for himself. While in jail, Jeffers found out that Cheney was cooperating with police and providing them with information against Jeffers. He wrote a note offering another inmate money to kill Cheney. The officer who was to deliver the note read it without delivering it. Later that year, after being released from jail, Jeffers met up with Cheney to provide her with heroin. He injected her with, in his words to a witness, "enough shit to kill a horse." While she was still alive, Jeffers choked Cheney with her own belt and then with his own hands until she was dead.

Continued

LEWIS v. JEFFERS 497 U.S. 764 (1990)—cont'd

Jeffers was convicted of first-degree murder. The trial court found two aggravating circumstances and no mitigating circumstances. In accordance with Arizona law, Jeffers was sentenced to death. On appeal, Jeffers contended that the aggravating factor of the crime being "especially heinous, cruel, or depraved" was unconstitutionally vague and broad. The Arizona Supreme Court rejected his claims and upheld the conviction and death sentence.

ISSUE: Is the aggravating circumstance that a crime is "especially heinous, cruel, or depraved" unconstitutional vague or overly broad? NO.

HOLDING: The aggravating circumstance that the crime was "especially heinous, cruel, or depraved" is not unconstitutionally vague or overly broad.

REASON: "... [I]f a State has adopted a constitutionally narrow construction of a facially vague aggravating circumstance, and if the State has applied that construction to the facts of the particular case, then the 'fundamental constitutional requirement' of 'channeling and limiting... the sentencer's discretion in imposing the death penalty,' *Cartwright*, 486 U.S. at 362, has been satisfied."

"In light of the Arizona Supreme Court's narrowing construction of the 'especially heinous... or depraved' aggravating circumstance, the Arizona Supreme Court could reasonably have concluded that respondent committed the murder in an 'especially heinous... or depraved manner.'"

CASE SIGNIFICANCE: In *Gregg v. Georgia* (1976),[77] guided discretion statutes were approved. These are statutes in which the sentencing decision is channeled and limited to ensure that only the most extreme cases result in death sentences. In this case, the aggravating factor upon which the death sentence rested was whether the crime was "especially heinous, cruel, or depraved." The defendant argued that this was too vague and broad to sufficiently limit the application of the death penalty. The Supreme Court disagreed and held that such an aggravating factor was valid. In a prior case (*Godfrey v. Georgia*, 1980[78]), the Court had held that aggravating circumstances must be adequately clarified and that their meaning must be applied independently to the facts of the case. The Court believed that the aggravating factor in this case was clear and relevant as applied. Many other statutes include aggravating factors that characterize the offense in similarly broad and vague terms. For example, in *Arave v. Creech* (1993),[79] the Court upheld an aggravating factor that the crime showed an "utter disregard for human life." Some have suggested that such sweeping phrases and characterizations could be applied to virtually any murder case and thus do not limit or channel the sentencing decision in any meaningful way. Nevertheless, the Court set a standard in this case that exists to this day—such imprecise aggravating factors remain common in state death penalty statutes.

MCKOY v. NORTH CAROLINA 494 U.S. 433 (1990)

CAPSULE: Capital juries need not be unanimous in their finding of mitigating circumstances.

FACTS: McKoy was convicted of first-degree murder. In the sentencing phase of the trial, the jury was, in accordance with North Carolina's death penalty statute, required to unanimously agree on the presence of mitigating factors in order for those factors to be considered in their sentencing decision. The jury unanimously found both the presence of aggravating and mitigating factors. They were then asked whether they unanimously agreed that the previously unanimously agreed-upon mitigating factors were insufficient to outweigh the aggravating factors. They answered yes and subsequently sentenced McKoy to death. McKoy challenged the death sentence, claiming the statute violated

Continued

---

[77]*Id.*
[78]*Godfrey v. Georgia, supra.*
[79]*Arave v. Creech, supra.*

MCKOY v. NORTH CAROLINA 494 U.S. 433 (1990)—cont'd

Mills v. Maryland (1988), which had previously held that jurors need not be unanimous in their finding of mitigating factors for those factors to be considered in sentencing. The North Carolina Supreme Court upheld the sentence.

ISSUE: Does a statute requiring a unanimous finding by the jury for a mitigating circumstance to be considered during sentencing violate the standard set in *Mills v. Maryland* (1988)? YES.

HOLDING: North Carolina's death penalty statute requiring unanimity among capital jurors regarding mitigating factors violates the U.S. Supreme Court's prior decision in *Mills v. Maryland.*

REASON: "Despite the state court's inventive attempts to distinguish *Mills*, our decision there clearly governs this case. First, North Carolina's Issue Four does not ameliorate the constitutional infirmity created by the unanimity requirement. Issue Four, like Issue Three, allows the jury to consider only mitigating factors that it unanimously finds under Issue Two. Although the jury may opt for life imprisonment even where it fails unanimously to find any mitigating circumstances, the fact remains that the jury is required to make its decision based only on those circumstances it unanimously finds. The unanimity requirement thus allows one holdout juror to prevent the others from giving effect to evidence that they believe calls for a 'sentence less than death' *Eddings v. Oklahoma*, 455 U.S. 104, 110 (1982). Moreover, even if all 12 jurors agree that there are some mitigating circumstances, North Carolina's scheme prevents them from giving effect to evidence supporting any of those circumstances in their deliberations under Issues Three and Four unless they unanimously find the existence of the same circumstance. This is the precise defect that compelled us to strike down the Maryland scheme in *Mills*. Our decision in *Mills* was not limited to cases in which the jury is required to impose the death penalty if it finds that aggravating circumstances outweigh mitigating circumstances or that no mitigating circumstances exist at all. Rather, we held that it would be the 'height of arbitrariness to allow or require the imposition of the death penalty' where 1 juror was able to prevent the other 11 from giving effect to mitigating evidence."

CASE SIGNIFICANCE: In *Mills v. Maryland* (1990),[80] the Supreme Court held that unanimity cannot be required for jurors to consider any particular mitigating circumstances. In that case, the issue was with jury instructions that implied that unanimity was required. In this case, the North Carolina instructions similarly indicated that unanimity was required for a mitigating circumstance to be considered in the sentencing decision. Unlike the instructions in *Mills*, however, the North Carolina jury instructions allow the jury the option of rejecting the death penalty, even if they do not unanimously find mitigating factors. The U.S. Supreme Court held the instructions to be in violation of the principles in *Mills* that each juror be allowed to consider the mitigating evidence as he or she sees fit. The Supreme Court ruled that North Carolina's instructions prevented individual jurors from appropriately assessing mitigating evidence and whether it should influence their sentencing decision. The Supreme Court reiterated that each juror should be given the opportunity to conclude on his or her own whether mitigating circumstances were present, regardless of the conclusions of other jurors.

PAYNE v. TENNESSEE 501 U.S. 808 (1991)

CAPSULE: Victim impact statements are admissible during the sentencing phase of capital trials.

FACTS: Payne was convicted of two counts of capital murder for killing Charisse Christopher and her two-year-old daughter, Lacie. He was also convicted of assault with intent to murder for his failed attack on Charisse's three-year-old son Nicholas. At the sentencing phase of trial, Payne called four witnesses: his mother and father; Dr. John T. Hutson, a clinical psychologist; and a friend he met at church, Bobbie Thomas. Each testified as to various mitigating factors regarding his capacity to commit such a crime. The prosecution called Nicholas's grandmother, who testified

Continued

---
[80]*Mills v. Maryland, supra.*

PAYNE v. TENNESSEE 501 U.S. 808 (1991)—cont'd

to the impact the murders had on Nicholas and the rest of the victims' family. The prosecution's closing arguments commented on the impact of the murders on the surviving family members. The jury sentenced Payne to death.

Payne argued that the admission of victim impact testimony violated his Eighth Amendment rights. He based his argument on the previous rulings in *Booth v. Maryland* (1987) and *South Carolina v. Gathers* (1989), which held that victim impact testimony was inadmissible in capital cases. The Tennessee Supreme Court disagreed.

ISSUE: Does the Eighth Amendment prohibit victim impact statements from being presented at the sentencing phase of a capital trial? NO.

HOLDING: The admission of victim impact statements in the sentencing phase of a trial does not constitute an Eighth Amendment violation as long as the information presented does not violate principles of fundamental fairness for the defendant. This applies only to statements regarding characteristics of the victim and the emotional impact of the crime on the victim's family, not to statements characterizing the crime or the defendant.

REASON: "There are numerous infirmities in the rule created by *Booth* and *Gathers*. Those cases were based on two premises: that evidence relating to a particular victim or to the harm caused a victim's family does not in general reflect on the defendant's 'blameworthiness,' and that only evidence of 'blameworthiness' is relevant to the capital sentencing decision. However, assessment of the harm caused by the defendant has long been an important factor in determining the appropriate punishment, and victim impact evidence is simply another method of informing the sentencing authority about such harm."

"Such evidence is not generally offered to encourage comparative judgments of this kind, but is designed to show instead each victim's uniqueness as an individual human being. In the event that victim impact evidence is introduced that is so unduly prejudicial that it renders the trial fundamentally unfair, the Fourteenth Amendment's Due Process Clause provides a mechanism for relief. Thus, a State may properly conclude that for the jury to assess meaningfully the defendant's moral culpability and blameworthiness, it should have before it at the sentencing phase victim impact evidence."

CASE SIGNIFICANCE: This case virtually overrules *Booth v. Maryland*, [482 U.S. 496] (1987), which held that victim impact statements (which typically describe a victim's characteristics and the effect of the crime on the victim's family) are not admissible in death penalty cases. The Court said that although the doctrine of stare decisis (adherence to decided cases) is usually the best policy, it is "not an inexorable command," particularly in cases in which the decisions are "unworkable or badly reasoned." Decided only four years earlier, the Court considered the rule in *Booth* to be unworkable and badly reasoned and overruled that part of the decision. The Court said that the *Booth* decision was based on two premises: "that evidence relating to a particular victim or to the harm caused a victim's family does not in general reflect on the defendant's 'blameworthiness,' and that only evidence of 'blameworthiness' is relevant to the capital sentencing decision." The Court rejected these statements, saying that "assessment of the harm caused by the defendant has long been an important factor in determining the appropriate punishment, and victim impact evidence is simply another method of informing the sentencing authority about such harm."

Decided by a six-to-three vote, this decision reflects the definite imprint of a conservative Court that has shown willingness to allow into the sentencing phase evidence that previously was considered inadmissible. The Court rejected the concept that such evidence must be kept out of death penalty cases because a capital defendant must be treated as a "uniquely individual human being," saying that because there are virtually no limits placed on the relevant mitigating evidence that may be introduced for the defendant in a capital offense, the same should be true with aggravating circumstances as well. The Court seeks to place the prosecution and the defense on the same level in the introduction of evidence in the sentencing phase, even in death penalty cases.[81]

---

[81]This case significance is taken from ROLANDO V. DEL CARMEN, SUSAN E. RITTER, AND BETSY A. WITT, BRIEFS OF LEADING CASES IN CORRECTIONS (5th ed. 2008).

KANSAS v. MARSH 548 U.S. 163 (2006)

CAPSULE: It is constitutional to impose the death penalty when aggravating and mitigating factors are found to be equal.

FACTS: Marsh was convicted of capital murder for the multiple-victim killing of a mother and her young child. During the sentencing phase of the trial, the jury found that mitigating and aggravating factors were exactly equal in weight (i.e., in "equipoise"). The Kansas death penalty statute stated that in such a circumstance, death was to be imposed. Accordingly, Marsh was sentenced to death. On appeal, Marsh challenged the Kansas death penalty statute, specifically section 21-4624(e), which reads: "If, by unanimous vote, the jury finds beyond a reasonable doubt that one or more of the aggravating circumstances enumerated in K.S.A. 21-4625... exist and, further, that the existence of such aggravating circumstances is not outweighed by any mitigating circumstances which are found to exist, the defendant shall be sentenced to death; otherwise the defendant shall be sentenced as provided by law." Marsh contended that the phrase "shall be sentenced to death" presents a presumption in favor of death when aggravating and mitigating factors are in equipoise and thus is unconstitutional. The Kansas Supreme Court agreed, holding that the statute was in violation of the Eighth and Fourteenth Amendments due to the fact that death becomes the default, required sentence in such circumstances.

ISSUE: Is it constitutional to impose the death penalty when aggravating and mitigating factors are unanimously found to be equal? YES.

HOLDING: It is constitutional to impose the death penalty when a unanimous jury finds aggravating and mitigating factors to be equal.

REASON: "Kansas' death penalty statute satisfies the constitutional mandates of *Furman* and its progeny because it rationally narrows the class of death-eligible defendants and permits a jury to consider any mitigating evidence relevant to its sentencing determination. The State's weighing equation merely channels a jury's discretion by providing criteria by which the jury may determine whether life or death is appropriate. Its system provides the kind of guided discretion sanctioned in, e.g., *Walton.* Contrary to Marsh's argument, § 21-4624 (e) does not create a general presumption in favor of the death penalty. A life sentence must be imposed if the State fails to demonstrate the existence of an aggravating circumstance beyond a reasonable doubt, if the State cannot prove beyond a reasonable doubt that aggravating circumstances are not outweighed by mitigating circumstances, or if the jury is unable to reach a unanimous decision in any respect. Marsh's contentions that an equipoise determination reflects juror confusion or inability to decide between life and death or that the jury may use equipoise as a loophole to shirk its constitutional duty to render a reasoned, moral sentencing decision rest on an implausible characterization of the Kansas statute—that a jury's determination that aggravators and mitigators are in equipoise is not a decision, much less a decision for death. Weighing is not an end, but a means to reaching a decision. Kansas's instructions clearly inform the jury that a determination that the evidence is in equipoise is a decision for death."

CASE SIGNIFICANCE: This was the first time the Supreme Court was confronted with the question of whether death can be the prescribed sentence when aggravating and mitigating factors are determined by the jury to be exactly equivalent or in equipoise. Based on the notion that "death is different," some might conclude that a tie should be decided in a direction less severe than a death sentence. However, the Court decided otherwise, holding that the Kansas statute was not unconstitutional and that when aggravating and mitigating factors are in equipoise, it is appropriate for a death sentence to result. This effectively establishes the standard for imposing death sentences at a point in which *mitigating factors do not outweigh aggravating factors,* as opposed to the previously assumed calculus of *aggravating factors outweighing mitigating factors.* The Court determined that this presumption in favor of death was not in violation of constitutional requirements in imposing the death penalty.

BREWER v. QUARTERMAN 550 U.S. 286 (2007)

CAPSULE: Capital juries must be allowed to consider all relevant mitigating factors, and jury instructions must adequately direct the jury to this effect.

FACTS: Brewer was convicted of murder in the act of a felony (robbery). At sentencing, Brewer introduced a variety of mitigating factors. Among these was evidence of a prior history of depression and drug abuse, domination and manipulation by his co-defendant, prior abuse at the hands of his father, and the witnessing of his father's abuse of his mother. At part of his counsel's trial strategy, no expert psychological or psychiatric testimony was presented. When the sentencing hearing concluded, Brewer submitted several proposed jury instructions pertaining to the mitigating evidence that was presented. The trial judge rejected Brewer's requested instructions, instead instructing the jury to consider only two particular issues in determining Brewer's sentence. These were the two special issues noted in the Texas statute: (1) that the defendant caused the death of the victim, and (2) that there is a probability, beyond a reasonable doubt, that the defendant would constitute a continuing violent threat to society. The prosecutor, in his closing argument, noted that Brewer's violent response to his father's abuse supported the fact that he was a future danger to society and argued that any mitigating effect was irrelevant to the jury's decision as to whether they should sentence Brewer to death. Brewer was sentenced to death and the conviction and sentence were affirmed on direct appeal.

ISSUE: Can a state's capital sentencing statute prevent a jury from giving, or being instructed to give, meaningful consideration to constitutionally relevant mitigating factors and evidence? NO.

HOLDING: It is unconstitutional for a state's capital sentencing statute to restrict the jury's consideration of relevant mitigating evidence. Such statutes must allow for the full consideration of mitigating factors by the jury, and jury instructions should reflect this.

REASON: "Brewer's trial was infected with the same constitutional error that occurred in *Penry* I, where the Court held that jury instructions that merely articulated the Texas special issues, without directing the sentencing jury 'to consider fully Penry's mitigating evidence as it bears on his personal culpability,' did not provide an adequate opportunity for the jury to decide whether that evidence might provide a legitimate basis for imposing a sentence other than death. The Court characterized Penry's mental-retardation and childhood-abuse evidence as a 'two-edged sword' that 'diminish [ed] his blameworthiness for his crime even as it indicat[ed] a probability' of future dangerousness. Brewer's mitigating evidence similarly served as a 'two-edged sword.' Even if his evidence was less compelling than Penry's, that does not justify the CCA's refusal to apply *Penry* I here. It is reasonably likely the jurors accepted the prosecutor's argument to limit their decision to whether Brewer had acted deliberately and was likely a future danger, disregarding any independent concern that his troubled background might make him undeserving of death."

"Under the narrowest possible reading of *Penry* I, Texas' special issues do not provide for adequate jury consideration of mitigating evidence that functions as a 'two-edged sword.' The Fifth Circuit's mischaracterization of the law as demanding only that such evidence be given 'sufficient mitigating effect,' and improperly equating 'sufficient effect' with 'full effect,' is not consistent with the reasoning of *Penry v. Johnson* (*Penry* II), which issued after Penry's resentencing (and before the Fifth Circuit's opinion in this case). Like the 'constitutional relevance' standard rejected in *Tennard*, a 'sufficient effect' standard has 'no foundation' in this Court's decisions. For the reasons explained in this case and in *Abdul-Kabir*, the Circuit's conclusions that Brewer's mental-illness and substance-abuse evidence could not constitute a *Penry* violation, and that troubled-childhood evidence may, because of its temporary character, fall sufficiently within the special issues ambit, fail to heed this Court's repeated warnings about the extent to which the jury must be allowed not only to consider mitigating evidence, or to have such evidence before it, but to respond to it in a reasoned, moral manner and assign it weight in deciding whether a defendant truly deserves death."

Continued

BREWER v. QUARTERMAN 550 U.S. 286 (2007)—cont'd

CASE SIGNIFICANCE: This case represents an ongoing conflict between the U.S. Supreme Court and the Texas capital sentencing procedure regarding jury instructions. Although the decision in this case (and its companion case, *Abdul-Kabir v. Quarterman*) is likely limited to the unique nature of the Texas statute and circumstances of capital sentencing in Texas, the Court reiterates the constitutional requirement that juries be given sufficient opportunity to fully consider all relevant mitigating factors and that they be instructed accordingly. Specifically, the Court reemphasizes that capital juries be allowed to give "full effect" to all mitigating evidence and that a standard of "sufficient effect" is not enough. From the Court's perspective, this requires that jury instructions specifically inform the jury of their duty to fully consider all relevant mitigating factors and not to resort to a verbatim reading of limited special issues such as those in the Texas statute.

Key Terms

aggravating factors
Ayers v. Belmontes
Barefoot v. Estelle
Brewer v. Quarterman
future dangerousness
Kansas v. Marsh
Lewis v. Jeffers
Lockett v. Ohio
McKoy v. North Carolina
mitigating factors
Payne v. Tennessee
Penry v. Lynaugh
Presnell v. Georgia
victim impact evidence
Woodson v. North Carolina

CRITICAL THINKING QUESTIONS

1. Why is a consideration of aggravating and mitigating factors required in capital cases? Identify and explain the key reasons the Supreme Court requires them.

2. The inclusion of victim impact evidence in capital trials is a controversial issue. Why is it controversial? Identify the pros and cons of allowing victims to give a statement in the sentencing phase of the trial. Based on these points, do you think such statements should or should not be allowed?

3. The issue of future dangerousness is a key aggravating factor in death penalty cases. Given what we know about our poor ability to predict future violence, do you think this is a fair factor on which to base decisions in capital cases? Why or why not?

4. This chapter identifies several mitigating factors in capital cases. Discuss several of these in terms of why they might warrant mercy (i.e., a sentence less than death) for the defendant. Can you think of other possible mitigating factors?

Internet Resources

Mitigation in Capital Cases
www.capitalpunishmentincontext.org/issues/mitigation

Capital Sentencing Guide
www.azcourts.gov/Default.aspx?alias=www.azcourts.gov/ccsguide

Conducting the Penalty Phase of a Capital Case
www.flcourts.org/gen_public/courted/bin/2001outlineWTOC.pdf

Texas Defender Service's Report on Future Dangerousness in Capital Trials
http://standdown.typepad.com/TDS-DeadlySpeculation.pdf

Effect of "Dr. Death" and His Testimony
www.chron.com/news/houston-texas/article/Effect-of-Dr-Death-and-his-testimony-lingers-1960299.php

Victim Impact Statements in Capital Trials: A Selected Bibliography
lsr.nellco.org/cgi/viewcontent.cgi?article=1005&context=cornell/clsops

Should Victims' Opinions Matter When Considering the Death Penalty?
http://deathpenalty.procon.org/view.answers.php?questionID=001005

States That Allow Victim Impact Statements
www.deathpenaltyinfo.org/article.php?did=575&scid=62

Appeals, Habeas Corpus, and the Death Penalty

10

CHAPTER OUTLINE

I INTRODUCTION

Appealing the decision of a trial court is a necessary component of our system of justice. Appeals serve to insulate innocent offenders from a wrongful conviction or protect those who have been subjected to a harmful error.[1] An appeal must be filed shortly after the termination of a criminal trial, because the privilege to file an appeal is subject to a statute of limitations.

An appeal is filed to reverse a conviction. It generally progresses through a legal hierarchical maze as defendants, unsatisfied with the outcome of a conviction or the decision of a lower court, seek relief

---

[1]A harmful error is an error that violates constitutional rights, such as the right to counsel and the right to trial by jury. Harmful errors necessitate a reversal of conviction.

from a higher court. If a defendant is convicted by a state court, an appeal is first filed with the state appellate court, followed by an appeal to the state supreme court. For a capital offender, the process of filing an appeal is similar—except that in some states, appeals are made directly to the highest state court, thus bypassing lower appellate courts. Capital defendants can be involved in a lengthy appellate process that can take them to the United States Supreme Court.[2]

Capital defendants who have exhausted their appeals have another legal recourse that may halt execution or lead to a new trial. This is through a petition called a writ of habeas corpus. Unlike an appeal, which is based on state law, a writ of habeas corpus is: (1) provided for in the suspension clause of the Constitution (Article 1, Section 9 [2]), (2) a constitutional right, (3) a separate case from the original criminal conviction, and (4) a civil proceeding.

A writ of habeas corpus is filed for the sole purpose of seeking release from prison. Therefore, it is usually filed after a capital offender begins serving his or her sentence. The writ must contain evidence that the capital offender is being held illegally or unconstitutionally. However, because a writ of habeas corpus must be filed with the court that originally tried the offender, a successful habeas corpus petition is a rarity.[3] In addition, federal legislation, such as the Antiterrorism and Effective Death Penalty Act of 1996 (AEDPA), severely limits the right of capital offenders to file successive petitions and thus weakens their repeated attempts to seek release from prison through a habeas proceeding.

This chapter first presents a brief overview of the appellate process, with special emphasis on capital defendants. Then it discusses the writ of habeas corpus. The origins of the writ are explored, from its use in England and its adaptation by the American colonists. This chapter also presents the limitations that both the legislative and judicial branches of government have placed on an inmate's ability to file a writ of habeas corpus, particularly those involving same-claim successive petitions and new-claim successive petitions. Also included is a brief overview of the AEDPA and consideration of its overall impact on the ability of inmates to file habeas petitions. Finally, various Supreme Court rulings on the AEDPA are discussed, as is the use of Section 1983 lawsuits by death row inmates.

‖ THE APPELLATE PROCESS

An appeal may be defined as an attempt, through intervention by a higher court, to seek a different court or jury decision. This happens when a defendant, dissatisfied with a lower court's decision, seeks reversal of a conviction based on a harmful legal or constitutional error. Generally, an appeal is filed shortly after the conclusion of a trial, although a special type of appeal called an interlocutory appeal may be filed during trial and before a verdict has been issued against a defendant. Although there are rights given to criminal defendants in the Constitution, the right to appeal is not a constitutional right. Nonetheless, the right to appeal a decision of a lower court has been firmly embedded in our system of justice through state and federal laws.

There are two characteristics of an appeal. The first is that a defendant's initial appeal cannot be denied, meaning that the court has no discretionary authority to refuse to hear the appeal. The second characteristic, however, restricts the number of times a defendant may appeal. For instance, defendants are permitted only one appeal. A defendant, dissatisfied with the appellate court's ruling, may file subsequent appeals with higher courts. However, such appeals are discretionary, meaning that the appellate

---

[2]The U.S. Supreme Court only considers cases that involve a constitutional or federal issue.
[3]del Carmen, Rolando, CRIMINAL PROCEDURE: LAW AND PRACTICE (6th ed. 2004).

courts may refuse to hear the appeal.[4] For capital defendants, appeals are usually filed directly with the state supreme court. Because it is the defendant's first appeal, the state supreme court cannot deny review.

Appellate courts, even in death penalty cases, do not review the facts of the case to determine whether the defendant is truly guilty or not. Instead, appellate courts review any legal or constitutional errors that may have occurred during the trial or sentencing. Appellate courts recognize two types of errors that may occur during trial or sentencing: harmless error and harmful error. A harmless error, also called a non-constitutional error, does not warrant the reversal of a conviction, because it does not affect the outcome of the trial. In other words, the error does not affect the finding of guilt by a judge or jury.[5] A decision by an appellate court to recognize an error as harmless generally occurs when there is enough evidence, without the error, to uphold the conviction. In *Kotteakos v. United States* (1946),[6] the Supreme Court created the following test for harmless errors: "If one cannot say, with fair assurance, after pondering all that happened without stripping the erroneous action from the whole, that the judgment was not substantially swayed by the error, it is impossible to conclude that substantial rights were not affected."

By contrast, harmful errors, also called constitutional errors, require the reversal of a conviction because the errors involved serious violations of constitutional rights, which prejudiced the verdict. Examples of harmful errors are denial of counsel and racial discrimination in the selection of a jury.

A reversal of a conviction does not mean that the capital defendant will not be tried again. The Court considers the defendant's decision to appeal as a waiver of her Fifth Amendment privilege against double jeopardy. Accordingly, the defendant may be granted a trial de novo (new trial). Another consequence of an appeal may be a reverse-and-remand decision whereby a defendant's conviction is reversed by the appellate court. However, the case is remanded, or sent back, to the lower court, usually for a new trial. If the defendant is dissatisfied with the decision of the lower court, he or she may appeal again. Such appeals are discretionary and must proceed through the same hierarchical court process, which again may reach the jurisdiction of the Supreme Court of the United States.

III THE GREAT WRIT

A History

Habeas corpus is a Latin term that means "you have the body." It is a judicial order directed at those detaining any person to bring the detainee to court and explain the reasons for detention. The writ of habeas corpus protects against the most arbitrary type of injustice—illegal detention or confinement—and is often referred to as the Great Writ. There are several reasons that the writ of habeas corpus is viewed with such reverence, but one reason stands out: The writ is a remedy for individuals who have been illegally, unjustifiably, and unconstitutionally confined and thus deprived of freedom.[7] The Great Writ thus "secures justice for those who at any particular moment find themselves

---

[4]Worrall, John L., Criminal Procedure: From First Contact to Appeal (2004).
[5]del Carmen, *Supra.*
[6]*Kotteakos v. United States*, 323 U.S. 750, 765 (1946).
[7]Hack, Peter, *The Roads Less Traveled: Post-Conviction Relief Alternatives and the Antiterrorism and Effective Death Penalty Act of 1996*, 30 Am. J. Crim. L. 171 (Spring 2003).

execrated by the dominant force in society."[8] It is a protective means or a "safety valve"[9] that bars abusive and arbitrary government action by providing a legal avenue for seeking release from injustice.

As with many of our legal traditions, habeas corpus has underpinnings in English law. Originating in England after the Norman Conquest of 1066, habeas corpus was a common law judicial procedure that required all criminal defendants to be brought before the judge for an inquiry regarding the legality of their detention. During the sixteenth century, the writ became an invaluable tool for those detained or imprisoned for voicing their displeasure against the monarchy.[10] In 1679, after much contention between Parliament and the English Crown, the writ was firmly and formally established as a legal right.

In view of the need to protect against illegal confinements, the writ of habeas corpus was quickly adopted by the American colonists. The writ was so significant that infringements against it were barred at the time of the writing of the Constitution. The delegates at the Philadelphia Convention debated whether there were any legitimate instances in which the writ should be suspended. The Federalists argued that a rebellion or invasion of the territory of the United States may require a brief suspension of the writ. Conversely, the anti-Federalists were concerned that allowing the government such authority could lead to abuse of power and serve as a means to oppress the citizenry. In the end, the delegates agreed to preserve the writ and allow its suspension only in rare instances.[11] As incorporated in the Constitution, Article I, Section 9(2) (known as the suspension clause), the delegates concurred that "the privileges of the Writ of Habeas Corpus shall not be suspended, unless when in cases of rebellion or invasion the public safety may require it."

Article I, Section 9(2) of the Constitution does not indicate which branch of government is vested with the authority to suspend the writ. Some legal scholars have inferred that the inclusion of the suspension clause in Article I indicated that Congress was vested with the sole authority to make such decisions. However, during the Civil War, President Abraham Lincoln assumed authority to suspend the writ, and since then Congress has legitimized the power of the executive to suspend the writ of habeas corpus in times of war or rebellion.[12]

As with all rights and privileges adopted by the delegates at the Philadelphia Convention, the writ of habeas corpus was exclusively a federal privilege. Accordingly, only federal inmates had the opportunity to use the writ to seek release from prison. In the Federal Habeas Corpus Act of 1867, Congress extended the right to petition courts using habeas corpus to any individual detained or incarcerated in violation of the Constitution. Habeas corpus was therefore extended to state prison inmates. Congress's decision to open a federal legal avenue to state prisoners was not well received by federal judges, who worried that their caseload would significantly increase as a result.[13] In *Ex parte Royall* (1886),[14] the Supreme Court eased such worries by ruling that judges had the discretion to deny state prisoners who had not exhausted state habeas corpus relief from seeking relief in federal court.

---

[8]Freedman, Eric M., *Federal Habeas Corpus in Capital Cases*. In Hugo Bedau and Paul Cassell (eds.), Debating the Death Penalty (2004), p. 553.

[9]Swafford, Tara L., *Responding to* Herrera v. Collins: *Ensuring That Innocents Are Not Executed*, 45 Case W. Res. L. Rev. 603 (1995).

[10]Peltason, J.W., and Sue Davis, Understanding the Constitution (15th ed. 2000).

[11]Freedman, *Supra*.

[12]Peltason and Davis, *Supra*.

[13]Stevenson, Bryan A., *The Politics of Fear and Death: Successive Problems in Capital Federal Habeas Corpus Cases*, 77 N.Y.U. L. Rev. 699 (2002).

[14]*Ex parte Royall*, 117 U.S. 241 (1886).

As is evident in this early ruling, there are two types of habeas corpus proceedings: state-level proceedings and federal-level proceedings. Since 1886, the Supreme Court has ruled that an inmate must first file a writ of habeas corpus in a state court (the court that originally convicted the inmate) before proceeding with a habeas petition at the federal level. Also, in *Ex parte Royall* (1886), the Court declared that any inmate seeking review in federal court must first exhaust state court habeas corpus remedies. Thus, the inmate must proceed through a court hierarchy where a denial of a habeas petition by the state district court must be appealed to a state appellate court, followed by an appeal to the state supreme court. If the inmate wants to proceed to the federal level, a petition must be filed in the hierarchy of federal courts, starting with the federal district court, federal circuit courts, and then the U.S. Supreme Court. A federal inmate seeking habeas review, however, need not file a petition at the state level but instead may directly file review with the federal district court that originally heard the case. Since 1886, the issue of the proper state and federal procedures to follow when filing habeas petitions has occupied much attention in both the legislative and judicial branches of government.

B The Battle Over Successive Petitions and the Road to the AEDPA
1 The Good Faith/Bad Faith Rule

With the exception of the ruling in *Ex parte Royall* in 1886, habeas corpus remained the most significant way, and perhaps the only way, in which state prison inmates, confined in violation of the Constitution, could have their confinement reviewed by the federal courts.[15] Until the early twentieth century, the Great Writ remained unaltered and inmates were allowed to file successive petitions, even for claims or issues already litigated (known as same-claim successive petitions) as well as successive petitions for claims not previously litigated (known as new-claim successive petitions). However, beginning in 1924, both the Supreme Court and Congress initiated actions that curtailed the freedom of prison inmates to file same-claim successive habeas corpus petitions. Curtailment of the use of the Great Writ by both the judicial and legislative branches of government was precipitated by the writ being used to delay the carrying out of state court decisions imposing the death penalty.[16]

In 1924, the Court was struck with two instances of blatant abuses of the Great Writ. Although not ready to believe that these two cases were representative of all petitions filed in federal courts, the Court nonetheless marveled at the ease with which inmates could manipulate the justice system. In *Salinger v. Loisel* (1924),[17] the Court created a discretionary rule that authorized federal judges to dismiss successive habeas corpus petitions based on the good faith or bad faith of the inmate's intention in filing such petitions. In other words, the Court allowed federal judges to deny habeas corpus relief to any inmate whom they believed may have filed such petition for disingenuous reasons, such as to impede the imposition of a sentence. In *Wong Doo v. United States* (1924),[18] the Court reiterated its subjective good faith/bad faith directive as a justification for denying successive petitions when it

---

[15]Duffett, Lisa R., *Habeas Corpus and Actual Innocence of the Death Sentence after* Sawyer v. Whitley: *Another Nail into the Coffin of State Capital Defendants*, 44 Case W. Res. L. Rev. 121 (1993).

[16]Stevenson, Bryan A., *The Politics of Fear and Death: Successive Problems in Capital Federal Habeas Corpus Cases*, 77 N.Y.U. L. Rev. 699 (2002).

[17]*Salinger v. Loisel*, 265 U.S. 224 (1924).

[18]*Wong Doo v. United States*, 265 U.S. 239 (1924).

realized that the petitioner in this case had successfully managed to delay the imposition of a court sentence for almost four years through the use of the writ.

2 New-Claim Successive Petitions Rule

In 1948, Congress reacted to the Court's decisions in *Salinger* and *Wong Doo* and codified its good faith/bad faith directive into law in the Judicial Code and Judiciary Act. The act permitted federal courts to "deny a successive federal habeas corpus petition if its claims had been previously presented and rejected and if the new petition presents no new ground not therefore presented and determined, and the judge or court is satisfied that the ends of justice will not be served by such inquiry."[19]

The Court in *Sanders v. United States* (1963)[20] placed further limitations on both same-claim and new-claim successive petitions. As for same-claim petitions, the Court again refused to permit inmates from manipulating the justice system by ruling that unless the ends of justice warrant an inquiry, dismissal of such claims was within the discretionary authority of the federal courts. For new claims not previously litigated, the Supreme Court ruled that federal courts may also dismiss or refuse to hear such petitions when the inmate had deliberately and strategically chosen not to include new issues in previous habeas petitions for the purpose of stalling or impeding a state court decision. The Court then said that if evidence was discovered at the time of an initial habeas corpus petition but was not filed in order to create another opportunity to seek the review of a court at a later date, the inmate's right to file such new claim was rescinded. In response to the Court's decision in *Sanders*, Congress revised its habeas corpus statutes in 1966 to include the high court's new rule on new-claim successive petitions.[21]

3 The Impact of Gregg on Successive Petitions

After the Supreme Court's decision in *Gregg v. Georgia* (1976),[22] the legal landscape for filing successive petitions, especially for death row inmates, changed to some extent. *Gregg* signified the Court's desire to ensure that death penalty statutes and practices are constitutional. The "death is different" jurisprudence initiated in *Gregg* meant that "capital litigation was not considered final until all available state and federal post-conviction review had been completed. The new prototype for capital litigation was a nine-step process that almost always included petitions for a writ of habeas corpus in federal court."[23] The Court's subsequent rulings on the death penalty after *Gregg* created new constitutional issues that only served to provide capital offenders with more opportunities to file new-claim successive habeas corpus petitions in federal court.

Although the Court in *Gregg* ended capricious and arbitrary death penalty sentencing schemes, it significantly increased the caseload for federal judges. This came about despite the Court not having created a federal constitutional right to counsel for capital offenders in state and federal habeas corpus proceedings. This oversight by the Court meant that most lawyers willing to represent capital offenders were overburdened and in some instances had to resort to filing habeas corpus petitions just hours before an execution was scheduled to take place.[24]

---

[19]Judicial Code and Judiciary Act § 2244, 62 STAT. at 966 (1948).
[20]*Sanders v. United States*, 373 U.S. 1 (1963).
[21]Stevenson, *Supra.*
[22]*Gregg v. Georgia*, 428 U.S. 153 (1976)
[23]Stevenson, *Supra at 717.*
[24]*Id.*

The last-minute attempts to halt executions, coupled with the volume of cases filed in federal court, prompted the Supreme Court to seek remedies. In *Rose v. Lundy* (1982),[25] the Court opined that state prison inmates must exhaust state court remedies before filing a writ of habeas corpus in federal court or else the privilege to file in federal court would be revoked. Although the ruling in this case was strikingly similar to one issued almost 100 years before in *Ex parte Royall*, the Court specifically addressed "mixed petitions." A mixed petition was one in which the inmate filed a habeas petition in the state court with two or more claims of illegal or unconstitutional confinement. However, when filing the same habeas petition in federal court, the inmate would include additional claims not previously litigated at the state level. In *Rose v. Lundy*, the Court barred inmates from filing mixed petitions, because it was a violation of the intent of the Great Writ and federal law.

The mixed-petition rule as well as the new-claim successive petition rule adopted by both the Supreme Court and Congress supplemented another rule created in 1977: the procedural default rule. According to the Court, a state prison inmate who failed to comply with procedural rules may not address issues of habeas relief in federal court because his or her petition was procedurally flawed and was therefore a defaulted petition. Failure to comply with procedural rules, whether at trial, during appeal, or in a post-conviction proceeding, virtually barred an inmate from filing a habeas corpus petition. The only way to circumvent this rule was if the inmate met the "cause and prejudice" test. The cause and prejudice test contains two opportunities to bypass the procedural default rule. For instance, the cause portion of the test required the inmate to demonstrate actual cause for failing to follow procedural rules, such as failure to follow procedures due to ineffective assistance of counsel. The inmate could also circumvent this rule by relying on the prejudice portion of the test. Thus, he or she could demonstrate that some other cause external to the defense (such as a constitutional violation) may have prejudiced the imposition of the sentence or created a miscarriage of justice.[26]

In 1988, Chief Justice William Rehnquist created the Ad Hoc Committee on Federal Habeas Corpus in Capital Cases to investigate ways to limit the filing of habeas corpus petitions. Justice Lewis F. Powell, who was appointed chair of the committee, noted that:

> *In some cases last-minute habeas corpus petitions have resulted from the unavailability of counsel at an earlier time. But in other cases attorneys appear to have intentionally delayed filing until time pressures were severe. In most cases, successive petitions are meritless, and we believe many are filed at the eleventh hour seeking nothing more than delay.*[27]

The Ad Hoc Committee agreed with the observation and recommended the passage of a congressional act that would severely limit successive petitions. However, the recommendations were not adopted by Congress. Because Congress refused to act, the Supreme Court proceeded to curtail successive petitions anyway. In *McCleskey v. Zant* (1991),[28] the Court held that the petitioner must prove that the failure to raise a claim during a prior habeas corpus petition was not an attempt to circumvent a court sentence. Thus, the petitioner must prove that the new claim was based on an objective factor external to the defense that necessitated the court's attention because it was prejudicial to the sentence imposed or would result in a miscarriage of justice. In essence, the petitioner had to provide factual evidence that

---

[25]*Rose v. Lundy*, 455 U.S. 509 (1982).
[26]See *Wainwright v. Sykes*, 433 U.S. 72 (1977).
[27]*Report on Habeas Corpus in Capital Cases*, 45 Crim. L. Rep. 3239, 3240 (1989).
[28]*McCleskey v. Zant*, 499 U.S. 467 (1991).

the petition for habeas corpus was worthy of proceeding through the maze of post-conviction review by either: (1) presenting new evidence that raised sufficient doubt about his or her guilt, or (2) showing that a constitutional violation had resulted when the sentence of death was imposed because the petitioner was "actually innocent" of a death sentence.

C The AEDPA

The Antiterrorism and Effective Death Penalty Act of 1996 (AEDPA) signaled a new era in habeas corpus petitions and provided new rules meant to limit the filing of successive petitions. The AEDPA was passed by Congress in the wake of the Oklahoma City bombing and was primarily designed to protect the country from future domestic terror threats. However, the act also contains explicit restrictions on habeas corpus petitions. Although much legal debate has surfaced regarding the connection between the tragic event in Oklahoma and habeas corpus petitions,[29] the AEDPA represents the most restrictive piece of legislation that affects inmates' ability to use the Great Writ. It has created an even more complicated and elaborate maze of legal technicalities than those previously imposed. To date, the Supreme Court has upheld the constitutionality of the provisions of the AEDPA and has narrowly interpreted its provisions to preserve the goals of the Act. Box 10.1 briefly outlines the significant provisions of the AEDPA.

The first significant provision of the AEDPA is the statute of limitations for filing an initial habeas petition with the state court that originally prosecuted the inmate. The AEDPA sets a one-year statute of

---

BOX 10.1 PROVISIONS OF THE ANTITERRORISM AND EFFECTIVE DEATH PENALTY ACT OF 1996

The AEDPA includes the following provisions:

- Sets a statute of limitations for filing an initial habeas corpus petition. A petitioner who fails to file within the specified time (one year) may be granted review only if the failure to file was: (1) the result of a state action, (2) the result of the Supreme Court's decision to apply a ruling retroactively, or (3) when evidence could not have been discovered through due diligence in time to file.
- Limits federal review of state convictions unless a petitioner can prove that the state court's decision was (1) contrary to, or involved an unreasonable application of federal law, or (2) was based on an unreasonable determination of facts in light of evidence presented in state court.
- Requires a petitioner to file a certificate of appealability before filing a second or successive petition of a previously unlitigated claim.

---

limitations for the filing of any initial habeas corpus petition. A statute of limitations is a legal rule that places a limit on the amount of time that an inmate is allowed to file a habeas petition. In essence, a statute of limitations is an "expiration date" that the court observes when considering hearing a petition. Generally, the one-year statute of limitations begins after the inmate has exhausted his or her state remedies. An inmate who fails to file within the specified time limit may be granted review only if the failure to file was: (1) the result of a state action, (2) the result of the Court's decision to apply a ruling retroactively, or (3) when evidence could not have been discovered through due diligence in time to file within the one-year timeframe.

---

[29]Worrall, *Supra.*

Another significant provision of the AEDPA limits federal review of state convictions unless the petitioner can prove that the state court decision was "contrary to, or involved an unreasonable application of, clearly established federal law, as determined by the Supreme Court or... was based on an unreasonable determination of facts in light of the evidence presented in the state court proceeding."[30] This provision, found in § 2254(d) of the AEDPA, gives significant deference to state courts. This deference was echoed by the Court in *Williams v. Taylor* (2000),[31] in which it held that an "unreasonable application" of law was not synonymous with a harmless error or a decision that was incorrect yet reasonable. The Court supplemented Congress's provision by creating a stringent standard for petitions where not even a reasonable though incorrect state decision would pass AEDPA's requirements. *Williams v. Taylor* reflected the Court's attempt to achieve some sense of finality with regard to state decisions rather than prolonging the imposition of a state decision due to lengthy post-conviction review.

Perhaps the most restrictive provision of the AEDPA applies to successive petitions. The AEDPA prohibits same-claim successive petitions but allows successive petitions for previously unlitigated claims. The Act requires inmates to obtain a certificate of appealability (COA) before filing a second or successive petition of a previously unlitigated claim. A COA must be obtained from a panel of three circuit court judges before the inmate is allowed to file the petition with the federal district court. Accordingly, the inmate must present evidence that a new rule, created by the Court, applies retroactively to the petitioner's case or must demonstrate that he or she, through due diligence, has discovered new evidence (a constitutional error or violation) that was previously unavailable during the first petition. The petitioner must demonstrate through clear and convincing evidence that, absent a constitutional error, he or she would have been found not guilty of the crime.

The decision to apply the ruling of one case retroactively to other cases is the exclusive domain of the Supreme Court. Traditionally, when the Court issues a ruling in one case, that ruling becomes controlling precedent for future cases only. Generally, automatic retroactivity is associated with appeals and not habeas corpus decisions. Habeas decisions issued by the Court may or may not apply retroactively. Under § 2244(b)(2)(A) of the AEDPA, an inmate cannot file a successive petition on the basis of "a new rule of constitutional law... that was previously unavailable," unless it has been "made retroactively to cases on collateral review by the Supreme Court."[32] Prior to the AEDPA, the Court had already explained the retroactivity rule in habeas decisions. In *Teague v. Lane* (1989),[33] the Court held that unless an inmate's claims are based on precedent made retroactive by the Court, he or she cannot use the writ of habeas corpus to seek review. Thus, claims that would result in a new ruling, thereby creating new law, were impermissible under habeas corpus. The essence of *Teague* was incorporated by Congress into the AEDPA. In 2001, the Court was asked to rule on the constitutionality of the AEDPA's "new rule" provision, and in *Tyler v. Cain* (2001),[34] the Court held that the AEDPA's provision was constitutional.

In 2005, the Supreme Court, in *Rhines v. Weber*,[35] addressed the issue of mixed petitions once again but this time clarified the role of the AEDPA and the statute of limitations for such petitions. Consistent with its ruling in *Rose v. Lundy*,[36] the Court confirmed that the AEDPA favors a "total exhaustion" of

---

[30]28 U.S.C. § 2254(d) (2000).
[31]*Williams v. Taylor*, 529 U.S. 362 (2000).
[32]28 U.S.C. § 2244(b)(2)(A) (2000).
[33]*Teague v. Lane*, 489 U.S. 288 (1989).
[34]*Tyler v. Cain*, 533 U.S. 970 (2001).
[35]*Rhines v. Weber*, 544 U.S. 269 (2005).
[36]*Rose v. Lundy*, 455 U.S. 509 (1982).

state court remedies before filing a habeas appeal in federal court. However, because *Lundy* was decided before the passage of the AEDPA, the Court acknowledged that "petitioners who come to federal court with mixed petitions run the risk of forever losing their opportunity for any federal review of the unexhausted claims" if the one-year statute of limitations expires.[37] Therefore, the Court noted that the statute does not bar federal district courts from practicing what is known as "stay and abeyance" of petitions. Under the practice of stay and abeyance, a district court may "stay the petition and hold it in abeyance while the petitioner returns to state court to exhaust his previously unexhausted claims. Once the petitioner exhausts his state remedies, the district court will lift the stay and allow the petitioner to proceed in federal court."[38]

Although the Court's decision in *Rhines v. Weber* seemingly relaxes the stringent rules of the AEDPA, the Court noted that the practice of stay and abeyance should be employed only in the rarest of circumstances, be available only in limited circumstances, and should not be used to stay a petition indefinitely, because otherwise it may encourage inmates to delay the resolution of their federal proceedings. Thus, both the AEDPA and the Court's decisions are stringent attempts to limit habeas corpus in an effort to accomplish three main goals: "a desire to promote 'comity' between state and federal systems; the need for finality in criminal convictions; and the goal of decreasing the burdens on federal court dockets."[39] In its totality, the AEDPA is a massive piece of legislation that severely restricts the original purpose of the Great Writ of habeas corpus. The Great Writ was originally intended to be unfettered and suspension issued only in times of war. The AEDPA seriously undermines the original purpose of the writ. Some argue that the AEDPA violates the suspension clause because it suspends or inhibits confined individuals from seeking to have their petitions heard by state and federal courts. The Court in *Felker v. Turpin* (1996)[40] responded by saying that the AEDPA does not violate the Constitution's suspension clause. Despite the Court's decision, the AEDPA has had several unintended consequences. For example, its legal maze of technicalities has added procedural rules, such as the certificate of appealability, with which inmates must comply before filing a petition. This has imposed an additional layer to the process and increased the caseload of the circuit courts.

IV CURRENT CONSEQUENCES OF THE AEDPA
A Current Debate Over Successive Petitions

Since the passage of the AEDPA, interpretation over the meaning of successive or second petitions has not subsided. The AEDPA, specifically 28 U.S.C. §2244(b)(1), prohibits habeas corpus petitions for claims previously filed/litigated but does not specifically clarify allowed subsequent petitions for unlitigated or unadjudicated claims. Although an inmate must first seek a certificate of appealability (COA) and pass several legal hurdles, such as the due diligence test and/or the clear and convincing evidence test, before filing a successive petition, the Court has refrained from placing a limit on the

---

[37]*Rhines v. Weber*, 544 U.S. 269, 272 (2005).
[38]*Id.*
[39]Swafford, Tara L., *Responding to* Herrera v. Collins: *Ensuring That Innocents Are Not Executed*, 45 Case W. Res. L. Rev. 603, 606 (1995).
[40]*Felker v. Turpin*, 518 U.S. 651 (1996).

numerical sequence of petitions. In *Stewart v. Martinez-Villareal* (1998),[41] for instance, the Court held that dismissal of a habeas petition for technical reasons does not bar a respondent from filing the same petition a second time. The facts of the case reveal that Martinez-Villareal filed multiple habeas corpus petitions in state court and in federal court, all of which were dismissed because state remedies had not been exhausted. He then filed another habeas petition in federal court on several grounds, including incompetence to be executed; Martinez-Villareal argued that according to *Ford v. Wainwright* (1986),[42] his life should be spared due to his mental impairment. Most of the claims in the latter petition were dismissed, but since his death warrant had not been issued, the *Ford* claim was judged to be premature by the Ninth Circuit Court. When the state of Arizona issued a death warrant and the Arizona Supreme Court ruled that Martinez-Villareal was competent to be executed, he then filed his successive petition arguing incompetence to be executed. The Ninth Circuit Court granted a stay of execution and concluded that he did not need a COA to file his petition with the district court. The court reasoned that since his original *Ford* petition was deemed premature and consequently dismissed on technical grounds rather than dismissed on merit, it did not consider his *Ford* claim a second or successive petition under the auspices of the AEDPA. The Court agreed with the Ninth Circuit Court's opinion and further noted that a literal interpretation of 28 U.S.C. §2244(b)(1) "would be far reaching and seemingly perverse."[43]

Two years later, in *Slack v. McDaniel* (2000),[44] the Court ruled that petitions that are unadjudicated on merit and dismissed because respondents have not exhausted all state remedies can make an appearance in a subsequent habeas corpus appeal; the refiling of a habeas corpus appeal, according to the Court, should not be considered as a second or successive petition because the first petition was dismissed without prejudice for failure to exhaust state remedies. In *Burton v. Stewart* (2007),[45] the Court issued a similar ruling when it opined that a respondent who incorporates both exhausted and unexhausted claims in a single habeas petition is entitled to file a subsequent petition on those never adjudicated by a state court. In this case, the Court also said it was permissible to interpret the meaning of successive petitions by looking at pre-AEDPA case law, since both case law on this matter and the AEDPA try to achieve a similar outcome: comity between state and federal systems plus finality of criminal convictions.

Much like the Supreme Court, most circuit courts, such as the First, Second, Third, Eighth, Ninth, and Tenth Circuits, rebuff a literal interpretation of the AEDPA's second and successive petition proviso and have taken a more liberal approach. Consistent with rulings in *Stewart v. Martinez-Villareal* and *Slack v. McDaniel*, these circuits "instead hold that the AEDPA's second or successive language is a term of art that incorporates pre-AEDPA abuse of the writ principles."[46] Therefore, rather than placing value in the numerical sequence of petitions, most circuit courts rely on the intention to file a successive petition. If it is determined that a petition was filed for a second time on an issue(s) that could have been discovered through due diligence during an initial filing of an appeal, the above-mentioned

---

[41]23 U.S. 637 (1998).
[42]477 U.S. 399 (1986).
[43]*Id.* at 6.
[44]529 U.S. 473 (2000).
[45]127 S. Ct. 793 (2007).
[46]Pavkov, Mark, *Does Second Mean Second? Examining the Split Among Circuit Courts of Appeals in Interpreting AEDPA's Second or Successive Limitations on Habeas Corpus Petitions*, 57 Case W. Res. L. Rev 4, (2007).

circuits will bar the second petition and deem it to be an abuse of the writ of habeas corpus. There are other circuits, however, that draw on the plain language of the AEDPA's provision to rule on second or successive petitions. The Seventh Circuit, for instance, in *In re Page*,[47] held that "a habeas petition was second or successive under the AEDPA even though the claim raised in the petition could not have been included in the petitioner's first habeas petition."[48] The Fourth, Fifth, Sixth, and Eleventh Circuits seem to vacillate between liberal and literal interpretations of the provision. In consequence, not only is there a divide among the circuits with respect to successive petitions, there is also an inconsistent application of the law. However, most recently in *Magwood v. Patterson* (2010),[49] the Court once again reiterated that the "phrase second or successive is a term of art" and therefore a more liberal interpretation is necessary. This has not stopped circuit courts from following their own precedents.

The Court's apparently broad interpretation of the AEDPA also extends to harmless errors in COA. In *Gonzalez v. Thaler* (2012),[50] for instance, it ruled that a circuit court has jurisdiction to hear a habeas petition even if the COA did not include a specific constitutional violation. In this case, Gonzalez filed a petition claiming a violation of the Sixth Amendment's right to a speedy trial since there was a 10-year lag between his indictment and his trial. His request for a COA did contain the constitutional violation plus a request for an exception to the AEDPA's one-year statute of limitations. The federal district court judge failed to mention his Sixth Amendment challenge when it granted the certificate. When the Fifth Circuit Court eventually heard Gonzalez's appeal, it issued a ruling with respect to the statute of limitations but did not address the Sixth Amendment violation nor mention the possibility of a procedurally defaulted COA. When Gonzalez filed a writ of certiorari with the Supreme Court, the state of Texas argued that the Fifth Circuit had no jurisdiction to hear the habeas appeal, because the COA did not list a constitutional violation, as required by the AEDPA (e.g., §2253(c)(2) reads: The COA may issue only if the petitioner has made a "substantial showing of the denial of a constitutional right"). The Court, however, held that "a COA's failure to indicate a constitutional issue does not deprive a Court of Appeals of jurisdiction to adjudicate the appeal."[51]

Although the Court held that failure to specify a constitutional issue in a COA did not bar a circuit court from adjudicating a habeas petition, in *Johnson v Williams* (2013)[52] the Court held that "for purposes of § 2254(d), when a state court rules against a defendant in an opinion that rejects some of the defendant's claims but does not expressly address a federal claim, a federal habeas court must presume, subject to rebuttal, that the federal claim was adjudicated on the merits."[53] Accordingly, when a state court expressly issues a ruling rejecting some of the petitioner's claims but remains silent on others, a federal court must assume that all of the other claims, even if not mentioned, were adjudicated and not simply overlooked. This ruling is consistent with the Court's prior ruling in *Harrington v. Richter* (2011).[54] In the latter case, the Court noted that even if a court issues a summary judgment denying

---

[47]179 F. 3d 1024 (1999).
[48]*Supra note* 45 at 1017.
[49]130 S. Ct. 2788 (2010).
[50]132 S. Ct. 641 (2011).
[51]*Id.* at 2.
[52]133 S. Ct. 1088 (2013).
[53]*Id.* at 2.
[54]131 S. Ct. 770 (2011).

habeas relief, other courts should assume that all claims encompassed with the habeas petition were adjudicated on their merits.

The above-mentioned case law on successive petitions is demonstrative of the Court's more moderate approach to some of the provisions of the AEDPA. The Court refrains from simply considering the sequential order of petitions in favor of a more subjective determination of a petitioner's intention to abuse the writ of habeas corpus. It also overlooks seemingly harmless errors in COAs and is not troubled by the specifics, or lack thereof, of summary judgments when deciphering adjudicated versus unadjudicated claims. But the Court's ostensibly liberal demeanor shifts to a more stern approach when clarifying the AEDPA's statute of limitations.

B Statute of Limitations and Actual Innocence
1 Statute of Limitations

A statute of limitation is a legal rule that places a limit on the amount of time that an inmate is allowed to file a habeas petition. The AEDPA, for example, places a one-year timeframe during which to file an initial habeas petition. But the Court does consider the "ripeness" when a petition is filed. In *Stewart v. Martinez-Villareal*, the Court recognized that habeas petitions may not become ripe until a death warrant, which specifies the date of execution, has been issued by the court. A death warrant can be issued after the statute of limitations has expired and thus an exception to the statute of limitations is warranted.[55]

In 2006, the Court heard oral arguments to determine whether the AEDPA's one-year statute of limitations is suspended or "tolled" while a state court reviews an inmate's application for state post-conviction relief. The AEDPA "tolls" the statute of limitations while a state prisoner seeks post-conviction relief in state court. Tolling, as defined in the AEDPA, is:

> *The time during which a properly filed application for state post-conviction or other collateral review with respect to the pertinent judgment or claim is pending... and this time shall not be counted toward any period of limitation under the AEDPA.*[56]

In *Lawrence v. Florida*,[57] a death row inmate filed for state post-conviction relief 364 days after his conviction became final. The trial court denied relief, as did the state supreme court and later the U.S. Supreme Court. However, while the post-conviction petition was pending in the U.S. Supreme Court, Lawrence filed a habeas corpus petition with the U.S. District Court—113 days after the state supreme court's decision in his post-conviction appeal. The Court held that the AEDPA does not suspend or "toll" the one-year statute of limitations if a defendant is awaiting a decision by the U.S. Supreme Court and then files a habeas corpus petition well after such limitation has expired. Thus, the Court reasoned that the statute of limitations may be suspended while an inmate awaits a response or decision by a state court, which is the final court to resolve post-conviction petitions, but not the U.S. Supreme Court, because the Court "rarely grants review of state post-conviction proceedings" and is thus not usually

---

[55]Sussman, Jake, *Unlimited Innocence: Recognizing an Actual Innocence Exception to AEDPA's Statute of Limitations*, 27 N.Y.U. Rev. L. & Soc. Change 343 (2001–2002).

[56]28 U.S.C. § 2244(d)(1)

[57]*Lawrence v. Florida*, 459 U.S. 327 (2007).

the final court to resolve a post-conviction petition.[58] The AEDPA statute of limitations is suspended only to await a decision by a state court.

The Court elaborated a bit more on the statute of limitations and the equitable tolling test under the AEDPA in the case of *Holland v. Florida* (2010).[59] Holland, when filing for habeas relief, was relying on his court-appointed counsel to file necessary documents. But he claimed that his attorney did not consult with him regarding strategy, did not frequently communicate with him, did not heed his advice on the statute of limitations, and did not submit paperwork on a timely basis. His habeas petition to the district court was subsequently denied for untimeliness. Holland filed a subsequent appeal to the Eleventh Circuit Court on grounds that his attorney was grossly negligent and that his case met the extraordinary circumstances prong of the equitable tolling test. The circuit court denied his petition, noting that his case did not involve extraordinary circumstances. It further stated that "when a petitioner seeks to excuse a late filing based on his attorney's unprofessional conduct, that conduct, even if grossly negligent, cannot justify equitable tolling absent proof of bad faith, dishonesty, divided loyalty, mental impairment, or the like."[60] The Court granted certiorari and held that equitable tolling is permitted under the AEDPA if a petitioner shows: (1) that he has been pursuing his rights diligently, and (2) that some extraordinary circumstance stood in his way.[61] But the Court argued that both the district court and the Eleventh Circuit Court applied incorrect legal standards and had also not truly considered the facts of the case. It thus reversed the circuit court's decision and remanded the case for further consideration. Justice Samuel Alito, who wrote a concurring opinion, agreed with the majority that legal standards were erroneously applied but felt that the Court should have provided more guidance as to the appropriate standards to consider. Justices Antonin Scalia and Clarence Thomas, on the other hand, dissented from the Court's opinion and argued that if Congress had intended for exceptions to the statute of limitations to be made for extraordinary circumstances, it would have outlined those exceptions in the AEDPA. Because it did not so specify, they reasoned, the Court should not entertain any exceptions.

The previously mentioned case of *Gonzalez v. Thaler* (2012)[62] also elaborates on the Court's opinion regarding the statute of limitations. In this case, the Court noted that the AEDPA, §2244(d)(1), establishes a one-year timeframe to file a habeas corpus appeal and the time begins tolling from the latest of four specified dates:

1. The date on which the judgment became final by the conclusion of direct review or the expiration of the time for seeking such review;
2. The date on which the impediment to filing an application created by State action in violation of the Constitution or laws of the United States is removed, if the applicant was prevented from filing by such State action;
3. The date on which the constitutional right asserted was initially recognized by the Supreme Court, if the right has been newly recognized by the Supreme Court and made retroactively applicable to cases on collateral review;

---

[58]*Id.*
[59]130 S. Ct. 2549 (2010).
[60]*Id.* at 1.
[61]*Id.* at 2.
[62]132 S. Ct. 641 (2011).

4. The date of which the factual predicate of the claim or claims presented could have been discovered through the exercise of due diligence.

Gonzalez v. Thaler (2012) involves the first of these dates, but since Gonzalez never appealed his case to the highest state court, the issue before the Court was when to start the AEDPA clock. According to Gonzalez, the clock on his statute of limitations for filing his federal habeas review should begin from the time the circuit court issues its ruling or mandate and not from the start of his purported opportunity to file an appeal to the highest court in the state. The Court disagreed and held that "for petitioners who pursue direct review all the way to this Court, the judgment becomes final at the conclusion of the direct review—when this Court affirms a conviction on the merits or denies a petition of certiorari. For all other petitioners, the judgment becomes final at the expiration of the time for seeking such review—when the time for pursuing direct review in this Court, or in state court expires."[63] Gonzalez fell under the latter prong, and his AEDPA clock was triggered not when the circuit court issued its ruling but rather when the window of opportunity to file a discretionary appeal to the state's highest court opened. If the triggering event was the circuit court's ruling, Gonzalez's appeal would have been timely. But the Court noted that that is not the proper triggering event; the clock begins to toll at the moment the opportunity to file a discretionary appeal to the state's highest court begins.

This case is salient because there were differing interpretations of the statute of limitations by circuit courts. Whereas the Fifth Circuit Court in *Gonzalez v. Thaler* (2012) took a very strict interpretation of the triggering mechanism, other circuit courts, such as the Eighth, used the issuance of a state court ruling or mandate to start the AEDPA clock. Although a significant clarification of the AEDPA, the ruling in *Gonzalez v. Thaler* (2012) raises other complications that will likely reach the Court in the future. For instance, although there is generally funding for indigent federal defendants filing habeas appeals, states vary with respect to funding for indigent state defendants filing appeals and, according to *Ross v. Moffitt* (1974),[64] states do not need to provide appointed counsel to indigent defendants in seeking discretionary appeals. Under *Gonzalez*, indigent defendants must be cautious of time limitations, and if counsel is not provided, it may bar their petition for lack of timeliness.

The strict interpretation of the AEDPA's statute of limitations is consistent with the Court's attempt to "balance the societal interests of finality, comity, and conservation of scarce judicial resources" by ensuring that inmates first exhaust all state remedies before filing a habeas petition in federal court and by encouraging inmates to file petitions on a timely basis.[65] According to the Court, allowing inmates to default on the statute of limitations period would motivate them to file petitions as a tactic to delay proceedings, which runs counter to the goal of the AEDPA.

2 Actual Innocence

Another area of legal challenge relevant to the AEDPA involves claims of innocence. Innocence, when viewed within the realm of the death penalty, is an ambiguous legal term. Its ambiguity stems from divergent constructs of innocence. For instance, innocence includes situations in which the inmate is actually innocent as well as situations in which an error occurred at sentencing. In the latter case,

---

[63]*Id.* at 15.
[64]417 U.S. 600 (1974).
[65]*Id.*

a claim of innocence (also known as a gateway innocence claim) can be established if the sentence was imposed because of a constitutional error at trial or when errors affected "the production and thus evaluation, of mitigating evidence at the sentencing stage of a capital trial—the site of the ultimate life/death decision."[66] With respect to the former category of innocence—actual innocence (sometimes also known as free-standing innocence claims)—an inmate may be truly innocent of the crime that he or she was accused of committing. The plain language of the AEDPA permits both types of innocence claims so long as petitions are filed before the statute of limitations expires and such claims are not raised in same-claim successive petitions, which are barred by the act. In fact, the innocence provision of the AEDPA was loosely adapted from the Court's ruling in *McCleskey v. Zant* (1991).[67] In *McCleskey*, the Supreme Court held that a court must entertain a defaulted petition when a petitioner could demonstrate that a miscarriage of justice would result if the court did not hear his petition because he was innocent. Although in *McCleskey* the Court ruled that a petitioner did not have to state why his petition failed to meet procedural rules (defaulted petition), Congress in the AEDPA modified this provision. Under the AEDPA, a petitioner must state why the petition was defaulted and also present evidence of innocence.

Since the passage of the AEDPA, the Court has added its own interpretation on innocence claims but continues to rely on its pre-AEDPA rulings. In *Sawyer v. Whitley* (1992),[68] for instance, the Court affirmed that the legal threshold of actual innocence claims is considerable; capital petitioners must show "by clear and convincing evidence that were it not for a constitutional error, no reasonable juror would have found the petitioner eligible for the death penalty under the applicable state law."[69] Thus, the Court required that a petitioner demonstrate, through clear and convincing evidence, that a constitutional error (proving actual innocence) would nullify his death penalty eligibility because such error would cancel out an aggravating factor used by the jury to elevate the defendant's status to "death eligible." Sawyer limited the ability of death row inmates to file a claim of actual innocence. Following this decision, the Court in *Herrera v. Collins* (1993)[70] further restricted claims of actual innocence when it held that:

> *Where a defendant has been afforded a fair trial and convicted of the offense for which he was charged, the constitutional presumption of innocence disappears. Federal habeas courts do not sit to correct errors of fact, but to ensure that individuals are not imprisoned in violation of the Constitution. Thus, claims of actual innocence based on newly discovered evidence have never been held to state a ground for federal habeas relief absent an independent constitutional violation occurring in the course of the underlying state criminal proceedings.*[71]

In 2006, the Court revisited the issue of actual innocence in *House v. Bell*.[72] This was a gateway case of innocence but also one that involved a defaulted petition because House did not raise his claim of ineffective assistance of counsel in prior post-conviction proceedings. In fact, in his prior-post conviction proceeding, which was heard by the U.S. District Court for the Eastern District of Tennessee,

---

[66]Duffett, Lisa R., *Habeas Corpus and Actual Innocence of the Death Sentence after* Sawyer v. Whitley: *Another Nail into the Coffin of State Capital Defendants*, 44 Case W. Res. L. Rev. 121, 136 (1993).
[67]*McCleskey v. Zant*, 499 U.S. 467 (1991).
[68]*Sawyer v. Whitley*, 505 U.S. 333 (1992).
[69]*Id.*
[70]*Herrera v. Collins*, 506 U.S. 390 (1993).
[71]*Id.* at 400.
[72]*House v. Bell*, 547 U.S. 518 (2007).

the court ruled that House's appeal was in violation of Tennessee law, which states that "claims not raised in prior post-conviction proceedings are presumptively waived." Even though the district court deemed the claim procedurally defaulted for this reason, the U.S. Supreme Court nonetheless held an evidentiary hearing to determine whether House fell within the purview of the actual innocence exception to procedurally defaulted claims (an exception previously created by the Court in *Schlup v. Delo*).[73] After hearing new evidence of innocence presented by House, the Court held that House fell within the procedural default exception and that "it is more likely than not that no reasonable juror would have found him guilty beyond a reasonable doubt"[74] had the juror heard the newly discovered evidence. The Court remanded the case to the state court for a new trial. The Court noted, however, that a gateway habeas corpus claim of actual innocence requires the habeas court to consider all evidence presented at the original trial as well as newly discovered evidence. The Court also clarified the position of the AEDPA under the procedural default exception in actual innocence claims. Because the claim did not involve a violation of the statute of limitations nor involve a same-claim successive petition but rather was only a defaulted claim, the Court held that the AEDPA and the *McCleskey* standard have no bearing on the case.

Recently, the Court addressed the AEDPA's statute of limitations in an actual innocence claim. Although not a death penalty case, in *McQuiggin v. Perkins* (2013), the Court suspended the statute of limitations and noted that a delay in filing a petition may serve to buttress the strength of the petition. That is,

> *Unexplained delay in presenting new evidence bears on the determination whether the petitioner has made a requisite showing [of actual innocence]. Taking account of the delay in the context of the merits of a petitioner's actual innocence claim, rather than treating timeliness as a threshold inquiry, is tuned to the exception's underlying rationale for ensuring that federal constitutional errors do not result in the incarceration of innocent persons."*[75]

The Court, nonetheless, reiterated that claims of actual innocence are rare and the petitioner bears a substantial burden in showing that "it is more likely than not that no reasonable juror would have convicted the petitioner in light of the new evidence."[76] The Court refrained, however, from determining whether it would also suspend the statute of limitations in freestanding claims of innocence. This case is salient because some circuit courts, such as the Fifth and Sixth Circuits, had narrowly interpreted the AEDPA and barred such petitions simply because of a violation of the statute of limitations. Although an inmate has recourse other than a habeas petition, such as clemency, in seeking a reversal of a conviction based on actual innocence, "clemency... has been described as arbitrary, lacking in both systematic rules and appellate review, and subject to the whims of the governor's personal preferences and the political pressures borne by him."[77] Moreover, although an inmate may also seek to file a petition directly with the U.S. Supreme Court under its original habeas corpus jurisdiction (created under the Judiciary Act of 1789), it is unlikely that the Court would hear the petition.

In sum, innocence is an elusive legal term, and whereas the AEDPA does not preclude petitions on this matter, it does not explicitly delineate issues such as actual innocence versus gateway innocence

---

[73]*Schlup v. Delo*, 513 U.S. 298 (1995).
[74]*Id.* at 327.
[75]*McQuiggin v. Perkins*, 133 S. Ct. 1924 (2013).
[76]*Id.*
[77]*Supra note* 54 at 368.

claims, the legal thresholds to prove innocence, or suspensions of the statute of limitations when there is a case of actual innocence. Justice Scalia, writing for the dissent in *McQuiggin v. Perkins*, warns that the Court overstepped its bounds by modifying the parameters of the AEDPA, especially in relation to the statute of limitations, since this is one of the hallmarks of the AEDPA. One legal commentator also noted that *McQuiggin* gives inmates a "get-out-of-habeas-procedure-free" card.[78] Yet other legal scholars contend that the Court is simply exercising its right to clarify the provisions of the AEDPA.

V HABEAS CORPUS AND 42 U.S.C. §1983

In 2004 and again in 2006, the Court was presented with two cases, *Nelson v. Campbell*[79] and *Hill v. McDonough*,[80] respectively, that challenged the constitutionality of two different methods of execution. In *Nelson*, the inmate sought to prevent the state of Alabama (by filing an injunction) from using a "cut-down" procedure, which would require making an incision into the arm or leg to gain access to veins in order to administer the lethal dose of drugs to effectuate his death. Although the standard technique for gaining intravenous access is through the use of a needle, Nelson's years of drug abuse, which severely compromised his veins, prompted the state to use the alternative cut-down procedure. Nelson argued, however, that such procedure would nonetheless cause him "gratuitous and unnecessary pain." In *Hill*, the inmate sought to prevent the state of Florida from using the three-drug lethal injection procedure because such procedure would cause "severe pain." Both cases alleged that the procedures violated the Eighth Amendment's prohibition of cruel and unusual punishment.

Individually, Nelson and Hill filed their claims under the federal statute known as Section 1983 (42 U.S. Code Section 1983). However, because both Nelson and Hill had already filed one unsuccessful habeas application to stay their executions before bringing their Section 1983 lawsuit, district courts in their respective cases dismissed the Section 1983 lawsuits under the belief that the latter lawsuit was the functional equivalent of a second habeas application, which is prohibited by the AEDPA.

As previously mentioned, when an inmate files a habeas corpus petition, he seeks release from prison because the incarceration is illegal or unconstitutional. It is filed after a criminal appeal, and the inmate must exhaust state court remedies and follow the provisions of the AEDPA before filing a habeas application in federal court. Conversely, when an inmate files a Section 1983 lawsuit, he seeks to improve or modify the conditions of incarceration and/or seeks monetary compensation from prison officials. A Section 1983 lawsuit originates from a federal law passed in 1871. It is part of a larger federal statute, known as the Civil Rights Act of 1871 or the Ku Klux Klan Act of 1871, which sought to protect southern blacks from the Klan by providing a legal remedy to alleged abuse. Section 1983 states:

> *Every person who, under color of any statute, ordinance, regulation, custom, or usage, of any state or territory, subjects, or causes to be subjected, any citizen of the United States or other persons within*

---

[78]Steiker, Jordan, Opinion Analysis: Innocence Exception Survives, Innocence Claim Does Not (Updated), SCOTUSblog (May 29, 2013). Available at: www.scotusblog.com/2013/05/opinion-analysis-innocence-exception-survives-innocence-claim-does-not/.

[79]*Nelson v. Campbell*, 541 U.S. 637 (2004).

[80]*Hill v. McDonough*, 126 S. Ct. 1189 (2006).

the jurisdiction thereof to the deprivation of any rights, privileges or immunities secured by the Constitution and laws, shall be liable to the party injured in an action at law, suit in equity, or other proper proceeding for redress.[81]

An inmate who files a Section 1983 lawsuit is therefore claiming that a person, acting under color of statute (meaning any person who has been vested with authority to enforce a law, ordinance, regulation, or custom such as a prison official), violated a constitutional right. To win, the inmate must not only prove that the person who deprived him of rights was acting under color of law but also that there was in fact a violation of rights. Table 10.1 summarizes the difference between habeas corpus and Section 1983 lawsuits.

The Court in both *Nelson* and *Hill* was forced to answer whether an inmate who seeks to prevent the state from administering the death penalty due to a procedure that he deems to be cruel and unusual can file under Section 1983 or whether this type of challenge falls within the purview of habeas corpus and the rules that govern this writ under the AEDPA. In *Nelson*, the Court declared that because he was not challenging the constitutionality of the death penalty per se nor challenging the fact of his impending execution but only the method used to administer it, a Section 1983 lawsuit is the appropriate vehicle to

Table 10.1 Difference Between Habeas Corpus and a Section 1983 Lawsuit

Habeas Corpus	Section 1983
1. Purpose is to seek release from prison or jail	1. Purpose is to improve prison or jail conditions and/or obtain monetary damages from prison or jail officials
2. Need to exhaust state judicial remedies before going to federal court	2. No need to exhaust state judicial remedies; the case may be filed directly in federal court
3. Begins in state court before it goes to federal court	3. Begins in federal court
3. Affects only one prisoner if it succeeds	4. Affects all prisoners if it succeeds
4. Filed by one prisoner seeking release	5. May be filed as a class action suit, meaning by a group of prisoners

Source: del Carmen, Rolando V., et al., Briefs of Leading Cases in Corrections *(4th ed., 2008: 6–7).*

use for such a challenge. Thus, the district court erred in classifying the challenge as the functional equivalent of a defaulted habeas corpus application. Furthermore, the Court noted that, although this case "falls within the margins of habeas,"[82] the fact that Nelson's successful Section 1983 lawsuit would only result in a change of the method used to execute him, as opposed to preventing the state from executing him, distinguishes this case from a habeas application. However, the Court, fearing that abuse of Section 1983 would impede the goals of the AEDPA, was quick to point out that the Prison Litigation Reform Act of 1995, which, among other things, establishes rules that inmates must follow when seeking to prevent the state from fully effectuating a court order, such as the particular method of execution, gives significant deference to the state. The Act states that before a court grants an inmate

[81]42 U.S.C. § 1983.
[82]*Nelson v. Campbell*, 541 U.S. 637, 645 (2004).

injunctive relief, it must "give substantial weight to any adverse impact on... the operation of the criminal justice system caused by the relief."[83] In addition, similar to the provisions of the AEDPA, inmates must exhaust available state administrative remedies prior to filing a Section 1983 lawsuit. The Act also grants courts the ability to dismiss suits that are "frivolous and/or malicious."

In *Hill*, the Court echoed its decision in *Nelson* and held that if an inmate challenges the lawfulness of his death sentence, then habeas corpus and the rules specified by the AEDPA govern such a challenge. However, if an inmate challenges only the method for which he is to be executed and only seeks to temporarily delay such execution, then Section 1983 is the appropriate remedy. It added that a Section 1983 lawsuit does not entitle inmates to permanently delay their execution but may provide them with a temporary delay of their execution to allow the state sufficient time to reconsider the method by which it executes inmates.

Section 1983 lawsuits have gained momentum in the death penalty legal arena since *Hill* and *Nelson*. In 2011, for instance, in the case of *Skinner v. Switzer*,[84] the Court held that a Section 1983 lawsuit can be used by a death row inmate to seek DNA testing of evidence that may prove his innocence. The facts of this case reveal that Skinner was sentenced to death in Texas for killing his girlfriend and her sons. In his defense, he argued that he was too intoxicated to have committed the crimes and alleged that his girlfriend's uncle was the likely perpetrator. When the case was tried, prosecutors ordered forensic testing of some evidence but not all. Skinner claimed that testing of all evidence would prove his innocence and thus filed multiple state and federal post-conviction appeals. All were denied. Six years after his conviction, Texas passed a law allowing inmates to seek DNA testing on evidence. The law states:

> To obtain DNA testing under Article 64, a prisoner must meet one of two threshold criteria. He may show that, at trial, testing either was "not available" or was "available, but not technologically capable of providing probative results." Alternatively, he may show that the evidence was not previously tested "through no fault" on his part, and that "the interests of justice" require a postconviction order for testing. To grant a motion for postconviction testing, a court must make further findings, prime among them, the movant "would not have been convicted if exculpatory results had been obtained through DNA testing," and "the [Article 64] request... [was] not made to unreasonably delay the execution of sentence or administration of justice.[85]

Because his appeals were denied, he pursued a Section 1983 lawsuit alleging that Texas had violated his Fourteenth Amendment due process rights by failing to test DNA evidence. Lower courts refused to hear his case, arguing that the proper mechanism to file suit is habeas corpus and not Section 1983. The Court granted certiorari and noted that Section 1983 can be an appropriate legal vehicle to file such claims. "Skinner has properly invoked Section 1983. Success in his suit for DNA testing would not 'necessarily imply' the invalidity of his conviction. While test results might prove exculpatory, that outcome is hardly inevitable; as earlier observed, results might prove inconclusive or they might further incriminate Skinner."[86] Thus, while Skinner was permitted to use Section 1983 to petition the state to test all evidence, the Court's ruling did not reverse his conviction.

---

[83]*Id*. at 647.
[84]131 S. Ct. 1289 (2011).
[85]*Id*. at 1291.
[86]*Id*. at 1292.

In fact, the Court was quick to state that Section 1983 is not an appropriate remedy for inmates seeking a reversal of their conviction.

Although this case provides a narrow window for death row inmates to seek some relief, the dissenting justices in this case, including Justices Anthony Kennedy, Clarence Thomas, and Samuel Alito, worried that the ruling in *Skinner* may have opened the window of opportunity too much. They argued that this may provide inmates with "a roadmap" to delay their execution and also to circumvent the AEDPA.

VI IN SUMMARY, WHAT DO THESE CASES SAY?

The writ of habeas corpus is an additional legal remedy for death row inmates, though they do not have unfettered access to file habeas petitions. As early as 1886, in *Ex parte Royall*,[87] the Court established firm jurisprudence with regard to habeas petitions by ruling that judges had the discretion to deny state inmates who had not exhausted state habeas corpus relief from seeking review in federal court. The Court also established the rule that any inmate seeking review in federal court must first exhaust state court habeas corpus remedies.

In the early twentieth century, the Court continued on its path to curtail the ability of inmates to file habeas petitions by creating the two additional rules—one pertaining to new-claim successive petitions and the other to same-claim successive petitions. These rules were created to address the problem of serial petitions, which the Court in *Salinger v. Loisel* (1924)[88] and *Wong Doo v. United States* (1924)[89] found to be abuses of the Great Writ. In these two cases, the Court authorized federal judges to deny successive habeas review to any inmate whom they believed may have filed the petition for disingenuous reasons. In *Sanders v. United States* (1963),[90] the Court placed further limitations on same-claim successive petitions and new-claim successive petitions. With regard to same-claim successive petitions, the Court opined that that unless the ends of justice warrant review, dismissal of such claims was within the discretionary authority of the federal courts. For new-claim successive petitions, the Court held that federal judges may also refuse to hear such petitions if it was discovered that an inmate had deliberately and strategically chosen not to include new claims in previous habeas petitions for the purpose of stalling the imposition of a state court decision. This was later reinforced by the Court in *Rose v. Lundy* (1983)[91] when it addressed mixed petitions. By 1991, the Court refined its jurisprudence on successive petitions when in *McCleskey v. Zant* (1991)[92] it ruled that an inmate must prove that the failure to raise a claim during a prior habeas petition was not an attempt to abuse the Great Writ. The inmate had to prove that an objective factor external to the defense prejudiced his or her conviction and that the failure of the court to hear the petition would result in a miscarriage of justice.

In 1996, the AEDPA introduced a new era in habeas corpus petitions by severely limiting the filing of successive petitions. The Court has upheld the constitutionality of the provisions of the AEDPA and

[87]*Ex parte Royall*, 117 U.S. 241 (1886).
[88]*Salinger v. Loisel*, 265 U.S. 224 (1924).
[89]*Wong Doo v. United States*, 265 U.S. 239 (1924).
[90]*Sanders v. United States*, 373 U.S. 1 (1963).
[91]*Rose v. Lundy*, 455 U.S. 509 (1982).
[92]*McCleskey v. Zant*, 499 U.S. 467 (1991).

has been interpreting its provisions. In *Williams v. Taylor* (2000),[93] for instance, the Court upheld the AEDPA's provision that a state court decision would be reversed only if it was "contrary to, or involved an unreasonable application of federal law...." In *Tyler v. Cain* (2001),[94] the Court upheld the AEDPA provision that an inmate cannot file a successive petition on the basis of a new constitutional law. But recent cases seem to indicate the Court is taking a more moderate approach to successive petitions. In *Stewart v. Martinez-Villareal* (1998)[95] it held that the numerical sequence of petitions does not necessary prevent an inmate from filing a successive appeal. What is salient, according to the Court, is whether previous petitions were dismissed on merit or dismissed without prejudice. If the latter is true, an inmate can file another petition. The Court is also not too concerned with technical deficiencies in COA. In *Gonzalez v. Thaler* (2012), it held that circuit courts had jurisdiction to hear a habeas petition even though the COAs did not contain a specific constitutional violation. This is in sharp contrast to the plain language of the AEDPA, which states that that a COA shall be issued only when there is a substantial showing of the denial of a constitutional violation.

The Court has also recently clarified the statute of limitations provision of the AEDPA. Whereas the Court is cognizant of the law's attempt to achieve finality with respect to state court decisions as well as an attempt to prevent any abuse of habeas corpus, it has seemingly relaxed the AEDPA's statute-of-limitations clock. Most recently, in *Holland v. Florida* (2010), the Court held that the clock can be tolled so long as the petitioner meets certain criteria, such as due diligence in pursuing evidence of constitutional violations and proof that there were extraordinary reasons for not doing so. *Gonzalez v. Thaler* (2012), however, elaborates on the triggering event that starts the AEDPA clock. According to the Court, the triggering event is the moment the opportunity to file a discretionary appeal to the state's highest court begins.

The Court's desire for finality and its interpretation of some of the provisions of the AEDPA have resulted in various problems for death row inmates, although the Court has been more moderate with its interpretation of the federal law. Under the provisions of the AEDPA, an inmate may file a claim of actual innocence as long as there is factual evidence of innocence, the claim is filed before the statute of limitations expires, and the claim is not raised in a same-claim successive petition. However, in *Herrera v. Collins* (1993),[96] the Court had previously prohibited inmates from filing claims of innocence under the purview of habeas corpus by ruling that "claims of actual innocence based on newly discovered evidence have never been held to state a ground for federal habeas relief absent an independent constitutional error...." Thus, although the AEDPA recognizes claims of actual innocence, the Court has curtailed the ability to file such claims if it is based on newly discovered evidence and no constitutional error occurred at trial. The Court does allow gateway claims of innocence, but there are varying standards for such claims. In *Sawyer v. Whitley*, the Court held that defendants must show by clear and convincing evidence that, but for a constitutional error, no reasonable juror would have found the defendant eligible for the death penalty. Recently, the Court has reiterated its stance on innocence claims but has provided a window of opportunity for inmates who file petitions after the statute of

---

[93]*Williams v. Taylor*, 529 U.S. 362 (2000).
[94]*Tyler v. Cain*, 533 U.S. 970 (2001).
[95]*Stewart v. Martinez-Villareal*, 523 U.S. 637 (1998).
[96]*Herrera v. Collins*, 506 U.S. 390 (1993).

limitations expires. In *McQuiggin v. Perkins* (2013), the Court expressed that petitions can be filed after deadline and that reasons for the delay can be used to substantiate a petition.

Section 1983 lawsuits have also been used by death row inmates as an alternate way to challenge execution. *Nelson v. Campbell* (2004) and *Hill v. McDonough* (2006) are two prime examples. In both cases, the Court ruled that inmates who challenge the methods used to administer a penalty of death can use Section 1983 to seek relief. The Court has been cautious, however, restricting the use of Section 1983 in death penalty cases; it does not permit its use when inmates are seeking a reversal of conviction and/or a permanent delay of their execution.

VII CONCLUSION

Habeas corpus, a constitutional right secured by the Framers of the Constitution in the suspension clause, was intended to ensure that individuals confined in violation of the Constitution or federal laws could petition the courts in order to obtain their freedom. Although the Great Writ remains an important vehicle for those unconstitutionally detained, both the legislative and judicial branches have limited the ability of detainees to file petitions. Those limitations are a response to inmate abuse of the writ. In 1924, the Court began to limit the occasions when inmates could use the writ by implementing a subjective test that allowed judges to decline to hear petitions if such petitions were filed for disingenuous reasons. The Court's decision was followed by congressional enactment that codified the ruling into federal law. In the next several years, the Court and Congress further limited habeas petitions by restricting same-claim successive petitions and new-claim successive petitions. In addition, the Court further restricted habeas corpus when it ruled on mixed petitions and procedural defaults.

In 1996, the Antiterrorism and Effective Death Penalty Act (AEDPA) was enacted by Congress, significantly limiting the ability of inmates to file habeas petitions. Provisions that include successive petitions, the statute of limitations, a certificate of appealability (COA), and the standard of proof to file petitions, especially related to innocence, have hampered granting of habeas corpus petitions. The Supreme Court, although cognizant of the goals of the AEDPA, has recently relaxed some of its provisions. Its holding in *Magwood v. Patterson* (2010) is demonstrative of the Court's more moderate interpretation of federal law with respect to successive petitions. It was in this case that the Court referred to the "phrase second or successive petition as a term of art." The Court's moderate approach changes when the issue involves the AEDPA's statute of limitations. Although it has clarified when equitable tolling is permissible, the Court cautions that allowing too many exceptions to the statute of limitations would motivate inmates to delay their punishment. Even in actual innocence claims, the Court has drawn limited exceptions to the statute of limitations. The narrow exceptions to the AEDPA also hold true for Section 1983 lawsuits. Although the Court has permitted the use of Section 1983 lawsuits by death row inmates, it does not allow inmates to use this remedy to impede their execution.

CASES BRIEFED IN CHAPTER 10

Case	Issue	Holding
Rose v. Lundy 455 U.S. 509 (1982)	Does federal law require a federal district court to dismiss a state prisoner's petition for habeas corpus if it contains claims that have not been exhausted in state court?	Under federal law, state prisoners must exhaust state court remedies before filing a writ of habeas corpus in federal court.
McCleskey v. Zant 499 U.S. 467 (1991)	Does the failure to include a claim of a violation of the Sixth Amendment in the first petition for a federal writ of habeas corpus preclude the same claim from being raised in a second habeas petition?	Failure to claim a violation of a constitutional right in the first habeas petition precludes the same claim from being raised in a second habeas corpus petition.
Sawyer v. Whitley 505 U.S. 333 (1992)	Does a claim of actual innocence, filed in a habeas petition, need a showing of clear and convincing evidence that were it not for a constitutional error, no reasonable juror would have found the petitioner eligible for the death penalty?	In claims of actual innocence, a petitioner must show through clear and convincing evidence that were it not for a constitutional error, no reasonable juror would have found the petitioner eligible for the death penalty.
Herrera v. Collins 506 U.S. 390 (1993)	Is a claim of actual innocence based on newly discovered evidence a ground for habeas corpus relief absent a constitutional error during a criminal proceeding?	A claim of actual innocence based on newly discovered evidence is not a ground for relief in the absence of a constitutional violation in the criminal proceeding.
Felker v. Turpin 518 U.S. 651 (1996)	Does the Antiterrorism and Effective Death Penalty Act of 1996 prohibit a court from accepting an application for habeas corpus relief? Does the Act violate the Constitution's suspension clause?	The Antiterrorism and Effective Death Penalty Act of 1996 does not prohibit a court from accepting an application of habeas corpus relief, nor does the Act violate the suspension clause.
Stewart v. Martinez-Villareal, 523 U.S. 637 (1998)	Can a capital defendant who has already filed a previous habeas corpus appeal on grounds that he is incompetent to be executed file a successive appeal on the same issue?	When a defendant's first habeas corpus petition is dismissed as premature, he or she may file a subsequent habeas petition on the same grounds. The second petition does not violate the AEDPA's successive petition rule, because the first petition was not adjudicated.
Nelson v. Campbell 541 U.S. 637 (2004)	Can a Section 1983 lawsuit be used by an inmate who wants to challenge only the method by which he will be executed but not the constitutionality of the death penalty per se and/or his impending execution?	A Section 1983 lawsuit is the appropriate legal remedy to use when seeking to temporarily halt an execution on grounds that the methods used to cause death violate the cruel and unusual punishment clause of the Eighth Amendment.

Continued

Case	Issue	Holding
House v. Bell 547 U.S. 518 (2006)	Is a petitioner barred from filing a habeas corpus petition on grounds of actual innocence because he failed to raise all claims in prior post-convictions proceedings?	If a petitioner has a defaulted petition due to not raising all issues in prior post-conviction petitions, habeas relief may be granted if the petitioner demonstrates cause for the default and presents new evidence that, if shown to the jurors, it is more likely than not that no reasonable juror would have found him guilty beyond a reasonable doubt.
Lawrence v. Florida 549 U.S. 327 (2007)	Is the AEDPA's statute of limitations suspended or "tolled" while a defendant awaits a decision of a habeas corpus petition by the U.S. Supreme Court?	Although the statute of limitations may be suspended while an inmate awaits a response or decision by a state court, which is the final court to resolve post-conviction petition, it is not "tolled" when an inmate awaits a decision by the U.S. Supreme Court, because the Court is not usually the final court to resolve a post-conviction petition.
Skinner v. Switzer 562 U.S. ___ (2011)	Can 42 U.S.C. §1983 be used by capital defendants to seek DNA testing of evidence that may prove their innocence?	A §1983 lawsuit can be used for claims of actual innocence so long as the inmate is not seeking reversal of his conviction and/ or release from prison.

CASE BRIEFS

ROSE v. LUNDY 455 U.S. 509 (1982)

CAPSULE: Under federal law, state prisoners must exhaust state court remedies before filing for a writ of habeas corpus in federal court.

FACTS: Noah Lundy was convicted in Tennessee of rape and crimes against nature and was sent to state prison. The Tennessee Court of Criminal Appeals affirmed his convictions and the Tennessee Supreme Court denied review. Lundy filed a petition for post-conviction relief in state court, which was denied. He then filed a petition for a writ of habeas corpus in federal district court under 28 U.S.C. § 2254, alleging the following: (1) that he had been denied the right to confrontation because the trial court limited the defense counsel's questioning of the victim; (2) that he had been denied the right to a fair trial because the prosecuting attorney stated that the respondent had a violent character; (3) that he had been denied the right to a fair trial because the prosecutor improperly remarked in his closing arguments that the state's evidence was uncontradicted; and (4) that the trial judge improperly instructed the jury that every witness is presumed to swear the truth. The federal district court granted the writ of habeas corpus, despite claims (3) and (4) not having been litigated in state court. The court of appeals affirmed the decision of the federal district court; the government appealed.

ISSUE: Does federal law (28 U.S.C. § 2254 [b] and [c]) require a federal district court to dismiss a state prisoner's petition for a writ of habeas corpus that contains claims that have not been exhausted in the state court? YES.

Continued

ROSE v. LUNDY 455 U.S. 509 (1982)—cont'd

HOLDING: A district court must dismiss "mixed petitions" (meaning petitions that contain claims that have been exhausted and others that have not been exhausted in state court) because such dismissal furthers the purpose underlying the federal habeas corpus statute.

REASON: "The exhaustion doctrine is principally designed to protect the state courts' role in the enforcement of federal law and prevent disruption of state judicial proceedings. Under the federal system, the federal and state 'courts [are] equally bound to guard and protect rights secured by the Constitution.' Because 'it would be unseemly in our dual system of government for a federal district court to upset a state court conviction without an opportunity for the state courts to correct a constitutional violation,' federal courts apply the doctrine of comity, which 'teaches that one court should defer action on causes properly within its jurisdiction until the courts of another sovereignty with concurrent powers, and already cognizant of the litigation, have had an opportunity to pass upon the matter.'

"The facts of the present case underscore the need for a rule encouraging exhaustion of all federal claims. In his opinion, the District Court Judge wrote that 'there is such mixture of violations that one cannot be separated from and considered independently of the others.' Because the two unexhausted claims for relief were intertwined with the exhausted one, the judge apparently considered all of the claims in ruling on the petition. Requiring dismissal of petitions containing both exhausted and unexhausted claims will relieve the district courts of the difficult if not impossible task of deciding when claims are related, and will reduce the temptation to consider unexhausted claims."

CASE SIGNIFICANCE: Despite the absence of a constitutional issue, this case is significant because it makes clear when state prisoners can file habeas corpus petitions in federal courts. Habeas corpus petitions are filed by inmates to gain freedom, alleging that something was wrong with their conviction and therefore they are in prison unconstitutionally. This is the prisoner's last hope of freedom after conviction has been affirmed by the courts. Although habeas corpus cases seldom succeed, they give prisoners another judicial avenue to pursue when they feel they have been wrongly convicted.

The "exhaustion of state court remedies" doctrine provides that remedies in state courts must be exhausted before a case can be heard in federal court. As this case states, "the exhaustion doctrine existed long before its codification by Congress in 1948." Although now codified, the "mixed petition" issue was not addressed in the codification, hence the need to clarify it in this case. The purpose of the exhaustion doctrine is to avoid piecemeal litigation. Its benefits are obvious. In the words of the Court, "[t]o the extent that the exhaustion requirement reduced piecemeal litigation, both the courts and the prisoners should benefit, for as a result the district court will be more likely to review all of the prisoner's claims in a single proceeding, thus providing for a more focused and thorough review."

There are two kinds of habeas corpus proceedings: state habeas corpus and federal habeas corpus. Both are available to prisoners, but this case states that issues brought to federal court on habeas corpus grounds must first be litigated in state court. In this case, the prisoner alleged four grounds for relief; two grounds were litigated in state court and the other two grounds were not litigated. The issue was whether such a "mixed petition" ought to be entertained by the federal court. The Court decided that 28 U.S.C. § 2254 "requires a federal district court to dismiss a petition for a writ of habeas corpus containing any claims that have not been exhausted in the state courts." This is significant because it lengthens the time of potential relief for state prisoners in habeas corpus proceedings. It usually takes a number of years for prisoner habeas corpus cases to be decided in state court. Only after that will the federal forum be available to a state prisoner. This therefore further delays the availability of the federal habeas corpus remedy because state prisoners must first go through the state process before taking their case to a federal court, even when some of the allegations have been litigated in state court. It is to be noted, however, that federal prisoners do not have to exhaust state proceedings, because they have been convicted under federal law and were tried in federal court.

McCLESKEY v. ZANT 499 U.S. 467 (1991)

CAPSULE: Failure to claim a violation of a constitutional right in a first federal habeas corpus petition precludes the same claim from being raised in a second habeas corpus petition.

FACTS: McCleskey was charged with murder and armed robbery. At his 1978 trial, the state of Georgia called Offie Evans, the occupant of the jail cell next to McCleskey, to rebut the petitioner's alibi defense. Evans testified that McCleskey had admitted to and boasted about the killing. Due to this testimony and other supporting evidence, the jury convicted McCleskey and sentenced him to death. After the Georgia Supreme Court affirmed the trial decision, McCleskey initiated post-conviction proceedings by filing a state habeas corpus petition, McCleskey alleging that his statements to Evans were acquired by the state creating a situation that induced him to make incriminating statements without the assistance of counsel, in violation of the Sixth Amendment. He was denied relief and filed his first federal habeas corpus and second state habeas corpus petitions, which did not contain the Sixth Amendment claim. Both petitions were also denied. He filed a second federal habeas corpus petition in 1987, challenging on Sixth Amendment grounds a 21-page statement that Evans had made to the police. The statement was made available to McCleskey just weeks before he filed his second federal petition. The document not only contained conversations that were consistent with Evans's trial testimony, but it also recounted the tactics used by Evans to engage McCleskey in conversation. At the petition hearing, a jailer who was present during McCleskey's pretrial incarceration gave testimony indicating that Evans's cell assignment had been made at the state's behest.

ISSUE: Does the failure to include a claim of a violation of a Sixth Amendment in the first petition for a federal writ of habeas corpus preclude the same claim from being raised in a second habeas petition? YES.

HOLDING: The failure to include a claim of a violation of a constitutional right in the first federal habeas corpus petition precludes a similar claim in the second federal habeas petition. Allowing the prisoner to do so constitutes an abuse of the writ.

REASON: "Much confusion exists as to the proper standard for applying the abuse of the writ doctrine, which refers to a complex and evolving body of equitable principles informed and controlled by historical usage, statutory developments, and judicial decisions. This Court has heretofore defined such abuse in an oblique way, through dicta and denials of certiorari petitions or stay applications and, because of historical changes and the complexity of the subject, has not always followed an unwavering line in its conclusions as to the writ's availability."

"Although this Court's federal habeas decisions do not admit of ready synthesis, a review of these precedents demonstrates that a claim need not have been deliberately abandoned in an earlier petition in order to establish that its inclusion in a subsequent petition constitutes abuse of the writ, see, e.g., *Sanders v. United States*, 373 U.S. 1, 18: that such inclusion constitutes abuse if the claim could have been raised in the first petition, but was omitted through inexcusable neglect... and that, because the doctrine of procedural default and abuse of writ implicate nearly identical concerns, the determination of inexcusable neglect in the abuse context should be governed by the same standards used to determine whether to excuse a habeas petitioner's state procedural defaults, see, e.g., *Wainwright v. Sykes*, 433 U.S. 72. Thus, when a prisoner files a second or subsequent habeas petition, the government bears the burden of pleading abuse of writ. This burden is satisfied if the government, with clarity and particularity, notes petitioner's prior writ history, identifies the claims that appear for the first time, and alleges that petitioner has abused the writ. The burden to disprove abuse then shifts to the petitioner. To excuse his failure to raise the claim earlier, he must show cause—e.g., that he was impeded by some objective factor external to the defense, such as governmental interference or the reasonable unavailability of the factual basis for the claim—as well as actual prejudice resulting from the errors of which he complains."

CASE SIGNIFICANCE: This case was decided on procedural grounds, but its implication is far reaching. Habeas petitions by prisoners seek release on the ground of unconstitutional confinement. Such petitions are first heard in

Continued

McCLESKEY v. ZANT 499 U.S. 467 (1991)—cont'd

state courts, and if denied, may be filed in a federal court under the Federal Habeas Corpus Act. The prisoner in this case went twice to state court and then filed a federal habeas corpus proceeding. In his first federal habeas corpus case, however, he failed to allege a violation of his Sixth Amendment rights. Having been turned down, he filed a second federal habeas corpus case, but this time he raised a violation of his Sixth Amendment rights as the basis for his release. The Supreme Court considered this an abuse of the writ and prohibited him from raising it in the second federal habeas corpus case. The Court said that "such inclusion constitutes abuse if the claim could have been raised in the first petition, but was omitted through inexcusable neglect." The Court added that "to excuse his failure to raise the claim earlier, he must show cause—e.g., that he was impeded by some objective factor external to the defense, such as government interference or the reasonable unavailability of the factual basis for the claim—as well as actual prejudice resulting from the errors of which he complains...." The prisoner failed to establish this in his second petition; thus the issue could no longer be raised.

The effect of this decision is to reduce successive filings of habeas corpus cases in federal court by state prisoners. In effect, the Supreme Court is saying that petitioners must include all constitutional claims in their first petition and not "serialize" them. Any claim not raised in the first petition cannot be raised in a subsequent petition. The only exception is if a prisoner can show that "a fundamental miscarriage of justice—such as the conviction of an innocent person—would result from a failure to entertain the claim."

SAWYER v. WHITLEY 505 U.S. 333 (1992)

CAPSULE: In claims of actual innocence, a petitioner must show through clear and convincing evidence that were it not for a constitutional error, no reasonable juror would have found the petitioner eligible for the death penalty under the applicable state law.

FACTS: Petitioner Robert Sawyer was prosecuted and found guilty of committing first-degree murder in the course of committing an aggravated arson. At sentencing, the jury found no statutory mitigating factors but found three aggravating factors, thus making the petitioner eligible for the death penalty under Louisiana law. The jury sentenced petitioner Sawyer to death. After having exhausted his state and federal judicial appeals, Sawyer filed his first habeas corpus petition alleging actual innocence. He said he was innocent because crucial mitigating factors (a claim of intoxication at the time of the murder and evidence of a deprived childhood) were deliberately withheld from the jury when making its determination of death eligibility. This was based on his original claim that due to ineffective counsel, such evidence was never fully presented to the jury. Sawyer claimed that, had such mitigating factors been allowed to be reviewed by the jury, he would not have been found death eligible and thus never sentenced to death.

ISSUE: Does a claim of actual innocence, filed in a habeas petition, need a showing of clear and convincing evidence that were it not for a constitutional error, no reasonable juror would have found the petitioner eligible for the death penalty under the applicable state law? YES.

HOLDING: In claims of actual innocence before a habeas court, the petitioner must demonstrate through clear and convincing evidence that, absent a constitutional violation, a reasonable jury would not have found the petitioner death eligible. Petitioner Sawyer failed to meet this burden because he could not prove that mitigating evidence was deliberately withheld from the jury when it considered his death eligibility. Thus, his death sentence was affirmed.

REASON: "The issue before the Court is the standard for determining whether a petitioner bringing a successive, abusive, or defaulted federal habeas claim has shown he is actually innocent of the death penalty to which he has

Continued

SAWYER v. WHITLEY 505 U.S. 333 (1992)—cont'd

been sentenced, so that the court may reach the merits of the claim... We affirm the Court of Appeals, and hold that, to show actual innocence, one must show by clear and convincing evidence that, but for a constitutional error, no reasonable jury would have found the petitioner eligible for the death penalty under the applicable state law... Under Louisiana law, petitioner is eligible for the death penalty because he was convicted of first-degree murder—that is, an intentional killing while in the process of committing an aggravated arson—and because, at the sentencing phase, the jury found two valid aggravating circumstances: that the murder was committed in the course of an aggravated arson and that the murder was especially cruel, atrocious, and heinous. The psychological evidence petitioner alleges was kept from the jury due to the ineffective assistance of counsel does not relate to petitioner's guilt or innocence of the crime. Neither does it relate to either of the aggravating factors found by the jury that made the petitioner eligible for the death penalty. Even if this evidence had been before the jury, it cannot be said that a reasonable juror would not have found both of the aggravating factors that make the petitioner eligible for the death penalty. Therefore, as to this evidence, petitioner has not shown that there would be a fundamental miscarriage of justice for the Court to fail to reexamine the merits of this successive claim."

CASE SIGNIFICANCE: This case is significant because it limited the ability of capital petitions to file a claim of actual innocence. It also established a standard for claims of actual innocence, which is as follows: A petitioner must show through clear and convincing evidence that were it not for a constitutional error, no reasonable juror would have found the petitioner eligible for the death penalty under the applicable state law. The rule on claims of actual innocence was first articulated by the Court in *Murray v. Carrier*,[97] when it said that despite the fact that the defendant could not show cause as to why he failed to meet procedural rules, the Court would nonetheless entertain a petition of an inmate who was unjustly incarcerated due to actual innocence because not doing so would be a miscarriage of justice. In *Smith v. Murray*,[98] the Court further acknowledged that innocence may also be claimed because of a constitutional error during sentencing that "precluded the development of true facts or resulted in the admission of false ones." Thus, the Court affirmed that any errors that affect the mitigation of evidence during the sentencing phase of a capital trial could be used to buttress a claim of actual "sentencing" innocence. However, in *Sawyer* the Court reconsidered its previous rulings and instead opined that capital petitioners must show "by clear and convincing evidence that were it not for a constitutional error, no reasonable juror would have found the petitioner eligible for the death penalty under the applicable state law." Thus, the Court now requires that a petitioner demonstrate, through clear and convincing evidence, that a constitutional error (proving actual innocence) would nullify his death penalty eligibility because such error would cancel out an aggravating factor used by the jury when deliberating whether to impose the death penalty.

HERRERA v. COLLINS 506 U.S. 390 (1993)

CAPSULE: A claim of actual innocence based on newly discovered evidence is not a ground for federal habeas relief in the absence of an independent constitutional violation in the criminal proceeding itself.

FACTS: Leonel Torres Herrera was charged with the capital murders of police officers Carrisalez and Rucker in the state of Texas. At his trial in 1982 for the murder of Carrisalez, Herrera was convicted and sentenced to death based on the testimony of two eyewitnesses, a significant amount of circumstantial evidence, and Herrera's handwritten letter admitting his guilt. Later that same year, Herrera pled guilty to the capital murder of Rucker. After filing a series of unsuccessful judicial appeals seeking a reversal of his conviction and sentence, Herrera filed for habeas corpus relief in 1991 on grounds that newly discovered evidence demonstrated that his brother

Continued

---

[97]*Murray v. Carrier*, 477 U.S. 478 (1986).
[98]*Smith v. Murray*, 477 U.S. 527 (1986).

HERRERA v. COLLINS 506 U.S. 390 (1993)—cont'd

had committed the capital murders. Herrera's claim of actual innocence was denied by the state district court. In 1992, Herrera filed a habeas petition in federal court alleging actual innocence, and thus, that his death sentence was in violation of the Eighth Amendment and Fourteenth Amendment. Although the federal district court dismissed most of Herrera's claims because of its belief that the petition was filed for disingenuous reasons and thus constituted an abuse of the writ of habeas corpus, the court granted a stay of execution so that Herrera could present his newly discovered evidence in state district court. However, the state district court dismissed his claim. On appeal, the Fifth Circuit Court of Appeals held that no evidence existed to exculpate Herrera and determined that the claim of actual innocence was disingenuous and therefore an abuse of the writ of habeas corpus. The court further held that, absent a constitutional error at trial, a claim of actual innocence was not grounds for habeas relief. Herrera appealed to the Supreme Court.

ISSUE: Is a claim of actual innocence based on newly discovered evidence a ground for habeas corpus relief absent a constitutional error during a criminal proceeding? NO.

HOLDING: A defendant's showing of innocence, and a constitutional claim for relief based upon that showing, must be evaluated in light of the previous proceedings. Absent an independent constitutional violation occurring in the state criminal proceeding, claims of actual innocence based on newly discovered evidence are not sufficient to constitute grounds for federal habeas relief.

REASON: "Claims of actual innocence based on newly discovered evidence have never been held to state a ground for federal habeas relief absent an independent constitutional violation occurring in the underlying state criminal proceeding. The rule is grounded in the principle that federal habeas courts sit to ensure that individuals are not imprisoned in violation of the Constitution—not to correct errors of fact. Petitioner is understandably imprecise in describing the sort of federal relief to which a suitable showing of actual innocence would entitle him. In his brief, he states that the federal habeas court should have an important initial opportunity to hear the evidence and resolve the merits of his claim. Acceptance of this view would presumably require the habeas court to hear testimony from the witnesses who testified at trial as well as those who made the statements in the affidavits that the petitioner has presented, and to determine anew whether or not petitioner is guilty of the murders. This is not to say that our habeas jurisprudence casts a blind eye toward innocence. In a series of cases, we have held that a petitioner otherwise subject to defenses of abusive or successive use of the writ may have his federal constitutional claim considered on the merits if he makes a proper showing of actual innocence. But this body of our habeas corpus jurisprudence makes clear that a claim of actual innocence is not itself a constitutional claim, but instead a gateway through which a habeas petitioner must pass to have his otherwise barred constitutional claim considered on the merits. Petitioner in this case is simply not entitled to habeas relief on the reasoning of this line of cases (see e.g., *Sawyer v. Whitley* [505 U.S. 333 (1992); *Smith v. Murray*, 477 U.S. 527 (1986)]. For he does not seek excusal of a procedural error so that he may bring an independent constitutional claim challenging his conviction or sentence, but rather argues that he is entitled to habeas relief because newly discovered evidence shows that his conviction is factually incorrect. The fundamental miscarriage of justice exception is available only where the prisoner supplements his constitutional claim with a colorable showing of factual innocence. We have never held that it extends to freestanding claims of actual innocence. Therefore, the exception is inapplicable here."

CASE SIGNIFICANCE: Claims of actual innocence may be made in habeas proceedings. These claims may include a factual showing that a petitioner is not guilty of the crime for which he or she is being prosecuted or a showing of innocence because of a constitutional error made during the criminal proceeding. However, claims of actual innocence must meet certain procedural rules. For instance, in *Sawyer v. Whitley* [505 U.S. 333 (1992)], the Court said that capital petitioners must show through clear and convincing evidence that had a constitutional error not been committed during trial or sentencing, a jury would have found the petitioner innocent of the crime. *Sawyer v. Whitley* required a showing that a constitutional error was committed during a criminal proceeding.

Continued

HERRERA v. COLLINS 506 U.S. 390 (1993)—cont'd

The significance of this case is the reaffirmation by the Supreme Court that claims of actual innocence, at least for habeas corpus review, must contain evidence that a constitutional error occurring during the trial or sentencing. Absent such showing, the petitioner is barred from using the writ of habeas corpus to file claims of actual innocence. The case is also significant because the Court said that a court in a habeas proceeding is not a trier of fact or one that corrects errors of fact but rather examines procedural constitutional errors in a criminal proceeding. The Court also reaffirmed its respect for the trial courts' proceedings, saying that "because the courts have considerable expertise in matters of criminal procedure... we have exercised substantial deference to legislative judgments in this area."

STEWART v. MARTINEZ-VILLAREAL 523 U.S. 637 (1998)

CAPSULE: A capital defendant who has already filed a previous habeas corpus appeal on grounds that he is incompetent to be executed can file a successive appeal on the same issue if his first appeal was dismissed as premature and therefore never adjudicated.

FACTS: Martinez-Villareal was convicted of murder and sentenced to death in Arizona. After filing several direct appeals, which were unsuccessful, he then sought habeas corpus relief in the state court but was denied. Then he filed three subsequent habeas corpus petitions at the federal level, and those too were denied on grounds that they contained claims that had not been exhausted at the state level. In his fourth habeas petition, Martinez-Villareal asserted, among other issues, that he was incompetent to be executed. He argued that according to *Ford v. Wainwright* (1986), his life should be spared due to his mental impairment. Most of the claims in the latter petition were dismissed, but since his death warrant had not been issued, the *Ford* claim was judged to be premature by the Ninth Circuit Court. When the state of Arizona issued a death warrant and the Arizona Supreme Court ruled that Martinez-Villareal was competent to be executed, he then filed his successive petition arguing incompetence to be executed. The Ninth Circuit Court granted a stay of execution and concluded that he did not need a certificate of appealability (COA) to file his petition with the district court. The court reasoned that since his original *Ford* petition was deemed premature and consequently dismissed on technical grounds rather than dismissed on merit, it did not consider his *Ford* claim a second or successive petition under the auspices of the AEDPA. The Supreme Court agreed with the Ninth Circuit Court's opinion and further noted that a literal interpretation of the AEDPA's successive petition provision (e.g., 28 U.S.C. §2244(b)(1)) would be too restrictive.

ISSUE: Can a capital defendant who has already filed a previous habeas corpus appeal on grounds that he is incompetent to be executed file a successive appeal on the same issue? YES.

HOLDING: When a defendant's first habeas corpus petition is dismissed as premature, he/she may file a subsequent habeas petition on the same grounds. The second petition does not violate the AEDPA's successive petition rule because the first petition was not adjudicated.

REASON: "This may have been the second time that respondent had asked the federal courts to provide relief on his *Ford* claim, but this does not mean that there were two separate applications, the second of which was necessarily subject to §2244(b). There was only one application for habeas relief, and the District Court ruled (or should have ruled) on each claim at the time it became ripe. Respondent was entitled to an adjudication of all of the claims presented in his earlier, undoubtedly reviewable, application for federal habeas relief. The Court of Appeals was therefore correct in holding that respondent was not required to get authorization to file a 'second or successive' application before his *Ford* claim could be heard. If the State's interpretation of "second or successive" were correct, the implications for habeas practice would be far-reaching and seemingly perverse."

Continued

STEWART v. MARTINEZ-VILLAREAL 523 U.S. 637 (1998)—cont'd

"We believe that respondent's *Ford* claim here—previously dismissed as premature—should be treated in the same manner as the claim of a petitioner who returns to a federal habeas court after exhausting state remedies. True, the cases are not identical; respondent's *Ford* claim was dismissed as premature, not because he had not exhausted state remedies, but because his execution was not imminent and therefore his competency to be executed could not be determined at that time. But in both situations, the habeas petitioner does not receive an adjudication of his claim. To hold otherwise would mean that a dismissal of a first habeas petition for technical procedural reasons would bar the prisoner from ever obtaining federal habeas review. Thus, respondent's *Ford* claim was not a "second or successive" petition under §2244(b) and we have jurisdiction to review the judgment of the Court of Appeals on the State's petition for certiorari. But for the same reasons that we find we have jurisdiction, we hold that the Court of Appeals was correct in deciding that respondent was entitled to a hearing on the merits of his *Ford* claim in the District Court."

CASE SIGNIFICANCE: The AEDPA has been described as one of the most restrictive pieces of legislation to affect the ability of death row inmates from filing habeas corpus petitions. One of the provisions of the AEDPA is a limit on the number of appeals that can be filed. Specifically, 28 U.S.C. §2244(b)(1) prohibits habeas corpus petitions of previously filed or litigated claims. However, the provision does not clarify subsequent petitions of unlitigated or unadjudicated claims. In several cases, including *Stewart v. Martinez-Villareal*, the Court has refrained from placing a limit on the numerical sequence of petitions. In the case of Martinez-Villareal, the issue before the Court was whether a successive petition could be filed or whether it would violate the provisions of the AEDPA. The Court ruled that an inmate may file a second petition of a previously filed claim because the first claim was dismissed as premature and thus not adjudicated. It further noted that not allowing a subsequent petition of a previous unadjudicated claim would be too restrictive. The dissenting justices, however, argued that allowing a second petition runs counter to the plain language of the AEDPA and allows inmates to delay their execution.

FELKER v. TURPIN 518 U.S. 651 (1996)

CAPSULE: The Antiterrorism and Effective Death Penalty Act (AEDPA) of 1996 does not preclude a court from accepting an application for habeas corpus relief, nor does the Act violate the Constitution's suspension clause.

FACTS: Felker was convicted of murder and other crimes in Georgia and was sentenced to death in state court. He was denied relief on direct appeal in two state collateral proceedings and in federal habeas corpus proceedings. While he was awaiting execution, the AEDPA of 1996 was enacted. It provides for dismissal of a claim presented in a state prisoner's second or successive federal habeas application if the claim was also presented in a prior application or dismissal of a claim that was not presented in a prior federal application, unless certain conditions apply.

Felker asked to file a second federal habeas petition, but his motion was denied by the Eleventh Circuit Court of Appeals on the ground that the claims raised had not been presented in his first petition and did not meet the conditions specified in sections of the Act. He then appealed to the U.S. Supreme Court.

ISSUES:
1. Does the Antiterrorism and Effective Death Penalty Act of 1996 preclude a court from accepting an application for habeas corpus relief? NO.
2. Does the AEDPA violate the Constitution's suspension clause, which provides that the privilege of the writ of habeas corpus shall not be suspended? NO.

Continued

FELKER v. TURPIN 518 U.S. 651 (1996)—cont'd

HOLDING:

1. The AEDPA does not preclude the Court from entertaining an application for habeas corpus relief, but it does affect the standards governing the granting of such relief.
2. The AEDPA does not violate the Constitution's suspension clause.

REASON: "[W]e conclude that Title 1 of the Act has not repealed our authority to entertain original habeas petitions, for reasons similar to those stated in Yerger. No provision of Title 1 mentions our authority to entertain original habeas petitions; in contrast, Section 103 amends the Federal Rules of Appellate Procedure to bar considerations of original habeas petitions in the courts of appeals. Although Section 106(b)(3)(E) precludes us from reviewing, by appeal or petition for certiorari, a judgment on an application for leave to file a second habeas petition in district court, in makes no mention of our authority to hear habeas petitions filed as original matter in this Court.

"The Act requires a habeas petitioner to obtain leave from the court of appeals before filing a second habeas petition in the district court. But this requirement simply transfers from the district court to the court of appeals a screening function which would previously have been performed by the district court as required by 28 U.S. Section 2254 Rule 9(b)... In *McCleskey v. Zant*, 499 U.S. 467 (1991), we said that 'the doctrine of abuse of the writ refers to a complex and evolving body of equitable principles informed and controlled by historical usage, statutory developments, and judicial decisions.' The added restrictions which the Act places on second habeas petitions are well within the compass of this evolutionary process, and we hold that they do not amount to a 'suspension' of the writ contrary to Article 1, Section 9."

CASE SIGNIFICANCE: The Antiterrorism and Effective Death Penalty Act was passed by Congress in 1996 and contains complex provisions. One provision requires the dismissal of any claim in a habeas corpus case that was raised in a prior application by the same petitioner. It also sets tough standards for claims that are presented to the court for the first time in a second petition. These standards provide for the dismissal of the claim unless: (1) the claim relies on a new, previously unavailable rule of constitutional law that has been made retroactive to cases, and (2) the factual basis for the claim could not have been discovered previously through the exercise of due diligence, and if proven, would be sufficient to establish by clear and convincing evidence that were it not for constitutional error no reasonable fact finder would have found the defendant guilty of the offense.

These provisions make it difficult for prisoners to file a second habeas case and were therefore challenged in this case. The Supreme Court concluded that these provisions did not affect the Court's jurisdiction to issue writs of habeas corpus under prior federal law (28 U.S.C. §§ 2241 and 2254); therefore, the Court still exercised jurisdiction over habeas cases. The Court also said that the law does not violate the suspension clause of the Constitution (which provides that the "privilege of the Writ of Habeas Corpus shall not be suspended") because the law "simply transfers from the district court to the court of appeals a screening function which would previously have been performed by the district court." The Court concluded, however, that the prisoner in this case did not meet the "exception circumstances" standard set by the Antiterrorism and Effective Death Penalty Act and therefore his habeas petition could not succeed.

NELSON v. CAMPBELL 541 U.S. 637 (2004)

CAPSULE: An inmate who challenges the method by which he is to be executed, and not the constitutionality of his death sentence, can use a Section 1983 lawsuit as a legal remedy to temporarily halt his execution.

FACTS: In 2004, with only three days before his impending death by lethal injection in Alabama, Nelson filed a Section 1983 lawsuit to temporarily halt his execution on grounds that the use of a "cut-down" procedure, which required making an incision into his arm or leg in order to gain access to his veins, violated the Eighth Amendment's ban against cruel and unusual punishment. Nelson, who severely compromised his veins with years of

Continued

NELSON v. CAMPBELL 541 U.S. 637 (2004)—cont'd

drug abuse, claimed that the procedure would cause him unnecessary pain. Because Nelson had already filed a habeas petition that was denied, the district court dismissed his Section 1983 lawsuit, saying it was the functional equivalent of a second or successive habeas appeal, which is prohibited under the AEDPA. The Eleventh Circuit Court of Appeals held that challenges to a method of execution fall under the domain of habeas corpus, and because Nelson had already filed an unsuccessful habeas petition, his most recent challenge was barred by the AEDPA.

ISSUE: Can a Section 1983 lawsuit be used by an inmate who wants to challenge only the method by which he will be executed but not the constitutionality of the death penalty per se and/or his impending execution? YES.

HOLDING: A Section 1983 lawsuit is the appropriate legal remedy to use when seeking to temporarily halt an execution on grounds that the methods used to cause death violate the cruel and unusual punishment clause of the Eighth Amendment.

REASON: "Section 1983 must yield to the federal habeas statute where an inmate seeks injunctive relief challenging the facts of his conviction or the duration of his sentence. Such claims fall within the core of habeas. By contrast, constitutional claims challenging confinement conditions fall outside of that core and may be brought under Section 1983. The Court need not reach here the difficult question of how method of execution claims should be classified generally. Respondents claim that because the cut-down is part of the execution procedure, petitioner is actually challenging the fact of his execution. However, that venous access is a necessary prerequisite to execution does not imply that a particular means of gaining such access is likewise necessary. A fair reading of the complaint leaves no doubt that petitioner sought to enjoin the cut-down, not his execution by lethal injection.

:Respondents are incorrect that a reversal here would open the floodgates to all manner of method of execution and last-minute stay requests. Because this Court does not here resolve the question of how to treat method of execution claims generally, the instant holding is extremely limited. And the ability to bring a Section 1983 claim does not free inmates from the substantive and procedural limitations of the Prison Litigation Reform Act of 1995."

CASE SIGNIFICANCE: This case is significant because it was the first time since the 1940s, in *Louisiana ex rel. Francis v. Resweber*, that the Court heard a method-of-execution case. In addition, it is significant because the Court held that a Section 1983 lawsuit may be used to challenge the manner in which an inmate will be executed, thus seemingly circumventing the rules of habeas corpus and the AEDPA. The Court held that because Nelson was only challenging the cut-down procedure and not the fact or constitutionality of his scheduled execution, a habeas petition would not be the appropriate legal remedy to use.

In anticipation that its decision would open the floodgates to all method of execution claims and pleas for last-minute stays of execution, the Court held that it is uncertain whether all method-of-execution challenges would fall under the domain of Section 1983 and that its ruling was "extremely limited." It also noted that Section 1983 challenges are not without substantive and procedural prerequisites. The Prison Reform Litigation Act of 1995 establishes rules that inmates must follow when seeking to prevent the state from fully effectuating a court order, such as the particular method of execution, and gives significant deference to the state. The Act states that before a court grants an inmate injunctive relief, it must "give substantial weight to any adverse impact on... the operation of the criminal justice system caused by the relief." In addition, similar to the provisions of the AEDPA, inmates must exhaust available state administrative remedies prior to using a Section 1983 lawsuit. The Act also grants courts the ability to dismiss suits that are "frivolous and/or malicious."

In 2006, the Court again heard a method-of-execution challenge in *Hill v. McDonough*. In *Hill*, the Court echoed its decision in *Nelson* and held that if an inmate challenges the lawfulness of his death sentence, then habeas corpus and the rules specified by the AEDPA govern such challenge. However, if an inmate challenges only the method by which he is to be executed and only seeks to temporarily delay such execution, then Section 1983 is the appropriate remedy. It added that a Section 1983 lawsuit does not entitle inmates to permanently delay their execution, but it may provide them with a temporary delay of their execution to allow the state sufficient time to reconsider the method by which it executes inmates.

HOUSE v. BELL 547 U.S. 518 (2006)

CAPSULE: A petitioner who fails to raise claims in post-conviction proceedings as to actual innocence is not barred from raising such claims under habeas corpus because they fall within the purview of the actual innocence exception to procedurally defaulted claims and not under the domain of the AEDPA.

FACTS: Paul Gregory House was convicted and sentenced to death for the murder of Carolyn Muncey. At trial, the state presented false statements made by House, FBI tests showing that semen consistent with House's was present on Mrs. Muncey's nightgown and underwear, and tests showing that small bloodstains consistent with Mrs. Muncey's blood type were found on House's jeans. House challenged the semen and bloodstains used at trial and presented other evidence, including an alleged confession that Muncey's husband committed the murder. The district court denied relief, holding that House had not demonstrated actual innocence nor had he presented new evidence that mitigated his death sentence. The Sixth Circuit Court of Appeals granted a certificate of appealability under the provisions of the AEDPA and denied relief because House's claim was procedurally defaulted because he had not raised all his claims (such as ineffective assistance of counsel and actual innocence) in prior post-conviction proceedings. Under Tennessee law, House's claims were barred because claims not raised in prior proceedings are presumptively waived.

ISSUE: Is a petitioner barred from filing a habeas petition on grounds of actual innocence because he failed to raise all claims in prior post-convictions proceedings? NO.

HOLDING: If a petitioner has a defaulted petition due to not raising all issues in prior post-conviction petitions, habeas relief may be granted if the petitioner demonstrates cause for the default and presents new evidence that, if shown to the jurors, it is more likely than not that no reasonable juror would have found him guilty beyond a reasonable doubt.

REASON: "To implement the general principle that comity and finality must yield to the imperative of correction a fundamentally unjust incarceration, this Court has ruled that prisoners asserting innocence as a gateway to defaulted claims must establish that, in light of new evidence, it is more likely than not that no reasonable juror would have found petitioner guilty beyond a reasonable doubt [*Schlup v. Delo*, 513 U.S. 298, (1995)]. Several features of the *Schlup* standard bear emphasis here... First, while the gateway claim requires new reliable evidence not presented at trial, the habeas court must assess the likely impact of all the evidence on reasonable jurors. Second, rather than requiring absolute certainty about guilt or innocence, a petitioner's burden at the gateway stage is to demonstrate that more likely than not, in light of the new evidence, no reasonable juror would find him guilty beyond a reasonable doubt. Contrary to the state's arguments, the standard of review in... the Antiterrorism and Effective Death Penalty Act of 1996 is inapplicable here."

CASE SIGNIFICANCE: This case is significant because the Court revisited the issue of actual innocence and clarified the gateway standard of proof, which is consistent with the Court's previous ruling in *Schlup v. Delo*. After hearing new evidence presented by House as to his innocence, the Court held that House fell within the procedural default exception and that "it is more likely than not that no reasonable juror would have found him guilty beyond a reasonable doubt." The Court also noted that a gateway habeas corpus claim of actual innocence requires the habeas court to consider all evidence presented at the original trial and newly discovered evidence. The Court further clarified the position of the AEDPA under the procedural default exception in actual innocence claims. Because the claim did not involve a violation of the statute of limitations nor involved a same-claim successive petition but rather was only a defaulted claim, the Court held that the AEDPA had no bearing on the case.

LAWRENCE v. FLORIDA 549 U.S. 327 (2007)

CAPSULE: The AEDPA does not suspend or "toll" the one-year statute of limitations if a defendant is awaiting a decision by the U.S. Supreme Court and then files a habeas corpus petition well after the statute of limitations has expired.

FACTS: Lawrence, a death row inmate, filed for state post-conviction relief 364 days after his conviction became final. The trial court denied relief, as did the state supreme court and later the U.S. Supreme Court. The statute of limitation was "tolled" during the time that the Florida courts heard Lawrence's petitions. However, while the post-conviction petition was pending in the U.S. Supreme Court, Lawrence filed a habeas corpus petition with the U.S. District Court—113 days after the state supreme court's decision in his post-conviction appeal. The district court dismissed the petition on grounds that it was untimely because the statute of limitation, per the provisions of the Antiterrorism and Effective Death Penalty Act of 1996, had expired. The Eleventh Circuit Court of Appeals affirmed the decision of the district court.

ISSUE: Is the AEDPA's statute of limitations suspended or "tolled" while a defendant awaits the decision of a habeas petition by the U.S. Supreme Court? NO.

HOLDING: Although the statute of limitations may be suspended while an inmate awaits a response or decision by a state court, which is the final court to resolve post-conviction petitions, it is not "tolled" when an inmate awaits a decision by the U.S. Supreme Court, because the Court is not usually the final court to resolve a post-conviction petition.

REASON: "Read naturally, the statute's [AEDPA] text means that the statute of limitations is tolled only while state courts review the application. A state post-conviction application 'remains pending' until the application has achieved final resolution through the state's post-conviction procedures. This Court is not a part of those procedures, which end when the state courts have finally resolved the application. The application is therefore not pending after the state court's post-conviction review is complete. If it were, it is difficult to understand how a state prisoner could exhaust state post-conviction remedies without filing a certiorari petition. Yet state prisoners need not petition for certiorari to exhaust state remedies."

CASE SIGNIFICANCE: This case is significant because the Court clarified the statute of limitations provision of the AEDPA. It held that the AEDPA does not suspend or "toll" the one-year statute of limitations if a defendant is awaiting a decision by the U.S. Supreme Court and then files a habeas corpus petition well after such limitation has expired. Thus, the Court reasoned that the statute of limitations may be suspended while an inmate awaits a response or decision by a state court, which is the final court to resolve post-conviction petitions, but not the U.S. Supreme Court, because the Court "rarely grants review of state post-conviction proceedings" and is thus not usually the final court to resolve a post-conviction petition. The AEDPA statute of limitations is suspended only to await a decision by a state court.

The case is also significant because the Court stood by the restrictions of the AEDPA and with its stance to halt tactics to delay proceedings. The strict interpretation is consistent with the Court's enduring attempt to "balance the societal interests of finality, comity, and conservation of scarce judicial resources" by ensuring that inmates first exhaust all state remedies before filing a habeas petition in federal court and by encouraging inmates to file petitions on a timely basis. According to the Court, allowing inmates to default on the statute of limitations period would only motivate them to file petitions as a tactic to delay proceedings, which runs counter to the goal of the AEDPA.

SKINNER v. SWITZER 562 U.S. ___ (2011)

CAPSULE: A capital defendant who seeks access to DNA evidence may file a civil claim under 42 U.S.C. §1983 to prove his innocence. However, a §1983 lawsuit cannot be used by inmates seeking reversal of a conviction and/or release from prison.

FACTS: Henry Skinner was convicted of murder and sentenced to death in Texas for the killing of his girlfriend and her children. He maintained his innocence, however, claiming that he was too inebriated and under the influence of several drugs to have committed the murders. Instead, Skinner accused his girlfriend's uncle as the murderer. Six years after his conviction, the state of Texas passed legislation allowing inmates to request DNA testing of previously untested evidence. Skinner petitioned the court to test evidence such as knives, an axe handle, vaginal swabs, fingernail clippings, and hair samples. His motion was denied and the ruling was affirmed by the Texas Court of Criminal Appeals. Skinner then sought relief under §1983, noting that the state had violated his Fourteenth Amendment right to due process by denying his request for DNA testing. The magistrate judge dismissed his §1983 lawsuit on grounds that §1983 cannot be used for such post-conviction requests and further stated that the appropriate vehicle should be a habeas corpus appeal. Both the district court and the Fifth Circuit Court affirmed the decision to dismiss his §1983 lawsuit. The U.S. Supreme Court reversed the decision and ruled that §1983 can be used to prove a claim of innocence.

ISSUE: Can 42 U.S.C. §1983 be used by a capital defendant to seek DNA testing of evidence that may prove his innocence? YES.

HOLDING: A §1983 lawsuit can be used for claims of actual innocence so long as the inmate is not seeking reversal of his conviction and/or release from prison. Due to the fact that Skinner was only using the civil lawsuit to request testing of DNA evidence and not a reversal of his conviction, a §1983 lawsuit is the appropriate remedy.

REASON: "When may a state prisoner, complaining of unconstitutional state action, pursue a civil rights claim under § 1983, and when is habeas corpus the prisoner's sole remedy? This Court has several times considered that question. Pathmarking here is *Heck v. Humphrey*, 512 U.S. 477 (1994). Plaintiff in that litigation was a state prisoner serving time for manslaughter. He brought a §1983 action for damages, alleging that he had been unlawfully investigated, arrested, tried, and convicted. Although the complaint in Heck sought monetary damages only, not release from confinement, we ruled that the plaintiff could not proceed under §1983. Any award in his favor, we observed, would "necessarily imply" the invalidity of his conviction. See *id.*, at 487. When 'a judgment in favor of the plaintiff would necessarily imply the invalidity of his conviction or sentence,' the Court held, §1983 is not an available remedy. But if... the plaintiff's action, even if successful, will not demonstrate the invalidity of [his conviction or sentence], the [§ 1983] action should be allowed to proceed...."

"Measured against our prior holdings, Skinner has properly invoked §1983. Success in his suit for DNA testing would not "necessarily imply" the invalidity of his conviction. While test results might prove exculpatory, that outcome is hardly inevitable; as earlier observed, results might prove inconclusive or they might further incriminate Skinner."

CASE SIGNIFICANCE: A habeas corpus appeal is generally the most common method for post-conviction relief. When filing such an appeal, inmates are seeking release from confinement. Recently, death row inmates are turning to 42 U.S.C. §1983 as an additional legal tool. However, §1983 is a civil lawsuit and is limited in scope. Inmates using this civil remedy cannot use it to seek release from prison but rather only to ask the court to review conditions of confinement. In the case of Skinner, he was asking the court to test DNA evidence in accordance to a Texas law that allowed for such actions. Thus, Skinner was not seeking release from prison and/or a reversal of his conviction. He was petitioning the court to test evidence. Both the district court and the Fifth Circuit Court ruled that Skinner's claim fell under the purview of a habeas petition and noted that his allegation that Texas violated his due process rights under the Fourteenth Amendment for refusing to test evidence is not cognizable under §1983. The Supreme Court disagreed and ruled that Skinner's claim was cognizable under §1983. The Court's ruling did not reverse Skinner's conviction. In fact, the Court was quick to state that §1983 is not an appropriate remedy for

Continued

SKINNER v. SWITZER 562 U.S. ___ (2011)—cont'd

inmates seeking a reversal of their conviction. In this case, even if Skinner won his §1983 lawsuit, it would not invalidate his conviction or sentence. The only result would be a new trial.

Although this case provides a narrow window for death row inmates to seek some relief, the dissenting justices in this case, including Justices Kennedy, Thomas, and Alito, worried that the ruling in Skinner may have opened the window of opportunity too much. They argued that this may provide inmates with "a roadmap" to delay their execution and to circumvent the AEDPA.

Key Terms

Antiterrorism and Effective Death Penalty Act of 1996 (AEDPA)
certificate of appealability (COA)
good faith/bad faith rule
harmful errors
harmless errors
Herrera v. Collins
innocence
Lawrence v. Florida
McCleskey v. Zant
Nelson v. Campbell
Sawyer v. Whitley
Section 1983 (U.S. Code Section 1983)
Skinner v. Switzer
statute of limitations
Stewart v. Martinez-Villareal
successive petitions
suspension clause
writ of habeas corpus

CRITICAL THINKING QUESTIONS

1. The writ of habeas corpus is found in the suspension clause of the U.S. Constitution. Explain why the writ has been described as a "safety valve."

2. Habeas corpus has remained one of the most significant ways in which state prison inmates, confined in violation of the Constitution, could have their confinement reviewed by federal courts. How do the cases of *Salinger v. Loisel* (1924), *Wong Doo v. United States* (1924), and *Sanders v. United States* (1963) impact inmates' ability to file habeas corpus appeals?

3. After the Supreme Court issued its decision in *Gregg v. Georgia* (1976), the legal landscape for filing successive petitions changed for death row inmates. How and to what extent did *Gregg* impact inmates' use of habeas corpus?

4. The AEDPA is perhaps the most significant piece of legislation that affects the ability of inmates to file habeas corpus petitions. Explain the provisions of the AEDPA with respect to successive petitions, the statute of limitations, and the certificate of appealability.

5. The Supreme Court has ruled on several cases since the passage of the AEDPA. Explain how *Stewart v. Martinez-Villareal* (1998), *Slack v. McDaniel* (2000), and *Burton v. Stewart* (2007) impacted the debate over successive or second petitions.

6. In *Holland v. Florida*, the Supreme Court elaborated on the AEDPA's statute of limitations and the equitable tolling test. What criteria does the Court use to determine when the statute of limitations should be tolled or temporarily suspended?

7. *Gonzalez v. Thaler* (2012) was a salient case because it explained the triggering event for the AEDPA's statute of limitations. What impact does this case have for state indigent defendants?

8. The AEDPA allows habeas corpus petitions on grounds of innocence. Explain the difference between gateway innocence claims and actual innocence claims. Also, what is the legal threshold for actual innocence claims as explained by the Court in *Sawyer v. Whitley* (1992)?

9. Recently, death row inmates have resorted to using Section 1983 lawsuits to challenge the constitutionally of methods of execution. Explain the Court's rulings in *Nelson v. Campbell* (2004), *Hill v. McDonough* (2006), and *Skinner v. Switzer* (2011). Also, explain the Court's view on whether Section 1983 can be used to overturn a conviction.

Internet Resources

Legal Information Institute, Cornell University Law School
www.law.cornell.edu/wex/habeas_corpus

Center for the Preservation of Habeas Corpus
www.habeascorpus.net/asp/

Legal Information Institute, Cornell University Law School
www.law.cornell.edu/uscode/text/28/2254

PBS, Frontline
www.pbs.org/wgbh/pages/frontline/shows/execution/readings/speed.html

Evolving Standards of Decency and the Eighth Amendment's Ban on Cruel and Unusual Punishment 11

CHAPTER OUTLINE

I INTRODUCTION

Probably the oldest and most persistent constitutional issue raised in regard to the death penalty is the Eighth Amendment's ban on cruel and unusual punishment. Throughout its history in the United States, the death penalty has faced challenges of being excessively cruel and unusual, evoking the use of such adjectives as "wanton," "freakish," "arbitrary," and "capricious."[1] Concern was initially focused on the method of execution. Early death penalty cases challenged firing squads, electrocution, and hanging as violating the Eighth Amendment's ban on cruel and unusual punishment. The Supreme Court decided that each of these methods was constitutionally permissible. Later cases were more concerned with the proportionality of the death penalty compared to the offense for which it was imposed. Anything less than murder (life for life) has historically been deemed unacceptable. The Court has recently reiterated this limitation by declaring that it is

---

[1]*Furman v. Georgia*, 408 U.S. 238 (1972); *Gregg v. Georgia*, 428 U.S. 153 (1976).

unconstitutional to impose the death penalty for the rape of a child when the victim is not killed. There has also been much recent concern over particular offenders for whom the death penalty may be excessive, including those who are "mentally retarded," mentally ill, or juveniles at the time of the offense. Some of the most recent attention, however, has been focused again on the method of execution, with lethal injection (both in general and in specific forms) being challenged as cruel and unusual punishment.

In this chapter, the Eighth Amendment's ban on cruel and unusual punishment as it applies to the death penalty is discussed. The chapter begins by considering the role the Eighth Amendment played in early death penalty cases that questioned the methods of execution. The issue of proportionality in the application of the death penalty is considered in light of the *Furman* and *Gregg* decisions in the 1970s. Finally, the concept of "evolving standards of decency," typically used to determine what constitutes cruel and unusual punishment, is analyzed. The Supreme Court in *Trop v. Dulles* (1958) stated that "[t]he Amendment must draw its meaning from the evolving standards of decency that mark the progress of a maturing society."[2] In this chapter, two primary factors in the contemporary assessment of this notion are considered: public opinion and international law. Both play increasingly important roles in shaping the ever-changing notion of "evolving standards of decency" and our understanding of what might constitute cruel and unusual punishment. Finally, the chapter concludes with a consideration of the recent trends in repealing the death penalty and what this might imply for future jurisprudence related to the Eighth Amendment's prohibition of cruel and unusual punishment.

‖ METHODS OF EXECUTION

The Supreme Court has historically refused to authoritatively consider whether particular execution methods are cruel and unusual and thus violate the Eighth Amendment. In two of the earliest death penalty cases heard by the Supreme Court, the Court deferred to state legislatures in the determination of appropriate execution methods. Table 11.1 indicates the various execution methods used in states that have the death penalty. The Court upheld statutes that provided for executions by shooting (*Wilkerson v. Utah*, 1878[3]), electrocution (*In re Kemmler*, 1890[4]), and hanging (*Andres v. United States*, 1948[5]) as permissible methods. Although refraining from a determination of whether particular methods might violate the Eighth Amendment, the Court did state that such punishments as "burning at the stake, crucifixion, breaking on the wheel, or the like"[6] are cruel and unusual. After many decades of silence about methods of execution, attention has more recently turned to lethal injection. Only in the last half-decade or so has the Court begun to consider this most modern of execution methods.

---

[2]*Trop v. Dulles*, 356 U.S. 86, 101 (1958).
[3]*Wilkerson v. Utah*, 99 U.S. 130 (1878).
[4]*In re Kemmler*, 136 U.S. 436 (1890).
[5]*Andres v. United States*, 333 U.S. 740 (1948).
[6]*Kemmler, supra* at 446.

A Modern Execution Methods (Lethal Injection)

Recently, questions concerning methods of execution have reemerged.[7] Members of the Supreme Court have expressed interest in considering the constitutionality of electrocution,[8] and the Ninth Circuit Court of Appeals' decision in *Fierro v. Gomez* (9th Cir. 1996) held that lethal gas was an unconstitutional method of execution.[9] Most recently, lethal injection, long considered the ultimate accomplishment in humane executions, has come under fire.[10] The three-drug protocol commonly used in executions by lethal injection (Box 11.1 describes such a protocol as previously used in Texas), a protocol typically prohibited for the euthanizing of dogs and cats under animal welfare laws due to causing excessive pain and suffering,[11] has begun to give way to a simplified single-drug protocol. In spite of such changes, controversy over, and legal challenges to, particular lethal injection drugs and methods have flourished in recent years. Moreover, availability of particular drugs has become an issue as international drug manufacturers discontinue them or refuse to sell them to states that use them for executions.

Although several stays had been granted because of issues pertaining to the constitutionality of lethal injection methods, in 2003 the Supreme Court refused to hear at least six separate appeals claiming that lethal injection was cruel and unusual in violation of the Eighth Amendment.[12] It was not until 2006 that the Court finally entertained the issue of the constitutionality of lethal injection. In *Hill v. McDonough* (2006),[13] the issue of constitutional challenges to lethal injection as a method of execution finally rose to the purview of the Supreme Court. Although lethal injection as an allowable method was not the central issue in *Hill v. McDonough*, the Court expressed increased willingness to consider the issue.[14] The decision in *Hill v. McDonough* stated that condemned inmates could challenge a state's method of execution (primarily lethal injection) under 42 U.S.C. Section 1983 in addition to seeking habeas corpus appeals. The Court finally decided to consider the constitutionality of lethal injection as an execution method in 2007 when it agreed to hear the case of *Baze v. Rees*.[15] From this point until the case was decided in April 2008, executions came to a virtual standstill as condemned inmates continued to challenge lethal injection as cruel and unusual punishment and as states awaited the Court's decision.[16] Furthermore, some states altered their statutes to allow other methods in the event that lethal injection was deemed unconstitutional (see Table 11.1).

The Court's decision in *Baze v. Rees* (2008),[17] a lengthy and fractured decision comprising seven different Justices' opinions, was that the three-drug lethal injection method under question

---

[7]Gee, Harvey, *Eighth Amendment Challenges After* Baze v. Rees: *Lethal Injection, Civil Rights Lawsuits, and the Death Penalty,* 31 B.C. Third World L.J. 217 (2011); Deborah W. Denno, *Getting to Death: Are Executions Constitutional?* 82 Iowa L. Rev. 319 (1996).

[8]*Denno, Supra.*

[9]*Fierro v. Gomez*, 77 F.3d 301 (9th Cir. 1996).

[10]Gee, *Supra.*

[11]Levine, Susan, *Death Row Appeal Over Method: Injection Is Cruel Punishment, Attorneys for Md. Killer Argue,* Washington Post, May 15, 2004 at B2.

[12]*Id.*

[13]*Hill v. McDonough*, 126 S. Ct. 2096 (2006).

[14]Greer, Megan, *Legal Injection: The Supreme Court Enters the Lethal Injection Debate*, 30 Harv. J.L. & Pub. Pol'y 767 (2007).

[15]*Baze v. Rees*, 553 U.S. 35 (2008).

[16]Greer, *supra.*

[17]*Baze v. Rees, supra.*

Table 11.1 Methods of Execution by U.S. State

State	Lethal Injection	Electrocution	Gas Chamber	Hanging	Firing Squad
Alabama	X	X			
Arizona	X		X		
Arkansas	X	X			
California	X				
Colorado	X				
Connecticut*	X				
Delaware	X			X	
Florida	X	X			
Georgia	X				
Idaho	X				X
Indiana	X				
Kansas	X				
Kentucky	X	X			
Louisiana	X				
Maryland*	X				
Mississippi	X				
Missouri	X		X		
Montana	X				
Nebraska	X				
Nevada	X				
New Hampshire	X			X	
New Mexico*	X				
North Carolina	X				
Ohio	X				
Oklahoma	X	x			x
Oregon	X				
Pennsylvania	X				
South Carolina	X	X			
South Dakota	X				
Tennessee	X	X			
Texas	X				
Utah	X				X
Virginia	X	X			
Washington	X			X	
Wyoming	X		x		

Note: A lowercase x indicates that the method is approved only if the current execution method is ever held to be unconstitutional.
*New Mexico, Connecticut, and Maryland have repealed the death penalty. However, the repeal was not retroactive, leaving inmates on death row.
Source: Death Penalty Information Center (2013). Available at: www.deathpenaltyinfo.org/methods-execution.

(see procedure in Box 11.1), which at the time was used by 30 of the 36 death penalty states, was not cruel and unusual and was thus constitutionally permissible. Upholding the most common execution method, the Court cleared the way for executions to resume across the United States. Although this decision seemed to close the door on the debate about the constitutionality of execution by lethal injection, the Court noted some potential standards regarding what might make an execution cruel and unusual and thus a violation of the Eighth Amendment. Chief Justice John Roberts, delivering the plurality opinion, noted that the mere risk of pain is not enough to violate the Eighth Amendment's prohibition on cruel and unusual punishment. Rather, the "wanton exposure to objectively intolerable risk" of pain is necessary to show such a violation.[18] Justice Clarence Thomas, in his own concurring opinion, went further, suggesting that an execution method is cruel and unusual "only if it is deliberately designed to inflict pain."[19] In the end, this was a relatively narrow decision applying only to the constitutionality of one particular execution method. Several Justices were quick to note that this was not a case about the constitutionality of the death penalty itself, but there seemed to be a suggestion by some that this broader issue was one they might be willing to consider in the future.

BOX 11.1 TEXAS LETHAL INJECTION PROCEDURE

Prior to July 18, 2012, lethal injection consisted of:

> Sodium thiopental (sedates person)
> Pancuronium bromide (muscle relaxant—collapses diaphragm and lungs)
> Potassium chloride (stops heartbeat)

The offender is usually pronounced dead approximately seven minutes after the lethal injection begins.
Cost per execution for drugs used: $86.08

After July 18, 2012, lethal injection consists of:

> Pentobarbital (barbiturate that causes death in large doses)

Cost per execution: Not reported

Source: Death Row Facts, *Texas Department of Criminal Justice (2013).*

Though the Supreme Court may have intended *Baze* to be its final say regarding the constitutionality of lethal injection, controversy over and challenges to this method of execution have not abated. Relying on the 28 U.S.C. Section 1983 claim raised in *Hill v. McDonough*, lethal injection was challenged again in *Brewer v. Landrigan*[20] on the grounds that Arizona's current lethal injection drug, obtained from a foreign source, was not FDA approved and would likely cause unnecessary pain and suffering. The district court had granted a restraining order barring the state from using the drug, but the Supreme Court dismissed the claim and vacated the restraining order. Landrigan was executed by lethal injection on October 26, 2010.

Since the *Landrigan* case, further issues with lethal injection drugs and procedure have emerged. Questions over whether particular drug protocols expose the inmate to undue risk of excessive pain and

---

[18]*Id.*
[19]*Id.*
[20]*Brewer v. Landrigan*, 131 S.Ct. 445 (2010)

suffering continue, and challenges to the methods by which lethal injection drugs are obtained and administered persist.[21] There continue to be concerns about the specific drugs being used, but we're also seeing challenges to the manner in which the drugs are chosen, obtained, and administered. California's Supreme Court has repeatedly rejected the state's lethal injection protocol as cruel and unusual.[22] And recently, Arkansas's Supreme Court struck down the state's death penalty law because it gives the state department of corrections the authority to determine the specific drugs used in lethal injection. This is something that, according to the state's Supreme Court, must be determined by the state legislature.[23] The way in which lethal injections are administered has also come under fire. Questions pertaining to the appropriate role of medical professionals (in one sense being necessary to avoid faulty application; in another sense being controversial, given the ethical standards of the medical professions) have recently been raised.[24]

Finally, as was the case in *Landrigan*, states' attempts to obtain lethal injection drugs have brought increasing scrutiny and constitutional challenges. In a recent stay of execution granted to Warren Hill in Georgia, not only was the inmate's mental status cited, but the state was rebuked for illegally obtaining the drugs to be used in his execution. Refusing to identify the source of the drugs being used (based on a recently passed state law mandating that execution methods be kept secret), Georgia had disallowed any third-party examination or inmate challenge of the execution method to ensure that it did not constitute cruel and unusual punishment in violation of the Eighth Amendment.[25] Georgia's Supreme Court granted Hill a stay, and as of this writing, the constitutional status of the state's law remains in question and Hill continues to await his fate on the state's death row.

Given the growing wave of challenges to lethal injection, several states began to change their protocols over the past several years. Many states have recently changed to a single-drug protocol rather than the historically predominant three-drug protocol. Texas, for example, changed its lethal injection method in 2012 from a three-drug protocol to a single dose of Pentobarbital, a barbiturate that is fatal in high amounts (see Box 11.1). This change brought Texas in line with standards for the humane euthanasia of animals. In spite of simplifying the drugs used for lethal injection, states continue to run into legal challenges based on the Eighth Amendment's ban on cruel and unusual punishment. But of greater emergent concern for states is the increasing difficulty in obtaining supplies of the drugs they wish to use. International (primarily European) countries are refusing to permit the export of drugs used for executions to the United States, and the few domestic manufacturers have, in some cases, halted or disrupted the production of the drugs.[26] In fact, as this is

---

[21]Gee, *Supra.*
[22]Dolan, Maura, *California will no longer pursue three-drug lethal injections*, LA Times (July 10, 2013). Accessed Aug. 5, 2013, at www.latimes.com/local/lanow/la-me-ln-lethal-injection-20130710,0,2844532.story.
[23]Brown, Robbie, *Arkansas court upends death penalty*, The New York Times (June 22, 2012). Accessed Aug. 5, 2012, at www.nytimes.com/2012/06/23/us/arkansas-justices-strike-down-death-penalty.html.
[24]Alper, Ty, *The Truth About Physician Participation in Lethal Injection Executions,* 88 N.C.L. Rev. 11 (2009-2010); Deborah W. Denno, *The Lethal Injection Quandary: How Medicine Has Dismantled the Death Penalty,* 76 Fordham L. Rev. 49 (2007–2008).
[25]Rankin, Bill, *Judge Upholds Stay of Hill's Execution,* The Atlanta Journal-Constitution (July 18, 2013). Accessed Aug. 5, 2013, at www.ajc.com/news/news/local/judge-upholds-stay-of-hills-execution/nYwF7/.
[26]Eckholm, Erik, and Katie Zezima, *States Face Shortage of Key Lethal Injection Drug,* The New York Times (Jan. 21, 2011). Accessed Aug. 5, 2013, at www.nytimes.com/2011/01/22/us/22lethal.html?_r=0.

being written, Texas (the state that uses more of these drugs than any other) is reporting that it will run out of its supply in less than a month.[27]

It may be ironic that states are experiencing greater difficulty with lethal injection, which was thought to be the most humane and noncontroversial method possible, than they have with prior techniques. Although the Supreme Court has consistently declared lethal injection constitutionally permissible, other challenges abound, and the future of lethal injection (and perhaps the death penalty) is more tenuous than many would have ever imagined. Suggestions that lethal injection may be cruel and unusual punishment raise difficult questions about the very nature of the death penalty and whether it can, in any form, comport with a desire to have humane executions.

B Botched and Failed Executions

Claims of cruel and unusual punishment in light of failed or botched executions have generally been rejected by the Supreme Court.[28] In *Louisiana ex rel. Francis v. Resweber* (1947),[29] after the first attempt at electrocution did not kill the condemned Francis, his execution was postponed to a later date. The Supreme Court declared that this was not a violation of the Eighth Amendment, calling the botched execution "an unforeseeable accident"[30] and "an innocent misadventure."[31]

Horror stories of botched executions remain today. The well-publicized botched execution by electrocution of Pedro Medina in 1997, in which the condemned's head burst into flames, spelled the end of electrocution as the most common method of execution.[32] Medina's was not an isolated case when it comes to botched executions, nor did lethal injection prove to be immune from such horrific "misadventures" (as the Court expressed it in *Resweber*).[33] There are numerous accounts of botched lethal injections, including cases in which adequate veins cannot be found, leading to repeated attempts at injection (in several cases resulting in the inmate helping to find a vein or even injecting himself), faulty injections leading to failure in the flow of drugs, violent reactions of agony when the drugs don't work properly, and even cases in which the needle has popped out and sprayed chemicals.[34]

Some have pointed to these incidents as proof that execution is equivalent to torture and thus constitutes cruel and unusual punishment. Others support the death penalty despite such occurrences and have even used botched executions to strengthen the legitimacy of the death penalty. For example, Robert Butterworth, the attorney general of Florida, made the following comment following a botched electrocution in which the condemned individual caught fire: "People who wish to commit murder,

[27]Kemp, Joe, *Texas Lethal Injection Drug to Expire, No Alternative Found: Officials*, New York Daily News (Aug. 2, 2013). Accessed on Aug. 5, 2013, at www.nydailynews.com/news/national/texas-lethal-injection-drug-expire-alternative-found-officials-article-1.1415862.
[28]Deborah W. Denno, *Execution and the Forgotten Eighth Amendment.* In James R. Acker, Robert M. Bohm, and Charles S. Lanier (eds.), America's Experiment with Capital Punishment, 547–577 (1998).
[29]Louisiana ex rel. *Francis v. Resweber*, 329 U.S. 459 (1947).
[30]*Id.* at 464.
[31]*Id.* at 470.
[32]Denno, *supra.*
[33]Radelet, Michael, Examples of Post-*Furman* Botched Executions. Accessed on Aug. 5, 2013, at www.deathpenaltyinfo.org/some-examples-post-furman-botched-executions.
[34]*Id.*

they better not do it in the state of Florida, because we may have a problem with our electric chair."[35] Though most don't sincerely wish to torture condemned inmates through execution, it's not uncommon for individuals to question any concern over the painfulness of the methods. In the words of Supreme Court Justice Antonin Scalia during oral arguments in *Baze*: "This is an execution, not surgery ... Where does that come from, that you must find the method of execution that causes the least pain?"[36]

Most politicians and policymakers, however, do not relish the horror of such execution incidents. Rather, attempts are made to "sanitize" executions and make them less dramatic, thus producing an "illusion of humaneness."[37] Stories of botched executions only serve to horrify the public and heighten concerns about the constitutionality of the death penalty under the cruel and unusual punishment clause of the Eighth Amendment. Steps have been taken to avoid this by using technology to effect increasingly reliable and "humane" execution practices.[38]

III **PROPORTIONALITY OF PUNISHMENT**

Although the Eighth Amendment's prohibition against cruel and unusual punishment has historically been applied primarily to the mode of punishment, the proportionality of punishment has also been invoked. In *Weems v. United States* (1910),[39] the Supreme Court interpreted the cruel and unusual punishment clause to include a proportionality requirement. The Court claimed that "it is a precept of justice that punishment for crime should be graduated and proportioned to the offense."[40] Proportionality has been a recurring concern in questions of constitutionality of punishment. In *Furman v. Georgia* (1972),[41] one of the primary factors that led to the temporary abolition of the death penalty was that it was applied "arbitrarily and capriciously" with little consideration of the particular crime for which it was being imposed. In 1976, when the Supreme Court considered statutes effectively reinstating the death penalty, it rejected mandatory death penalty statutes,[42] saying that the death penalty should only be imposed in response to the most extreme crimes, because this most extreme punishment is only proportional to the most extreme crimes. The Court approved only "guided discretion" statutes that contained several procedural safeguards to ensure heightened standards of reliability in the application of the death penalty.[43] One of these safeguards was a review process to ensure proportionality.

In this section, several aspects of proportionality in the context of the death penalty are considered in light of Supreme Court decisions. First, the crimes for which the death penalty has been deemed appropriate (proportional) are considered. Second, the defendant's degree of involvement in the capital murder and eligibility for the death penalty are considered. Third, the issue of proportionality review,

---

[35]Cited in Austin Sarat, WHEN THE STATE KILLS: CAPITAL PUNISHMENT AND THE AMERICAN CONDITION, at 61 (2001).
[36]www.oyez.org/cases/2000-2009/2007/2007_07_5439.
[37]Garland, David, PECULIAR INSTITUTION: AMERICA'S DEATH PENALTY IN AN AGE OF ABOLITION (2010); Robert Johnson, DEATHWORK: A STUDY OF THE MODERN EXECUTION PROCESS (2005).
[38]Sarat, *supra*.
[39]*Weems v. United States*, 217 U.S. 349 (1910).
[40]*Id.* at 367.
[41]*Furman v. Georgia, supra*.
[42]*Woodson v. North Carolina*, 428 U.S. 220 (1976); *Roberts v. Louisiana*, 428 U.S. 325 (1976).
[43]*Gregg v. Georgia, supra*; *Jurek v. Texas*, 428 U.S. 262 (1976); *Proffitt v. Florida*, 428 U.S. 242 (1976).

a procedural safeguard among those suggested in *Gregg v. Georgia* (1976), is discussed. A fourth area of proportionality issues in death penalty jurisprudence will not be discussed here; this is the issue of the type of offender for which the death penalty is appropriate. The Supreme Court has held the death penalty to be cruel and unusual when used on the mentally retarded and mentally ill as well was juveniles under a certain age. These issues are addressed in other chapters of this book.

A Types of Crimes

The earliest post-*Furman* cases to deal with proportionality of the death penalty followed closely after *Gregg* and focused on the types of crimes for which the death penalty was an appropriate punishment. Prior to *Furman*, the death penalty had been imposed for a variety of crimes, including rape, kidnapping, espionage, and treason.[44] Although some states today have statutes allowing the death penalty for crimes other than murder, no executions have been carried out for such crimes since the death penalty was reinstated.[45] Since *Gregg*, the Supreme Court has continued to maintain that the death penalty should be reserved only for murder, with the Court's strongest statement in this regard coming in its most recent decision in *Kennedy v. Louisiana* (2008).[46]

In a pair of cases decided in 1977, the Supreme Court ruled that the death penalty was disproportionate and thus violated the Eighth Amendment's prohibition of cruel and unusual punishment for the crimes of rape (*Coker v. Georgia*, 1977)[47] and kidnapping (*Eberheart v. Georgia*, 1977).[48] Coker had escaped from prison, where he was serving multiple life sentences for murder, rape, kidnapping, and aggravated assault. Subsequent to his escape, he raped a woman during the commission of a robbery. Under Georgia's statute, rape was a capital crime if committed by a person with previous felony convictions or during the commission of another felony. Coker was sentenced to death. The Supreme Court held that Georgia's statutory allowance of the death penalty for crimes other than murder was excessive and in violation of the Eighth Amendment. Coker's death sentence was overturned. The Court applied the same rationale in *Eberheart*, in which it struck down the death sentence for the crime of kidnapping. More recently, the Court has acknowledged that "[a]rmed robbery is a serious offense, but one for which the penalty of death is plainly excessive; the imposition of the death penalty for robbery, therefore, violates the Eighth and Fourteenth Amendments."[49]

The 30-year precedent that the death penalty be reserved only for murder was recently challenged in the case of *Kennedy v. Louisiana* (2008).[50] Amid increasing public outcry for harsher punishment of sex offenders and the movement in several states to amend death penalty statutes to allow for the death penalty for the rape of a child, the Court considered whether the death penalty is constitutional in such cases if the victim is not killed. Kennedy had committed a particularly brutal rape against his then-eight-year-old stepdaughter and, under Louisiana's statute allowing the death penalty for the rape

---

[44]Bohm, Robert M., DEATHQUEST: AN INTRODUCTION TO THE THEORY AND PRACTICE OF CAPITAL PUNISHMENT IN THE UNITED STATES. (2012).
[45]*Id.*
[46]*Kennedy v. Louisiana*, 554 U.S. 407 (2008).
[47]*Coker v. Georgia*, 433 U.S. 584 (1977).
[48]*Eberheart v. Georgia*, 433 U.S. 917 (1977).
[49]*Tison v. Arizona*, 481 U.S. 137, 148 (1987).
[50]*Kennedy v. Louisiana, Supra.*

of a child under 12 years old, was sentenced to death. The U.S. Supreme Court, in a five-to-four decision, held that Louisiana's statute violated the Eighth Amendment and that the death penalty could not be extended to crimes against persons in which the victim was not killed. Relying on the original notions of proportionality and limiting the use of the death penalty to only the most severe cases of murder as expressed in *Gregg* as well as the national consensus against using the death penalty for the crime of rape (it was reported that only six states have laws allowing this penalty), the Court made its strongest statement yet that the death penalty be reserved only for cases of murder.

B Degree of Involvement in Killing

In addition to being limited only to the crime of murder, the Supreme Court has considered the degree of a defendant's involvement and responsibility (meaning culpability) as important to ensuring that the death penalty is applied proportionally. In *Enmund v. Florida* (1982),[51] the Supreme Court held that the death penalty is disproportionate (and therefore in violation of the Eighth Amendment) for offenders who do not do the actual killing in the commission of a murder (such as those who only aid and abet in the commission of the murder). Again, the Supreme Court adhered to the position that the death penalty is only proportionate and therefore is constitutional when imposed on a defendant who killed someone.

However, in *Tison v. Arizona* (1987),[52] the Court retreated slightly from this stance, holding that it is constitutional to impose the death penalty on an individual who participated in a major way in the commission of a felony that resulted in murder and who acted with reckless indifference to human life. The case involved two brothers who assisted their father in his and his cellmate's escape from prison and subsequent armed robbery and murder of a family. Although the brothers did not directly participate in the actual killing of the family, their participation in the felony that led to the murder resulted in death sentences for them.

Most recently, the Court, in *Bradshaw v. Richey* (2005),[53] has held that a defendant may be given the death penalty in cases in which he fails to kill his intended victim but instead causes the death of an unintended victim. This flows logically from the *Tison* decision in that such a defendant would be causing the death of another in the process of committing a felony. The Court noted that "transferred intent" applied in this case and thus the defendant was eligible for the death penalty.[54] Citing the state death penalty statute, which states that aggravated murder requires that the defendant "intended to cause the death of *another*"[55] (emphasis added), the Court held that the intent to kill was present and thus the fact that the actual victim was not the intended victim did not reduce the murder to a non-capital one.[56]

Currently, several states are attempting to expand the death penalty to include those who, though not doing the actual killing in murder cases, participate in a way (i.e., as an accomplice) that makes them at least partially responsible for it. This challenges the *Enmund* decision but seems aligned with the more

---

[51]*Enmund v. Florida*, 458 U.S. 782 (1982).
[52]*Tison v. Arizona*, 481 U.S. 137 (1987).
[53]*Bradshaw v. Richey*, 546 U.S. 74 (2005).
[54]*Id.*
[55]Ohio Rev. Code Ann. § 2903.01 (D).
[56]*Bradshaw v. Richey, supra.*

recent *Tison* and *Bradshaw* decisions. In Virginia, for example, in each of the last five legislative sessions the legislature has considered a bill that would expand the death penalty to accomplices. Though in Virginia it has either been vetoed by the governor (as was the case under Governor Tim Kaine) or failed in committee (which was the most recent disposition),[57] expansion of the death penalty continues to be a legislative initiative in Virginia and several other death penalty states. Whether such expansions would be constitutionally permissible is yet to be debated.

C Proportionality Review

In *Weems v. United States* (1910),[58] the Supreme Court interpreted the cruel and unusual punishment clause to include the notion of proportionality of punishment in regard to the gravity of the crime. Proportionality was of primary concern to the Court when approving the new death penalty statutes in 1976. One of the important safeguards approved in *Gregg v. Georgia* (1976)[59] was proportionality review. Proportionality review constitutes the systematic review of a death sentence by comparing the particular case and its characteristics and circumstances to other similar capital cases to determine whether similar sentences were applied. The objective of such proportionality review is to ensure that like cases receive like penalties and that the death penalty is not being discriminatorily or arbitrarily imposed. Similar cases should have similar results.

In *Pulley v. Harris* (1984),[60] the Supreme Court ruled that proportionality of this form is not constitutionally mandated. The Court said that the proportionality review requested by Harris was infeasible, unnecessary, and beyond that required by the Eighth Amendment. The Court held that the more common concept of whether the punishment is appropriate for the crime, in general, is sufficient to satisfy the proportionality requirement. The Court explained the apparent contradiction of *Gregg* by noting that "[proportionality review] was considered an additional safeguard against arbitrary or capricious sentencing... [w]hile... some form of meaningful appellate review is required... those Justices did not declare that comparative review was so critical that without it the Georgia statute would not have passed constitutional muster."[61] The Court then concluded that *Gregg* and the Eighth Amendment did not require proportionality review in capital cases.

IV THE ROLE OF PUBLIC OPINION

In *Weems v. United States* (1910), the Supreme Court suggested that what constitutes "cruel and unusual punishment" evolves "as public opinion becomes enlightened by a humane justice."[62] More than 60 years later, in the landmark case of *Furman v. Georgia* (1972), Justice William J. Brennan stated: "A severe punishment must not be unacceptable to contemporary society. Rejection by society,

---

[57]http://washington.cbslocal.com/2012/02/08/bill-to-expand-death-penalty-in-virginia-dies/.
[58]*Weems v. United States, supra.*
[59]*Gregg v. Georgia, supra.*
[60]*Pulley v. Harris,* 465 U.S. 37, 45 (1984).
[61]*Id.* at 45.
[62]*Weems v. United States, supra* at 378.

of course, is a strong indication that a severe punishment does not comport with human dignity."[63] Justice Thurgood Marshall elaborated: "Where a punishment is not excessive and serves a valid legislative purpose, it still may be invalid if popular sentiment abhors it."[64] The cruel and unusual punishment clause of the Eighth Amendment is unique from other constitutional rights and mandates in that it rests on mutable standards that are representative of the population at a given time. Thus, what we deem cruel and unusual punishment changes over time. Moreover, the Supreme Court's determination of what constitutes cruel and unusual punishment at any time depends upon some sense of a national consensus, a notion driven in large part by public opinion. Indeed, since *Furman*, public support has consistently been used as a marker of evolving standards of decency and the legitimacy of capital punishment in the United States.

Since the 1970s, a majority of Americans have been in favor of capital punishment.[65] Public opinion polls show that more than 60 percent of Americans support the death penalty for the crime of murder, though there has been a general decline in that number over the last decade and a half.[66] It is important to recognize, however, that attitudes about the death penalty are not as cut-and-dried as such numbers might suggest.[67] Research has found that the public is much more conflicted about this most extreme form of punishment than once thought. Although supporting the death penalty in general, the public is less likely to support its use on certain populations, such as juvenile, mentally ill, or mentally retarded offenders.[68] Furthermore, support tends to diminish markedly as people become confronted with certain realities of the death penalty system.[69] The increasing availability of sentences of life without parole (LWOP) has added another dimension to public opinion about the death penalty. Recent data reveal that when given the alternative of LWOP, support for the death penalty drops below 50 percent.[70]

As stories of the exoneration of innocent people sentenced to death, botched executions, incompetent lawyers, possible wrongful executions, and other failures of the system are increasingly publicized, the public will likely become more ambivalent and conflicted about the death penalty.[71] This is what Supreme Court Justice Marshall suggested in his *Furman* opinion when he proposed what has come to be known as the "Marshall Hypothesis." He hypothesized that if Americans actually knew about the realities of the death penalty, they would no longer support it. In his opinion, considering the notion of the constitutionality of the death penalty resting on majority support for it, Marshall proclaimed, "[T]he question with which we must deal is not whether a substantial proportion of American citizens would today, if polled, opine that capital punishment is barbarously cruel, but whether they would find it to be so in light of all information presently available."[72] He further asserted that if the public was made aware of this information, "the great mass of citizens would conclude . . . that the death penalty is

---

[63]*Furman v. Georgia, supra* at 277.

[64]*Id.* at 332.

[65]Bohm, *supra.*

[66]See, for example, Gallup Poll results at www.gallup.com/poll/1606/death-penalty.aspx.

[67]Bohm, Robert M., Louise J. Clark, and Adrian F. Aveni, *Knowledge and Death Penalty Opinion: A Test of the Marshall Hypotheses*, 28 J. Res. in Crime & Delinquency 360 (1991).

[68]www.gallup.com/poll/1606/death-penalty.aspx; See also Ellsworth and Gross, *supra.*

[69]Bohm, Clark, and Aveni, *supra.*

[70]www.gallup.com/poll/1606/death-penalty.aspx.

[71]Baumgartner, Frank R., Suzanna L. De Boef, and Amber E. Boydstun, The Decline of the Death Penalty and the Discovery of Innocence (2008).

[72]*Furman v. Georgia,* 408 U.S. 238, 362 (1972).

immoral and therefore unconstitutional."[73] In the years following Marshall's argument in *Furman*, volumes of research have been devoted to testing his hypothesis. Much of the early research supported Marshall's hypothesis,[74] but findings became more mixed as researchers began examining the deeper foundations of death penalty attitudes and death penalty support.[75] On balance, Marshall's hypothesis appears to be only partly correct. Information and knowledge about the realities of the death penalty do, indeed, appear to impact support for its use, but that impact is found to be relatively weak and short-lived. Furthermore, a significant proportion of support for the death penalty remains resistant to information. In other words, there is a portion of death penalty supporters among the American public who will continue to support the death penalty regardless of what they learn about it. These are folks who support the death penalty more out of deeply held values or ideological principles than out of a rational consideration of its effectiveness as public policy. As some scholars have put it, support of the death penalty has a "value-expressive" function for these individuals.[76]

In spite of the findings that a portion of the U.S. citizenry supports the death penalty for more symbolic, nonrational reasons, it is undeniable that changes in the perceived effectiveness and practicality of the death penalty have effected changes to aggregate support for its continued use. As previously noted, death penalty support has been declining since the early 1990s; it would be misguided to think this had nothing to do with increasing exposure to and awareness of many of the concerning issues about the death penalty and its administration. One of the most impacting factors has no doubt been the increasing awareness of wrongful convictions and possible wrongful executions in death penalty cases (such errors in capital cases are further discussed in Chapter 12).[77] Moreover, as states' budgets are increasingly strained and as the cost of the death penalty becomes more apparent, opposition not only grows but comes from some groups not historically opposed to the death penalty.[78] A 2004 study of Texans, arguably the staunchest supporters of capital punishment, revealed that a majority supported a moratorium on the death penalty so that the system could be studied for potential flaws.[79] In some states, it has been conservative and Republican leaders (individuals historically found to be likely to support the death penalty) who have initiated efforts to abolish the death penalty for a variety of reasons, including the cost associated with administering the death penalty and errors in its application.[80] Indeed, broad-based efforts to curb the use of the death penalty are spreading across the United States.[81] Most states are seeing moratorium legislation proposed virtually every

---

[73]*Id.* at 363.

[74]Bohm, *supra.*

[75]Vollum, Scott, and Jacqueline Buffington-Vollum, *An Examination of Social-Psychological Factors and Support for the Death Penalty: Attribution, Moral Disengagement, and the Value-Expressive Function of Attitudes,* 35 AMERICAN JOURNAL OF CRIMINAL JUSTICE 15 (2010).

[76]*Id.*

[77]Baumgartner, et al., *supra.*

[78]Steiker, Carol S., and Jordan M. Steiker, Cost and Capital Punishment: A New Consideration Transforms an Old Debate, University of Chicago Legal Forum, Vol. 2010, No. 1; Harvard Public Law Working Paper No. 12-04; U. of Texas Law, Public Law Research Paper No. 208 (2010).

[79]Vollum, Scott, Dennis R. Longmire, and Jacqueline Buffington-Vollum, *Confidence in the Death Penalty and Support for Its Use: Exploring the Value-Expressive Dimension of Death Penalty Attitudes,* 21 JUSTICE QUARTERLY 521 (2004).

[80]https://www.aclu.org/blog/capital-punishment/conservative-commentators-speak-out-against-death-penalty.

[81]Bessler, John D., *Revisiting Beccaria's Vision: The Enlightenment, America's Death Penalty, and the Abolition Movement,* 4 NORTHWESTERN J. LAW AND SOC. POLICY 195 (2009).

year and, as previously mentioned, five states have abolished the death penalty in the last half-decade. In spite of some ambivalence, however, the fact remains that a majority of Americans continue to support the death penalty in principle if not in practice. This support remains a statement about standards of decency in our society, providing some foundation for Eighth Amendment jurisprudence regarding the death penalty.

In spite of the role of public opinion in Eighth Amendment jurisprudence, the Supreme Court has typically rejected public opinion polls as the actual benchmarks for a national consensus on the death penalty. The Court has opted instead for the use of state and federal legislation as indicators of what the public perceives and values.[82] The thought is that legislators act on behalf of the populace in voting for and enacting legislation, thus such legislation is an extension of public will. It follows, then, that with a majority of states (currently 32 out of 50) having laws allowing for the death penalty, there is a consensus that the death penalty is neither cruel nor unusual and thus does not violate the Eighth Amendment. With more states considering abolition of the death penalty, the question remains whether this calculus will change.

V INTERNATIONAL PERSPECTIVES

If we take the notion of evolving standards of decency beyond our borders to the realm of international law and opinion, a different view emerges. The measurement of evolving standards of decency and what constitutes cruel and unusual punishment today plays out in an increasingly global context. The policies and practices of the United States can no longer remain restricted to the purview of those within the United States. With the increasingly potent global emphasis on international law and international treaties and the added political and economic presence of coalitions like the European Union, international perspectives on actions occurring within the United States can no longer be ignored.

In 2012, the United States executed the fifth highest number of people in the world, trailing China, Iran, Iraq, and Saudi Arabia in number of executions.[83] It is estimated that over 90 percent of all executions in the world were carried out in these five countries.[84] As the international trend moves toward the abolition of the death penalty (see Box 11.2), the United States, over the last several decades, increased its use to some of the highest levels in the world.[85] These and other facts have generated a tremendous amount of criticism from human rights groups and other Western countries. In fact, the United States' use of the death penalty has been cited as one of the top international human rights concerns in recent decades.[86] The United States' execution of juveniles and foreign nationals has threatened its status in international treaties and in some cases prohibited its inclusion in such treaties altogether.[87] In 2004, the International Court of Justice (ICJ) held that the United States had violated

---

[82]Vollum, Longmire, and Buffington-Vollum, *supra.*

[83]Amnesty International. *Death Sentences and Executions 2012.* Available at: www.amnesty.org/en/library/asset/ACT50/001/2013/en/bbfea0d6-39b2-4e5f-a1ad-885a8eb5c607/act500012013en.pdf.

[84]*Id.*

[85]Hood, Roger, and Carolyn Hoyle, The Death Penalty: A Worldwide Perspective (4th ed. 2008).

[86]Trail, Rebecca, *The Future of Capital Punishment in the United States: Effects of the International Trend Toward Abolition of the Death Penalty,* 26 Suffolk Transnat'l L. Rev. 105 (2002).

[87]*Id.*

BOX 11.2 ABOLITIONIST AND RETENTIONIST COUNTRIES (AS OF DECEMBER, 2012)

Abolitionist for all crimes	97
Abolitionist for ordinary crimes only	8
Abolitionist in practice	35
Total number of abolitionist countries	140
Retentionist countries	58

Number of Countries That Have Abolished the Death Penalty (for All Crimes), by Year, 1991–2012

Countries with Executions in 2011
(in Alphabetical Order)

Afghanistan	Pakistan
Bangladesh	Palestinian Authority
Belarus	Saudi Arabia
Botswana	Somalia
China	South Sudan
Gambia	Sudan
India	Taiwan
Iran	United Arab Emirates
Iraq	USA
Japan	Yemen
North Korea	

Source: Amnesty International, Death Sentences and Executions 2012, *www.amnestyusa.org/sites/default/files/worlddpreport2012.pdf.*

the Vienna Convention by failing to allow Mexican nationals charged with capital crimes to speak to a Mexican consul.[88]

As a result of the ICJ's finding that the United States had violated the Vienna Convention, in 2008 the U.S. Supreme Court decided the case of *Medellin v. Texas*.[89] The ICJ had held that the United States violated international law in accordance with the Vienna Convention by failing to inform foreign nationals—51 of them, including Medellin, a Mexican citizen—of their Vienna Convention rights. Specifically, Medellin argued that he had not been afforded his right to contact the Mexican consulate. The ICJ ordered the United States to review the cases. Texas refused to do so in Medellin's case. Before the U.S. Supreme Court could decide the case, President George W. Bush ordered all states to review the cases as ordered by the ICJ. Texas courts rejected the President's order, maintaining that he had no authority to give such an order. The Supreme Court agreed with the Texas courts, holding that neither the President's order, the ICJ's ruling, nor the Vienna Convention hold authority over states' rights to carry out criminal procedure and, in this case, the death penalty.

In spite of recent decisions supporting U.S. sovereignty in the international arena, factors surrounding international law and opinion appear to have had some, albeit limited, impact on the Supreme Court's consideration of Eighth Amendment issues surrounding the death penalty. In *Trop v. Dulles* (1958), the case in which the Court established the notion of evolving standards of decency, international practices and perspectives were taken into account.[90] More recently, in *Atkins v. Virginia* (2002) and *Roper v. Simmons* (2005), in which the court held that the execution of the mentally retarded and juveniles, respectively, is cruel and unusual, international opinion and trends were cited as support for the contention that the death penalty has become contrary to evolving standards of decency. The dissenting justices rejected international practice or opinion as being irrelevant to the United States' use of the death penalty.[91] It has been opined, however, that as political and economic interests become more global and as more pressure is placed on the United States by the European Union and the international community in general, such factors will become increasingly relevant.[92] Indeed, as of this writing, two states (Ohio and Texas) are currently facing shortages of their lethal injection drugs in part because European countries put pressure on pharmaceutical companies, persuading them to no longer supply such drugs to the United States.[93]

VI STATES REPEALING DEATH PENALTY STATUTES

In the past six years, five states (New Jersey, New Mexico, Illinois, Connecticut, and Maryland) have abolished the death penalty. Another (New York) declined to challenge its state supreme court's decision that its death penalty statute is unconstitutional. Other states have come close to abolishing the

[88]*Mexico v. United States of America*, International Court of Justice (March 31, 2004).
[89]*Medellin v. Texas*, 552 U.S. 491 (2008).
[90]*Trop v. Dulles*, 356 U.S. 86 (1958).
[91]*Atkins v. Virginia*, 536 U.S. 304 (2002).
[92]Trail, *supra.*
[93]Kitamura, Makiko, and Adi Narayan, *Europe Pushes to Keep Lethal Injection Drugs from U.S. Prisons*, BLOOMBERG BUSINESSWEEK (Feb. 7, 2013). Available at: www.businessweek.com/articles/2013-02-07/europe-pushes-to-keep-lethal-injection-drugs-from-u-dot-s-dot-prisons.

death penalty. In California a referendum that would have abolished the death penalty failed, narrowly missing the majority needed to pass (48% of voters supported it). Several other states have had repeal bills narrowly fail to pass (see, for example, Colorado, where a bill passed the state house but not the senate), and numerous states currently have bills before their legislators.

By all measures, the death penalty is on the decline in the United States. Though executions have plateaued following a decline from the late 1990s, death sentences and death row populations continue to decline. In fact, death sentences have declined more than 75% since 1996. [94] Moreover, fewer of the states that maintain the death penalty seem to be using it. In 2012, only nine states carried out executions. Of the 32 states with the death penalty, only 20 have executed anyone in the last five years, and 13 of them have executed fewer than 10 people in the more than 35 years since *Furman*.[95] Remarkably, the states of North Carolina, South Carolina, and Virginia (the state with the second most executions in the post-*Furman* era, after Texas) had no death sentences and no executions in 2012.[96]

Assuming that these trends continue, we must ask whether and how they might bear on the Supreme Court's Eighth Amendment jurisprudence pertaining to the death penalty. In attempting to answer this question, it is important to recall the Court's reasoning in *Atkins v. Virginia* (discussed in Chapter 4) and *Roper v. Simmons* (discussed in Chapter 5). In *Atkins* and *Roper*, the Court declared the death penalty cruel and unusual for "mentally retarded" and juvenile offenders, respectively. Importantly, in each case, the Court used a calculus based on the number of states that did not allow executions of individuals in these populations. In the former, 18 of the (then) 38 states with the death penalty prohibited the execution of mentally retarded offenders. In the latter, this number was 17. When you add these numbers to the (then) 12 states that did not allow execution of *anyone*, you have a majority of states prohibiting executions of individuals from these particular populations. This, according to the Court, represented a national consensus marking currently evolved standards of decency and thus was an appropriate signifier of what constitutes cruel and unusual punishment. Using this logic, it is not difficult to determine a potential tipping point at which the death penalty, in general, may become cruel and unusual. Currently, with 32 states maintaining the death penalty, an argument could be made that it would only take eight more states repealing the death penalty (leaving a majority of states *not* allowing the death penalty) for the Eighth Amendment tide to turn and for the death penalty to be potentially deemed "cruel and unusual." This is, of course, speculative and relies on the assumption that the future Court will rely on the logic used in *Atkins* and *Roper*. And, as noted in Chapter 1, some Justices have said that only state legislatures should have the authority to abolish the death penalty. Whether this means that each state must decide this issue for itself or whether the broader consensus of states' legislatures may warrant intervention by the Court is unknown. In any case, the current trends signify changes for the death penalty in the United States. It remains to be seen where these changes might take us in the future.

---

[94]Death Penalty Information Center, *Facts About the Death Penalty* (2013). Available at: www.deathpenaltyinfo.org/documents/FactSheet.pdf.

[95]*Id.*

[96]Death Penalty Information Center, *The Death Penalty in 2012: Year-End Report* (2012). Available at: http://deathpenaltyinfo.org/documents/2012YearEnd.pdf.

VII IN SUMMARY, WHAT DO THESE CASES SAY?

Because the Eighth Amendment is inherently malleable, evolving with changing sensibilities and "standards of decency" in American society, the Supreme Court has taken steps to ensure that the death penalty does not violate current sensibilities. In an effort to maintain proportionality of punishment, the Court has remained steadfast in reserving the death penalty for only the most severe crimes of murder. Less severe crimes of rape, kidnapping, and aggravated robbery traditionally have been flatly rejected by the Court as crimes justifying the death penalty. Indeed, in its most recent case (as of this writing), the Court has once again made a strong statement against using the death penalty for crimes against persons that do not result in the death of the victim, striking down a statute allowing the death penalty for the rape of a child. Finally, the Court has held in several cases that a person may be eligible for the death penalty even if they do not commit the actual act of killing or do not kill their intended victim but cause these deaths through their commission of or participation in a felony resulting in that murder.

In spite of its concern with proportionality of punishment, the Supreme Court held that proportionality review in which a particular death sentence is systematically compared to sentences in other similar cases is not required by the Constitution. Although the death penalty should be reserved for the most serious crimes of murder, the actual sentence in an individual case is to be determined by the jury and a consideration of the individual facts and circumstances of that particular case. Proportionality of punishment is not guaranteed at this more minute level.

One area involving the Eighth Amendment and "evolving standards of decency" in which the Court has been more "hands off" is the acceptable method of execution. Hanging, firing squads, electrocution, gas chambers, and lethal injection are all currently permissible methods of execution used in the United States. The Court has not explicitly ruled against any particular method of execution but has indicated that more torturous methods such as burning, crucifixion, and breaking on the wheel violate standards of decency and thus are prohibited by the Eighth Amendment's prohibition of cruel and unusual punishment. The Court's decision in *Baze v. Rees* (2008) followed in this "hands-off" tradition. The Court, with seven Justices writing their own opinions, held that the then predominant three-drug lethal injection protocol was constitutionally permissible. Some Justices did, however, add qualifications regarding standards for cruel and unusual punishment when it comes to execution methods. The plurality opinion noted that avoidance of all risk of pain is not required for an execution method to comport with the Eighth Amendment; rather, there must be "wanton exposure to an objectively intolerable risk" or a "wanton infliction" of pain and suffering in order to be cruel and unusual. In the years since *Baze*, these standards have been and continue to be tested, with lethal injection procedures throughout the country being subjected to increasing scrutiny and state legislatures scrambling to adjust their protocols to keep up with rapidly emerging legal and practical developments.

VIII CONCLUSION

Challenges related to the prohibition of cruel and unusual punishment pervade death penalty jurisprudence and to this day continue to face the Supreme Court. The death penalty, the ultimate and most extreme punishment, will always be at the forefront as we contemplate the parameters of "evolving standards of decency." Although we continue to refine the methods of execution, attempting to imbue the death penalty with the appearance of humaneness, stories of botched executions and the unavoidable messiness of killing other human beings always lurk on the periphery of our collective vision. The death penalty, more than any other criminal justice policy, evokes stark images—images of ultimate retribution and of brutality. It has always brought controversy and polarized feelings, often exposing deep contradictions in American culture. The majority of the American public supports the death penalty, but at the same time, that majority has shrunk over the past few decades, calls for moratoriums and abolition are surging, death sentences are declining, and support for alternatives such as life in prison without parole is rivaling support for the death penalty. Moreover, the controversy about the death penalty now plays out not only within our borders but in the international arena as well.

We cannot be sure what the future holds for the death penalty, but we can be certain that the U.S. Supreme Court will continue to be confronted with the question of whether the death penalty is cruel and unusual. This becomes especially salient as more and more states abolish the death penalty. Amidst an ever-changing calculus, the Court will continue to be asked to define and redefine the evolving standards of decency as they apply to this most extreme of criminal penalties.

CASES BRIEFED IN CHAPTER 11

Case	Issue	Holding
Pulley v. Harris 465 U.S. 37 (1984)	In capital cases, does the Eighth Amendment require states to implement comparisons of particular sentences to those imposed in other similar cases?	The Eighth Amendment does not require that a state compare the sentence in the case before it with the sentence imposed in similar cases, even if asked to do so by the prisoner.
Tison v. Arizona 481 U.S. 137 (1987)	Is it constitutional to sentence to death defendants who did not do the actual killing in a capital murder?	Defendants who participate in a major way in a felony murder and who act with reckless indifference to human life, even though they do not directly inflict the act of killing, may be given the death penalty.
Baze v. Rees 553 U.S. 35 (2008)	Does Kentucky's three-drug protocol for executions by lethal injection violate the Eighth Amendment's prohibition of cruel and unusual punishment?	Kentucky's three-drug lethal injection protocol, also used by 29 other death penalty states, does not constitute cruel and unusual punishment and is thus constitutionally permissible.
Kennedy v. Louisiana 554 U.S. 407 (2008)	Is it constitutional to impose the death penalty for the crime of sexual assault against a child when the crime does not result in the victim's death?	It is a violation of the Eighth Amendment to sentence a defendant to death for the rape of a child when the crime does not result in the victim's death.

CASE BRIEFS

PULLEY v. HARRIS 465 U.S. 37 (1984)

CAPSULE: Proportionality review is not required in death penalty cases.

FACTS: Harris was convicted in a California court of the kidnapping, robbery, and first-degree murder of two boys. Having been convicted of multiple felonies, including murder, the "special circumstance" required by California law was met and a capital sentencing hearing was held to determine whether Harris would receive a death sentence or life without the possibility of parole. The jury, finding several aggravating factors, sentenced him to death. Harris challenged the sentence, maintaining that the death sentence was unconstitutional due to the fact that no proportionality review had been implemented. He argued that such a review, in which his sentence was compared with those imposed in similar capital cases, was required.

ISSUE: In capital cases, does the Eighth Amendment require states to implement comparisons of particular sentences to those imposed in other, similar cases? NO.

HOLDING: "The Eighth Amendment does not require as an invariable rule in every case that a state appellate court, before it affirms a death sentence, compare the sentence in the case before it with the sentence imposed in similar cases, even if asked to do so by the prisoner."[97]

REASON: "At the outset, we should more clearly identify the issue before us. Traditionally, 'proportionality' has been used with reference to an abstract evaluation of the appropriateness of a sentence for a particular crime. Looking to the gravity of the offense and the severity of the penalty, to sentences imposed for other crimes, and to sentencing practices in other jurisdictions, this Court has occasionally struck down punishments as inherently disproportionate, and therefore cruel and unusual, when imposed for a particular crime or category of crime. The death penalty is not in all cases a disproportionate penalty in this sense.

"In *Gregg*, six Justices concluded that the Georgia system adequately directed and limited the jury's discretion. The bifurcated proceedings, the limited number of capital crimes, the requirement that at least one aggravating circumstance be present, and the consideration of mitigating circumstances minimized the risk of wholly arbitrary, capricious, or freakish sentences. In the opinion announcing the judgment of the Court, three Justices concluded that sentencing discretion under the statute was sufficiently controlled by clear and objective standards. In a separate concurrence, three other Justices found sufficient reason to expect that the death penalty would not be imposed so wantonly, freakishly, or infrequently as to be invalid under *Furman*.

"Both opinions made much of the statutorily required comparative proportionality review. This was considered an additional safeguard against arbitrary or capricious sentencing. While the opinion of Justices Stewart, Powell, and Stevens suggested that some form of meaningful appellate review is required, those Justices did not declare that comparative review was so critical that without it the Georgia statute would not have passed constitutional muster.

"Any capital sentencing scheme may occasionally produce aberrational outcomes. Such inconsistencies are a far cry from the major systemic defects identified in Furman. As we have acknowledged in the past, 'there can be "no perfect procedure for deciding in which cases governmental authority should be used to impose death."' As we are presently informed, we cannot say that the California procedures provided Harris inadequate protection against the evil identified in Furman. The Court of Appeals therefore erred in ordering a writ of habeas corpus to issue."

Continued

---

[97]This is taken from Rolando V. Del Carmen, Susan E. Ritter, and Betsy A. Witt, Briefs of Leading Cases in Corrections (5th ed. 2008) at 296.

PULLEY v. HARRIS 465 U.S. 37 (1984)—cont'd

CASE SIGNIFICANCE: "The Supreme Court ruled in this case that state appellate courts are not constitutionally required to provide, upon request by the defendant, a 'proportionality review' of death sentences in which the court would compare the sentence in the case before it with penalties imposed in similar cases in that state. Proportionality reviews are constitutional and are provided for by law or judicial practice in some states, but such reviews are not required by the Constitution. For example, the Court found the Texas death penalty statute to be constitutional even though neither the law nor judicial practice provide for any form of proportionality review. The Court did not completely close the door to a proportionality review, however, in some extreme cases. It said: 'assuming that there could be a capital sentencing scheme so lacking in other checks or arbitrariness that it could not pass constitutional muster without comparative proportionality review, the California statute involved here is not of that sort.'"[98]

TISON v. ARIZONA 481 U.S. 137 (1987)

CAPSULE: The death penalty may be imposed on a defendant who did not actually kill the victims but participated in a major way in a felony that resulted in their murder.

FACTS: Brothers Ricky and Raymond Tison, along with other family members, planned and effected the escape of their father from prison, where he was serving a life sentence. The Tison brothers entered the prison with an ice chest filled with guns and armed their father and another convicted murderer. They later helped abduct, detain, and rob a family of four and watched their father and the other convict murder the members of that family with shotguns. Although the brothers later stated they were surprised by the killings, neither of them attempted to help the victims. Instead, they drove away in the victims' car along with the rest of the escape party. Ricky and Raymond Tison received the death penalty under Arizona's felony murder and accomplice liability statutes. They appealed their death sentences, alleging that the Supreme Court decision in *Enmund v. Florida*, 458 U.S. 782 (1982), required reversal of their sentences because they were merely accomplices and not principals.

ISSUE: Is it constitutional to sentence to death defendants who did not do the actual killing in a capital murder? YES.

HOLDING: Defendants who participate in a major way in a felony murder and who act with reckless indifference to human life, even though they do not directly inflict the act of killing, may be given the death penalty.

REASON: "The issue raised by this case is whether the Eighth Amendment prohibits the death penalty in the intermediate case of the defendant whose participation is major and whose mental state is one of reckless indifference to the value of human life. *Enmund* does not specifically address this point.

"Like the *Enmund* Court, we find the state legislatures' judgment as to proportionality in these circumstances relevant to this constitutional inquiry. The largest number of States still fall into the two intermediate categories discussed in *Enmund*. Four States authorize the death penalty in felony-murder cases upon a showing of culpable mental state such as recklessness or extreme indifference to human life. Two jurisdictions require that the defendant's participation be substantial and the statutes of at least six more, including Arizona, take minor participation in the felony expressly into account in mitigation of the murder. These requirements significantly overlap both in this case and in general, for the greater the defendant's participation in the felony murder, the more likely that he acted with reckless indifference to human life. At a minimum, however, it can be said that all these jurisdictions, as well as six States which *Enmund* classified along with Florida as permitting capital punishment for felony murder simpliciter, and the three States which simply require some additional aggravation before imposing the death penalty upon a felony murderer, specifically authorize the death penalty in a felony-murder case where, though the defendant's mental state fell short of intent to kill, the defendant was a major actor in a felony in which he knew death was highly likely to occur."

Continued

---

[98]*Id.* at 211.

TISON v. ARIZONA 481 U.S. 137 (1987)—cont'd

CASE SIGNIFICANCE: The *Enmund* Court ruled that accomplices to a crime who participated in a minor role and had no prior knowledge that lethal force might be used in the commission of a felony could not be held responsible for that lethal force. It held that punishment by death in such a case is disproportionate to the crime and thus is prohibited by the Eighth Amendment. The Tison brothers attempted to use that ruling to overturn their death sentences, claiming that the death penalty was disproportionate to their participation in the crime committed. The Court disagreed and concluded that the Tison brothers played a major role in the killing of four family members and that their actions during the commission of the crime also suggested a reckless indifference to life. Based on these findings, the Court stated that it could not find fault with the sentences handed down by the trial court and that a survey of other state procedures in similar cases showed that society was also in agreement with severe punishments for accomplices who actively participated in violent crimes.[99]

BAZE v. REES 553 U.S. 35 (2008)

CAPSULE: The currently predominant three-drug protocol for executions by lethal injection, as represented in Kentucky's execution method, does not violate the Eighth Amendment's prohibition of cruel and unusual punishment.

FACTS: Ralph Baze was convicted of a double homicide and sentenced to death under Kentucky's capital murder statute. Baze, joined by Thomas C. Bowling, filed suit against Kentucky, contending that the state's lethal injection process constitutes cruel and unusual punishment because it can result in unnecessary pain and suffering. Petitioners did not challenge the constitutionality of the death penalty itself, just the particular method currently used. Specifically, petitioners believed that the current method carried an unnecessary risk of error or improper administration and thus caused severe pain and suffering. They proposed an alternate method of lethal injection—one that had not been yet adopted or tried in any state. The Kentucky Supreme Court upheld the state's execution method and the U.S. Supreme Court agreed to hear the case.

ISSUE: Does Kentucky's three-drug protocol for executions by lethal injection violate the Eighth Amendment's prohibition of cruel and unusual punishment? NO.

HOLDING: Kentucky's three-drug lethal injection protocol, also used by 29 other death penalty states, does not constitute cruel and unusual punishment and is thus constitutionally permissible.

REASON: "We begin with the principle, settled by *Gregg*, that capital punishment is constitutional. It necessarily follows that there must be a means of carrying it out. Some risk of pain is inherent in any method of execution—no matter how humane—if only from the prospect of error in following the required procedure. It is clear, then, that the Constitution does not demand the avoidance of all risk of pain in carrying out executions... Simply because an execution method may result in pain, either by accident or as an inescapable consequence of death, does not establish the sort of 'objectively intolerable risk of harm' that qualifies as cruel and unusual."

"Reasonable people of good faith disagree on the morality and efficacy of capital punishment, and for many who oppose it, no method of execution would ever be acceptable. But as Justice Frankfurter stressed in *Resweber*, '[o]ne must be on guard against finding in personal disapproval a reflection of more or less prevailing condemnation.'[100] This Court has ruled that capital punishment is not prohibited under our Constitution, and that the States may enact

Continued

---

[99]*Id.* at 216–217.
[100]*Louisiana ex rel. Francis v. Resweber*, 329 U.S. 459, 471 (1947).

BAZE v. REES 553 U.S. 35 (2008)—cont'd

laws specifying that sanction. '[T]he power of a State to pass laws means little if the State cannot enforce them.'[101] State efforts to implement capital punishment must certainly comply with the Eighth Amendment, but what that Amendment prohibits is wanton exposure to 'objectively intolerable risk,'[102] not simply the possibility of pain.

"Kentucky has adopted a method of execution believed to be the most humane available, one it shares with 35 other States. Petitioners agree that, if administered as intended, that procedure will result in a painless death. The risks of maladministration they have suggested—such as improper mixing of chemicals and improper setting of IVs by trained and experienced personnel—cannot remotely be characterized as 'objectively intolerable.' Kentucky's decision to adhere to its protocol despite these asserted risks, while adopting safeguards to protect against them, cannot be viewed as probative of the wanton infliction of pain under the Eighth Amendment. Finally, the alternative that petitioners belatedly propose has problems of its own, and has never been tried by a single State.

"Throughout our history, whenever a method of execution has been challenged in this Court as cruel and unusual, the Court has rejected the challenge. Our society has nonetheless steadily moved to more humane methods of carrying out capital punishment. The firing squad, hanging, the electric chair, and the gas chamber have each in turn given way to more humane methods, culminating in today's consensus on lethal injection. The broad framework of the Eighth Amendment has accommodated this progress toward more humane methods of execution, and our approval of a particular method in the past has not precluded legislatures from taking the steps they deem appropriate, in light of new developments, to ensure humane capital punishment. There is no reason to suppose that today's decision will be any different."

CASE SIGNIFICANCE: In this case, the Court continues a longstanding tradition of refusing to declare any particular execution method in violation of the Eighth Amendment's prohibition of cruel and unusual punishment. Nevertheless, the Court does weigh in on some key standards for assessing the potential cruelty of such methods, noting that they must be "humane" and not exhibit "wanton infliction of pain." This is not groundbreaking but is about as unequivocal from the Court as one can expect in regard to the constitutionality of particular methods of execution. The Court also addresses the "unusual" component of the Eighth Amendment's ban on cruel and unusual punishment, noting that 30 of the 36 states that have the death penalty have determined the method under question to be the preferred and most humane method available.

This case resulted in a lengthy opinion in which seven justices rendered opinions (the decision and holding resting on a plurality opinion penned by Chief Justice Roberts). Most concurring Justices agreed that this case should not be interpreted as about the constitutionality of the death penalty itself but one that is limited to a very specific execution protocol. However, Justice John Paul Stevens, in his concurring opinion, took the opportunity to challenge the constitutionality of the death penalty itself as excessive and presenting an unnecessary risk. Others noted the controversial nature and potential risks of the death penalty as well. These statements perhaps open the door for a later consideration of the very constitutionality of the death penalty. At the very least they entertain the validity of such a debate.

Perhaps the greatest significance of this case, however, occurred before it was decided. During the time in which the Court was considering this case, the United States saw what was the functional equivalent of a moratorium on executions—the longest such hiatus since executions resumed after *Gregg*. Moreover, the pending decision drove some states to amend their death penalty statutes to allow for alternate methods of execution in the event that lethal injection was declared unconstitutional. In the end, the Court's decision was not as impactful as it might have been. With the Court declaring the currently predominant mode of execution constitutional, executions were allowed to resume as they had in the wake of past challenges based on the Eighth Amendment.

[101]*McCleskey v. Zant*, 499 U.S. 467, 491 (1991).
[102]*Farmer v. Brennan*, 511 U.S. 825, 846 (1994).

KENNEDY v. LOUISIANA 554 U.S. 407 (2008)

CAPSULE: It is unconstitutional to impose the death penalty for the rape of a child when the crime does not result in the victim's death.

FACTS[103]: On March 2, 1998, Patrick Kennedy called 911 and reported that his stepdaughter had been raped. He told the 911 operator that he had heard her scream and ran outside to find her in the yard. Kennedy reported that two neighbor boys had dragged her from the garage to the yard and had forced her down and raped her. He claimed he saw one of the boys fleeing on a bicycle. When police arrived at the scene, they found the victim on her bed wrapped in a bloody blanket and bleeding profusely from the vaginal area. Kennedy claimed to have carried her in from the yard and to have washed her with a wet cloth. Injuries to the victim were excessive and required emergency surgery. An expert in pediatric forensic medicine later testified that the injuries were the worst he had seen in a case of sexual assault in his four years of practice.

In the week following the attack, both Kennedy and his victim reported that the assault had been perpetrated by two neighborhood boys. The victim relayed this account several times but also reportedly told a family member that Kennedy was the one who raped her. Additionally, investigators found blood under the victim's mattress, indicating that the assault had taken place in the victim's bedroom and not in the yard, as reported by Kennedy and the victim. Eight days after the crime, in spite of the victim's continued refusal to implicate Kennedy, Kennedy was arrested for the rape. On June 22, 1998, the victim told her mother that Kennedy was the one who raped her. This accusation was recorded and videotaped much later in an interview at the Child Advocacy Center. She later told authorities that Kennedy had told her to say that the two neighborhood boys had raped her. Kennedy was convicted and sentenced to death for the assault under Louisiana's statute authorizing the death penalty for the rape of a child who is under 12 years old. The Supreme Court of Louisiana affirmed the death sentence.

ISSUE: Is it Constitutional to impose the death penalty for the crime of sexual assault against a child when the crime does not result in the victim's death? NO.

HOLDING: It is a violation of the Eighth Amendment to sentence a defendant to death for the rape of a child when the crime does not result in the victim's death.

REASON: "[Forty-four] States have not made child rape a capital offense. As for federal law, Congress in the Federal Death Penalty Act of 1994 expanded the number of federal crimes for which the death penalty is a permissible sentence, including certain nonhomicide offenses; but it did not do the same for child rape or abuse. Under 18 U.S.C. § 2245, an offender is death eligible only when the sexual abuse or exploitation results in the victim's death."

"The evidence of a national consensus with respect to the death penalty for child rapists, as with respect to juveniles, mentally retarded offenders, and vicarious felony murderers, shows divided opinion but, on balance, an opinion against it. Thirty-seven jurisdictions—36 States plus the Federal Government—have the death penalty. As mentioned above, only six of those jurisdictions authorize the death penalty for rape of a child. Though our review of national consensus is not confined to tallying the number of States with applicable death penalty legislation, it is of significance that, in 45 jurisdictions, petitioner could not be executed for child rape of any kind. That number surpasses the 30 States in *Atkins* and *Roper* and the 42 States in *Enmund* that prohibited the death penalty under the circumstances those cases considered."

Continued

---

[103]In the U.S. Supreme Court's written opinion, the facts of the case are preceded with the following: "Petitioner's crime was one that cannot be recounted in these pages in a way sufficient to capture in full the hurt and horror inflicted on his victim or to convey the revulsion society, and the jury that represents it, sought to express by sentencing petitioner to death." The facts of the case as relayed in this brief represent only the facts that were included in the written opinion.

KENNEDY v. LOUISIANA 554 U.S. 407 (2008)—cont'd

"There are measures of consensus other than legislation. Statistics about the number of executions may inform the consideration whether capital punishment for the crime of child rape is regarded as unacceptable in our society. These statistics confirm our determination from our review of state statutes that there is a social consensus against the death penalty for the crime of child rape. Nine States—Florida, Georgia, Louisiana, Mississippi, Montana, Oklahoma, South Carolina, Tennessee, and Texas—have permitted capital punishment for adult or child rape for some length of time between the Court's 1972 decision in *Furman* and today. Yet no individual has been executed for the rape of an adult or child since 1964, and no execution for any other nonhomicide offense has been conducted since 1963."

"The constitutional prohibition against excessive or cruel and unusual punishments mandates that the State's power to punish "be exercised within the limits of civilized standards." *Trop*, 356 U.S., at 99, 100 (plurality opinion). Evolving standards of decency that mark the progress of a maturing society counsel us to be most hesitant before interpreting the Eighth Amendment to allow the extension of the death penalty, a hesitation that has special force where no life was taken in the commission of the crime. It is an established principle that decency, in its essence, presumes respect for the individual and thus moderation or restraint in the application of capital punishment."

"The rule of evolving standards of decency with specific marks on the way to full progress and mature judgment means that resort to the penalty must be reserved for the worst of crimes and limited in its instances of application. In most cases justice is not better served by terminating the life of the perpetrator rather than confining him and preserving the possibility that he and the system will find ways to allow him to understand the enormity of his offense. Difficulties in administering the penalty to ensure against its arbitrary and capricious application require adherence to a rule reserving its use, at this stage of evolving standards and in cases of crimes against individuals, for crimes that take the life of the victim."

"Our concern here is limited to crimes against individual persons. We do not address, for example, crimes defining and punishing treason, espionage, terrorism, and drug kingpin activity, which are offenses against the State. As it relates to crimes against individuals, though, the death penalty should not be expanded to instances where the victim's life was not taken."

"Based both on consensus and our own independent judgment, our holding is that a death sentence for one who raped but did not kill a child, and who did not intend to assist another in killing the child, is unconstitutional under the Eighth and Fourteenth Amendments."

CASE SIGNIFICANCE: The Court, in this case, makes one of its strongest statements in limiting the use of the death penalty in line with the Eighth Amendment notion of "evolving standards of decency" and cruel and unusual punishment. This case reiterates the Court's stance that the death penalty be reserved for cases in which the victim is killed by the perpetrator. Relying, as they did in the recent *Roper* and *Atkins* cases, on consensus among the states based on legislation, the Court determined that executing an offender who does not kill his victims counter to "evolving standards of decency." The Court also notes that such a punishment is disproportionate in cases in which the victim does not die and thus is excessive in terms of the Eighth Amendment's prohibition of cruel and unusual punishment.

This case is important in that it communicates the Court's unwillingness to allow any expansion in the use of the death penalty. In spite of the movement of several states to allow the death penalty for sex offenses committed against children, as well as growing public support for such measures, the Court refused to open any new doors in the use of the death penalty. In the majority opinion (written by Justice Kennedy), great reluctance was expressed in regard to broadening the scope of crimes for which the death penalty could be imposed, with some verbiage even bordering on abhorrence at the idea that the death penalty might become more widely used. Recalling the original notion from *Gregg* that the death penalty be extremely limited in use, the Court has put an ostensible end to attempts to expand the applicability of the death penalty to crimes in which the victim is not killed. The majority was careful to point out, however, that the decision does not apply to crimes against the state such as treason, espionage, and terrorism, thus leaving the death penalty available in such cases.

Key Terms

Baze v. Rees
botched executions
Coker v. Georgia
cruel and unusual punishment
Eberheart v. Georgia
Eighth Amendment
electrocution
evolving standards of decency
firing squad
gas chamber
hanging
Hill v. McDonough
Kennedy v. Louisiana
lethal injection
Marshall Hypothesis
proportionality review
public opinion
Pulley v. Harris
Tison v. Arizona
Trop v. Dulles

CRITICAL THINKING QUESTIONS

1.   The Supreme Court has consistently held that the death penalty is only appropriate in cases of murder (more specifically, "aggravated" murder). Briefly explain the Court's reasoning behind this. Do you think the death penalty is justified for crimes other than murder? If so, which crimes? Explain your reasoning. If not, explain why you think the death penalty should remain only applicable to murder.

2.   The Court refers to "evolving standards of decency" in determining what violates the Eighth Amendment's prohibition of cruel and unusual punishment. What does the Court mean by this? What are the primary factors that the Court relies on in establishing the evolving standards?

3.   Think about where the United States stands in the world in terms of its use of the death penalty. Why do you think the United States differs in terms of the death penalty in comparison to other Western countries? What possible impacts do you think the United States' use of the death penalty has on international relations? What, if any, role do you think the United States' standing internationally should play in future policy and legal decisions about the death penalty?

4.   Considering the reasoning in *Atkins v. Virginia* and *Roper v. Simmons*, think about what it would take for the Supreme Court to consider the death penalty, in and of itself, cruel and unusual punishment. Consider and explain the calculus that the Court might employ in determining this.

Internet Resources

The Death Penalty: Public Opinion Trends
www.gallup.com/poll/1606/death-penalty.aspx

Abolitionist and Retentionist Countries
www.amnesty.org/en/death-penalty/abolitionist-and-retentionist-countries

Botched Executions
www.deathpenaltyinfo.org/some-examples-post-furman-botched-executions

State-by-State Lethal Injection
www.deathpenaltyinfo.org/state-lethal-injection

The Execution Tapes
www.soundportraits.org/on-air/execution_tapes/

International Death Penalty Database
www.deathpenaltyworldwide.org/index.cfm

State-by-State Lethal Injection Information
www.deathpenaltyinfo.org/state-lethal-injection

Other Issues, Trends, and the Future of the Death Penalty

12

CHAPTER OUTLINE

I INTRODUCTION

Public support for the death penalty in the United States has changed over time. From virtually total support in early Colonial times to the abolition of its use by several states during the early twentieth century, culminating in the *Furman* and *Gregg* decisions of the early 1970s.[1] The death penalty has endured varying levels of support throughout its existence in this country. Although the death penalty continues to be an acceptable and constitutional penal sanction, support for it has declined over the last few decades, and there seems to be growing support for another sanction: life without the possibility of parole (LWOP). According to recent polls, U.S. citizens were almost evenly divided between support for the death penalty and support for LWOP.[2] However, a 2012 Gallup Poll showed that 63 percent of Americans surveyed were in favor of the death penalty.[3] Although this is a slight increase from 2011, when support was at 61 percent, attitudes toward the death penalty have been fairly stagnant for the past several years and have diminished substantially since 1994, when support for the death penalty was at 80 percent.[4]

---

[1]*Furman v. Georgia*, 408 U.S. 238 (1972); *Gregg v. Georgia*, 428 U.S. 153 (1976).
[2]Death Penalty Information Center, *Public Opinion: American Values Survey Shows Even Split on Death Penalty, with More Catholics Opposed*, Aug. 14, 2013. Available at: www.deathpenaltyinfo.org/public-opinion-american-values-survey-shows-even-split-death-penalty-more-catholics-opposed.
[3]Gallup Politics, *U.S. Death Penalty Support Stable at 63%*. Available at: www.gallup.com/poll/159770/death-penalty-support-stable.aspx.
[4]*Id.*

Support for the death penalty can also be gauged by examining other trends. At present, 32 states plus the federal government retain the statutory right to impose a penalty of death, whereas 18 states have abolished it. Notably, within the past six years, five states have abolished the death penalty; additionally, one state (New York) has not revised its penal code to rectify constitutional concerns addressed by a federal court, and another state (California) has not executed an inmate due to legal issues regarding lethal injection.[5] Moreover, in most of the states that retain the death penalty, there has been a marked decline both in the number of death sentences imposed and in actual executions.[6] Nevertheless, since 1976, the year the death penalty was reinstated, 1,343 individuals have been executed in the United States[7] (as of September 3, 2013), with another 3,125 inmates currently awaiting death[8] (see Table 12.1). By international standards, the United States joins 21 countries around the

Table 12.1 Number of Inmates on Death Row by State (As of April 1, 2013)

State	Number of Inmates	State	Number of Inmates	State	Number of Inmates
California	731	South Carolina	52	Utah	9
Florida	412	Missouri	48	Washington	8
Texas	298	Mississippi	46	U.S. Military	5
Pennsylvania	198	Arkansas	38	Maryland*	5
Alabama	197	Oregon	37	Colorado	4
North Carolina	161	Kentucky	34	South Dakota	3
Ohio	147	Delaware	18	Montana	2
Arizona	126	Idaho	13	New Mexico*	2
Georgia	95	Indiana	13	Wyoming	1
Louisiana	88	Nebraska	11	New Hampshire	1
Nevada	80	Connecticut*	11		
U.S. Government	58	Virginia	10		
Oklahoma	58	Kansas	10		

*State has abolished the death penalty, but repeal was not retroactive, so inmates already on death row remain there.
Source: Death Penalty Information Center. Available at: www.deathpenaltyinfo.org/article.php?scid=9&did=188#state.

[5]Death Penalty Information Center, *States With and Without the Death Penalty*, Aug. 8, 2013. Available at: www.deathpenaltyinfo.org/states-and-without-death-penalty.
[6]Death Penalty Information Center, *The Death Penalty in 2012: Year End Report*, Aug. 14, 2013. Available at: http://deathpenaltyinfo.org/YearEnd2012.
[7]Death Penalty Information Center, *Death Penalty By Year*, Sept. 3, 2013. Available at: www.deathpenaltyinfo.org/executions-year.
[8]Death Penalty Information Center, *Size of Death Row By Year*. Sept. 5, 2013. Available at: www.deathpenaltyinfo.org/death-row-inmates-state-and-size-death-row-year#year.

world that executed inmates in 2012 and ranked fifth among countries, following only China, Iran, Iraq, and Saudi Arabia in terms of number of executions in 2012.[9]

The basic and most prominent legal issues surrounding the death penalty were addressed in the preceding chapters. This concluding chapter presents other issues and trends regarding the continued use of the death penalty in this country. This chapter first explores penological justifications for punishment, with a focus on the death penalty. It then examines the Court's reasons for the continued use of the death penalty. Flaws in the administration of the death penalty are also discussed, with particular focus on the execution of innocent offenders and wrongful convictions, issues that have produced the most potent controversy surrounding the death penalty in recent years. Finally, future trends in the death penalty are explored and its future is considered.

II PENOLOGICAL JUSTIFICATIONS FOR PUNISHMENT AND THE DEATH PENALTY

There are four penological justifications or rationales for punishing a person who has committed a crime. These include retribution, deterrence, incapacitation, and rehabilitation. Although rehabilitation has no bearing on the continued use of the death penalty, the other three justifications have been used to support the death penalty, not only in the United States but also in other countries. Retribution and deterrence constitute the main reasons the death penalty has survived as a form of punishment in the United States. In fact, giving inmates their just desserts was cited as the primary reason to support the death penalty in the 2012 American Values Survey.[10] Opponents of the death penalty, however, argue that retribution does not accord with the provisions of the Constitution, particularly the Eighth Amendment. The Supreme Court, with the exception of several Justices in *Furman v. Georgia*,[11] has consistently held that the penalty of death is not cruel and unusual per se and defers judgment about the peculiarities of the cruel and unusual nature of the penalty to juries, state legislative bodies, and state executive branches.[12] That is, the Court looks to juries, state legislative bodies, and state governments to determine the evolving standards of decency that mark the progress of a maturing society with respect to the proportionality of a given punishment. Opponents further contend that the death penalty is not an effective deterrent to crime and also argue that sentencing alternatives such as LWOP can have the same incapacitating effect as the death penalty.[13] In terms of the latter alternative, the Court once again will allow states to define the boundaries of acceptable punishments for crimes.

[9]Amnesty International, *Death Sentences and Executions in 2012*, Sept. 6, 2013. Available at: www.amnestyusa.org/research/reports/death-sentences-and-executions-2012.
[10]Death Penalty Information Center, *Public Opinion: American Values Survey Shows Even Split on Death Penalty, with More Catholics Opposed*, Aug. 14, 2013. Available at: www.deathpenaltyinfo.org/public-opinion-american-values-survey-shows-even-split-death-penalty-more-catholics-opposed.
[11]408 U.S. 153 (1972).
[12]Bessler, John D., *Tinkering Around the Edges: The Supreme Court's Death Penalty Jurisprudence*, AMERICAN CRIMINAL LAW REVIEW (2012).
[13]Fagan, Jeffrey, *Death and Deterrence Redux: Science, Law, and Causal Reasoning on Capital Punishment*, OHIO STATE JOURNAL OF CRIMINAL LAW, vol. 44, 255–320 (2006).

A Retribution and the Death Penalty

Retribution is the oldest form of punishment and one of the main reasons for the use of death penalty in ancient times and today. However, retribution is also the most misunderstood form of punishment, largely due to conflicting definitions. The traditional definition of retribution contains the element of revenge. This vengeful form of retribution has its origins in the Mosaic Code of the Old Testament and is captured in the idea of lex talionis ("an eye for an eye"). Lex talionis was the foundation of the Code of Hammurabi, which permitted the victim or the victim's family to seek revenge for injurious behavior. Thus, capital punishment, the ultimate form of vengeful retribution, was a private matter between individuals as well as a civil matter during the reign of King Hammurabi, approximately 1900 years B.C.

The evolution of retributive punishment has naturally produced variants from the classic definition. Some legal scholars maintain that retribution is not synonymous with revenge because revenge is "imposed at the whim of the revenger" who derives "pleasure in the suffering of another."[14] Scholars who subscribe to this differentiation between retribution and revenge also contend that retributive punishment restricts the amount of punishment that is imposed and also restricts the justification for its imposition. Thus, they argue that retributive punishment must be proportionate to the amount of harm inflicted by the offender. They also believe that punishments for vengeful purposes have no internal limitation on the amount of pain to be imposed, and justifications for its use need not be consistent with the doctrine of proportionality.[15]

Despite scholarly effort to differentiate the notions of revenge and retribution, the merging of these two elements of punishment constitutes the main reason for the continued use of the death penalty in the United States. Although the death penalty is certainly not imposed at the "whim of the revenger" due to constitutional constraints or limits, there is some truth to the notion of deriving pleasure in the suffering or death of an offender. As one source notes, "Indeed, there have been public celebrations outside prisons during executions. The viciousness of some of these displays can hardly be exaggerated."[16] It is not uncommon for relatives of the victim to express their need to witness the execution of the individual in their desire for closure. However, the death penalty is not a private act that allows families to exact revenge on those who inflict harm and thus must be justified under the Constitution.

From a purely legal standpoint, however, justifying the death penalty under the Constitution has caused problems. Some scholars say that despite numerous cases, the Court has yet to fully and explicitly articulate that this ultimate sanction can be imposed for retribution. For instance, in *Furman v. Georgia* (1972),[17] several Justices examined the retributive nature of the death penalty, but there was no consensus among the Justices that retribution is an acceptable reason for the death penalty. Justice Potter Stewart, who ruled that the death penalty was unconstitutionally imposed on minorities, opined that the retributive nature of the death penalty was not contradictory to the mandates in the Constitution. According to Justice Stewart, states are given the authority to impose the death penalty

---

[14]Sigler, Mary, *Contradiction, Coherence, and Guided Discretion in The Supreme Court's Capital Sentencing Jurisprudence*, 40 Am. Crim. L. Rev. 1177 (2003).

[15]*Id.*

[16]Vandiver, Margaret, *The Impact of the Death Penalty on the Families of Homicide Victims and of Condemned Prisoners*. In James R. Acker, Robert M. Bohm, and Charles S. Lanier (eds.), America's Experiment with Capital Punishment: Reflections of the Past, Present, and Future of the Ultimate Penal Sanction (2003), pp. 613–647.

[17]*Furman v. Georgia*, 408 U.S. 238 (1972).

on the most violent offenders to seek retribution for crimes committed (just deserts), as long as this ultimate sanction was not imposed arbitrarily or capriciously in violation of the equal protection clause of the Fourteenth Amendment. However, Justice Thurgood Marshall, who also wrote a concurring opinion in *Furman*, reached a different conclusion about the retributive aspect of the death penalty. He argued that retribution violated the Constitution, specifically the Eighth Amendment. Acknowledging that retribution has been historically used as a justification for the death penalty in the United States, Justice Marshall argued that "retaliation, vengeance, and retribution have been roundly condemned as intolerable aspirations for a government in a free society" and further stated that "the history of the Eighth Amendment supports only the conclusion that retribution for its own sake is improper."[18]

Justice William J. Brennan, who in *Furman* supported the abolition of the death penalty on grounds that it violated the cruel and unusual punishment clause of the Eighth Amendment, abhorred the fact that "naked vengeance"[19] was used by states to justify the death penalty. He also insisted that retribution could not be accepted as a contemporary reason for the continued use of the death penalty. In *Gregg v. Georgia* (1976),[20] only four justices concurred that retribution was an acceptable reason for the death penalty. In *Gregg*, Justice Stewart, who wrote the plurality opinion, reiterated that retribution was acceptable under the provisions of the Constitution. He further clarified that the retributive quality of the death penalty was essential to an ordered society because it reflected society's desire to punish those who engaged in morally outrageous and offensive conduct. He underscored the importance of bestowing upon the government the authority to impose the death penalty and the consequences that would result if this form of punishment was not legally permitted. Reiterating his previous opinion in *Furman*, Justice Stewart said:

> The instinct for retribution is part of the nature of man, and channeling that instinct in the administration of criminal justice serves an important purpose in promoting the stability of a society governed by law. When people begin to believe that organized society is unwilling or unable to impose upon criminal offenders the punishment they deserve, then there are sown the seeds of anarchy—of self-help...[21]

Although Justice Stewart presented a uniquely pragmatic reason for imposing the death penalty based upon the preservation of an ordered society, there is no conclusive evidence that the death penalty significantly contributes to such order or that the abolition of the death penalty would lead to anarchy. Accordingly, not only does the lack of evidence discredit arguments for the death penalty based on the notion of retribution, it also brings into disrepute arguments about the deterrent effect of the death penalty.

B Deterrence and the Death Penalty

In *Gregg*, Justice Stewart noted that one of the social purposes of the death penalty is to permit society to exact retribution on those who engage in the most serious offenses. However, he also conceded that the death penalty was a useful method of deterring the behavior of potential offenders. Deterrence, which is a derivative of eighteenth-century classical criminology, is a sentencing goal or a crime

---

[18]*Id.* at 315.
[19]*Id.* at 258.
[20]*Gregg v. Georgia*, 428 U.S. 153 (1976).
[21]*Furman v. Georgia*, 408 U.S. 238, 308 (1972).

prevention strategy that seeks to inhibit criminal behavior in either the offender (specific deterrence) or in others (general deterrence) by using punishment or the threat of punishment to outweigh any beneficial or profitable outcomes that may result from the commission of a crime. Theoretically, deterrence is based on the notion that offenders or would-be offenders rationally consider the consequences of their actions and will be dissuaded if punishment or the threat of punishment is more costly or painful than law-abiding behavior. Deterrence is also based on the premise that punishments must be administered by the legal system with swiftness and certainty, as well as administered to the degree that is proportional to the crime committed.

Deterrence represents the most logical reason for imposing this ultimate sanction on those who commit the most serious crimes in our society. Because "potential offenders are aware of the death penalty and regard it as a more severe sanction than imprisonment... murder is discouraged because the threat of one's own death presumably outweighs the rewards gained from killing another."[22] However, this argument, used by proponents of the death penalty, may be flawed in several respects. First, some criminologists argue that offenders may not rationally consider the consequences of their actions. Specifically for the crime of first-degree murder, some criminologists maintain that premeditation does not generally precede the commission of this capital crime because most murders of this degree are committed out of anger or passion[23] rather than after a rational consideration of the legal penalties likely to be imposed if one is convicted.

Second, for the death penalty to be an effective deterrent, it must be administered with swiftness and certainty—two elements that do not characterize our current system of criminal justice, especially with the numerous appeals that are available to capital offenders. In 2012, the average time between sentencing and execution was 14.8 years.[24] However, there have been cases of inmates spending more than three decades on death row. The case of *Valle v. Florida* (2011),[25] for example, involves an inmate (Valle) who spent 33 years behind bars waiting for his execution. While the Court denied certiorari in this case, Justice Stephen Breyer wrote a dissenting opinion in which he argued that being held prisoner for so many years under the threat of execution is cruel and invalidates the penalty's deterrent value. Additionally, the infrequency with which the death penalty is imposed conflicts with the basic tenets of deterrence theory. This is salient today since there seem to be fewer and fewer penalties being imposed by juries, and when examining state-level data by those who continue to use the death penalty, impositions of death are concentrated in only certain counties of every state that retains the death penalty.[26] Also, when the death penalty is inflicted arbitrarily on minority members of our society, the deterrent effect of this sanction becomes a moot issue. This has been a consistent finding and one that has prompted states in recent years to implement racial justice acts.

[22]Peterson, Ruth D., and William C. Bailey, *Is Capital Punishment an Effective Deterrent for Murder? An Examination of Social Science Research*. In James R. Acker, Robert M. Bohm, and Charles S. Lanier (eds.), AMERICA'S EXPERIMENT WITH CAPITAL PUNISHMENT: REFLECTIONS OF THE PAST, PRESENT, AND FUTURE OF THE ULTIMATE PENAL SANCTION (2003), pp. 251–258.
[23]Bowers, W.J., and G. Pierce, *Deterrence or Brutalization: What Is the Effect of Executions?* CRIME & DELINQUENCY 26:453–484 (1980).
[24]Death Penalty Information Center, Time on Death Row, www.deathpenaltyinfo.org/time-death-row.
[25]564 U.S. ___ 2011.
[26]Liebman, James S., and Peter Clarke, *Minority Practice, Majority's Burden: The Death Penalty Today*, OHIO STATE JOURNAL OF CRIMINAL LAW, 9 (2011).

A third flaw of deterrence theory and the death penalty involves the so-called brutalization effect—or the notion that the death penalty cannot deter the killing of human beings because state-authorized executions "demonstrate that it is correct and appropriate to kill those who have gravely offended us."[27] Some opponents of the death penalty challenge its deterrent effect by stating that the continued use of the death penalty sends conflicting messages about the authority of government to exact revenge on those who commit crimes while at the same time attempting to deter the same vengeful behavior in members of society. Finally, another significant flaw of the belief in the deterrent effect of the death penalty is the lack of empirical evidence to support the contention that this ultimate sanction decreases the number of crimes committed. Although extensive empirical research has been undertaken to determine whether the death penalty has any deterrent effect, only a handful of studies have demonstrated a marginal deterrent effect.[28] Several of these studies have been challenged as methodologically flawed.[29] Most recently, the National Research Council conducted a meta analysis of studies on the deterrent value of the death penalty and concluded that the research is at best inconclusive, noting the following:

> The committee concludes that research to date on the effect of capital punishment on homicide is not informative about whether capital punishment decreases, increases, or has no effect on homicide rates. Therefore, the committee recommends that these studies not be used to inform deliberations requiring judgments about the effect of the death penalty on homicide. Consequently, claims that research demonstrates that capital punishment decreases or increases the homicide rate by a specified amount or has no effect on the homicide rate should not influence policy judgments about capital punishment.[30]

The value of the death penalty as a deterrent is yet to be conclusively ascertained. Despite the failure to find an empirical link between deterrence and the death penalty, the Court has used this penological rationale to buttress the death penalty. In *Spaziano v. Florida* (1984), for example, Justice White noted that:

> [T]he majority of the Court has concluded that the general deterrence rationale adequately justifies the imposition of capital punishment at least for certain classes of offenses for which the legislature may reasonably conclude that the death penalty has a deterrent effect.[31]

C Incapacitation and the Death Penalty

Incapacitation is the third penological justification for the death penalty. Indeed, the death penalty is the ultimate form of incapacitation because it completely and permanently removes the offender from society. According to one scholar, incapacitation, although generally not first on the list of articulated

---

[27]Bowers, W.J., and G. Pierce, *Deterrence or Brutalization: What Is the Effect of Executions?* CRIME & DELINQUENCY 26:453–484 (1980), at 456.

[28]See, for example, Joanna M. Shepherd, *Deterrence Versus Brutalization: Capital Punishment's Differing Impacts Among States*, 104 MICHIGAN L. REV. 203 (2005).

[29]Donohue, J.J., and J. Wolfers, *The Ethics and Empirics of Capital Punishment: Uses and Abuses of Empirical Evidence in the Death Penalty Debate*, 58 STANFORD L. REV. 791 (2005).

[30]Nagin, Daniel S., and John V. Pepper, editors; Committee on Deterrence and the Death Penalty; Committee on Law and Justice; Division on Behavioral and Social Sciences and Education; National Research Council, at p. 2.

[31]*Spaziano v. Florida*, 468 U.S. 447, 479 (1984).

reasons for the continued use of the death penalty, is at the forefront of rationales. He argues that jurors deliberate on the future dangerousness of an inmate prior to imposing a penalty of death, and thus incapacitation does enter jurors' determination of life versus death:

> *Future dangerousness determines the outcome of capital sentencing determinations because (1) it is a required inquiry for the jury under some states, (2) it is explicitly or implicitly part of the determination of the presence of certain aggravating factors, and (3) it is often one of the factors, perhaps the most important, considered by jurors making their capital punishment decisions.*[32]

Advocates of the death penalty quickly use incapacitation to justify the death penalty, pointing to how effective the death penalty is in eliminating those who inflict the most harm on society.[33] But opponents of the death penalty are also quick to indicate that incapacitation, particularly a life sentence, is just as effective at preventing even the most serious offenders from committing crime. Thus, they argue that the death penalty has become an obsolete form of punishment.

Life imprisonment has been used as an alternative to the death penalty in many countries, including the United States. However, for some, a life sentence has not been a sufficiently appealing alternative to the death penalty. Admittedly, incapacitation in the form of a life sentence historically has not fully incapacitated an offender from engaging in future criminal behavior, because he or she may be released from prison after serving only a portion of a life sentence. Unless specified by statute, a life sentence historically has not necessarily meant that the capital offender would remain in prison until death. Under an indeterminate sentencing scheme, an inmate sentenced to life may have had his or her sentence reduced, depending on good time credit and evidence of rehabilitation while in prison. However, under a mandatory sentencing scheme, true life without parole (LWOP) may be as effective as death in incapacitating capital offenders. At present, all states that currently retain the death penalty also reserve the right to impose definite life sentences without the possibility of parole. As mentioned, current public opinion polls show an even split between those who support the death penalty and those who favor LWOP.[34]

D Justifying the Death Penalty: The Supreme Court

Among the three reasons for the continued use of the death penalty, retribution is the most controversial because the execution of a capital offender is justified on the basis that the offender deserves to die due to the crime committed. However, retribution remains one of the prime reasons for the continued use of the death penalty. Deterrence has fallen out of favor with many in advocating the death penalty as public policy. Nevertheless, deterrence remains a part of the political justification in spite of the fact that empirical research has failed to sufficiently and consistently demonstrate an actual deterrent effect.

---

[32]Berry III, William W., *Ending Death by Dangerousness: A Path to the De Facto Abolition of the Death Penalty*, Arizona Law Review, 52, 889–924 (at p. 893).

[33]Sigler, Mary, *Contradiction, Coherence, and Guided Discretion in the Supreme Court's Capital Sentencing Jurisprudence*, 40 Am. Crim. L. Rev. 1157 (2003).

[34]Death Penalty Information Center, *Public Opinion: American Values Survey Shows Even Split on Death Penalty, with More Catholics Opposed*, Aug. 14, 2013. Available at: www.deathpenaltyinfo.org/public-opinion-american-values-survey-shows-even-split-death-penalty-more-catholics-opposed.

Incapacitation, though carrying significant weight in political rhetoric and with juries, has become less prevalent in justifying the death penalty as LWOP has become a more ready option across the country.

Between these three reasons or justifications for the death penalty, the Supreme Court has explicitly commented on two: retribution and deterrence. The Court's vacillation between retribution and deterrence, and at times complacency in indicating whether retribution or deterrence (or both) are constitutionally permissible as justifications for the death penalty, has led some critics to argue that the failure or unwillingness of the Court to articulate a concrete reason for the continued use of the death penalty makes such a sanction arbitrary. Other critics contend that "the Court has never undertaken any systematic review of the legitimate constitutional rationale justifying the death penalty... and in the absence of a legitimate purpose for capital punishment, imposing the death penalty is irrational and unconstitutionally arbitrary."[35]

Although it is true that the Court has not reached a definitive conclusion about the justifications for the death penalty, critics of the Court's death penalty jurisprudence are doubtless cognizant of the counterarguments. It starts with the reality that the Court, as the judicial enforcer of the provisions of the Constitution, must adhere to principles of federalism that allow states, through the legislature, to decide issues regarding the appropriateness and legitimacy of penal sanctions. Because matters of criminal justice, including the imposition of proportionate sanctions, are issues that primarily concern the states, the Court must respect the decisions of legislatures and the people they represent. As noted by Justices Powell, Blackmun, and Rehnquist in *Furman v. Georgia* (1972),

> The designation of punishments for crimes is a matter peculiarly within the sphere of the state and federal legislative bodies. When asked to encroach on the legislative prerogative we are well counseled to proceed with the utmost reticence. The review of legislative choices, in the performance of our duty to enforce the Constitution, has been characterized as the gravest and most delicate duty of the Court.[36]

The Court is conscious of its duty and is generally unwilling to interfere in state matters, but it has set aside states' rights when state sanctions are capriciously, freakishly, and wantonly imposed.[37] But it has done so on a case-by-case basis and has not overturned the legislative judgments of all the states that continue to use the death penalty.

What one scholar finds interesting, however, is the fact that the Court has been seemingly indifferent to the death penalty while explicitly using the Eighth Amendment to protect inmates from harm within correctional settings.[38] For example, the Court has used the cruel and unusual provision of the amendment to bar prison officials from using excessive force, corporal punishment, or bodily harm. Yet it upholds the ultimate sanction as constitutional. He concludes: "The Court has never adequately explained how the Eighth Amendment can protect prisoners from harm and intolerable conditions yet simultaneously permit their execution."[39]

---

[35]Sigler, Mary, *Contradiction, Coherence, and Guided Discretion in the Supreme Court's Capital Sentencing Jurisprudence*, 40 Am. Crim. L. Rev. 1157 (2003).

[36]*Furman v. Georgia*, 408 U.S. 238, 258 (1972).

[37]*Gregg v. Georgia*, 428 U.S. 153 (1976).

[38]Bessler, John D., *Tinkering Around the Edges: The Supreme Court's Death Penalty Jurisprudence*, Am. Crim. L. Rev. 2011–2012.

[39]*Id.* at p. 9.

As mentioned in Chapter 1, Supreme Court Justices have personal views regarding the death penalty but maintain judicial composure when deliberating about its constitutionality and/or legal parameters. It is often after retiring from the bench that sentiments about the penalty are revealed to the public. Retired Justice Stevens, who served more than 35 years on the Supreme Court, argued in favor of limiting prosecutorial discretion in capital cases. He said there should be more oversight on prosecutors' decisions to seek the death penalty. He also favored the abolition of the death penalty.[40] Justice O'Connor, who has since retired after serving 24 years on the bench, noted that the death penalty continues to be imposed arbitrarily and there continues to be inadequate representation of indigent defendants. She was also concerned about the possibility of executing innocent individuals due to flaws in the administration of justice.[41]

At times, however, Justices' personal feelings about the death penalty are exposed prior to stepping down from the court. Justice Ginsberg, for instance, wishes for the abolition of the death penalty but understands that the penalty is used by several states, and thus she will continue to respect a state's right to impose the ultimate sanction. Though considering the review of death penalty cases a "dreadful part of the business," she believes that more resources should be devoted to defendant representation, particularly for indigent defendants.[42] Justice Scalia is perhaps the most vocal about state rights. He said:

> The Constitution that I interpret and apply is not living but dead—or, as I prefer to put it, enduring. It means today not what current society (much less the Court) thinks it ought to mean, but what it meant when it was adopted. For me, therefore, the constitutionality of the death penalty is not a difficult, soul-wrenching question. It was clearly permitted when the Eighth Amendment was adopted (not merely for murder, by the way, but for all felonies—including, for example, horse-thieving, as anyone can verify by watching a western movie). And so it is clearly permitted today.[43]

III FLAWS IN THE ADMINISTRATION OF THE DEATH PENALTY

As has been expressed by the Court, the death penalty is different from any other penal sanction that can be imposed on criminal offenders because, unlike any other form of punishment, death is final and irreversible. This reality necessitates that all means must be employed to avoid wrongfully convicting the innocent or, worse, executing an innocent offender. However, as noted by Justice Marshall in *Furman*, "no matter how careful courts are, the possibility of perjured testimony, mistaken honest testimony, and human error remain all too real." Justice Marshall further stated that "we have no way of judging how many innocent persons have been executed, but we can be certain there were some."[44] This statement, however, remains contested because, according to leading scholars on this issue, "no capital jurisdiction in this country has ever admitted to executing an innocent person in this

---

[40]Death Penalty Information Center, Statements on the Death Penalty by Supreme Court Justices, Sept. 15, 2013. Available at: www.deathpenaltyinfo.org/statements-death-penalty-supreme-court-justices.
[41]*Id.*
[42]*Id.*
[43]*Id.*
[44]*Furman v. Georgia*, 408 U.S. 238, 367–8 (1972).

century."[45] But, as they further noted: "Obviously, the government's failure or refusal to acknowledge that an innocent defendant has been executed is hardly evidence that none have been executed."[46]

Since Marshall's opinion in *Furman*, several studies have looked into the number of innocent offenders who have been executed or wrongfully convicted. In an early preliminary study conducted by researchers Bedau and Radelet, evidence of 23 innocent offenders executed between 1900 and 1990 was uncovered.[47] Bedau and Radelet have further discovered that 400 individuals had been wrongfully convicted in capital cases.[48] The Death Penalty Information Center, which maintains a database of exonerations in capital cases, reports that, as of September 1, 2013, there have been 142 exonerations in 26 different states (see Table 12.2) since the reemergence of the death penalty after *Furman*. Most of these individuals had spent many years on death row before exoneration and some had come within days and even hours of being executed. Had these executions occurred, an innocent person would have been killed by the state.

Studies of wrongful convictions have found the most common reasons for error to be eyewitness misidentification, false confessions, faulty forensic evidence, unreliable or perjured informant or "jail-house snitch" testimony, prosecutorial or police misconduct, and incompetent attorneys.[49] In their study of wrongful convictions in capital or potentially capital cases, Bedau and Radelet found that the common causes of error were similar to these. Table 12.3 presents their findings.

Table 12.2 Exonerations by States as of September 1, 2013

Florida	24	Massachusetts	3
Illinois	20	Missouri	3
Texas	12	Mississippi	3
Oklahoma	10	Tennessee	3
Louisiana	9	Indiana	2
Arizona	8	South Carolina	2
North Carolina	7	Idaho	1
Pennsylvania	6	Kentucky	1
Ohio	6	Maryland	1
Alabama	5	Nebraska	1
Georgia	5	Nevada	1
New Mexico	4	Virginia	1
California	3	Washington	1

Source: Death Penalty Information Center. Available at www.deathpenaltyinfo.org/documents/FactSheet.pdf.

[45]Radelet, Michael L., and Hugo Adam Bedau, *The Execution of the Innocent.* In James R. Acker, Robert M. Bohm, and Charles S. Lanier (eds.), AMERICA'S EXPERIMENT WITH CAPITAL PUNISHMENT: REFLECTIONS OF THE PAST, PRESENT, AND FUTURE OF THE ULTIMATE PENAL SANCTION (2003), p. 333.
[46]*Id.*
[47]Bedau, Hugo, and Michael Radelet, *Miscarriages of Justice in Potentially Capital Cases*, 40 STANFORD L. REV. 21 (1987).
[48]*Id.*
[49]Acker, James R., and Allison D. Redlich, WRONGFUL CONVICTION (2011).

Table 12.3 Factors Contributing to Wrongful Convictions in Capital Cases

Type of Error	% of Cases
Witness Error	**55.1%**
Mistaken eyewitness identification	16.0%
Perjury by prosecution witness	33.4%
Unreliable or erroneous prosecution testimony	5.7%
Police Error	**23.4%**
Coerced or other false confession	14.0%
Negligence	3.1%
Other overzealous police work	6.3%
Prosecutor Error	**14.3%**
Suppression of exculpatory evidence	10.0%
Other overzealous prosecution	4.3%
Other Error	**59.7%**
Misleading circumstantial evidence	8.5%
Incompetence of defense counsel	2.9%
Judicial denial of admissibility of exculpatory evidence	2.0%
Inadequate consideration of alibi evidence	12.8%
Erroneous judgment on cause of death	4.6%
Fraudulent alibi or false guilty plea made by defendant	4.9%
Conviction demanded by community outrage	20.0%
Unknown	4.0%

Source: Acker, James R., and Allison D. Redlich, Wrongful Conviction, *at p. 16 (2011).*

Though errors happen throughout the criminal justice system, there is evidence that such errors are more likely in capital cases. Research has indicated that this increased likelihood may be attributable to heightened publicity in capital cases and its influence on the opinion of prospective jurors; the biasing effect of death-qualification predisposing juries to finding defendants guilty; and limited resources and ill-prepared or ineffective counsel for what is often an exceedingly complex and arduous process.[50] One of the co-authors of this book has summarized this elsewhere as follows:

> First, capital murders are, by nature, particularly brutal crimes which evoke horror and outrage on the part of the public. This heightened outrage produces a situation in which there is great pressure on police to make an arrest and on prosecutors to secure a conviction. This pressure creates a situation ripe for overzealous investigation and prosecution which in turn exacerbates a lot of the already common factors that contribute to wrongful convictions. Police officers under great pressure

---

[50]Dieter, Richard C., *Innocence and the Death Penalty: The Increasing Danger of Execution the Innocent,* Death Penalty Information Center, Sept. 23, 2013. Available at: www.deathpenaltyinfo.org/article.php?scid=45&did=292.

to make an arrest are more likely to take short-cuts or circumvent rigorous investigative due dili-gence. They are also more likely to pursue a confession beyond normal bounds. A prosecutor under great pressure to secure a conviction is more likely to ignore exculpatory evidence or engage in ques-tionable legal practice surrounding evidence and witnesses. The horrific nature of the crime and associated public outrage that puts such pressure on police and prosecutors also spills over to capital juries who may be driven toward findings of guilt in part by a strong desire to see justice done in such cases. These are not simply hypothetical suppositions; they are well-documented realities in capital cases, which contribute to a heightened risk of error.[51]

BOX 12.1 CASES OF PROSECUTORIAL MISCONDUCT IN CAPITAL CASES

The Case of Randal Dale Adams

In 1977, Adams was sentenced to death for killing a Dallas, Texas, police officer during a traffic stop. In 1989, Adams was given a new trial due to evidence that the prosecution had withheld exculpatory evidence (evidence proving that Adams was innocent) from the defense.

The Case of Clarence Brandley

In 1980, Brandley, an African American janitor, was sentenced to death in Texas for the murder of a 16-year-old girl. In 1990, Brandley was given a new trial due to evidence that the prosecution had suppressed exculpatory evidence and used perjured witness testimony.

The Case of Daryl Atkins

In 2002, Daryl Atkins, the defendant in the Virginia case in which the Supreme Court declared the execution of mentally retarded offenders a violation of the U.S. Constitution, had his sentence reduced from death to life without parole not because of his mental limitations but because it was discovered that prosecutors coaxed a co-defendant to lie about some of the circumstances surrounding the crime.

The Case of John Thompson

After spending 18 years in a Louisiana prison (14 of them on death row), John Thompson was retried and acquitted by a jury after only 35 minutes of deliberation. He was subsequently awarded $14 million in damages after a successful lawsuit of New Orleans prosecutors, only to have the case overturned by the Supreme Court in *Connick v. Thompson* (2011). The fact that prosecutorial misconduct occurred was uncontested; prosecutors had intentionally withheld exculpatory evidence. But the Supreme Court held that the prosecutor's office could not be held liable for this misconduct.

Critics claim that, as a result of this heightened outrage and pressure, "some prosecutors place so much importance on securing a conviction that doubts about the person's guilt or innocence become second-ary."[52] As such, accounts of blatant prosecutorial misconduct have surfaced as sources of error in numerous death penalty cases (see Box 12.1). In the case of *Banks v. Dretke* (2004),[53] for example, the Court reversed the Fifth Circuit Court of Appeals' decision to deny petitioner Banks a certificate of appealability on the ground that the prosecution had suppressed an interrogation transcript that revealed that a paid informant of the police was coached to testify against Banks at trial. More recently,

---

[51]Vollum, Scott, *The Death Penalty: Ultimate Punishment or Failed Public Policy?* pp. 134–135. In Reddington and Bon-ham, FLAWED CRIMINAL JUSTICE POLICIES: AT THE INTERSECTION OF THE MEDIA, PUBLIC FEAR AND LEGISLATIVE RESPONSE (2012).
[52]American Civil Liberties Union, *Three Decades Later: Why We Need a Temporary Halt on Executions: Report on the Anniversary of* Furman v. Georgia, Sept. 4, 2004. Available at: www.aclu.org/DeathPenalty/DeathPenalty.cfm?ID=13028&c=17.
[53]*Banks v. Dretke*, 540 U.S. 668 (2004).

in the case of *Connick v. Thompson* (2011), it was established that prosecutors in Louisiana intentionally withheld evidence of John Thompson's innocence from the defense and continued to do so throughout the 18 years Thompson spent behind bars, at one point coming very close to execution. If it hadn't been for an investigator working for Thompson's attorney who turned up the withheld evidence, Thompson would have been executed. Today he is free and exonerated. Subsequently, he successfully sued the prosecutor (Harry Connick, Sr.) and was awarded a $14 million settlement. However, in *Connick v. Thompson*, the Supreme Court overturned the award, asserting that the prosecutor's office could not be held liable for the errors.

There are also factors associated with the way capital cases are tried that contribute to the uniquely heightened risk of error in capital cases. Specifically, the process of death qualification in jury selection (see Chapter 6) has been found to predispose a jury toward guilt. The death qualification process asks prospective jurors to *assume a guilty verdict* in responding to questions about whether or not they could vote for a death sentence. This presumption of guilt prior to the actual trial produces a bias toward guilt in the minds of jurors and thus increases the likelihood of a defendant being found guilty, sometimes in spite of a lack of evidence of guilt or the prosecution proving guilt beyond a reasonable doubt.[54]

In terms of errors, of greatest concern in capital cases is the possibility of executing an innocent person. Though no case of wrongful execution has been acknowledged officially by any state, there is no doubt that they have occurred. Bedau and Radelet, in their classic study, identified 23 such cases prior to 1991. With the explosion of attention to errors in capital cases and the proliferation of innocence projects in states across the country, as well as other organizations aimed at investigating wrongful convictions, it has become increasingly clear that there have continued to be executions of people who were most likely innocent, some of which have happened relatively recently. Box 12.2 highlights two cases of possible wrongful execution in Texas: Carlos DeLuna (executed in 1989) and Cameron Todd Willingham (executed in 2004).

The realization that the administration of the death penalty is fallible and that errors occur has been a significant contributing factor in the increase in moratorium and repeal legislation. A moratorium, which is an order to stop the executions of capital offenders pending further investigation into the administration of the death penalty, was first considered by the Supreme Court in *Furman v. Georgia* (1976).[55] Since *Furman*, there have been no more formal Court-ordered moratoriums on the death penalty. However, several state governors have issued such moratoriums due to errors discovered in the administration of the death penalty. In 2000, then-Governor George Ryan of Illinois, a known supporter of the death penalty, issued a moratorium to stop further executions until a thorough assessment of the administration of the death penalty could be conducted. The moratorium was issued to ensure that no innocent individual was put to death. After a lengthy investigation by a committee appointed by the governor, several recommendations to improve or fix the administration of the death penalty were proposed. Some of these recommendations are as follows:

* Custodial interrogations of alleged capital offenders by the police should be videotaped and/or electronically recorded.

---

[54]Sandys, Marla, and S. McClelland, *Stacking the deck for guilt and death: The failure of death qualification to ensure impartiality.* In J.R. Acker, R.M. Bohm, and C.S. Lanier (eds.), America's Experiment with Capital Punishment: Reflections on the Past, Present, and Future of the Ultimate Penal Sanction (2nd ed., 2003, pp. 385-411). Durham, NC: Carolina Academic Press.

[55]*Furman v. Georgia*, 408 U.S. 238 (1976)

BOX 12.2 WRONGFUL EXECUTION? THE CASES OF CARLOS DELUNA AND CAMERON WILLINGHAM

The Case of Carlos DeLuna

Carlos DeLuna was executed in Texas in 1989. Though his case had drawn some attention as DeLuna maintained his innocence all the way to the death chamber, it wasn't until 2012 that it received substantial attention as a case of likely wrongful execution. In 2012, Columbia Law School scholar James Liebman published a lengthy article (over 200 pages) in the *Columbia Human Rights Law Review*[1] that thoroughly documented the case for DeLuna's innocence.

In 1983, Carlos DeLuna was apprehended in the vicinity of a robbery and homicide at a gas station in Corpus Christi, Texas. About 30 to 40 minutes after the crime, DeLuna was found hiding shirtless under a truck and was taken into custody as a possible suspect in the murder. In spite of the crime scene being extremely bloody (the murder was committed with a knife), DeLuna had no blood on him. There were two eyewitnesses in the case; they had seen a man hanging around the gas station with a knife. Both eyewitnesses identified DeLuna as the killer (one identified him at the scene while DeLuna sat in the back of the police car).

In the years since his execution, a substantial amount of evidence has emerged showing that another man, Carlos Hernandez, who bore a striking resemblance to DeLuna, had committed the robbery and murder. Hernandez was known to carry a knife that matched the murder weapon and had bragged to others that he had killed the victim and that someone else had taken the fall for it. Those close to Hernandez have subsequently come forward and submitted that he, not DeLuna, committed the murder.

Liebman's report reveals that police and prosecutors knew about and had initially pursued Hernandez for the murder but failed to tell the defense about this other likely suspect. The report also revealed several other failures and errors by police in their investigation, which turned up no DNA or other physical evidence tying DeLuna to the crime. Liebman concludes that "the DeLuna case was flawed at virtually every level" and that had the prosecution and police done their jobs appropriately, DeLuna would still be alive.

For a more thorough review of this case, see: Cohen, Andrew, Yes, America, We Have Executed an Innocent Man, *The Atlantic* (2012). Available at: www.theatlantic.com/national/archive/2012/05/yes-america-we-have-executed-an-innocent-man/257106/.

The Case of Cameron Todd Willingham

The case of Cameron Willingham, executed in Texas in 2004, provides one of the most striking and compelling cases of likely wrongful execution. Willingham was executed for killing his three young children by burning his house down while they were asleep inside. He was convicted based primarily on an arson investigation that has since been discredited and scientifically refuted. In fact, recently another defendant sentenced to death based on virtually identical evidence has been exonerated and released from death row due to the flaws of this forensic evidence.

Cameron Willingham's case came the closest to reaching an official conclusion. In 2005, the Texas Forensic Science Commission was convened to examine Willingham's case, resulting in several experts and officials revealing that there was no scientific basis for a conclusion that the fire was arson, instead concluding that Willingham did not intentionally start the fire that killed his children. The commission itself never released its report, because the commission was disbanded and its analysis (which had been completed, leaving only the final report to be done) was terminated. Though most agree that Willingham did not murder his children, the case fell short of official acknowledgment.

For a more thorough review of this case, see: Grann, David, Trial by Fire: Did Texas Execute an Innocent Man? *The New Yorker* (2009). Available at: www.newyorker.com/reporting/2009/09/07/090907fa_fact_grann?.

[1]Liebman, James, et al., Los Tocayos Carlos: An Anatomy of a Wrongful Execution. 43 Colum. Hum. Rts. L. Rev. 711 (2012). Available at: http://www3.law.columbia.edu/ hrlr/ltc/print-version.html.

- Police must give prosecutors access to all investigatory materials in their possession.
- Police must ensure that lineups are not biased against suspects.
- Police officers working on homicide cases should receive extensive training on matters such as risks of wrongful convictions as well as investigation and interrogation methods.
- An independent state forensic laboratory should be created.
- Minimum standards for DNA evidence should be established.
- A DNA database should be developed.
- Bar the death penalty in cases in which there is only one eyewitness, an in-custody informant, or testimony from an uncorroborated accomplice.
- After a jury decides to impose a death sentence, the trial judge must also agree that death is an appropriate sentence.
- Ensure that the death sentence is proportionate to the crime committed.[56]

As a result of errors in the administration of justice, Governor Ryan commuted the sentences of all 156 death row inmates. Other states followed suit, several of which (including Illinois) have since completely repealed the death penalty, partially as a result of not being able to adequately protect against such errors.

IV CURRENT DEATH PENALTY TRENDS IN THE UNITED STATES

There are several notable trends with respect to the current state of the death penalty in the United States. The first and most significant involves a movement to abolish the sanction. Within the past six years, five states—New Jersey (in 2007), New Mexico (in 2009), Illinois (in 2011), Connecticut (in 2012), and Maryland (in 2013)—have eliminated the death penalty.[57] Currently, there is a de facto moratorium in the state of New York. New York has a long tradition with the death penalty dating back to Colonial times and was the state whose legislative branch proposed the electric chair as a more humane alternative in the late 1880s. Although it had abolished and reinstated the death penalty several times throughout its rich history with the sanction, in 2004 a federal court struck down the state's death penalty statute, ruling it unconstitutional.[58] At the center of the court's decision was New York's so-called "deadlock instruction." Jurors, during deliberation, were given two options in capital cases: (1) impose the penalty of death, or (2) impose life without the possibility of parole. Either decision had to be unanimous. In the event of a deadlock, however, the state would assume responsibility over sentencing and impose life *with* the possibility of parole. The court held that these options, including the lesser alternative imposed by the state if jurors were deadlocked, ostensibly compelled jurors to rule in favor of the death penalty for fear that the defendant would be given life with the possibility of parole. "The court found that under New York's current death penalty scheme, whether a juror

---

[56]State of Illinois, *Report of the Governor's Commission on Capital Punishment, Recommendations Only.* Sept. 20, 2004. Available at: www.idoc.state.il.us/ccp/ccp/reports/commission_report/index.html.
[57]Death Penalty Information Center, *States With and Without the Death Penalty*, Aug. 8, 2013. Available at: www.deathpenaltyinfo.org/states-and-without-death-penalty.
[58]Death Penalty Information Center, New York. Available at: www.deathpenaltyinfo.org/new-york-1.

chooses death or life without the possibility of parole, the choice is driven by the fear that a deadlock may result in the eventual release of the defendant."[59] The state of New York was given the option to revise its statute, and to date it has neglected to do so, resulting in what appears to be de facto abolition.

As was discussed in previous chapters, California is grappling with changes to its lethal injection protocol. In May 2013, a court invalidated the state's three-drug lethal injection practice because the state failed to properly follow administrative procedures when it implemented the lethal concoction. Rather than appealing the decision to the California Supreme Court, the state is now searching for a single drug that can extinguish life. However, this may take some time since another trend related to the death penalty involves searching for alternative methods of execution.[60] Similar to California, other states are exploring a single drug potent enough to cause death without excessive pain or cruelty. The search or exploration for alternate means to end life was prompted by the reluctance of drug manufacturers to sell their product(s) for executions. The manufacturer of pentobarbital, for example, which is an anesthetic and the first drug used in the three-pronged lethal injection protocol, refuses to allow the sale of its product in executions.[61] States such as Texas and Ohio, which are running out of their available supply of pentobarbital, are now searching for alternatives. Missouri has already decided to use propofol, which has not been used in any executions in the United States.[62] Time will tell whether propofol will be deemed inappropriate for executions.

Another significant trend is the number of studies conducted by various legislative committees inquiring into the administration of the death penalty. The most significant development could be states' seemingly earnest acknowledgment that errors plague the administration of this ultimate sanction and their resolve to minimize, if not completely eliminate, such errors. This high resolve is significant because in the not-too-distant past, states were willing to overlook a few errors (the possible execution of one or two innocent capital offenders) in order to retain the death penalty. Findings by various legislative and executive committees as well as judicial officers and independent organizations, however, have revealed errors that cannot be easily overlooked. These flaws in the administration of the death penalty have prompted states to pass moratoriums and issue safeguards against their recurrence. For instance, Ohio is considering a blue-ribbon panel of former prosecutors to decide whether the state should seek the death penalty.[63] Rather than allowing the prosecutor of the jurisdiction to make such a determination, the panel would weigh aggravating and mitigating factors before seeking a penalty of death. Several states have also implemented racial justice acts after studies showed racial disparity in the imposition of the death penalty.

An additional trend is the use of DNA testing. Although the use of DNA tests has been relied on by the courts in the past to exonerate innocent offenders charged with sexual crimes, there has been a significant increase in the use of these tests in death penalty cases. In Texas, for instance, Senate Bill 1292

---

[59]DPIC, New York's Death Penalty Law Declared Unconstitutional: *People v. Stephen LaValle*; www.deathpenaltyinfo.org/node/1199.

[60]www.mercurynews.com/crime-courts/ci_23635792/california-death-penalty-state-abandons-defense-three-drug.

[61]Death Penalty Information Center, Lethal Injection. Available at: www.deathpenaltyinfo.org/lethal-injection-moratorium-executions-ends-after-supreme-court-decision.

[62]Death Penalty Information Center, Lethal Injection: Missouri Intends to Use Propofol in One-Drug Lethal Injection. Available at: www.deathpenaltyinfo.org/lethal-injection-missouri-intends-use-propofol-one-drug-lethal-injection,

[63]Death Penalty Information Center, Ohio Committee Makes Preliminary Recommendations for Death Penalty Reform. Available at: www.deathpenaltyinfo.org/ohio-committee-makes-preliminary-recommendations-death-penalty-reform.

now requires DNA testing of all biological evidence in capital murder cases. The law was meant to reduce instances of innocent people being convicted and sentenced for crimes they did not commit. However, the law does have its critics. Opponents of the law argue that testing will delay time to case prosecution and will increase the cost of prosecution and that DNA tests are not foolproof.[64] DNA tests are only as good as the evidence left behind at the scene of the crime, and thus not all capital offenders benefit from this technological advance. Because this procedure depends on the effectiveness of the police in gathering information, capital offenders will not have the opportunity to prove their innocence through DNA evidence if the police destroy evidence or fail to collect enough evidence. If the offender was known to the victim and regularly visited the location of the victim's eventual death, DNA evidence would not be able to fully exonerate the offender. The most damaging criticism of DNA tests continues to be the reliability of the crime laboratory that analyzes the DNA. In recent years, much has been learned about careless mistakes committed by DNA analysts throughout the United States. Investigations by the FBI have even indicated that some crime laboratories fabricate DNA results.[65]

One of the most significant trends is the decline in death sentences and executions. As mentioned in prior chapters and noted at the beginning of this chapter, there has been a sharp drop in the number of sentences imposed since the late 1990s. Support for the death penalty hovers at around 60 percent, but only 76 new death sentences were imposed by jurors in 2012. Additionally, even in traditionally death-prone states such as North Carolina, South Carolina, and Virginia, no new sentences were issued in 2012. This trend was also noticed in death-prone counties. Harris County, which includes the city of Houston, has few sentences imposed.[66] According to some legal scholars, the disproportionate imposition of the death penalty among counties is related to several factors. Money is often a decisive factor in seeking the death penalty. More populated counties equate to more fiscal resources for prosecutors, including resources to seek the penalty of death in certain cases.[67] However, parochialism may also be an influential factor. James Liebman and Peter Clarke define parochialism, within the context of studying the irregularity of the death penalty in several counties, as an affinity for local and traditional values.[68] Communities that espouse such parochialism place a high premium on quality-of-life issues such as security, safety, and low crime rates. Although being town-centered can be advantageous to the fulfillment of the above listed quality-of-life issues, it can also lead to shared fears and anxiety over the same issues. This is particularly evident in communities that are geographically in close proximity to minority neighborhoods. "The combination of a large African-American population nearby and a large proportion of the risk of homicide being borne by whites relative to blacks has a particularly strong association with more frequent resort to the death penalty and higher rates of reversible error in death verdicts imposed."[69] Thus, the perceived risk predisposes certain counties to resort to the death penalty.

---

[64]www.news-journal.com/news/local/law-could-curb-death-penalty-cases-in-texas/article_7924d503- b863-5a2d-a12c-6c8af53d1ef3.html.

[65]American Civil Liberties Union, *Three Decades Later: Why We Need a Temporary Halt on Executions: Report on the Anniversary of* Furman v. Georgia, Sept. 4, 2004. Available at: www.aclu.org/DeathPenalty/DeathPenalty.cfm?ID=13028&c=17.

[66]Death Penalty Information Center, *The Death Penalty in 2012: Year End Report*, Aug. 14, 2013. Available at: http://deathpenaltyinfo.org/YearEnd2012.

[67]Gershowitz, Adam M., *Statewide Capital Punishment: The Case for Eliminating Counties' Role in the Death Penalty*, 63 VANDERBILT L REV 307 (2010).

[68]Liebman, James S., and Peter Clarke, *Minority Practice, Majority's Burden: The Death Penalty Today*, OHIO STATE JOURNAL OF CRIMINAL LAW, 9 (2011).

[69]*Id.* at p. 271.

In a way, parochialism has a spiraling effect since community residents will expect law enforcement to abide by their values as well as hold the same expectations for prosecutors and judges.

Another explanation proffered by Liebman and Clarke is related to libertarian views about crime and punishment. They argue that more pronounced support for the death penalty is related to stronger sentiments about individual liberties and restrained state power. It is also related to a belief that states either unwilling or incapable of exerting enough fortitude to address crime tend to translate into vigilantism. Thus, the combination of a community's belief in a weak or limited government, people's willingness to take law enforcement matters into their own hands, and fervent opinions about retributive justice yields strong support for the death penalty. According to Liebman and Clarke, however, the reality regarding the uneven use of the death penalty in some communities is related to an amalgamation of both parochial and libertarian views. Since it is rare that communities will solely espouse one view over another, the more common arrangement is that communities will blend aspects of both parochialism and libertarianism. With this combination of views comes ardent support for the death penalty and an explanation as to why some communities are more insistent in the imposition of the penalty. As Liebman and Clarke put it, "[T]he mixture of conspicuous fear of outsider crime, demand for harsh punishment when the community is invaded and autonomy is threatened, and doubts about government's intestinal fortitude when it comes to punishment can be a toxic brew."[70]

V THE FUTURE OF THE DEATH PENALTY IN THE UNITED STATES

Of the three justifications for imposing a legal sanction on a criminal offender, retribution and deterrence are the reasons the Supreme Court has typically invoked as rationales for the continued use of the death penalty in the United States. Retribution, however, has many variants, one of which includes strong elements of vengeance and revenge. Although this would seem inconsistent with the mandates of the Eighth Amendment's proscription against cruel and unusual punishment, members of the Court have used this form of retribution to justify the use of the death penalty. No doubt there are members of society who subscribe to this justification for the most severe form of punishment. Due to a lack of conclusive evidence that the death penalty deters crime, deterrence, as a justification for the death penalty, has fallen out of favor with many groups, including scholars, law enforcement officials, policy makers, and even many politicians. Nevertheless, deterrence continues to emerge in legal and constitutional reasoning in defense of the death penalty. There is no arguing that the death penalty is an effective form of incapacitation. However, with the increasing availability of true life sentences (LWOP), there are serious questions about whether the death penalty is necessary to sufficiently incapacitate dangerous offenders. In spite of any debate over the validity of these justifications for the death penalty, they do remain, both in the legal and public spheres, potent and persuasive rationales for its continued use.

Regardless of the justifications for the death penalty, consideration must be given to the inherent flaws in the administration of the death penalty; there is growing evidence that wrongful convictions and the execution of innocent capital offenders have occurred far more often than many would have ever imagined. As a result of the growing evidence of such errors, efforts are afoot to prevent their recurrence. Some states have issued moratoriums as they investigate errors or flaws, but these states are in the minority. Other states, as we have discussed, have gone to the length of simply abolishing the

---

[70]*Id.* at p. 278.

death penalty, sometimes after determining that there is no way to fix the system so that errors are avoided. Still other states have expressed concern that improving the administration of the death penalty may be too costly, particularly when it involves the creation of independent DNA laboratories and DNA databases.

Given the current state abolition trends, the question of whether the Supreme Court will abolish the death penalty countrywide is more open than it has been in a long time. There is no indication that the Court is currently entertaining any possible decision that would do so. But, when we look at the Court's prior logic in deciding what constitutes cruel and unusual punishment and recognize that we are only eight states away from a minority of states having the death penalty, it is tempting to speculate what the Court might do. Are we likely to arrive at this point anytime soon? No. But it is a foreseeable future where the death penalty no longer comports with "evolving standards of decency that characterize a civilized society." Only then might the Court consider whether the death penalty, as a form of punishment, deserves its own legal death.

Key Terms

abolition
brutalization
Connick v. Thompson
deterrence
DNA evidence
exoneration
incapacitation
innocence
life without possibility of parole (LWOP)
moratorium
prosecutorial misconduct
racial justice acts
retribution
wrongful conviction
wrongful execution

CRITICAL THINKING QUESTIONS

1.   Of the three primary rationales or justifications for the death penalty, which do you believe is the most compelling and important? Explain and defend your answer. Discuss how current evidence or knowledge impacts the strength of this justification.

2.   Public support for the death penalty has declined over the last few decades. Based on the material in this chapter (and previous chapters), offer some explanation for why this might be the case. Should this decline play a role in the Supreme Court's determination of the constitutionality of the death penalty? Why or why not?

3.   In the last six years, five states have abolished the death penalty, leaving 32 states with this sanction. Based on logic used by the Supreme Court in other cases (e.g., *Atkins v. Virginia; Roper v. Simmons*), what likely has to happen for the Supreme Court to declare the death penalty, in and of itself, cruel and unusual punishment? Explain the logic that underpins your answer to this question

Internet Resources

Pros and Cons of Abolishing the Death Penalty
www.balancedpolitics.org/death_penalty.htm

Death Penalty Opinion Poll
www.gallup.com/poll/1606/death-penalty.aspx

Death Penalty Due Process Review Project
www.americanbar.org/groups/individual_rights/projects/death_penalty_due_process_review_project.html

Wrongful Execution? The Liebman Report on Carlos DeLuna
www3.law.columbia.edu/hrlr/ltc/

Witness to Innocence
www.witnesstoinnocence.org/

The Innocence Project
www.innocenceproject.org/

Righting Wrongful Convictions
www.northwestern.edu/magazine/northwestern/spring99/convictions.htm

Index

Note: Page numbers followed by *b* indicate boxes, *f* indicate figures, *t* indicate tables and *np* indicate footnotes.